Dorothy Day and the Catholic Worker Movement

Centenary Essays

Edited by

William J. Thorn
Phillip M. Runkel
Susan Mountin

Marquette University Press

Marquette Studies in Theology
No. 32

Andrew Tallon, Series Editor

Library of Congress Cataloguing in Publication Data

Dorothy Day and the Catholic worker movement : centenary essays / edited by William Thorn, Phillip Runkel, Susan Mountin.
p. cm. — (Marquette studies in theology ; no. 32) Includes bibliographical references and index.
ISBN 0-87462-682-X (pbk. : alk. paper)
1. Day, Dorothy, 1897-1980—Congresses. 2. Catholic Worker Movement—Congresses. I. Thorn, William J. II. Runkel, Phillip M. III. Mountin, Susan, 1949- IV. Marquette studies in theology ; #32.
BX4705.D283 D67 2001
267'.182'092—dc21
2001005357

Cover Design by Andrew J. Tallon

Photo of Dorothy Day on back cover first published in the *New York World-Telegram & Sun* in 1934. Original held by the Library of Congress.

Marquette University Press
Milwaukee

The Association of Jesuit University Presses

Dana Konopka
portrait from photograph

Dedicated to

Bill Miller

&

Jeremiah O'Sullivan

Acknowledgements

The editors have been sustained by the support of their colleagues, students, families, and friends.

In particular, they wish to thank Nicholas C. Burckel, Charles B. Elston, Lydia R. Runkel, Susan B. Stawicki-Vrobel, and Rebecca L. Tress.

They are grateful as well to the members of the Marquette University Religious Commitment Fund Committee for a grant to defray the costs of publication.

CONTENTS

PART V
Work and the Economy

PART VI
Dorothy Day's Writings and Rhetoric

PART VII
DOROTHY DAY'S SPIRITUALITY

PART VIII
PETER MAURIN AND CATHOLIC WORKER FARMS

PART IX
AMMON HENNACY

PART X
CATHOLIC WORKER PACIFISM, 1933–1945

PART XI
ECUMENICAL PERSPECTIVES

PART XII

PERSONAL NARRATIVES

Preface

In 1995 colleagues in the Marquette University Archives encouraged me to start planning a national conference to commemorate the centenary of Dorothy Day two years hence. This seemed to be a task for which I was suited as curator of her papers; my lack of any experience in organizing academic symposia notwithstanding. Suffice it to say that my limitations in the latter department soon manifested themselves—to me, at least, and probably to the others on the Dorothy Day Centenary Committee as well. With a *lot* of help from these friends, however, and the generous support of the Raskob Foundation and other donors, the conference took place as planed, on October 9-11, 1997 (one month before the actual 100th anniversary of Day's birth, to avoid a conflict with celebrations organized by Catholic Workers in New York City and Las Vegas, Nevada). It featured workshops, roundtable discussions, and paper presentations by more than 60 scholars and Catholic Workers. More than 500 participants came from 26 states, Canada, England, The Netherlands, and New Zealand. The conference was dedicated to the memory of William D. Miller (1916-1995), pioneer historian of the Catholic Worker movement, biographer of Dorothy Day, and esteemed colleague, mentor, and friend to generations of Workers, scholars, and archivists.

The essays and poems included in this volume were presented at the Dorothy Day Centenary Conference, most for the first time. We offer them now in the hope that they will contribute to that ongoing "clarification of thought" so dear to Peter Maurin's heart. Anyone seeking additional information about Dorothy Day and the Catholic Worker movement is most welcome to contact the Department of Special Collections and University Archives, Marquette University Libraries, in Milwaukee, Wisconsin.

Phil Runkel
Curator, Dorothy Day-Catholic Worker Collection
Chair, Dorothy Day Centenary Committee

Introduction

Still Provoking Us after All These Years: Dorothy Day of and outside Her Time

William J. Thorn, Ph.D.

Director, Institute for Catholic Media
Marquette University

Today, tomorrow, next year and throughout this new century Dorothy Day provokes us, pricks our consciences, upsets the comfort of middle class Christianity, and challenges our assimilation in contemporary American life by bearing witness to the possibility of living a life guided solely by the principles Christ proclaimed. Even though she began her work among the poor almost 70 years ago and died 20 years ago, she remains a modern presence, a voice which rises out of *The Catholic Worker*, her autobiographies, and the recollections of those who worked with her in the Catholic Worker movement. It is a voice which challenges us about the way we live our lives, that is to say, the way we live out our faith.

To members of Generation X and their younger counterparts searching for a meaningful faith and community, Day offers the vision of a community of faith which actively reaches out to the poor, the hungry, the alienated, as well as to those blinded to the suffering by their own comfort. For those who had to jettison their church in order to find God in the world, Day and the Catholic Worker movement provide a point of connection, a way of resolving the struggle. In this, she provokes both the young and their parents.

Founding *The Catholic Worker* would surely bring her to our attention as a farsighted publisher and journalist. Founding the Catholic Worker movement would commend her work and organizational strategies for further study. Founding and sustaining the houses of hospitality in order to feed the hungry, clothe the nearly naked, and provide shelter for the homeless warrants close study as the Sermon on the Mount put into action. Standing for justice in wages and protection of workers and against their exploitation by wealthy employers urges examination of social justice in the workplace as a Christian construct. Challenging government to give special attention to the plight of the poor and disadvantaged generates examination of strategies for political organization. Unwavering opposition to war and military expenditures, including World War II and the air raid drills of the '50s draws students of American pacifism. Her role as a woman draws examination in the light of the feminist movement. Her vision, drawn from and with Peter Maurin, of a more humane society linked with communitarian farming and suspicion of the dark tendencies of industrialism resonates with movements of the '70s and even post-industrial thinking.

Day's major activities stand out in Depression era America as a beacon of hope for the poor and hungry and in sharp contrast to the two dominant trends of the ethnic Catholicism in America prior to World War II: defense against anti-Catholicism and assimilationist patriotism. The Catholic Worker became a voice for the powerless which challenged those who ignored or dismissed them —the wealthy, churches, government, and employers.

In contemporary America the context is very different for Catholicism, but the need for Day's provocation remains. Although Catholicism has proclaimed a "preferential option for the poor" and social justice stands as a little disputed orientation within the church, the church is no longer dominated by immigrants. Affluent and successful, the children and grandchildren of immigrants have become insulated in suburban life, removed from the plight of the poor and dispossessed. It is precisely among middle and upper class Catholics that Day's ideas and the Catholic Worker movement remain provocative—when encountered. Afflicting those comfortable in their faith and affluence remains the role of the Catholic Worker movement and the enduring legacy of Dorothy Day.

Her faith journey from parental Protestantism to Communism and to Catholicism, reported in her autobiographies and other accounts, seems to draw rather less interest. But the religious philosophy which underlies Day's world view needs close examination within the Christian tradition and in comparison with other religious traditions. All of these factors seem likely to produce scholarly works, even artistic works in poetry and the plastic arts.

The Marquette University commemoration of the centennial of Day's birth was in turn calm and reflective, intellectually combative, touchingly reminiscent, contentious, and poetic—that is, thoroughly alive.

Thus the question remains: why does Dorothy Day retain the power to provoke us after all these years? Why, after all these years, does Dorothy Day retain the power to generate heated controversy in a society and culture seven decades past the one in which she began the Catholic Worker and nearly a quarter century past her death? Why are Dorothy Day and the Catholic Worker movement cited authoritatively in discussions of the internet, computers, low power radio stations, and Microsoft, Inc.?

To my mind, Dorothy Day's power continues undiminished for the same reasons that St. Francis of Assisi retains the power to move people 800 years after his death: a life of Christian integrity and a moral vision shaped by her faith. Dorothy Daythoughtfully lived out her life in accord with the most demanding proclamation of the Good News—Christ's Sermon on the Mount—and in accord with the doctrines and beliefs of the Catholic Church. In living a life of voluntary poverty and selfless devotion to the least of her brothers and sisters, Dorothy Day speaks to us even today as a sign of contradiction to self centeredness and to many aspects of contemporary society and its culture of consumption and disposability.

Moral vision allowed Dorothy Day to see things and people from a perspective different from most of her contemporaries. In her vision, the moral dimension was the foreground and the other aspects moved to the background of the individuals and situations she encountered. Where others first saw bums, alcoholism, failures, the shiftless and the lazy, she saw the face of Christ. Where others saw patriotic self defense, she saw the Mystical Body torn and shattered on the battlefield. Where others saw unruly and obnoxious strikers, she saw laborers and their families denied a living wage and labor stripped of its dignity. This is the moral vision of the prophets. It provokes reflection; it provokes conversion; it provokes puzzlement. It also provokes resentment and hostility. Part of her power comes from the way she taught this moral vision to others. In their recollections in this volume, those who worked with her comment on how they had to learn to see people from Day's perspective. John Cort recounts how all stood equal, and Jim Forest states that Day more than anyone taught him what it means to follow Christ.

The lives of Francis and Day provoke reflection and even heated debate because they lived their lives in the most radical Gospel tradition, embracing Lady Poverty, serving the poorest, and gently challenging all. This is perhaps best understood in light of a quotation from Cardinal Emmanuel Suhard of Paris that Day inscribed in her journal: "To be a witness does not consist in engaging in propaganda or even in stirring people up, but in being a living mystery; it means to live in such a way that one's life would not make sense if God did not exist."

What makes Dorothy Day's life cohere is her faith, her profound understanding and dedication to Catholicism. As in other things, Day's perception was acute and precise. She understood clearly the difference between Catholicism as a system of belief and the Catholic Church as an institution. Moreover, she understood the intimate relationship between Catholic faith and Catholic leaders. In challenging the wage policies of the Archdiocese of New York, she was prepared to both pray for change and peacefully demonstrate at the cathedral. Once Day encountered Catholicism's radical call to serve the poor, she studied, then embraced, and finally came to exemplify the call of the Gospel.

The modern tendency, one all too easy to adopt so many years after Day's death, seems to focus on one or another aspect of Day's life and work—feeding the poor, providing shelter and clothing, pacifism, communitarianism, worker's rights, opposition to corporate domination, journalism in service to the movement, a woman leader, religious ideals as motivation—and ignore or downplay faith as her central organizing principle. While valuable in its own right, study of individual aspects of the Catholic Worker movement always runs the risk of diminishing our ability to see Dorothy Day whole. Her power comes from the absolute integrity of her faith and her lifestyle. From her days as a student at the University of Illinois, Day showed concern for the poor. Communism became for her a solution to society's injustice toward the poor and the workers. But it was her conversion to Catholicism that provided her with the complete rationale and motivation for serving the poor and developing her own inner life. In examining Day apart from her Catholicism, one risks examining the trunk and its branches but ignoring the root system. In examining one aspect of Day's life, for example pacifism, it is necessary to include the religious belief which provided Day with the *raison d'etre*. Hers was hardly a blind or passively obedient faith, for she was prepared to confront bishops and cardinals on social justice. Rather, it was a reasoned and deeply held faith which sustained and directed everything she did. Day attended Mass daily, and accounts of the depth of her faith, while less fulsome than those of other aspects of her life, create a paradox for American categorical thinking: religiously orthodox and socially radical. Contrary to the categories of contemporary political and social thought, the wellspring and source for Day's social radicalism is traditional Catholic doctrine.

Dorothy Day went beyond a personal commitment to a life of service to the least of God's children by inviting everyone else to join her, even if only for a short time. Her invitation, like her life, touched the idealism in many, some of whom joined her in the Catholic Worker house in New York and some of whom started Worker houses in other cities. I chaired several panels at this conference, including one on radio and another on computers. The intense debate over how to approach modern technology drew directly from the vision of Peter Maurin and Dorothy Day, and it demonstrated that part of the power of Dorothy Day and the Catholic Worker movement is that they dealt with the fundamentals of life in contemporary America: technology, capitalism, wealth, and the power of individuals over and against the powerful. Thus integrity and the willingness to take up the most important and profound issues of the day provide twin sources for Day's power to prod and challenge.

Throughout the 1930s, Day was a regular guest journalist in Marquette's College of Journalism, invited by the Dean, Jeremiah O'Sullivan, a former Associated Press editor who admired both her journalistic skill and her life of total dedication to her Catholic faith. *The Catholic Worker* differed dramatically from the rest of the Catholic newspapers of its time because it developed the principles and ideals of the Catholic Worker movement. In fact, its design, language, and style were directly related to the *Daily Worker*, the Communist newspaper. Well written, *The Catholic Worker* was not a vehicle of Church hierarchy, but the voice of social justice. It presented Catholic teaching in direct application to the poor and oppressed, not in abstract theological categories or in the apologetic forms of the Baltimore Catechism.

Marquette journalism students followed Day to New York, moved by her vision and her work. Some started a Catholic Worker house in Milwaukee. Others opened stores of religious art and books with a special room for discussing the ideas in *The Catholic Worker* and books. Day's clarion call touched the idealism of many beyond the circle of Catholicism.

What drew these students? Michael Harrington shared her passion for economic social justice and, after leaving the Catholic Worker, he went on to write *The Other America.* Accounts of how Dorothy Day changed the lives of those who worked with her in any capacity are bountiful. Less bountiful are the other stories of those who just could not bring themselves to such a total dedication to a life of poverty. In the late 1980s I had in a conversation with an elderly New York woman who wanted to donate some memorabilia of Dorothy Day acquired during her years of working with Day and financially supporting her work. In the course of the conversation she told of taking Dorothy Day shopping at least twice a year for a new dress to replace the worn and patched one. Day always insisted on shopping at second hand stores. And, when this good woman tried to lead Day to the nearly new dresses, Day always rummaged through the dresses to find the most worn one. Fifty years later, this woman still had trouble understanding Day's complete fidelity to the life of voluntary poverty.

On a much larger scale, Day's radical Catholicism stood in sharp contrast to the ethnic Catholic culture of the immigrants. Explicitly linking Catholicism with principles of social justice, the Catholic Worker movement opened up a form of Catholicism not previously visible in America, a Catholicism which addressed the social realities of the day and encouraged working to resolve them. Radical as Day's approach seemed in the '30s, it drew more liberally oriented Catholics, especially those active in the union movement and oriented to social issues.

Day's vision become less well received when America entered World War II and *The Catholic Worker* continued its absolute pacifism and opposition to all elementsof the military machine. For Catholics who fought nativist anti-Catholicism by working constantly to prove they were thoroughly American, this aspect of the Catholic Worker movement went too far, and many dismissed Day as a false convert, a communist at heart. Suspicion about Day and her paper even led the Catholic Press Association to drum The Catholic Worker out as a member, a step which was reversed years after World War II ended.

Day stood by her principles, even through the Civil Defense era of the early Cold War when disaster drills were the norm in schools and in cities. Viewing this as an extension of militarism which took money away from the poor, Day expressed her pacifism by sitting in city parks during New York's disaster drills. She and other Catholic Workers were arrested for civil disobedience.

By the 1960s Day was celebrated as a Catholic visionary, a role model for Catholic concern about the poor. In fact, American Catholics had only begun to catch up to the Catholic Worker ideals, and by the 1980s Catholics accepted that the "preferential option for the poor" was a central principle of Catholic thinking in the United States. And when she died, Dorothy Day was celebrated as a visionary and model Catholic, placed on a par with Mother Teresa. Today, the cause of canonization of Dorothy Day as a saint moves forward with great support. This, in itself, is hardly an uncommon pattern for radicals like Day.

Day's power to stimulate controversy and debate in the 21st century, however, has something to do with those things which made her controversial during her life, but not within Catholic circles. What seems to make her controversial now are the fundamental aspects of her life and their link to the Catholic Worker movement. Today's scholars, concentrating on one aspect of Day or the Catholic Worker movement, contribute to the division when they encourage separation of Day's integrity by studying only her works.

The Catholic Worker movement is today profoundly divided over its Catholicity. Some argue catholic meaning universal, others argue Catholic meaning rooted firmly in Catholic doctrine and religious practice. No such division was possible while Day was alive. Articles in this volume reveal the depths of that division. One group argues that Day's Catholicism and the very name of the movement means that the Catholic Worker movement must remain faithful to Catholic doctrine and practice, even if opposing abortion contradicts the popular position of social liberals. The other group argues that while Catholicism was fine for Day, it holds no special place nor obligates those in the movement to refrain from supporting abortion. In some respects this differs not at all from the issues which confronted other movements when the founders passed on. In another respect, this cuts to the core of the integrity of the Catholic Worker movement. Can it continue to call itself Catholic when it proclaims positions directly contrary to the Catholic Church?

Scholarly work on specific aspects of Day's life, on Peter Maurin and Ammon Hennacy, and the Catholic Worker movement provide significant and interesting insights from various perspectives. For example, a feminist perspective on Day highlights the uniqueness of her position amidst a hierarchical structure that was completely male. While not different in ways from that of every female religious leader of the past 2 millennia in the Catholic Church, Day did not found a religious community nor seek official Church affiliation. Debate and research on the Catholic tradition of nonviolence and pacifism will continue to bring up the ideas of Day and the Catholic Worker movement.

Papers and panels at this conference recall life with Dorothy Day, celebrate her life and vision in poetry, analyze the context and implications of Day and the Catholic Worker movement, and take up the issues of the day in the context of Catholic Worker thinking. Through these papers one can see how Day's integrity gives rise to study of different aspects of her work and life: pacifism, social justice, worker's rights, and the like.

When she thought about it, which was probably not that often, Day opposed being put forward for canonization as a saint on the grounds that saints are old figures easily dismissed and forgotten, disconnected from contemporary life. The power of her life to prod and challenge us demonstrates that, like others who lived lives of total dedication to the most radical understanding of the Gospel, formally sainted or not, Dorothy Day will continue to inspire and confront those who are concerned about our personal obligations to the poor, the homeless, the prisoners, the hungry, and all who suffer from injustice.

This book contains some of the marvelous poetry which was read during the Marquette conference. To bring it more fully to the attention of the readers, we chose to highlight each work by placing one at the end of each section. Indeed, Dickey's profoundly moving poem opens the book. Powerful works by M.L. Liebler and Jeff Poniewaz were located in sections which seemed most appropriate. The book also contains the work of Ade Bethune and Rita Corbin, lest we ignore the role that visual art has played in Catholic Worker publications and Day's impact on the modernization of Catholic religious art. Indeed, the conference section of the art of the Catholic Worker included displays of the art which contributed so much to the impact of *The Catholic Worker.*

The essays in each section provide a diverse set of perspectives on Dorothy Day, the Catholic Worker movement, and its singular prophets, Peter Maurin and Ammon Hennacy.

David O'Brien's examination of Dorothy Day's role in American Catholicism over the past half century concludes with a clarion call for reestablishment of a liberal Catholicism which fully corresponds to the vision of the Catholic Worker movement which contributed so significantly to its emergence. Louise and Mark Zwick recount the results of the Houston Catholic Worker's close study of the roots of the Catholic Worker movement. They carefully review the religious, philosophical, and social writings which provided inspiration for a "Revolution of the Heart" against the bourgeois spirit which blinded so many to the poor and oppressed. As they note, much research remains to be done on the roots of the movement.

Part II offers some of the most exciting and challenging essays in this collection. Michael Baxter's essay develops the wonderful image of blowing the dynamite of the Church, extending O'Brien's conclusion that the radical vision of the Catholic Worker movement must once again revolutionize the current complacency of Catholics and institutional Catholicism. In addition, Baxter reminds us of the importance of public theology, of the fundamental integration of theological vision and public policy. Fred Boehrer examines the anarchist component of the Catholic Worker movement, noting that this is precisely the component which urges a constant revolution against institutional complacency while encouraging the movement to be ecumenical. Ann O'Connor and Peter King, the foremost advocates of Catholicism's essential role in all Catholic Worker activities and public positions, review the Catholic nature of the Catholic Worker movement and Day's own faith in addressing the controversy over Catholic Worker positions on issues like abortion. Brian Terrell offers a somewhat different perspective on Day's Catholicism, reminding us that she was not a meek and subservient Catholic but one who lived in permanent dissatisfaction with that part of institutional Catholicism which stands with the rich and powerful. Matthew Smith adds to the portrait of Dorothy Day a more contemporary issue of liberation theology, noting the many points of correspondence between the underlying ideologies of the Catholic Worker movement and liberation theology.

Two major scholars, Patrick Coy and Stephen Krupa, examine nonviolence in the Catholic Worker movement. Coy identifies the five aspects of the Catholic Worker movement which made it congenial to nonviolent action: biblical seriousness, personalist politics, solidarity with the poor, living in community, and turnover of members. Krupa provides a deep and thorough historical and philosophical analysis of nonviolence as but one aspect of Day's prophetic role as a biblical witness standing in direct and open contradiction to the dominant American moral standards and a kind of Christian militarism that pervades the national mythic system.

The essays in Part IV provide different approaches to understanding Dorothy Day's political and social thought. Geoffrey Gneuhs takes issue with those who would simply locate Dorothy Day and the Catholic Worker as the Catholic part of America's left, identifying the multiple reasons for which she should be more accurately understood as a profoundly orthodox Catholic who went to the roots of Catholic belief and lived out its social doctrine. Bill Kauffman provides a fascinating study which supports the unconventional view that Dorothy Day, on the basis of shared values and ideology, may have been more at home with Catholics on the American Right than with the socialists and communists. Keith Morton and John Saltmarsh employ the method of cultural construction, including Dorothy Day's construction of her life story, in order to identify her political and social ideas before her conversion to Catholicism and then the links to her early years in the Catholic Worker movement. They conclude that even today Day's approach offers a life of integrity and authenticity.

Five essays specifically address work and the economy as Dorothy Day and Peter Maurin understood them and took them up as issues. John Cort, one of the early Catholic Workers, recounts Dorothy Day's deep involvement with workers, particularly those laid off or on strike during the Depression, and her encouragement when he and others established the Association of Catholic Trade Unionists (ACTU). Paul Miller's essay provides a larger portrait of John Cort in tracing the history of the ACTU and Cort's work and then setting it in the context of Catholic culture. David Gregory, drawing from an extensive law journal study of Dorothy Day and labor, identifies the lessons for workers on the transformation of labor from mindless drudgery to a task conveying human dignity to both employers and employees. Nicholas Lund-Molfese explores how the Distributists' view of the nature of work affected Maurin's own view of labor as a potential means to freedom, and leads to a call for both a restoration of dignity to domestic work and protection of the dignity of those who are unable to work. Eugene McCarraher draws from Day's work and writing on labor and technology a means for addressing the "wrenching transformation in the nature of work and technology" America faces at the turn of the 21st century.

Journalism played a central role in Day's life and in the development of the Catholic Worker movement. Essays by Carol Jablonski and Markha Valenta deal directly with her writing and rhetoric, although in markedly different ways. Carol Jablonski's analysis of Day's rhetorical style centers on the problem reformers and prophets face in trying to persuade the audience, especially that of toning down the radical aspect to make the message palatable, and she concludes by pointing out that Day's use of irony, which worked well in communicating her message, also explains why Day resisted sainthood: it is hard to think of an ironical saint. Markha Valenta provides a completely different approach, concentrating on the community of diverse voices which emerge in Day's writing, including ancient Catholic voices which challenge the very foundational perspectives of a capitalist society.

Part VII brings together three essays on the spirituality of Dorothy Day, a topic which is both broader and more personal than her Catholicism. Catherine Faver's outstanding study of the crises of identity and community which accompanied Day's conversion provide insight for contemporary women whose spirituality takes them into the same crises of identity and community. Julie Leininger Pycior offers an insightful and tantalizing overview of her long term research project, a comparison of the shared aspects of the lives of Dorothy Day and Thomas Merton, including their prolific writings which revealed so much of their inner lives. Roger Statnick uncovers the complex roots of Day's religious vision and lifestyle in the context of Christian tradition and her own spiritual journey to a level of spiritual reality where nature and grace interact cooperatively.

Peter Maurin brought a distinctively European and communitarian world view which complemented and enriched Day's vision and shaped much of the Catholic Worker movement. William Collinge's essay thoroughly explores the conceptual basis for Maurin's ideal of the farming commune, which the movement proposed as a solution to the alienation and unemployment problems created by industrial capitalism, and he notes in conclusion that those problems remain with America as does Maurin's ideal as part of the solution. Paul Magno takes up perhaps the most troubling question, "why does Peter Maurin matter?" Magno's analysis of Maurin's role in the life, thought, and spirituality of Day and the Catholic Worker movement leads him to conclude that it is essential to know Maurin in order to understand the other two. Jeffrey Marlett examines Catholic Worker farm communes as a demonstration of the "Catholic agrarian theology" which emerged from the National Catholic Rural Life Conference, and tracks the development of both to the postwar return to the farm movement of the 1950s. Frank Sicius' excellent essay reconstructs Day's thoughts about Peter Maurin, and through her words demonstrates that he was the spiritual companion who deepened her understanding of Catholicism and taught her to see Christ in the face of the poor: "Peter's arrival changed everything; I finally found a purpose in my life and the teacher I needed."

The other major figure associated with Dorothy Day and the Catholic Worker movement is Ammon Hennacy, an anarchist whose admiration of her work led him to Dorothy Day and whose spiritual longing led him into the Catholic Church despite his opposition to organized religion. James Missey, employing the fruit of his careful study of Hennacy's correspondence, provides an intriguing account of the ideological admiration of Day which turned to romantic hopes and of his aspiration to radicalize the church to which he had converted.

During the war in Vietnam, Catholic men seeking exemption from the draft on the grounds of conscientious objection to war based on religion found that draft boards demanded written justification drawn from church teaching and history. While not a difficult task for Quakers and members of the other peace churches whose theological objection to war was well known, it was difficult for Catholics because of the almost unknown tradition of pacifism which ran through early Christianity and Catholicism. Dorothy Day's writings and the Catholic Worker movement provided the justification. Four essays examine Catholic Worker pacifism before and during World War II and the opposition which Day faced within Catholic circles for encouraging what was judged an unpatriotic, even treasonous position for an American. John LeBrun traces Day's development of Just War

Theory and of nonviolent Christianity through her articles in *The Catholic Worker* and her testimony before Congress opposing a peacetime draft, concluding that it was the "fountainhead of Catholic pacifism in the United States," which fully developed pacifist theology during the Cold War. William Cavanaugh's analysis of *Catholic Worker* editorials and articles provides a moving and insightful assessment of Day's understanding of the Catholic doctrine of the Mystical Body of Christ, which led her to see the Church as the true body of Christ, torn and suffering on the battlefields of Europe as well as starving and homeless in the alleys of New York. Sandra Yocum Mize's study clarifies the pacifist commitment of *The Catholic Worker* during the early years of World War II and its impact on the paper, on Day, and on the movement. This essay also examines how Day's understanding was clarified with the help of Fr. Pacifique Roy and Fr. John Hugo. John O'Sullivan examines the establishment of the Civilian Public Service program as an alternative to the draft for members of the peace churches and its relationship to those Catholics who claimed conscientious objector status on account of their faith. His profile of the resulting social situation in CPS camps and the Catholic corporate witness against war and military service justifies his conclusion that these Catholics planted mustard seeds.

One of the more complex and fascinating areas of scholarship on the Catholic Worker movement and Dorothy Day has explored them from the perspective of other religious traditions. The four essays in this section provide historical accounts and comparisons of beliefs. Walter Chura compares the historical development of the Shakers with that of the Catholic Workers, focusing in particular on the special role Mother Ann Lee and Dorothy Day played in their respective communities. Chura illustrates from his personal experience the shared communal values and world view. Marc Ellis summarizes the Jewish approach to Christianity as background for his profoundly challenging analysis of Dorothy Day and Peter Maurin's "assertion of the importance of Jews and Judaism to the fidelity of Christians" which then and now allows proclamation of "a radical center to their faith" to which the Catholic community can be called and an elaboration of the mystery which Judaism and Catholicism share. Mel Piehl, in analyzing the Protestant reception of Dorothy Day and the Catholic Worker movement, broadens the perspective by beginning with Day's conversion to the Episcopal Church in 1907 and her youthful encounters with classic Protestantism. His analysis points out that while

Day has much more to say to Catholics about social justice based on their faith, history, and customs, she is equally challenging to Protestants, not on matters of social justice and personalism, but on "discipline, prayer, and especially the centrality of church and community." John Sniegocki proposes to bring the Catholic Worker movement into dialogue with Buddhism in one of the most challenging essays in this collection. Working from primary authors on socially engaged Buddhism, he aligns the points of common vision to create a foundation for further dialogue, centering on two points: a "deepened appreciation of spiritual discipline and a broader understanding of nonviolence."

This book would be incomplete without the personal reflections of those who knew and worked with Dorothy Day. John Cort, in recalling the now amusing challenges living and working in the Catholic Worker house brought to his middle class sensibilities, sketches a portrait of Day which emphasizes her leadership style and the power of her personal vision. Tina Sipula, in an essay which borders on poetry, leads us to understand how encounters with Day inspired so many to follow her lead—in looking first to God for direction and then in keeping a house of hospitality faithful to the Catholic Worker vision. Rosalie Riegle, analyzes the conversion narratives which emerged in her interviews for *Voices for the Catholic Worker* and concludes that unlike Dorothy Day, whose conversion led to the formation of the Catholic Worker community, contemporary Catholic Workers are drawn to the community which provides "an impetus for conversion." Jim Forest's experience with Dorothy Day led him to describe her as a saint and a troublemaker, the most Christ centered person he has ever known, one who continues to touch his life more than 20 years after her death.

This bibliography which concludes this book is a compilation of all the citations from all of the essays. Each entry was verified against authoritative listings in the following libraries: Marquette University (including the archives), the Library of Congress, the New York Public Library, the University of Wisconsin-Madison, the University of Minnesota-Twin Cities, and Notre Dame University, and the special archives cited by the authors.

Contemporary Students and Dorothy Day

Dr. Susan Mountin

Marquette University

What is it about Dorothy?

What is it about a turn-of-the-twentieth-century person that enraptures turn-of-the-twenty-first-century college students? Why do these college students bury themselves in decades-old archival records, spend hours in snowy 10-degree-weather serving sandwiches and soup to the poor and homeless of their campus neighborhood, and present research and theological reflection on the church and society that one might expect from seminary students?

For the past three years Marquette University's Theology Department has offered a course on Dorothy Day and the Catholic Worker Movement. I have been privileged to teach the 35-40 students who have taken it each semester as they grapple with concepts and life choices that most college students in this technological world of ever-expanding "stuff" will never broach. In spite of complaining about heavy course requirements, tough grading, and too much reading, the students will add on their course evaluations that "Dorothy" was the best theology class they have taken. Why?

{Because} There is something about Dorothy. It may be elusive, but there is enough of something special in Dorothy that she has been raised by the Vatican to "Servant of God" on the path to sainthood, which raises all sorts of questions and issues for college students in a society clearly lacking in positive role models.

The course, "Dorothy Day and the Catholic Worker," has four components which compel students: 1) the Dorothy Day-Catholic Worker Collection at Marquette; 2) the service learning component; 3) theological reflection based on the Gospels, Church history, social justice teaching, and the writings of Dorothy; and 4) the contemporary spin {perspective} on many of the timeless issues that Dorothy and the movement addressed: poverty, hunger, justice, violence, war, materialism, community, faith, religious expression, spiritual growth. The list goes on and on and will be developed in the remainder of this essay.

Marquette University's Dorothy Day–Catholic Worker Collection

Marquette University boasts of more than 200 cubic feet of archives on Dorothy Day and the Catholic Worker which contain everything from original manuscripts to letters, videos and even articles of clothing. Spending hours in the archives does not normally rank as a fun idea for most college students, but I have found that students find Dorothy and her story so compelling that they quickly warm to her and dig deeply in the archives to discover clues about her life and choices, many of which are the same the students face today.

Imagine being a twenty-year-old female student who knows that Dorothy is on the track to sainthood. Like Dorothy the student has struggled with intimate relationships outside of marriage. Perhaps she, too, or someone she knows has had an abortion, has left school, has tried to get a job to support herself or has had gnawing questions about the meaning of life and her role in the world.

Or perhaps think about a male ROTC student watching the escalation of the Balkan War and worrying about what it might mean to his future. Suddenly issues of war and peace become real in a way they have not before.

Holding in one's hands the original manuscript of a handwritten or typed article, chapter, or letter produced by Dorothy or Peter Maurin is a moving experience. Carefully reading the material takes a researcher to new places and understanding.

The students in the class are required to do a major oral presentation and paper based on that archival research. Their initial groans become whispers of excitement as they find new ideas, and share information, which they are encouraged to do: cooperation not competition is encouraged for these research projects and the students readily find ways to share information and watch for tidbits that might help a classmate.

The students produce publishable papers in this course. Topics can be current. Some examples include: nonviolent resistence (a la the School of the Americas protest in November of each year), a comparison of Ani de Franco (a contemporary music performer who has had an abortion) and Dorothy, the Just War Theory as looked at through the experience of Kosovo, sainthood today, the current Catholic Worker movement—the list goes on and on.

The archival research has another dimension: providing background for the roundtable discussions which occur in class when there is time. The students love Peter Maurin's phrase, "You share a piece of your mind and I will share a piece of my mind. Then together we will both have more in our minds." The discussions are free expressions in which inquiry takes shape as the teacher stays out of the picture allowing the students to speak freely and openly. They show a remarkable respect for each other and really work on listening to another perspective rather than biding time waiting to present their own argument. They talk about learning a skill that they find themselves taking into their daily lives.

Service Learning

Dorothy Day is one of more than 150 Marquette courses which incorporate an official "service learning" component. That means that as part of the course requirements, students participate in some type of community service. They get credit not for the service itself, but for the *learning*, in this case the theological reflection, which flows from the experience of service. Students in " Dorothy" volunteer at shelters and meal programs, particularly at an on campus noon time meal program in which students make sandwiches and take them along with soup and beverages and desserts in a van to a parking lot on the edge of campus, providing lunch for 40 -100 people a day.

The service is important. It gives students an inkling of what Dorothy and the founders of the Worker experienced when they fed thousands. At the same time, like the Worker, student coordinators of the program, lovingly referred to as "Noon Run," must find the money to buy the food and support the program through donations and simple fund-raisers, costing several thousand dollars each semester. I recall a simple request that came from one of the Noon Run guests and conveyed by the students: "Could we have some lettuce and tomato to put on the sandwiches instead of just bologna for the last day of the semester?"

Noon Run, like Dorothy, takes its inspiration for existence from the Gospel, specifically Matthew 25: "When I was hungry, you gave me to eat...when I was thirsty, you gave me to drink...." Students who have before scoffed at the homeless people who grace the Marquette campus, call them "friends" by the end of the semester. They share stories about their lives with each other, not just bread. The students are surprised some of the homeless have college educations, and some of the guests have regular jobs, but can't make ends meet. The students say that when they meet someone who "looks homeless" on the street, they stop, smile and say "hi" instead of pretending the person is not there. At the same time the "guests" say they are inspired by the students and their care and they come to know their concerns. Community takes place in ways unimaginable.

The learning takes place when students study the Gospels (particularly Matthew 25), the social encyclicals, the works of mercy, the Bishops' pastoral letter on the economy. They begin to ask questions about the dignity of the human person, why a rich society is able to send people to the moon but not house our mentally ill sisters and brothers, or why our shelters are full every night. It extends when they begin to see themselves taking roles in the future in which they can work for change and use their education to make a difference in a social service agency, in government, in policy making. It is in these times that the *Pastoral Constitution on the Church in the Modern World* becomes a reality. John Courtney Murray would be proud, because this kind of activity is what he envisioned writing about the role of the laity in the modern world: bringing the Gospel into daily life.

Theological reflection/Theology

The Dorothy Day course is not a course in social work; it is a theology course. So at its core is the research and theological reflection on service, coupled with a healthy dose of church history, scripture, and tradition. The course is part of both the Catholic Studies Program and the Women's Studies program.

Trying to understand the historical development of the Catholic Church in the United States, especially as thousands of immigrant Catholics poured into New York seeking housing and jobs, needing education and language skills, seeking faith and future, students begin to tell the stories of the grandparents and great-grandparents or what they know about the founding of their parish communities.

They raise questions about the growth of the Church and building of parishes and schools at a time when so many Catholics lived in poverty. They are stunned to learn of Pope Leo XIII's teaching on the rights of workers in the late 1800s and the subsequent documents on labor and the economy. They are surprised to study the Church's views on capitalism, Marxism, and communism. They learn about a social gospel, perhaps for the first time. One woman proclaimed that since she discovered the church taught all these radical ideas, she might come return to the church which is not now as repugnant.

Students learn terms many have never heard before: "encyclical" and "benediction." They hear through Dorothy's heart the "Te Deum" and "Salve Regina" she loved so much. They are drawn into the idea of "retreat" and several went on retreats in the course of the semester. Students see the inherent consistency in Dorothy's religious expression and acts for justice. They love her lack of hypocrisy. Dorothy does not just read and pray what is in the Gospels and Catholic Social Teaching: she lived it and it challenges them to do the same.

Dorothy invites students to read the Gospels in a new way, the way Dorothy read them: not just in words but in action. The students, like Dorothy and Peter, ask tough questions about what the church is doing for the poor, about the dignity of the human person, about prayer without works, and about what poverty and riches really are. The Beatitudes take on new meaning. They struggle with the tenets of Catholic Social Teaching and what it might mean for them and the career track they are on. Suddenly their definition of "success' takes on new meaning. A bank account and great clothes are no longer important.

One student commented that when she went home for spring break and went shopping, she found herself picking up one item after another and saying to herself, " I don't really need this." Dorothy would be proud. Another student changed his plans for after graduation to join a post-graduate volunteer project in a large city. Another student spent the summer at a Catholic Worker house. The choices they made were inspired by Dorothy.

Contemporary Issues

Today's students are remarkably ignorant of contemporary history. Thus, Dorothy's life and activities, covering the greater part of twentieth century, immerses students in areas they may have only heard passing reference to before.

Like Dorothy who, as a journalist was constantly interacting with the times, the students each semesters confront varied issues. Dorothy started with the Depression, and the war in Spain, with joblessness, and housing and labor issues. She confronted war and its effects and the tremendous growth of the military and defense industries and nuclear weapons, with Vietnam and the School of the Amercias.

The issues of the day provided grist for the mill, topics for roundtable discussions, inspiration for articles for *The Catholic Worker* newspaper.

The students also saw issues coming to the fore which Dorothy and Peter faced. In the first semester, they attended the Dorothy Day conference, meeting more than 500 participants including many who had known and worked with Dorothy. They heard from Tom Cornell in class and had so many questions. They used the Internet to access materials about Dorothy, but also wondered what on earth Peter would say if he knew!

The second time the course was offered, the United States led its assault on Kosovo two weeks prior to the point on the syllabus which listed "Theology of Non-Violence." Flipping the syllabus was easy and necessary. The discussion of nonviolent response and Dorothy's continued protests of war became fodder for lively discussion, especially with an ROTC student in class. Learning about the Just War Theory and trying to understand the Church's position was a challenge, but the students had some incredibly poignant discussions. The class also learned via a *New York Times* article that the property on Staten Island which was the site of Dorothy's cottage would become luxury condos, providing more fodder for great discussion.

The most recent offering of "Dorothy" had an entirely different cast. A few weeks into the class notice of Cardinal John O'Connor's proposal to begin canonization processes hit the press, and in the middle of the semester the announcement was made about Dorothy being named "Servant of God." What an opportunity for theological questions and growth. What does sainthood really mean? Does it mean anything today? What is holiness? Who is called to holiness? Can someone who smoked and had an abortion be a saint? Why does the church make people saints anyway? What would Dorothy say? Peter?

Is Dorothy outmoded or outdated? No, there is something about Dorothy. Her compelling story lives on and needs to be told. Several students commented that they had been changed forever by studying Dorothy. A few plan to live simpler lives. Some have joined small communities for volunteer work after graduation. But most say they will keep in their hearts this challenging woman who taught them a different value system, a different way to make choices and decisions, a different respect for people they had before rejected, and a new love of Jesus Christ and his Gospel.

Dorothy Day and the Catholic Worker Archives

Phillip M. Runkel

Assistant Archivist
Marquette University Libraries

The presence of the Dorothy Day-Catholic Worker Collection here at Marquette University is largely due to the foresight of William Ready, director of libraries from 1956 to 1963, whose forte was the acquisition of book and manuscript collections. Soon after his arrival Ready joined forces with Raphael Hamilton, S.J., long-time professor of history, to establish the archives department in the new Memorial Library. Among those he solicited for donations was Dorothy Day, whom he had met when she spoke at Stanford University during his tenure there.

For her part, Day had reasons other than the presence of an admiring librarian to be favorably disposed toward Marquette. The dean of the College of Journalism, Jeremiah O'Sullivan, had provided moral and material support to the Worker movement in its early days, and several of his students had been active in the Milwaukee Catholic Worker community before the Second World War; one of them—Nina Polcyn Moore—remained one of Day's closest friends. The university's Jesuit ties did not hurt either, as she thought well of that order. Perhaps most of all, Marquette benefited—given Day's inclination to behave impulsively at times—from being the first archival suitor. In any event, Dorothy Day readily agreed to send her papers and the records of the New York Catholic Worker community to the university, and the first shipment arrived in March 1962.

Father Hamilton had been appointed to the newly created position of university archivist the year before, but William Ready continued to actively participate in the management of the manuscripts program. So it was to Ready that Dorothy Day confided, in a letter of May 22, 1962, that she was "having a fearful attack of cold feet" for having sent the records, "what with so many personal letters from people in them." She asked that the papers remain closed until she could "come and go over them a bit." Ready quickly dashed off a note of reassurance, reiterated in his next note to her, two months later, which contained the rather chivalrous promise, "I shall guard your files against all." True to her word, Day made her first "tour of inspection" that November. How much time she spent in the library is unknown, but she reportedly "showed great pleasure at the handling of her papers."

When Ready left Marquette, his role as Dorothy Day's principal contact at the university was assumed by William Miller of the History Department. Recognizing the significance of the Worker papers and the need for a scholarly history of the movement, Miller had written Day as soon as he learned of the records' arrival to request permission to use them, which she promptly granted. A lengthy correspondence and close friendship ensued. The historian aided the Archives by urging Dorothy Day and her colleagues at the New York Catholic Worker to regularly transfer office records to the repository without a prior culling of the material. This they faithfully proceeded to do—though Day expressed some qualms in a Christmas 1973 note to Father Hamilton:

> Dr. Miller kept telling me to send "everything" to the Archives and as we answered my mail we just bundled up the mail and sent it on. I have been thinking we have put you to a great deal of unnecessary work. We should have eliminated a lot of useless material ourselves.

Before she had time to act on her good intentions, the archivist hastened to assure her that the burden was a welcome one. So the New York Catholic Workers have continued to "bundle up" their mail and send it on to the Archives, following the Catholic Worker "non-filing system," and leaving to their archivist the task of creating a semblance of order out of what seems, at times, pretty chaotic.

Today the Catholic Worker Archives comprise more than 300 boxes of records, including the personal papers of Dorothy Day, Peter Maurin, and others involved in the movement; records of past and present CW communities; photographs; tape-recorded interviews and speeches; television programs on film and videotape; and a wide variety of publications. Although confidential materials—such as Day's diaries— have been restricted at the donors' request, most records are now open to research use, which the archivists encourage and strive to assist. They hope and trust that the resources in the CW Archives will inspire others to work toward a world "where it is easier to be good."

The Archives is open weekdays from 8 a.m. to 5 p.m., and at other times by appointment. Inquiries, requests, and encouraging words are appreciated. Please write the

Department of Special Collections and University Archives
Marquette University Libraries
PO Box 3141, Milwaukee, WI 53201-33141;
telephone 414-288-7256;
or visit the Web site at
www.marquette.edu/library/ collections/archives/index.html.

Angeli tui sancti habitent en ea, qui nos in pace custodiant

– Compline

I had not met her
but went to Maryhouse
where aged, she was
cloistered in her room.
She doesn't come down much
these days we were told.

Downstairs, I made conversation
with a woman in the hallway
stationed guard with an umbrella.
At dinner she heard the lavendar laughter
of three saints in her prune dish.

She sat next to a man who,
rocking back and forth,
peered into an empty soup bowl
and chanted with monklike reverence:
Is this a room
or a womb
or a tomb?

I am not a whore! she shouts for dessert.
Then chin on breast
lowers her voice
to take me into her confidence:
her favorite husband
committed suicide
by eating an omelet
scrambled with shattered glass.

I imagine Dorothy
in the upper room
with Mozart on the radio,
a pen, a bookmark, a book, a candle.
Her lips genuflect to the breviary
as she unhooks thick black
reading glasses from her ears.

She closes her eyes.
She seeks solitude
the way soldiers
took to monasteries after battle.
A lifetime of the poor, the mad, the lonely
burns like a war zone in her.
Like Mary, she has held faithful to
what is precious in her womb.

Downstairs as we gather for evening prayer
I miss seeing the way candlelight heaves
shadows in the hollows of her high cheekbones
as she mouths the *noctem quietam.*
I miss the holy harbor of dark spaces
inside fingers rounded in supplication.
This is her work now in the great cloud of witnesses:

Leave the dishes undone
to end the night in prayer.
The breadlines are ours now–
In manus tuas Domine.

Jacqueline Dickey
South Bend, IN

PART I

THE CATHOLIC WORKER AND HISTORY

The Significance of Dorothy Day and the Catholic Worker Movement in American Catholicism

David J. O'Brien

I gather we have come together today to discuss Dorothy Day and the Catholic Worker movement because we honor her memory and share the concerns that were central to her life and remain central to the movement she founded. This is not a museum, and we are not curators discussing Dorothy Day and her work as we would the bones of some dead dinosaur. Nor is it a convocation called to examine some odd aberration in church and society. In life Dorothy surely refused to become a dinosaur and, as for academic gatherings, she seemed to regard them with some suspicion, particularly if held in her honor. The few times I saw her in a college setting, she seemed envious of students with their opportunity for study and reflection and she seemed as deferential toward professors as she sometimes was toward bishops. Yet, when she spoke, to my amazement, she seemed simply to assume that those who had gathered were a kind of family groping to discover how to live properly while making a better world. So in her unassuming way she would tell stories and talk about books and conduct a kind of conversation. If I knew how, I would talk in that kind of spirit today. But lacking her gift, I can only try to tell you something from my work about the American Catholic Church and where Dorothy and her movement fit in.

Now, that paragraph is a paraphrase pretty accurately of the opening paragraph from a paper I delivered here at Marquette 16 years ago on the occasion of a previous symposium held not long after Dorothy's death. Much has changed since that day, not least the tremendous expansion of Catholic Worker scholarship evident in the wonderful program we have before us today and tomorrow. When we gathered in 1981, Bill Miller was still among us. Bill Miller was such a friend and such a warm supporter for me when I was young. To him I am enormously grateful. I almost came to Marquette in 1968. I taught summer school at Marquette that year and was ready to accept an invitation to teach here. Then Bill decided to leave, and teaching here seemed less attractive when he was gone. He was a wonderful man.

I thought I would do my usual thing, that is, set a context by offering a correct view of United States Catholic history. There are incorrect views around. One view is that Catholic history is the story of immigrant outsiders who are now insiders and should be grateful and keep religion in church and get on with being good Americans. An incorrect view from the left sees immigrant outsiders who became insiders by pursuing the false gods of materialism and Americanism, sins they should repent.

On occasion I try to offer the correct view that immigrant outsiders chose to become insiders while remaining true to themselves and that their success in becoming insiders, that is, achieving a degree of economic well-being, educational advancement, and access to the institutions and culture of this society, is an experience of liberation. It may be a little murky, as all liberation experiences probably would be. But it is an experience of liberation badly in need of theological reflection and pastoral response.

The other part of history is that there are still many outsiders among us, Catholic outsiders, who want the same thing. They are not well served by those who hold to the incorrect views I just noted above. At its best, our Church tells them that it's okay to seek liberation in ways that the United States makes available, and it's okay to try to remain true to yourselves in doing so, recognizing and hoping to learn from all the false terms and murky parts of that earlier experience.

In this view Dorothy Day and the Catholic Worker were not a counter-story running along in the footnotes. H.G. Wells' *Outline of History*, the best seller of the 20s, held up the image of academic historians who didn't like the book constantly running along in the footnotes yelling, "Stop! Stop!" Well, this is a way we might think about the Catholic Worker—a kind of counter-cultural story in the history of American Catholics. Imagine the Catholic Worker running along and saying, 'Stop! Stop! You're making a mistake!"

I don't think we should do that. But Dorothy Day stood as a reminder of the many who were left behind in that story. It was and remains a cruel process.

She was a witness to the responsibilities of freedom, asking what to do when one gets the ability to choose, freed from economic necessity.

What does one do with that freedom? She stood as a sign to the church, perhaps a sacramental sign of a vital Christian truth like the mystical body of Christ.

Certainly the Worker was a place, a network of communities, where people had the opportunity to think as Catholics about what was going on in their lives.

I thought I would help to stir things up a bit at the beginning of the conference and try to place the Worker and Dorothy Day in the context of the history of the Catholic Left, a fairly recent history. Let me begin with a brief history of the Catholic Left. The Catholic Left made attention-grabbing headlines in 1968 as the American press picked up on the enormous public interest sparked by the surprising appearance of priests and nuns in dramatic protests against the Vietnam War. But a few years earlier prominent Catholics had taken to the streets with Martin Luther King, first in Selma, later in Chicago. One of their number, Fr. James Groppi entered the ranks of civil rights heroes as he marched for open housing with youthful black activists in hostile ethnic Catholic neighborhoods right here in Milwaukee. He had counterparts in many American cities where Catholics were shocked and some angered by priests and religious who seemed to switch sides in disputes over open housing, educational reform and public employment. Race was the first wedge to shape what really was a new Catholic Left.

Vietnam was the next. A growing number of priests, religious, and lay people joined long-time Catholic pacifists like Dorothy Day and Gordon Zahn in protesting nuclear weapons, the arms race, and especially the escalating American war in Indo-China. What caught press attention in 1968 of course was the raid on the Catonsville, Maryland, draft board by a group of Catholics. They seized draft records, burned them in the parking lot with homemade napalm, sang hymns and awaited arrest. The group's leaders, Philip and Daniel Berrigan, imprinted themselves on national consciences as The Berrigans. They were the leaders of the most radical wing of the anti-war movement. I remember when Holy Cross produced an issue of its alumni publication on the Berrigans, which caused all kinds of stir. It was later published as a book under the title *The Berrigans* (Casey and Nobile 1971). From that moment on, the phrase, "Catholic Left" had a fairly vivid meaning as a broad movement of Catholics who on the basis of their faith challenged national policy and sought to bring about substantial social change.

The radicals were no longer alone; backing them up were growing numbers of priests, sisters and religious orders called to renewal by the Second Vatican Council. Many orders thought deeply about their work in light of the Gospel and the needs of the church in the world. The coincidence of this renewal movement and the conflicts of the 60s drew substantial numbers of religious priests, brothers and sisters to support work for peace and justice either by enlisting directly in activist work or by supporting those causes in their existing ministries.

While religious orders occupied the cutting edge of the conflict, diocesan clergy were not far behind. The National Federation of Priests' Councils (NFPC), founded in 1967 to represent the new senates and associations of diocesan clergy, soon adopted a very progressive social agenda. The NFPC's Mike Gannon, a priest historian, later with the University of Florida, lined up dozens of priests volunteer to go to North Vietnam and take the place of the POWs. A marvelous spirit of idealism swept through these groups of priests and religious. While there were murmurs of conservative dissent, the momentum stirred by racial conflict, assassinations, and Vietnam created a powerful current to the left. Advocacy of racial justice and opposition to the Vietnam War topped the peace and justice agenda, but there were other causes. Among them was the organizing movement of Cesar Chavez among Mexican American farm workers in California, which drew church support locally and nationally and then through a nationwide boycott of table grapes enlisted the backing of thousands of lay people.

At the same time, urban disorders, sometimes extremely violent, spawned a wide variety of reform efforts with churches at the core. While less inclined to nonviolent direct action than the Berrigans, the activists in these causes increasingly shared the radicals' pessimism about reform, suspicion of government, and alienation from mainstream American culture. This process of radicalization received support from liberation movements in Latin America and from the new liberation theology these movements spawned. As we moved into the 1970s, we got a sense that this was part of the worldwide upsurge in the church that had tremendously significant historical and public importance. Returning missionaries familiar with these currents confirmed suspicions that the deep poverty of the Third World was systemic and that the U.S. government helped sustain authoritarian regimes determined to crush popular movements for social change, many of which were led by priests, sisters, and lay catechists.

This rapid transformation of attitudes toward American society was also supported by the seemingly permanent national commitment to ever more dangerous weapons of mass destruction. In addition, in 1973 as American participation in the Vietnam War ended, the Supreme Court struck down state laws limiting abortion, opening yet another window on what a growing number of Catholic radicals perceived as deeply rooted violence and injustice in American society. The belief that reform had failed and that only systemic structural change, even revolution, would open the way to social justice and world peace became almost a unifying conviction across the Catholic Left.

In the 1960s Catholic social action across the country had the character of an authentic movement aimed at working with other groups to bring about substantial change in the economic and social institutions of the country. The experience of the war on poverty, the failure of civil rights in northern cities, the discovery of deeply rooted sources of poverty, particularly institutional racism, and the terrible violence that punctuated the decade climaxing in the outbreaks that followed the assassination of Dr. King in 1968 all contributed to a radicalization of social discourse, secular and religious, Catholic and non-Catholic.

The presence of a New Left and a Catholic Left shifted the center of society in the Church, at least for a moment. A social gospel spirit influenced many groups within the church and brought in a more radical language. The major Catholic provider of social services, Catholic Charities, represents diocesan and social welfare agencies. Their self-study concluded that while the Church should continue to offer direct social services, it should work to decentralize service delivery, strengthen its capacity to serve as an advocate for the poor before public and private institutions, and rebuild parish capacity to deliver services and serve as a catalyst for social change. Almost Peter Maurin's dream of shelters in parishes. This resulted a few years later in a major effort by Catholic Charities to bring about parish based community organizing aimed at challenging racism, systemic poverty and structural injustice

In 1974 the Bishops themselves launched a national consultation on the theme of liberty and justice for all to mark the national bicentennial. This process climaxed with a Call to Action Conference in Detroit in October of 1976, when delegates from all the nation's dioceses and almost all of its organizations approved recommendations urging pastoral leaders to help the Church better confront racism, economic inequality, global injustice and the arms race. The delegates also urged the bishops to consider problems of injustice within the Church and to examine controversial teachings on women, marriage and sexuality, and divorce. When the bishops ignored the appeals for Church reform and shared responsibility, the stage was set for a period of internal Church conflict which would divide moderates and activists. In the end, it all but destroyed the Catholic Left.

But the Catholic Left never disappeared. Through the late 1970s and the 1980s, the radical edge of the peace movement persisted in actions against nuclear weapons installations by the Plowshares groups linked together in a number of informal networks, many associated with Catholic Worker communities. Many priests, religious and lay people worked openly to oppose the war in Central America, a war America sponsored.

The most active leaders came from religious communities of men and women responding in part to three symbolic moments which seemed to demand a prophetic response: first, the assassination of four religious women in El Salvador; second, the assassination during Mass of El Salvador Archbishop Oscar Romero; and third, the murder of the six Jesuit priests, their housekeeper and her daughter at the University of Central America by an arm of the El Salvador military which was trained in the United States.

Congregations across the country responded to the arrival of Central American refugees by declaring their churches to be sanctuaries. Throughout the period almost every center of poverty and homelessness in the United States saw the creation and re-creation of soup kitchens and shelters sponsored by parishes and independent groups of apostolic laity and religious as well as the Catholic Worker. When the general assault against the social welfare programs picked up steam in the 1980s Catholic leaders, sometimes alone, spoke out strongly and consistently in opposition. The Catholic bishops, even against opposition among their own people, stood out consistently in opposition to capital punishment.

In short, there is no shortage of groups and actions that together might constitute a Catholic Left. If the Catholic Left is defined by faith-based opposition to violence, racism and social injustice, and by a structural rather than reformist interpretation of these issues, and by a determination to work actively to transform society, then the Catholic Left is probably alive out there in the country, although more narrow than it was at the end of the 1960s. What is missing now compared to the 1960s and early 1970s are the alliances, especially the alliance with liberal Catholics which gave the Catholic Left the character of a social movement.

Use of the phrase "left" in any setting raises the question, left of what? The Catholic Left emerging in the 1960s had a pretty quick answer to that usually. The Catholic Left was left of liberal Catholicism. The reform bishops, clergy and religious who dominated post-conciliar American Catholicism seemed to represent the moderate center of Catholic life, linking the radical demands of social and political activists to the pastoral life and organizational dynamics of mainstream Catholicism.

This was surely the image of John Cardinal Dearden, an old school bishop converted at Vatican II to an understanding of the faith that demanded shared responsibility within the Church and disciplined engagement with contemporary social problems. Presiding over the Call to Action Conference, he served as an honest broker between Catholic activists of all sorts and clergy and lay Catholics worried about the Church's apparent shifts to the left. Later, Joseph Cardinal Bernardin would embody a similar liberal center most dramatically when he drew a powerful pastoral letter on nuclear weapons from a committee which included former military chaplain Cardinal John O'Connor on the right and nonviolence activist Thomas Gumbleton on the left. Such leaders, and there were many, were not ordinarily included in the ranks of the Catholic Left but in a real sense they made the Catholic Left possible.

For support they could draw on a distinguished tradition of liberal Catholicism, long a minority stance in Catholic life but vindicated at Vatican II. The Council finally approved church-state separation, renounced a specifically Catholic political agenda, and endorsed human rights including religious liberty. Foundational theological changes, approval of ecumenical dialog, and sharp criticism of the arms race and global economic injustice signaled a new stance for the Church, not counter cultural but incarnational within and not aloof from the struggles of the human family.

In the United States, liberal Catholicism, long known as Americanism, provided a body of ideas which sanctioned the assimilation of European immigrants by affirming the positive values of American democratic institutions and mainstream culture. In the years before the Council, Catholic liberals advocated support for religious liberty, greater intellectual and cultural freedom in the Church and a vigorous lay apostolate directing newly mobile Catholics toward the cause of social reform. As renewal began after the Council, it invariably intersected with the problems of the 1960s, directing pastors and parishioners away from the historic role of maintaining the Catholic subculture and hierarchical compliance toward a new role as active participant in the culture and a more democratic process. Within the church I think that reached its climax at the Call to Action Conference. The Catholic Bishops by that time seemed to embody the agenda of liberal Catholics.

During the Council and in its aftermath they endorsed equal rights for African-Americans, and many encouraged their clergy and religious to work for racial integration. When the cities exploded in riots, the hierarchy responded by launching its own creative war on poverty, the Campaign for Human Development. As the council ended with a document affirming conscientious objection and condemning the arms race and total war, the United States began its massive bombing in North Vietnam and introduced American troops into South Vietnam. Despite the war- time situation, the bishops, for the first time, endorsed the right of conscientious objection and even called for legal protection for selective conscientious objection.

At Vatican II the U.S. bishops had lobbied against the more critical texts on war and peace, but as the Vietnam conflict escalated a growing number of bishops cautiously challenged specific decisions and gradually began to question the war itself. In a remarkable move in 1971 the hierarchy concluded that the war could no longer by justified, using the standard Catholic teaching on a just war. In subsequent years a growing number explored the responsibility of the Church for peacemaking. Over 100 joined Pax Christi, the International Catholic Peace Movement. Others regularly pushed the moral questions surrounding nuclear deterrence. After the Call to Action Conference the bishops, while shelving its proposals for internal reforms, continued to offer critical moral commentary on public policy, from abortion to economic justice to nuclear arms. They stood against American policy in Central America and challenged the drift of foreign and domestic policy during the Reagan administration. This was evident in the two remarkable pastoral letters of the mid 1980s. In *The Challenge of Peace* (1983) the bishops set strict moral limits on deterrence while affirming in the strongest language the Church's responsibility for peace making. In *Economic Justice For All* (1986), they offered a stinging criticism of social policy based on a preferential option for the poor. In both texts, they argued for reform, specified concrete steps they thought should be taken, and urged their fellow Catholics to take up the cause of social justice and world peace.

While their theological analysis and spiritual advice echoed the radical voice of the Catholic Left—nonviolence and the option for the poor—their proposals were moderate, urging limits on the arms race, affirming job creation, supporting government programs on welfare, housing, and medical care. Similarly, while the bishops regularly endorsed specific reform legislation, they made little effort to mobilize popular support, in contrast to their activism on the abortion question. In theory they supported the idea that the pursuit of justice and peace were integral elements of Christian life. But in practice their priorities seemed to lie elsewhere. Close followers of the bishop's conference knew the progressive stands the bishops took on controversial policies, but many more knew of their opposition to abortion, which seemed at times to ally the Church with conservative politicians opposed to Catholic teaching on many other questions.

One of the many ironies of American Catholic history is that the National Conference of Catholic Bishops adopted a great deal of the liberal Catholic agenda, but when they had done so they found that liberal Catholicism as a coherent movement and a compelling set of ideas no longer enjoyed substantial public support. The only people out there interested were the remnants of the Catholic Left. The liberal support group that mediated between the radical wing and the Church at large had shrunk if not disappeared.

Instead, liberal Catholics came under attack from the left because its Americanist reform solutions seemed religiously and politically inadequate. They were attacked from the right because these social reform proposals seemed unnecessary and their religious stance seemed compromised by undue adaptations to secular culture. Perhaps most important, liberal Catholics among the hierarchy, clergy and Church employees found it increasingly difficult to negotiate their way through an organization whose leaders required acceptance of or silence on theological and ecclesiastical issues which were growing in importance and moral force, particularly those dealing with women and with the use of power.

As Catholic piety in the Church at large became more evangelical and as clerical and religious activists found themselves in conflict with Church authorities over a range of issues with women at the center, liberal Catholicism seemed not wrong but simply irrelevant. Similarly, as national politics moved away from the New Deal legacy to policies anchored in the marketplace, liberal Catholicism learned how dependant it had been on: A) secular liberalism with its social reform agenda, B) broad-based social movements like those for peace and civil rights, and C) trade unions, the only sturdy defenders of working people and the strongest bulwark of economic policies the bishops supported such as full employment and a living wage. As each of those lost its hold on public opinion and popular politics, liberal Catholics were left isolated with limited backing within the Church and a sense of political homelessness in the wider society.

This meant a major shift for the more radical Catholic Left which had defined itself in part by its differences with Catholic liberals: nonviolence as opposed to just war, structural analysis and systemic change as opposed to moral commentary and legislative reform, counter cultural witness as opposed to dialog, coalitions and compromise. Still, the two groups needed each other more than they knew. Catholic radicals helped keep liberals from too quick or too close an accommodation with power by continually insisting on radical fidelity to the Gospel. Catholic liberals, in return, forced Catholic radicals to be a bit more responsible. They gave Catholic radicals dialog partners within the Church, provided them with access to the Catholic sub-culture, and translated the radical message into language middle class Catholics might understand.

Community organizing is an approach of the left because it takes the side of the poor and calls for more grassroots participation in deciding social and economic arrangements. But it has a local base and a practical orientation that allows for maximum flexibility. Most importantly, it seeks to integrate have-nots into the existing social and economic system, thereby accepting that system and indeed seeking to strengthen it at least at the local level. When the time comes to solve problems, they seek active government help and partnership in local institutions and community development corporations. I would argue that in trying to reconstruct the sense of movement, the relationship between Catholic radicalism, the Catholic Worker and community organization might be what it was between Catholic radicalism and trade unionism in the 30s. There needs to be a sense of critical partnership.

A lot of good work at peace and justice is going on, then. There are a lot of ideas which give that work legitimacy in the Church. All the elements of a powerful and important social movement akin to the Catholic Left of the 1960s which once gave us so much hope remain. Where better to begin regeneration of the movement than here? I have argued in the past that Dorothy Day stood at the center and not on the margins of the American Catholic Church. It is the rest of us who gravitate away from the center of things. When I met Catholic Workers in 1960, when I read the paper, when I met Dorothy Day and when I run into my Catholic Worker friends, I feel as I did two summers ago in Assisi. Yes, this is my Church and here I am at home. So I can think of no better place to begin rebuilding the Catholic Left as an honorable movement contending for the mind and heart of our Church than here. The Assisi thought is not accidental. Religious orders shrink and die, religious orders are reborn, and new religious orders appear with their own particular charisma and zealous members and faithful non-member friends who find that in renewing themselves they help renew the Church. Our Franciscan-like renewal could draw several themes from Dorothy Day, themes that might be convergent and might help restore a sense of movement. The themes are those I spoke about in 1981.

1. Love for the poor. *The Catholic Worker* began addressing itself to the poor and unemployed in its first issue. Dorothy's love for the poor was never naíve nor sentimental. Nor was it a love of "us" for "them." We should go to the poor, it seemed, not to relieve their woes through our generosity, not for the sake of the Church as a form of evangelization, but for the sake of ourselves so we might live with integrity. It was what the great Jane Adams once called "the subjective necessity of settlement." If you believe noble things and never do noble deeds, those noble thoughts fade and die, die with your spirit. For the young who stopped in at the Worker for a time and then went on to other things, their Worker period was a bright light, not because they worked, which they did, not because they eliminated poverty, which they didn't, but because for a brief time they lived with a kind of integrity never to be recaptured. They had given of themselves and practiced the works of mercy, not to gain merit in heaven, but to be brothers and sisters to other men and women and thus be at peace with themselves.

The older life long Catholic Workers have a serenity, a strength, a wholeness about them which is mysterious and altogether unique. It arises from the fact they have lived according to their values as best they could. Blessed are those who do that, if only for a time. This is no small thing to live and work in ways that bear some relationship to our beliefs. That work is vocation, useful work done for the common good and thus good for us. Once Catholic Workers and their friends talked seriously about the meaning, not just the ethics of work.

Today in Latin America liberation theologians speak of the need for liberation agronomists and economists and specialists. There is no area in which we in Catholic higher education could do more good. Dorothy always spoke of work to student groups. Many of my fine students yearn for work that makes sense. It's an area in which we can work together and build bridges between lay Catholics and Catholic radicals to renew a sense of movement. So the work of the Worker goes on, benefitting the Workers themselves and those folks who visit, donate and cook because it provides a way for many to practice the message of the Gospel and perhaps in the process develop a real solidarity with the poor. For the way of the Worker and the way of the modern Church is not "us" helping "them," not reaching down from our elevated status to uplift the poor, but discovering a love for the poor which illuminates our common humanity and leads us to express with them our shared responsibility for our Church and the world.

I have this constant frustration that we never find ways of helping students who make contact with the Catholic Worker and Catholic Worker-like experiences when they're young to find ways to integrate that experience into the vocation that they then pursue. It is that old syndrome of what to do after JVC (Jesuit Volunteer Corps), as they say on Jesuit campuses all the time. The lack of a home, lack of community, lack of support, lack of an ability to sustain a vision of useful work that should be convergent ground between people in pastoral ministry, people in education and people in social service and social action.

2. Love for the non-poor. The Christian commitment to people is a commitment to real people. John Paul said men and women must be loved for their own sake. Dorothy Day could be angry, and she could be tough, but in the end she trusted in people and knew that it was wrong to judge others. In her life in the Church there was no contempt for those who feared the message of Christ by which she was trying to live. If we are to love the poor as they are, we must love Catholics as they are: "Their perseverance in worship week after week, holyday after holyday has always impressed me and filled my heart with a sense of love for all my fellow Catholics, even Birchites, bigots, racists, priests and lay people alike, whom I can term 'my enemies' whom I am bided to love," Dorothy wrote. "Our worst enemies are of our own household," Scripture says. We are united, however, as people are united in marriage, by the deepest spiritual bond, participation in the sacraments, so that we have become "one flesh" in the Mystical Body. (CW 5/1967:2)

Robert Coles pointed again and again to that attitude toward ordinary people. He thought that Dorothy loved St. Therese because she was so much like the rest of us in her ordinariness. Coles argued

> *The Catholic Worker* was meant to address plain, ordinary working-men and women....She never wanted to lose contact with these people; never wanted to lead them, either, or tell them that they were being tricked, duped, fooled—and so, by implication, tell them they were dumb and gullible; never wanted to look upon herself as knowing, as "mature" and "responsible," an example to benighted, illusion-saddled "masses" who needed to be uplifted by their betters....Radical as Dorothy Day has been, she has never wanted to sever her connection with those who don't think, let alone act or, more broadly, live as she does, but who submit to life's everyday demands....(Coles 1973: 55)

Coles offers an important point. I would argue that the biggest civil problem we have in the country is our distrust, our enormous distrust of other people. How many conversations do you have with people—students, faculty and others—in which everyone in the room is okay but everyone outside is really no good anymore? We've lost the connectedness with others. The enormous distrust of people runs all through the Church, and it's just awful. This is not a democratic spirit; you can't build a democratic movement with such massive distrust.

3. Love for the Church. How Dorothy loved the Church, its traditions and odd structures, its rich assortment of persons and personalities, its saints and its martyrs. So much did people like Dorothy love the Church that, like Daniel Berrigan, they "could not recognize themselves apart from it." Envision a ragged and dirty Peter Maurin sleeping on a bench in the station while a respectable Holy Name president searches the station for his speaker. Dorothy Day traveling on buses like a nomad between Catholic oases. Ammon Hennacy trying to make an enemy into a friend. Each of them were saying in their own eccentric way, "Wherever the Lord leads us, let us go, and let us go together."

The Church changes as we change, Dorothy wrote. More that most, Dorothy helped moved the Church through her life and her writings. Increasingly, we know that our Church depends upon the personal decisions of ordinary members. Dorothy Day was there early, inviting everyone to consider what they were doing with their lives. For herself, she knew the dramatic moments of conversion were rare and grace-filled. At least as important were the daily experiences of life. None defined the responsibilities of Christian commitment in more dreadful and demanding ways; none bore those demands with greater wit, modesty and courage. Dorothy had no wish to challenge the institutionalized Church or make life uncomfortable for anybody in it, even Bishops. "I didn't ever see myself as posing a challenge to church authority." she told Coles.

> I was a Catholic then, and I am now, and I hope and pray I die one. I have not wanted to challenge the church, not on any of its doctrinal positions. I try to be loyal to the church—to its teachings, its ideals. I love the church with all my heart and soul. I never go inside a church without thanking God Almighty for giving me a home. The church *is* my home, and I don't want to be homeless. I may work with the homeless, but I have had no desire to join their ranks. (Coles 1987: 82)

Many have said from time to time that Dorothy was too docile, too respectful. Perhaps she was. Those who are born Catholic take the Church for granted, and they feel freer than she did to challenge the authorities and demand reform. But Dorothy was no patsy. For years people worried about her oft quoted remark that if Cardinal Spellman demanded that *The Catholic Worker* close down, she would quickly do so. In fact, in 1951 a request did come from the chancery to remove the name Catholic from the masthead. Dorothy refused, pointing out that the Catholic War Veterans used the name and no one identified their views with those of the hierarchy. But she admitted later she was concerned that the pressure would continue, and she had thought about what to do. For one thing, she respected Cardinal Spellman as, "our spiritual leader—of all of us who live here in New York."(Coles 1973: 82) "But he is not our ruler," she quickly added. "No one in the Church can tell me what to think about social, political and economic questions without getting a tough speech back." Coles asked her one time what would she have done if the 1951 inquiry had been pursued.

> I never believed that the monsignor who wanted us to shut down or delete the word *Catholic* from our paper was acting on his own. I'm sure at least a few monsignori were in on the act. Maybe his eminence, the cardinal. Maybe not. I think they realized that we were going to pray *very hard*, to pray and pray: in churches and in homes and even on the streets of our cities. We were ready to go to Saint Patrick's, fill up the church, stand outside it, in prayerful meditation. We were ready to take advantage of America's freedoms so that we could say what we thought and do what we believed was the right thing to do: seek the guidance of the Almighty. (Coles 1987: 84)

So they always prayed for the Cardinal, and "If he had ordered us closed, we might have gone right to Saint Patrick's Cathedral and continued our praying there, day and night, until the good Lord took us or settled the matter."(Coles 1987: 85)

But witness, not conflict, was her normal style: "It took me some years to find my place in the church," Dorothy recalled.

> It wasn't mine by birth or even youth. I came to it at the onset of my middle years, I guess you could say. I wasn't going to rush all over telling people what *I* thought *they* should be thinking and saying and doing. I felt like a lucky guest for a while, then at home, and then I did decide to try to be as loyal as possible to the example set by the head of the household and let that loyalty, if it was achieved, be my testimony, my critique. (Coles 1987: 88)

Maybe we could call this the common ground approach: loyal, grateful, articulate but not demanding, ready for dialog, getting on with the work with the hand of fellowship always extended, and in the end, trusting the Spirit.

Finally I'd like to say a word about Catholic Worker politics. National politics need reconstructing. In light of the need for national political reconstruction, people might take more seriously the reading of modern history of Peter Maurin and Dorothy Day, especially the latter's understanding of what democracy requires. Miss Day had her own well thought out version of the former Speaker of the House Tip O'Neil's dictum that all politics is local. Responsibility, like justice and charity, begins at home and requires not only the Catholic Worker's gentle personalism, but decentralization of power and continuing experiments in participation. Without such communitarian strategies—political and economic—Christian and American ideas of human dignity and democratic self government become meaningless language covering the continuing atrocities of the twentieth century. "A good citizen uses the Bill of Rights, says what he believes to be true and shares his thoughts with others," Dorothy said. "A good citizen *takes part in democracy*, doesn't leave it to others—some big-shots—to speak for him, to act for him."(Coles 1987: 107) This is the language of American radicals, a language with which we American Catholics have had too few conversations. For Dorothy, who knew well some of the century's leading intellectuals, Peter Maurin was a man whose good intellectual food, as she called it, was to be taken seriously. She meant to launch no "cute little experiment," but a movement to explore better ways of human living and working. Ways which could and should attract and convince serious people. She was also democratic to her bones; this is the heart of the politics, I think.

What we miss most of all is her democratic spirit. On his first visit to the New York Worker house as a troubled medical student, Robert Coles found Dorothy Day engaged in a long one-sided conversation. She, silent, was nodding in response to another woman's alcoholic "ranting." Finally she politely excused herself, came over to Coles and asked, "are you waiting to talk with one of us?"

With those last three words, Coles recalls, she had cut through layers of self importance, of a lifetime of bourgeois privilege, and scraped the hard bone of pride. Later she told him, as a youngster "there was something in me...that made me stop and look at people, at certain people, and wonder and wonder about their lives, how they lived, and wonder if I could ever do it, live the way they did."(Coles 1987: 19)

Day felt a joy and pride in the courage of men who marched on Washington in 1932: "I wanted to go and *be* with the people I heard all those learned folks talking about." She did, and in the process she discovered "a neighborliness that is both spiritual and political in nature."(Coles 1987: 102-103) She liked people. It was this concrete form of human love, not guilt or middle class alienation, which filled her with an outrage which worried her. Recalling her feelings at the time of her conversion, she told Coles that she felt that charity was a word to choke over. "Who wanted charity? And it was not just human pride but a strong sense of man's dignity and worth, and what was due him in justice, that made me resent, rather than feel proud of so mighty a sum total of Catholic institutions."(Coles 1987: 58)

Coles observed that it was Maurin who taught her "that the spirit of the Catholic church has to be fought for," and "that it is foolish and sinful to accept the reality of a particular society by sitting back and railing against its great power and awesome resources, thereby abdicating one's responsibility to use one's God-given capacity for independent initiatives."(Coles 1987: 72)

So the Church, its culture and its symbols, as well as those of the nation, have to be fought for, especially by people who share Dorothy Day's democratic confidence in ordinary people. Understanding that and acting on it by entering the cultural and political struggle in Church and society would not be a bad place to begin the reconstruction of the Catholic Left.

So there we are. Let's try to reinvent a Catholic Left by claiming a place in and sharing responsibility for the Church we love. Let's begin by loving the poor and the democratic way of Dorothy Day and Peter Maurin and welcoming all those who work to empower the poor, especially those in labor unions, community organizations. Let's begin by loving the non-poor, especially our newly liberated well-to-do Catholic brothers and sisters and their children. Let's not write them off or leave them by default to the right, Catholic or secular. Let's contend for their minds and hearts. Let's begin by loving them with the same respect we extend to the poor, then by renewing in unapologetic ways our attention to politics—to the use and abuse of power, to the reality not just the choice of political responsibility—and trust and work with our people to renew our Church.

At Holy Cross we have a first year program, the theme of which is, marvelously, "How then shall we live?" Every year faculty spend a lot of time talking to students about that."The way people live was of enormous interest to Dorothy Day," Coles wrote. "She thought hard and long about how one ought to live this life and how one ought to respond to others as they struggle with the same question."(Coles 1987: xxi) That was her central question, he thinks: how then should we live this life?

Elements of an answer are found in her work. Coles clearly recalled Day's answer when he asked her how she wanted to be remembered:

> She first made sure I remembered her pleasure in appreciating this life's contradictions and its inevitable inconsistencies....She then took up the challenge and repeated what I had heard before—her wish to be defined and remembered as a member of a particular

Christian community, as an ardent seeker after God who, with some devotion, had followed His example "after a few false starts." Then after pausing to look out the window, after retreat into silence, she said slowly, quoting the archbishop of Paris, Cardinal Suhard, "To be a witness does not consist in engaging in propaganda or even in stirring people up, but in being a living mystery; it means to live in such a way that one's life would not make sense if God did not exist." (Coles 1987: 159-160)

Roots of the Catholic Worker Movement: Saints and Philosophers Who Influenced Dorothy Day and Peter Maurin

Mark and Louise Zwick

Founders, Casa Juan Diego
Editors, *Houston Catholic Worker*

Dorothy Day and Peter Maurin developed a unique synthesis of ideas, faith and radical witness in the Catholic Worker movement. They created something with deep roots in the richness of the Catholic tradition and Catholic social teaching, combined with their own originality, insight, prayer and commitment to the poor and peace.

The Houston Catholic Worker has been engaged in intensive research and study over the past several years on saints, philosophers, theologians, radical social thinkers and literary figures who influenced Dorothy and Peter as they put together the vision of the Catholic Worker. These influences included Emmanuel Mounier, Nicolas Berdyaev, Fr. Virgil Michel, O.S.B., Jacques and Raissa Maritain, Fr. John Hugo, Fyodor Dostoevsky, Peter Kropotkin, Fr. Vincent McNabb, O.P., G. K. Chesterton and Saints Benedict, Teresa of Avila, Catherine of Siena, Francis of Assisi, Thomas Aquinas and Therese of Lisieux. The vision of Dorothy Day and Peter Maurin which included the ideas that came from these thinkers and saints provides a model for living as a radically committed Catholic in the world one hundred years after the birth of Dorothy Day. How and why did we at the Houston Catholic Worker decide to focus on the formative forces in the lives of Peter Maurin and Dorothy Day?

We had been in touch with the Catholic Worker movement since we were teenagers, when we were in the seminary and seventeen years old. Jim Clarke, also a seminarian, was a captain in the New York fire department who became one of Dorothy's favorite pacifists and later a Capuchin. He gave us our first copies of *The Catholic Worker* after World War II. When we visited the New York Worker decades later, Jim celebrated the Mass.

We had gotten to know Fr. John Hugo, Fr. Louis Farina, and Fr. Urban Gerhart over the years; their lives were restricted because of their involvement in the retreat that influenced Dorothy so much. We had made the retreat recently. Mark had made the retreat at age 20 and 40 years later we made it again. We also knew Bishop John Dearden, Mark's seminary rector, who was sent to Pittsburgh to manage the controversy around Fr. Hugo, who was Dorothy Day's spiritual director.

In the '60s we were involved with the civil rights movement and the peace movement.

In the early 70s we read William Miller's book, *A Harsh and Dreadful Love* (1973), and thanks to Dan Berrigan we read most of what Jacques Ellul had published; he influenced the later CW movement. Mark, who attended graduate school at the University of Chicago, worked in mental health services during this time as a psychiatric social worker, gaining valuable experience. We organized and helped the United Farm Workers in California. And we related to Catholic Worker houses in Northern California. During this time Louise attended graduate school at the University of California at Berkeley in library science, children's literature and children's librarianship.

In 1977 we moved to El Salvador to learn Spanish, to learn about the Hispanic culture and base communities. Archbishop Oscar Romero was made archbishop while we were there. We did not know the war would be starting and that for the safety of our young children we would be forced to leave before our time was up.

Our time in El Salvador was a powerful experience in living with the poor in a level of poverty most Americans have not observed. As we saw the Church standing with the poor in the midst of oppression, we had a different picture of the institutional church. It drove us to our knees and deeper into our faith. We remembered again the Catholic Worker and were challenged to do more.

In 1980 we started the Casa Juan Diego Catholic Worker in Houston to provide hospitality to refugees from the wars in Central America. People were pouring into Houston from these wars, sleeping in used car lots because they had no place to stay. Other Catholic Workers soon came to join in the work. Immediately we also began publishing the *Houston Catholic Worker* in Spanish and English.

Our children were in the fourth and sixth grade when Casa Juan Diego began; Louise worked as a children's librarian at Houston Public Library for eleven years while Mark ran the CW house and cared for the children after school. When the children grew up, Louise was able to leave her job and join Mark full-time at the Worker.

We prayed and studied as we provided a home for refugees who had no home, hoping to grasp the essence of the Worker movement and read most of the literature in print. We read Miller's biography of Dorothy Day,(1982) we read *By Little and By Little,* now published as *Selected Writings of Dorothy Day* (Day, 1983, 1992). We read Mel Piehl's book, *Breaking Bread* (1982). We read *Revolution of the Heart* (Coy 1988). We read *The Long Loneliness* (Day 1952) and *Loaves and Fishes* (Day 1963). We meditated and reflected again on Matthew 25 and the Sermon on the Mount. We didn't know from day to day whether or not we would be jailed for receiving undocumented immigrants and refugees in our houses, as had happened to others in the sanctuary movement.

The Houston community translated into Spanish Robert Ellsberg's introduction to *By Little and By Little,* so highly praised by Robert Coles, Eileen Egan's pamphlet, *The Permanent Revolution* (1983), and chapters on Peter Maurin and Dorothy Day from John Mitchell's book, *Critical Voices in American Economic Thought* (1989). We attended a number of Catholic Worker gatherings in various parts of the country. As the Central American wars waned, we began receiving immigrants from Mexico and South America as well as Central America.

None of this prepared us for the bombshell of Ann O'Connor's article in the *New Oxford Review* (March 1994) on "Dorothy Day's Crumbling Legacy." She protested the rebellion of many Catholic Worker houses and individuals against Church doctrines and disciplines, insisting that much of the CW had become "incoherent, if not downright dishonest in claiming the name *Catholic* Worker." It did not prepare us for the follow-up letters like that of Geoffrey Gneuhs, declaring the Worker movement dead. It didn't prepare us for Rosalie

Troester's book, *Voices from the Catholic Worker* (1993), in which Marc Ellis says that the Worker "made its intellectual and cultural contributions to the Catholic Church in the thirties. And then again in the sixties and seventies." And then Ellis declared, "It will never again be a major force in the same way; the movement that informs the North American church is liberation theology. That's where the cutting edge is." It didn't prepare us for David Stein's saying in *Voices:* "I don't see the Catholic Worker as having the remotest thing to do with being Catholic."

We tried to respond to the *New Oxford Review,* but they wouldn't publish our responses, nor those of our friends. We only would have liked to say that if the CW is dead, it is only partly dead, because we knew it was alive and well in a number of places. What could we do? We weren't comfortable taking an approach of attacking others in the movement. We couldn't imagine who would listen to us if we tried to convince everyone that the Catholic Worker movement really was a great movement, that there were no problems. We wanted people to know of the greatness of the founders and what the movement had to offer in pulling together a vision for our times.

At this moment there came to us a book that changed our lives: Sr. Brigid Merriman's *Searching for Christ: the Spirituality of Dorothy Day* (1994).We were fascinated by Merriman's study of the various influences on Dorothy Day's spirituality. We thought it so good that we used it to counteract the negative publicity of O'Connor, Gneuhs and Ellis. We wrote to the bishops of the United States to see if they were interested in the book and 60 cardinals, archbishops and bishops responded in the positive.

From Merriman we received the inspiration to go to the roots of the movement, to do a serious study of the thought of the Catholic Worker which would help ourselves as much as anyone to discover what was really at the heart of the thought of Peter and Dorothy. It was so clear that the richness of the movement was not just a few thoughts out of the heads of Peter and Dorothy. It was not just a social action movement to help the poor or work for peace.

We discovered again that Peter and Dorothy were thoroughly founded in the best of Catholic tradition. They were a part of the great movement in this century in the Church of *ressourcement,* retrieving the tradition, going back to the sources. This *ressourcement* and that of the personalist movement were both rooted in France. Peter, an undocumented immigrant from France, was a part of this and brought this thought to the United States; his French was very important to the movement. This *ressourcement* included Peter's emphasis on making the social encyclicals click, studying and quoting the Fathers of the Church, early Church Councils (especially one requiring parishes to have houses of hospitality), and retrieving the insights of both well-known and more obscure saints throughout the history of the Church. In addition, Dorothy Day brought insights from literature, especially Dostoevsky, and from pacifism and anarchism.

As our research proceeded, we discovered Anne Klejment's index to *The Catholic Worker* (1986) in the local university library. In addition to excellent references from Merriman's and other books, we were able to identify articles from the *Worker* itself through this index and receive copies through the kind assistance of Phil Runkel at the Marquette University Archives.

The idea of a series on the figures who influenced the movement developed, with the plan of printing some of their original ideas, encyclicals or other writings about saints which Dorothy and Peter and the early Workers read as they studied these thinkers and saints. Since many of the books we needed were out of print and not available locally, we requested them on interlibrary loan from other cities. The library of the local Catholic university, the University of St. Thomas in Houston, allowed Louise, a librarian, to climb among dusty volumes in the basement to find old issues of *Orate Fratres* and other periodicals.

All during this time we have continued receiving immigrants and refugees in our houses. They arrive from a terrible, dangerous journey crossing several countries, hiding out, going through many days and nights of walking (often without food or water), facing robbery, rape, wild animals and snakes as they walk or try to sleep outside at night. Our guests arrive with only the shirts on their backs, shoes in tatters, feet swollen, legs bitten and often covered with allergic reaction to plants. As they tell us about their journey, they say, "God did not abandon us in the worst times." Others, of course, do not make it through at all. Some have been shot, others have drowned in the river. Some have died from lack of water in the desert.

We listened to the arguments and acrid debates between liberals and conservatives in the Church and found them more and more irrelevant. As we continued our research on the profound roots of the Catholic Worker movement, we saw that it goes far beyond these debates. It provides a Catholic vision that not only incorporates the best of the tradition and the living out of the Sermon on the Mount and Matthew 25, but also insists on the construction of a more just social order.

Roots of the Catholic Worker Movement

Our research acquainted us with Emmanuel Mounier, whose *Personalist Manifesto* (1938) was one of Peter Maurin's favorite books. He arranged for the monks of St. John's Abbey to translate it into English. It is to Mournier that we owe the Catholic Worker emphasis on personal responsibility in history (not withdrawal from the world). It was Mournier who said, "One does not free a man by detaching him from the bonds that paralyze him; one frees a man by attaching him to his destiny."

The personalist view had an amazing early understanding and harsh critique of the consumerism that so plagues our society today: "On the altar of this sad world there is but one god, smiling and hideous: the bourgeois... For him there is only prosperity, health, common sense, balance, sweetness of life, comfort. Comfort is to the bourgeois world what heroism was to the Renaissance and sanctity to medieval Christianity—the ultimate value, the ultimate motive for all action."

Peter Maurin, in his special style of distilling difficult writings and the profound thought of the age and of the tradition into his Easy Essays, captured Mounier's ideas in his Easy Essay, "The Personalist."

A personalist
is a go-giver,
not a go-getter.
He tries to give
what he has,
and does not
try to get
what the other fellow has.
He tries to be good
by doing good
to the other fellow.
He is altro-centered
not self-centered.
He has a social doctrine
of the common good.

He spreads the social doctrine
of the common good
through words and deeds.
He speaks through deeds
as well as words
for he knows that deeds
speak louder than words.
Through words and deeds
he brings into existence
a community,
the common unity
of a community. (Maurin 1984: 116-117)

The emphasis here on the common good is from St. Thomas Aquinas, frequently quoted by Dorothy and Peter. The article on St. Thomas in our series on the roots of the movement, in the November 1997 issue of the *Houston Catholic Worker,* is by Michael Dauphinais, a doctoral student at Notre Dame.

As that example shows, we did not personally write all the articles in the series. Other authors include Jim Allaire of the Winona Catholic Worker, who wrote about Dorothy and St. Therese of Lisieux, and Joe Peabody of Houston, who wrote two articles, one on Dostoevsky and the other on Peter Kropotkin. Rosemary Hugo wrote about her uncle, Fr. John Hugo, who gave the retreat Dorothy loved so much, that she called the "Bread of the strong," giving insight into the depth of the thought and spirituality of Fr. Hugo. Fr. Hugo's retreat was more than a retreat: it was an introduction to all the classic spiritual writers, e.g., St. John of the Cross, Teresa of Avila, St. Francis de Sales, DeCaussade, Lallemont. It was also an introduction to spiritual direction and penance. The retreat continues to be given today in Pittsburgh and Detroit. Fr. Hugo was restored to respect when Cardinal Wright went to Pittsburgh.

The second article in the series took us to research the work of Fr. Virgil Michel, a Benedictine who was a great friend of the Worker. He brought to Dorothy and Peter his emphasis on the relationship of social action and the communal nature of worship united in the concept of the Mystical Body of Christ, which was affirmed in 1943 by the encyclical *Mystici Corporis* of Pius XII. Fr. Michel carried on the anti-bourgeois spirit of Mounier, but is well-known as the person who tried to popularize participation in liturgy as the transforming action needed to transform society. Like Mounier, he insisted on engagement with the world, teaching that the liturgy is the source of the true Christian spirit and must be the source of the application of the principles of solidarity in our common life and civilization. He was anything but sectarian, but he was against the Americanist trend which instead of challenging American culture with the Gospel, accommodated to it. His essay in *Orate Fratres* on the bourgeois spirit (the emphasis on profit and accumulation of goods and wealth above all which undermines all Christian renewal) is classic. Fr. Michel also helped to bring the Benedictine spirit to the movement. This recalls Stanley Vishnewski's famous quote: "I am sure that without the influence of the Benedictines that there would be very little in the Catholic Worker Movement—for from the Benedictines we got the ideal of Hospitality–Guest Houses–Farming Communes–Liturgical Prayer. Take these away and there is very little left in the Catholic Worker Program." (Merriman 1994: 107)

From Virgil Michel we went to Nicolas Berdyaev, one of the great personalists and a "particular prophet" of the Catholic Worker movement. With the gift of his genius he explored the meaning of the life of the spirit in the twentieth century, as William Miller stated in *A Harsh and Dreadful Love* (1973).

> Nicholas Berdyaev (1874-1948), A Russian philosopher exiled for his opposition to the Russian Revolution, saw the central historical problem of his age as the ascendancy of the bourgeois spirit. For Berdyaev, the word "bourgeois" designated not a social, economic, or ethical condition but rather a spiritual state and a direction of the soul. In essence, the bourgeois spirit was a pursuit of the material aspects of life and an endless search for the expedient and the useful. The bourgeois was an "idolater" of this world.... The center of life, the spiritual had been exiled to the periphery.... Berdyaev lamented that the will to power and affluence had triumphed over the will to holiness and genius. (Ellis 1981: 87)

Another important theme in Berdyaev's works which found an echo in Peter Maurin and in the CW movement was an understanding of history quite different from that of most historians and political philosophers of the nineteenth and twentieth centuries. Berdyaev's view of history is beyond time. For him history has nothing to do with material success, with progress or achievement, or with seeking the idolatries of power, lust or comfort. Berdyaev understood that in the Incarnation and Redemption, Christ stands at the center of history and that the human person, made in the image and likeness of God, is meant to participate with God in the building of the New Creation.

The Bourgeois Spirit Continues Today

We saw this "bourgeois spirit" all around us. We spoke to immigrants every day who had left their homes and their families because they could not survive on the pittance foreign and multinational companies paid them in maquiladoras placed in their countries to take advantage of labor so cheap it was slave labor. Manufacturing jobs in the United States that paid $14.00 an hour were replaced by maquiladoras in Honduras that paid $14.00 per week. We had thought progress had cured the abuses of the Industrial Revolution, of slave labor, child labor, chimney sweeps described by Dickens, but all these abuses have returned in the global economy. Immigrants and refugees who came to live in our houses of hospitality over the past seventeen years told us about these jobs; on these salaries they could either eat or pay housing expenses, not both. Immigration to the United States by at least one family member often seemed the only solution. A new Dickens was needed.

As we observed suburban life styles and the accumulation of goods in the United States, we identified very much with these great thinkers who were so outspoken about the destructiveness of the bourgeois spirit. We commented on these things as we continued to publish the *Houston Catholic Worker*. They brought accusations of being Communists.

We also began to absorb the religiosity of our guests from Latin America. We have Mass every week; Spanish-speaking priests from the Galveston-Houston diocese come in to celebrate it, in turn. We process through the streets to our various houses on Good Friday for the Way of the Cross. A great celebration occurs on December 12, the Feast of Our Lady of Guadalupe, when she appeared to Juan Diego in 1531. Liberation theologians, except for Gustavo Gutierrez, would be disappointed in the way we have been seduced by the popular piety, the color, of the Latin culture.

We learned of the importance of the beautiful story of Our Lady of Guadalupe, who appeared to Juan Diego, a poor Native American person of great faith, a symbol of a people despised and considered less than human by the *conquistadores*. She chose him to evangelize the Native Americans and the Spaniards, the Bishop and the middle management of the Church, even though this person of great faith did not speak Spanish. This poor Native American not only was not familiar with the historical-critical method, or with United States democracy, he didn't even know how to read and write in his own language—a language forbidden by the *conquistadores*.

Mary, the mother of Jesus, now known in Mexico and throughout the world as Our Lady of Guadalupe, appeared to Juan Diego as a brown-skinned Aztec princess and spoke to him in his native tongue, the forbidden Nahuatl. She had a mission for Juan Diego. This appearance of Juan Diego changed the face of that Church and radically renewed it. There was a new-found, unheard of dignity in the choice of Juan Diego as a messenger.

We visited the Basilica of Our Lady of Guadalupe each time we went to Mexico City as we worked to found houses in Mexico and later Guatemala to help immigrants as they made their difficult journey to the United States, and also battered and homeless or pregnant women in Mexico. Each time we went to "La Villa," as it is affectionately called by all in Mexico, we were struck again by the powerful message of this great event.

Our life with Hispanic immigrants made us realize again the greatness of the saints who had been at the very least marginalized in the euphoria after Vatican II in the '60s and ''0s.

We were thus better prepared to appreciate the importance of the saints as models for Dorothy Day and Peter Maurin.

Saints as Models

St. Francis of Assisi was one of the most important models for the Catholic Worker because of his radical commitment to the Gospel. The heart of the Worker movement, expressed in love and service of the poor, personalism, voluntary poverty, pacifism, and participation in manual labor, had been brought to the world in a dramatic and unique way by St. Francis many centuries earlier. Dorothy and Peter and the early Workers studied especially the Johannes Jorgensen biography of St. Francis (1912) and the encyclicals about him, especially those of Pius XI and Leo XIII. They read books like Jorgensen's during mealtimes.

St. Francis, like the Catholic Worker, saw pacifism as the living out of the Gospel, especially the Sermon on the Mount. He made the refusal to bear arms a condition of membership in his Third Order, and thus changed the face of Europe without firing a single shot—there were few people left to fight battles for the nobles. We might say that Francis wrote the book on reform and revolution. His was a great reformation, and like Attila the Hun he decided not to sack Rome to accomplish it. Dorothy Day quoted St. Francis in several articles in *The Catholic Worker* in the '30s when she wrote against violence; Peter Maurin quoted him often regarding voluntary poverty. St. Francis is one of those saints who speak to people of all ages and centuries. His life was a very radical adherence to the Gospel and is a continuing challenge to the Catholic Worker movement and to all Christians.

Dorothy frequently mentioned three great women saints in her writings: St. Catherine of Siena, St. Teresa of Avila and St. Therese of Lisieux. In her earlier years as a Catholic it was the first two that were her inspiration, and later she turned to St Therese of Lisieux and her Little Way. It is most interesting to note that all three of these women are now doctors of the Church.

A study of Dorothy's writings shows that she was familiar with biographies of these great women and also with their own writings. One of her favorite quotes from St. Catherine was "All the way to heaven is heaven because He said I am the way." This saying relates to Catherine's idea of Christ as the bridge between heaven and earth, by reason of his having joined himself with our humanity.

Dorothy had read Catherine's dialogue with God during ecstasy, *The Dialogue*, and quoted it. Some of the passages resonate closely with passages of Dostoevsky which Dorothy often quoted:

> If you have received my love sincerely without self-interest, you will drink your neighbor's love sincerely. It is just like a vessel that you fill at the fountain. If you take it out of the fountain to drink the vessel is soon empty. But if you hold your vessel in the fountain while you drink, it will not get empty: Indeed, it will always be full. So the love of your neighbor, whether spiritual or temporal, is meant to be drunk in me, without any self-interest. I ask you to love me with the same love with which I love you. But for me you cannot do this, for I love you without being loved....So you cannot give me the kind of love I ask of you. This is why I have put you among your neighbors: so that you can do for them what you cannot do for me—that is, love them without any concern for thanks and without looking for any profit for yourself. And whatever you do for them I will consider done for me. (1980)

Dorothy tells us in *The Long Loneliness* that she was first introduced to Teresa of Avila when years before her conversion to Catholicism she read William James' *The Varieties of Religious Experience* (1902). James was skeptical on religion, but he presented Teresa as one of the ablest women on record—even though he felt it was "a pity that so much vitality of soul should have found such poor employment." James' emphasis on the correlation between personal prayer and personal life and action drew Dorothy Day to Teresa.

In the 1920s and 30s she read Teresa's autobiographical *Life* and her *Foundations*. Dorothy concentrated on the great mystic's teachings regarding the fruits of prayer, not on her visions and extraordinary experiences. She related to Teresa's struggle with mediocrity for seventeen years, even while she was in the convent. Dorothy speaks about this in *From Union Square to Rome* (1938):

> "I wished to live," [Teresa]wrote, "but I saw clearly that I was not living, but rather wrestling with the shadow of death; there was no one to give me life, and I was not able to take it...."
> The shadow of death that she spoke of was the life she was leading, purposeless, disordered, a constant succumbing to second-best, to the less-than-perfect which she desired. As a convert I can say these things, knowing how many times I turned away, almost in disgust, from the idea of God and giving myself up to Him. (154-55)

This is the fear of conversion and its consequences that Dorothy Day, like Teresa, had to face.

Dorothy Day's devotion to St. Joseph originally came from her reading of St. Teresa, who counted on his prayer for practical help for her foundations. Dorothy also relied on St. Joseph as her banker and asked his help in all kinds of practical situations.

A central theme of St. Teresa's writings is that all are called to the summit of the mountain in prayer, that the mercy of God is reaching out to every soul, even though it may take a long time for a person to respond. What is required of each one is a change of heart, a change so profound that a person will be able to perceive and follow the voice of the Holy Spirit. Great saints and mystics like St. Teresa helped to convince Dorothy of the universal call to holiness of the Gospel, a call which includes lay people as well as priests and religious. The Catholic Worker embraced these ideas long before the Second Vatican Council promulgated them.

Dorothy's interest in and devotion to St. Teresa was evident when she named her child for her.

Around the time of her becoming a Catholic, Dorothy found St. Therese of Lisieux's *The Story of a Soul* to be "colorless, monotonous, too small in fact for my notice." Dorothy dismissed the book as "pious pap." She preferred the more heroic saints like Teresa of Avila and Catherine.

But by the early 1950s, after doing the Works of Mercy in Catholic Worker houses for twenty years, Dorothy saw the wisdom of "The Little Way" and actually wrote a book about St. Therese of Lisieux.

We have to remember that Dorothy was a part of the Catholic renaissance earlier in this century, which included a new approach to hagiography. Dorothy wrote strongly on this subject, insisting on a more realistic view to replace the romanticized and embroidered, sweet books previously available on many saints. She, like many today, was offended by saccharine descriptions of these great women and men who had offered so much during their lives of faith and struggles to create a new heaven and a new earth where justice dwells.

Jim Allaire, in his article in the *Houston Catholic Worker* asked, "What was it in the life and teachings of Therese of Lisieux that Dorothy Day found so compelling?" He answered, "First and foremost, of course, was Therese's Little Way, the way of absolute abandonment of ourselves to the love and mercy of God, trusting that God will sustain us in all that we are and do....In Therese's understanding, no act, however apparently insignificant, is without meaning when done within the awareness of God's loving presence. The Little Way is the ordinary way we can all become saints." (5-6/96:1,6)

Dorothy was very aware of the redemptive value of suffering and quoted St. Paul often on how our sufferings were meant to fill up the sufferings of Christ. She related to Therese's idea of bringing redemptive love to bear on the pain of this Earth through the acceptance of one's own suffering joined to the cross of Christ. As Allaire commented in his article, "These teachings are not easy to assimilate. No wonder Dorothy once spoke of Therese as a saint we should dread." (5-6/96:6)

Dorothy herself was committed to becoming a saint, and she expected that all who follow Christ should want to become saints as well. She wrote, "We are all called to be saints, St. Paul says, and we might as well get over our bourgeois fear of the name. We might also get used to recognizing the fact that there is some of the saint in all of us." Allaire further quoted Dorothy from a notebook in the Archives from November 1951, where she insisted that becoming a saint was not merely a matter of personal salvation, but that the work of social transformation requires saints: "Sanctity alone will meet the crisis of the day. Nothing else matters. One can feed the poor, shelter the homeless, comfort the afflicted, but if you have not charity, the Love of God, Sanctity, it is worthless." (DD-CW:W-4,Box 2)

Dostoevsky

Dorothy Day also had a great love of literature, and she brought her insights from literature to her synthesis of faith and ideas. When we studied Dorothy Day and Dostoevsky, we were already familiar with the latter's story about the society woman who wanted to be immediately thanked for any help she gave to the poor. This included Fr. Zossima's famous reply, so often quoted by Dorothy: "Love in action is a harsh and dreadful thing compared to love in dreams." This parable of Dostoevsky was used over and over by Dorothy and many other Catholic Workers in facing the day to day difficulties of working with the poor and desperate, who came to houses of hospitality after a life of failure. As late as May 1973 Dorothy Day wrote in *The Catholic Worker*, "I do not think I could have carried on with a loving heart all these years without Dostoevsky's understanding of poverty, suffering and drunkenness."

We had not been so conscious of Dorothy's frequent quoting of one of Dostoevsky's other themes: "The world will be saved by beauty." Some would say, "How could she talk that way about beauty when she was in the midst of the suffering and the poor, seeing every day the disfigured face of Christ?

We understood much better because we had been studying the theology of Hans Urs von Balthasar, who emphasized so much, beauty and the glory of God. Von Balthasar, along with Dostoevsky and Dorothy Day, knew that "the world will be saved by beauty."

Von Balthasar characterizes beauty as "the disinterested one, without which the ancient world refused to understand itself." Von Balthasar's insistence that "whoever sneers at the name of beauty as if she were the ornament of a bourgeois past—whether he admits it or not—can no longer pray and soon will no longer be able to love."

We at Casa Juan Diego, like Dorothy Day, saw beauty shining through even in the midst of the harsh and dreadful love of hospitality houses. In the lives of people who have suffered too much, who don't always act appropriately, moments of grace and beauty appear unexpectedly and one knows with Peter Maurin that they are the ambassadors of God.

Those who come to us have suffered too much. Lucille Evans, who spent many years in the Milwaukee CW house, told us that she had never met people like the undocumented guests of Casa Juan Diego, who literally have only the shirts on their backs, and no possibility of assistance from welfare.

They have suffered, working at tiresome jobs (if lucky enough to find a job—otherwise selling things on the street) many hours at a day for wages insufficient to maintain an individual, let alone a family. We have found that the philosophers to whom Dorothy and Peter turned have much to tell us about our social order and how we can approach the justice issues facing us in the person of the exploited and the poor who are its victims.

Kropotkin

One of the most interesting influences on the Worker movement was Peter Kropotkin, a Russian prince who was an anarchist, whose social and economic theories were known and endorsed by both Peter Maurin and Dorothy Day before they knew each other.

Joe Peabody, who wrote the article on Kropotkin for the July-August 1997 *Houston Catholic Worker,* reminded us that Kropotkin lived through a period of European history that featured barbaric exploitation of the poor by the wealthy—in particular, of workers by their employers. Entire generations were forced to leave their farms and small workshops to work in factories. There were, for the most part, no minimum wage laws, no child labor laws, no regulation of the length of the workday, no days off, and no laws governing workplace health or safety. Workers became "wage slaves," making only enough money to keep alive until they could produce the next generation, so that the system could continue.

Kropotkin traced the source of this problem to the factory system of production. One man, because he owned the factory and the machines, could profit by the work of many laborers, without having to actually produce anything himself. The workers, by contrast, produced all the wealth of the society, but were allowed to keep almost none of it, because they did not control the means of production (namely the factory and the raw materials). Individual artisans could not make things as cheaply as factories could, so they were forced to go out of business and seek work in the factory, for a wage. Under this system, a small minority was allowed to attain fabulous wealth, while the vast majority of people endured grinding poverty, malnutrition, hellish working conditions, and a polluted environment. This description might have been written today of the maquiladoras, factories of the United States, Japan, South Korea, and Europe placed in many Third World countries to take advantage of cheap labor.

Kropotkin advocated small factories and workshops so that whatever a community might need could be made locally and for local consumption. Instead of competition between manufacturers driving the prices down and tempting them to mistreat workers for the sake of their profit margin, each cooperative would produce its own food, clothing, shelter, and luxury items to the best of its ability. Each local group could have its own set of small factories to meet its own needs. He also thought it would be best if each community grew its own food. In his view, there was no barrier to self-sufficiency, and therefore no need for speculators, middlemen, or brokers. However, while Kropotkin wrote about these theories, there is no evidence that he himself implemented them, although Peter Maurin visited the south of France to see the workshops set up there on his model.

The early Catholic Workers sought to implement theories such as these in their lives. Their faith taught Dorothy Day, Peter Maurin, and the first Catholic Workers that whatever good they hoped to do in the world had to be accomplished by pure means. No matter how bad the system was, or how badly they wanted to change it, they could not use or advocate violence. They could not coerce. Furthermore, they committed themselves to "poor means." They could not propagandize in the way that Kropotkin suggested without taking the initiative in their own lives. As long as anyone was suffering poverty and want, the Catholic Workers would embrace voluntary poverty. Further, they would work to alleviate the involuntary poverty of others.

The Maritains

This emphasis on "Pure Means" at the Catholic Worker came from Jacques Maritain. His "Pure Means" article, from which Peter Maurin made a lengthy Easy Essay, is a classic, which is very relevant today. According to Stanley Vishnewski, "His teaching on the use of pure means was one of the cornerstones of the philosophy of the Catholic Worker. His maxim: 'Victory or defeat with pure means is always victory,' was imbedded in our way of thinking and our activities."

(Vishnewski 1984: 130) Unfortunately, today's morality no longer asks if the end justifies the means, because the consumer mentality says the end justifies the end.

Jacques and Raissa Maritain were friends of Peter Maurin, Dorothy Day and the Catholic Worker in its earliest years. Both converts, Jacques from a Protestant background and Raissa from a Jewish family, they joined the Church under the influence of Leon Bloy, who provoked them into believing that life was worth living. As university students they were in despair and had made a pact to commit suicide together if they didn't find meaning in life. Thank God, along came Bloy who wrote and spoke with a sword instead of a pen, shouting at people, "Wake up, do something with your life, for God's sake."

At the center of French Catholic thought, the Maritains had Sunday afternoons at home where leading intellectuals came to share and discuss ideas—not all participants were Catholic. Personalists Emmanuel Mounier and Nicolas Berdyaev were among those who attended regularly. Dorothy Day learned from the Maritains that the Revolution must come, but it begins with a Revolution in one's heart. The goal of the Maritains and of Dorothy and Peter was to transform society by bringing Christian values to society and to ordinary people. Credit must be given to Maritain, as well as to Mounier, for promoting the concept of the primacy of the spiritual.

One cannot conclude writing about the Maritains without mentioning the famous quote from Leon Bloy that influenced them so much:

> At bottom what should you do to avoid being an idiot or a swine? Merely this: you should do something great, you should lay aside all the foolishness of a more or less long existence, you should become resigned to the fact you will seem ridiculous to a race of janitors and bureaucrats if you are to enter the service of Splendor. Then you will know what it means to be the friend of God.
>
> The Friend of God! I am on the verge of tears when I think of it. No longer do you know on what block to lay your head, no longer do you know where you are, where you should go. You would like to tear out your heart, so hotly does it burn, and you cannot look upon a creature without trembling with love. You would like to drag yourself on your knees from church to church, with rotten fish strung from your neck, as said the sublime Angela of Foligno. And when your leave these churches after speaking to God as a lover speaks to his beloved, you appear like those poorly designed and

> poorly painted figures on the Way of the Cross, who walk and gesticulate full of pity, against a background of gold. All the thoughts that had been pent up unknown within you, in the caverns of your heart, run out in tumult suddenly like virgins who are mutilated, blind, starving, nude and sobbing. Ah! Surely at such moments the most horrendous of all martyrdoms would be embraced, and with what rapture. (*Mon Journal,* quoted in Jacques Maritain's article, "The Secret of Leon Bloy")

We have by no means exhausted the roots of the CW movement. We recently discovered Anne Klejment's and Nancy Roberts' book on *American Catholic Pacifism* (1996) and wrote about Dorothy Day and the Catholic roots of her pacifism. At the moment we have articles in the works with several authors on St. Philip Neri and Peter Maurin, Distributist economics, and one of Dorothy's very favorite books, *The Imitation of Christ.*

There seems to be no end to the depth of this movement. In today's world with so little commitment to the poor on the left or the right, rhetoric has replaced commitment and service. It is a joy to see attempts at bringing together workers and scholars in the profound vision of Dorothy and Peter. We are so pleased that the University of St. Thomas in St. Paul, Minnesota, hopes to establish a program in Catholic Studies based on Catholic Worker thought and with a CW house of hospitality as an integral part. We know there are other serious and exciting efforts taking place in other Catholic Worker houses and in Catholic universities.

Meanwhile, the social crisis for so many has not improved. Immigrants and refugees and battered immigrant women continue to come to Casa Juan Diego. The Bishop of Torreon, Mexico, recently respectfully requested an Encyclical on Ethics and the Global Market. So much remains to be done in constructing a more just world order. May the work and the study continue!

PART II

THE CATHOLIC WORKER AND THE CATHOLIC CHURCH

Pax Christi, by Ade Bethune, first appeared in the June 1936 issue of *The Catholic Worker.*

"Blowing the Dynamite of the Church": Catholic Radicalism from a Catholic Radicalist Perspective

Rev. Michael J. Baxter, C.S.C.

University of Notre Dame

In the wake of their momentous encounter in December 1932, Peter Maurin subjected Dorothy Day to a pedagogical program that he dubbed "indoctrination," which, from Day's account, consisted of Maurin coming over to her apartment and expounding to her on God, the Church, the Church Fathers, the saints, the poor, hospitality, liberalism, capitalism, fascism, communism, personalism, distributism, anarchism, Aquinas, Catherine of Siena, Chesterton, Belloc, Maritain, Berdyaev, Kropotkin, and so on, until she had heard enough for one day and sent him away (Day 1952: 169-174; Day 1963: 3-9, 14-16). Maurin liked to compose and recite "easy essays," clever, laconic commentaries on the Church and the world, and it is likely that one of the first easy essays he recited in Day's presence (her memory was not so clear on this)(Day 1952: 172) was entitled "The Dynamite of the Church," which goes as follows:

> Writing about the Catholic Church,
> a radical writer says:
> "Rome will have to do more
> than to play a waiting game;
> she will have to use some of the dynamite
> inherent in her message."
> To blow the dynamite
> of a message
> is the only way
> to make the message dynamic.
> If the Catholic Church

is not today
the dominant social dynamic force,
it is because Catholic scholars
have taken the dynamite
of the Church,
have wrapped it up
in nice phraseology,
placed it in an hermetic container
and sat on the lid.
It is about time
to blow the lid off
so the Catholic Church
may again become
the dominant social dynamic force. (Maurin 1977: 3)[1]

The notion of the Church as "dynamic" and having "dynamite" in its possession is worth lingering over for a moment. Both words are derived from the Greek *dynamis,* meaning power or might. It appears many times in the Septuagint (the Greek translation of the Hebrew Old Testament) in reference to the mighty acts of God, and in the New Testament in reference to Jesus, who also is an agent of God's power and might, when he casts out demons and heals the sick, and commissions his disciples to do the same. After the resurrection, the apostles bear witness to Christ "with great power," especially Paul, who delivers the Gospel "not with persuasive words of wisdom, but with a demonstration of spirit and power."(I Cor 2:4) This same power will prevail at the end of time, when Christ destroys all other sovereignties and powers and hands over the kingdom to God the Father (I Cor 15:24) (Wink 1984: 161-162).

Peter Maurin's point is this: God unleashed a power, a *dynamis,* in the life, death, and resurrection of Christ, which was to be shared by his followers in their spreading of the Gospel message, but Catholic scholars have taken this dynamic message, cordoned it off, kept it under wraps, and rendered it socially impotent. They have done so in the way that scholars know best, by means of "nice phraseology."

In its own quipping way, the essay points to the fact that in the world of Catholic scholarship in the thirties, theology and social theory functioned as separate, unrelated disciplines. I elaborate on this separation in the first part of this article. In the second part, I draw on writings of Maurin and Day to show that they did not separate theology from social theory, but espoused a social theory suffused with theological terms and categories. In the third part, I argue that many Catholic scholars today fail to appreciate this integration because they continue to work under an assumed separation between theology and social theory, a separation that privileges the ethical agenda of the nation-state and unfairly marginalizes the radicalist ethical vision of the Catholic Worker. In the fourth and final part, I briefly describe the difficulty in presenting the Catholic Worker from its own radicalist perspective given the disciplinary lines which currently separate theology from social theory, and the nature of the task that is immediately before us.

Theology, Hermetically Sealed

Maurin's description of theology "in an hermetic container" was not a critique of any particular Catholic scholar, but of how all Catholic scholars—or almost all—collectively went about their work. It was a critique of discourse, that is, of the paradigms, institutions, disciplines, practices, rules, regulations, and unexamined assumptions making up the frame of reference out of which a group of scholars works (Bove 1995: 50-65). The questions and problems taken up by a given group of scholars emerge within this frame of reference, but the frame of reference itself often goes unquestioned, unproblematized. In his essay, Peter Maurin contends that the discourse or frame of reference of Catholic scholarship unwisely treats theology and social theory as if they constitute two separate fields of inquiry, and inaccurately views theology as asocial and social theory as having little to do with theology.

Peter Maurin was right. If we look at the theoretical paradigm dominating the discourse of Catholic scholarship in these years, we see that it divided all fields of knowledge according to two fundamentally distinct realms: the natural and the supernatural. Derived from a misreading of Aquinas, this neo-Scholastic paradigm held that the natural desires of the human person—the desire to meet one's physical needs, to live in society, to marry and raise children, to produce and consume goods, to establish forms of governments which enable such natural activities to be performed in accord with justice and the common good—that these natural desires can be fulfilled without the aid of the supernatural life of Christ in the Church. In this view, there were two separate realms or tiers of human existence, the natural and the supernatural, and it was possible to confine the study of society, economics, and politics to one of those two realms, the natural (McPartlan 1995: 45-60; Duffy 1992: 50-84; Kerr 1997: 159-184). Hence the separation between theology and social theory.

Any critique of discourse entails a critique of institutions; in this instance, a critique of the standard institutional arrangement in U.S. Catholic higher education in the pre-conciliar era. With few exceptions, Catholic colleges and universities placed philosophy at the center of the curriculum as the discipline that would organize and place into proper perspective knowledge gained from all other academic fields, the arts, the natural sciences, and the newly emergent social sciences. Theology, by contrast, had virtually no place in the standard curriculum. It was studied in the seminaries, which were organizationally separate from the colleges and usually free-standing institutions. Dogma, christology, moral theology, sacramental theology, mystical theology, and scripture, were reserved for the training of future priests. What religious instruction was available at the colleges was catechetical in nature, and did not relate directly to the knowledge pursued and produced at the colleges and universities. This institutional arrangement reinforced the idea that the study of politics, economics, and society deals with natural activities and should be governed by philosophy, not theology (Baxter 1996: 123-147).

Admittedly, the situation was not as clear cut as this account implies, but I believe the picture I have painted, big brush and all, is accurate as regards Catholic social theory in the early twentieth century. John Ryan, for example, the most prominent Catholic social theorist of this era, wrote almost nothing on sin and grace, the sacraments, christology, soteriology, or eschatology, or scripture (Curran 1982: 84-87). The same is true of Moorhouse F.X. Millar, a colleague of Ryan's, whose extensive writings in philosophy and political theory propose no more than a marginal role for theology (Baxter 1996: 323-353). The same is true of the many lesser known social theorists whose journal articles about political, economic, and social matters are by and large devoid of substantive theological reasoning and argumentation. And the same is true, with qualifications, of the most influential U.S. Catholic social theorist of this century, John Courtney Murray.

How to read Murray is a hotly contested and complex matter these days, too complex to give a full account here, so let me sum up my reading of him in a nutshell. Murray was more ready and able than his predecessors to import theological terms and categories into his social theory (Komonchak 1996: 60-81), but he did so in such a way that his theology effaced itself as it moved into the realm of the natural and the social. In *We Hold These Truths,* he invokes the incarnation, but only to say that it established a spiritual, not temporal, order (Murray 1960: 202-204). This spiritual/temporal distinction dictates (and mutes) the significance of other theological terms and categories. Thus he refers to redemption, but only to note in passing that the Western constitutional tradition may be seen as redemptive in a terrestrial sense (155). He mentions providence, but only to suggest that it was operative at the U.S. founding (30, 67-68). He even brings up the Sermon on the Mount, but only to insist that its precepts, or any other precepts drawn directly from scripture, have no direct bearing on the morality of public policy (275ff.). In each case, Murray's use of theological terms and categories only serves to reinforce the premise of the primacy of the spiritual order, a premise that serves to reinforce the existence of another order set aside solely for temporal affairs—the affairs of politics, the state, civil law, public discourse—wherein the language of faith and revelation yields to the language of reason and natural law. The overall effect is to lend support to the presiding contention of *We Hold These Truths,* that this spiritual/temporal distinction received full-fledged endorsement by the U.S. founders and was granted legal recognition in the First Amendment of the Constitution of the United States.

It is important to note the connection between the neo-Scholastic division of the natural from the supernatural and the exigencies of liberal democratic political order in the United States of America. Murray set out to provide a basis for a "public philosophy" that would appeal to all parties in a religiously pluralistic setting; this meant a philosophy not grounded in the beliefs and practices of any specific ecclesial body, a philosophy not referring to the ultimate ends of human existence (Murray: 54, 73); and the neo-Scholastic natural law, autonomous from the supernatural and accessible by means of reason alone, was perfectly suited to this task. [2]

The problem with natural law conceived apart from its supernatural end is that it perpetuates the myth of the modern liberal state as a religiously neutral institutional arrangement. In fact, this is a debased, unnatural law that should rather be understood as a rival to true religion (in the Augustinian sense), and its emergence in the seventeenth and eighteenth centuries dissipated the authority of the Church not only among the networks of social and political power but also within its own membership (Cavanaugh 1995: 377-420). Furthermore, when natural law is not ordered to its supernatural end, it lacks the linguistic and conceptual resources needed to challenge existing configurations of political power from a perspective other than the realm of "the political." In this sense, the neo-Scholastic enclosure of the natural within an autonomous sphere precluded a fundamental theological critique of the modern liberal state. Thus, while Murray was an accomplished theologian, theology had little direct and substantive effect on his political theory. The same is true of Catholic social theory in general. It is remarkably bereft of references to Christ, the sacraments, scripture, the saints, and other tradition-specific theological terms and categories which do not easily conform to the discursive protocols of the modern liberal state.

This is what Peter Maurin put his finger on in "Blowing the Dynamite of the Church." What we need to put our finger on is that much the same is true of Catholic social theory today. But before commenting on the contemporary scene, I want to take up the Catholic Worker from its own non-state-centered, theologically informed, radicalist perspective.

The Dynamite of the Church

The social theory to which Maurin referred in his essay was dynamic because it possessed an explosive ingredient: Jesus Christ. The image of dynamite jolts the listener/reader into imagining Christ and the Church in temporal rather than in purely spiritual terms. This is not to say that Maurin denied that the Church's mission is "spiritual"; no Catholic intellectual of that era would have denied that; but, for Maurin, "spiritual" signified specific practices and a specific form of social life. In contrast to standard Catholic social theory, his social theory was, in a word, ecclesial.

Consider, for example, his three-pronged vision of a society based on cult, culture, and cultivation. Together with culture and cultivation he lists as an indispensable element "cult," the practice of the worship of God (and he had a specifically Catholic form of worship in mind) (Day 1952: 171). Consider his designation of parishes and dioceses as sites for the practice of hospitality; not the "muni," not state-run shelters, but the Church (Maurin 1977: 8-12). Consider his view of St. Francis as one who lived the kind of life that could spark social reconstruction, not personal piety or ecclesiastical reform alone, but the reconstruction of *society* (Maurin 1977: 37-38). For Peter Maurin, society is not built on a "pure nature"; rather, society flows out of a "nature" ordered to and fulfilled by Christ in the Church, a nature that is, to paraphrase both Father John J. Hugo and the English theologian John Milbank, "supernaturalized."(Milbank 1991: 206-255)

This supernaturalism permeates the writings of Dorothy Day, particularly *The Long Loneliness.* Think of the scene at the outset: "Confession"—the practice of bringing one's sins into the light of day, also writing about "all the things which had brought [her] to God," about how she "found faith" and "became a member of the Mystical Body of Christ."(Day 1952: 9-12, 10) Think of the scene in the postscript: people sitting, talking, dividing up loaves and fishes, welcoming the poor into houses with expanding walls, knowing God and each other in a Eucharistic banquet joining heaven and earth (285-286). Confession, then communion: here we have the story of a practicing Catholic who like Augustine (whom she cites in depicting her own task as a writer)(10-11) feels compelled to tell how God has taken possession of her life.

This supernaturalist perspective is written into the structure of the overall narrative of *The Long Loneliness,* as it moves from the second to the third part. Dorothy Day's time on Staten Island with Forster Batterham, walking the beach, reading, cooking, eating together, sleeping together, bearing a child, this consoling time of "natural happiness" draws her into an overflowing supernatural love. With Forster she had a child she loved, and he made the physical world come alive, awakening in her a flood of gratitude. But, she writes, "the final object of this love and gratitude was God. No human creature could receive or contain so vast a flood of love and joy as I often felt after the birth of my child. With this came the need to worship, to adore."(Day 1952: 135) Natural happiness could not satisfy. It expands one's desire beyond what the natural itself can ever fulfill. Nature, in other words, produces a lack. It is like salt on the tongue, leaving us thirsting for something more; not for more salt, but for the water which alone quenches our thirst (Lubac 1998: 31). So the story moves on, painfully, to the baptism of her daughter, to the break-up with Forster, to her own baptism, and at length, to her life at the Worker: the story of natural love transformed into the love of the cross.

A theology of the supernatural comes in Day's account of the Retreat. She describes Fr. Pacifique Roy as talking "of nature and the supernatural, how God became man that man might become God, how we were under the obligation of putting off the old man and putting on Christ." This, he said, is done by "acting always for the 'supernatural motive,' by "supernaturalizing all our actions every day."(Day 1952: 247) Fr. John J. Hugo, director of many Catholic Worker retreats, stressed that as Christians "we have been given a share in the divine life; we have been raised to a supernatural level."(256) "Grace is a share in the divine life," he said, "and the law of this supernatural life is love, a love which demands renunciation."(257) Significantly, she wrote this chapter shortly after the promulgation of *Humani generis* (1950), the encyclical that defended the neo-Scholastic notion of "pure nature" as necessary to preserve the integrity of nature and the gratuity of grace. This pronouncement called into question the *nouvelle theologie* of Henri de Lubac and others for arguing that the notion of a purely natural end was a distortion of Aquinas' belief that the human person has a *natural* desire for God and thus a single, supernatural end. Given this context, it is significant that Day alludes to the controversy, mentions de Lubac favorably (258), and offers a brief formulation of her own supernaturalist theology: "Body and soul constitute human nature," she writes. "The body is no less good than the soul. In mortifying the natural we must not injure the body or the soul. We are not to destroy it but to transform it, as iron is transformed in the fire."(257) This is clearly a defense of Hugo against his critics, and also perhaps her own homespun attempt to allay official suspicion.

All of which goes to show that Day's integrated understanding of the natural/supernatural relation ran counter to the neo-Scholastic two-tier paradigm that dominated the discourse of Catholic scholarship during the pre-conciliar era. She envisioned society not as enclosed within an autonomous "natural" realm of human activity, but as radically open and dynamically oriented toward the supernatural. Two scholars associated with the Worker, Virgil Michel, O.S.B. and Paul Hanly Furfey, articulated this perspective in books, academic journals, and articles in popular periodicals including *The Catholic Worker*: Michel, by rooting all social regeneration in the liturgy (Baxter 1997: 499-528); Furfey, by showing that all true society flows from participation in the inner life of the Trinity (Furfey 1936). But it was Day who was able to articulate it in terms of specific practices that make up a supernaturalized life. Her thick descriptions of feeding the hungry, clothing the naked, giving hospitality to the stranger, instructing the ignorant (that is, picketing), growing food on the land (or trying to), and so on, all showed that Peter Maurin's "new society within the shell of the old" where "it is easier for people to be good" (Day 1952: 170) was thoroughly realizable in the here and now, through the power of the Holy Spirit and the intercession of the saints.

But this "new society" never figured into the work of Catholic social theorists. It did not register as a "society" as they understood the term. It was "spiritual" rather than "temporal," "supernatural" rather than "natural," "ecciesial" rather than "social." It embodied "charity" rather than "justice." These are false oppositions, of course, produced by the separation of theology and social theory that dominated Catholic scholarly discourse in the pre-conciiar era, but the effect, as Peter Maurin saw so clearly, was to confine the power or *dynamis* of Christ to an asocial sphere where it lay dormant.

The situation is not fundamentally different now. Even though the Catholic Worker has received plenty of scholarly attention lately (something that Catholic Workers should fear because, as Stanley Hauerwas has observed, academics study religious movements that are dead or that they are trying to kill), it remains marginalized in the discourse of Catholic social ethicists. Some social ethicists exclude it willingly; others, against their best intentions; but in any case, the problem is not so much with the ethicists themselves as with the discursive structure of their field, which still posits a division between theology and social theory.

Public Theology As Ideology

Permit me to make a sweeping generalization about Catholic social ethics which is too complex to explain or defend fully here, but which needs to be made anyway: Catholic social ethics today continues to posit a separation between theology and social theory, and it does so in two ways: first, by extending John Courtney Murray's project of providing the nation with a "public philosophy" (or now, a "public theology") to which all in a pluralistic society can appeal; and second, by reinforcing that project with a theoretical paradigm quite distinct from the neo-Scholastic one that shaped Murray, a paradigm inherited from Max Weber.

The genealogy of this Weberian paradigm is long and complex, tracing from Ernst Troeltsch, to H. Richard and Reinhold Niebuhr, and to James Gustafson, whose influence in the field of Catholic social ethicists today is pervasive (Troeltsch 1931; Niebuhr 1924, 1951; Gustafson 1985: 83-94). For our purposes, we should note that this paradigm is structured along the lines of an antinomy between religion and politics, each of which performs a distinct ethical function (Weber 1994: 309-369; Bauerschmidt 1997: 78). Religion, for Weber, furnishes an ideal vision that forms the basis for an "ethic of ultimate ends," while politics determines how ethical ideals may be approximated in a world of conflict and violence, thus functioning as an "ethic of means." These two ethical functions complement each other, Weber maintains, but they operate within distinct life-spheres governed by distinct laws. It is the task, indeed the "vocation," of the politician, working within the domain of the state, to ensure that ethical means be appropriate to real-life circumstances. The politician must ensure that the harsh realities of necessary means be segregated from the lofty vision of ultimate ends, thus avoiding irresponsible attempts to put religious ideals such as, say, the Sermon on the Mount into practice in the "real world" of politics—which is, as Weber himself acknowledges, a world of ethical compromise. It is this religion/politics antinomy, along with the dualism between ends and means, that has given rise to the litany of antinomies that shape the discourse of social ethics in the Troeltsch-Niebuhr-Gustafson tradition: ideal/real, absolute/relative, individual/social, sect/church, love/justice, Christ/culture, kingdom/history, and so on. My point in identifying this paradigm, along with that of Murray, is to emphasize that in the field of Catholic social ethics they have combined to form the distorted lens through which the Catholic Worker is read.

This distortion is evident in the readings of *The Catholic Worker* offered by two very different thinkers, George Weigel and Charles Curran. In *Tranquillitas Ordinis,* George Weigel, a neo-conservative, presents what he calls "The John Courtney Murray Project" over the course of 150 pages and then he pauses to deliver an overtly hostile critique of, among others, Dorothy Day and the Catholic Worker (Weigel 1987: 148-173). "Given the Weberian choice between an 'ethics of responsibility' and an "ethics of absolute ends," he writes, "Dorothy Day unhesitatingly chose the latter." There is no problem with this in itself for Weigel; the problem is that "Dorothy Day and the Catholic Worker did not heed Weber's advice to eschew politics. The movement may have rejected 'politics as a vocation,' but it eagerly embraced politics as an avocation." This was especially the case regarding its approach to Soviet communism, which was "distorted by the apocalyptic horizon and its failure to distinguish relative evils." As regards Day herself, Weigel grants that her religious intuitions were sincere and intense, but this does not detract from her shortcomings as an absolutist unwilling to make the compromises and prudential judgments necessary in the political arena. She should have avoided politics altogether. Thus Weigel assures us that "Dorothy Day's life and witness remains a powerful sign in modern American Catholicism," but finally, "the enduring truth of [her] life rests...not in her political judgments, but in her faith."(152-153)

A surprisingly similar reading of the Catholic Worker has been offered by the liberal Catholic moral theologian and social ethicist Charles Curran. In *American Catholic Social Ethics,* Curran focuses on one of the Catholic Worker's leading theological spokesmen, Paul Hanly Furfey (Curran 1982: 130-171; Piehl 1982: 126-128). The primary positive feature of Furfey's "radicalism," says Curran, is that it is "prophetic" and thus has "the ability to see the problems." Whereas "Catholic liberals at times might tend to overlook some problems...the Catholic radical possesses a methodological approach which makes one sensitive to the real problems facing our society." And yet, while the methodology of Catholic radicalism serves to make "Catholics and others in our society aware of the dangers of conformism," it is deeply flawed, as Curran sees it, in that it has not been "effective in helping the lot of the poor and oppressed in our society." The problem here is that it has a "one-sided emphasis on the change of the heart of the person with comparatively little or no stress on the need for the change of institutions or of structures."(Curran 1982: 166-167) Thus, while the work of Dorothy Day and the Catholic Worker has been "awe-inspiring and of great spiritual beauty," their program "has not been effective. They have concentrated only on the derelicts and have done little or nothing to help the poor of the ghetto change the conditions in which they live."(170) Nevertheless, Curran affords Day and the Worker a limited place within his "catholic and universal church," to wit: "within the total church there must always be room for a radical Christian witness. Individual Christians, but not the whole church, can be and are called to a radical vocation and witness within the church."(169)

Notice here the similarities between Weigel's and Curran's reading of the Worker. Both find it lacking in responsibility when it comes to institutional change. Both appeal to criteria of effectiveness. Both extol the Worker for its inspiring example, but its significance is restricted to the realm of individual witness. Both are indebted to the Weberian paradigm of politics. Differences in tone and emphasis notwithstanding, the readings of the Catholic Worker offered by Weigel and Curran are equally condescending and misleading.

And this is true, I would submit, of a host of social ethicists dedicated to developing a "public philosophy" or a "public theology," whose considerable differences give way to a common reading of The Catholic Worker's ecclesiology as "sectarian." This is a key word in the lexicon of Catholic social ethics done in the Troeltsch-Niebuhr-Gustafson lineage. It is invoked as a way to dismiss the claim that Christian discipleship entails a form of life that is embedded in the beliefs and practices of the Church and therefore cannot serve as the basis for universal, supra-ecclesial ethical principles that are then applied in making public policy (Gustafson: 83-94; Hauerwas 1988: 1-21).[3] In this dismissal, it is possible to detect the lineaments of the kind of Weberian critique of the Catholic Worker offered by Weigel and Curran, namely, that Gospel ideals do not pertain to politics and must therefore be translated from ends into means, from absolute into relative terms, so as to have a more direct bearing in the world of pragmatic policy making. But such a translation reproduces the former neo-Scholastic separation of theology and social theory that Peter Maurin criticized in his easy essay. It also runs counter to the consistent claim of Maurin and Day that true society is rooted in the supernatural life of Christ and cannot be abstracted from the beliefs and practices of the Church. Most importantly, this "public theology" approach fails to take seriously a contention that has been central to the life of the Catholic Worker from the beginning, namely, that the modern nation-state is a fundamentally unjust and corrupt set of institutions whose primary function is to preserve the interests of the ruling class, by coercive and violent means if necessary—and there will always come a time when it is necessary.

Those working out of the Murray tradition of "public theology" find this assessment of the modern nation-state to be intolerably negative. And indeed it certainly is negative, but Day would add that this is for good reason. After all, she was formed politically by the Old Left during and after the Great War. This was the era of the Committee on Public Information, the suppression of journals such as *The Masses,* the Palmer Raids, the shut-down of the Wobblies, and the Red Scare of the twenties. The history of state-sponsored political repression was very much intertwined with Dorothy Day's personal history (as is especially clear from the first part of her autobiography), and it left her forever wary of the claims of the state, as she herself indicates with the title of the chapter in *The Long Loneliness* on anarchist politics: "War Is the Health of the State."

The title comes from a phrase in an essay written by Randolph Bourne as the Great War was drawing to a close (Bourne 1964: 65-104, esp. 69, 71). It was well-known among the Old Left in the years after the war, and it is worth reviewing at length because it obviously reflects Day's worldview. The essay decries the way in which a nation's population during war is transformed into a single herd that conforms to the aims and purposes of the state. In times of war, Bourne observes, the state realizes its "ideal," which is "that within its territory its power and influence should be universal." It makes a claim on "all the members of the body politic," for "it is precisely in war that the urgency for union seems greatest, and the necessity for universality seems most unquestioned. The State is the organization of the herd," Boume continues, and "war sends the current of purpose and activity flowing down to the lowest level of the herd, and to its most remote branches." Thus the state becomes "the inexorable arbiter and determinant of men's businesses and attitudes and opinions."(69) As an open supporter of the International Workers of the World (I.W.W.) or "Wobblies," an anarchist union that was subjected to intense governmental scrutiny and repression during and after the war, Bourne was concerned with the ways in which control is exercised over the population by means of the police, courts, prisons, and other state-sponsored institutions. But he is particularly insightful about the subtle mechanisms by which conformity is ensured through a complex network of symbols, attitudes, and customs that produce what he calls "State-feeling" or "State-enthusiasm."(77-78) Old symbols are taken out and dusted off. Old slogans are brought back into circulation. "Public opinion, as expressed in the newspapers, and the pulpits and the schools, becomes one solid block. And 'loyalty,' or rather war orthodoxy, becomes the sole test for all professions, techniques, occupations."(70) This is true in the academy, when the "herd-instinct" becomes the "herd-intellect"(3-14, 7), and also in the churches, "when Christian preachers lose their pulpits for taking more or less in literal terms the Sermon on the Mount."(71) The mechanisms that produce this "State-feeling" are so subtle, so well dispersed, reaching each cell in the body politic, that conforming to it feels natural and right, so much so that it feels natural and right to kill for it.

By using Bourne's provocative aphorism as a chapter title in her autobiography at a time when the nation was in the throes of the cold war, Day reminded her readers that the Catholic Worker is "radical" in two related senses. It is radical in the sense that it addresses the roots of social reconstruction by grounding it in the person and work of Christ, and also in the sense that it refuses to conform to the order—or disorder—imposed by the modern nation-state. This second sense of radicalism is crucial for reading the Catholic Worker from its own radicalist perspective, for it challenges public theology's state-centered understanding of politics by disclosing the possibility of reading "public theology" as ideology, that is, as a constellation of ideas that legitimate the dominant power relations of capitalist order by depicting particular forms of social and political life as natural or universal.[4]

One way to begin reading "public theology" as ideology would be to examine the word "public," which is supposed to signify the inclusive nature of the workings of liberal democracy in the United States. From the perspective of the Catholic Worker, the mechanisms of the state have never really been "public" for much of the population, the ones who live in shelters and S.R.O.'s, who work the fields or sweep the floors at McDonald's, who live a paycheck away from eviction, who are not counted in the census, who live in constant economic depression. Similar criticisms could be made of notions like "freedom," "justice," "the common good," "civil society," and "the limited state," words or phrases that conceal the dehumanizing world of those who live in the bottom fifth of "our society." Public theologians, of course, respond that this is the situation that they seek to reform, which would seem to be a worthy task; but this kind of reformist agenda only serves to reinforce the assumption that the only effective mechanism for implementing justice in the modern world is the modern state. It is this assumption that Dorothy Day, with the help of Robert Ludlow, rejects in her chapter on the state and Christian anarchism, in favor of a localist understanding of government and politics grounded in the power of the cross (Day 1952: 268; Coles 1987: 89-109).

The power of the cross moved Dorothy Day beyond the pale of the Old Left, where religion was seen only as part of the ideological superstructure that kept capitalism running smoothly. In her journey from natural happiness to supernatural love, she discovered another kind of religion, with a social program at least as radical as any she had encountered among the Marxists, socialists, and anarchists of her youth. Having been singed by "the dynamite of the Church," she could pose the startling question, in the first issue of the New York paper, "Is it not possible to be radical and not atheist?" The question pointed to a crucial flaw in the standard critique of religion put forth by radicals of the Old Left, namely, that it was a critique of *bourgeois* religion, religion that conforms to norms established by the social relations of capitalist production, religion that is designed to legitimate the workings of the state and market. That critique failed to consider the possibility of another religion, one founded on a Lord who preached love of enemies and good news to the poor, who healed the sick and welcomed the outcast, who made the rulers of this world tremble, and who bestows upon His followers the power to do the same. This is the religion that was proclaimed by Day in the first issue of *The Catholic Worker* and, as has been amply demonstrated by Catholic Workers ever since, it was—and is—a genuinely radical religion.

But this theological claim can be explicated only from a radicalist perspective. Given the present configuration of the field of Catholic social ethics, this requires distinguishing the radicalist perspective of the Catholic Worker from the bourgeois perspective of Public Theology and unmasking Public Theology as a discourse which legitimates the nation-state. It requires a demolition of public theology using "the dynamite of the Church."

No More Playing a Waiting Game

Unmasking public theology as ideology is a theoretical task, a scholarly task, and one would expect that one place where such a task might be accomplished is the Catholic college or university. But here we run into a problem. The theoretical paradigms and institutional structures shaping Catholic colleges and universities today continue to separate theology from social theory and therefore militate against a supernaturalized social theory such as that embodied in the Worker. It is by no means a coincidence, therefore, that these Catholic schools all too often function as production sites of capitalist theory and training centers for capitalist practice. At times, the ethos of these schools is so drenched in late-twentieth-century capitalist culture as to lead one to conclude, in darker moments, that the shepherding being done at these schools is the kind that raises sheep not for the Church, but for the market (Lentricchia 1983: 88).

But resisting capitalism is a problem we face not only in our schools. It is a problem for everyone everywhere, as some Leftist theorists of hegemony began to recognize earlier this century. One of the first such theorists in this country is mentioned in *The Long Loneliness,* very briefly. He was the brother-in-law of Forster Batterham (Day's English, anarchist common-law husband), and when Day first met him, he was "writing the first of his strange books."(Day 1952: 114) This was Kenneth Burke, the Marxist literary critic who informed the radical left of the thirties that revolution is a cultural as well as an economic struggle, and that (in the words of Frank Lentricchia) "a revolutionary culture must situate itself firmly on the terrain of its capitalist antagonist, must not attempt a dramatic leap beyond capitalism in one explosive, rupturing moment of release, must work its way through capitalism's language of domination by working cunningly within it, using, appropriating, even speaking through its key mechanisms of repression."(Lentricchia 1983: 24) If the point provides a helpful corrective to Peter Maurin's image of dynamite (perhaps the image of termites is more appropriate), it only heightens the urgency of the message of Peter Maurin's easy essay.

Catholic scholars will have to do more than play a waiting game.

Acknowledgment

This paper was originally given at the conference on Dorothy Day and the Catholic Worker at Marquette University, 10 October 1997. I am grateful to Frederick C. Bauerschmidt, William T. Cavanaugh, Michael Dauphinais, Michael Garvey, Stanley Hauerwas and Thomas Hibbs for reading and commenting on subsequent drafts of this essay.

Notes

[1] The 1977 edition uses the title, "Blowing the Dynamite."

[2] This summary raises the possibility of developing a philosophy that does make adequate reference to ultimate ends, a philosophy that points beyond itself and thus acknowledges its own insufficiency in providing a full account of society and politics. Such a task clearly goes beyond the purposes of this paper, but it is important at least to acknowledge that the position I am setting forth calls for the developing of precisely this kind of philosophy.

[3] The most frequent target of this critique is Stanley Hauerwas. For a critique of Hauerwas, see James Gustafson, "The Sectarian Temptation," 83-94; for Hauerwas' response, see "Introduction," in *Christian Existence Today: Essays on Church, World, and Living In Between* (Durham: Labyrinth Press, 1988), 1-21.

[4] Ideology can be understood in a multitude of ways, as has been noted by Terry Eagleton in *Ideology: An Introduction* (London: Verso, 1991), 1-3. Here I am combining several of these possible uses, though not, I hope, in a self-contradictory way.

Diversity, Plurality and Ambiguity: Anarchism in the Catholic Worker Movement

Fred Boehrer

Albany Catholic Worker Community

> [A]narchism - the word, first used as a taunt by its Marxists opponents, best brings to mind the tension always existing between the concept of authority and freedom which torments man to this day.
>
> Dorothy Day

Introduction

Within the Catholic Worker movement anarchism not only critiques the state's use of power, but extends to identity and authority issues within Catholic Worker communities, the movement, and the Roman Catholic Church. Frequently articulated or redefined as "personalism,"(Murray 1990: 212) the anarchist thread of the Catholic Worker movement is a curious influence. Surfacing in a variety of forms, anarchism finds expression in the individual's relationship to government bodies and to fellow Catholic Worker community members. Anarchism is also present in the relationships among the numerous Catholic Worker communities which constitute today's "movement."

In Section I, I review the secular and religious roots of anarchism in Peter Maurin (1877-1949) and Dorothy Day (1897-1980), the cofounders of the Catholic Worker movement. A review of three expressions of Catholic Worker anarchism, 1933-1980, is offered in Section II. In the following section, I compare these three expressions within the contemporary Catholic Worker (1980-present). In Section IV, I suggest a fourth stage of Catholic Worker anarchism has become more pronounced within the movement since the death of Day: the Catholic Worker individual or community in conflict with the institutional Roman Catholic Church. The final section is an opportunity to explore the issues of Catholic identity and authority within today's movement.

One purpose of this essay is to provide clarity with regard to the multiple usages of the term "anarchism" within the Catholic Worker. Numerous texts about this movement relegate "anarchism" to footnote status, or at best a minor factor in the Catholic Worker history. Similarly, most texts about anarchism treat religion as problematic and de-emphasize any religious expressions of anarchism, especially those derived from a group identifying itself as Roman Catholic (DeLeon 1978: 150-151).[1] Indeed, most readers with Roman Catholic sentiments would have difficulty finding a convergence between Catholicism and *anarchism,* just as most readers with anarchist sentiments would have difficulty finding a convergence between anarchism and *Roman Catholicism.* By examining both Catholicism and anarchism, I am suggesting that anarchism is integral, not merely supplemental, to the Catholic Worker.

It is a challenge to write about the contemporary Catholic Worker: as a "movement," the Catholic Worker lacks a leader, a headquarters and a set of policies. It is difficult to make broad statements about this movement since each community is autonomous. And it is difficult to make generalizations about a particular community because each person within a community is an individual operating within his/her own Catholic Worker anarchist framework. For example, the term "membership" is rarely used to describe people within this movement, since this term presumes an agreed-upon set of criteria which does not exist within the Catholic Worker. I offer a portrait of the complexities within today's movement, examining the various anarchist threads, while trying not to reduce the expressions of individuals and communities which comprise the Catholic Worker.

I. Anarchist Roots in the Catholic Worker Movement

The anarchist thread of the Catholic Worker movement has roots in co-founders Dorothy Day and Peter Maurin, who were influenced by both secular and religious writers in this theme.

As a student, teacher, and farmer, Peter Maurin aspired to integrating the ideas of great anarchist and personalist writers into everyday life. Upon withdrawing from the Sillon movement, Maurin took to the writings of Peter Kropotkin, especially *Fields, Factories and Workshops* and *Mutual Aid* (Sheehan 1959: 70). In his studies of

Kropotkin, Maurin developed his anarchist-based "Green Revolution" in opposition to the ideas and spirit behind Marx's Red Revolution (Sheehan: 70). Maurin's proposals were influenced by Kropotkin's "farming communes," Nicholas Berdyaev's notion of "freedom," and the "personalism" of Emmanuel Mounier (Gneuhs 1988: 44ff.). In addition to European thinkers, Maurin saw parallels between his anarchist views of America and those of a "founding father:"

> Thomas Jefferson says that the less government there is, the better it is. If the less government there is, the better it is, then the best kind of government is self-government. If the best kind of government is self-government, then the best kind of organization is self-organization.[2]
>
> "Self Organization," *Easy Essays*

Maurin's three-point program of hospitality houses, agronomic universities and roundtable discussions (for the clarification of thought) suggests opportunities for an anarchist lifestyle.

Prior to her conversion to Roman Catholicism, Day studied anarchism. In high school, she read a biography of one of the Haymarket anarchists and considered Peter Kropotkin one of her "companions at that time."(Day 1952: 38) At the University of Illinois, Day continued to study anarchist writers while joining the Socialist party (Day 1952: 39). As a journalist for two radical papers, the *Call* and *The Masses,* Day encountered several anarchist groups. She became a member of the I.W.W. and met Alexander Berkman while studying and discussing a variety of anarchist thinkers: Proudhon, Kropotkin, Tolstoy, and Zeno. In *The Long Loneliness*, Day's autobiography, she reflected about her life circa 1917:

> I wavered between my allegiance to socialism, syndicalism (the I.W.W.'s) and anarchism. When I read Tolstoi [sic], I was an anarchist. Ferrer with his schools, Kropotkin with his farming communes, the I.W.W.'s with their solidarity, their unions, these all appealed to me....The I.W.W. had an immediate program for America so I signed up with them. (Day 1952: 62)

The religious dimension of anarchism for Maurin and Day is distinctively Roman Catholic. Beyond the apparent inconsistency between anarchism and a religious tradition which boasts an authoritative and hierarchical structure, Maurin and Day saw parallels between Catholic social teaching and a society functioning according to the decentralized principles of mutual aid and cooperation. Particular principles offered in Catholic social thought, which bridge anarchist principles, include: dignity of the human person, the concept of the common good, the rights of workers, the principle of subsidiarity and primacy of conscience. Of this list, I contend that the last two ideas, the principle of subsidiarity and primacy of conscience, have played the greatest role in bridging Roman Catholicism and anarchism within the Catholic Worker movement.

While critiquing the government for officially recognizing works of charity through granting tax-exempt status, Day wrote that "there is a principle laid down, much in line with common sense and with the original American ideal, that governments should never do what small bodies can accomplish...Peter Maurin's anarchism was on one level based on this principle of subsidiarity."(*CW* 5/1972: 3, 5) Subsidiarity, formally introduced into Catholic social teaching by Pius XI's *Quadragesimo Anno* (1931), has its origins in the New Testament Gospels, according to Maurin and Day. Day reflected about the biblical roots of subsidiarity:

> We were taught in the Gospel to work from the bottom up, not from the top down. Everything was personalist, we were our brothers' keepers, and we were not to pass by our neighbor who has fallen by the wayside and let the State, the all encroaching State, take over, but were to do all we could ourselves. These were the anarchist and pacifist teachings Peter Maurin, our founder, taught us. (*CW* 5/1958: 1)

Day insisted upon this bridge between Roman Catholicism and anarchism: "Popes and anarchists have emphasized the principle: subsidiarity. The State should never take over the functions that could be performed by a smaller body."(Terkel 1970: 304)

In addition to subsidiarity, the primacy of conscience played an important role in articulating the notion of anarchism within the Catholic Worker movement. In "Non-Catholic Catholics" in his *Easy Essays*, Peter Maurin (1984: 154) wrote: "Non-Catholics say that Catholics are led by the nose by the clergy. Real Catholics follow their consciences."

Both Maurin and Day were very familiar with the writings of Thomas Aquinas and John Henry Newman on this matter. According to Aquinas

> The obligation of conscience has the force of a divine precept... therefore, since a divine precept is binding when it is contrary to the precept of a prelate, and has a greater binding force than such a precept, the bond of conscience is superior to the bond arising from the precept of a prelate, and conscience will bind in spite of the existence of a prelate's precept to the contrary. (Aquinas 1875: Vol. XV, q. 17, a.5)

Aquinas's description of conscience had an influence on Day, who invoked "the primacy of conscience" during several disagreements she had with Catholic bishops on social issues (*CW* 7-8/1964: 1,6,8; 12/1965: 1,2,7).

The fallibility aspect of conscience formation was known to Day, who was influenced by Newman (*CW* 7-8/1964: 6,8). Newman wrote

> [C]onscience is ever to be obeyed whether it tells truly or erroneously, and that, whether the error is the fault of the person thus erring or not....Of course, if a man is capable of being in error, which he might have escaped, had he been more in earnest, for that error he is answerable to God, but still he must act according to that error, while he is in it, because he in full sincerity thinks the error to be the truth. (Newman 1866: 259)

Day recognized the importance of a Catholic individual to follow one's conscience, "[e]ven when one is following a wrong or illinformed conscience." (*CW* 12/1965: 1) As a lay person within the Roman Catholic Church, Day's interpretation of the primacy of conscience was unique. June O'Connor observes

> Dorothy Day's reading of the centrality and supremacy of conscience as characteristic of the Catholic Church is intriguing. Although the claim can indeed be defended in the history of Catholic theology, rooted in the thought of St. Paul and explicated in the theology of Thomas Aquinas, it is a claim that many nontheologically oriented practicing Catholics would find surprising. (O'Connor 1991: 82)

Of Day, O'Connor contends that it is "likely that her esteem for conscience as central was originally rooted in her anarchist commitments" and did not initially come from her reading of Paul or Aquinas (O'Connor 1991: 82). However, the writings of Paul, Aquinas, Newman and Church councils helped Day to bridge her secular anarchist beliefs through a particular understanding of the primacy of conscience in Roman Catholicism.

As a supplement to the principle of subsidiarity and the primacy of conscience, I suggest that the principle of nonviolence also played a role in the anarchism developed within the Catholic Worker movement. Although not formally recognized in Catholic social teaching until 1983, nonviolence has become a valued principle and lifestyle in Roman Catholicism (U.S.Catholic Conference 1983: para. 78, 117-121).

In the anarchist critique of the state, there is the belief that governments function on the basis of coercion. The unequal distribution of wealth can only be maintained in a society through the use of force, especially when there are members of society who lack certain material necessities (food, clothing, shelter, etc.) while others are prospering with excess. The maintenance of both wealth and poverty in a nation requires an organized effort to threaten violence against anyone who wishes to disrupt this state of order (or structured disorder). This organized effort takes the form of law, whereby a militia, an armed force of people, is trained to protect the status quo. This militia is funded, generally, through taxation.

Both Day and Maurin saw nonviolence as an important principle in the Gospels. They agreed with the aforementioned anarchist critique of government, and found an inconsistency with them, as nonviolent Christians, supporting a government based to some extent upon coercive power. The decisions of Maurin and Day to not vote or pay federal taxes or serve on jury duty or to apply for tax-exempt status is rooted in this commitment to Christian nonviolence.

II. Expressions of Anarchism in the Catholic Worker Movement (1933-1980)

When we examine the history of the Catholic Worker, we see the word "anarchism" is used in a variety of ways by Catholic Workers. "Anarchism" is used to reflect "anti-State" sentiments or the desire for a lack of organization, or is twinned with "personalism" to express the initiative of the individual to assist others directly through the works of mercy. I will clarify the multiple uses of the term "anarchism"and, by doing so, bring to the surface the extent to which anarchism is embedded in the fabric of Catholic Worker praxis and thought.

Anarchism As an Alternative to State Definitions of Social Life

Committed to the principle of nonviolence, as interpreted from the New Testament gospels as well as the lives of various saintly people, the Catholic Worker is at odds with the use of coercive power, which is thought to be at the basis of all government. The presence of the military, along with its funding through taxation, is problematic for a group of people committed to nonviolence. A variety of Catholic Workers have chosen to live in opposition to state sanctioned violence. This expression of anarchism is clearly articulated in the writings of Kropotkin and others: the individual and /or community in opposition to the government.

Throughout Dorothy Day's life, the Catholic Worker refused to accept the definitions of social life set forth by government. Frequently raising their voices against the state, Catholic Workers engaged in numerous demonstrations which included varying degrees of civil disobedience. The protests against Civil Defense drills is but one example of anti-State anarchism.

Beginning in 1953, Catholic Workers protested the annual Civil Defense drill in New York City. A group of ten Catholic Workers, led by Ammon Hennacy, were arrested on June 15, 1955 when they refused to take shelter amidst the blare of air-raid sirens. Mel Piehl refers to this as "the first significant pacifist civil disobedience campaign of the post-Korea period." (Piehl 1982: 214) Each year, more people joined the Catholic Worker protest. By 1961, 2,500 people protested the Civil Defense drill in New York City. Shortly thereafter, the public air-raid drills were terminated by the Office of Emergency Preparedness (Piehl 1982: 215).

It is beyond the scope of this essay to describe many other examples of refusing to accept State definitions for social arrangements. I might add that Catholic Workers were actively engaged in protesting the Nazi Party government of Germany, World War II, wars in Korea and Vietnam, the Cold War as well as supporting the effort to unionize migrant farm workers in California. Less publicly recognizable alternatives to the state pervade the fabric of the Catholic Worker at the time.

The decision to not be incorporated or to become a 501-C-3 (statesponsored non-profit organization) speaks of the grassroots commitment to performing works of mercy. The Gospel example of helping one's sister, brother, neighbor or enemy, is grounded in taking personal responsibility for the "other." The bureaucratizing and systematizing of "helping" and the creation of professions to assist others leads to stripping away the precious dignity left for so many who are considered "least" in society. Stated bluntly, the Catholic Worker perspective is that the government is unable to legislate compassion or dignity (Murray 1990). Practicing an anarchism which refuses the privileges of cooperating with the state, Day explained the Catholic Worker position:

> Governments should never do what small bodies can accomplish: unions, credit unions, cooperatives, St. Vincent de Paul Societies....We believe also that government has no right to legislate as to who can or who are to perform the Works of Mercy. Only accredited agencies have the status of tax-exempt institutions. After their application has been filed, and after an investigation and long delays, clarifications, intercession, and urgings by lawyers—often an expensive and long-drawn-out procedure—this tax-exempt status is granted. As personalists, as an unincorporated group, we will not apply for this "privilege." (*CW* 5/1972: 3,5)

Refusing 501-C-3 status meant refusing the governmental (and capitalist) effort to treat charity as a commodity. However well-intentioned the offer, a financial donation to a tax-exempt organization is frequently partnered with the benefit of a tax-deduction. The Catholic Worker perspective on such a donation begs the question: how much of a sacrifice is involved when a donor benefits from a tax "write-off?" Peter Maurin stated, "To feed the hungry *at a personal sacrifice* [emphasis added] is what God wants us to do."(Maurin 1984: 58) Maurin compared today's Christians with those of the early centuries, when "the pagans used to say about the Christians 'See how they love each other'":

> In our own day
> the poor are no longer
> fed, clothed and sheltered
> at a personal sacrifice,
> but at the expense of the taxpayers.
> And because the poor

are no longer fed,
clothed and sheltered
the pagans say about the Christians
"See how they pass the buck." (Maurin 1984: 110-111)

The refusal of practicing usury (the charging or acceptance of financial interest) is not just an indictment against capitalism, it is also a form of resistance against a government that offers its blessing, according to Maurin (1984: 19). The following incident exemplifies the Catholic Worker refusal to accept money which has its source in both the government and bank interest. In 1960, the New York Catholic Worker received $3,579.39 from the City of New York. The money was interest earned from the sale of a former Catholic Worker building to the city, which planned to demolish the building to construct an elevated subway line. In a letter to the City's Treasurer, accompanied by the $3,579.39 check, Dorothy Day explained,

> We are returning the interest on the money we have recently received because we do not believe in "money lending" at interest....We do not believe in the profit system, and so we cannot take profit or interest on our money. People who take a materialistic view of human service wish to make a profit but we are trying to do our duty by our service without wages to our brothers as Jesus commanded in the Gospel (Matthew 25). (Day 1983: 294)

The commitment to war tax resistance is yet another example of such anti-state anarchism. Members of the Catholic Worker contend that a large portion (more than 50% during wartime) of federal income taxes support the U.S. military budget (Hedemann 1986: 15-23).[2] By living in voluntary poverty (earning less than the taxable level of income), Catholic Workers are free to not pay federal and state income taxes, which support war, the preparations for war, capital punishment, etc.

Anarchism As the Practice of Personalist Community

When the Catholic Worker movement shifted in its very early days, from solely a newspaper to include a soup kitchen and place of hospitality for many of New York City's poor, a live-in community was formed comprised of writers, food servers, people without homes, cooks, people to sort through donations, etc. Whether it be farms or hospitality houses, Catholic Worker communities frequently have had few or no rules. In community, an individual strives to live out the "Gentle Personalism" espoused by Peter Maurin—taking personal responsibility for the other person in need, instead of shirking it off to someone else or to an impersonal institution. The practice of a personalist community is another expression of anarchism—it describes the complex set of expressions between an individual and his/her fellow community members at a Catholic Worker house or farm.

Oral history provides us with many examples of how Catholic Workers have dedicated themselves to creating personalist communities. The frequent lack of rules and clearly defined expectations created an environment which permitted individuals to freely express their own views—sometimes consistent, other times incompatible with the views of other community members. One example, from the late 1930s, involved several Catholic Workers of the Easton, Pennsylvania Farm, who decided to go "on strike" until Peter Maurin told them what to do. Peter maintained his anarchist vision of individuals taking responsibility for themselves and for each other to the point of not "requiring" others to help in particular ways. Dorothy recalled one of the "strikers:"

> I remember one fellow, who used to sit under the trees and watch Peter work. Peter always carried his point so far that he would never ask anyone to help him, or tell anyone to do a lot of work... But Jim used to say, "I'll work when I'm told to. I want someone to give me orders." So he would sit under the tree and do nothing all the day[...] But Peter never gave an order. He will sacrifice material success any day, in order to drive home his ideas in regard to personalism. (Miller 1982: 296)

This example reflects the anarchism within a personalist community, in which one Catholic Worker is at odds with the rest of that community's Catholic Workers. Countless examples of this expression of anarchism pervade this movement, which hosted such strong personalities as Ammon Hennacy, the self-proclaimed "Catholic Anarchist" and "one-man revolution."(Hennacy 1994: xix)

Anarchism As a Personalist Social Movement

As the Catholic Worker movement expanded beyond the boundaries of New York City, another type of anarchism can be observed. "The Catholic Worker" was no longer just a newspaper, or just a single community, but now a network of communities—a personalist-based social movement. Although Peter Maurin and Dorothy Day served as co-founders for the movement, they were not clearly "in charge" of each and every community. Lacking a corporate structure, the Catholic Worker was woven together by an anarchist thread. This expression of anarchism may be described as the relationships among the different Catholic Worker communities with each other, ultimately forming what is referred to as the "movement." This is anarchism functioning on a macro-level.

While Dorothy Day was alive, the relationships among the various Catholic Worker communities with each other was complex, but Day's influence was powerful and constant. While the Catholic Worker was anarchistic in organization (more like an "organism," according to Peter Maurin) the physical presence of Peter Maurin (until 1949) and, especially Dorothy Day (until 1980) had an impact which seems impossible to calculate. The opinons and views of these co-founders were for the most part sought out and, once enunciated, held in high esteeem. But powerful and profound differences of opinion cropped up between Day and other members of the Catholic Worker movement. For example, when Day reiterated the pacifist position of the Catholic Worker shortly after the U.S. government declared war on Japan and Germany, 70% of the Catholic Worker communities closed within two and a half years (*CW* 10/1944:7). The Los Angeles Catholic Worker community went so far in their disagreement with Day as to burn all of their issues of *The Catholic Worker* newspaper (Roberts 1984: 133).

In a technical sense, the Catholic Worker lacks organizational structure, hierarchical leadership, and clearly defined rules or policies. But in a practical sense, it was not needed because Day's influence was tremendous. Some people remember Day as the benevolent dictator of an anarchist movement. Her decision to emphasize the principle of nonviolence in the midst of the U.S. entry in World War II elevated a mutually understood notion to the level of a clearly defined policy for the whole Catholic Worker movement, not just for the New York community (Sicius 1996: 65-76).

Prior to 1980, only a blurred line differentiated various Catholic Worker communites vis-a-vis Dorothy Day. Each community generally functioned independently within this anarchist movement. However, Day's presence had a profound impact on the practices of each Catholic Worker community in varying degrees. The degree to which

Day's impact was experienced in individual communities is a worthwhile research project, but beyond the boundaries of this paper.

III. The Anarchist Thread in the Contemporary Catholic Worker Movement (1980-present)

The individual or community's refusal to participate in the coercive powers of the state manifests itself in a variety of ways in today's movement. Many Catholic Worker communities still mount public demonstrations, frequently accompanied by civil disobedience. Since the early 1980s, Plowshares actions have involved many Catholic Workers saying "no" to the state's commitment to creating and deploying weapons of destruction. Plowshares actions have involved trespassing into military bases, with the intention of "turning swords into plowshares" by hammering and spilling blood on weapons. This limited form of violence, directed against military property (not people), is not new in the movement. In the 1960s, many Catholic Workers took part in demonstrations against the Vietnam War, which sometimes destroyed government property, but never harmed people. For example, the first person to violate the Rivers Amendment, making it illegal to burn draft cards, was Catholic Worker David Miller (Klejment and Roberts 1996: 160-166).

More subtle forms of critiquing the state, such as refusing tax-exempt status or incorporation, seem to be questioned and debated more by people in today's movement. Dorothy Day House of Syracuse, NY, provides an example of the issues currently being discussed. Begun in the early 1980s as a Catholic Worker house of hospitality for homeless women and children, it was neither incorporated nor holder of 501-C-3 (tax-exempt, non-profit) status. The Catholic Workers, those providing hospitality, did not receive a wage and they lived in voluntary poverty with the families they served. Dorothy Day House refused to receive any governmental funds to reimburse them for their efforts (DD-CW, W- 45, Box 1).

By the late 1980s, Dorothy Day House was not raising enough money to pay for food, rent, utilities, etc. An offer of help was received from Catholic Charities of the Roman Catholic Diocese of Syracuse. Initially, the offer was limited to free Catholic Charities staff time and limited funding. In the midst of this limited form of help, the diocesan Catholic Charities office made changes which they felt were "necessary" for the continuation of the house. Paid staff were hired specifically for Dorothy Day House and both government and corporate grants were received to fund the staff's salaries. Quickly, the original visionaries of Dorothy Day House saw their Catholic Worker home turned into yet another 501-C-3 institutional shelter. In the end, Dorothy Day House's founders were not welcomed to participate in critical decision making because of their refusal to accept the state definitions for performing works of mercy. They refused to be certified by the state as social workers and counselors. They refused to accept a salary (due to voluntary poverty and war tax resistance) and thus were not recognized as "staff" by the Catholic Charities employees receiving a salary. Until recently the Catholic Charities staff of Dorothy Day House claimed a Catholic Worker identity. This is a curious claim, considering that Dorothy Day House is comparable to all other Catholic Charities shelters, with one exception: Dorothy Day House has a picture of Dorothy Day hanging in their living room.

The example of Dorothy Day House illustrates a variety of issues confronting today's movement: there are benefits to not practicing typical anarchism. Many of today's Catholic Worker communities have debated whether to receive tax-exempt status, FEMA funding or other governmental assistance, etc. (McKenna 1987: 6-9)[3] his topic is not new: the St. Joseph's House of Hospitality in Rochester, NY is incorporated as a 501-C-3, receives food through governmental programs, and hosts a board of directors which has the power to make a variety of decisions. St. Joseph's House has maintained its tax-exempt status since 1941. This early exception to the Catholic Worker "tradition" proves the rule, as a Catholic Worker from St. Joseph's wrote to Day to defend the "necessity" of their incorporation and tax-exempt status (Murray 1990: 128-129). Harry Murray observes:

> They... took a step at this point that branded them a deviant Worker house, a house that was "looked at askance" by the New York house. On the advice of a lawyer, they incorporated and formed a board of directors... Incorporation was viewed as a dangerous compromise with the capitalist system by other Worker houses, which had not incorporated.

Anarchism As Practice of Personalist Community

The complex set of relationships between an individual and his/her respective Catholic Worker community continues today in the movement. The struggle to live as a community, while acknowledging the different needs of community members easily leads to disagreements and sometimes to open conflict. There is not much difference between the intra-community anarchism today and during the days of Maurin and Day. This is due, in part, to the lack of structure which continues to permeate most Catholic Worker communities today.

It should be noted, however, that since the late 1960s, more non-Catholics and nonpracticing Catholics joined the Catholic Worker. Inspired by the movement's public demonstrations against the Vietnam War, many secular-minded persons joined the Catholic Worker for their political radicalism. Such a group did not join because of a shared sense of traditional Catholic piety espoused by Day and many others. To a certain degree, the attraction of non-Catholics and nonpracticing Catholics has had an impact on the dynamics in some of today's Catholic Worker communities. The extent of of this impact would be a valuable research project for the future, however, it falls beyond the parameters of this essay.

Anarchism As Personalist Social Movement

The set of relationships between and among various Catholic Worker communities, comprising what we call the "movement," has significantly altered since the death of Dorothy Day. As previously noted, while the Catholic Worker has developed with an anarchist thread, the influence of Dorothy Day, until her death, was enormous. Prior to 1980, some communities chose paths which were directly or indirectly in disagreement with the perspective of the co-founder. I contend, however, that the types of disagreements with Dorothy Day's intentions have both increased in frequency and changed in intensity, since her death.

In various Catholic Worker roundtable discussions, newsletters, gatherings and publications, the issues of feminism, abortion and gay/lesbian lifestyles in the Catholic Worker have become more pronounced (Troester 1993: 518-560). While these issues were discussed in the Catholic Worker toward the end of Day's life, they played a peripheral role in how Catholic Workers identified themselves. Since Day's death, I contend that discussions about these three topics have increased in both frequency and importance for the Catholic Worker. For more and more Catholic Worker individuals and communities, the issues of feminism, abortion and gay/lesbian sexuality in the Church have become essential in the development and maintenance of their Catholic Worker identities.

In addition to the aforementioned topics, it should be noted that there are two additional issues being debated among today's Catholic Worker communities. These issues include organizational status and the role of technology. There is enormous diversity of opinion about how a Catholic Worker community should be organized. In spite of Maurin's and Day's original vision, some of today's communities opt to become incorporated, tax exempt or even to receive direct government assistance. This appears to contradict the expression of anarchism of the co-founders. The matter of decision making varies from community to community. Some maintain a more anarchist "spirit" by using consensus models for decisions; others use a democratic vote or a board of directors.

The role of technology stimulates significant deliberation in today's Catholic Worker communities. A fundamental concern is the way technology further separates the poor from the affluent. Another is the link between technology and the consumer mentality being pressed on society. Thus, each community must decide about use of the following: computers, word processors, credit cards, bank accounts (with or without interest), televisions, microwave ovens, etc.

Since the death of Dorothy Day, the Catholic Worker has no leader, no headquarters, no clearly defined policies, and no membership requirements. Dorothy Day's presence influenced and shaped the expression of anarchism as a personalist social movement. Although there was diversity within the Catholic Worker during Dorothy's life, Catholic Worker communities in recent years have broadened the spectrum of diverse views. The fundamental issues of identity and authority in the Catholic Worker community surface whenever strong differences of opinion arise. While Maurin contended that "we have no party line," Day oprovided some responses to questions of Catholic Worker identity and authority (*CW* 4/52: 1,7).

Now, nearly two decades after Day's death, the movement continues. Without Day as a leader, without New York City as the headquarters, today's movement lacks a mechanism to mediate the issues which raise questions about Catholic Worker identity or authority. Insofar as community decisions had been influenced by Day's presence, today each community is truly on its own, in terms of decision making. This leads to a more open form of anarchism as a personalist social movement. There is no such thing as "membership" with the Catolic Worker. Individuals can become Catholic Workers without meeting any requirements, and communities can declare themselves to be Catholic Worker houses without meeting a standard or a requirement.

IV. The Newly Developed Anarchist Thread in Today's Catholic Worker Movement

Day's death also opened the way for wide diversity—anarchism—regarding the relationship between the Catholic Worker movement and the Roamn Catholic Church. Another aspect of more open engagement of anarchism as a personalist social movement arises in conflicts with the institutional aspects of the Roman Catholic Church. Some Catholic Workers and their communities have taken positions or engaged in practices openly at odds with both the doctrines and hierarchy of the Catholic Church.

These conflicts fall into two distinctive categories: calling on the Church to better fulfill explicit biblical or Church teachings or, on the other hand, calling on the Church to change its teaching. The former is done in a spirit of Church renewal; the latter results from a progressive-radical view of Church. Both expressions of anarchism are displayed publicly and lead to questions of identity and authority not only in today's Catholic Worker, but in the Roman Catholic Church as well.

Issues of Economic Justice

The Dorothy Day-Catholic Worker Collection at Marquette University contains several examples of recent Catholic Worker community actions which explicitly challenged Catholic leaders to more faithful fulfillment of their teachings on the poor:

– In Los Angeles, a Catholic Worker community protested on Church property in front of the Cardinal and other leaders over plans to construct a $100 million cathedral and archdiocesan center. The Los Angeles Catholic Workers contended that the poor had greater need for the funds.

– In Philadelphia, a Catholic Worker community protested the diocesan decision to close several inner city Catholic schools by organizing a "sit-in" outside the bishop's office.

– The Hartford, CT, Catholic Worker community publicly demonstrated against the bishop's decision to suspend a soup kitchen

> by serving meals to poor people on the stoop of the bishop's office. The bishop suspended the soup kitchen because it was in a neighborhood experiencing gentrification, and Church leaders believed the kitchen's presence might deter upwardly mobile Catholics from joining the parish.
>
> – The Dorothy Day Catholic Worker community in Washington, DC publicly demonstrated against the expenditure of $50 million for the Pope John Paul II Cultural Center on the grounds that the poor should be given preference over a $50 million "think tank."

While Dorothy Day had disagreements with Church leadership, usually on matters of economics and nonviolence, she was opposed to using the newspaper to criticize individual Church leaders. Day went so far as to refuse the publication of some of Peter Maurin's ideas, which she felt were too critical of particular Catholic clergy. Mel Piehl observed:

> Maurin... exhibited a mild anticlericalism of a sort not uncommon among European, and especially French, Catholic social activists. Day made sure no hint of this got into *The Catholic Worker*. "I do indeed keep out some of his stuff which attacks the bishops," she told one correspondent. "I just don't think it's politic. There are quite a number of priests who think Peter just quaint when he verbally attacks the clergy, but who would hold up their hands in horror if we printed the stuff." (Piehl 1982: 62)

It might be concluded that the recent actions were inconsistent with Day's approach. Today's Catholic Worker communities in Los Angeles, Philadelphia, Hartford and Washington, demonstrated openly against their diocesan leaders. I think these contemporary protests have a parallel in the conflict between Day and New York's Francis Cardinal Spellman over a gravedigger strike. In 1949 employees of New York's Calvary Cemetery formed a union and began a strike with the hopes of better wages and resting one day a week. Because it was a Church cemetery, the workers were employees of the archdiocese. Spellman refused to participate in negotiations, referring to the strike as "Anti-American, anti-Christian evil" and "a strike against the Church." (O'Connor 1991: 72) The cardinal was enraged when *The Catholic Worker* supported the gravediggers' strike. Day, citing *Rerum Novarum* and *Quadragesimo Anno,* explained to the stikers that "their action was Christian and that they themselves were the Church." Day publicly criticized the cardinal for contradicting Catholic social teaching on the right of workers to form unions and strike (*CW* 4/ 1949: 1,2).

Day specifically called Church leaders to fulfill what the explicit Church teaching of *Rerum Novarum* and *Quadragesimo Anno*, which state that workers have the right to form labor associations and the right to strike. Cardinal Spellman acted contrary to this Church teaching, and Day confronted him. Regarding this and other troubling encounters with Spellman and other Archdiocesan officials, Day reflected:

> But the Church has never told its flock that they have no rights of their own, that they ought to have no beliefs or loyalties other than those of the pope or one of his cardinals. No one in the Church can tell me what to think about social and political and economic questions without getting a tough speech back: please leave me alone and tend to your own acreage; I'll take care of mine. (Coles 1987: 81)

Day did not call for revolution; she merely asked Church leaders to live up to the teachings they expounded for others.

Thus there may be less difference between Day's approach and that of the aforementioned Catholic Worker communities who called upon Church leadership to set their actions in accord with their teachings. U.S.bishops have articulated in Catholic social teaching the concept of the common good and the preferential option for the poor (U.S. Catholic Conference 1986).[4] Today's Catholic Worker communities are demanding that leaders follow these principles of Catholic social teaching. For example, archdiocesan leaders must explain how spending $50 million for a Catholic "think tank" benefits the residents of Washington, DC, a city with one of the highest rates of poverty in the country.

Issues of Gender & Sexuality

The other category of conflict, the call for the Church to change its teaching, emerges among those Catholic Workers who reject Catholic teachings on gender and sexuality, particularly feminism, abortion, and gay/lesbian sexuality. This form of anarchism, an anti-institutional position, has generated concern about the identity of the Catholic Worker movement and individual Catholic Workers.

In this context, multiple answers emerge to the central questions: What makes an individual a Catholic Worker? What makes a Catholic Worker Catholic?

This essay examines only two of the most popular responses, which fall into these categories: those Catholics who find great meaning in obeying the Church hierarchy and those Catholics who have become discouraged by Church teaching (usually on gender and sexuality issues) and no longer find Church hierarchy to have much importance in their lives.

Eugene Kennedy's identification of two distinctive "cultures" of American Catholics may help distinguish the divisions with the Catholic Workers on issues related to the Church. In *Tomorrow's Catholics, Yesterday's Church*, Kennedy (1988) describes the majority of U.S Catholics falling into one of two groups: Culture One or Culture Two.

Culture One Catholics share a strong commitment to the institutional Church. Kennedy remarks, "Culture one is intrinsically dependent on the Church *as institution* for its existence." (Kennedy 1988: 9) Many left-wing and right-wing Catholics share a home as Culture One Catholics. While their opinions may differ over controversial issues, what binds them together is that both groups depend upon what the institutional Church states about matters of faith and morality. It is clear that, with their traditional Catholic piety, both Day and Maurin would be considered Culture One Catholics according to Kennedy's categories. Catholic Workers calling for Church practices to better reflect biblical or Church teachings seem to be Culture One Catholics. If they disagree with Church teachings, they wait with the hope that the hierarchy will change the Church's position.

Culture Two Catholics, by contrast, have their faith primarily influenced by the experience of sacraments in their local parish community. Culture Two Catholics are not influenced by pronouncements from bishops or popes. Church statements with which a Culture Two Catholic disagrees are of no consequence. Unlike Culture One Catholics who will read (about) the latest papal encyclical, magisterial pronouncement or bishop's pastoral letter, Culture Two Catholics proceed with their faith regardless of the institutional Church.

Catholic Workers who engage in a more radical form of Church critique do not fall into either of Kennedy's categories. Culture One and Culture Two Catholics may be thought of as institutional Catholics and non-institutional Catholics, respectively. What distinguishes those Catholic Workers openly challenging Church authority is that they are neither institutional Catholic nor non-institutional Catholics. Rather, these Catholic Workers are *post-institutional Catholics.* Most of them were active Culture One Catholics, but through a series of experiences, chose to leave behind their dependence on the institutional Church. It is this post-institutional quality which distinguishes this group of Catholic Workers from those who were lifelong non-institutional Culture Two Catholics.

For Catholic Workers, being "Catholic" involves an identity which is distinguishable from the other expressions of Catholic Worker anarchism. Progressive Church anarchism reflects a post-institutional Catholic identity. In challenging Church authorities as an expression of anarchism, Catholic Workers may also be thought of as *parainstitutional.* Catholic Workers calling for reform within Church leadership ask only that institutional leaders of the Church live up to explicit Church or biblical teachings, thereby recognizing the authority of the Catholic hierarchy. But Catholic Workers who radically challenge the Church do not simply disagree with Church leaders; they publicly embrace beliefs and practices which are explicitly denounced by the institutional Church.

The presence of post-institutional Catholics in today's Catholic Worker has led many to question whether there are limitations to critiquing the institutional Church beyond which one ceases to be a faithful Catholic Worker in the movement and a faithful member of the Catholic Church. Open challenges to Church teachings these days arise on the issues of feminism, abortion, and homosexuality

Feminism

One dimension of the feminism issue takes up the ordination of women to priesthood and the role of women in the celebration of Mass. Since 1983, Casa Maria, the Catholic Worker community in Milwaukee, has permitted women to preside at their prayer gatherings which they call Eucharist and which have sometimes been labeled "Mass." The community's decision to celebrate liturgy in this way is explained by longtime Casa Maria member Don Timmerman:

> It has always been the contention of the Milwaukee Catholic Worker house that wherever we see injustice or unfairness that we

> speak out against it or act against it in some way. In this instance, we think it is unfair or unjust for the Church to lay down a law that says that only men who have been ordained are allowed to lead or celebrate the Eucharist. (Jasperse 1988)

Timmerman compares this act of protesting Church policy with protesting non-religious social policies:

> We feel that it is wrong to forbid women the opportunity to preside at Mass, since it is wrong; we refuse to follow the Church mandate which states that only men may preside at Mass. If we accuse our society of being unjust and, thus, refuse to cooperate with it, then we also have an obligation to see the injustice in the Church and refuse to cooperate with it also. (Timmerman 1988: 460)

Timmerman's refusal to cooperate with social policy and violation of Church policy breaks the traditional boundaries of Catholic Worker communities during Day's lifetime. Day was very particular about public criticism of the institutional Church: she insisted that it be limited to cases where the Church was not living up to explicit Church and biblical teachings.

Casa Maria's commitment to allow lay women and men to preside at in-house Eucharist reflects the community's post-institutional Roman Catholicism. This is evident in another way. Not only do women preside, Casa Maria functions outside Church authority, because, like most Catholic Worker communities, it is not formally related to the local Church. Rev. Ralph Gross, Chancellor for the Archdiocese of Milwaukee, acknowledged that the Church had no official authority over Casa Maria:

> Gross said the archdiocese could do little if the group flouted the Church's teaching. Archbishop Rembert G. Weakland could counsel or reprimand the group *but could not discipline it,* Gross said, because the Catholic Worker movement is an organization independent of the Catholic Church. 'What jurisdiction do we have over them?' Gross said. 'The jurisdiction we have over them as a Catholic group is different than the jurisdiction we have over a Catholic parish.' (Jasperse 1988, emphasis added)

Since the institutional Church is unable to discipline Casa Maria, the Catholic Worker community is able to continue its post-institutional form of Catholicism.

Yet another way Casa Maria may be seen as a post-institutional community is in their self definition of "Catholic." Many of those protesting Casa Maria's actions have asked why they maintain the name *Catholic* Worker if they celebrate liturgies which are non-canonical. Timmerman explains:

> We still claim to be Catholic Workers since we believe strongly in the philosophy of the Catholic Worker movement. We try to practice the spiritual and corporal works of mercy. We take in families and single women, give food to the hungry...give clothing to the needy.... and, of course, we realize that God is the cause and reason of our work. (Timmerman 1988: 460)

Missing from Timmerman's description of being a Catholic Worker is any mention of the institutional Church. To be a Catholic Worker (and a *Catholic*?) means to practice the works of mercy and recognize that God is the ultimate source of these deeds, according to Timmerman. In place of popes, bishops, magisteria, or chanceries are God and the poor.

Many critics of Casa Maria may be seen as Culture One Catholics. In discussing women's ordination, as well as birth control and celibacy, Kennedy observes

> These are the issues, par excellence, in Culture One, for it is in this setting that they are endlessly and inconclusively debated. Culture One seems obsessed if not possessed, one way or the other, by these matters. These are, literally, very telling controversies, for they tell us that control is the central dynamic of institutional Catholicism. (Kennedy 1988: 15)

The matter of control is at stake in many of the protesters' arguments, especially controlling the definition of Catholic identity. Commenting upon the "invalid liturgies" celebrated by Casa Maria, Gross remarks

> If somebody claims that they are Catholic, then we would expect that they are acting according to the Catholic beliefs, teaching and practices. If they claim they are Catholic, we would expect that they are following this. (Jasperse 1988)

While Timmerman formulates the community's Catholicism in practicing the works of mercy, Gross defines Catholicism as "acting according to" the institutional Church.

Gordon Zahn, a Roman Catholic and longtime friend of Dorothy Day and the Catholic Worker, publicly took issue with the Casa Maria liturgies. Using Culture One reasoning, Zahn argued that Casa Maria continues "to reject or defy established ecclesiastical authority by disregarding rules and procedures relating to the most sacred core of Catholic belief, the liturgy itself."(Timmerman 1988: 461) In response to Timmerman's emphasis on the works of mercy, Zahn states that by condoning invalid liturgies, "they depart from the full service to the spiritual works of mercy." Unlike Timmerman, Zahn links practicing the spiritual works of mercy to the institutional Church. Zahn defines the *Catholic* in Catholic Worker vis-a-vis the spiritual vision of the movement's founders. Zahn applies Culture One reasoning to the Catholic Worker and cites Day as the official authority of the movement, even after her death. Much of Zahn's argument with Casa Maria depends upon the notion that Day's views during her lifetime set the parameters which constitute the definition of a Catholic Worker. Zahn's view is shared by other Catholic Workers who uphold Day as the teaching authority on the Catholic Workers and the movement, in much the same way Culture One Catholics see the institutional Church as a teaching authority. Zahn explains:

> [Dorothy Day] would have been the first to reject changes that threatened or weakened the movement's basic commitment to the recognized and legitimate teaching authority of the Church. She would not deny the faults and failures that call for correction, but she would insist that the correction must come through the efforts of true believers guided by love and respect for the Church as it is, imperfections and all—and as God's grace, we can help it become...the Catholic Worker she founded could do no better than to accept and follow her guidance. (461)

Zahn maintains that Day's life should be the permanent benchmark for Catholic Worker individuals and communities. He implies that Day's life should continue as the controlling force within the contemporary Catholic Worker.

The anarchism expressed by the post-institutional Catholic Workers at Casa Maria seems closely related to the primacy of conscience.

Their primary intentions are to do what they perceive as being just and right, not to disagree or disobey the institutional Church. Timmerman explains, "The reason... is not that we want to be disobedient to Rome, but the reason is that we feel it is just that other people who feel called to a particular priesthood... should be allowed to do so."(Jasperse 1988)

Abortion

In the summer of 1991, Haley House, a Catholic Worker community in Boston, hosted a gathering for Catholic Worker communities throughout the U.S., Canada, Europe and Australia. Amidst the ongoing workshops, many Catholic Workers discussed abortion and the Catholic identity of the Catholic Worker movement. This debate was sparked by an open letter from Unity Kitchen Community of the Catholic Worker in Syracuse, NY, which was intentionally absent from the gathering. In the "Open Letter" to Catholic Workers gathered in Boston, Unity Kitchen Community stated

> What is at stake here is the Catholic identity of the Catholic Worker. This identity, given to the Catholic Worker by Dorothy Day and Peter Maurin, shapes its vocation and gives meaning and coherence to its witness. (Unity Kitchen 1991: 1)

The Unity Kitchen Community letter pointed out the loss of Catholic identity on several issues, including abortion and submission to the teaching authority of the Church. The "Open Letter" was photocopied and distributed to each of the participants in the Boston gathering along with a letter signed by "Deidre," a member of the Haley House community, in response to Unity Kitchen's concerns. The author, a self-described pro-choice feminist, wrote, "I do not wish to engage in dialogue with anyone who is convinced that abortion is murder and that it is okay for them to confront women at clinics, whether it is with physical blocking or prayer or other activity."(Deirdre 1991) The writer continued, "Abortion is not murder for many of us." The writer saw Church teaching on abortion as oppressive to women and concluded, "The question is about power, and unless that power is being challenged in the State and the Church and on the streets, I have a hard time believing we are in the same revolution."

Response to both letters was expressed throughout workshops and impromptu "soap-box preaching," reminiscent of Maurin's teaching style in New York's Union Square. Diverse and passionate opinions about abortion, and to a lesser extent Catholic identity, were expressed.

Conversations and speeches about abortion led to the topic of the Catholic identity of the contemporary Catholic Worker. In "Open Letter," the Unity Kitchen Community criticized the lack of Catholicism in Haley House's identity. The Haley House newsletter carried the community's description of their approach to religion: "[W]hile our spirituality is open and at times incorporates insights from other traditions, the communal spiritual life is fundamentally Christian in form and content." In response to a previous critical letter from Ann O'Connor of Unity Kitchen, Haley House printed the following self description:

> We are, we suspect, a religiously more diverse community than the Unity Kitchen. We happily count Quakers, Jews, Protestants, Deists and Agnostics as well as devout and not so devout Roman Catholics as partners in our endeavors. And, we have experienced "Church," those called to be people of God, as wider than any specific faith community....We seek to remain open to truth wherever it may be found: in the teachings of the popes or the silence of the mystics or the words of M.K. Gandhi. (Haley House 1985: 7)

Within these two remarks, one can observe the tensions regarding the issue of Catholic identity for the Haley House community. The remarks speak of a "Christian" center (with Roman Catholic deemphasized to a certain extent) in which members gather to be part of a religiously diverse community.

O'Connor took issue with this approach by a Catholic Worker community. Referring to Unity Kitchen as "an orthodox Roman Catholic community," O'Connor criticized the (mis)use of the word "Catholic" by Catholic Worker houses like Haley House:

> Some houses have no Catholics as Workers, and/or have Workers who are ex-Catholics or anti-Catholics. Much of the Catholic Worker has become incoherent, if not downright dishonest, in claiming the name *Catholic* Worker. (O'Connor 1994: 6)

O'Connor went on to define Catholic in the context of a Catholic Worker house as meaning "holding Catholic convictions in union with the Magisterium." The Unity Kitchen Community claimed that it is dishonest for Catholic Workers at Haley House and other communities to claim a Catholic identity while being supportive of abortion rights.

Gay/Lesbian Sexuality

During her life, Day never publicly discussed or wrote about the topic of homosexuality. Privately, it was understood that Day supported the Church's teaching on homosexuality. Chris Montesano, a former New York Catholic Worker, recalled: "Dorothy would not open up the issue to discussion because she felt it was too volatile. She was clear that her stand was traditional Church. I don't agree with that, but that was clearly her stand. I think Dorothy definitely loved many gay people and loved them very well."(Troester 1993: 526)

In the summer of 1984, the New York Catholic Worker community sponsored its first round table discussion on the topic: "Church's Ministry to the Gay Community." New York Catholic Worker community member Jane Sammon expressed concern about raising the topic: "Dorothy would not have liked the talk to be given. In the past, she would not let anyone put articles in the paper on homosexuality. In many ways on political and social issues, she was radical, but when it came to Church doctrine, she was conservative."(Aronica 1987: 121)

In January 1985 Peggy Scherer, an editor of *The Catholic Worker*, submitted an article for publication entitled, "Homosexuality: Searching for Understanding." The thrust of this article was that the continued silence about gay and lesbian issues perpetuate homophobic forms of violence. Scherer's article was not published until the October-November 1985 issue after, she later wrote in a letter, eight months of "innumerable hours praying, studying, talking 1-to-1, in small and large groups, plus in days of reflection led by priests, and numerous re-writes and compromises."(Scherer 1987: 2) In the published article, Scherer called for "dialogue" to begin breaking the cycle of gay-bashing in our society. Scherer affirmed Church teaching on the issue of homosexuality: "The Catholic Worker has always accepted the Church as authority on matters of faith and morals, and continues to do so."(*CW* 10-11/1985: 3)

Despite this affirmation of official Church teaching, the New York Catholic Worker community was sharply divided through much of 1985 and 1986. Scherer observed, "The key concerns which have led to division among us... are those which caused pain and division in the Church around the country: questions about dissent, orthodoxy, and authority."(Scherer 1987: 1)

This division was expressed through two new editorial policies formulated by some but not all of *The Catholic Worker* editors in the summer of 1986. First, "no article on any topic (economics, politics, etc. as well as religious matters) can include any 'deviation' from what is understood as the Catholic Worker view." Second, "no one who disagrees with any Church teaching (by implication, on women's ordination, whatever) publicly—no matter if they do so as an individual, in conscience, sensitively & nonviolently—can be an editor of the *C.W.*" (Scherer 1987: 2) These policies, determined by some editors in the absence of others, led to the removal of two gay Catholics on the editorial board: Ernesto de la Vega and Gary Donatelli. Longtime Worker and *Catholic Worker* associate editor Geoffrey Gneuhs resigned because of the editorial decisions. Peggy Scherer, a member of the New York Catholic Worker community for 12 years, also left the community over these policies. Donatelli, an editor who was not present at these decision-making meetings, later recalled

> Some of the editors felt that someone who publicly questioned the *Magisterium* on Catholic teaching couldn't be an editor of the *Catholic Worker.* I'm out in California thinking, "Now wait a minute! I never heard this before. This isn't something Dorothy talked about." (Troester 1993: 530)

Donatelli implied a lack of such policy during Day's life at the Catholic Worker. Ultimately, the issue of authority and decision-making is at the core of this division. Donatelli noted, "One thing that I really fault the editors for is not writing about it in the paper... this community functioned in this mysterious way, with decisions made without anybody knowing them." Scherer elaborated on the issue of authority:

> A very basic problem was that there was no real resolution on the question of authority—who had the authority to make decisions, who is the community. There was just a lot of confusion. Because it wasn't clear how decisions were made and by whom, making a decision, especially about a very difficult topic, became next to impossible. (Troester 1993: 532)

Gneuhs also observed that authority and decision-making are at the heart of this division within the New York Catholic Worker Community. In his letter of resignation Gneuhs wrote: "A kind of autocracy and individualism become the norm with one or a few arrogating to themselves power and authority—but neither ever given or delegated. The result of not having clear and fair procedures can only lead to confusion and division." (DD-CW: W-52, Box 1)

Conclusion

> It's good to criticize the Church. The way Dorothy criticized the Church was with love, and you felt that. But there is a lot of very trenchant, unloving criticism now. - Eileen Egan (Troester 1993: 522)

In Section I, the anarchist roots of the Catholic Worker were presented through both secular and religious formulations. Through their interpretations of the principle of subsidiarity and the primacy of conscience, Maurin and Day introduced a distinctively Catholic approach to anarchism.

In the second section, three different expressions of anarchism were examined in the Catholic Worker during the life of Maurin and Day. These were: first, the refusal to accept state definitions of social life; second, the practice of a personalist community; and third, anarchism as a personalist social movement.

In Section III, the contemporary Catholic Worker movement was compared with the movement during Day's life (1933-1980) through the three expressions of anarchism. While the sentiments of anti-state anarchism continue in today's movement, governmental support of Catholic Worker houses of hospitality has become an issue. In today's movement, numerous Catholic Worker communities are incorporated, have tax-exempt status, or receive financial or food assistance through federal government programs. This contrasts with the majority of Catholic Worker communities between 1933 and 1980 and Day's expressed position.

The anarchist practice of personalist community continues with little difference in most of today's communities. It was noted, however, that since the late 1960s more non-Catholics and nonpracticing Catholics have joined the Catholic Worker. To a certain degree, the attraction of such persons has had an impact on the dynamics in some of today's Catholic Worker communities.

Since the death of Day, the third expression of anarchism has significantly altered in the movement. Lacking an organizational structure (i.e. no headquarters, no leader, no clearly defined policies, no membership requirements, etc.) today's Catholic Worker wrestles with disagreements on such issues as feminism, abortion, gay/lesbian sexuality in the Church, organizational status, and technology.

Section IV examined a more contemporary form of anarchism: the Catholic Worker individual or community in conflict with the doctrine of the Roman Catholic Church. This anti-Church anarchism is grounded in two distinctive perspectives. Catholic Workers seeking reform within the Church respect the validity of the Church leadership, as did Day and Maurin. A more revolutionary perspective is adopted by Catholic Workers who simply disregard Church teachings. In fact, I contend that these latter Catholic Workers are using Catholicism, vis-a-vis the primacy of conscience and the principle of subsidiarity, to not only critique but to deconstruct Catholicism. This is a deconstructive process because the post-institutional Church position is informed by notions embraced by the institutional Church. Catholic Workers engaging in this anti-Church anarchism are using elements of Church teaching (e.g. principle of subsidiarity, primacy of conscience, and nonviolence) to unravel the fabric of the institutional Church.

The same Catholic roots of the co-founders' anarchism (conscience and subsidiarity) have become reinterpreted by many of today's Catholic Workers who deconstruct Catholicism to create a "post-institutional" Catholic identity within the movement. Primacy of conscience, used by Day and Maurin to critique the economic and social teachings of the Church, is now used to override papal and magisterial teachings on such topics as women's ordination, abortion, and homosexuality. James Fisher observed, "Though Day was essentially a devoutly Catholic separatist, her movement launched a process which by the 1960s would find, much to her sorrow, millions of American Catholics exalting private conscience over the claims of the Church of Rome."(Fisher 1989: xiv) Likewise, the principle of subsidiarity, used by Day and Maurin to primarily critique government and economic systems, is now invoked against the hierarchical structures of the Roman Catholic Church.

Although a spectrum of opinions existed on a variety of issues during Day's lifetime, post-institutional members of today's Catholic Worker have increased this spectrum by geometric proportions. The issues of identity and authority have never been more blurred within the Catholic Worker. Fisher concluded

> The Catholic Worker movement survived, although after Day's death in 1980, it resembled more a peace group dedicated to the memory of a charismatic individual than a Catholic movement in the sense Day herself would have insisted upon. There was, to be sure, no longer a mass base of working-class Catholics wary of upward mobility. As Donald Meyer succinctly wrote [...], "The 'individualization' of Catholicism has, of course, swelled the precincts of basic middle-class life immeasurably." By the 1960s and 1970s it seemed that American Catholics were free of the identity concerns which plagued many of their parents. (Fisher 1989: 253)

Fisher raised two important issues: today's Catholic Workers' views of Dorothy Day and the complicated category of identity in American Catholicism, as well as today's Catholic Worker movement.

In reviewing the diverse opinions on feminism, abortion and homosexuality in the Church, Catholic Workers continue to invoke Dorothy Day's name to justify their respective positions on these controversial issues. Those Catholic Workers appear to function in the same way as Kennedy's description of Culture One Catholics. Catholic Workers who invoke Day's views to defend a particular position are appealing to Day as an "authoritative" source within today's movement. Like the Culture One Catholics who embrace the teaching authority of Church hierarchy, some Catholic Workers similarly embrace Dorothy Day's views as "authoritative" for today's movement. In making decisions these Catholic Workers ask questions like: What would Dorothy Day do? What would Dorothy Day say? It is quite common in social movements, following the death of a charismatic founder, to raise similar questions when the movement encounters new situations or re-visits old ones. But these questions, within the anarchist context of the Catholic Worker only yield further questions.

The question, "What would Dorothy think about this?" raises the question of who has the authority to answer.

There are those Catholic Workers who oppose using Day's writings or positions as a measuring rod for today's Catholic Worker communities. David Stein, a Chicago Catholic Worker, took this position:

> I'm real sick of hearing about Dorothy and reading about Dorothy. There's too many damn books about Dorothy Day. Too many posters of Dorothy Day, that icon the Claretians put out makes me want to lose my dinner [...] I admire Dorothy Day and Peter Maurin and I thank God that they started the Catholic Worker. I don't know how many times I've listened to someone give a rap to a bunch of students about the Catholic Worker. They'll start out, "Well, in 1933 a woman named Dorothy Day met a man named Peter Maurin and they..." Who cares? (Troester 1993: 416-417)

The perspectives on how to apply Day's life to today's Catholic Worker raises the issue of identity. David Tracy wrote, "Roman Catholic identity is far more complex and pluralistic than in the past but remains recognizably Catholic."(Tracy 1994: 93) In many ways, today's Catholics have been fully embraced by U.S culture and vice versa. Today's U.S. Catholic Church is no longer that of the poor, working class, undereducated European immigrants of the 1920s and 1930s. While Latin American immigrants comprise the fastest growing group within the U.S. Catholic Church, they are joining a Church which is fully integrated in mainstream America. College education and family income frequently match or exceed other Christians in the United States, while shopping malls have replaced church halls as meeting places for today's Catholics. The influences of America's individualistic thinking on economic, social, and gender issues has had an impact on Catholics. A 1993 nationwide Gallup survey revealed that 72% of Catholics agree "it would be a good thing if married men were allowed to be ordained as priests," and 64% felt the same way about the ordination of women (D'Antonio 1996: 178). The same survey reported the following percentages feel individuals should have more moral authority than Church leaders alone on decisions dealing with

> abortion (44%-21%),
> homosexuality (39%-26%)
> contraceptive birth-control(57%-14%).

The heterogenous views of sexuality and gender in today's Catholic Worker reflect the opinions of the larger Catholic population.

In addition to disparate views on Catholicism, politics, as well as the role (if any) of Dorothy Day in today's movement, David Stein questioned whether Catholicism has *anything* to do with the Catholic Worker: "I don't see the Catholic Worker as having the remotest thing to do with being Catholic. I justify the Catholic Worker on logical and rational terms."(Troester 1993: 415) Stein describes himself as both Jewish and a Catholic Worker. David Tracy depicts "Roman Catholic identity as both fundamentally Catholic and genuinely, i.e. inclusively catholic."(Tracy 1991: 454-455)

Today's Catholic Workers come from a variety of religious backgrounds: non-Catholics, former Catholics, traditional Catholics, reform-minded Catholics and post-institutional Catholics. Given this pluralism amidst a movement with neither mechanisms nor procedures to define and reinforce identity issues, Tracy's concept of analogical imagination provides some assistance on the matter of religious pluralism: "We understand one another, if at all, only through analogy. Who you are I know only by knowing what event, what focal meaning, you actually live by[...] That analogical imagination seems and is a very small thing. And yet it does suffice."(Tracy 1981: 454-455)

Catholic Workers have an opportunity to engage these issues of identity by recognizing the various forms of religious "otherness" which pervades today's movement. Despite not having structured modes of discussion as a movement, it may be suggested that those Catholic Workers wrestling with these issues engage in conversation:

> Conversation remains the ideal of any analogical imagination in any tradition. Conflict is just as often the reality. Nor should conflict be feared as the analogical imagination's own internal demand for ever-new negations of its always tentative order, its similarities-in-difference, must recognize. (Tracy 1981: 453)

Tracy explained the fundamental value of conversation lies in self revelation. Only through exposing one's self can one enter the "backand-forth movement of the conversation itself" into the delicate issues of identity and authority.

The multiple anarchist expressions in the Catholic Worker movement continue to complicate the issues of identity and authority. I contend that the ambiguity resulting from these anarchist threads has helped to maintain the fabric of the movement. By not developing an authoritative body or mechanism to resolve issues of identity, the Catholic Worker remains a diverse, personalist social movement.

However, a continual sense of dissatisfaction will accompany any sense of hope for future conversations within and about the Catholic Worker movement regarding identity and authority. As Tracy wrote, "The attempt to understand remains an effort to interpret well. But to interpret as pluralistic, ambiguous and important a phenomenon as religion is to enter a conflict of interpretations from which there can often seem no exit."(Tracy 1987: 112-113)

Notes

[1] David DeLeon, *The American as Anarchist: Reflections on Indigenous Radicalism* (Baltimore: Johns Hopkins University Press, 1978), 150-151. Here, the author states the difficulty of placing the Catholic Worker into his "elastic" categories of anarchism. Lawrence Holben is a Catholic Worker who has written the following in his *All The Way To Heaven* (Marion, SD: Rose Hill Books, 1997): "The Catholic Worker's claim to anarchistic credentials has often exasperated traditional philosophical anarchists, who are inclined to argue that the 'Christian anarchism' touted by the movement is an oxymoron. A venerable anarchist rallying cry, they point out, was 'Neither God nor Master,' and the deity affirmed by the Worker as the ultimate ground of its meaning was sometimes scorned as the 'tyrant in heaven' by early anarchist polemicists." (p. 51).

[2] According to the War Resisters League, the proportion of federal taxes used for military spending depends upon the intensity of U.S. involvement in war and/or preparations for war. For example, the following list includes percentages of federal dollars used in military spending: 1963 (63%), 1970 (4 1%), 1975 (29%), 1986 (64%). Ed Hedemann, ed. *Guide to War Tax Resistance,* 3rd ed. (New York: War Resisters League, 1986), 15-23.

[3] For example, members of Haley House, Boston, decided to accept FEMA funding as part of their outreach to the homeless and hungry. Throughout much of 1986-1987, members of Haley House debated on the pros and cons of this arrangement. For specific issues raised in these discussions, see Kathe McKenna, "To Apply or Not to Apply," *Haley House Newsletter,* Easter 1987: 6-9. For a Catholic Worker opinion against receiving FEMA funding, from a Christian and anarchist perspective, see Scott Schaeffer-Duffy's response letter in *Haley House Newsletter,* Summer 1987: 3-4. Schaeffer-Duffy is a founding member of the Ss. Francis & Therese Catholic Worker Community in Worcester, MA.

[4] The concept of the common good goes back to Aquinas' social writings, reiterated in papal encyclicals and bishops' pastoral letters in the twentieth century. The "preferential option for the poor" originated in liberation theology during the late 1970s, but has been included in a variety of Church writings, including the U.S. Catholic Bishops' *Economic Justice for All,* 1986.

What's Catholic about the Catholic Worker Movement? Then and Now

Ann O'Connor and Peter King

Unity Kitchen Community of the Catholic Worker
Syracuse, New York

Mel Piehl states in his book, *Breaking Bread: The Catholic Worker and the Origin of Catholic Radicalism in America*, "Beginning almost inadvertently out of the publication of the Catholic Worker (paper) the Catholic Worker movement became one of the first Roman Catholic efforts since the Reformation to advocate a thorough going radical Gospel perfectionism in social life." And he further adds, "The (Catholic) Workers' religious orthodoxy is crucial to its identity and social outlook."(Piehl 1982)

The Catholic Worker movement was an expression of the Catholic faith of its founders, Peter Maurin and Dorothy Day. They were of one heart and one mind in their Faith. Although their roots and pilgrimages in the Faith were amazingly different, they were brought together by the Holy Spirit to form the Catholic Worker movement. Peter Maurin had formulated a Catholic social philosophy for the reconstruction of the social and economic order, which was collapsing under the evils of industrial capitalism, communism and Modernism. Day later said that Maurin was the theorist and she, as a journalist, was the propagandist.

Maurin was a French peasant, born in 1877 into a large family in southern France. He was educated by the Christian Brothers and entered the order in Paris at age 16. It was with the Christian Brothers that he was introduced to the idea of Christian personalism and the relationship between the Gospel and the social, economic order. Before his final vows, he left the order. It was 1903 and he was 26 years old. At that time, he was involved in Le Sillon, a pacifist Catholic lay group started by Marc Sangnier, which was committed to social and political reform through Christian democracy. Its personalism and its critique of bourgeois values attracted Maurin. It was decentralist: no dues, no rules, no elections and no salaries. Maurin included decentralism in his Catholic Worker principles. But when Le Sillon began to move out into the realm of secular politics to accomplish its goals, and also compromised its commitment to nonviolence, he left them-the Catholic Worker has no use for large political movements. Yet, Maurin's developing thought about the meaning of Christian personalism and the relationship between the Gospels and the social, economic order was further nurtured during this period.

He left France and traveled to Western Canada where he homesteaded. After a few years, he came to the United States (illegally) and for about eight years worked at various menial jobs as a miner, a gandy dancer and janitor; he also worked on a freighter on Lake Michigan. But all the while he was working at these jobs, he was continuing his more important task of clarification of his social philosophy. His life during those years is otherwise sketchy.

During the early 1920s, he tutored French in Chicago, and then in 1925 he came to New York State. In the Catskill Mountains in upstate New York, he worked without pay at a boys' camp and went to the libraries in New York City on his time off. It was in New York City in 1932 that he met Dorothy Day through George Shuster, then editor of *Commonweal*, a Catholic journal. And so began the Catholic Worker.

Dorothy Day

Dorothy Day followed a different route on her Faith pilgrimage. She was an urban creature, Maurin a peasant. He was born into a Catholic family with 21 siblings. She was born into an Episcopalian family with Presbyterian connections who weren't strong in practicing their religion. Her father was a newspaperman. The family moved from Brooklyn, where she was born in 1897, to San Francisco; but after the earthquake in 1906 they moved to Chicago. She was eight at the time, one of four siblings. She attended the University of Illinois at Urbana where, she said, she rejected all religion and became a socialist. After two years, she left college and went to New York. But she never lost her religious sensibilities and longings of her childhood. In New York, she became a denizen of Greenwich Village where she entered into the life of the artists and writers. Playwright Eugene O'Neill spent hours reciting "The Hound of Heaven" to her from memory. This long poem by Francis Thompson describes God's unrelenting pursuit of a soul. It seems that just as O'Neill was leaving the Catholic Church Dorothy Day was being drawn to it.

From girlhood, she had developed a concern for the poor and working class, which led her to her experiments with socialism and communism; in the 20s in New York, she wrote for socialist and communist publications. In her moral wanderings, she was involved in relationships with several men. One led (some say) to an abortion, another to a brief marriage; but the most important was a common-law marriage to Forster Batterham, an anarchist and naturalist, who fathered their daughter, Tamar. But as an anarchist he rejected marriage and religion. So, when Day decided to have their baby baptized into the Catholic Church and eighteen months later she also joined the Church, they separated.

Day's compassion for the poor and oppressed deepened, and though she looked for solutions in socialism and communism for the oppression of workers, she was attracted to the Church and came to see it as the Church of the poor and immigrants and the working class. In spite of the Church's apparent failures, Day entered it at a great personal cost, losing a fulfilling human love and many friends who did not understand her joining the Church which they saw as a collaborator with the powers-that-be in oppressing the poor.

From the time of her conversion to the Church in 1927, she embraced the Catholic faith heart and soul. She saw the Church for what it is, at once transcendent *and* fallen: transcendent in that it was founded by Christ, is animated by the Holy Spirit, and provides salvation and sanctity through its teachings and worship; fallen in the weak and sinful relationships of its members (you and me) who are so easily seduced by the world, the flesh, and the devil and given in to greed and selfishness. She recognized the Church as a consecrated community created by Jesus who gave it its mission to continue His work of salvation to all people down through the ages until He returns. For Day, it was the Body of Christ, a community of loving sacrifice and service, a counter-sign in a chaotic world.

Because of her great love and gratitude for the Church, Day was grieved at its human failures. She was scandalized by the leadership, which failed to live out its own teachings. But she trusted in Christ's promises that the Church would endure to the end of time and that even "the gates of hell will not prevail against it."(Mt.16:18) She remained faithful in the face of its human failures—the sometimes "angry but obedient daughter of holy Mother Church."(Piehl 1982) It was through her obedience that she was able to recognize her prophetic vocation and to develop, with Peter Maurin, a prophetic movement. She continually called the Church, which she loved, back to its radical vocation by her example and witness.

When Peter Maurin first met her in 1932, she was a relatively new Catholic. He became her teacher. Day commented that he was the master and she the disciple. He opened up to her the broad intellectual life of the Church. He introduced her to the rich tradition of the Church's social teachings, and he taught her that the best way to study the history of the Church is through studying the lives of the saints. The doctrine of the Communion of Saints, which unites Christians on earth, in purgatory and in heaven, gave her many great saints to befriend her: to name a few, St. Catherine of Siena, St. Francis of Assisi, St. Teresa of Avila, and St. Thérese of Lisieux, about whom she wrote a biography—all companions with her through her struggles. She was deeply affected by the great Russian writers, especially Dostoevsky whom she read over and over.

Dorothy Day never developed a coherent synthesis of her theological or socio-economic thought. Her theology was a concern for the individual person and a call for the transformation of the social order. She wanted to demonstrate the relationship between the person and the common good (traditional St. Thomas Aquinas), and, like Peter Maurin, the relationship between Christian personalism and socioeconomic reform. She offered no clearly defined program. Rooted in the Catholic faith, she and Maurin came to see that the best response for the deepening social and economic chaos in America was a revolution of the heart. Jesus' Sermon on the Mount and the practice of the works of mercy were her synthesis for a new social order. She said, "Together with the works of mercy (feeding, clothing, and sheltering our brothers) we must indoctrinate. We must give the reason for the faith that is in us..."(Day 1983: 91) This was the cornerstone of Dorothy Day's legacy. Day's revolution of the heart meant that she urged people to abandon the hedonistic and materialistic cultural values and to refuse to participate in the nation's militarism, as well as to refuse to participate in whatever threatens the dignity of the person and violates justice. She hoped more Catholics and other Christians would take Jesus seriously and follow him, living out the Sermon on the Mount and practicing the works of mercy "at a personal sacrifice," as Peter Maurin said.

Dorothy Day understood the Eucharist's social and economic implications. In the Eucharist, she found a model for the creation of a new socio-economic order in which people come together to share the Bread of Life—a school for the creation of a new moral consciousness in every age. In the Eucharist, the believer experiences the meaning of Jesus' suffering for the sake of all humankind. As Jesus suffered and sacrificed His life for the redemption of all, the Eucharist invites Catholics to a life of sacrifice and suffering for the sake of others. She saw the celebration of the Mass as the fullest expression of community: people worshipping together as one body for the common good while not blurring or confusing the identity of each person.

Dorothy Day said many times, "The Mystical Body is the doctrine which is behind all our efforts."(Miller 1973) The doctrine of the Mystical Body of Christ found in St. Paul's First Letter to the Corinthians and other letters teaches us that the Church is the Body of Christ with Christ as its head and the Holy Spirit as its soul, analogous, as St. Paul says, to the human body: each one who is baptized into the Church becomes a member of the Body. Members are given varying functions, i.e., vocations with compatible spiritual gifts to assist in living out their vocation for the good of the whole body, the Church.

Maurin's Social Theory and Program

Peter Maurin would quote Lenin's observation, "You can't have a revolution without a theory." His social theory is based on the Church's social teachings which are rooted in the Gospels, the early Church Fathers, and Saint Thomas Aquinas' teaching on the dignity of the person and the common good. Also, St. Francis' love and practice of voluntary poverty became for Maurin a keystone in his program. Maurin's synthesis included the encyclicals of Pope Leo XIII (*Rerum Novarum*, 1891), and of Pope Pius XI (*Quadragesimo Anno*, 1931). At the heart of his social philosophy is Christian personalism.

Maurin was a European and utilized the thought of Europeans. But he syncretized it into his analysis and critique of American society and the entire industrialized West. He drew from French Catholic thinkers of his day such as the personalists Jacques Maritain and Emmanuel Mounier, and the philosophers Charles Peguy and Leon Bloy. The Russian personalist, Nicolas Berdyeav, who emphasized the intrinsic freedom of the person, contributed to Maurin's development of personalism. Three French Catholics representing European social Catholicism who had a great influence on Peter Maurin's thought were René de la Tour du Pin and Albert du Mun, founders of Catholic Study Groups in Paris and elsewhere, and Leon Harmel. Their ideas were, like Maurin's, rooted in monasticism and medievalism. But he did not share their positions on anti-Semitism, militarism and politics (Novitsky 1976). He was also influenced by the English Catholic Distributists: Hilaire Belloc, G.K. Chesterton, Fr. Vincent McNabb, and Maurin's favorite, Eric Gill, who was also a pacifist. Distributists believe in decentralism and cooperative relations between people that focus attention on the needs of the common good in economic affairs. The decentralization of economic affairs was supported by Popes Leo XIII and Pius XI. Distributists are anti-capitalist, anti-industrialist and anti-statist. They favor a decentralized economy of property owning farmers, artisans, and shopkeepers. The Distributists articulated 1) the spiritual nature of work, 2) the necessary connection between property and responsibility, and 3) the quality of daily life.

Others who were not Christian contributed to Maurin's synthesis. Prince Peter Kropotkin, the nineteenth century anarchist, emphasized cooperation vs. competition. Maurin found him helpful in developing his ideas about the cooperative sharing between scholars and workers—that is, the worker's need to study and the scholar's need to work. Also, Pierre Joseph Proudhon, the French anarchist and communitarian, reinforced Maurin's views with his advocacy of decentralized political arrangements.

Maurin's ideas on the organization of the Catholic Worker were taken from St. Philip Neri and the oratory. Irish monasticism was the source for his definition of the mission of the Catholic Worker movement.

Catholic Workers have no faith in the reformability of capitalism which upholds the primacy of the material over the spiritual, because that leads eventually to its own self-destruction. Rather, Catholic Workers uphold cooperatives as part of a Christian social order; they promote farming communes, credit unions, leagues of mutual aid, and voluntary land reform.

Leon Bloy's relentless critique of bourgeois "culture and religion" was very important for Maurin, who wrote a great deal about the nature of bourgeois culture. He saw that the bourgeois mentality had the shallowest understanding of human life. It is elitist and economically competitive; it exalts rigid individualism and self-centeredness. Bourgeois acquisitiveness leads to impoverishment of the many, so that a few can live in affluence. Maurin thought it tragic that even Catholics became caught up in these destructive tendencies—an enormous threat to Christian life, a form of moral amnesia which renders Christians unable to address the needs of their brothers and sisters.

Modern society remains under the curse of the ideology of a bourgeois capitalism, which severs the bond between economic life and Christian faith. Maurin saw the bourgeois mentality generated among Catholics to be every bit as bad as the economic injustices of industrial capitalism. This mentality stands in contradiction to the Gospel and Catholic tradition. However, many Catholics are unable to see the danger this mentality poses for their Christian faith. The privatized faith of bourgeois religion is a corruption of Jesus' love. A socialized Catholic faith, on the other hand, will give birth to the politics of service, the economics of sharing, and a social life based on cooperation, not on competition and individualism. Bourgeois culture is the consequence of a secular, capitalistic society. Catholics wanting to enjoy the benefits of capitalism have severed their tie to the moral principles of Catholic social tradition.

Maurin wanted a complete repudiation of capitalism and the creation of a new social and economic order founded on Christian principles. He never claimed that his vision for social economic reform was uniquely his own. He was only reaffirming principles of Catholic social tradition. His solution to the present crisis rested, not in establishing new Catholic social principles, but in reestablishing Catholic social principles trampled by industrial capitalism. Maurin urged the following:

- returning to Jesus' model in the Gospels,
- returning to the socio-economic principles extolled by St. Thomas Aquinas,
- embracing Christian personalism, and
- returning to the social teachings of Popes Leo XIII and Pius XI.

Maurin died in 1949. He would have been heartened by the development of the Church's social teachings since Pius XI, but he would be equally disheartened by the global dominance of capitalism and the massive social disintegration. Yet his personalist and communitarian revolution is more pertinent today than ever.

Maurin's body of thought is not hard to study. One does not need to search libraries or scan computer screens. His thought is contained in his "Easy Essays," which are concise, cogent, verse-like writings, most of which are collected into one volume titled simply, *Easy Essays* (Maurin 1984). These pithy essays are simple, full of wisdom and direct. He wrote them, he said, "to be understood by the man in the street." They form the handbook of the Catholic Worker movement.

Maurin's social philosophy was not only radically Catholic, his program for implementing it was aimed primarily at Catholics. Christian personalism is at the heart of Maurin's vision and the cornerstone of his social program. He insisted that reform must begin with each person. Personalism means that God creates each and every human being in God's image; therefore human life is sacred and not to be harmed or killed. Each person bears a personal moral responsibility for him/ herself and others. The roots of Christian personalism are in Scripture, especially in the Gospels. A new economic order would be built on the counsels of the Gospel of Jesus Christ, who offered the model for economic and social life: voluntary poverty, loving service to others, non-violence, and love of enemies. Justice is to love God and love others in God.

From personalism and voluntary poverty flow Maurin's three-fold program for the reconstruction of the social and economic order:

–Round Table Discussions (Clarification of Thought) to give a new awareness of the relationship between Catholic faith and economic conditions in society. Maurin wanted Round Table Discussions to provide a new vehicle to enable Catholics to break away from bourgeois ideology (Maurin 1984: 36-37).

–Houses of Hospitality to help the poor by the practice of Christian personalism.

–Farming communes to bring workers and scholars together through cult, culture, and agriculture. Cult is worship; culture means literature and study; and agriculture means working the land so that workers can study and scholars can work.

Maurin was a loyal son of the Church, and he drew his vision from Catholic tradition. In the concordance to the *Easy Essays* (a wonderful help that Kevin Craig gave the Catholic Worker movement)(Craig n.d.), the word "Catholic" appears 18 times, more than any other word. Yet Maurin, like Dorothy Day, was disappointed by the Church's unwillingness to live up to her own social teachings.

Nevertheless, Maurin always defended the Church for that rich tradition.

Dorothy Day called Maurin her teacher, a genius and the theoretician of the Catholic Worker. "I was a journalist, a doer, but without the theory, I would have gotten nowhere."(Miller 1973) Although she brushed aside the suggestion that she was a saint, she said that Maurin "was a saint and a great teacher."(Day 1963: 101) He wanted a Christian personalist revolution. He called himself an "idea man." No doubt he was very saintly, and it is expected and "devoutly to be hoped" that both he and Day will one day be raised to the altars of the Church.

So, we have here a clearly radical, Catholic, social movement founded by two charismatic Catholics, a teacher and a disciple, saints both. As Mel Piehl wrote in *Breaking Bread,* the Catholic Worker is a movement, "first and foremost, Roman Catholic." (Piehl 1982: 137)

The Catholic Worker Today

The Catholic Worker is today in crisis. We know that there have been crises of various kinds throughout Catholic Worker history, and varying degrees of disagreements within the movement over issues such as unions, decentralism, anarchy (which is often misunderstood within the Catholic Worker), and pacifism/nonviolence, which created a serious split during World War II. Even before Dorothy Day died tensions and difficulties were growing among Catholic Workers concerning fidelity to the Church and the Catholic Worker vision. But there was never a question about the Catholic basis and identity of the movement. It was a given.

The current Catholic Worker crisis is profound: a crisis of its Catholic identity and its vocation in the Church. The question at hand is: Is the Catholic Worker Catholic? Catholic as the Church defines Catholic, for that is the only valid measure, the measure by which Day and Maurin identified themselves and their movement. To be Catholic, Roman Catholic, means submitting to the teaching authority and discipline of the Church which comes down to us from the Apostles to today's Pope and bishops, and to worship in only valid Catholic worship forms. There is a unity to the Faith and doctrine of the Church which cannot be selectively divided into categories: this I accept, that I reject.

For 15 years or so, Unity Kitchen Community of the Catholic Worker has been warning the Catholic Worker movement of its increasingly visible signs of cracking under the pressure of Modernism. Now it appears to be caving in. This can no longer be denied, ignored or glossed over.

Many houses and individual Catholic Workers have abandoned the Faith, or are in varying degrees of rebellion against one or more of the Church's doctrines or disciplines. Some houses have no Catholics as workers, or have workers who are ex-Catholics and anti-Catholics. Some Catholics have lost their Faith after coming to a Catholic Worker house, which is a tragedy and a bad fruit for the Catholic Worker movement. The Catholic Worker movement should be an occasion for Catholic Workers to grow in faith and holiness.

When we speak of a loss of Catholic identity within the movement, we are speaking of a significant number of Catholic Workers. We know, of course, of Catholic Workers who claim adherence to the Church, but they are a small minority considering the number of houses which claim to be Catholic Worker houses. Oh, would that more Catholic Workers would come forth to witness to being faithful Roman Catholics!

Some Catholic Workers claim to live by the Gospels without the Church, but that is not Catholic. And some Catholic Workers who claim the Gospels without the Church are often very selective as to which of Jesus' teachings they follow, and how far they will follow them. For example, they may strongly profess Jesus' teachings on poverty, and love of others, including enemies, while they ignore Jesus' teaching on chastity and marriage. The sexual values and mores of our hedonistic culture pervade the Catholic Worker movement, and too frequently are accepted as the norm. But our Lord Jesus requires of His followers wholehearted obedience to His law of love and life, just as He was obedient even to death, death on a cross (cf. Phil. 2: 8).

Much of the Catholic Worker movement has become incoherent, if not misleading and downright dishonest in claiming the name "Catholic" because they give scandal to fellow Catholics and others outside the Church.

It should be made clear that the Catholic identity for Catholic Worker houses does not exclude non-Catholics from the work and life of the house. Yes, it is true that Day and Maurin welcomed people of other faiths to work as Catholic Workers, but there was never any doubt for anyone that they were clearly Catholic and that the movement was the *Catholic* Worker. Non-Catholics who came did not try to deny or change the Catholic identity; they subsisted within it, usually with no trouble, or they left. Certainly people of different or no faith can be part of the life of a Catholic Worker house as long as they can accept the identity and practice of Catholicism within the house. Catholic members must be clear on the gifts and roles of everyone in the house. At Unity Kitchen Community of the Catholic Worker, everyone who comes to volunteer or to live and work with us knows who we are. We have had living and working with us a Gandhian, Anabaptists, and uncertain Catholics struggling with some of the life issues which we proclaim. Among our volunteers we have had Protestants, agnostics, Unitarians, Mormons, non-pacifists, a defense engineer, and others not necessarily of one mind with us on our Faith and witness. We have some excellent discussions on our differences.

But if in a Catholic Worker house there are no Catholics willing to uphold the Catholic identity of the house, at least until Catholics come along, we suggest that the name be changed or the house close down.

Why is it that so many Catholic Workers who reject the Church's teaching authority and, worse, bash the Church in their newspapers and other ways, still claim the name "Catholic"? Frequently the justification given for this misuse of the name "Catholic" is that they put into practice the Catholic Worker program of Houses of Hospitality, Round Table Discussions, and farming communes. Or that they adhere to certain Catholic Worker practices such as voluntary poverty, eschewal of governmental privileges, resistance, and serving the poor. Some claim to be in the "tradition" of the Catholic Worker, which is questionable, depending on whether it is Day's and Maurin's tradition or that of someone else. In any case, it is an arrogation of the name "Catholic" without authenticity. Of course, the Catholic Worker movement is best known for its practice of the corporal works of mercy, most commonly feeding the hungry, clothing the naked, sheltering the homeless (or as Dorothy Day said, drawing from the older tradition, "harboring the harborless"). But there are seven spiritual works of mercy which one rarely hears about in Catholic Worker circles any more, even though personalism stresses the primacy of the spiritual.[1]

Without its union with the Church and without a clear and strong witness for the unity and sanctity of all human life from conception until natural death, the Catholic Worker movement may have already lost its unique transcendent dimension and have become irrelevant in our "culture of death."

Schismatic trends in the Catholic Worker movement, its confusion and dissent, are a reflection, a microcosm of the Catholic Church in America. Modernism has permeated and infected the Church in America and seduced the Catholic Worker movement as well.

Modernism is, in truth, a religion that rejects the Graeco-Judeo-Christian morality that for 1600 years has provided the basis of Western culture, morality, and polity. Polity is the set of social institutions and civic virtues that enable a people to live with one another in reasonable internal harmony and public order.

The current crisis within the Church and the Catholic Worker movement has its roots in Modernism which is essentially an anti-Christian world view. On the philosophical level it espouses materialism that denies God, or if it espouses a belief in God, it acts as if there is no God. Being materialistic, it is preoccupied with matter and technology, and it idolizes mammon, that is, money and the power it can give. It is hedonistic; it glorifies "me and nowism" purveying sensuality and self-indulgence. This exaggerated individualism leads to moral relativism, and it makes people easy candidates for the mass mind control dominating our society. Modernism rejects the sanctity of all human life and personal moral responsibility for the common good. It makes true communality impossible.

Doesn't this sound familiar? Aren't these some of the very evils Maurin and Day struggled against by way of the Catholic Worker movement? And now it appears that many in the Catholic Worker movement are giving themselves over to them. The Catholic Worker movement, originally a radical Catholic movement whose values contradicted the American culture, has adopted the American liberal agenda which values individual rights over the common good, extols tolerance to the point of denial of objective truth or binding moral order, and rejects any higher moral authority other than individual choice and opinion. It even rejects the Church's teaching authority and discipline in the area of Faith and morals as well as its authority over Catholic worship. Many Catholic Workers have assumed the liberal agenda of deathmaking through abortion and euthanasia and even selective wars of liberation. So instead of being able to prophetically speak to the Church's unholy alliances with Caesar and the culture, the Catholic Worker movement is itself seduced.

How did this state of affairs in the Catholic Church, and now in the Catholic Worker movement, come about? As part of the seduction of the Church by our modernistic society, we are seeing the fruit of weak and confusing catechesis, which goes back at least two generations. Modern catechesis has offered little doctrinal substance and has been very short on instilling discipline and a sense of sin. Today's catechesis and religious education is infected with New Age and relativism about life and death issues. Where are the believers who have experienced the power which Faith gives, even to martyrdom, and who are willing to lay down their lives for Christ and the Church? H. Richard Niebuhr describes American liberalism as having "a God without wrath (who) brought men without sin into a Kingdom without judgment, through the ministration of a Christ without a Cross."

As a result of inadequate catechesis, modern Catholics fail to understand the nature and vocation of the Church, for example, its teaching office and what it implies; or the Church as Priest, Prophet, and King; or the exalted doctrine of the Mystical Body of Christ and what membership in it offers and requires of us. This can lead to misinterpretation of ecumenism and misguided efforts toward overcoming differences.

Poorly formed Catholics who are confused by the surrounding pagan values are not, of course, the only, nor the biggest reason for the confusion and dissent within the Church and within the Catholic Worker movement. Many of those who received clear and strong teaching have later in life rejected the Church with full understanding of the implications.

But all the signs of the times that have been mentioned have their root causes in a more profound, cosmic reality. The Church exists in the midst of the Fall as does all creation and all life, and it is subject to the unrelenting assaults of the Power of Death (a.k.a. Satan) who, as St. Peter reminds us, "prowls about like a roaring lion seeking someone to devour." (1Peter 5:8) But Christ promised to be with the Church "always to the end of the world."(Mt. 28:20) He doesn't promise that the Church will never fail the test, only that it will be ultimately victorious and vindicated.

One of the most crucial failures in Church history is the Constantinian Arrangement in the fourth century, by which the Empire co-opted the Church. We live with that unholy alliance down to this day. The Church's accommodation to American society, or as

Fr. Michael Baxter calls it, "the Americanization of the Church," simply reiterates the Constantinian Comity.

Yet throughout the history of the Church, and usually at its darkest moments, the Holy Spirit raises up saints and prophets to challenge the faithful and point to the Way. Filled with the gifts of the Holy Spirit, these charismatic figures typically gather a community of followers. Such was the case, it would seem, with Peter Maurin and Dorothy Day.

The true prophet always comes from within the Church and is obedient and subject to the authority of the Church. Without these credentials, a claimant is a false prophet.

Day and Maurin are pre-eminent prophetic voices in this chaotic century, calling the Church, including all its members, out of Babylon back to the Gospel imperatives. Their stance against usury, the lifeblood of capitalism, reiterates the Old Testament prophets and Jubilee laws fulfilled in the Sermon on the Mount as well as the Church's unchanging teaching against usury.

Some Hard Questions Facing the Catholic Worker Movement

It is an empirical reality, and it is to be expected, that when a movement loses its charismatic founders it tends to lose its way for a time, betraying its charismatic gifts and abandoning its communal vocation. It happens to religious orders and other charismatic groups in Church history. Providentially, some such groups disappear, but many of the surviving movements continue on as a perversion of the founder's vision—shells of a lost vocation. They become secular distortions with a Catholic name and trappings. In a parallel vein, once a charismatic movement or religious order initiated by the Holy Spirit has accomplished its Spirit-given mission, the Spirit will leave it and raise up new efforts to meet the needs of the time. As members of a Catholic movement whose saintly founders have died and is now suffering a crisis of identity and vocation, Catholic Workers face some serious questions. One question is: has the Catholic Worker movement accomplished the mission given by the Holy Spirit to Dorothy Day and Peter Maurin? Or is it being seduced by our Modernistic culture into betraying its vocation? Or has the Holy Spirit already moved on from the Catholic Worker movement?

Serious discernment is required here. If the Catholic Worker movement has accomplished its mission, then how does the movement address that? If the movement is being co-opted by our pagan society, how can we hope for conversion and restoration to the founders' intended mission and role in the Church? Can we even hope for conversion and restoration? If the Holy Spirit has left the Catholic Worker movement, how can we know? By what signs can we know? On the other hand, if the Holy Spirit continues to work within the Catholic Worker movement, where can we recognize the signs of the Spirit?

There is strong denial among many Catholic Workers about the seriousness and meaning of the present crisis of identity and vocation, along with indifference which forms a big obstacle to facing it fearlessly. Another obstacle to confronting the crisis is the confused understanding of anarchism: many Catholic Workers misperceive anarchism as simply no authority and no leadership. Unless the Catholic Worker movement acknowledges the crisis and deals with it creatively, we will be reading the writing on the wall.

If we develop a willingness to face these hard questions, then only through communal, Christian discernment can the Catholic Worker movement hope to receive light in the present moment on these issues. Communal, Christian discernment is so little understood and so rarely practiced that it would certainly be a sign of the Holy Spirit at work in the Catholic Worker movement if Catholic Workers came together to seek through discernment God's will. This could begin with just a few houses, perhaps within a region, who would come together to prayerfully and humbly submit to the Holy Spirit's leading.

In the meantime, we must take the critical first step. Unity Kitchen Community of the Catholic Worker calls our Catholic Worker brothers and sisters to decision! If you are a faithful Catholic as the Church defines Catholic, simply say so! Do not hide your light under a bushel. If you are not Catholic in union with the Church, don't call yourself a Catholic Worker, because you are not one. Read Peter Maurin's Easy Essay, "Non-Catholic Catholics." Call yourself anything you want, but don't call yourself Catholic Worker if you are not Catholic. Be coherent! Be honest! Our age of confusion hungers for clarity, honesty, and coherence. Integrity demands it. Be what you want, but don't call yourself what you are not.

In conclusion we would like to share with you another easy essay from another wisdom tradition. (As Christians, we believe that all wisdom points to and converges in Christ.) It is from Confucius

(Fifth Century BC), who says that "The beginning of wisdom is calling things by their right names."

> If language is not used rightly,
> Then what is said is not meant.
> If what is said is not what is meant,
> Then that which ought to be done is left undone.
> If it remains undone,
> Morals and art will be corrupted.
> If morals and art are corrupted,
> Justice will go awry.
> And, if justice goes awry,
> The people will stand about in helpless confusion.

Added note: During the discussion which followed the above talk, a young woman stood up and said that she had seen our workshop listed in the conference material, and that she came to it because of her confusion at a Catholic Worker house where she had spent two years. During that time, she said, only twice did a priest actually lead the weekly Eucharist liturgy. The other times ex-priests, nuns, and lay people celebrated "Mass." While she was a Worker at the house, a young pregnant woman was a guest. Half the Workers in the house, without informing the other Workers, helped the pregnant woman obtain an abortion. The woman sharing her story was visibly upset by her experiences in the Catholic Worker house, and she had since left it and was living alone.

[1]

The Corporal Works of Mercy	**The Spiritual Works of Mercy**
Feed the Hungry	Counsel the doubtful
Give drink to the thirsty	Instruct the ignorant
Clothe the naked	Admonish the sinner
Visit the imprisoned	Forgive all injuries
Shelter the homeless	Bear wrongs patiently
Visit the sick	Pray for the living and dead
Bury the dead	Comfort the sorrowful

Dorothy Day, Rebel Catholic: Living in a State of Permanent Dissatisfaction with the Church

Brian Terrell

Strangers and Guests Catholic Worker Farm
Maloy, Iowa

> I was just as much against capitalism and imperialism as ever, and here I was going over to the opposition, because of course the Church was lined up with property, with the wealthy, with the state, with capitalism, with all the forms of reaction. This is what I had been taught to think and this is what I still think to a great extent...I loved the Church for Christ made visible. Not for itself, because it was so often a scandal to me. Romano Guardini said that the Church is the Cross on which Christ was crucified; one could not separate Christ from His Cross, and one must live in a state of permanent dissatisfaction with the Church.
>
> Dorothy Day

No biographical note on Dorothy Day, co-founder of the Catholic Worker movement with Peter Maurin, is complete without mention of her faithfulness and deep devotion to the Roman Catholic Church. The apparent contradiction that a person so radical in questions of labor and of war and peace should identify herself with the Church of Rome is often noted; the irony of her situation was not lost to Dorothy herself.

Some voices from within and without the CW movement warn that dissent from Church discipline and doctrine by many Catholic Workers since Dorothy's death in 1980 is evidence of a falling away and abandonment of Dorothy's and Peter's founding principles. It is feared that our dissent attacks the integrity of the movement, even threatening its continuing existence. These friends call upon Dorothy as a witness, and they portray her as "totally submitted to the Magisterium." In this depiction, Dorothy is "conservative from her mantilla to her rosary beads," and "*totally, irrevocably* faithful to the teaching authority of the Catholic Church"... a person who had "not deviated in one iota!"

Such characterizations are, except for the bit about the mantilla, mostly true, I think. However, they so oversimplify both Dorothy's spirituality and her relationship to the Church that this image is almost false and demands clarification.

It is only, I believe, because the Church at its best today has been marked by the courageous efforts at reform by people like Dorothy and Peter that in retrospect they are no longer seen for the dissenters they clearly were. As dissidents they stood in loving defiance to the highest authorities in the hierarchy when those authorities denied the teaching and example of Jesus. They were at the same time faithful and obedient to the Church in as much as they held to its truths, even those doctrines that had been abandoned, obscured or suppressed through the cowardice or ignorance of those who had been ordained to proclaim them. These two good Catholics leave us a rich tradition of faithful dissent. Here are only a few examples from the life and writings of Dorothy Day.

The Tremendous Freedom

When Dorothy set out at Peter Maurin's urging to begin to publish *The Catholic Worker* newspaper in 1933, she sought the advice of two friends, one a Jesuit, the other a Paulist, two priests experienced in editing and publishing. A recent convert at that time, Dorothy was concerned whether permission from Church authorities might be required for such a venture. "... in no uncertain terms: No, it was not necessary to ask permission," Dorothy was counseled, "The thing to do was to go ahead on one's own, and if the work were of God it would continue." All her life Dorothy rejoiced in and promoted "the tremendous freedom there is in the Church, a freedom most cradle Catholics do not seem to know they possess!" The Church authorities in 1933 were equally ignorant of the tremendous freedoms Dorothy's advisors assured her Catholic lay folk possess.

Until the *Index of Forbidden Books* was repealed in 1966, *The Catholic Worker* was published in defiance of Canon 1385: "Without prior Church censorship, even laymen are not allowed to publish:...books (including periodicals) concerning the Bible, theology, Church history, canon law, natural theology, ethics or other religious and moral sciences."

When, during the McCarthy era, government burglars stole the mailing list of the Communist paper, *The Daily Worker*, Dorothy offered the subscription list of *The Catholic Worker* to replace it. *The Daily Worker*'s editors refused Dorothy's gracious gesture of solidarity. The Church's *Index* banned under pain of mortal sin the possession of any publication "... defending as lawful or harmless Freemasonry, divorce, Socialism, suicide, dueling," without written permission from one's Bishop. Love knows no law, and to help her besieged comrades ("the mass of bourgeois smug Christians who denied Christ in His poor made me turn to Communism, and it was the Communists working with them that made me turn to God...") Dorothy was ready to send their condemned paper willy nilly into thousands of Catholic homes, convents, seminaries and parochial schools!

Many of the books read and recommended by Peter and Dorothy at least fell within the *Index*'s broad categories for condemnation. Dorothy's beloved French and Russian authors were not above suspicion and her King James Bible and her Book of Common Prayer would have been enough to send her to Hell, if God could be imagined to take such stuff seriously.

I am not aware if Peter and Dorothy ever responded to the attempted suppression of some of their favorite books and authors by the hierarchy. My guess is that they ignored it, overlooking it as too silly and embarrassing to the Church to mention. They were in any case being neither disobedient nor challenging to Church authority. Popes, bishops and theologians, telling fellow Catholics what they may not read, obstructing the tremendous freedom God gives to the people of the Church, were trying to exercise authority they simply did not have.

While it is often recounted that Dorothy's obedience to the Church went to the extreme that she said that she would stop publishing *The Catholic Worker* if Church authorities so ordered, it is less often told how Dorothy responded when in 1951 Cardinal Spellman demanded that *The Catholic Worker* change its name or cease publishing. This order may have had something to do with Dorothy and other Catholic Workers picketing the Cardinal's offices two years previously when he ordered seminarians to scab on striking grave diggers. Dorothy had taken the part of these archdiocesan workers against their eminent employer, writing of them as "victims of that most awful of all wars, the war between clergy and laity."

To this arch episcopal crack down Dorothy answered that while she herself would happily obey, the paper's associate editors, more rebellious souls than she, objected and in effect out-voted her. With loving apologies to His Eminence, *The Catholic Worker* would continue. I was an associate editor of *The Catholic Worker* in the free wheeling 1970s: the notion that we had any such power to override Dorothy Day on an important issue of policy was simply not entertained. My own opinion is that Dorothy copped out. In any case, the Cardinal blinked and Dorothy had again claimed and preserved the tremendous freedom enjoyed by the Catholic laity from those powerful but misguided men who would deprive us of it

Pacifist Doctrine

The *New Catholic Encyclopedia* (1967–1969) offers a most thorough treatment of the topic "Pacifism", concluding with the final judgment, "It is clear from what has been said that absolute pacifism is irreconcilable with traditional Catholic doctrine." "Conscientious objection (to military service) is morally indefensible," this entry quotes Pope Pius XII, "a Catholic citizen may not appeal to his own conscience as ground for refusing to give his service to the state, and to fulfill duties affixed by law!" Pius XII is well known for his services rendered to the combatant states during World War II, particularly the service of his silence during the Holocaust.

The writers mention and dismiss the words of Pope John XXIII, "In this age of ours that glories in atomic might, war cannot any longer be regarded as an apt means of repairing violated rights," but gives great weight and authority to the claim of Pius XII (again) that "the right to stand on the defensive cannot be denied to the state even today." That Pius XII refused to deny the right of the state to use thermo-nuclear weapons in extreme circumstances is made much of in *The New Catholic Encyclopedia.*

Dorothy Day consistently defended Catholic doctrine, the teaching of Jesus and practice of the Apostolic Church, against the errors of almost every post-Constantinian pope and council. When she insisted that the draft was contrary to Church teaching, that conscientious objection fulfilled a Christian duty, that the Catholic Church forbids its members to take part in warfare, that the nuclear arms race was a sin and a crime, she was simply catechizing, evangelizing, spreading the Gospel.

Marriage and Celibacy

In *Therese*, Dorothy wrote this about the parents of one of her most beloved saints, St. Therese of Lisieux: "Louis and Zelie were whole man and woman, with a proper balance of soul and body, and to them the marriage act was as truly a sacrament as Holy Orders." Dorothy recognized that marriage is of equal dignity with Holy Orders and with celibacy. She knew that God was served and glorified as much through the cohabitation of Louis and Zelie Martin as by their daughter's contemplation and labor in a Carmelite monastery.

The new *Catechism of the Catholic Church* agrees with Dorothy: "Esteem of virginity for the sake of the kingdom and the Christian understanding of marriage are inseparable, and they reinforce each other: 'Whoever denigrates marriage diminishes the glory of virginity. Whoever praises it makes virginity more admirable and resplendent,' Pope John Paul II." The catechism that was approved for use in 1950 when *Therese* was written, however, told Dorothy in no uncertain terms that *any* Christian was better off unmarried, just as years before it had taught the Martins that their lives were less holy, less acceptable to God, than if they had remained virgins, undefiled by the marriage act.

Pope St. Gregory the Great had long ago proclaimed with the authority of his office that there could be no sexual act without sin. St. Augustine said this sin could be mitigated only if the act were open to conception. Augustine regarded intercourse by married couples after menopause and those practices now promoted by the Church as "natural family planning" as being far more perverse and evil than incest or prostitution. Thomas Aquinas in his *Summa Theologica* suggests that there are five sacraments for all Christians plus one more for the strong (Holy Orders) and one lesser sacrament (Matrimony), a consolation for weaker Christians. Dorothy loved St. Thomas for his doctrine of the Common Good. Would she recommend him as a marriage counselor?

The Council of Trent solemnly proclaims: "If anyone says that it is not better and more godly to live in virginity or in the unmarried state than to marry, let him be anathema!" NB: *Anathema*, a Greek word meaning "accursed" or "separated", is used to denote those excluded from the Church and sacraments on account of heresy or contumacious behavior. It thus signifies excommunication.

Cardinal Ratzinger of the Holy Office has warned that relativism in the 1990s is an even greater danger to the Church than was liberation theology in the 1980s, so we must point out that neither John Paul II nor Dorothy are suggesting that God's mind has changed on the dignity of marriage. They cannot be saying that God valued celibacy over marriage in the past and that God formerly inspired the Church to teach this as truth but that now, perhaps upon reviewing the polls, God changes the truth to suit the 1990s. This would make the current Pope and Dorothy into relativists.

No. God has always honored and blessed sexual love. The hierarchy of vocations has always been false. No one has ever been accursed or separated from the Church for honoring the marriage of their parents as a vocation as holy as that of their parish priest. Misogynous lies have long been pawned off as Christian doctrine by men who may have been holy and great but on this subject badly screwed up. The errors of popes, preachers and catechism teachers have heaped ridicule and scandal on Christ's Church, scarring the lives of all her people. May we all experience the joy of God's healing power.

What now?

Dorothy Day lived as a Catholic in a state of permanent dissatisfaction with the Church, in critical faithfulness to the Church—the cross on which Christ was crucified. If we come to the Church in a spirit of docility and subservience, then we do not love the Church as much as Dorothy did. If we are not scandalized, but are blind and silent to the Church when it takes the part of wealth and power, then we are not obedient to the Church as Dorothy was.

Editor's note: This article was published in *the catholic radical*, Rock Island, IL:Rock Island Catholic Worker (Autumn 1996).

The Catholic Worker Movement: Toward a Theology of Liberation for First World Disciples

Matthew R. Smith

Most Catholics have never heard of the Catholic Worker movement; the rest have mixed reactions to it. Dorothy Day, the first editor and publisher of *The Catholic Worker*, had been a reporter for communist and socialist papers. *The Catholic Worker* would often address issues of social justice, human rights, civil rights, and economic justice (labor strikes, unemployment, etc.), themes that are often addressed in communist and socialist papers. In addition, the title of their paper is similar to the famous communist paper, the *Daily Worker*.

Similarly, the typical Catholic in the United States likely knows little about liberation theology. Among those who recognize the term, it seems to have left a negative impression, perhaps from association with the civil wars in Nicaragua and El Salvador in the 1980s or with barely recollected reports of fanatic priests in Latin America who mixed Christianity with Marxism, Communism, and violent revolution. Some may recall that Pope John Paul II and the Curia expressed concern over it, and that the Vatican cautioned or silenced priests who wrote and taught about liberation theology.

Addressing the claim that liberation theology is a communist movement falls outside the scope of this essay. However, the comment of the late Archbishop Helder Camara is apt: "When I fed the poor, they called me a saint. When I asked, 'Why are they poor?' they called me a Communist."

Although liberation theology and the Catholic Worker movement are unknown or misunderstood by the average Catholic in the pew, they are in fact two of the most beautiful, powerful and inspiring examples of Christian discipleship of our age. They challenge us with prophetic words to care for the poor and to work for peace and social justice. Like John the Baptist, both of these movements are "voices calling from the wilderness," asking us to repent and prepare the way. Those who fail to hear their prophetic voices may miss the coming of the saving hand of the Lord in our time.

As the title of this essay suggests, there is a close relationship between the Catholic Worker movement and liberation theology. I will argue the following hypothesis:

The Catholic Worker movement is a form of liberation theology that has emerged in the North American or first world context.

In his analysis of the driving forces of Catholicism, Charles R. Morris saw a connection between the two movements:

> Liberation theology is mostly indigenous to Latin America, although with genetic links to Canon Cardijn and Dorothy Day through American and European missionaries. The lines converged in the United States in the antiwar protests led by nuns and priests like the Berrigan brothers in the 1960s and 1970s. (1997: 339)

June O'Connor's assessment of Day's moral vision included a stronger connection:

> Day's views and values anticipated those voiced in the liberation theologies of Latin America, Africa, and Asia: a decision to see life from the standpoint of the poor and to stand with the poor in a struggle for justice, an approach to theology rooted in praxis, and a view of religion as a spur to revolutionary action, a desire to help bring about the transformation of society grounded in the values of justice, peace, freedom and love. (1991: 98)

Here are some of the similarities, or contextual and thematic links, between the Catholic Worker movement and liberation theology as practiced in Latin America:

1. Both groups were born out of poverty.
2. Both groups are responding to the abuses of capitalism.
3. Both groups seek economic and social justice.
4. Both groups emphasize a preferential option for the poor.
5. Both groups encourage solidarity with the poor.
6. Both groups view life from the standpoint of the poor.

7. Both groups are movements which work for peace, justice, and freedom.
8. Both movements arose in the Western Hemisphere.
9. Both movements began during the twentieth century.
10. Both movements emphasize the importance of community.
11. Both movements are grass roots or lay based.
12. Both movements meditate on, study, and pray with scriptures.
13. Both movements find direction from the life and teaching of Jesus Christ.
14. Both movements are a form of Christian discipleship.
15. Both movements emphasize orthopraxis, i.e. right action.
16. Both movements believe service to others is integral to Christian life.
17. Both movements arose from within the Roman Catholic Church.
18. Both movements influence and are influenced by Catholic social teaching.
19. Both movements engage in theological reflection.
20. Both movements believe work for God's reign begins on earth.
21. Both movements seek to transform society.
22. Both movements support a "praxis cycle" of prayer, study, and action.
23. Both movements were influenced by the social sciences.
24. Both movements were influenced by socialism
25. Both groups stress the social dimension of the Gospel message.
26. Both groups follow Gospel precepts in light of the "signs of the times."

Differences

The major differences between the Catholic Worker movement and some practitioners of liberation theology have to do with practical questions of application. In concrete terms, what are the best political and economic solutions to the violence, oppression, and suffering faced by so many? What is the best way to work for a just and peaceful society?

Due in large measure to the guidance and direction of Dorothy Day and her reading and interpretation of Sacred Scripture, the Catholic Worker movement consistently and prophetically advocated the Christian nonviolent tradition, whereas some liberation theologians, in response to oppression, support the Church's "just war" tradition. Another central difference rests in the question of who or what is responsible for the transformation of society. To what extent should we rely on governments and large institutions or should we depend on small groups, community organizations, and individuals? The Catholic Worker movement stresses a "personalist" approach, whereas some liberation theologians support socialism and structural solutions to social or governmental problems. Should Christians work to transform the world from within or from without, bringing about a revolution of the heart or on the streets? Or both?

Theology and Method

After seeing these differences one may be inclined to question the central premise of this study. That is, can one still claim that the Catholic Worker movement is a form of liberation theology? Are socialism, Marxist analysis or the "just war" theory integral to liberation theology? If so, it would be incompatible with the Catholic Worker movement.

Therefore, what are the defining characteristics of liberation theology? The Catholic Worker movement shares many key traits, but does it share the core values or the necessary and sufficient conditions to practice liberation theology? Which elements are essential and which are incidental? For example, can one still practice liberation theology if they disavow the use of violence to achieve justice? Can one still practice liberation theology if they do not engage in Marxist analysis?

Theology and method provide assistance in answering these questions through analysis of both a "theology of liberation" and the "liberation of theology."This involves looking at the task of theology and how it works.

Central to the analysis is discussion of not only the poor and oppressed who are in need of liberation but also *theology* itself. Often theology is understood as "the queen of sciences," removed from the world, static, academic, imparting "ivory tower" speculation from on high. When understood properly, according to liberation theologians, theology is a dynamic, practical and engaging process of the People of God.

The description of *liberated theology* requires a brief look at the philosophy of hermeneutics, which contends that the interpratation of Scripture is influenced by the interpreter, their circumstance, location, culture, and the like. The hermeneutical circle, sometimes called praxis cycle or pastoral circle, which lies at the heart of liberation theology, is central to this analysis.

Liberation theology cannot be seperated from this method, for it is this method that determines the defining features of liberation theology and makes it possible to determine whether the Catholic Worker movement shares the necessary and sufficient conditions to practice liberation theology.

The Theology of Liberation

In the beginning of his book *A Theology of Liberation*, Gustavo Gutiérrez explains that theology is present in every believer and in every community of faith:

> Theological reflection—that is, the understanding of the faith—arises spontaneously and inevitably in the believer, in all those who have accepted the gift of the Word of God. Theology is intrinsic to a life of faith seeking to be authentic and complete and is, therefore, essential to the common consideration of this faith in the ecclesial community. There is present in *all believers*—and more so in every Christian community—a rough outline of a theology. There is present an effort to understand the faith, something like a pre-understanding of that faith which is manifested in life, action, and concrete attitude. It is on this foundation, and only because of it, that the edifice of theology—in the precise and technical sense of the term—can be erected. This foundation is not merely a jumping-off point, but the soil into which theological reflection stubbornly and permanently sinks its roots and from which it derives its strength. (1973: 3)

In a "pre-understanding of faith" a community may give expression to a theology through "life, action, and a concrete attitude" before they even give a name to it themselves. In an interview with Kathleen Hayes for *The Other Side* magazine, Fr. Gutiérrez explained that people can practice liberation theology without calling it that by name.

> **The Other Side**: Do the poor in Latin America know about "liberation theology"? Is that a word the base Christian communities use themselves?
>
> **Gustavo Gutiérrez**: The question is not really one of the explicit name. For example, in my parish in Rimac, I never mention liberation theology in my homilies. I was not taught in seminary to teach liberation theology but to preach the gospel. Many poor people have experienced liberation theology, but my interest is not that they know the term itself.
>
> So maybe my answer to your question is, "I don't know." But if you ask the poor, "Do you think poverty is against the will of God?" "Do you think that a Christian must struggle for justice," they say yes, yes. Well, this is liberation theology. Our interest is the content, the ideas, the goals of this theology, not the expression *liberation theology*. (November 1987: 11)

The words of Fr. Gutiérrez lead to the conclusion that there is a theology present in the "life, action, and concrete attitude" of the Catholic Worker communities. And although this theology has not been fully articulated on the professional level, it certainly has been described on the popular and pastoral levels.

The Liberation of Theology

Having looked briefly at the "theology of liberation," it is necessary to look at the "liberation of theology." How does one engage in a "critical reflection on praxis?" How does one "do" theology? How can a theology also be a movement?

That which makes liberation theology a *movement* can be found in the relationship between the parts or themes just examined. The themes previously mentioned are neither static nor independent from one another, rather they are dynamic parts of an interactive system. Together the whole is greater than the sum of the parts. Together there is a dynamism or "synergy." They are not "structural elements" of an inanimate object like a building or even a machine; rather a better analogy would be they are like parts of a living organism.

Theologian Juan Luis Segundo, S.J. explains that the challenge before us is to discover how to make theology dynamic. He called for the liberation of theology:

> Liberation is not merely a theme. It is the central message of Christ. The Good News of Liberation. Unfortunately, theology lost sight of this basic fact through the years and became something like an "archaeological science." It lost sight of its main task which is to liberate. Thus, it would be better to say Teologia Leberadora, Liberating Theology or Liberation Theology. The problem is how theology can once again become liberating; not how to make a theology of liberation but how to make theology liberating. (Reilly, n.d.: 95)

Similarly, Peter Maurin called for a more dynamic theology. He asked people to engage in works of mercy daily. He called for roundtable discussions. Peter Maurin was critical of scholars and theologians for being too passive. He felt they concealed or masked the strength of the Gospel message. He thought theology should be liberated. In his famous "Easy Essay" entitled "Blowing the Dynamite" we are reminded of his views on this subject:

> Writing about the Catholic Church,
> a radical writer says:
> "Rome will have to do more
> than to play a waiting game;
> she will have to use
> some of the dynamite
> inherent in her message."
> To blow the dynamite
> of a message
> is the only way
> to make the message dynamic.
> If the Catholic Church
> is not today
> the dominant social dynamic force,
> it is because Catholic scholars
> have failed to blow the dynamite
> of the Church.
> Catholic scholars
> have taken the dynamite
> of the church,
> have wrapped it up
> in nice phraseology,
> placed it in a hermetic container
> and sat on the lid.
> It is about time

to blow the lid off
so the Catholic Church
may again become
the dominant social dynamic force. (Maurin 1984: 3)

This "Easy Essay" calls Catholic scholars to help the Church become the dominant social force. Theology can stifle a living faith rather than liberate it. Maurin knew that ofen there is a disparity between words and deeds—i.e., between orthodoxy and orthopraxis. In a *Commonweal* article Dorothy Day explained, "Peter liked to talk of making a message dynamic, and that meant with him putting into practice. There was simple common sense in his argument that if you want to reach the man in the street, you go out on a park bench with him..."(Day 1949: 99-102)

Peter Maurin called for direct action; he asked people to put ideas into practice (praxis); he called for scholars to talk to workers so that scholars would not become too academic and workers would not become too superficial (anaylsis). He wanted to take theology out of "a hermetic container."His solution was not unlike what theologians call a "hermeneutic circle."

Hermeneutic Circle

The word "hermeneutics" comes from the name Hermes, who "was the 'messenger of the gods' in the Greek pantheon; it is easy to see why they derived the word for 'interpreter' from his name."(Myers 1988: 4) *A Concise Dictionary of Theology* defines the hermeneutic circle as

> A notion developed, at times differently, by Martin Heidegger (1889-1976), Rudolf Bultmann (1884-1976), Hans Georg Gadamer (b. 1900) and others apropos of the interpreter's search for meaning. In a particular historical situation and with some prior understanding of what a given text is about, the interpreter begins a "dialogue." The text will modify questions put to it, challenge expectations and even radically correct our presuppositions. In the dialogue with the interpreter, the text and its message retain their priority. A 1989 document of the International Theological Commission ("The Interpretation of Dogmas") proposed a "metaphysical hermeneutics" as a solution to the risk of relativism involved in the hermeneutical circle. (O'Collins and Farrugia 1991: 90)

The Pontifical Biblical Commission's document, *The Interpretation of the Bible in the Church*, addresses the philosophy of hermeneutics:

> Based upon various forms of the philosophy of hermeneutics, the task of interpretation involves, accordingly, three steps: 1. To hear the word from within one's own concrete situation; 2. To identify the aspects of the present situation highlighted or put in question by the biblical text; 3. To draw from the fullness of meaning contained in the biblical text those elements capable of advancing the present situation in a way that is productive and consonant with the saving will of God in Christ. (Catholic Church. Pontificial Biblical Commission 1994: 521)

Thus, according to the philosophy of hermeneutics, theology becomes dynamic when these themes are seen and understood in relationship to one another. They are all aspects or elements of a method of liberation theology.

In *Social Analysis: Linking Faith and Justice* (1983), Joe Holland and Peter Henriot, S.J., provide a wonderful illustration that they call "the pastoral circle." The pastoral circle illustrates not only the strong link to Scripture, but also the relationship to other themes we have discussed such as social analysis and praxis.

> The first moment in the pastoral circle—and the basis for any pastoral action—is insertion. This locates the geography of our pastoral responses in the lived experience of individuals and communitities. What are people feeling, what they are undergoing, how they are responding—these are the experiences that constitute the primary data. We gain access to these by inserting our approach close to the experiences of ordinary people.
>
> These experiences must be understood in the richness of all their interrelationships. This is the task of social analysis, the second moment in the pastoral circle. Social analysis examines causes, probes consequences, delineates linkages, and identifies actors. It helps make sense of experiences by putting them into the broader picture and drawing connections between them.
>
> The third moment is theological reflection, an effort to understand more broadly and deeply the analyzed experience in light of living faith, scripture, church social teaching, and the resources of tradi-

> tion. The Word of God brought to bear upon the situation raises new questions, suggests new insights, and opens new responses.
>
> Since the purpose of the pastoral circle is decision and action, the fourth moment in the circle is crucial: pastoral planning. In the light of experiences analyzed and reflected upon, what response is called for by individuals and by communitities? How should the response be designed in order to be most effective not only in the short term but also in the long term?
>
> A response of action in a particular situation brings about a situation of new experiences. These experiences in turn call for further mediation through insertion, analysis, reflection, and planning. Thus, the pastoral circle continues without final conclusion because it is more of a "spiral" than a "circle." Each approach does not simply retrace old steps but breaks new grounds. (Holland 1983: 8-9)

Clearly the Catholic Worker movement also experiences the dynamic circle. Through the establishment of houses of hospitality the communities are *inserted* into impoverished locations. Through roundtable discussions and publications the communities engage in social analysis of the economic, political, and cultural causes of suffering they witness and endure. Members also engage in *theological reflection* analyzing the "experience in light of a living faith." They also take action, *plan responses*, practice spiritual and corporal works of mercy, engage in civil disobedience and protest.

Now to answer the question: Does the Catholic Worker movement have the necessary and sufficient conditions to practice liberation theology? Yes, for the preceding material shows that the Catholic Worker movement and liberation theology not only emerged from a similar context, they share essential themes, and they employ the same method. While the "just war" theory and socialism are supported by some liberation theologians, they are not supported by all, and these subjects are not integral to liberation theology.

Discipleship in the First World

> "There is still one thing left for you: sell all you have and distribute it to the poor, and you will have a treasure in heaven. Then come, follow me."
>
> (Luke 18:22)

Over the last thirty years many in North America have been inspired and moved by the insights of liberation theology in Latin America. But the challenges to practicing liberation theology in a North American context are daunting. Theologian Robert McAfee Brown states the problem:

> Liberation theology is about "the God of the poor"—and we are not poor. It's about "the view from the poor"—and we're on top. It's about "good news to the poor"—and that's bad news to the rich. It's about the third world—and we live in the first world. It's about social structures as carriers of evil—and those same social structures are very beneficial to us. It's about "subversion"—and that's simply an unacceptable word in our circles. (Brown 1993: 89)

Is it possible to practice liberation theology in the first world? If so, what would liberation theology look like in a first world context? What themes would characterize this theology?

Theologians and biblical scholars who admire liberation theology caution that one can not simply transplant liberation theology as practiced in Latin America into North America. Ched Myers observed, "A midweek Bible study group in our local parish does not become a 'base community' just because it is so renamed, nor are we in solidarity with the poor simply by declaring we are."(1994: 20) Those who engage in liberation theology must take their context, or the concrete situation in which they live, into consideration. Brown points the way: "The task is not to decide that liberation theology is the way of the future, and seek to import it. The task is rather to discover where our own areas of need for liberation are located, and begin to create a liberation theology for North America."(Brown 1989: 494)

Liberation theologians and biblical scholars in North America have attempted to formulate how liberation theology would be expressed in a North American context. In this section of the essay we will look to the themes expressed by these scholars and see if the Catholic Worker movement manifests these characteristics.

In the letter to the Galatians, Paul declares our freedom in Christ enables us to overcome the racism, economic exploitation, and sexism that have plagued humanity for ages: "There is neither Jew nor Greek, there is neither slave nor free, there is neither male nor female; for you are all one in Christ Jesus. For freedom Christ has set us free; stand fast therefore, and do not submit again to the yoke of slavery." (3:28, 5:1) Interestingly, liberation theologians in North America have focused on these areas too.

> Since becoming a North American and worldwide movement in theology, liberation theology has appealed primarily to people committed to addressing situations of economic, racial and sexual exploitation. In the U.S. liberation theology may be divided into three major streams: (1) white, male liberation theologians, among whom Robert McAfee Brown and Federick Herzog are prominent; (2) feminist liberation theologians, among whom Rosemary Radford Ruether and Elizabeth Schussler Fiorenza are well known; and (3) African-American liberation theologians...among whom James H. Cone and Gayraud S. Wilmore are recognized leaders. In addition to these major streams, the influence of liberation theology can be seen in the writing of Asian-American, Native American and Hispanic-American church leaders. (Adeney 1990: 469)

Although the Catholic Worker movement has spoken to the evils of racism and sexism, we will focus our attention on the first "major stream," economic justice. We do this for two reasons. First, the Catholic Worker movement has given most of its attention to this area. And secondly, as we have seen, liberation theology in Latin America also focuses on the area of economic justice.

A theology of liberation for the first world will need to emphasize the themes and methods we have already discussed. But in addition, it will also emphasize themes directed to the majority population that enjoys wealth, power, status, and influence.

In the anthology *The Future of Liberation Theology*, Robert McAfee Brown addressed some of the issues North Americans "must confront realistically, if we are to come within hailing distance of a meeting place between ourselves and the liberation struggles of others."He raised five thematic areas of confrontation: being an oppressor, being a traitor to one's class, speaking truth to power, working within church structures, and broadening the base (1989: 495-500).

In Brown's view a theology of liberation for the first world not only says, "Blessed are you poor," but it will also say, "Woe to you that are rich." The rich are called to recognize they are "*being an oppressor*."Here the rich are called to compassion (to suffer-with). They are called to conversion, to turn toward God and their brothers and sisters in need. They are called to repentance: "repent and believe the good news."(Mark 1:15) They are called to atonement (at-one-ment) and solidarity. The rich are called to live and work in solidarity with the poor, and to share their wealth.

By rejecting the greed of capitalism and the idolatry of materialism and entering into solidarity the rich become a "*traitor to their class.*" They are not only turning away from these false gods, they are also invited to follow Jesus and "believe the good news" of God's Kingdom. First world disciples are invited to join with other committed Christians in faith—the base ecclesial communities—"*working within church structures*" in the struggle for peace and justice. These communities of conscience will "*speak truth to power*" and challenge the systems that perpetuate oppression. And finally, although small faith sharing communities give strength, direction and vision, they must avoid becoming sectarian, parochial, or insular. Rather they need to "*broaden the base,*" collaborating with other base communities and movements for peace and liberation, and working with all people of good will who seek a better world.

Here we argue that the Catholic Worker movement gives its members a lens through which first world Christians can view the world and Scripture. This unique vantage point enables Catholic Workers to practice liberation theology in a first world context. The "Sermon on the Plain" gives us a key to understanding the unity and differences of liberation theology throughout the Americas. While those in Latin America are comforted by Christ's words, "Blessed are you poor," those in North America need to hear Christ's warning, "Woe to you that are rich."

> And he lifted up his eyes on his disciples and said:
> "Blessed are you poor, for yours is the kingdom of God.
> "Blessed are you that hunger now, for you shall be satisfied.
> "Blessed are you that weep now, for you shall laugh.
> "Blessed are you when men hate you, and when they exclude you and revile you, and cast out your name as evil, on account of the son of man! Rejoice in that day, and leap for joy, for behold, your reward is great in heaven; for so their fathers did to the prophets.
> "But woe to you that are rich, for you have received your consolation.
> "Woe to you that are full now, for you shall hunger.
> "Woe to you, when all men speak well of you, for so their fathers did to the false prophets.

> "But I say to you that hear, love your enemies, do good to those who hate you, bless those who curse you, pray for those who abuse you." (Luke 6:20-28)

Although on the surface Jesus' sermon appears to have two different messages, it is really two parts of the same message. Freedom and responsibility go hand in hand; they are two sides of the same coin. Both rich and poor are called to be part of God's kingdom.

Jesus' famous sermon is a promise of salvation and liberation to those who suffer, and it is also a forewarning of suffering and sorrow for those who refuse to share. The first part of the sermon is a message of hope for the oppressed. The second part of the sermon is a call for conversion of the oppressor. In this sermon, Jesus "comforts the afflicted and afflicts the comfortable."

Liberation theology speaks of freedom for the oppressed; the Catholic Worker calls us to voluntary poverty, service and work. "(For the poor) God's love will take the form of liberation, but for their oppressors it will take the form of a call to conversion and disempowerment."(Downey 1993: 598)

Why Does It Matter?

Now that the case has been made that the Catholic Worker movement is a model of liberation theology for first world disciples, questions remain: Why is it beneficial to demonstrate the relationship between the Catholic Worker and liberation theology? What does this mean? Where do we go from here? Who cares? Why does it matter?

1) *It builds a common language.* The vocabulary of liberation theology gives a voice and a contemporary language to articulate the meaning of the Catholic Worker movement today. Liberation theologians are developing a systematic theology that gives a common theological lanaguage for faith communities who are working for peace and social justice.

2) *It builds a bridge.* There is a huge gulf between North and South America. There is a large gap between the rich and poor in the Western Hemisphere. Understanding the common aspects of both movements may strengthen ties and help us work together in solidarity. Seeing these connections will also foster a dialogue between the Catho-

lic Worker movement and liberation theology movements throughout the world. Together they will be stronger.

3) *We can learn from one another.* As both groups talk and work together, wisdom will also be shared. Both movements have insights to share.

4) *It is important for the future.* Dialogue and collaboration between ecclesial communities dedicated to peace and social justice in the North and the South will influence both movements and the Church as a whole.

5) *To connect first world advocates of liberation theology with the Catholic Worker movement.* Some who have read, understand and appreciate liberation theology do not see how it relates to a first world context. Some may be inspired by liberation theology but not know how they could be involved. This study may convince such readers that liberation theology is as close as their local Catholic Worker community.

6) *Lessons for the Catholic Worker.* Important priorities emerge when one sees the Catholic Worker movement in relationship with liberation theology. These priorities can be found in the lives of the founders and leaders of the movement (if not in the stated aims and means). The Catholic Worker must never forget the crucial role Scriptures played in the life of the movement—members need to cultivate the same love and knowledge of the Bible as Dorothy Day. Following Dorothy Day's example, it is necessary to form base communities which are ecclesial—that is, open and in service to all, and at the same time profoundly connected and faithful to the Church. One way to strengthen the connection to both the Church and liberation theology is to focus on a goal that was mentioned in the first issue of *The Catholic Worker*: to promote Catholic social teaching.

Toward a Catholic Worker Theology

The Catholic Worker movement has been described through autobiography, biography, history and anthologies, but few have tried to express the theology of the Catholic Worker movement. Dorothy Day and Peter Maurin were not theologians; they did not try to articulate the meaning and method of the Catholic Worker movement through systematic theology. I think the Catholic Worker movement was ahead of the theology of its day. Insights from liberation theology can help describe the dynamism and theological underpinnings of the Catholic Worker movement. This study points to the importance of Catholic Worker communities around the world beginning to consciously articulate a systematic theology of liberation for a first world context.

Gustavo Gutiérrez posed the fundamental questions: "What does it mean to do theology? What is the meaning of poverty in biblical revelation? How can we witness resurrection in a context of poverty and death?"(Dwyer 1994: 548)

These seem to be important questions for the Catholic Worker movement to ponder as well, and may serve as a common ground for dialogue. What does it mean for a Catholic Worker to do theology? What is the meaning of poverty in biblical revelation for Catholic Workers? And how does the Catholic Worker witness resurrection in a context of poverty and death in the United States?

Why does it matter if we compare these two movements? In short, it will help both groups communicate with one another and help span the gulf between North and South. It will help both movements work together and learn from one another so they both can be stronger, wiser and more effective.

M.L. Liebler

Roll Away the Stone

Today I walked free
Out of the dark tomb of myself.
Resurrected and thoroughly connected
Back to the Holy Spirit of life.

All of my years amassed
Like crows on rows and rows
Of telephone wires filling the lonely
Fields in the America of my nights.

Alone, too long, I've tasted
Darkness; my feast to the emptiness
of my hollow, pale soul that once was
Shallow and forbidden-prayerless and uneasy.

Today I claim victory over
The death of this world.
Greater love I've not known
Than One Lord-One Faith-One Baptism.

PART III

THE NONVIOLENCE OF DOROTHY DAY AND THE CATHOLIC WORKER

Works of Mercy and Works of War, by Rita Corbin, is dated 1966.

Beyond the Ballot Box: The Catholic Worker Movement and Nonviolent Direct Action

Patrick G. Coy

Kent State University

In the fall of 1983, I joined the St. Louis Catholic Worker community at Karen House, and lived there in community for seven years. In those days the community gathered together Wednesday nights in an apartment near by the house. There was a meal and socializing, some prayer, and something called "tradition," where one member of the community would lead a discussion or make a short presentation on some aspect of Catholic Worker life and thought. There was also a discussion about the weekly business: the guests and their various struggles, their status in the house, the needs of the old convent that served as our hospitality house, and our shared economics. Since everything was done by consensus, and since this was a group of Catholic Workers, the 3-hour meetings often went considerably past the time limit.

The second meeting I attended finished on schedule at 9 p.m. so that the community could adjourn to the downtown bus station. The Greyhound bus drivers were on strike, and they were maintaining a 24-hour picket line in front of the station. This was still in the early years of the so-called Reagan revolution, in the days before deregulation gave Greyhound the green light to run all of its competition out of the national market. A strike by Greyhound drivers back then meant not just a temporary loss of riders to Greyhound, but the potential long-term loss of customers who went to competing bus lines. So, for the driver's union, the strike was a nonviolent tactic of considerably more import than it is in these post-regulation days where competition in interstate bus travel is more the exception than the rule.

When the Catholic Worker cummunity's weekly meeting adjourned, the members gathered up thermoses of coffee and hot chocolate, a large sack of sandwiches, and some picket signs, made up earlier that day. Unannounced, the Worker community went down to the bus station to stand vigil with the picketing drivers for a few hours, pouring coffee and hot chocolate and passing out sandwiches to the cold and hungry strikers.

Although it was far from a commonplace event, this simple act of solidarity was still not a dramatic form of nonviolent action. All it involved was walking a picket line and serving up some food and drink. Aside from some interesting political discussions with the drivers, it was a rather uneventful action. Nevertheless, it somehow made a deeper and much more lasting impression on me than any of the many nonviolent actions taken by our community and its members during my years with the St. Louis Catholic Worker. Had I been on my own, I am quite sure that I would not have ventured to a largely deserted downtown street corner in St. Louis to stand with and serve food to the striking Greyhound drivers on a weeknight at 9 p.m. But now, as a member of this Catholic Worker community, it seemed like a natural, even ordinary thing to do.

The naturalness of it can be made more specific. Walking the picket line seemed directly tied to the community business meeting that had adjourned moments before. Pouring coffee and standing vigil looked an awful lot like an extension of the community's prayer at the meeting. Serving sandwiches and hot chocolate passed quite nicely for the final course in the community's meal, even while it also complemented the hospitality work done at the Worker house during the day with the homeless, including the neighborhood soup line. And finally, the whole experience felt like a living embodiment of the "tradition" component of the community's meeting. It was something like putting flesh on the bone of Catholic Worker theory.

Nonviolent Action and the Catholic Worker

The Worker movement's philosophical foundations are found in its statement, "Aims and Means of the Catholic Worker Movement," where a commitment to nonviolent action is clearly stated. In fact, the movement says it is called

> to fight against violence with the spiritual weapons of prayer, fasting and noncooperation with evil. Refusal to pay taxes for war,

> to register for conscription, to comply with any unjust legislation; participation in nonviolent strikes and boycotts, protests or vigils; withdrawal of support for dominant systems, corporate funding or usurious practices are all excellent means to establish peace. (*CW* 5/1999:50

Catholic Worker communities employ all of these nonviolent tactics and many others. Most house newsletters regularly carry articles about that community's involvement in various nonviolent direct action campaigns regarding war, homelessness, capital punishment, labor issues, or, to a lesser extent, abortion. The whole of Catholic Worker history reveals that the tactics of nonviolent action give both form and substance to the outward expression of the Worker's personalist politics. For example, most Worker communities do little or no traditional lobbying of elected representatives, no matter the social issue or political problem involved. We are more likely to find a Catholic Worker carrying a sign at a demonstration, and perhaps even more likely to find one sitting-in at a congressional office than picking up the phone and calling their congressperson. This rejection of politics in traditional, structured forms is a current that runs strong and deep through the Worker movement. The relatively well known aversion of movement co-founder Dorothy Day to voting in elections is something that many contemporary Workers also share, and it is another expression of the movement's alternative approach to political action.

Depending upon the community, the context, and the calendar, Catholic Worker nonviolent action takes many forms and even meanings. For some communities, political protest and nonviolent direct action are a significant part of the community's collective identity, as important in its own way as the work of providing hospitality for the hungry and the homeless. Even more rare, but nonetheless present, are those Worker communities where resistance in the form of nonviolent action has supplanted hospitality as the primary charism, and where nonviolent action comes to define the community's orientation to personalist politics more so than do soup lines and shelters.

The Catholic Worker movement's commitment to nonviolence includes the outwardly political sphere whenever and wherever the Worker movement intersects with the public commonweal. What may be less often understood is that this holds true in equal proportion within the movement's many houses of hospitality. Although not the focus here, this commitment to nonviolence in the houses is also worthy of note and study. Nonviolence is used with mixed results in the often crisis-ridden and occasionally contentious interactions between community members and resident guests, between volunteers and soup line guests, and between the guests themselves (O'Gorman and Coy 1988: 239-271).[1]

In what follows, I will offer some answers to two related questions. What contributes to the Catholic Worker movement's commitment to nonviolent direct action? What makes it possible for its individuals and for the movement as a whole to continually embrace and endure the many demands and varied costs of nonviolence? Before moving on to analyze these factors in more detail, a caveat regarding generalizations is in order. Like its members, the particular communities and houses that make up the Catholic Worker movement are idiosyncratic. There are no party lines in the movement, and in the event someone would try to put one forward, there is no individual or movement structure capable of enforcing it.

During much of the 1990s, for example, the Unity Kitchen Catholic Worker community in Syracuse, New York, has used what they call the principles of a "Catholic Worker orthodoxy" to define the Catholic Worker in a theologically conservative and narrow fashion. Unity Kitchen claims that Worker communities that do not adhere to this "orthodoxy" should not be allowed to call themselves Catholic Workers (Unity Kitchen: 1995). The problem with this approach is that it runs afoul of the genius of the Catholic Worker movement: the fact that nobody ever had to get permission from anybody else to open up a Catholic Worker house. By the same token, no one has the authority to close down someone else's house or to deny them the use of the Catholic Worker name. This largely held true even when Dorothy Day was alive, with only a few exceptions. There simply is no structural basis for decision making of this sort, to say nothing of the existence of actual enforcement mechanisms (Zahn 1988).[2]

The idiosyncratic nature of the houses and the intentional lack of a movement-wide structure puts even the nuanced generalizations of social scientists and historians on thin ice (Murray 1990). Although the ice may be thin in spots, it can support some weight. For while there is no party line in the Catholic Worker, there are some general principles that are widely if not universally subscribed to. Moreover, there are some characteristic patterns to Catholic Worker life and thought that those who are familiar with the movement can readily recognize as being valid. It is those general principles and characteristic patterns that I hope to engage in what follows. One basis for generalizability, therefore, is the degree to which the basic principles and patterns that I describe are recognizable and meaningful to those who are familiar with particular Worker communities.

There are five discrete aspects of Catholic Worker life and thought that in large measure contribute to and sustain the movement's commitment to nonviolent action: biblical seriousness, personalism, solidarity with the poor through hospitality, living in community, and membership turnover. A discussion of each of these factors follows.

Biblical Seriousness

Whatever else it may be, the Catholic Worker movement is a lay religious movement whose members tend to take the religious dimensions of life extraordinarily seriously. For example, house newsletters frequently carry columns written by quite recent arrivals to the community. They may be likened to a religious coming-out column where new Workers discuss their reasons for joining the movement. The search for spiritual growth and meaning often figures prominently in their motivations. Moreover, many come to the Worker to live out the demands of the Christian Gospels in what they hope will be less morally compromising ways. But many of these new Workers are in the throes of having their idealized bubbles burst all around them as they confront the contradictions of community life and the realities of the soup line. The new arrivals frequently confess to arriving with a shockingly idealized and romanticized notion of life at the Worker. For the reader, what is equally striking (and occasionally inspiring) is the religious meaning and sustenance that these new Workers invariably mine from these profound and multiple discrepancies between their dashed expectations and the reality of life at a Worker house.

At the center of Catholic Worker life are the Scriptures, most especially the Christian Gospels. The scriptures have always been read, studied, prayed and even discussed in the Catholic Worker movement to a degree that, at least until very recently, was far above the norm for Catholic lay people. Although neither fundamentalist nor literal in its approach to Scripture, the search for religious meaning that characterizes many members revolves around trying to transfer Gospel principles to daily life in a sustained and uncommonly direct manner. The importance of this point can scarcely be overestimated.

That is why Fritz Eichenberg's wood engravings "Christ of the Breadlines," where Christ is depicted as a lonely figure standing in a breadline, and "The Lord's Supper," where those gathered around the table are the homeless and the hungry, are so very popular and frequently reproduced in movement newsletters. They symbolize the movement's effort to take the ethical demands of the Christian Gospel seriously in ordinary, daily life; e.g. if Christ said feed my neighbor, then that is what we must do. But it would be a misreading of the Worker movement to equate this stance with biblical literalism. It is not so much literalism as plain seriousness.

Many other examples would fill in the details of the picture I am trying to paint here of the movement's serious approach to the Scriptures. They include the biblical exegesis frequently published in house newsletters, and the popularity of Matthew 25, the story of the Last Judgment, where Christ concludes his lesson with the words, "Whatever you do for the least of these you do for me." The doctrine of the Mystical Body of Christ, rooted in Pauline theology, has also been a central notion in Catholic Worker theology and reinforces the Gospel idea that everyone is linked together as sister and brother in Christ (Coy 1986). Of course, the ultimate biblical foundation of Catholic Worker life is found in the nonviolent love ethic of the Sermon on the Mount, which the Worker movement has often and tellingly referred to as its "Manifesto."(*CW* 1/1942: 1; *CW* 10/1939: 4; Coy 1988: 134-173)

The prescription to serve, protect, and act for justice on behalf of the least of those among us is one of the more clear and uncontested injunctions in the Gospels. It animates and serves as a primary motivator for Catholic Worker action, including a variety of forms of nonviolent action.

Personalist Politics

The philosophy of personalism was first brought to the Worker by co-founder Peter Maurin (Mournier: 1938; Hellman 1981).[3] Originally fashioned in France as a religious but nevertheless politically engaged alternative to both existentialism and Marxism, personalism provided tenets which Maurin and Dorothy Day embraced even while they and their movement eventually fashioned a distinctively American version stamped with the Catholic Worker imprint. The result for the Catholic Worker movement is a remarkably defined sense that each person must become concretely involved in and take personal responsibility for three things in life: 1) directly coming to the aid and service of those in need, 2) working to change the social and political conditions that are creating the problems in the first place, and 3) fashioning viable alternatives while openly resisting and confronting current conditions. This is the heart of the Catholic Worker's version of personalist philosophy.

One of the hallmarks of personalist politics is its unabashed affirmation of the dignity of each and every human being. No person is expendable; indeed, no one is taken for granted. Personalism refuses to put a price tag on any human life, to say nothing of tagging one life as more valuable than another. This differential valuing of one human life over another is, of course, standard operating procedure not only in various forms of authoritarianism but in the negotiated compromises that always define representative democracy. Yet the distinctive nature of the personalist approach to politics taken by the Catholic Worker movement is even more striking on the level of human action.

So much of what makes up mainstream approaches to political action is wedded to particular notions of practicality and effectiveness. The value of individual human action is largely discounted in favor of building coalitions that can get the message out, get the job done, get the bill based, or get the bacon delivered to the home district. Never mind that these coalitions usually run no deeper than the topsoil on a dust bowl farm. Never mind also that the required compromises include violations of fundamental principles all around, from the largest coalition partner to the smallest and least powerful. Unfortunately but perhaps predictably, more compromises are required by the latter than by the former. While the personalist approach does not completely abandon the politics of compromise or the need for coalitions, it has a decided bias toward individual action and the presumed morally superior character of that action, especially when it is taken on behalf of others. The Worker movement's statement of "Aims and Means" reflects this approach:

> We move away from a self-centered individualism toward the good of the other. This is to be done by taking personal responsibility for changing conditions, rather than looking to the state or to other institutions to provide impersonal "charity." (*CW* 5/1999:5)

The commitment to personalism serves as a conceptual springboard for engaging in nonviolent action. If we look closely enough inside Worker personalism, we find a bias toward taking direct, personal action. Just as there is a *spiritual immediacy* in the Worker movement arising from its serious approach to the Gospels (e.g., the poor are Christ, and therefore I simply cannot turn away from them), there is also a *political directness* arising from its personalist philosophy (e.g., I must take action to right the wrong, not wait and hope someone else will, including my congressperson or the state). Worker personalism and the directness if so values results, in a pronounced tendency to favor extra-institutional forms of politics. We might, with equal accuracy, call it direct action politics, or even nonviolent action politics. In any case, this kind of action can be recognized by two defining characteristics: 1) it is direct and unmediated, and 2) it relies primarily upon the grand triumvirate of nonviolent tactics: protest, noncooperation, and resistance.

For these reasons, to cite but one among many possible examples, the Nuclear Weapons Freeze Campaign of the 1980s, was not a political vehicle that caught the Catholic Worker fancy. There simply was no bandwagon effect in the Worker movement toward the Freeze campaign as there was in so many other sectors of the liberal or even the progressive U.S. This was in spite of the fact that Catholic Workers were just as upset about the Reagan administration's massive arms build up as anyone else, perhaps more so given their daily work with its victims. The Freeze campaign was by and large rejected as too reformist and too institutionalized to merit sustained political energy.

Solidarity with the Poor through Hospitality

A third source of Catholic Worker nonviolent activism is the experience of daily living and working with the poor and homeless. By far the most significant aspect of that experience is the solidarity with the poor that it encourages in the Workers. Providing hospitality is a central aspect of Catholic Worker life, and its influence on why and how the Worker movement engages the outward political sphere is profound enough that it transcends both time and space within the movement. In other words, the importance of hospitality and its effects on the Worker's emphasis on nonviolent action is widespread across the bulk of Worker communities, both in the present and in the past. Here the ice is probably thick enough for historians and social scientists to make less nuanced generalizations.

Worker house newsletters regularly report on the trials of various community members arrested for civil disobedience or for other forms of nonviolent direct action. Many include all or part of the formal statements that the members made in court justifying their actions. We find in these statements a recurring theme: workers repeatedly explain their nonviolent activism as being directly related to their hospitality work. Workers write, sometimes eloquently, about acting on behalf of the guests, about not being able to ignore social problems, political policies, and economic systems precisely because they live with and serve those who are hurt or victimized by those systems and policies. In other words, nonviolent direct action becomes the political expression of the Gospel injunction to love thy neighbor. The following comment by Mary West of the Detroit house reflects this.

> We really struggle in our own hearts and in our own minds to make the connection between the work that we do at the soup kitchen and at the house, and the work that we do in jail. In some respects we are going to jail to protest the way that poor people are treated. All these resources go into armaments and so there is nothing, or next to nothing, going for poor people. (Troester 1993: 195)

Biblical seriousness and personalism lead to a very concrete and direct involvement in the works of mercy, and the unmediated nature of those works leads in turn to doing politics in the direct, unmediated fashion of nonviolent action. Many Catholic Workers take to the streets as quickly and as easily as they take to serving the soup. Consider this explanation from Char Madigan of St. Joseph's House in Minneapolis:

> It's a systemic thing. And so a lot of my work is not just standing at Honeywell but talking in the churches. I only talk if they let me talk about St Joe's [House of Hospitality] and the Honeywell project, and [make] the connection. But [to answer] your question about why we keep doing it: perhaps we are using energy senselessly. We had hoped eight years ago that we would grow to be thousands and thousands resisting Honeywell, and we haven't. And yet many other peace movements have broken off from the Honeywell Project.
>
> We really are mosquitoes on an elephant. It's how you spend your energy. Is this band-aid at St. Joe's a good way to spend your

energy? Is nonviolent resistance at Honeywell?" (Troester 1993: 194-195)

Here we see the close connection between hospitality and resistance that is so common in the Worker movement. This Worker member will not speak in churches about the hospitality work unless she can also speak about the nonviolent direct action campaign at Honeywell headquarters in the Twin Cities. They are so interconnected as to require a compromise of principle if one is presented or done without the other. One project leads to and informs the other. Madigan sees the problems as systemic, meaning that the entire system must be engaged. Furthermore, she concludes that the direct, unmediated way that she and the Worker movement respond to the problems of homelessness (soup lines and shelters) and massive military budgets (nonviolent action) are also closely related. She tags them both as a band-aid approach, and implicitly criticizes them as little more than "mosquitoes on an elephant." But she does not discount the ultimate meaning of personal hospitality or nonviolent direct action. Nor does this longtime member of the movement abandon it or its methods. More important for our purposes is the fact that the personal, direct, and unmediated nature of Worker hospitality leads to and informs a sustained, direct and unmediated nonviolent engagement with the weapons industry in the form of the Honeywell Project. The Catholic Worker does politics in the same extra-institutional manner as it does hospitality.

A popular conception of nonviolent action is that of "speaking truth to power." Although a phrase originally made popular in the United States. by the American Friends Service Committee in the 1950s, when they published an influential booklet by that name, this formulation is much used within the Worker movement, especially in regard to nonviolent action. There is a dual presumption in the phrase.

It first presumes that the nonviolent actionist actually knows the truth, and second that the actionist is somehow empowered to speak. While those presumptions have always made some people uncomfortable, in today's deconstructed and postmodern world that is even more often the case. The questions are by now familiar: How am I to know a truth, and who am I to speak of it anyway? Yet these hesitancies are much less common within the Worker movement. A close analysis suggests that the reason has more to do with the solidarity experience arising out of doing hospitality than anything else.

The experience of living in a Catholic Worker house in solidarity with the poor softens the aversions many people have to presuming to know a "truth," and to speaking that truth to the world through nonviolent action. The first-hand experience Workers get regarding the effects of public policies on the poor shapes and in some cases sharpens their political analysis of those policies (discerning the truth). It also emboldens them to act on that analysis (speaking the truth) through public, dramatic nonviolent action, which is a form of political action that is decidedly not postmodern as it is often designed to paint stark contrasts and create a crisis of moral choice.

In short, the Catholic Worker house of hospitality is a source of political knowledge leading to nonviolent action. We might usefully see hospitality and the solidarity it engenders as the grounding of a Catholic Worker epistemology. Karl Barth, the great Swiss theologian of the first half of this century, said that one should regularly read the Bible with the newspaper in the other hand. We can also profitably extend Barth's insight by asking, if the newspaper illuminates the Bible, what will illuminate the newspaper? The history of Catholic Worker nonviolent activism suggests that the answer is a soup kitchen. The newspaper's reports on public events and political policies will take on new meanings given the radical consciousness formed by the hospitality experience and perhaps lead to different kinds of nonviolent political engagement.

Living in Community

Living in community at a Catholic Worker house engenders nonviolent action in many ways, and this factor is also hard to overestimate even if it is less easy to pin down. But, we can begin with the power of tradition. The traditions of a community have a way of making claims on human action, and the members have a way of wanting to enact, pass on, and honor the traditions of the community. Beginning in 1939 with the ill-fated "Non-participation League," which was partly organized by the Worker to boycott World War II-related products and jobs, there is a very well established tradition within the movement of engagement in nonviolent activism and resistance of various sorts. Put plainly, nonviolent activism is part of the air one breathes in a Catholic Worker community. The St. Louis Worker community served the sandwiches and walked the picket line with the striking Greyhound drivers in 1983 partly because we knew the long history of Catholic Worker support for union struggles, and we wanted to live out that part of our tradition just as we were trying to live out the other parts.

Another way to approach the relationship between community life and nonviolent action is to recognize that people gain all sorts of things from small group memberships, especially from their membership in intentional and intensive communities like the Catholic Worker. The benefits may be easily broken down into two kinds: affirmations and challenges.

Regarding affirmation, life in community brings to an individual the strength and safety of numbers, including a sense of affinity in holding unpopular political positions or spiritual values. In short, members gain affirmation for their views coupled with refuge from their doubts, a powerful elixir. They also develop a personal identity that is rooted partly in their group membership, which is of course tied to the collective identity of the group.

For relatively marginalized communities like the Catholic Worker, these benefits and affirmations arising from community membership can be quite important. This is even more so in the realm of nonviolent direct action, which tends to have the effect of setting its participants apart from the mainstream (Epstein 1991; Berrigan and McAlister 1989). Nonviolent action is for most citizens of the United States. far enough from their own political experiences that it may easily serve to highlight differences between them and the nonviolent activist. The common result is a form of social isolation borne largely by the practitioner of nonviolence. The proclivities of an independent rebel like Ammon Hennacy notwithstanding, most people no doubt appreciate acting in the context of a community of nonviolent activism and resistance. Relatively few, including most Catholic Workers, are going to embark on lengthy public fasts or sustained pickets and campaigns apart from a community context. Nonviolent action is not only politically but also socially taxing, and membership in a Catholic Worker community reduces those many costs while adding various affirmations into the mix.

More practically, life in a Catholic Worker community may free the individual from all or part of the need to financially support themselves, opening the way for nonviolent actions that involve considerable planning, implementation, or even jail time. This is true for two reasons peculiar to the Worker: the shared economics of many communities, and the ethic of voluntary poverty and simple living that marks the movement.

Turning toward the challenges that come with living in a Worker community and that impact the doing of politics primarily via nonviolent direct action, a number of things should be noted. Community members participate in open forums and in informal discussions over coffee or a beer in the community's quarters about the meanings of nonviolent action and the need for engaging in it relative to a particular issue. People with open minds and hearts can expect to be challenged in such discussions and perhaps to be changed in one way or another. This social process was, after all, the purpose behind Peter Maurin's idea of roundtable discussions for clarification of thought.

People with open minds and hearts can also expect to be challenged not only by words but also by deeds, especially by the activities of those fellow community members whom they know and respect. This is born out by the fact that one of the most often researched and widely established theses in social movement research is that recruitment into social movements occurs primarily through pre-existing networks and along lines of social relationships. In other words, friends influence and recruit their friends to social movement organizations and activities while business people are recruiting their business associates to join in on the activities of the social movement to which they belong. Relative to participation in social movement activities like the nonviolent actions of a Worker community, people are most influenced by those they already know and are in relationship with. Furthermore, there is a culture of engaging in nonviolent political action in Catholic Worker communities; as with all cultures, it manifests itself through the words, deeds and values of its individual members. All of this serves to influence other members, and if it was characterized as a mix of loving challenges and relatively simple peer pressure, we would not be very far from the truth.

Perhaps the following quotation from a Detroit member best reflects both the preceding discussion and the reality of human relationships in a Worker community. Here we see that the affirmations and the challenges that come with living in community are actually bundled up together and not easily separated.

> Our house has been real blessed inasmuch as it's always had people who have expected going to jail as both necessary and desirable. No

> one has ever been forced to do civil disobedience if they were in the house, and yet it's been kind of a common understanding that it was desirable and that there would be openness to people going to jail and taking time away from the house. So that's supported, and when people come into the house, they implicitly agree to shouldering the extra work if someone goes away. (West in Troester 1993: 195)

Membership Turnover

The final contributor to the Worker's long-standing and absolutist commitment to nonviolence is the fact that the formal membership of a Catholic Worker community turns over relatively frequently. Many Workers come to the movement when they are young, and leave after five years or less. Others come somewhat later in life. In any case, it is quite unusual for a member to live in a Worker community for more than ten years. The reasons for leaving are multiple. Many move on to raise families in what are considered "healthier" environs or develop career goals that provide little room for community life and the demands of hospitality houses. Still others leave partly because their views and values have changed and they no longer embrace key aspects of the Catholic Worker idea. Some leave because they are burned out, tired of the mandates of hospitality or the costs of nonviolent action.

In any event, community turnover is a fact of life at the Worker. In some ways this turnover no doubt inhibits and hinders nonviolent action because it disrupts the social processes and community dynamics discussed above. In other ways it probably contributes to the Worker movement's sustained use of nonviolent action in the political arena over 65 years because fresh souls continue to arrive to bear the costs and to take up where others left off.

Taken together, these five factors provide more than a congenial climate for Catholic Worker nonviolent action. They work together in a manner that has insured that Catholic Workers primarily engage in political action in the same non-institutionalized and unmediated way that they work with the hungry and homeless. In this way, the hundreds of Catholic Worker houses have developed an uncommonly integrated and wholistic approach to alternative politics, and fashioned a fertile seed bed for an ongoing experiment in nonviolent direct action.

Acknowledgement

Jay Kelly, Harry Murray, Mark Scheu, and Karin Tanquist provided good advice and helpful comments on this paper, which I gratefully acknowledge.

Notes

[1] Many Workers find the practice of nonviolence within the house of hospitality even more challenging and personally demanding that its use in the public, political sphere. Still, the movement's commitment to nonviolence means that Worker houses have themselves been a daily, living laboratory of experiments in nonviolence for 65 years. Unfortunately, the insights and lessons have been too little identified and reflected upon by either Workers or historians. It is a rich and important history waiting to be written and studied.

[2] The lack of enforcement mechanisms was especially striking in 1988 in a series of events involving the Casa Maria Catholic Worker House in Milwaukee, which allowed women, laymen, and non-Catholics to preside at their weekly liturgies instead of a priest. After an exchange of letters between New York and Milwaukee Catholic Workers failed to end the practice, a few publicly prominent "fellow travelers" of the Catholic Worker, most notably Eileen Egan and Gordon Zahn, became involved. The issue was larger than non-clergy presiding at liturgies; it was the lack of an institutionalized structure or mechanisms by which Egan and Zahn could pressure the Milwaukee house. Zahn eventually wrote an article exposing and criticizing the practice in the lay Catholic periodical, *Commonweal.*

[3] The European personalist movement that influenced Maurin had its heyday in France in the 1930s, and was closely associated with Emanuel Mounier and the journal *Espirit.*

American Myth and the Gospel: Manifest Destiny and Dorothy Day's Nonviolence

Stephen T. Krupa, S.J.

John Carroll University

> Fundamentally, human history is a struggle between myth and gospel.
>
> Gil Bailie, *Violence Unveiled*

The warring nations of the world would not begin to hear a consistently critical voice in opposition to war and the use of force from within American Catholicism until Dorothy Day made pacifism central to life in the Catholic Worker movement. In the crucible of world war members of the Catholic Worker and their faithful followers would come to realize the high price of fidelity to Catholic pacifism and the uncompromising commitment of Dorothy Day to absolute nonviolence. The Catholic Worker was the only group in the history of the American Catholic Church that refused to view the nation's wars as the moral crusade of Christianity against the evil forces of tyranny or Communism. The meek and unquestioning obedience which characterized the devotional Catholicism of the immigrants, on the one hand, left most Catholics in nineteenth and twentieth century America submissive even unto death to a Church hierarchy which instructed them to submit to civil authority. The socially active spirituality of the Americanists, on the other hand, surely was closer to the energetic spirit of the modern papal social encyclicals and the urgent statements of several popes calling for peace and disarmament among the nations. But the influential Americanist leaders in the Church like Orestes Brownson, Isaac Hecker, Archbishop John Ireland, and Cardinal James Gibbons were also ready to go along with the judgments and policies of the nation's political and military leaders. In response to the government's war policies, the Americanists converted themselves and their following into models of conformity and compliance. In time of war the progressive social reformers were no different than their conservative peers in the American Catholic Church.

The Catholic Worker's active nonviolence and pacifism was due largely to the spiritual vision of Dorothy Day. From the beginning of the movement in 1933, absolute nonviolence was an essential element of the Catholic Worker vocation to personal and social transformation as Day conceived it. For Day nonviolence was a way of life. While Catholic Worker nonviolence included *pacifism*, or "antiwarism,"(Teichman 1986: 2-5) its common exercise, Day emphasized, was through a life of voluntary poverty in community with the poorest members of society and the daily practice of the works of mercy. The radicalizing force of Dorothy Day's spirituality of nonviolence in the Church challenged the blind patriotism and, in some cases, militant nationalism of Catholics in the United States. But Day's resolute stand on nonviolence and pacifism confronted, as well, the entrenched myths that have structured life and social consciousness for most Americans.

The Myth of Manifest Destiny

When Dorothy Day was born in 1897, the United States was the most powerful nation in the Western Hemisphere. The next year the United States became a world power with the Spanish-American War (1898). By Armistice Day 1918, the United States had become the greatest power in the world (Lukacs 1993: 46). America's rise to world power and domination has been considered by many of its citizens as the work of divine Providence. America, in this hallowed view, is the "redeemer nation" chosen by God to govern and guide the millennial war between good and evil in the world and to extend to all nations the benefits of freedom and democracy (Tuveson 1968). At the beginning of a new millennium many Americans still claim as their destiny the anointed leadership of the forces of freedom and civilization throughout the world.

The myth of American exceptionalism dates back to the founding of the nation if not to the time of the first colonists on North American shores (de Tocqueville 1953: v.2, 36-38; Lipset 1996; Tyrell 1991:1031-1055; Weaver 1995: 231-247). In the ideology of English colonialism North America was the Promised Land, the New Israel, and the Puritans were God's new Chosen People. In this sacral view of history the triumph of English civilization on new soil was ordained and guided by Providence. The conquest of the immense territory of North America, and eventually of its "disordered pagan inhabitants," represented the culmination of the Protestant Reformation (Miller 1957: 12). Since the fiercest phalanx within the Reformation, the Puritans, had failed to realize their spiritual destiny in England, divine Providence directed the creation of a new and uncorrupted humanity in a new land. According to Edward Johnson, writing in 1650, the New England of the New Elect would be the place "where the Lord would create a new heaven and a new earth, new churches and a new commonwealth together."(Niebuhr 1962: 25; Johnson 1650)

The sense of divine mission among the early colonists was regarded as proof of their virtue. Neither the violence of the European settlers against the native Indian populations, nor the southern and western push into Florida, Texas, Mexico, California, and Oregon in the seventeenth and eighteenth centuries, nor the racial domination by whites of the African slaves, nor the American imperialism of the Spanish-American War of 1898 in any way threatened the pretension of American innocence because the sons and daughters of Europe had come to American shores as the divinely appointed bearers of civilization and salvation. Racial chauvinism and righteous violence were justified by religious rationalization.

Christian imperialism was supported by biblical sanction, in particular, by the Old Testament narratives concerning Israel's conquest of Canaan (Cave 1988: 277-297; Kadir 1992). In the ideology of early English colonialism North America was viewed biblically as England's Canaan and the American Indians as the North American Canaanites. A few examples from the colonial period are illustrative. The Virginia Company (1606-1624) hired preachers to deliver sermons which presented its mercantile enterprise in the New World in the light of a preordained providential design. To this end William Symonds delivered the first official sermon of the Company in 1609 based on Genesis 12:1-3, a text in which Abraham is instructed by the Lord to leave his country to form a new nation, one in which he will have the authority to bless those who support him and curse those who do not (Kadir 1992:126-27). Similarly, in a sermon from 1609 celebrating the founding of Jamestown (1607) the Anglican Robert Gray took as his text Joshua 17:14-18, a passage in which the Lord assures the tribe of Joseph that they will "drive out the

Canaanites." On their departure from England the Puritan founders of the Massachusetts Bay Colony were encouraged by the sermon of the Reverend John Cotton based on 2 Samuel 7:10, wherein God assures the Israelites that He has "appointed a place" for them where the "children of wickedness" will no longer "afflict" His chosen ones. Finally, in 1609, Robert Johnson, a prominent entrepreneur in the Jamestown venture, declared that since the Indians were a "wild and savage people" who lived in a "beastly and brutish manner," they were obligated to accept English occupation and allow Christians to make them "tame and civil." The English are justified, Johnson claimed, to subject to "just conquest by the sword" those savages who might behave as "unbridled beasts" and "obstinately refuse to unite themselves with us."(Cited in Cave 1988: 283, 289, 284)

Like the Israel of old, the United States claimed a messianic role at birth of the nation. Both the Declaration of Independence and the Constitution of the United States defined this mission. The nation was born "to exemplify the virtues of democracy and to extend the frontiers of the principles of self-government throughout the world."(Niebuhr and Heimert 1963: 123) A recommendation by Thomas Jefferson, author of the Declaration of Independence, illustrates the pervasiveness of the idea of the nation as God's American Israel. In 1785 Jefferson proposed that the Great Seal of the United States should depict the children of Israel led by a pillar of light (Chinard 1957: 428).

By the time of the push into Mexican territory during the U.S.-Mexican War (1846-1848) the notion of America as the new Chosen People with a God-given mission had become the official ideology of the new nation. Violence was permissible as a means to advance the ideals of liberty and civilization. In 1848, Ashbel Smith, an official of Texas, declared that the Mexican War was the beginning of "the destiny allotted to the Anglo-Saxon race . . . to Americanize this continent. . . The sword is the great civilizer, it clears the way for commerce, education, religion and all the harmonizing influences of morality and humanity."(Kohl 1914: 74-75) In 1850 Herman Melville would write: "We Americans are the peculiar, chosen people—the Israel of our time...the political messiah has come in us."(Weaver1995: 235) The providential theory of Empire, sanctioned biblically by the saga of Israel's conquest of Canaan, was bolstered by the secular principle of *vacuum domicilium*, which endorsed the right of the civilized to seize underutilized lands from savage natives

(Stephanson 1995: 25; Cave: 279, 283, 289; and Kadir: 100, 102, 127). The Promised Land and Vacant Land motifs, woven into the fabric of American exceptionalism, accorded England's pursuit of economic interests in North America both a divine and legal sanction.[1] Christian messianism was implicit in the idea of Manifest Destiny.[2] In 1845 the businessman and publisher John O'Sullivan coined the phrase "Manifest Destiny" to signify the divine right of territorial expansion and the missionary task of spreading the forces of order and civilization (Lukacs 1984: 212-214). Writing in defense of President James K. Polk's aggressive policy against Mexico and his termination of the 1818 agreement with Great Britain which provided for the joint occupation of the Oregon territory, O'Sullivan argued that the government's expansionist claims were based on "the right of our manifest destiny to overspread and to possess the whole of the continent which Providence has given us for the development of the great experiment of Liberty and federated self-government entrusted to us."[3] Manifest Destiny became popular as a slogan during the expansionist U.S.-Mexican War of 1846-1848. In 1847 O'Sullivan wrote: "The Mexican race now see in the fate of the aborigines of the north their own inevitable destiny."(Kohn: 183) From the mid-nineteenth century, however, the slogan was used to express a sense of national purpose and direction in the United States in a number of increasingly ambitious government initiatives. The phrase which was used by O'Sullivan to defend continental expansion in 1845 was used three years after his death in 1895 in a wider sense to anoint foreign expansionism by the United States into the colonial territories of Spain. Hence, a term used in 1845 to refer to the continental push of democratic nationalism became by the 1890s the slogan for the rise of American imperialism. On the eve of the Spanish-American War, the Washington *Post* gave expression to the renewed sense of Manifest Destiny in the United States at the end of the nineteenth century as the nation prepared to spread its influence overseas.

> A new consciousness seems to have come upon us—the consciousness of strength—and with it a new appetite, the yearning to show our strength....Ambition, interest, land hunger, pride, the mere joy of fighting, whatever it may be, we are animated by a new sensation. We are face to face with a strange destiny. The taste of Empire is in the mouth of the people even as the taste of blood in the jungle. It means Imperial policy, the Republic, renascent, taking her place

> with the armed nations. (Lukacs 1984: 204; Pletcher 1978: 532-33)

In 1898, one month after the battle of Manila Bay, President William McKinley justified the taking of Hawaii with these words: "We need Hawaii just as much and a great deal more than we did California. It is our manifest destiny."(Weinberg 1958:263) McKinley's successor President Theodore Roosevelt, who had created an American epic on San Juan Ridge with his "Rough Riders" in the capitulation of Santiago, Cuba, in 1898, insisted throughout his life that expansionism represented the advance of civilization over barbarism as well as an imperative of patriotism, and that pacifists and anti-imperialists were in fact devoid of true love for their country. Roosevelt wrote to Massachusetts Senator Henry Cabot Lodge that the anti-expansionists were "barbarian." (Weinberg: 299) He publicly reviled pacifists as "cravens, cowards, poltroons, and eunuchs," and as "the most undesirable citizens this country contains." (Abrams 1933: 34)

No one, however, expressed the imperialist imperative of the United States at the end of the nineteenth century as well as Senator Albert J. Beveridge of Indiana. Like O'Sullivan before him Beveridge developed a suitable moral narrative for American expansionism through the use of biblical rhetoric. Discussing the conquest of the Philippines, Beveridge declared that since Americans were marked by God as "His chosen people to lead the regeneration of the world" they had a divine mission to "establish system where chaos reigns" and to "administer government among savage and senile peoples."(Tuveson 1968: vii; Burns 1957: 218)

Manifest Destiny, a distinct expression of American exceptionalism, has functioned as a "charter myth" for Americans from the middle of the nineteenth century, and it is not yet "tired."[4] The central idea of Manifest Destiny, namely, the divine mandate to spread American institutions throughout and beyond the North American continent, has appeared throughout the twentieth century in various forms: the crusade of President Woodrow Wilson to "make the world safe for democracy" in World War I, the anti-fascism and anti-Communism of World War II and of the post-War McCarthy era in the United States, the quasi-religious fervor that Americans attributed to capitalism during the Cold War, the effort to halt Communism in Vietnam, and the shift of the American animus from the Soviet Union to the relatively defenseless nations of the Middle East and Third World, to name a few obvious examples. What was a catch phrase for the notion of a divinely sanctioned right to continental expansionism in the nineteenth century became, by the time of the presidency of Harry Truman, a warrant for the United States to act as the world hegemon. Truman's assertion that "if history has taught us anything, it is that aggression anywhere is a threat to peace everywhere in the world" still arouses the moral passion of Americans intent on uplifting humanity through the export of free political institutions, even if by force (Stephanson 1995: 125).

Manifest Destiny was damaged but not defeated by the war in Vietnam and the clear evidence of racism in America during the civil rights movement in the 1960s and 1970s. For a short time, "the realities of Vietnam and the ghetto turned the messianic shibboleths of cold-war ideology into absurdities."(Stephanson: 126) But American messianism was resuscitated by Presidents Ronald Reagan and George Bush only a few years later. The election of Ronald Reagan in 1980 demonstrated the enthusiasm and receptivity in the American public for the ideas of *exceptionalism* and *destiny* (Stephanson: 127-29). As Stephanson notes, in Reagan's view America had temporarily lost the vision of its original faith and mission after the cultural upheavals of the 1960s and the war in Vietnam. Reagan began his political career in 1964, therefore, with a call to courage in the "rendezvous with destiny," and came into the White House in 1981 proclaiming that the nation was "a beacon of hope to the rest of the world" and "the last best hope of man on earth."[5] Religious and mythic references to "Armageddon" and the "Evil Empire" accompanied Reagan's staggering military buildup and renewed vision of a showdown with the Soviet Union. These apocalyptic references were matched by President George Bush's demonizing rhetoric as the U.S. military won a lopsided victory in 1991 against the "Hitler" of the Middle East, Saddam Hussein. On 4 August 1988, exactly two years before making preparations to send U.S. troops to the Persian Gulf, candidate Bush delivered a campaign speech on foreign affairs in which he seconded the declaration of Manifest Destiny made by President John F. Kennedy in his 1961 Inaugural Address: "We shall bear any burden, meet any hardship, support any friend or oppose any foe to assure the survival and success of liberty." President Bush made good on Kennedy's "anys" in the defense of Kuwait in the 1991 Persian Gulf War.[6]

The myth of *Manifest Destiny* has not been "an idle rhapsody" in the history of the United States but a highly potent "cultural force."(Malinowski 1954: 97) A myth, in general, is a unique fiction which both expresses and creates the reality it describes (Doty 1986: 6). When viewed as a "pragmatic charter" for society, myth provides both a model *of* society, setting forth an ideal mirror image of the culture, and a model *for* society, setting forth the standards which guide the organization of relationships and action within a society.[7] Charter myths establish social roles and patterns of relationship, and they validate a society by relating the established social structure to divine or mythic prototypes.[8] With its foundation in a Judeo-Christian "myth of origin," namely, the Exodus and the Promised Land, Manifest Destiny became for America a most effective charter issued from on high. It helped to create national unity from a diverse ethnic population, and it supplied Americans with a motive and guide for moral and practical action. Supplemented by the myths of "frontier" and "wilderness,"[9] the myth of Manifest Destiny provided the descendants of the first European visitors to America with a warrant which both guided and justified their settlement and eventual conquest of continental lands and the territories of enemies abroad.

Manifest Destiny expresses, simultaneously, both moral potential and responsibility and national egoism. There are both virtues and pretensions in the charter. It is the nature of myth to simultaneously reveal and conceal reality. The etymological root of the Greek word for myth, *muthos*, is *mu* which means "to close" or "to keep secret." The myth of Manifest Destiny, at best, has disclosed the enlightened humanitarianism of the American spirit in the desire to uplift the human community through the spread of democratic ideals. Such positive interpretations of the myth, like Merk's (1963), have not survived the scrutiny of most scholars, however. They conceal the fact that America's attempts to fulfill a providential destiny, on and off of the American continent, have been fraught with violence, religious arrogance, and racial superiority.

The nationalism represented by Manifest Destiny at its best, then, has been a humanitarian nationalism based on the natural rights enshrined in the founding documents of the nation: equality, liberty, and pride in a government based on popular sovereignty. An earlier understanding of nationalism in the United States reflected this humanitarian impulse. Allegiance to the nation in the early history of America required "the submission of the selfish strivings of the individual in favor of the collective effort to advance the good of the national community as a whole."(Weinberg 1958: xi) But the affirmation of equality among diverse peoples and the foundation of the government on the consent of the governed was violated in the years after the founding of the Republic, as it had been in the years preceding nationhood, by the exercise of rule over both native and alien peoples without their consent. The attainment and spread of natural rights developed at the expense of the rights of other people. Dispossession, war, and ethnic slaughter were inserted over time into the overarching myth of Manifest Destiny (Stephanson 1995: 24-25). Accordingly, the historical development of the expansionist arguments from a mere warrant to fill in the empty spaces (viz. *vacuum domicilium)*, to annexations, and, finally, to colonization overseas provides a lucid study of the evolution of American nationalism. From an initial pride in *nationality* there developed an aggressive *nationalism* which "regards the nation as the supreme value, the source of all life's meaning, as an end-in-itself and a law to itself."[10] National might and glory became for many in the land, including many Christians, their true religion. For a long time in the Roman Catholic Church in America there was no distinction between the Gospel and this nationalist faith.

Day Opposes the Myth

The early Anglican and Calvinist ministers in the New World were not the only religious leaders in the country who got caught up in the myths of American exceptionalism and Manifest Destiny. The providential theory of Empire that Protestants once used in claiming domination over Catholic settlers in North America, (Pletcher 1978: 527-28; Stephanson 1995: 30,49) was used eventually by Catholics to justify their own participation in American expansionism "by the sword." America's Roman Catholic prelates and priests, on the whole, enthusiastically embraced the idea of the providential origin and mission of the United States. During the Civil War, Archbishop John Hughes of New York (1797-1864) inflamed the patriotism and martial ardor of Roman Catholics with rousing sermons at St. Patrick's Cathedral in New York City. While opposed to revolutions in principle and the French Revolution in particular, Hughes claimed "the invisible but real agency of a divine Providence" in the American Revolution: "the American revolutionists . . . trusted to heaven for its approving smile on their righteous cause."(Hughes 1865: 85, 87)

Archbishop John Ireland and James Cardinal Gibbons, even if unwittingly, became Catholic advocates for American destiny by supporting government policies of military preparedness and conscription. The support by Ireland and Gibbons for the nationalist cause of the United States over Catholic Spain in the Spanish-American War fueled the strong response against Americanism, reflected in Leo XIII's *Testem Benevolentiae* (1899), by a European hierarchy fearful of the growing power and reach of the United States at the end of the nineteenth century. Francis Cardinal Spellman (1889-1967) of New York represented the epitome of religious nationalism, the worship of the nation. According to his most recent biographer, Spellman was "an ardent nationalist who came to view the aims of his Church and those of his country as being the same."(Cooney 1984: xvi) Six of the seven published works of Cardinal Spellman are on patriotic themes and contain a resolute and uncritical defense of the nation's goals and purposes. Spellman was the leader of the Catholic Church in New York City during 28 of the 47 years which Dorothy Day spent living in the New York Catholic Worker community. Throughout his tenure as the Ordinary of the New York Archdiocese and the Military Vicar of the Armed Forces of the United States, Spellman offered an unashamed benediction on America's destiny.[11]

While Cardinal Spellman chanted hymns to the nation, Dorothy Day announced her objections to the social order in America and asserted that violence and war could not be reconciled with the spirit of Christ. Though she was unrelenting in her and the Worker's pacifism throughout the Spanish-American War and World War II, Day did not fail to acknowledge the evils committed by the Loyalists in Spain and by Hitler in Germany, and by Stalin and the Russians during the Cold War. She became the perennial sign of contradiction within and outside of the American Catholic community, however, by always drawing attention to evils right at home.

> I think the Kremlin is just what the cardinal [Spellman] said it was, a center of atheism and of totalitarianism and of hatred and persecution: a center of evil. Of course, we've got plenty of evil here, too. Capitalism and communism—strangely alike in ways: the callousness, the arbitrariness, the militaristic passion, justified by talk of history and of *manifest destiny* [emphasis added]. (Coles 1987: 82)

Through her writings as well as through her actions Day tried to bring about nonviolent social change. Day used the pages of *The*

Catholic Worker to inveigh against capitalism and militant nationalism, twin evils in the American system, in her view, because they mistakenly emphasized individual economic gain and national rights over the rights and needs of the human family. Upon declaring herself and the newspaper pacifist, Day informed her readership that there were alternatives within Roman Catholic teaching to the absolute and unreserved obedience to country called for by the Church hierarchy. Although it was generally believed by most Catholics and their draft boards that Catholics could not refuse a call to arms by the leaders of government, Roman Catholic doctrine had never discarded the belief that there ought to be limits to the use of brute force. Orthodox Catholicism from the time of St. Augustine (d. 430) contained a strong foundation for a religiously based opposition to war in its teaching on the "just war." *The Catholic Worker* became, if not the first, one of the first Catholic publications to counter the common opinion that "good Catholics" never opposed a call to arms by legitimate authority, through the presentation in its pages of an explanation of the just war theory during the 1930s.[12]

Personally, Day went beyond the principles of the just war, however, and recovered the earlier teaching of the Church on war and peace. Day herself could not abide the doctrine of the just war. Killing, so often motivated by hatred and self-interest, was clearly against the life and teachings of Christ, Day believed, and the "just war" was usually a euphemism in the rhetoric of militant nationalism for economic and political gain. A note fragment from the late 1950s reveals Day's mind on the matter of the just war.

> Just war theory dead. St. Thomas in trying to quiet consciences of Princes—is ruler justified in laying an ambush. Theologians go to incredible lengths to justify war. Acrobatics. . . . Hierarchy seems determined to follow state. (Miller 1982: 345)

Day held to the absolute pacifism of Jesus and the primitive Christian Church, adding to the nonresistance of the early Christians tactics of nonviolent resistance and direct action that she had learned during her years as a young leftist radical. The pacifist tradition had been the constant, but more silent, partner of the just war tradition in the Church since the time of Augustine, but it had largely disappeared from Catholicism after the Protestant Reformation. Day took it to the streets on picket lines and in jail and to the common man and woman through her writing and public speaking. Readers of *The*

Catholic Worker learned through Day's writing and personal example that along with the just war there was another moral and intellectual tradition within Roman Catholicism which provided solid ground for a religiously based antiwar stance.[13]

Inspired by the life and teaching of Jesus Christ, Day attempted to render the law of love into countless situations of conflict. When the nation and the Church sanctioned war, Day refused to abandon her deep-seated pacifism. When society and the Church ignored the lynching of black Americans in the South, Day denounced the hangings and racial violence on the front page of her newspaper.[14] When labor demonstrations grew violent, Day called for nonviolent tactics of resistance and fed and housed striking workers. When the secular press neglected to report the hiring by factory owners of scabs to incite violence at strikes, Day reported on the brute tactics used by management in industry.[15] When the nation and Church overlooked the persecution of the Jews by Hitler, Day denounced the German atrocities.[16] When the Church ignored or disowned Catholic conscientious objectors during and after World War II, Day helped them to organize.[17] When the government consigned Japanese-Americans to internment camps during World War II, Day was one of few American newspaper editors to criticize the injustice in print (*CW* 6/1942: 1,3). When President Truman delighted in the success of the atomic missions over Japan, Day took him on in *The Catholic Worker* with a caustic commentary: "Mr. Truman was jubilant. President Truman. True Man. What a strange name, come to think of it. *Jubilate Deo.* We have killed 318,000 Japanese."(*CW* 9/1945: 1) When the American masses in large cities ran for shelter during the Civil Defense air raid drills of the 1950s and '60s, Day sat down in a New York City park in protest of the government's nuclear war propaganda and awaited arrest for civil disobedience.[18] When the government and the Catholic Church refused to support conscientious objectors to the Vietnam War, Day backed the young Americans who burned their draft cards (Gray 1970: 50). When the government and Church disregarded the misery of non-unionized farm workers, Day left a scheduled speaking engagement in San Francisco in the summer of 1973 to join Cesar Chavez and striking farm workers in a Fresno jail. This was her final jail sentence before her death in 1980.[19] All of these actions were inspired, fundamentally, by the life and teaching of Jesus. When asked to explain her actions, Day quoted the Gospel-based principle which so often was included in the newspaper's listing of

"Catholic Worker Positions": "We believe that Christ went beyond natural ethics and the Old Dispensation in this matter of force and war and taught non-violence as a way of life."(*CW* 11/1968: 6)

Gospel Challenges Myth

Prophetic and saintly people do for society what the Gospel does: *they reveal a truth which makes it impossible for us to keep forgetting what myth exists to help us forget* (Bailie 1995: 34). It was in the face of the powerful national myths of American exceptionalism and Manifest Destiny, supported by prominent Roman Catholic leaders, that Day made her nonviolent stand. Day's position on nonviolence and pacifism was grossly unpopular in the nation and among Catholics in the middle decades of the twentieth century. Her uncompromising stand against the use of force confronted Americans with the possibility of a dark side to the national character. Detractors accused her of claiming moral superiority or simply dismissed her as a Communist.

Still, Day, armed with the biblical witness of a nonviolent Christ and the words of the Sermon on the Mount, continued to speak out against the violence, racial supremacy, will-to-power, and self-interest which were written in between the lines of the nation's charter myths. Day was willing to be a *signum cui contradicetur*, a sign of contradiction, to those who believed in war as "a useful and justifiable engine of national purpose."[20] In her declaration of absolute nonviolence and pacifism Day stood in opposition to the moral narratives Americans had constructed to justify their periodic bloodlettings. These narratives, enshrined in the national myths of exceptionalism and destiny and supported by both political and ecclesiastical leaders, were based, in good part, on religious claims and biblical rhetoric. When Day quoted the Bible it was not to lay claim to a unique status conferred by God or to put God on one side or the other in the battle over rights and possessions. When Day used the Bible to address America it was to condemn the nation's violence and wars. In confronting those in the country who would take up arms, Day simply quoted Jesus: "You know not of what spirit you are."(Lk. 9:55)

Notes

[1] The expansionists in America also drew upon Darwin's study of evolution published in 1859. The theory of natural selection provided the expansionists

with a scientific rationale for the predestined nature of racial and cultural expansion in North America. Thus, "the survival of the fittest" seemed to be not only the law of nature but also the law of nations. On Social Darwinism and Manifest Destiny, see Albert K. Weinberg, *Manifest Destiny: A Study of Nationalist Expansionism in American History* (Gloucester, MA: Peter Smith, 1935, 1958), 212; and Edward McNall Burns, *The American Ideal of Mission: Concepts of National Purpose and Destiny* (New Brunswick, NJ: Rutgers University Press, 1957), 241.

[2] On the concept of Manifest Destiny, in addition to the works of Tuveson, Stephanson, and Weinberg cited above, see David M. Pletcher, "Manifest Destiny," in *Encyclopedia of American Foreign Policy*, vol. 2, ed. Alexander DeConde (New York: Charles Scribner's Sons, 1978), 526-34; Julius W. Pratt, *Expansionists of 1898* (Baltimore, MD: Johns Hopkins Press, 1936); Julius W. Pratt, "The Ideology of American Expansion," in *Essays in Honor of William E. Dodd*, ed. Avery Craven (Chicago: University of Chicago Press, 1935), 335-353; and Frederick Merk, *Manifest Destiny and Mission in American History: A Reinterpretation* (New York: Alfred A. Knopf, 1963).

[3] This quotation from an 1845 article by John L. O'Sullivan provides the original definition of "Manifest Destiny." See Hans Kohn, *American Nationalism: An Interpretative Essay* (New York: Macmillan, 1957), 183; and Pletcher, p. 526. Also, see Julius W. Pratt, "John L. O'Sullivan and Manifest Destiny," *New York History* 14 (July 1933): 213-34. On the flamboyant nationalism of O'Sullivan's periodical *United States Magazine and Democratic Review*, see Kohn, 107, 152f., and 182f. On the relationship of the term "Manifest Destiny" to the rich complex of millennial and religious ideas in early America, see Tuveson, 91-136.

[4] Sidney E. Mead maintains that "destiny under God," the religious root of American national identity, has become "a part of the common consciousness" among Americans and has passed into the realm of "motivational myths." See Sidney E. Mead, *The Lively Experiment: The Shaping of Christianity in America* (New York: Harper & Row, 1963), 74-75. Bronislaw Malinowski argues that myth arises not only in the realms of magic and religion but in relationship "to any form of social power or social claim." See Bronislaw Malinowski, "The Art of Magic and the Power of Faith," in *Magic, Science and Religion and Other Essays* (Garden City, NY: Doubleday, 1948, 1954), 84. On the notion of myths as charters for social orders, see Malinowski, "Myth in Primitive Psychology," ibid., 93-148. On "charter myths" in contemporary culture, see Raphael Patai, *Myth and Modern Man* (Englewood Cliffs, NJ: Prentice-Hall, 1972); and Herbert I. London and Albert L. Weeks, *Myths That Rule America* (Washington, DC: University Press of America, 1981). On the sociofunctional approach to myth, see William G. Doty, *Mythography: The Study of Myths and Rituals* (University, AL: University of Alabama Press, 1986), 41-71. Doty also raises the issue of the "functional vitality" of myths and provides a developmental model (viz. "levels of operational vitality") for myths through different periods of a society's evolution. See Doty, 8, 37, 49-51. When a myth no longer serves to shape and inform a culture, Waardenburg claims that it has become "tired." See Jacques Waardenburg, "Symbolic Aspects of Myth," in *Myth, Symbol, and Reality*, ed. Alan M. Olson (Notre Dame, IN: University of Notre Dame Press, 1980), 56.

[5] The phrase "the last, best hope of earth" as an expression of America's destiny and mission has a long pedigree in American history. Ronald Reagan borrowed it from Abraham Lincoln's "Annual Message to Congress, December 1, 1862." See Abraham Lincoln, *The Life and Writings of Abraham Lincoln*, ed. Philip Van Doren Stern (New York: Random House, 1940), 745. Lincoln's thought, in turn, reflects the words of Thomas Jefferson from 1801. Jefferson considered America "the world's best hope." See James D. Richardson, ed. *A Compilation of the Messages and Papers of the Presidents, 1789-1897,* vol. 1 (Washington, DC:United States Congress, 1896), 322. Sidney E. Mead treats Lincoln's phrase as an expression of American destiny and uses it to explain and evaluate critically the essential "religious roots and heart of America." See Mead, 72-89.

[6] Nevertheless, many critics and historians share Michael Kramer's skeptical view of Kennedy's ringing declaration of America's messianic mission as a standard for American foreign policy at the end of the twentieth century: "After nearly three decades of convulsive history, that single Kennedy paragraph, with its repetitive 'anys,' is one that many historians identify as representing a misplaced sense of Manifest Destiny." See Michael Kramer, "Read My Ships," *Time* 136 (20 August 1990): 20.

[7] Quotation from Malinowski, "Myth in Primitive Psychology," 101. Malinowski comments: "[M]yth is not only looked upon as a commentary of additional information, but it is a warrant, a charter, and often even a practical guide to the activities with which it is connected." Ibid., pp. 107-08. On myths as models *of* and *for* society, see Clifford Geertz, "Religion as a Cultural System," in *the Interpretation of Cultures*. New York: Basic Books, 1973, 93, 118; and Doty, 44-45.

[8] On the function of myth to validate the social order by relating the human realm to divine forces and powers, see W. Richard Comstock, *The Study of Religion and Primitive Religions* (New York: Harper & Row, 1972), 38-39. See, also, Malinowski, "Myth in Primitive Psychology," 107-108: "The myth comes into play when rite, ceremony, or a social or moral rule demands justification, warrant of antiquity, reality, and sanctity. . . . [Myths are] a statement of a primeval, greater, and more relevant reality, by which the present life, fates, and activities of mankind are determined."

[9] See Richard Slotkin, *Regeneration Through Violence: The Mythology of the American Frontier, 1600-1860* (New York: Harper Perennial, 1973, 1996); and Francis Jennings, *The Invasion of America: Indians, Colonialism, and the Cant of Conquest* (Chapel Hill, NC: University of North Carolina Press, 1975). Slotkin and Jennings have drawn attention to historical realities overlooked in the standard presentations of the frontier and wilderness myths. Slotkin emphasizes the racism and violence used in the conquest of the West, while Jennings argues that there was no "wilderness" when the Europeans arrived on the shores of North America. The European settlers, rather, created a wilderness through the diseases and demoralization they brought to the Indians. Also, see Stephanson, 25-27, and Weinberg, 85-89, who discuss the problem for the expansionists posed by Indians who were basically farmers. In the standard frontier and wilderness narratives the Indians are typically presented as landless nomads, as hunters and gatherers, so that it appears that no land was taken unjustly from them. Landed and literate agriculturalists, like the members of the Cherokee nation, therefore,

posed a real problem for the expansionists. Their subjugation and relocation could not be justified by the myths of the Europeans. Also, see Weaver, 236-239. Weaver challenges Reinhold Niebuhr's "ironic" view of American history on the basis of Niebuhr's virtual neglect of the history of the subjugation and slaughter of America's original inhabitants.

[10] See H. Richard Niebuhr, "Toward the Independence of the Church," in H. Richard Niebuhr, Wilhelm Pauck, and Francis P. Miller, *The Church Against the World* (Chicago: Willett, Clark & Co., 1935), 133. Similarly, see Carlton J. H. Hayes, *Essays on Nationalism* (New York: Macmillan, 1926), 6. Hayes defines nationalism as "a condition of mind in which loyalty to the ideal or to the fact of one's national state is superior to all other loyalties." Hayes notes further: "Syncretism of nationalism and religion is strikingly noticeable in the United States." See Carlton J. H. Hayes, *Nationalism: A Religion* (New York: Macmillan, 1960), 180.

[11] See, for example, Spellman's speech calling America to leadership in the fight against the spread of Communism by the Soviet Union after World War II. Francis Cardinal Spellman, "Address of His Eminence Cardinal Spellman at Dinner of the Society, March 17, 1948," *In Memoriam: Francis Cardinal Spellman* (New York: The Society of the Friendly Sons of St. Patrick in the City of New York, 1968), 44-52. Also, see Spellman's poems and prayers in Francis Cardinal Spellman, *What America Means to Me* (New York: Charles Scribner's Sons, 1953).

[12] See, for example, "Not Pacifism" *The Catholic Worker* [hereafter, *CW*] 2 (November 1934): 4; William M. Callahan, "Ethics of Modern War Discussed in Brooklyn," *CW* 3 (December 1935): 3, 7; Paul Hanly Furfey, "Maximum—Minimum" *CW* 3 (May 1935): 5; and "For the New Reader," *CW* 6 (December 1936): 6.

[13] For examples of Day's thinking on Catholic pacifism, see Dorothy Day, *The Long Loneliness* (New York: Harper and Brothers, 1952), 253-273; [Dorothy Day and Editors], "Pacifism," *CW* 4 (May 1936): 8; Day, "The Use of Force," *CW* 4 (November 1936): 4; Day, "Explains *CW* Stand on Use of Force," *CW* 6 (September 1938): 1, 4, 7; Day, "Fight Conscription," *CW* 7 (September 1939): 1; and [Day], "Our Stand—An Editorial," *CW* 7 (June 1940): 1.

[14] For example, see "Lynching is Scored at Big Meeting of the Layman's Union," *CW* 1 (November 1933): 1; "Anti-Lynch Bill Up Before Senate," *CW* 1 (March 1934): 1; "Poverty in South Leads to Negro Lynching Orgy," *CW* 2 (December 1934) : 1, and 8; and "Lynchings Increase," *CW* 3 (January 1936): 8.

[15] See [Dorothy Day], "Strikes and Violence Two Separate Things," *CW* 1 (September 1933): 6-7; "N.Y. Milk Strikers Ask for Greater Share of Profits," *CW* 1 (September 1933) : 1, 4; "Ohrbach and Klein Violate NRA Codes and Jail Pickets," *CW* 2 (February 1935) : 1, 6; and "Nabisco Strike Enters Fifteenth Orderly Week With Victory Close Ahead," *CW* 3 (May 1935): 1, 6.

[16] See "Germany," *CW* 1 (November 1933): 1; also, the comment on the persecution of Jews and Negroes in "Anti-Lynch Bill Up Before Senate," *CW* 1 (March 1934): 1; and "Catholic Pickets Protest German Fascist Terror" and "Campion Propaganda Committee," *CW* 3 (September 1935): 1 and 6, respectively.

[17] See [Dorothy Day], "C.W.'s Position" and "C.W. Fights Draft at Senate Hearing," *CW* 7 (July-August 1940): 1, 4; and 1-2, respectively. Also, see Arthur

Sheehan, "Work Camp Offered to Catholic C.O.'s," *CW* 8 (April 1941) : 1, 3; Dwight Larrowe, "The Association of Catholic Conscientious Objectors," *CW*, 8 (September 1941): 2; and Gordon Zahn, "Leaven of Love and Justice," *America* 127 (11 November 1972): 383-385.

[18] See Day 1963: 160-78; "Where Are the Poor? They Are in Prisons, Too," *CW* 22 (July-August 1955) : 1, 8; Day, "Dorothy Writes From Jail," *CW* 24 (July-August 1957): 3; and Day, "Vocation From Prison," *CW* 24 (August 1957): 1, 2, 6.

[19] In late July 1973 Day traveled to California where she had been invited to participate at both the 50th anniversary conference of the War Resisters League and the Institute for the Study of Non-Violence founded by folk-singer and peace activist Joan Baez. When Day learned of the mass arrests of farm workers who were defying an injunction against picketing in the vineyards and lettuce fields of California's central valley, she left the conferences to join the workers. Day reported: "Cesar Chavez' union of Farm Workers has everything that belongs to a new social order, so my path was clear. I had come to picket where an injunction was prohibiting picketing, and I would spend my weeks in California in jail not at conferences." See Dorothy Day, "On Pilgrimage," *CW* 39 (September 1973): 1-2, 6; and Eileen Egan, "50 Years of Non-Violent Resistance," ibid., 1, 8. The now famous photograph by Bob Fitch of Day sitting on her folding chair-cane prior to her 1973 arrest with the Farm Workers is included in Robert Cooney and Helen Michalowski, eds., *The Power of the People: Active Nonviolence in the United States* (Philadelphia: New Society Press, 1987), 180.

[20] See Herbert Croly, *The Promise of American Life* (Cambridge, MA: Belknap Press of Harvard University Press, 1909, 1965), 255. Croly's book, a critical assessment and elaboration on Theodore Roosevelt's presidency (1901-1909), relied on Alexander Hamilton's idea of an energetic and intelligent use of national power. Croly argued for an America which would take the lead in the emerging democratic world order through the exercise of a strong nationalism and a government committed to a clear and rational national purpose. Roosevelt was so impressed with Croly's book that it became a primary resource when he returned to political life after 1910. Also, Burns, "War as an Instrument of National Mission," 1957, 234-258.

M.L. Liebler

The Anti-War Politics of Christ

In the garden, He made it
All so simple, "He who lives
By the sword shall die
By the sword." And He
Healed His enemy's
Wounded ear.

PART IV

DOROTHY DAY'S POLITICAL AND SOCIAL THOUGHT

Drawing by Rita Corbin) is ca. 1987, from her 1988 *Cathoic Worke*r calendar.

Radical Orthodoxy: Dorothy Day's Challenge to Liberal America

Geoffrey Gneuhs

Dorothy Day and the Catholic Worker movement, which she and Peter Maurin founded in 1933, are generally thought of by popular writers, academics, historians, liberal Catholics, and some Catholic Workers themselves as a manifestation of leftist ideology and its attendant understanding of history. This gross misreading not only reveals a lack of understanding of the theological and philosophical foundations of the Catholic Worker but also diminishes the radical critique of modernity and the liberal bourgeois world that is at the heart of the Catholic Worker and the orthodox Catholic faith of Dorothy Day.

What are the reasons for such a misperception? Without question Day emerged from her teens as a self-proclaimed leftist certified by her declaration while still a student at the University of Illinois that she was an atheist. Although never formally a communist (the party was not organized in the United States at this time around 1917), she associated with various leftist groups, talked the politically correct line of the moment, and led a free and easy life—a lot of talking and a lot of drinking. She wrote for *The Masses* and later for *The Liberator.* She participated in demonstrations against World War I, opposing not only U.S. involvement in that war but the war itself as "imperialistic." Favoring woman suffrage, she participated in demonstrations advocating the vote for women, even getting herself arrested in Washington, DC She counted Malcolm Cowley, Caroline Gordon, Kenneth Burke, and Mike Gold as her friends, and Eugene O'Neill in a drunken stupor could recite to her verbatim Francis Thompson's poem "The Hound of Heaven." Her loose, bohemian life by today's standards would hardly be noticed.

Day liked falling in love; she did with Lionel Moise, a leftist journalist. When she told him she was pregnant, he told her to get an abortion, otherwise he would leave her. Madly in love, and not wanting to lose her man, she had the abortion. He walked out on her anyway. A lost love, a lost life. For the rest of her life Day would be haunted by that abortion and hounded by God.

Some 60 years later in December 1980 at her wake at Maryhouse in New York City, she was given the final anointing as a leftist when Abbie Hoffman, an icon of the radical left, declared while waiting in line to view the coffin: "Dorothy was the first hippie!"

History and Humanity in Leftist Ideology

Liberal ideology is the epistemological framework of the modern world. It is the construct out of which the media functions, and the media is the message and the messenger of our world. Beginning with the Protestant revolt in the sixteenth century, a new understanding of individuals, their role in society, and of society itself began to take place. Individualism and nationalism began to take on an importance previously unknown.

This focus on individualism and nationhood was a fundamental shift in thought and in the conception of the world and a human's role in it. This emphasis on the individual and rights continued in the thought of Locke and Kant. The individual, viewed as autonomous, was objectified; in the thought of Aquinas, rejected by Enlightenment thinkers, the person is subject whose being is realized in the Transcendent Being. In the development of liberal thought, the individual is a player on the world stage, but liberal ideology is hard pressed to give any substantive reason for the value of the player. Under liberal thought the autonomous individual is unrelated and ultimately shares no common source of existence. The most glaring example of the implication of this thinking is abortion. The autonomous individual can destroy human life. Human life viewed as object is, therefore, expendable. That which is inconvenient, intrusive, bothersome—in the case of abortion—a baby, can be removed, eliminated, and destroyed. In liberal thought there is no intrinsic worth to life.

Jeremy Bentham, who stressed that the individual good is self-interest, certainly has aided contemporary liberal thought with its extreme promotion of "rights." One's individuality is realized in the fulfillment of one's interest. Whatever is useful for the individual is good; whatever is inconvenient is bad. This rejects a transcendent, metaphysical understanding that is at the heart of a Thomistic understanding of the human being, of one's place in society, and of an understanding of society itself. In this milieu the Industrial Revolution occurred in the early nineteenth century, paving the way for capitalism, which is not an economic theory but rather the natural expression of a philosophy that exalts the individual and sees the good in terms of self-interest.

Having done away with a transcendent grounding for existence and a recognition that the human being is not autonomous but relational, liberal ideology resorts to government and political power as the guarantor of rights, and ultimately the originator of rights. This is called positivism. Consequently, what is moral is determined by the government, for there is no longer an objective truth grounded in ultimate reality, the transcendent. Under positive, liberal thought what is law is the good. Morality, right and wrong, therefore, is determined by the state. What the law permits is deemed morally right and, therefore, allowable. There is no higher law, no divine law, not even natural law. One of the great absurdities of the twentieth century is the outright dismissal by liberal culture of natural law. Smug liberal culture finds it now impossible to acknowledge a commonality in human nature. Each individual is self-created; each has their own truth; each has their own reality. The result can only be conflict and division: ultimately a breakdown of community, a fragmentation of culture, and the death of civilization.

Of course, in such chaos, a Pandora's box set in a maze, leftist ideology resorts to government authority to ensure order. It is one of the paradoxes of liberal ideology, or perhaps hypocrisies, that it resorts to state authority, which is a collective authority, to promote individual autonomy. But in doing so it must necessarily impose an ideological conformity that is destructive of a creative, free person. The liberal state becomes the manager and engineer of individuals.

It is not surprising, although it is quite disturbing, that liberal ideology can not tolerate a diversity of ideas. It can only tolerate those ideas that it has deemed acceptable in its world view. There are multitudes of examples. In recent years in New York City as in other places there has been argument over sex education programs, specifically in regard to AIDS prevention. Consistently and loudly, liberals vehemently object to inclusion of any mention that self-control and abstinence can be a way of preventing disease. The liberal media never criticizes the cruelty of their intolerance of letting this natural, self-evident truth be included in an educational program. There no longer is truth; the liberal world is a world of relativity. It is beyond the scope of this paper, but such a world view begs the question: can we know?

Liberal ideology has in this century created two economic systems: state capitalism, which began in the more fluid, laissez-faire capitalism of the nineteenth century, and state socialism, whose major proponent was Marx. The former could be called the politics of greed, the latter the politics of envy. In either case, the human being as a free and creative person is no longer the subject of activity but the object. Hannah Arendt commented that state capitalism and state socialism are "twins each wearing different hats."(Arendt 1972: 214)

Both liberal economic systems see history as linear. The doctrine of progress sees human activity only in terms of the future in which time the individual can achieve self-fulfillment, material satisfaction, and a comfortable, convenient existence. The past has no significance; the present is but a moment on the way to the future. The liberal doctrine of progress is incapable of dealing with reality, with the tragedy of time—imperfection, sin, cruelty, hatred, suffering, and death itself are ignored. The realization of the self is all-important. This liberal understanding of history is eloquently critiqued by Ernest Becker in his *The Denial of Death.*

American liberal ideology finally achieved dominance after World War II. Earlier, two liberal presidents took us into wars; something they had vociferously said they would never do. Harry Truman dropped the atom bomb. A month later in the September 1945 issue of *The Catholic Worker*, Day wrote: "Mr. Truman was jubilant. President Truman. True man; what a strange name, come to think of it. We refer to Jesus Christ as true God and true Man." But in the twentieth-century liberal world there is no truth.

Catholic Liberals and Their Faustian Wager

Orestes Brownson and Isaac Hecker were two major figures in nineteenth century Catholic America. They sought a dialogue with the American experiment in democracy as well as a certain accommodation with the liberal culture that was evolving. They both retained a solid confidence in their Catholicism despite their concern for an engagement in the American reality. The so-called Americanism of the late nineteenth-century, though in several ways different from twentieth century Catholic liberalism, nevertheless prepared the way for the latter.

In the early twentieth-century Monsignor John A. Ryan, later called by his biographer the "Right Reverend New Dealer," attempted to synthesize Thomistic doctrine and Catholic social teaching with liberal concepts of economics and government. He became an adviser of the American bishops and the National Catholic Welfare Conference and authored *A Living Wage* (1906) and *Distributive Justice* (1916). There was a great concern on his part and that of the bishops to speak to the social and economic problems of the day. They did with certain eloquence, but in so doing they had to accept many of the premises of liberal thought and as time went the distinctive critique of Catholic doctrine became minimized.

Ryan favored government intervention, a centralized directing of the economy, and the welfare state itself. It is a grand irony, for the welfare state began in Prussia under Bismarck some fifty years earlier. Bismarck in his *Kulturkampf* closed Catholic social agencies such as schools, orphanages, hospitals, nurseries—the very stuff of a decentralized, personalist approach to social problems based on the Catholic principle of subsidiarity—and he abolished the religious orders staff of the institutions, replacing them with a state-controlled welfare system.

Ryan's accommodationist approach continues today. Acceptance of federal monies has compromised Catholic institutions, imposing controls and bureaucratic interference. As the bishops accept so much money for Catholic charities, it becomes harder and harder for them to offer a critical, prophetic, Christ-centered analysis of government policies, social as well as economic. The bishops, in a February 1997 New York *Times* op-ed piece regarding the welfare reform debate then dominating Congress, offered no new ideas. Rather, they pleaded basically that the failed system of sixty some years be maintained.

How does one explain the paucity of ideas on the part of the bishops? Their advisers remain firmly rooted in the liberal, statist approach to human problems. I also think that the popular perception fostered by the media is that liberals care, liberals look to government to institutionalize and bureaucratize their care, and that therefore anyone who seeks other ways is uncaring. And no one wants to be seen as uncaring; certainly not the American bishops.

Last year the liberal group Call to Renewal was formed, comprised of various religious leaders of several denominations; it included several Catholic bishops, Thomas Gumbleton and Milwaukee's Rembert Weakland. Call to Renewal's response to social issues is the usual statist approach. The insistent secularism of contemporary liberal ideology is such a blatant and even vitriolic rejection of the fundamentals of Catholicism that it is at best baffling that Catholic leaders continue to ally themselves with this ideology.

It is not surprising that in this mode of intellectual and spiritual equivocation and accommodation that Frances Kissling, president—self-appointed, I believe—of Catholics for Free Choice, a pro-abortion group, is often quoted and interviewed by the liberal media as a valid representative of Catholicism. "Choice" we are told by liberals is a basic right, an expression of freedom; however, when it comes to the freedom of choice to choose a school for one's child, this right evaporates under liberalism, as does the right to privacy, other than the right to destroy defenseless human life. Thus does liberal ideology limit rights and diversity of opinion. Kenneth Woodward, religion editor of *Newsweek*, points out that in his 30 years of reading the New York *Times,* the liberal journal of record, that he has seen only four op-ed pieces criticizing the pro-choice position, which, he writes, "the *Times* defends about four times a week." Not much diversity there. Liberal ideology does not permit an unborn child to be called a baby; it is a fetus, or neutral biological tissue, contrary to all scientific and medical knowledge. Woodward asks, "When was the last time you heard someone ask an expectant mother, 'How's your fetus?' Do Liberals really think that a fetus becomes a baby only when the mother chooses not to abort it?"(Woodward 1997)

Matthew Lamb, a theologian at Boston College, sums up the accommodationist position of Catholic liberals: "Rather than providing critical scholarship of the culture, it seems to promote soft dissent from the Church and conformity to the culture. Does not the culture have enough messengers?"(Lamb 1997) It is a Faustian wager.

Dorothy Day's Conversion: A Choice for the Transcendent

For the first 30 years of her life Day lived this liberal ideology. She did not find it hard, but she found it wanting, and she made a choice for the Transcendent. G. K. Chesterton, also a convert, once made the pithy observation that Christianity has not been found wanting but has been found hard. Despite hardships, Day never regretted her decision to convert. Like Chesterton and a convert of our own time, Bernard Nathanson, a physician, former atheist and founder of the National Abortion Rights Action League (NARAL), she recognized her sinfulness and her need for forgiveness and healing. She turned to the Church for such healing. To recognize such a need, such existential angst, was a supreme act of humility on her part but in so doing she opened herself up to hope and to love that is God. She wrote that she "had reached the point where I wanted to obey...I was tired of following the devices of my own heart, of doing what I wanted to do, what my desires told me to do, which always seemed to lead me astray."(Day 1983: 168) The Latin root for "to obey," means to listen and to follow what one has listened to. Day listened to God and followed, and there was no turning back.

One day in early 1927 while taking a walk in Tottenville, Staten Island, Day saw two nuns across the street and approached them, asking how one could become a Catholic. For a moment picture that scene. In all likelihood, it would not occur today as so many nuns have abandoned any form of religious garb, including crucifixes, wearing instead fashionable secular garb, including earrings and necklaces. They have done so thinking that by accepting the ways and styles of liberal culture they will be more relevant; who would recognize them today? How would a latter-day Dorothy Day know whom to approach? Another Faustian wager.

Liberal culture has promoted and funded Andres Serrano, a so-called artist, for his "Piss Christ." He was paid by the National Endowment for the Arts to put a crucifix in a bucket of urine. Protest? What protest was there? If the liberal nuns have so cavalierly discarded this most sacred of Catholic symbols, why should we be surprised that liberal culture has found another use for it?

Day was also attracted to the Church for the physicality: for her symbols, signs, and rituals. The crucifix sums up the essence of Catholicism—divinity in humanity realizing forgiveness, love, and redemption. It is the most counter cultural symbol in the last two thousand years of history. It is the symbol of truth. In Catholic belief truth is a person—Christ. Day wrote: "I wanted to be poor, chaste, and obedient. I wanted to die in order to live, to put off the old man and put on Christ. I loved in other words, and like all women in love, I wanted to be united to my love....I loved the Church for Christ made visible."(Day 1952: 149) The Church was the church of the poor, she said. Day would never have discarded a crucifix.

Peter Maurin's Personalist Vision

The meeting of Dorothy Day and Peter Maurin is one of the grand instances of Divine Providence: he, a somewhat shabby man of French peasant stock, she, a single-parent, Catholic convert of leftist background. Twenty years older than she, he had been a Christian Brother in Paris at the turn of the century. In the early 1900s he did not renew his vows and eventually immigrated to Canada, where he homesteaded for several years. During World War I he was in Chicago, where he gave French lessons, later moving to New York, where he worked upstate at a boys' camp and did manual labor. He never spoke much about his past, but for a period of his life he was out of the Church, only later to undergo an intense conversion of renewed faith. A voracious reader, he had a keen intelligence and clarity of thought. On December 8, 1932, Day, who was in Washington, DC, reporting on the Bonus March of World War I veterans, found herself praying in the crypt of the Shrine of the Immaculate Conception. A Catholic for five years, she was at a low period in her life. How could she, she prayed, serve the poor and work for social justice? The next day, back in New York City, Peter Maurin arrived at her apartment on Fifteenth Street. She later recalled that he was the man "whose ideas and spirit would dominate the rest of my life." He became her teacher—in Russian, her *staretz*, and in Hindi, her *kalyanamitra*. Maurin opened her eyes and showed her that there was an answer to the "liberal and radical blah" as Daniel Berrigan wrote some forty years later. Maurin insisted on the "twinning of justice and mercy." (*CW* 5/1977)

Maurin introduced Day to personalism, a philosophy of the person, freedom, and history that radically confronts liberal ideology with an understanding drawn from Thomas Aquinas. Aquinas explained human destiny as the *exitus* and the *reditus*. We come from God and are called to return to God. We are creatures whose creatureliness is grounded in God; we are created in the image and likeness of God and willed by God for happiness. The person is free because only in freedom can one love, choose to love, live love, and act in love. According to Aquinas, we are most free then when we love, when we act for the good, because then we are acting in God, the source of our being and the one to whom we are called to return. Our being resides in the Divine Being. We are becoming who we truly are when we love: "God is love, and he who abides in love abides in God."

Day embraced this transcendent understanding, rejecting the linear, this-world explanation of reality in liberal ideology. By revealing himself in history God destroyed history in the conventional understanding. The Incarnation is the ultimate revelation of God. Time is shattered, if you will, as Nicholas Berdyaev, the twentieth-century Russian philosopher, pointed out in *The Meaning of History* and *The End of Our Time.* Christ is the incarnation of Spirit, eternity breaking through time. Aquinas described this truth as *aeternitas nunc*—eternity now. Day grasped this profound insight. She lived *aeternitas nunc.* She realized that love is not measured in *doing* but rather in *living* the eternal now. Every moment thus is the Incarnation. Liberals, on the other hand, see history as acts making progress (a rather relative notion indeed) over time. Religious liberals also accept this limited notion. They believe they can make the Kingdom of God in time, in history; but for Day one does not *make* the Kingdom of God but rather *lives* it. Tolstoy, a great favorite of Day, expressed this radical understanding of the Incarnation in his book *The Kingdom of God Is Within You,* although Christ Himself said it first!

Dostoyevsky, another major influence in Day's thinking, said that modernity presses toward mediocrity and vulgarization. American culture as we conclude the twentieth century has certainly confirmed his observation of a hundred years ago! Only beauty, he wrote in *The Idiot,* will save the world. He meant beauty in the sense of love, grounded in God. The ancient Greeks considered beauty, truth, and goodness as Transcendental. The relativism of liberal culture does not allow for an objective understanding of beauty, truth, and goodness, and thus we have ended up with very little beauty, truth, and goodness; to do so would offend some individual or group. And the French mystic Simone Weil wrote: "Beauty is eternity below." For Berdyaev spirit is reality, more real than the material. Modernity, he said, had disembodied the spirit from the life of the world, resulting in the sacrifice of true freedom and the disintegration of society.

Dostoyevsky's passage of the Grand Inquisitor in *The Brothers Karamazov* aptly dramatizes these contrasting views of history. The Inquisitor, a Jesuit, confronts Christ who appears fifteen centuries after having walked the earth. The Inquisitor does all the talking. Christ remains silent. He accuses Christ of giving men freedom when all they want is bread and comfort: "Dost thou know that the ages will pass, and humanity will proclaim by the lips of their sages that there is no crime, and therefore no sin; there is only hunger. In the end they will lay their freedom at our feet, and say to us, 'Make us your slaves, but feed us.'" He continues: "Mankind as a whole has always striven to organize a universal state."

Christ's silence is haunting, as is the silence of the crucifix. Truth does not always have to speak words; our media age is an age of words but not one of truth. In leftist ideology materialism replaces spirit. The nature of the person is understood only as matter—physical matter—like technology a machine to be manipulated by the state, which offers technocratic solutions to the human dilemma.

Dorothy Day and Peter Maurin explicitly founded the Catholic Worker in response to this crisis of modernity, a crisis of the spirit. They rejected the welfare state because it offered a materialistic vision of human existence, destroyed freedom, and denied personal responsibility for the good of the other. Dorothy derisively referred to this twentieth century reality as "Holy Mother the State," or "Servile State" in the words of Hilaire Belloc. The state had taken over what was rightly the responsibility of the Church and the duty of the person. Day wrote in *The Long Loneliness*: "Peter did not wish to turn to the government for funds. 'He who is a pensioner of the state is a slave of the state.'" (Day 1952: 225) They advocated a decentralized society, where the dignity and creativity of the person could be realized.

One of Maurin's criticisms of the labor movement, Day wrote, was that "it was aiding in the creation of the Welfare State, the Servile State, instead of aiming for the ownership of the means of production and the acceptance of the responsibility that it entailed."(222) This idea is the key to Catholic Worker economics. Worker ownership, employee ownership of businesses, is a nonstatist solution to the injustice of extreme capitalism, the term used by Pope John Paul II. It respects the principle of subsidiarity: that which can be done at a lower level is best done at that level. Hannah Arendt saw the problem as "how to arrange matters so that the masses...dispossessed of property can regain property."(Arendt 1972: 214) Since the mid-1980s the Center for Economic and Social Justice in Washington, DC, has been promoting worker ownership and participatory rights of workers. Under the present mentality of owners versus workers there is the inevitability of conflict, very graphically played out in the August 1997 strike at United Parcel Service.

The common good, another key element of Catholic Worker philosophy as well as of Catholic social teaching, according to Aquinas has to do with persons not with the state. Aquinas goes so far as to say that the end of all law is the common good, and that any law that is not good is not true law and need not be obeyed (Aquinas 1948: III, 90-97). This notion of law, by the way, becomes a cogent defense for one engaged in civil disobedience—that is, if one accepts that all law ultimately derives its power from divine law. Mahatma Gandhi, Martin Luther King, and Dorothy Day understood this. So too did Franz Jagerstatter, the Austrian who was beheaded by the Nazis in 1943 for refusing to serve in the military and for refusing to acknowledge the Nazi state. He said he was obligated to obey God's law, which is higher than man's law. Liberal ideology does not acknowledge divine law. There is no law other than the law of the state; there is no objective truth. That which is true is that which the state declares to be true. By denying a higher law, a divine law, liberalism undercuts the ability to have a moral and just society, which it purportedly advocates. For Aquinas the analogue for the common good is the Trinity, the *summum bonum* (Aquinas 1948: I-II, 19:10). The Godhead is like an atom, three persons intertwined; it is the energy of complete love. Pope John Paul II speaks of the "civilization of love" as being lived out in the common good. In a message to the American bishops in 1934, Maurin wrote: "According to St. Thomas Aquinas man is more than an individual with individual rights; he is a person with personal duties toward God, himself, and his fellow man. As a person man cannot serve God without serving the Common Good."(Maurin 1984: 44) Such service necessarily entails self-sacrifice, not the self-fulfillment and self-indulgence of liberal ideology. While liberalism speaks of rights it is unable to speak of duty, as there is no greater good than the self. The common good is principally a moral good. In *Gaudiem et Spes* the Second Vatican Council declared: "Man's social nature makes it evident that the progress of the human person and the advance of society itself hinge on each other."

One of Day's most familiar quotations comes from *The Brothers Karamazov:* "Love in action is a harsh and dreadful thing compared to love in dreams. Active love is labor and fortitude." The French personalist philosopher Emmanuel Mounier, whose articles appeared in *The Catholic Worker*, expressed it: "I love, therefore being is, and life is worth the pain of having been lived."(Amato 1975: 22)

The Disappointment of Politics and the Spirituality of Dorothy Day

Day's disappointment with the cant and vacuity of leftist ideology brought her to Catholicism; Peter Maurin in turn gave her a way to articulate the faith that spoke to the human condition in which there is injustice, inequality, and poverty. From Maurin she realized that the greatest poverty is the poverty of spirit and that no good society can exist unless it is founded on the spiritual. She spoke of the "joys of the spiritual life" and the "duty of delight." Her program for living was the Beatitudes and the twenty-fifth chapter of the Gospel of Saint Matthew. Her radical orthodox Catholicism resists any secular, political, ideological hegemony. Day's vision of the world is Christ-centered. She could not conceive of speaking about any social or economic issue without reference to Christ. When she spoke in the public sphere she never hedged from speaking directly about Christ and the truths of the faith as the basis and motivation for her unstinting dedication to the poor, social justice, and pacifism. She made no accommodation to secular audiences. In fact, she could not speak in any language other than the language of faith. Committees, organizations, and so forth did not interest her. The Gospel was a joy to her; it was the duty of delight. Of Christ she wrote: "He died between two thieves because He would not be made an earthly King. He lived in an occupied country for thirty years without starting an under-ground movement or trying to get out from under a foreign power." He never advocated a system or a political party, she wrote. "He had set us an example and the poor and the destitute were the ones we wished to reach."(Day 1952: 205) She unabashedly spoke of the Church as the "one true Church." Is there even a bishop today in our over-sensitized, so-called tolerant world who would speak of the Church as the "one true Church"?

The material world disembodied of the spiritual presses toward mediocrity and vulgarization. Day reached to holiness and beauty. She saw beauty in New York City's ubiquitous ailanthus tree or a green weed sprouting from a crack in the sidewalk. She once reflected that her early disposition to beauty, to nature, to human beauty was the foundation for her conversion.

The Church makes all life a sacrament, an encounter with God. In a journal entry she wrote, "The Mass is the most important thing we do." Typically, she saw a connection between the spiritual and the material, real union. "Ritual, how could we do without it?" she wrote.

"And just as a husband may embrace his wife casually as he leaves for work in the morning, and kiss her absent-mindedly in his comings and goings, still that kiss on occasion turns to rapture, a burning fire of tenderness and love....We have too little ritual in our lives," she lamented in *The Long Loneliness* (Day 1952: 200).

Day's spirituality challenges those who seek to redress the injustices and the failings of the political system by means of ideology and politics. She had tried those ways in her youth. What system did Christ ever challenge? she would ask. She pointed out that his revolution was a revolution of the heart. Changes in systems will never effect a personalist society. Christ never told Caesar to create a bureaucratic welfare system. The "new social order" advocated by the Catholic Worker was explained by Day in these words: "When we receive the Bread of Life each day, the grace we receive remains a dead weight in the soul unless we cooperate with the grace. When we cooperate with the grace we 'work with' Christ in ministering to our brothers." Dorothy used traditional language; she had no use for the "inclusive language" crowd. For her such concerns were frivolous indulgences of the liberal bourgeois world. She was about more important matters: feeding the hungry, sheltering the homeless, and comforting the abandoned.

Contrary to modernity's emphasis on autonomy, Day fully embracing Catholicism's understanding of the person as one in relationship to God and others, lived and encouraged community. She saw the Incarnation as pouring forth in the Eucharist: nourishment so that we may nourish others. Her life was structured around daily Mass, reading the Psalms, praying vespers, regular confession, and frequent retreats. She fasted not just as a penance but as a form of spiritual cleansing. Fasting was a powerful spiritual weapon for her. She herself lived a life of voluntary poverty and encouraged others to do likewise. Why? First, Christ lived a life of detachment, simplicity; second, the mass consumption of contemporary culture was deadening to the spirit and also the cause for so many not having enough; third, voluntary poverty allowed her to be an immediate presence with the poor. Hers was a *living* not a *doing,* as I noted above. Thus when she spoke, she spoke with authenticity.

Day endured many trials, not just civil, but spiritual. In the mid-1940s she took time away from the Catholic Worker. But remembering her conversion, she wrote, "most cradle Catholics have gone through, or need to go through, a second conversion which binds them with a more mature love and obedience to the Church." In a conversation with Robert Coles, the eminent child pyschiatrist at Harvard, Day said, "I have never wanted to challenge the Church....I was trying to be a loyal servant of the Church Jesus had founded."(Coles 1987: 84)

Day engaged in civil disobedience for the last time in 1973 protesting injustice with Cesar Chavez in Fresno, California. She taught nonviolent resistance, for it was the method advocated by Christ. She also believed in overcoming evil with good (Romans 12). Never would she have countenanced any kind of protest or demonstration against the Church or during Mass or outside a church as has become the tactic of many liberal Catholics in promoting their issues. In a journal entry she wrote: "It makes me sick to see priests go all romantic over revolution...knowing nothing of genuine nonviolence.... Every revolution has first led to another revolt down through the centuries. People are losing sight of the primacy of the spiritual."(Miller 1987: 183)

Day did not subscribe to confrontational tactics; they only breed more violence. She quoted Maurin: "Appeals not demands." He wanted concordances, she recalled, and to build a new world "within the shell of the old." She became very disheartened with the vulgar and violent methods of the antiwar movement of the 1960s, which the Catholic Worker had helped get started. The first draft card burners were Catholic Workers who committed the act in Union Square in 1965, with Day watching. In the mid-1970s Day admitted to her dear friend Maisie Ward, who often needled Dorothy that she was "too damn precious" about "her pacifism," that she would never do it again. She saw too many lose their faith and turn against the Church (Sheed 1980).

Dorothy Day also regretted many of the changes in the Church after Vatican Council II (many not prescribed or intended but which nevertheless occurred). In a letter to her friend Father Neudecker, she wrote: "I miss...Tenebrae, for instance, and Ember Days, Benediction...when I'm driving around with Stanley[Visnewski] on a shopping trip we sing the hymns to our Lady in Latin so as not to forget them. They take so much breath that I wonder why my grandchildren have to go in for Zen breathing exercises."(Miller 1987: 188) She wanted priests to wear clerical garb and nuns to wear their habits. Quite frankly Day liked being Catholic, liked Catholic culture, and liked "things Catholic." The downplaying of such by liberal Catholics dismayed her.

Moreover, she was dismayed by the internal rancor in the Church and by the casualness and hedonism in American society. She found herself meditating on this in a letter to Daniel Berrigan, S.J., in 1972: "And so when it comes to divorce, birth control, abortion, I must write in this way: The teaching of Christ, the Word, must be upheld. Held up, though one would think that it is completely beyond us—out of our reach, impossible to follow....We may stretch toward it, falling short, failing seventy times seven, but forgiveness is always there...I believe in the sacraments. I believe the priest is empowered to forgive sins."(Miller 1982: 506) Day never lost confidence in being an orthodox Catholic.

Her favorite saint was Saint Therese de Lisieux. Dorothy was born in the year the Little Flower died. How fitting and providential that this symposium is being held within the octave of the proclamation of St. Therese as a doctor of the Church by His Holiness Pope John Paul II. Day wrote a book about Therese, published in 1960. One of the things that attracted her to Therese was that the devotion to Therese was spread by the masses, the poor. She was also inspired by Therese because she was "so much like the rest of us in her ordinariness." Like Therese's life, Day's life was a "path of total abandonment and confidence."

Day's relationship to the Church in her more institutional sphere is eloquently illustrated in two episodes. The first occurred in 1949. The gravediggers at the Catholic cemeteries in the Archdiocese of New York went on strike. Francis Cardinal Spellman reigned, and he was their boss. Day and the Catholic Worker supported the strikers. She felt that the cardinal could at least have spoken with them. How did she express her support? By going out and standing on line with them and feeding them soup, bread, and coffee. No shouting, no stridency, no insults, only a quiet prayerful presence. That was her way, that was the way of Christ.

There was at least one instance when the hierarchy sought, feebly I might add, to take action against Day and the Catholic Worker during Spellman's tenure as archbishop. On March 3, 1951 Dorothy was asked to "stop by" the chancery by Monsignor Edward Gaffney, who informed her that she would have to cease publication of *The Catholic Worker* or change the name. She could not use Catholic in the title. In her journal Day wrote, "Mike Harrington [later author of *The Other America*] urges me to fortitude and the fighting of obscurantism in the Church." (Leftists like Harrington have always accused the Church of obscurantism.) Several days later Day gave her response to the monsignor. She wrote: "First of all I wish to assure you of our love and respectful obedience to the Church, and our gratitude to this Archdiocese, which has so often and so generously defended us from many who attack us." Then she astutely and cogently pointed out that "I am sure no one thinks the Catholic War Veterans (who also use the name Catholic) represent the point of view of the Archdiocese any more than they think the Catholic Worker does." She then requested any scholarly criticism and any theological or spiritual censures of theological or spiritual errors; none ever came. Then she added shrewdly that if *The Catholic Worker* ceased publication that "would be a grave scandal to our readers and would put into the hands of our enemies, the enemies of the Church, a formidable weapon." She concluded the letter by saying she would try to do better as an editor. Day never heard again from Monsignor Gaffney (Miller 1982:427-429).

In a conversation with Robert Coles, Day said that if the cardinal had insisted that she close down *The Catholic Worker* she would have obeyed. But she added that she would have also invited the readership of *The Catholic Worker*, some 100,000, to come and pray and fast with her for a day at St. Patrick's Cathedral! (Coles 1987: 84)

In an entry in one of her retreat notebooks of the 1940s, Day wrote: "Jesus was not class conscious…never objectivized social evils….St. John is in prison by Herod. Does Our Lord protest? Does he form a defense committee? Collect funds? Stir up public opinion?"(Miller 1982:362) In other words, Day believed that injustice would be ended by living *aeternitas nunc,* by living the spiritual and corporal works of mercy: instructing, advising, consoling, comforting, forgiving, bearing wrongs patiently, feeding the hungry, clothing the naked, sheltering the homeless, and giving alms to the poor. Day often used to say that the works of mercy are the works of peace. This was her way. She believed in the power of truth; she lived her life truthfully. Gandhi spoke of *satyagraha,* or truth force. For Day, the truth force was Christ. She knew that she looked foolish to the bourgeois world, where self-realization not self-sacrifice was the norm, the world of cliches and comfort, the liberal world of autonomy and rights, of capitalistic plutocracies. She gladly was a fool for Christ.

Day never considered herself a feminist. She never identified with feminist issues. She was a Christian personalist living out her baptismal vows. She gratefully called herself a "daughter of the Church." She wrote: "As for me I love the Church who has room for saints and sinners, for the mediocre, the lame, the halt, the blind....I still like the expression Holy Mother the Church."

Her orthodox faith and selfless love remain prophetically radical, radical in the true sense of that word, whose Latin root means "root." With Peter Maurin she went to the roots of Catholic social doctrine and gave a luminous vision of a world lived as the common good. Her lived commitment to life with the poor, the rejects of society, the lonely, and her rejection of an all-powerful state and the liberal culture of convenience remain an eloquent witness to Christ Crucified, Christ Redeemer.

The name of the nun who instructed Day in the Catholic faith was Aloysia. Curiously, it is the feminine form of the name of the young Russian monk-hero of *The Brothers Karamazov,* Alyosha. At the end of that novel, which is key to Day's outlook, Alyosha cries out: "How good life is when one does something good and just!" Day showed how good life is.

In her journal she quoted Cardinal Emmanuel Suhard of Paris: "To be a witness does not consist in engaging in propaganda or even in stirring people up, but in being a living mystery; it means to live in such a way that one's life would not make any sense if God did not exist." Day's life made utter sense.

"The Way of Love"–Dorothy Day and the American Right

Bill Kauffman

Elba, NY

The title of my talk is "Dorothy Day and the American Right," so you think you're in for a short paragraph, maybe two, before I sit down, but not so fast. There is more to the "Right" than a dollar bill stretching from the du Ponts to Ronald Reagan, just as the "Left" is something greater than the bureau-building and bomb-dropping of Roosevelts and Kennedys. I shall contend—no, contend is too certain a word—I shall entertain the possibility that just maybe Dorothy Day had a home, if partially furnished and seldom occupied, on the American Right.

The Catholic reactionary John Lukacs, after attending the lavish 25th anniversary bash for *National Review* in December 1980, held in the Plaza Hotel, hellward of the Catholic Worker house on Mott Street, wrote:

> During the introduction of the celebrities a shower of applause greeted Henry Kissinger. I was sufficiently irritated to ejaculate a fairly loud Boo!...A day or so before that evening Dorothy Day had died. She was the founder and saintly heroine of the Catholic Worker movement. During that glamorous evening I thought: who was a truer conservative, Dorothy Day or Henry Kissinger? Surely it was Dorothy Day, whose respect for what was old and valid, whose dedication to the plain decencies and duties of human life rested on the traditions of two millennia of Christianity, and who was a radical only in the truthful sense of attempting to get to the roots of the human predicament. Despite its pro-Catholic tendency, and despite its commendable custom of commemorating the passing of worthy people even when some of these did not belong to the conservatives, *National Review* paid neither respect nor attention to the passing of Dorothy Day, while around the same time it published a respectful R.I.P. column in honor of

> Oswald Mosley, the onetime leader of the British Fascist Party (Lukacs 1990: 192-193).

Lukacs was echoed by Garry Wills, who wrote: "Bill Buckley calls himself a radical conservative. But Dorothy Day has a better claim to that title, going all the way back to the Gospel through that higher hero worship called hagiography."(Wills 1980: 217)

National Review, dreadnought of postwar American conservatism, occasionally aimed its scattershot at Day. Founder William F. Buckley, Jr., referred casually to "the grotesqueries that go into making up the Catholic Worker movement." Of Miss Day, he chided "the slovenly, reckless, intellectually chaotic, anti-Catholic doctrines of this good-hearted woman who, did she have her way in shaping national policy, would test the promise of Christ Himself, that the gates of Hell shall not prevail against us."(Buckley 1960: 307)

The grotesqueries he does not bother to itemize; nor does Buckley, whose only memorable witticism was "Mater, Si; Magistra, No," explain just what was anti-Catholic about a woman who told a friend, "The hierarchy permits a priest to say Mass in our chapel. They have given us the most precious thing of all—the Blessed Sacrament. If the Chancery ordered me to stop publishing *The Catholic Worker* tomorrow, I would."(Macdonald 1957: 353) Perhaps Buckley's hostility to Day had roots in Michael Harrington's stupid and splenetic review of *God and Man At Yale* which appeared in the November 1951 issue of *The Catholic Worker*.

If Buckley and Kissinger were the sum of the American Right, mine would be a very brief paper indeed. But there is another American Right—or is it a Left, for praise be the ambidextrous—in which Miss Day fits quite nicely. Indeed, I think she's more at home with these people than she ever was with Manhattan socialists. They are the Agrarians, the Distributists, the heirs to the Jeffersonian tradition. The keener of them, particularly the Catholics, understood their kinship with Day. Allen Tate, the Southern man of letters and contributor to the 1930 Southern Agrarian manifesto, *I'll Take My Stand*, wrote his fellow Dixie poet Donald Davidson in 1936:

> I also enclose a copy of a remarkable monthly paper, *The Catholic Worker*. The editor, Dorothy Day, has been here, and is greatly excited by our whole program. Just three months ago she discovered *I'll Take My Stand*, and has been commenting on it editorially. She is ready to hammer away in behalf of the new book. Listen to

> this: *The Catholic Worker* now has a paid circulation of 100,000! [Tate neglects to say that the price is a penny a copy.]....She offers her entire mailing list to Houghton-Mifflin; I've just written to Linscott about it. Miss Day may come by Nashville with us if the conference falls next weekend. She has been speaking all over the country in Catholic schools and colleges. A very remarkable woman. Terrific energy, much practical sense, and a fanatical devotion to the cause of the land! (Fain and Young 1974: 297)

The program that so excited Miss Day was summarized in the statement of principles drawn up at the Nashville meeting of Southern Agrarians and Distributists. Mocked as reactionary for their unwillingness to accept bigness as an inevitable condition, the conferees declared, (*inter alia*):

> – The condition of individual freedom and security is the wide distribution of active ownership of land and productive property.
> – Population should be decentralized as well as ownership.
> – Agriculture should be given its rightful recognition as the prime factor in a secure culture. (Chamberlain 1946: 3)

Though Day was absent from Nashville, she was to speak the language of the Southern Agrarians, without the drawl, many times over the years. "To Christ—To the Land!" Day exclaimed in the January 1936 issue. "*The Catholic Worker* is opposed to the wage system but not for the same reason that the Communist is. We are opposed to it, because the more wage earners there are the less owners there are....how will they become owners if they do not get back to the land."(*CW* 1/36)

Widespread ownership was the basic tenet of the Agrarians' Catholic cousins, the Distributists. *The Catholic Worker* published all the major Distributists of the age, among them Chesterton and Belloc, Vincent McNabb, Father Luigi Ligutti, and the Jesuit John C. Rawe, a Nebraska-born "Catholic version of William Jennings Bryan." (Southern 1996: 87) Father Rawe, as Peter McDonough notes, "evoked images of eighteenth-and early-nineteenth-century America without the trappings of gothic Catholicism," unlike many of the Distributists, with their laments for the vanished Middle Ages (McDonough 1992: 89).

On numberless occasions Dorothy Day called herself a Distributist. Thus her gripe with the New Deal: "*Security* for the worker, not ownership," was its false promise; she despaired in 1945 that "Catholics throughout the country are again accepting 'the lesser of two evils'...They fail to see the body of Catholic social teaching of such men as Fr. Vincent McNabb, G.K. Chesterton, Belloc, Eric Gill and other distributists. . .and lose all sight of *the little way*."(*CW* 7-8/ 1945: 1,3)

Dorothy Day kept to the little way, and that is why we honor her today. She understood that if small is not always beautiful, at least it is always human.

Property Is Proper

The Catholic Worker position on economics was expressed quite clearly:

> We favor the establishment of a Distributist economy wherein those who have a vocation to the land will work on the farms surrounding the village and those who have other vocations will work in the village itself. In this way we will have a decentralized economy which will dispense with the State as we know it today and will be federationist in character...
>
> We believe in worker ownership of the means of production and distribution as distinguished from nationalization. This to be accomplished by decentralized co-operatives and the elimination of a distinct employer class. (*CW* 5/1949: 2)

The American name for this is Jeffersonianism, and the failure of Distributism to attract much of a stateside following outside of those Mencken derided as "typewriter agrarians" owes in part to its Chesterbellocian tincture. "Gothic Catholicism" never could play in Peoria.

Nor could it stand upon the Republican platform. Garry Wills recalls this exchange during his first visit with William F. Buckley, Jr.:

> "Are you a conservative, then"? [Buckley asked]. I answered that I did not know. Are distributists conservative? "Philip Burnham tells me they are not." It was an exchange with the seeds of much later misunderstanding. (Wills 1980:5)

Were the Distributists conservative? Was Day conservative? Depends. Herbert Agar, the Kentucky Agrarian and movement theorist, wrote in *The American Review*, "For seventy years, a 'conservative' has meant a supporter of Big Business, of the politics of plutocracy," yet "the root of a real conservative policy for the United States must be redistribution of property." Ownership—whether of land, a crossroads store, a machine shop—must be made "the normal thing."(Agar 1934: 2, 15)

"Property is proper to man,"(*CW* 6/1948: 7) insisted Dorothy Day, though she and the Distributists—and much of the Old American Right—meant by property something rather more substantial than paper shares in a Rockefellerian octopus. "Ownership *and* control are property" declared Allen Tate (1936: 610), making a distinction between a family farm—or family firm—and a joint stock corporation, the artificial spawn of the state.

Like Tate and the Southern Agrarians, Day was no collectivist, eager to herd the fellaheen onto manury unromantic Blithedales. "The Communists," she said, sought to build "a sense of the sacredness and holiness and the dignity of the machine and of work, in order to content the proletariat with their propertyless state."(*CW* 11/1946: 4) So why, she asked, "do we talk of fighting communism, which we are supposed to oppose because it does away with private property. We have done that very well ourselves in this country." The solution: "We must emphasize the holiness of *work*, and we must emphasize the sacramental quality of *property* too."(*CW* 12/1946: 4) "An anti-religious agrarian is a contradiction in terms," according to Donald Davidson (1933: 241).

Day described the Catholic Worker program as being "for ownership by the workers of the means of production, the abolition of the assembly line, decentralized factories, the restoration of crafts and the ownership of property,"(Coles 1987: 90) and these were to be achieved by libertarian means, through the repeal of state-granted privileges and a flowering of old-fashioned American voluntarism.

During the heyday of modern American liberalism, the 1930s, when Big Brother supposedly wore his friendliest phiz, Day and the Catholic Workers said No. They bore a certain resemblance to those old Progressives (retroprogressives)—senators Burton K. Wheeler, Gerald Nye, and Hiram Johnson—who turned against FDR for what they saw as the bureaucratic, militaristic, centralizing thrust of his New Deal. The antithetical tendencies of *The Catholic Worker* and the 30s American Left were juxtaposed in the November 1936 issue of the *CW*. Under the heading "Catholic Worker Opposition to Projected Farm-Labor Party," the box read:

Farm-Labor Party stands for:	**Catholic Worker stands for:**
Progress	Tradition
Industrialism	Ruralism
Machine	Handicrafts
Caesarism (bureaucracy)	Personalism
Socialism	Communitarianism
Organizations	Organisms

(*CW* 11/1936:2)

And never the twain shall meet.

In the flush and heady first year of Mr. Roosevelt's Caesarism, Day comrade Peter Maurin lectured in the Easy Essay "Self-Organization":

> 1. People go to Washington, asking the Federal Government to solve their economic problems, while the Federal Government was never intended to solve men's economic problems.
> 2. Thomas Jefferson says: "The less government there is the better it is."
> 3. If the less government there is, the better it is then the best kind of government is self-government. (*CW* 9/33: 1)

An anarchistic distrust of the state, even in its putatively benevolent role as giver of alms, pervaded the Catholic Workers, as it did the 1930s Right. But then as the late Karl Hess, onetime Barry Goldwater speechwriter turned Wobbly homesteader, wrote, the American Right had been "individualistic, isolationist, decentralist—even anarchistic,"(Hess 1969: 30) until the Cold War reconciled conservatives to the leviathan state.

The 1930s dissenters—the old fashioned liberals now maligned as conservatives; the unreconstructed libertarians; the cornbelt radicals—proposed cooperatives and revitalized village economies as the alternative to government welfare. The Catholic Workers agreed. Peter Maurin asserted that "he who is a pensioner of the state is a slave of the state."(Day 1952: 220) Day, in her memoir *The Long Loneliness*, complained, "The state had entered to solve [unemployment] by dole and work relief, by setting up so many bureaus that we were swamped with initials....Labor was aiding in the creation of the Welfare State, the Servile State, instead of aiming for the ownership of the means of production and acceptance of the responsibility that it entailed."(Day 1952: 217-218)

"Bigness itself in organization precludes real liberty," wrote Henry Clay Evans, Jr. in the Distributist journal *The American Review* (Evans 1936: 563).

The home—the family—was the right size for most undertakings. And so the home must be made productive once more. In the April 1945 *Catholic Worker*, Janet Kalven of the Grailville Agricultural School for Women in Loveland, Ohio, called for "an education that will give young women a vision of the family as the vital cell of the social organism, and that will inspire them with the great ambitions of being queens in the home." By which she did not mean a sequacious helpmeet to the Man of the House, picking up his dirty underwear and serving him Budweisers during commercials, but rather a partner in the management of a "small, diversified family farm," who is skilled in everything "from bread-making to bee-keeping." For "the homestead is on a human scale"—the only scale that can really measure a person's weight (*CW* 4/1945: 4).[1]

The Agrarians and Distributists dreamed of a (voluntary, of course) dispersion of the population, and Day, despite her residence in what most decentralists regarded then and now as the locus of evil, agreed: "If the city is the occasion of sin, as Father Vincent McNabb points out, should not families, men and women, begin to aim at an exodus, a new migration, a going out from Egypt with its flesh pots?" asked Day in September 1946 (*CW* 9/1946: 1). This revulsion against urbanism seems odd in a woman whose base was Manhattan, symbol of congestion, of concentration, of cosmopolitanism rampant. Yet she wrote of the fumes from cars stinging her eyes as she walked to Mass, of the "prison-gray walls" and parking lots of broken glass. "We only know that it is not human to live in a city of ten million. It is not only not human, it is not possible."(*CW* 7-8/1948: 6) The Southern Agrarians would not demur. Day was unenthusiastic about the New Deal's rural resettlement program. "We do not expect to see the government moving people out to subsistence homesteads. It is not the place of the government so to regulate the lives of its citizens."(*CW* 1/1936: 2)

The Health of the State

The Second World War destroyed agrarianism as an active force in American intellectual life, just as it fortified the urban citadels of power and money. Foes of U.S. involvement in the war, heirs to the non-interventionist legacy of George Washington, were slandered, most notably Charles Lindbergh, whom the *CW* defended against the smears of the White House.

Despite Day's disavowal of the "isolationist" label, *The Catholic Worker* of 1939-1941 spoke the diction of the American antiwar movement, which, because it was anti-FDR, was deemed "right-wing."

Sentences like "We should like to know in just what measure the British Foreign Office is dictating the foreign policy of the United States!" could have come straight from the pages of Colonel McCormick's Chicago *Tribune*. So could the objection to the "*English and Communist Propaganda*"(*CW* 2/1939: 2) of the New York papers, and the reverence toward the traditional "neutrality of the United States" and the keeping of "our country aloof from the European war."(Roberts 1984: 126)

"*The Catholic Worker* does not adhere to an isolationist policy," editorialized the paper in February 1939, though in fact its position, and often its phraseology, was within the American isolationist grain. The editorial sought to distinguish the paper from the bogeymen "isolationists" by urging "that the doors of the United States be thrown open to all political and religious refugees"(*CW* 1/ 1939: 2) a position also taken by many isolationists, for instance H.L. Mencken, who wanted our country to be a haven for the persecuted Jews of Europe.

Day and the Workers dug in for a tooth-and-nail fight against conscription as "the most important issue of these times," as they saw it (*CW* 4/1945: 5). Day replied to those who noted that Joseph and Mary went to Bethlehem to register with the census that "it was not so that St. Joseph could be drafted into the Roman Army, and so that the Blessed Mother could put the Holy Child into a day nursery and go to work in an ammunition plant." (*CW* 1/1943: 1)

Or, as Peter Maurin put it

> The child does not belong to the state;
> it belongs to the parents.
> The child was given by God to the parents;
> he was not given by God to the state. (*CW* 1/1943: 1)

This was by now a quaintly reactionary notion. What were children if not apprentice soldiers? Like their isolationist allies, the Catholic Workers suffered years of "decline, suspicion, and hatred" during the Good War. (O'Brien 1965: 323) Circulation of *The Catholic Worker* plummeted from 190,000 in May 1938 to 50,500 in November 1944. By 1944, only 9 of 32 houses of hospitality were operating.

The Cold War transmogrified led the American Right: anti-communism became its warping doctrine, yet a remnant of cantankerous, libertarian, largely Midwestern isolationists held on, though the invigorating air of the 1930s, when Left and Right might talk, ally, even merge, was long gone. The fault lies on both sides.

The unwillingness of *The Catholic Worker's* editors to explore avenues of cooperation with the Old Right led them, at times, to misrepresent the sole popular anti-militarist force of the late 1940s. In denouncing the North Atlantic Treaty which created NATO, the *CW* claimed that "the only serious opposition in the Senate is from a group of the old isolationist school, and their argument is that it costs too much."(*CW* 5/1949: 1) This is flatly untrue—the isolationist case was far more sophisticated and powerful, and it rested on the same hatred of war and aggression that underlay the Catholic Worker's. But to have been honest and fair would have placed the *CW* on Elm Street and Oak Street, whose denizens might have taught the boys in the Bowery a thing or two.

When Nebraska Congressman Howard Buffett, stalwart of the "far right" in the House of Representatives, denounced the Truman Doctrine, saying, "Our Christian ideals cannot be exported to other lands by dollars and guns. Persuasion and example are the methods taught by the Carpenter of Nazareth...We cannot practice might and force abroad and retain freedom at home. We cannot talk world cooperation and practice power politics,"(Rothbard 1964: 222) did he sound all that different than Dorothy Day asking "what are all these Americans, so-called Christians, doing all over the world so far from our own shores?"(Roberts 1994: 164)

To call the isolationist journalist John T. Flynn an exponent of "semi-fascism," as Michael Harrington did in *The Catholic Worker* (*CW* 11/1951: 5), is both odious and ignorant, and it suggests that the blindness, the refusal to see beyond the boxes labeled "left" and "right," afflicted Catholic Worker eyes as well. (Flynn, parenthetically, was among the tangiest critics of the maldistribution of wealth in our country; he was expelled by Mr. Buckley from the *National Review* in 1956 for submitting an essay lacerating the "racket" of militarism) (Flynn 1995; 129-134).

Postwar Catholic isolationists would be condescended to as parochial morons by the Cold War liberal likes of James O'Gara, managing editor of *Commonweal,* who snickered at those mossbacks who refused to recognize that "American power is a fact"(O'Gara 1954:

106) and that "modern science has devoured distance and made neighbors of us all."(O'Gara 1954: 111) What good is personalism in a world of atomic bombs? What mattered the small? Father John C. Rawe's experimental school of rural knowledge, Omar Farm, near Omaha, was shattered when all but two of its students were drafted to fight WWII. Liberal Catholics continued to support the conscription against which pacifists and right-wingers railed, although, as Patricia McNeal has written of the League of Nations debate, "the majority of American Catholics supported the popular movement towards isolationism and rejected any idea of collective security." (McNeal 1973) But the League aside, we all know which side won. The state side. The liberals who do not know us but, as they so unctuously assure us, have our best interests at heart.

"The greatest enemy of the church today is the state," Dorothy Day told a Catholic audience in 1975 (Coy 1988: 93), sounding much like the libertarian Right that was her natural, if too little visited, kin.

The powerful libertarian strain in *The Catholic Worker* was simply not present in other postwar magazines of the "Left," excepting *politics,* edited by Day admirer Dwight Macdonald. American liberals had made peace with—had made sacrifices to Moloch on the Potomac. As *Catholic Worker* editor Robert Ludlow argued in 1951,

> we are headed in this country towards a totalitarianism every bit as dangerous towards freedom as the other more forthright forms. We have our secret police, our thought control agencies, our overpowering bureaucracy....The American State, like every other State, is governed by those who have a compulsion to power, to centralization, to the preservation of their gains. And it is the liberals—*The New Leader*, *New Republic*, *Commonweal* variety—who have delivered the opiate necessary for the acceptance of this tyranny among 'progressive' people. It is the fallacy of attempting social reform through the State, which builds up the power of the State to where it controls all avenues of life. (*CW* 1/1951: 1)

To which the *New Republic*-style liberals replied: welcome to the real world.

The inevitable Arthur Schlesinger, Jr., in *The Vital Center* (1949), his manifesto of Cold War liberalism, wrote, "One can dally with the distributist dream of decentralization," but "you cannot flee from science and technology into a quietist dream world. The state and the factory are inexorable: bad men will run them if good abdicate the job."(Schlesinger 1949: 7)

Alas, most on the "Right" crawled into the devitalizing center. A dispersion of property, a restoration of ownership, the reclaiming of the land, a foreign policy of peace and non-interference: these were the dreams of losers, of fleers from reality, of shirkers of responsibility. Of, most damningly, *amateurs*. Non-experts. In 1966, in the just-as-inevitable *National Review*, Anthony T. Bouscaren mocked Day and other "Catholic Peaceniks" because, "sinfully, their analysis of the situation [in Vietnam] goes directly counter to that of the distinguished list of academicians…who support U.S. defense of South Vietnam."(Bouscaren 1966: 202) Grounds for excommunication, surely.

In all this worry about the other side of the world few partisans bothered to notice the dirt under their feet. Distributism was dead. Or was it? For in 1956, long after the Agrarian dream had been purged from the American Right, supplanted by the Cold War nightmare, Dorothy Day insisted that "distributism is not dead." It cannot "be buried, because distributism is a system conformable to the needs of man and his nature."(*CW* 7-8/1956: 4)

Conforming to their decentralist principles and presaging a later strategy of "right-wing" tax resisters, the Workers refused payment of federal taxes, though as Day wrote, we "file with our state capital, pay a small fee, and give an account of monies received and how they were spent. We always comply with this state regulation because it is local—regional," and "because we are decentralists (in addition to being pacifists.") This resistance, she explained, was

> much in line with common sense and with the original American ideal, that governments should never do what small bodies can accomplish: unions, credit unions, cooperatives, St. Vincent de Paul Societies. Peter Maurin's anarchism was on one level based on this principle of subsidiarity, and on a higher level on that scene at the Last Supper where Christ washed the feet of His Apostles. He showed the new Way, the way of the powerless. In the face of Empire, the Way of Love. (Day 1983: 313-314)

It is only in the local, the personal, that one can see Christ. A mob, no matter how praiseworthy its cause, is still a mob, said Day, paraphrasing Eugene Debs, and she explained, in Thoreauvian language, her dedication to the little way:

> Why localism?...For some of us anything else is extravagant; it's unreal; it's not a life we want to live. There are plenty of others who want that life, living in corridors of power, influence, money, making big decisions that affect big numbers of people. We don't have to follow those people, though; they have more would-be servants—slaves, I sometimes think—than they know what do with. (Coles 1987:105)

> We don't happen to believe that Washington, DC, is the moral capital of America... If you want to know the kind of politics we seek, you can go to your history books and read about the early years of this country. We would like to see more small communities organizing themselves, people talking with people, people *caring* for people...We believe we are doing what our Founding Fathers came here to do, to worship God in the communities they settled. They were farmers. They were craftspeople. They took care of each other. They prayed to God, and they thanked Him for showing them the way—to America! A lot of people ask me about the influence on our [Catholic] Worker movement, and they are right to mention the French and the Russian and English writers, the philosophers and novelists. But some of us are just plain Americans whose ancestors were working people and who belonged to small-town or rural communities or neighborhoods in cities. We saw more and more of that community spirit disappear, and we mourned its passing, and here we are, trying to find it again... (Coles 1987: 107-108)

Dorothy Day found it. Not on the Left, and not on the Right, but in that place where Love resides. In the face of Empire, the Way of Love.

Note

[1] Anthony Novitsky has argued that Peter Maurin is understandable only "in the context of reactionary social Catholicism." Anthony Novitsky, "Peter Maurin's Green Revolution: The Radical Implications of Reactionary Social Catholicism," *The Review Of Politics* (Vol. 37, No. 1, January 1975): 103. Among the manifestations of this reactionary social Catholicism was the *The Catholic Worker*'s support for a family wage. "What about paying a living family wage to men so that the wives can stay home and raise the children?" the paper editorialized during one labor dispute. "Working Wives Opposed by Priest in Mill Town," *The Catholic Worker* (December 1935): 8. See also Tim O'Brien, "The Family Wage," *The Catholic Worker* (October 1943): 6.

A Cultural Context For Understanding Dorothy Day's Social and Political Thought

Keith Morton

Providence College

John Saltmarsh

Brown University

Dorothy Day remains a compelling mystery, a person whose life invites deep and persistent inquiry and instills a haunting desire for understanding. The power of her legacy and the need to grasp its significance is evidenced by a conference like this one.

This conference also reflects the tendency to follow Day's autobiographical lead to frame her life in a Catholic perspective. Her 1952 autobiography *The Long Loneliness,* her influence on the biography by William Miller, and interviews and writings from late in her life all prescribe an understanding of her life from the point of view of her devotion to the Catholic faith and her need to protect an increasingly rarefied image. As she wrote in *The Long Loneliness,* she was recounting her religious journey, not her life story. "I have never intended to write an autobiography," she claimed, but "wanted instead to tell of the things that brought me to God."(Day 1952: 94) Whether through *The Long Loneliness* or an earlier autobiographical account, *From Union Square to Rome* (1938), Day framed her life story in a way defined by her conversion and devotion to Catholicism.

A different perspective, we argue, is warranted. What we describe as a cultural context for understanding Day's life allows for an exploration of both her political and social thought prior to her conversion to Catholicism and asks the question of how her earlier life relates to the religious faith and social activism of her Catholic years. We are interested in reaching a clearer understanding of the origins of the political and social thought expressed through *The Catholic Worker* in the years of Day's life after 1932. To do so we want to grasp the full contours and deeper implications of her political thought by better understanding its relation to her personal struggles. A cultural context provides a framework that connects, in an intimate and closely-woven way, the personal and the political, raising a series of questions aimed at understanding her personal politics and the development of her religious sensibilities.

A cultural context also requires an examination of Day's construction of her life story. It requires, contrary to her vehement disclaimers, that we take seriously *The Eleventh Virgin*, her 1924 autobiographical novel, which provides important details of her life that are conspicuously absent in her later autobiographical writings (Coles 1987: 37-38). The novel itself is a reminder that the personal was so much intertwined with her political identity—the politics of "personalism"—that she attempted on three occasions in her life to set down her autobiography: *The Eleventh Virgin*, *From Union Square to Rome*, and *The Long Loneliness*. Arguably it is the first of these, the only one she later regretted writing, which is the key text for understanding the formative experiences of her life.

The period of Day's life recounted in *The Eleventh Virgin* is not part of the story of what brought her to God or the Catholic faith. It is instead the details of a rough, raw, and intensely joyful and painful life laid bare, telling the story of a young woman's coming of age, with great difficulty, grasping toward maturity. It is divided into three sections: "Adolescent," "Still Adolescent," and "Not So Much So." The veneer of fiction is perhaps protection against the intense vulnerability she must have experienced from such overt exposure. It is an intimate telling of her personal struggles confronting the cultural tensions surrounding vocation, gender, sexuality, spirituality, and politics in the Teens and Twenties. She was coming of age (she is 22 years old when the novel ends) at a time of cultural fragmentation, experiencing all the disconnections of modern existence: mind from body, theory from practice, work from labor, intellect from spirit, knowledge from morals, the individual from community. In her youth, "all beauty, all joy, all music touched my heart and my flesh, so that they cried out for fulfillment, for union."(Day 1952: 55) Day experienced cultural fragmentation as a lifelong search for what she would come to call "a synthesis."(Day 1952: 187) The sense of wholeness, of striving for a life of integrity, meant experiencing the painful struggle for a way in which she could practice a vocation of a journalist as a woman, where she could engage in a politics of social justice, and where she could live according to her desire for a deep and sustaining relation with another where she would be loved and not be exploited. "I wanted," she wrote of her early years in *The Long Loneliness,* "though I did not know it then, a synthesis: I wanted life and I wanted an abundant life."(Day 1952: 39) The difficulty of achieving this is the story of *The Eleventh Virgin.*

A thinly veiled retelling of Day's own life, *The Eleventh Virgin* details a young woman's search for a life of integrity, a problem Day was only able to resolve years later with the creation of the Catholic Worker. It is woven of five searches: for a true vocation, a fulfilling sexuality, a politics of social justice, a deep spirituality, and a sustaining community. June Henreddy, Day's fictional "self" in the novel, experiences the cultural tensions of the early part of the century that lead her to be divided against herself, and her response to them illustrates not only Day's personal values and political commitments, but her religious sensibilities. June is a young woman drifting among disconnected vocations. She has an increasingly fragile and problematic understanding of her gender and her sexuality. Her suffering increases as she observes and experiences injustice, some of her own making. Her sense of belonging to any place or human relationship diminishes and she grows fearful that there is no moral order in the world. Taken one at a time, the threads describe the ways in which Day perhaps felt her own life was coming unraveled, reflecting the changes and pressures wrought by the broader culture.

Clearly much of Day's adult life was concerned with the problem of finding meaningful work integrated into a meaningful life. In the novel, Day tells of her work as a journalist, an activist, a nurse, and a writer. She describes failed attempts to be a wife and homemaker. All these vocations are unsatisfying, failing as they do to help her become whole, achieve some kind of justice, or tie her to a sustainable community. Collectively they suggest that for Day the search for a vocation was a creative, almost aesthetic process. It was not about putting food on the table, but about finding one's self in work. And no single pursuit could satisfy.

Not surprisingly in a story of a young woman coming of age written by an author who had been impressed by the urban realism of

Theodore Dreiser in *Sister Carrie* (1899) and Jack London in *Martin Eden* (1909), many of the abandonments Day experiences are related to gender and sexuality. In work, and especially in romance, she suffers because she is female, and because she believes she needs a man to be whole. As she wrote in *The Long Loneliness,* "a woman does not feel whole without a man." (Day 1952: 236) In *The Eleventh Virgin,* Day describes a succession of relationships, beginning with her father, that violate her being and leave her abandoned and alone. June's relationships with men received substantial treatment, and they are not pleasant reading, especially for those accustomed to Day as strong and clear and whole in herself. In the disturbing "Monologue" with which Day ends the novel, June explains:

> I thought I was a free and emancipated young woman and I found out that I wasn't at all, really. I got excited over socialists and the I.W.W.'s, and anarchists and birth controlists and suffragists, and if I had not been working on a newspaper and bumped into them all at once, I would have gone from one to another of them and joined them all, and kept on being fervent for years....It looks to me that this freedom is just a modernity gown, a new trapping that we women affect to capture the man we want. (Day 1924: 312)

This ending suggests Day's complex and conflicting beliefs: that she needed a man in her life to be whole and that men would, in all likelihood, betray her. Clearly Day perceived enormous tension between her desires for a man and family, and meaningful, creative work.

Throughout the novel Day is compelled in response to each disappointment to search more deeply and thoroughly for political and social justice, only to be disappointed again and hurt even more deeply. There seems to have been a pivotal moment in Day's life with respect to justice, a moment when she had to face it squarely and honestly. She describes the moment in both *The Long Loneliness* and *The Eleventh Virgin.* In both versions (much of the language is the same in the two) the moment comes when she is imprisoned for the first time, following a demonstration in support of women's suffrage in Washington, DC in late 1917. The immediate consequence is that she has to face up to reality: how badly people can treat one another, and how poorly the progressive political interests cooperate. In *The Long Loneliness,* Day asks, "What was good and evil? I lay there in utter confusion and misery.... it is rarely that such a realization of the horror of sin and human hate can come to you."(Day 1952: 78-79)

After a 10-day hunger strike, she leaves her jail cell not as a committed radical but as a witness to the extremes of human nature and the limits of her own fiercely independent self-reliance. "To be so degraded was to be shamed and humbled," she wrote, "but I rejected the humiliation. I had seen myself as too weak to stand alone. I was ashamed and again rejected religion that had helped me when I had been brought to my knees by suffering."(Day 1952: 83) In the novel, Day's character faces up to the reality of how compromised she feels by singular devotion to "causes." June says to her friend and mentor in prison, the strong-willed suffragist Billy, "I'd feel as though I were of some use in the world if I believed in socialism or I thought working for the birth control league of suffragists I could benefit the world in some way. But I don't feel that any of these things are solutions and if I worked among these people with their single-track minds I'd go crazy. I'm ignorant and I feel that all these people with their causes are one-sided. I either want to retire from the world and study for the sake of acquiring wisdom or else I want to do something simple and useful."(Day 1924: 217)

Day has come to radical politics because she has explicitly rejected charity in her quest for justice, and she has been disappointed. In *The Long Loneliness,* jail is simply one more time when she postponed her conversion and faith commitment. But in *The Eleventh Virgin* it is a moment in which a naive faith in justice is shattered, leaving behind only confusion and pain. It is a moment when June realizes that she cares about the persons and stories she encounters in prison more than the issues or causes or politics that lead her there. Yet there is no alternative path opened to her by this realization. She is alienated, despairing, still hungering for a type of justice she cannot articulate, and knowing of no way to live with integrity of mind, body and spirit.

The thread of community, or more precisely of not belonging and not being part of a sustained community, runs through the entire novel, beginning with her home life as a child. Further, her search for community is inextricably linked to her spiritual quest. These threads of the novel are ultimately about the search for a "center," a moral home, what the religious historian William Clebsch has called a "way of being at home in the universe."(Clebsch 1973: 187) *The Eleventh Virgin* describes at length her childhood home as emotionally strained, if not explicitly abusive, soured by the failed middle class aspirations of her parents, the alcoholism of her father and the melancholy of her mother. She recalled that "there was never any kissing in my family, and never a close embrace...we kept ourselves to ourselves, as the saying is....It is the way we were as a family....We could never be free with others, never put our arms around them casually....We were never handholders. We were always withdrawn and alone."(Day 1952: 35)

All of Day's attempts to join or create other communities, places of belonging defined by work (journalist, nurse) or politics or aesthetics, or by finding the right man, failed. This thread lends drama and organization to the novel as Day lurches from one experience of abandonment and disappointment to another that will be worse: more punishing, more diminishing, more isolating.

June's fragmented life reflects what Day and many of her contemporaries perceived as the crisis of community: the fragmentation of a unified American culture by the combined forces of industrialization, urbanization, and immigration, and by the increasing centralization of political and economic power in the hands of a private, industrial elite. The most immediate symptom of this fragmentation was a devolution of the ordinary person's role as a citizen and the emergence of a new role as an individual consumer of goods and services. The most direct consequence of cultural fragmentation was the threat to democracy. For many cultural critics, this cultural shift was marked by the intersection of capitalism and democracy: on the one hand, a culture of consumption and the economic hegemony of an industrial elite, and on the other a technocracy of managers and physical and social scientists. Thus joined, they redefined individuals as consumers rather than citizens and shrank the public realm altogether. The result was the disappearance of community. And the question for Day was how to respond powerfully and authentically to this crisis.

In the nine years between the publication of *The Eleventh Virgin* and the founding of the Catholic Worker, Day experienced this crisis of community in ways both personal and political. While she sensed fragmentation and longed for unity in restoration, she could not locate existing institutional structures that would relieve her felt trauma or offer a place of synthesis. Further, she experienced this crisis in moral terms that required, in part, a deeply spiritual response which raised unavoidable questions about equality, justice, and citizenship in a democratic culture.

Over time, Day became less concerned with the diminishment of political democracy and more concerned with the basic issue of human relationships; it was these relationships that defined community. As she wrote after her conversion to Catholicism, "we cannot love God unless we love each other, and to love we must know each other."(Day 1952: 285) Her position became unencumbered by social theory and progressive politics and was increasingly simple and direct: "we have learned that the only solution is love and that love comes with community." (Day 1952: 286)

As Day became less concerned with theory and politics, she could not accept the practice of charity. Charity, more than anything else, distorted one's ability to know others, and thus endangered community. In the period of her bohemian youth, she claimed that "our hearts burned with the desire for justice and were revolted at the idea of doled-out charity. The word charity had become something to gag over, something to shudder at."(Day 1952: 87) She did not know then—and she would struggle to define her life by her attempt to know—"the true meaning of the word." That would come with the "personalism" and "voluntary poverty" at the heart of the Catholic Worker movement she founded with Peter Maurin in 1933. By then she had created for herself a Catholic identity founded on the communalism of the medieval Church. But her version of Catholicism, her faith, was not consistent with the modern institution of the Church, and the point of contradiction was the issue of charity. Wherever she distances herself from the Catholic Church in her autobiography, it is done so in the context of charity.

She lived, she wrote, in a state of "permanent dissatisfaction with the Church" because, in part, she "felt that charity was a word to choke over. Who wanted charity?" And, she explained "it was not just human pride but a strong sense of a man's dignity and worth, and what was due him in justice that made me resent rather than feel proud of so mighty a sum total of Catholic institutions."

The church, she claimed "was so often a scandal to me," "the scandal of businesslike priests, of collective wealth, the lack of a sense of responsibility for the poor, the worker, the Negro, the Mexican, the Filipino, and even the oppression of them by our industrial-capitalist order." "There was plenty of charity," she observed, "but too little justice."(Day 1952: 150)

"Suddenly," she wrote, "a succession of incidents and the tragic aspects of life in general began to overwhelm me and I could no longer endure the life I was leading."(Day 1952: 87) This passage from *The Long Loneliness* refers to the 2-month period from early December 1917, when she returned to Greenwich Village from her prison experience in Washington, until late January 1918, when the inconsistencies in her life became so intolerably conflicting that she could "no longer endure" them. Day's life during these months which culminated in the death by a heroin overdose of a bohemian comrade and her concealing the heroin from the police, was primarily defined by her love affair with the playwright Eugene O'Neill. It is a part of her life that she would never write about and arguably her moment of deepest despair.

Whereas there are significant events in Day's life that appear in one version of her autobiography and not another, this period in her life stands out for having been omitted from all her autobiographical writing. Even the destructively painful and emotionally tumultuous relationship with Lionel Moise, left out of *From Union Square to Rome* and *The Long Loneliness,* is revealed in tragic detail in *The Eleventh Virgin.* Not so her winter of discontent, 1917-1918. It is a brief but enormously significant episode in Day's struggle to find purpose in her life. This time provided evidence of her difficult struggle toward a life of authenticity and her deep failure among the radicals and bohemians with whom she associated to resolve her needs in social justice, vocation and gender, sexuality, spirituality, and community. The hopes she had for true love, for right causes, for belonging in a supportive community, for meaningful journalism, all of these collapse, as symbolically the dying comrade collapsed in her arms, signifying the banality and hollowness of all in which she believed.

The bitter cold of the winter of 1917-1918 was matched only by the bitter reality of the collapse of radical dreams. America was embroiled in the war in Europe. Political radicals faced domestic repression. *The Masses,* which Day worked for, had been suppressed; even as she worked on its successor, *The Liberator,* the heady days of exuberant rebellion were long past. Writers and artists retreated to the refuge of Greenwich Village to act out the last gasps of a quickly vanishing personal and cultural innocence.

Shortly after being released from jail in Washington, Day arrived in Greenwich Village and was introduced to Eugene O'Neill by their mutual friend, Mike Gold. Day was unsettled, moving frequently from apartment to apartment, and working infrequently in the office of *The Liberator.* It is apparent that what she describes as the "mad rush of living" (Day 1952: 84) at this time was as much a quest for intense experience as it was a means for denying the weightlessness of utopian ideals and the destruction of romantic dreams. O'Neill, perhaps, faced similar denial, yet he was more overtly distraught over the loss of Louise Bryant. Bryant, with whom he had been passionately in love, had left for Russia to join her husband, John Reed, who was gathering what would become first-hand accounts of the Russian Revolution. While O'Neill had achieved some notoriety as a playwright for the success of his *Bound East for Cardiff* in 1916, he was now depressed and drinking heavily. Day was nine years younger than O'Neill and was one of several women vying to fill the void left by Bryant. Together, Day and O'Neill spent long hours together, closing down the saloon known by its patrons as the Hell Hole. They drank the night away, walked endlessly through the streets into the early morning hours, and flaunted all moral strictures and cultural conventions (Gelb and Gelb 1962; Ranald 1984).

When she wasn't hanging around the Provincetown Playhouse with O'Neill, Day was with him at the Hell Hole, where she had gained somewhat of a reputation for hard living. Malcolm Cowley noted that "the gangsters admired" her "because she could drink them under the table."(Cowley 1951: 69) O'Neill and Gold were her "constant companions" and after long nights and many drinks she and O'Neill would end up clutching each other in bed. Day recalled that this was a time when "no one ever wanted to go to bed and no one ever wanted to be alone."(Day 1952: 84) When O'Neill evidenced an attraction for Agnes Boulton, whom Day knew, Day befriended her and convinced her that the three of them should share an apartment together.

In many ways this was a desperate time for Day personally and politically. Reflecting on this period of her "wavering life" without providing any details of her experience, she explained that "the life of the flesh called to me as a good and wholesome life, regardless of man's laws, which I felt rebelliously were made for the repression of others...satisfied flesh has its own laws." "It is easy," she concluded, "to stifle conscience for a while."(Day 1952: 85)

While she struggled to uphold the fallacy of maintaining personal integrity while absorbed in reckless hedonism, political delusions surfaced. In their blinding innocence, Day and her fellow Village radicals "lived in one world and it was a world where dreams come true, where there was a possibility of the workers beginning to take over the means of production and starting to build that kind of society where each received according to his need and worked according to his ability."

In the end it was all a dangerous illusion. She could only stifle her conscience for a time. Day and her circle of radicals "had never examined the fundamental principles" of their revolutionary creed. They "belonged to that school of youth which lived in the present, lived in the life of the senses."(Day 1952: 85) It would be only a matter of time before she would have to face her conscience, until something would permanently shatter the illusion of her existence, until something would lead her to claim, as her character in *The Eleventh Virgin* does, that "I hate being Utopian and trying to escape reality."(Day 1924: 222)

The events of the evening of January 22, 1918 were similar in many respects to the typical routine of Day's life in the Village that winter. What was unique was the revelry surrounding the return to the village of one of its denizens, a friend of O'Neill's, Louis Holladay. Holladay had been on the West Coast for a year to dry out from alcohol and drugs as he had promised the woman he hoped to marry. The anticipated climax of the evening was to be the announcement of their wedding. All went according to the plan until late in the evening when Holladay's fiancé-to-be arrived at the Hell Hole to tell him that she was planning to marry another man. Holladay announced to all his change of fortune and for the next hour, until the Hell Hole closed down, he ended his abstinence and bought rounds for the house.

The crowd moved to Romany Marie's, the saloon around the corner, where Holladay's gaze caught O'Neill and Day. Upon seeing them together, he took a glass bottle of heroin from his pocket and downed the contents. As he lapsed into unconsciousness and began to foam from the mouth, the party goers fled, including O'Neill. Day went to Holladay's aid, recovering and concealing the bottle with the remains of white powder. He died in her arms. She was with him still when the police and the coroner arrived. Then she went looking for O'Neill to tell him what had happened. At 3 a.m. she arrived at their apartment to find O'Neill in bed with Agnes Boulton. According to Boulton, Day appeared to be in shock: she "gave the appearance of being disheveled, as though she had forgotten about herself and even who she was. Her coat was unbuttoned, her hair damp, her face very pale...there was an emptiness in her face, as if some sudden knowledge had shocked her into awareness."(Boulton 1958: 86)

Day convinced Boulton, but not O'Neill, to return with her to the scene of Holladay's death. It was dawn by the time the two arrived at Romany Marie's. Day spoke to the police, and Boulton saw Holladay's body. They went from there to the Hell Hole where they found the door unlocked and O'Neill drunk. By mid-morning Day and Boulton left O'Neill and walked several blocks together, when suddenly Day turned down a side street. She walked away, literally and figuratively, from a period in her life that she "could no longer endure." In all likelihood she walked that morning to her family's townhouse for comfort and support from her mother and sister and in spite of her terror of her father. She would not return to the Village until 1924. And she would not revisit her life there in any of her autobiographical writing, insisting, as William Miller has written, "on exorcizing the Village from her past."(Miller 1982: 103)

When Day left the Village her life was shattered: "the tragic aspects of life began to overwhelm me."(Day 1952: 87) She was not writing because her political dreams were destroyed by the war, her community of idealists had proven false, she had chased after a relationship with a man that was destined to fail, and she had found no home for her religious sensibilities. Her life demanded a drastic reordering. In early April she began training as a nurse at King's County hospital. As much as such work addressed the question of "what am I doing for my fellow men?" it also enforced structure and order upon her disordered life. For a year she submitted to the "twelve hour days on the ward, beginning work at seven in the morning." The job required "strict etiquette" and she was taught "almost military deference and respect for" her superiors (Day 1952: 88). It was extreme compensation for her life in the Village.

While her work at the hospital provided structure in her life and time for healing, it could not resolve her fundamental struggles. She wanted to write and came to the realization that nursing, while suited to the cultural acceptability of her gender, was "a second choice, and not my vocation."(Day 1952: 93) While her need for a meaningful vocation eliminated nursing, she actually left the hospital to move in with Lionel Moise, having entered into another emotionally destructive and constitutionally unstable relationship. Her relationship with Moise, a hard-living, rough and unstable newspaperman, would end like the one with O'Neill, tragically. Yet there was something about it that left her quest for an authentic life intact. At least it was a part of her life which she could later recount about her preconversion life in *The Eleventh Virgin.* Recalling that winter in the Village, on the other hand, was just too much to endure.

The Eleventh Virgin ends at the time Day underwent a late term abortion in a failed attempt to maintain an emotionally abusive relationship with Moise. Even as June Henreddy expressed unfounded optimism about the hope of a future life—stable, grounded, and fulfilling—with her lover and with a child, she recognized that she was "poised on the edge of an abyss of unhappiness."(Day 1924: 306) In *The Long Loneliness,* Day glossed over this turmoil with a reference to her "wavering life." The abyss that followed 1919 is barely mentioned, though it went deep. It was during this period of further disintegration of her life that she writes *The Eleventh Virgin.*

The optimistic ending of the novel aside, it is only a few months after Moise leaves Day in New York and heads to Chicago that she marries Berkeley Tobey, a self-styled promoter and something of a confidence man who is also eminently unstable, eventually going through eight marriages. He and Day traveled to Europe, separated while there, and then divorced after returning to New York in the summer of 1920. The details of the time in Europe are sketchy. She spent some time in Italy, possibly alone. During this time she wrote *The Eleventh Virgin.* She wrote in a way that came naturally: "I have always been a journalist and diarist pure and simple."(Day 1952: 160) During one of the lowest periods in her life, the book project was perhaps an attempt to write herself whole, to create meaning from the chaos of her life. Hoping to re-establish her relationship with Moise, she followed him to Chicago in late 1920, and she finally gave up the hope with which the novel ends.

In the winter of 1923–1924 Day surfaced as a writer for the New Orleans *Item*. Having not practiced her journalism since 1918, she had written one piece for *The Liberator* while in Chicago, and she wrote regularly for the *Item* through February 1924. At this time *The Eleventh Virgin* was published, and a Hollywood studio bought the rights to the book for $5,000; Malcolm Cowley claimed that it was not for its merits but for the racy title. In *The Long Loneliness* she recalled her life from 1919–1925 in a 15-page chapter entitled "A

Time of Searching." Of these years she wrote that "I find I have little to say."(Day 1952: 94) Her marriage and travels are referred to as "a trip to Europe," writing *The Eleventh Virgin* as "a year I spent writing," and her chasing after Moise as "I went to Chicago."(95) Moise is identified only as "a man with whom I had been deeply in love for several years."(107) Her abortion and its aftermath she refers to only as "for a long time I thought I could not bear a child."(135) Day returned to New York City in 1924. Encouraged by Malcom Cowley's wife, Peggy, Day used her royalties to purchase a beach house on Staten Island. This is where "Part Two" of *The Long Loneliness* begins.

Day not only experienced barriers to her vocation presented by her gender, but she struggled, too, with a sense of belonging within a larger group of radicals who shared her political sympathies. More importantly, she endeavored to attain those values, quite conventionally bourgeois, with which she ends *The Eleventh Virgin*:

> [June envied] those women who were buying things to take home to their husbands, probably to their babies as well. Why couldn't she too have a home, a husband, and babies? A dull resentment smouldered in her breast...I know what I want. It's [a husband] and marriage and babies! And I'll have them yet."(297, 312)

Most of all, she sought a child. It would bring her wholeness, purpose, and perhaps, a sense of absolution. Thus, there is the inescapable connection, emphasized by Day, between the birth of her daughter and her religious conversion to Catholicism. Having a child and becoming a Catholic led Day toward realizing a "synthesis" in her life. This emergent synthesis began with her return to New York in the spring of 1924, and it continued with new tensions after Day's baptism in December of 1927.

Day entered fully into the cultural milieu of Greenwich Village upon her return to the city, re-established old contacts in radical and bohemian circles and wrote sporadically. Mostly she was concerned, obsessed in Malcolm Cowley's view, with having a child. Of this time in her life she wrote in *The Long Loneliness*: "the longing in my heart for a child was growing."(Day 1952: 35-36) The single-mindedness of purpose, with apparent concurrent intention not to be caught in the passionate attachment that had proved so tragic with Moise, led to behavior that was viewed, at least by some, as recklessly promiscuous. As Cowley noted, at this time Day seemed "almost contemptuous of the flesh."(Cowley 1951: 165)

Not long after her return, she entered into a relationship with Forster Batterham, a political radical and philosophical anarchist. He was a deeply introverted individual who abhorred convention and loved solitude, preferably in natural surroundings. After Day decided to use her earnings from *The Eleventh Virgin* to purchase a beach cottage on Staten Island, Batterham was enthusiastically supportive. The period from 1925 through the beginning of 1927 was perhaps the most stable and tranquil in her life. She was settled, content, and reflective to the point that she started keeping a journal, something she had not done in years. The peacefulness and beauty that she experienced is amply conveyed in the middle section of *The Long Loneliness* which she titles "Natural Happiness." In fact, she felt that "this period of my life was so joyous and lovely, I want to write at length about it."(Day 1952: 116) There is a stability and consistency in her life that is evermore preciously recalled when placed in the perspective of her years since 1917.

Her relationship with Batterham ultimately gave Day two things essential to the eventual sense of personal resolution of the crises that haunted her. One was a child. The other was, as she writes in *The Long Loneliness,* "my new found sense of religion." Day explained, "I always felt that it was life with him that brought me natural happiness, that brought me to God. His ardent love of creation brought me to the creator of all things." Otherwise, their relationship was overtly superficial and emotionally unfullfilling. "We did not talk much," claimed Day, "but 'lived together' in the fullest sense of the phrase."(Day 1952: 114) While she claims that after one year they "contracted" a common law marriage, it was with a man who "had always rebelled against the institution of the family and the tyranny of love." Batterham, she noted, "lived with me as though he were living alone...this was a comradeship rather than a marriage."(Day 1952: 120)

Batterham was a consummate witness to the natural surroundings of the seashore which fed his need for solitude, escape, and his scientific curiosity. When Day found a place in this experience, it opened up for her a new world, illuminating the wonders of nature in a deeply spiritual way. When Day discovered spiritual awareness through nature she underwent a conversion to spirituality through an awakening to nature as sacred. The wonder of nature provided an opening to her spiritual self. As she wrote, "the very love of nature, and the study of her secrets...was bringing me to faith."(Day 1952: 134) As she planted her garden along the seashore at her beach house on Staten Island in 1925, she said to herself:

> I *must* believe in these seeds, that they fall into the earth and grow into flowers and radishes as and beans. It is a miracle to me because I do not understand it. Neither do naturalists understand it. The very fact that they use glib technical phrases does not make it any less of a miracle, and a miracle we all accept. Then why not accept God's mysteries? (Day 1952: 133)

Her discovery of a "love of creation brought me," she continued, "to the Creator of all things." Before she converted to a God-centered religion, she converted to natural religion, opening the way to faith in a Creator.

The uncomplicated happiness of this period in Day's life began to unravel in June of 1925 when she became pregnant. One can surmise that Batterham's objections to bringing a child into the world, along with the demand of personal responsibility, led to suggesting another abortion. Batterham rebelled against marriage, family and fatherhood. Day undoubtedly tried to persuade him otherwise. Only a child would provide her with the wholeness she needed. "No matter how much one loved or was loved," she wrote, "that love was lonely without a child. It was incomplete."(Day 1952: 136) Not only would Day, "awed by the stupendous act of creation," go through with the pregnancy, she determined resolutely to baptize her child in the Catholic Church. By the time her daughter was born she "knew I was going to have my child baptized, cost what it may. I knew I was not going to have her floundering through many years as I had done, doubting and hesitating, undisciplined and amoral." She "felt that 'belonging' to a church would bring order into" her daughter's life "which I felt my own had lacked."(Day 1952: 136) If she could convince Batterham to become father as well as husband, if he would accept her spiritual longing and accede to the baptism, Day could make her past wrongs right. Even her first marriage could be voided if she married Batterham in the Church. She knew at the same time that it was not to be. Batterham was, she conceded, "averse to any ceremony before Church or state. He was an anarchist and an atheist and he did not intend to be a liar or a hypocrite."(Day 1952: 148)

Their relationship became increasingly volatile and personally destructive through the fall of 1927. Finally, after another explosive argument, Day locked Batterham out of the cottage and on the following day was baptized herself. Increasingly, her life would be shaped by Catholicism. And there would be continual and tormenting turmoil.

An initial look at Day's conversion to Catholicism suggests that it was counterintuitive. While much in her past seems to have prepared her for and precipitated a crisis of faith, her early history, including the nominal Episcopalianism of her family, would seem to have prepared her for one form or another of liberal, socially progressive Protestantism. But these various forms of Protestantism, expressed through the Social Gospel movement and through emergent institutions such as the Salvation Army and the YMCA, for example, shared a belief (common among Progressive Era reformers) in the perfectablity of the world and of the people in it. This is a dominant motif in American Protestantism, prevalent in the urban Protestant churches associated with the Social Gospel from the 1880s through the 1920s.

A significant part of Day's decision to embrace Catholicism rather than the radical politics or Protestant expressions of the Social Gospel seems to have been an acceptance that the world and the human beings in it, including herself, were flawed and not perfectable. This perspective helps to explain, as well, her politics of witness. It is evident that the impetus for conversion was deeply personal and spiritual and had more to do with fundamental questions of moral philosophy and human nature than social justice. Why didn't she choose other options than the Catholic Church, many open to her within Protestant denominations, if the issues presented were those of social religion and social justice alone?

The spiritual awareness that had been heightened by nature provided her with an understanding, or a confirmation, that nature reveals a world that, while beautiful, is neither perfect nor perfectible. This view locates for her a place in the world for her own experiences. It is a world that accepts and accommodates sin and offers forgiveness. It is a world where moral disorder is countered by a vision of moral order in a disordered existence. It is deeply personal and social only to the extent of sharing solidarity with those whose imperfections dominate their perfectibility. It is a world view explained and embraced by, as Day saw it, the teachings of the Catholic Church. In Catholicism, Day found a vision of the interconnectedness of all things, an ecological metaphor for the sacredness of creation. But this view also accepted, where the Protestant alternatives did not, the flawed and corrupt aspects of nature, of humanity, which Day needed. She would explain her adherence to Catholicism as the need for acceptance and belonging for herself and her daughter, and she would claim allegiance to the Church in terms of solidarity with the poor in the ideal of the medieval Church, open to all, at the center of the community.

By all accounts, Day's relationship with Batterham was strained even before her resolve to have their daughter baptized exacerbated any tensions. Day's devotion to Catholicism was the cause for deep disruption in other parts of her life as well. Through her conversion to Catholicism she cut herself off from the only sense of community and larger sense of belonging that she had known, the social and political fabric of the radicals, bohemians, and intellectuals who were now bewildered by her religious commitment. In her younger years family and friends seemed bemused by her "religious pose"(Day 1924: 91) as she describes it, her "always pretending" about things religious. Later, during her time with Eugene O'Neill, her early morning visits to a Catholic Church led some of her friends to question her odd behavior. One close friend noted Day's "sudden and unexplainable impulses to go into any nearby Catholic church and sit there. She had no religious background, and probably this impulse was as obscure to her then as it was to her friends, who only considered it amusing."(Boulton 1958: 75) But this time it was different; this was authentic and sincere.

In addition to "the misery of leaving one love," Day felt the sting of the loss of "another love too, the life I had led in the radical movement." Her "experience as a radical, my whole make-up," formed the essence of her political identity. This same experience led her to associate with the masses, and the Catholic Church had "claimed the allegiance of the masses of people in all the cities where I had lived." It wasn't just her friends who were suspect of the Catholic Church. Day herself was uncertain how she would reconcile her allegiance to a community of believers with the Church as an institution that oppressed them. She was, she explained "just as much against capitalism and imperialism as ever, and here I was going over to the opposition, because the course of the Church was lined up with property, with the wealthy, with the state, with capitalism, with all the forces of reaction."(Day 1952: 149)

At the end of August 1927, the Italian-born anarchists, Nicola Sacco and Bartolomeo Vanzetti, were executed in Boston. Their case caused an international furor and went right to the heart of Day's dissatisfaction with the Church. She thought of the case as "the war of the classes," and wondered "where are the Catholic voices crying out for these men?"(Day 1952: 151) "No wonder," she confessed, despite motherhood and her conversion, "there was such a strong conflict going on in my mind and heart."

Catholicism did not resolve the tensions in Day's life, did not provide the "synthesis" she longed for. It grounded her spirituality but seemingly contradicted her politics and created confusion with regard to satisfying sexuality. Neither did it address her struggle toward a vocation. Further, while the birth of her daughter gave Day a tremendous sense of wholeness, the circumstances of her being an unwed mother raised doubts for others about the "validity" of her quest for community and personal responsibility (Day 1952: 235).The threads of the struggles in her life were not coming together, nor was it clear how they could be woven into a sustainable and authentic whole.

After her conversion, Day remained in New York, staying on the West Side during the winter and summering at the cottage on Staten Island. She worked for the Anti-Imperialist League and the Fellowship of Reconciliation, remaining active in radical politics. She wrote a play and sold stories and articles to the Catholic weekly, *Commonweal.* During the summer of 1929 the play she had submitted to Metro-Goldwyn led to a contract. She went to California, found Hollywood shallow and unstimulating, and saved just enough money to go to Mexico early in 1930. She admitted that she would have returned to New York instead but she "hungered too much to return to Forster...to me at that time New York was an occasion of sin." She "had to stay away for a while longer" and went to Mexico. This was not a joyful time for Day despite her writing, the success of her play, the strength of her faith, and the fulfillment of motherhood. Of this period she recalled that she "was lonely, deadly lonely. And I was to find out then, as I found out so many times, over and over again, that women especially are social beings, who are not content with just husband and family, but must have a community, a group, an exchange with others."(Day 1952: 158)

After six months in Mexico, Day left due to her daughter's ill health. She spent an apparently unhappy time with her parents in Florida before returning to New York in the spring of 1932. She kept on writing, working on a novel "about the depression, a social novel with the pursuit of a job as the motive and the social revolution as its crisis."(Day 1952: 161) Her spiritual life deepened; she began going to daily communion for the first time. As the politics of social justice intensified with the deepening of the Depression, Day noted that "it was a time for pressure groups, for direct action, and radicalism was thriving among all groups except the Catholics."(Day 1952: 158-159) While her heart burned for justice, she admitted that she "felt out of it" politically.

In late November 1932 Day used an advance from *Commonweal* to travel to Washington to cover the Hunger March, organized by the Unemployed Councils to dramatize the plight of the poor. Farmers and tenants protesting economic conditions were also assembling in the Capital. Day encountered friends that she had known from her days at *The Masses* and *The Liberator.* It had been 15 years since her imprisonment for the suffrage demonstration in the city. Her life had taken a course very different from that of her fellow radicals, and the culminating result of all her struggles produced considerable dismay. She "could write," and she "could protest," but ultimately she was left with the question of "where was the Catholic leadership in the gathering of bands of men and women together, for the actual works of mercy that the comrades had always made part of their technique in reaching the workers?"(Day 1952: 165)

Had all her struggle been for naught? Where had her choice of faith led her? "How little, how puny," she despaired, "my work had been since becoming a Catholic."(Day 1952: 165) Before leaving Washington, she went to the national shrine at Catholic University and prayed for guidance, "a prayer which came with tears and anguish, that some way would open up for me to use what talents I possess for my fellow workers, for the poor."(Day 1952: 166) With both great doubt and unshakable faith, Day returned to New York to find Peter Maurin waiting for her in her apartment. Five months later the first edition of *The Catholic Worker* went to press, and three years later houses of hospitality were started. Day had found a way to weave the threads of her struggle into a life of integrity.

When she met Peter Maurin he offered her a way to bring her "self" together. She found in his vision of the medieval Church a way to integrate her faith and her spirituality; and her life with Tamar and Maurin, and then with the growing circle of the Catholic Worker, met her need for community based on love, family, and belonging. In the Catholic Worker she was able to draw on all of her chosen vocations: journalist, activist, nurse, writer and worshiper. It resolved her struggles with gender and sexuality, which were made moot as the Worker gave her a role of "mother." Her relationship with Peter was deep, passionate and profoundly celibate. The Catholic Worker also gave her a new way to approach the problem of justice by allowing her opportunity to move back and forth between hospitality, seeing and reaching out to God's image in every person, and witness, speaking truth to power. With the Catholic Worker, her politics were transformed from the politics of social change to the politics of witness. The Catholic Worker signifies Day's resolution of her searches, of her difficult struggle toward authenticity, her solution to a "synthesis," a way to be whole and to be at home in the universe.

Certainly the crisis of community continues today, characterized by an evolving culture of consumption, increasing individualism and consumerism, and by the increase and strengthening of economic, religious, social, racial and political boundaries that separate people one from another. Young people increasingly report the expectation that theirs will be a fragmented, compartmentalized life in which meaning is only occasionally found, and then fleetingly. Day and the Catholic Worker offer a way and a place in which people can seek and experience integrity, authenticity. But it is largely Day's integrity, her authenticity, that is alive in the Catholic Worker, and its hospitality is the invitation, ultimately, that we must each search for our own integrity, as harsh and dreadful as this search might be.

M.L. Liebler

Mass Production

When we look closely inside
The tunnel of the American
Factory, we see gears turning
In disorienting prophecy, it is not
Salvation that first catches our eye.

Diego Rivera said "Industry is
Our Salvation!" What he dreamed
Was a much different nightmare
Of wires and gears and smoke
Stack lightening than the burning sleep
Deep within the cavernous factories
Of our broken hearts. We are left hollow,
And alone on a cold highway
Of separation and pressing discrimination.

The American spirit has long been
Strangled at some untraceable point
Between the ideal and the real. Now,
We are hungry and we are waiting
For our justice to pass through
This system of mass production. The wheels
Grind slowly in a world of industrial darkness
Where the murderous dollar suffocates
Our hope with progress, and where
Our dreams twist in fitful sleep.

Our futures lie stricken in
Inanimate blankness as we wait
And wait, like our ancestors did,
For a change that surely moves
As slow as blood through the thick
Grease heart of oil fed machines.

PART V

WORK AND THE ECONOMY

This masthead by Ade Bethune first appeared in the May 1935 *Catholic Worker*.

Dorothy Day, The Catholic Worker, and the Labor Movement

John Cort

Association of Catholic Trade Unionists

I joined the Catholic Worker in July 1936 and had to leave in November 1938. This was an exciting time in American history, exciting and terrible. Dorothy and Peter Maurin had founded the movement in New York City in May of 1933, almost in the middle of a May Day parade, which ended, as usual in those days, with a massive rally of Communists and Socialists in Union Square.

They founded the movement in the middle of the Great Depression. Unemployment was about 30 percent, and there was no unemployment compensation, no social security, no minimum wage, no mandatory overtime pay after 40 hours, no prohibition of child labor, no protection for the workers' right to organize. There was hunger to the point of starvation. There was massive homelessness. There was talk of revolution.

The American Federation of Labor (AF of L), which was supposed to be the workers' champion, was almost moribund, dead. Gangsters were sucking money and blood out of many of the old craft unions that remained alive. Major industries were totally unorganized, totally at the mercy of ruthless bosses. Then came John L. Lewis and the Congress of Industrial Organizations (CIO). Lewis, with the head and voice of a lion, was only one step short of a megalomaniac, but with the help of Roosevelt and a Democratic Congress, he proved to be a great organizer of unorganized workers.

When roused, Lewis was magnificent in battle. His talent for abusing bosses was a catharsis for workers who had seen the lords of industry go unchallenged for so many years. After the Republic Steel Massacre of 1937 Lewis called Tom Girdler, the president of Republic, "a heavily armed monomaniac, with murderous tendencies, who has gone berserk." It took a megalomaniac to give a monomaniac the name he deserved. During the negotiations to settle the Chrysler strike, Lewis became irritated by the supercilious attitude of K.T. Keller, Chrysler vice-president. Lewis said to him, "I am 99 percent of a mind to come around this table and wipe that damned sneer off your face." Keller wilted visibly. When this story got around, we all rejoiced with loud Alleluias, and our backs correspondingly stiffened as Keller's wilted.

By 1937 Lewis and the CIO were on the way to organizing the great mass of workers in the steel, auto, electrical, radio, rubber and other mass production industries.

At the Catholic Worker our founders had two different reactions to these developments. Peter Maurin was negative. He used to say, "Strikes don't strike me." In one of his Easy Essays he wrote a classic non-sequitur, "When the organizers organize the unorganized, the organizers don't organize themselves." Peter's solution was to let the factories rust away and get everybody back on the land in farming communes.

Dorothy's reaction was more positive. Coming out of the socialist/communist movements, she had a natural sympathy for the labor movement, on which she grafted her new Christian and Catholic convictions. About the time I joined in 1936 she was writing in the paper: "When workers are striking they are following an impulse, often blind, often uninformed, but a good impulse, one could even say an inspiration of the Holy Spirit. They are trying to uphold their right to be treated not as slaves but as human beings. They are fighting for a share in the management, for their right to be considered as partners in the enterprise in which they are engaged." Which is good Catholic social doctrine.

She went out to Chicago and interviewed the workers at Republic Steel who had been shot in the back by police. She went to Flint, Michigan, where, to show her solidarity with the strikers, she climbed through the window of a General Motors plant that had been shut down by a sitdown of members of the United Auto Workers.

Dorothy didn't just stop at these vivid supporting reports in the paper. In December 1936 thousands of seamen struck the New York waterfront in a wildcat strike against both their corrupt union, the AF of L, and the ship owners. Dorothy rented a vacant storefront one block off the waterfront, and we spent $4000 feeding the seamen. This is the equivalent of $47,000 in 1999 dollars, and we begged that money from *The Catholic Worker*'s readers. This support was crucial in helping the CIO to organize the seamen into a more honest and effective trade union.

Dorothy's vivid reports in the paper and actions like feeding the seamen on strike brought the class struggle alive for us at the Catholic Worker. Thus inspired, nine union men and Bill Callahan and I from the Worker staff, sitting around the kitchen table, founded the Association of Catholic Trade Unionists (ACTU). Its purpose was to encourage Catholic workers to join the unions in their trade or industry, to assist those unions in securing and defending their members' rights as against oppressive employers, and to defend also the integrity of the unions as against racketeers and Communist infiltration.

Dorothy encouraged us. She wrote in the paper, "Christ our Brother started with twelve men. Let us not lose sight of that fact. A few strong and ardent Catholic men can save the trade union movement in this country. Join your union and see that it is a workers' union and not a company union. Work for it. Study the history of the labor movement."

Eventually the ACTU had chapters in most of the major cities of the country. ACTU members and ACTU priests organized hundreds of labor schools, often at the parish level, at which we taught labor history, labor ethics, the rights and duties of the worker. Also practical subjects like organizing, grievance procedure, labor law, contract negotiating, and the like.

We published newspapers: *The Labor Leader* in New York and *The Wage Earner* in Detroit. We also got out on picket lines in support of various labor struggles. For example, as that quote of Dorothy indicated, in the '30s the labor movement was pretty much a man's world, but even then women were beginning to organize. Saleswomen at the Woolworth stores in New York, many of them little more than girls, had joined a CIO union and gone on strike. Heywood Broun wrote about it in one of his columns, calling attention to the miserable pittance that the salesgirls were getting for a six-day week, and contrasted that with the fabulous fortune of Barbara Hutton, the Woolworth heiress. Barbara, or Babs, as she was known to the American public, was young and beautiful then, and her face, and love-life, were frequently featured in American newspapers.

A New York society columnist, feeling that Broun had been unfair to Ms. Hutton, came to her defense, pointing out that she was really a nice person and, to the columnist's personal knowledge, had given $11 million to charity.

That was all we needed. At one of our ACTU meetings at the Worker we discussed the strike, voted to support it, made up some crudely lettered signs, and went uptown to picket the big store on 14th Street, just a brick's throw from Union Square. One of our signs informed the world:

> BABS GAVE $11 MILLION TO CHARITY, BUT "THE WORKER IS NOT TO RECEIVE AS ALMS WHAT IS HIS DUE IN JUSTICE."
>
> Signed, POPE PIUS XI

Since this was the first time that the Pope had appeared on a picket line in the U.S., this made something of a sensation, even among the more jaded lefties over in Union Square.

That was then. This is now. I have given you this small slice of Catholic Worker and ACTU labor history to make several points that are relevant here today. Those points are:

> * Dorothy and the Catholic Worker movement, Peter Maurin excepted, and the ACTU, which grew out of the CW, gave wholehearted support to the labor movement at a critical stage in the history of that movement.
>
> * There is a strong case to be made for the claim that it was this kind of support, the spearhead of a whole movement on the part of lay and clerical members of the Catholic Church, that made labor a major player in the life of this country. In Europe, as Pius XI lamented, the Church lost the working class to the socialists and communists. That did not happen here. What happened here was that much of the Catholic working class remained Catholic but became middle class, not only in economic status, which wasn't so bad, but in attitude, which was.
>
> * Labor leaders began to think like the men they bargained with across the table. Business unionism replaced the crusading spirit of the 30s and 40s. Pragmatists like George Meany and Lane Kirkland replaced idealistic visionaries like Philip Murray and Walter Reuther. And the labor movement, which once represented over 30 percent of the work force, gradually shrunk to about half of that.

However, labor is still a movement of 15 million men and women. Irving Howe used to say that the labor movement is a sleeping giant, but it is still a giant, and we need a giant. And today there is evidence that the giant is waking up. John Sweeney, who looks like your favorite Irish uncle, has become president, and beneath that pink cheeked exterior lurks a real fighter and a man who is determined to restore the AFL-CIO to the role of a major player once again. He is doing it by organizing the unorganized and going out to march himself on picket lines all over the country. He has said, "We will extend to management the open hand of cooperation, but if the hand is brushed aside, it will turn into a fist." We are talking about non-violent belligerence, of course. After all, Leo XIII said that "Christians are born for combat."

Like the labor movement over the past 30 or 40 years, the Catholic Church in America has to a great extent gone from working class to middle class, as has the clergy, not only in economic standing, but also in attitudes. Of the hundreds of labor schools ACTU once ran, only one remains, that run by the Labor Guild of the Archdiocese of Boston, a somewhat more prudent offspring of the ACTU, which died in the late 60s about the time we Catholics were becoming middle class.

Like the labor movement, the Catholic Church has been something of a sleeping giant. But it is a giant, and we need a giant. You might say the same for the whole religious community of America, which still makes up a substantial majority of the population.

The Christian Coalition has been trying, with some success, to wake the religious giant and persuade it that Christian faith demands a vote for a conservative Republican. Another group is trying with some success to wake the giant. That group is the National Interfaith Committee for Worker Justice, which includes Catholics, Protestants, Jews and Muslims. Under the leadership of Kim Bobo, a dynamite organizer, a kind of Protestant Dorothy Day, the Committee has, over just the past two years, organized and brought together, under the umbrella of the Committee, interfaith organizations in 45 of the major and minor cities of the country, including Milwaukee.

I called Kim last Tuesday at the committee's headquarters in Chicago and urged her to get some of her literature up here so that those of you who might be interested could learn about the work of this excellent committee and, I hope, join up and lend it your support. At the Catholic Worker in Baton Rouge, Steve Donahue and Tim

Vining are setting a good example with their support of various labor struggles.

I would also hope that some of today's young CW's are moved by Dorothy's words to become directly involved in the labor movement as organizers, shop stewards, officers, editors, research directors.

We need a labor movement that is not only strong but wide awake, intelligent, progressive, visionary. We need it especially now because the rich are getting richer, more powerful, more greedy and more arrogant every day. At the same time, the workers are getting downsized and thrown out on the street in order to increase the profits of the rich. And the poor are getting poorer and more desperate every day, as their safety net is shredded by a president who sometimes looks more like a Republican than a Democrat.

We need Catholic Worker houses, farms and soup kitchens to feed the hungry and shelter the homeless. But we also need the things that only a strong labor movement can accomplish, such as the election of a president and a Congress that will pass legislation like the Living Wages, Jobs for All Act (HR 1050). This Act, now sponsored by 41 members of the House, led by the Minority Whip, a pro-life fighter named David Bonior, would provide jobs at living wages, job training, child care and health care so that when government insists that those welfare mothers go to work there will be jobs for them, the training to qualify them for those jobs, the child care and health care necessary to provide for themselves and their children.

It all starts with jobs and the recognition of the real right to work, for without decent jobs at decent pay there can be no right to life, liberty and the pursuit of happiness. And no just society.

"Jobs for All." There's a slogan that rings with great resonance in the inner ear and the lower bowels. Another slogan, "Tax the rich to employ the unemployed," rings with even greater resonance. Did you realize that Bill Gates alone is sitting on money bags worth $36.4 billion? One study has shown that this amount of money could fund for one year a federal job guarantee that would reduce unemployment to 2 percent! And Bill would still have $6 billion left over. Did you realize that the six richest families in America are sitting on $125.6 billion, and that would fund a federal job guarantee for four years?

Money is not the problem. This country has money coming out of its ears. Did you realize that under Republican presidents Eisenhower, Nixon and Ford the income tax on the very rich was 70 percent, and that if it was raised back up there, and if the loopholes were plugged and corporate welfare eliminated and defense spending reduced to a reasonable level, we could balance the budget in three years, get all our people working, including the teen-age mothers and the self-destructive fathers, make sure their children are properly cared for, get our cities and slums and environment cleaned up, provide some decent housing for the poor, fix our decaying infrastructure, get both black and white youth off the mean streets, and save our national soul.

Not a bad bargain. But first, in answer to Dorothy's appeal, we must build a strong, intelligent, progressive labor movement.

John Cort and Catholic Social Action since the New Deal

Paul Miller

Empire State College

This paper traces developments in Catholic social action from the 1930s to the 1960s. Building my narrative around a biography of John Cort, a former member of the Catholic Worker, I argue that after World War II Catholic interest in papal social reconstruction waned while Catholic activism made greater accommodations with secular liberal reform. Throughout the paper, when I use the term "Catholics," I am usually not speaking about all the members of the American Church, but those activists who applied Catholic social thought to problems like unemployment and poverty. During the Great Depression, these Catholics, guided by Pope Pius XI's encyclical *Quadragesimo Anno* (1931), unionized workers and promoted the Pope's vocational group plan. With post-World War II prosperity, however, they increasingly believed that liberalism could solve America's social problems. For Catholics and Americans in general, Keynesian economics and Great Society welfare programs promised to lift up the poor. Before and after World War II, these Catholics rejected the social philosophy of the Catholic Worker. Few believed that dispensing with modern industry and settling proletarians in agrarian communes was realistic. Still, historians have been more intrigued with the Catholic Worker, and we have few studies of Catholic social action since 1945.

The studies we have stress the Church's anti-communism. The issue of communism in the labor movement, according to Douglas Seaton and Steve Rosswurm, became an obsession with Catholics after 1945. Moreover, these authors claim that in the process of driving communists out of unions Catholics gave up their support for progressive social reform: "As purely negative anti-communism became all consuming to Catholic laborites, radicalism of any sort became increasingly suspect and pro-capitalism became a political and religious litmus test," writes Rosswurm (Rosswurm 1992: 120; Seaton 1981). Such an argument is untenable, however, given Catholic opposition during the 1940s and 1950s to the Taft-Hartley Act (1947) and state-sponsored right-to-work-laws.

Yet even sympathetic observers have tended to misinterpret the history of recent social Catholicism. For example, one scholar has claimed that 1950s and 1960s Catholic social action was merely an extension of programs conceived by Catholic progressives half a century earlier. Anthony Sean Pastor-Zelaya argues that "[in] order to interpret the development of social Catholicism during the New Deal and post-New Deal eras, one must explore the Catholic social gospel that emerged toward the end of the nineteenth century."(Pastor-Zelaya 1988) The problem with this argument is that it fails to acknowledge new trends after World War II, a watershed event in American and Catholic history. Post-1945 Catholics were just as conditioned by secular politics as other Americans. As a result, Catholic social thinking began to take on a more liberal cast. Catholic activists became solid Democrats. Few had even heard of *Quadragesimo Anno,* or the vocational group plan.

This was not true during the 1930s and 1940s when the vocational group plan was more popular among Catholics. In *Quadragesimo Anno,* Pius XI offered some principles concerning the vocational group idea that were intended to guide activists. Michael O'Shaughnessy, Raymond McGowan, and Edward Parsons, S.J. designed elaborate applications for America. The CIO's Phil Murray and John Brophy, however, submitted what most thought was the most practical application of the plan. Called the Industry Council Plan (ICP), Murray and Brophy's scheme established councils of labor, management, and the government in the defense industry. These councils were authorized to set wages and prices, decide working conditions, and settle shop-floor grievances. Supporters predicted that the ICP would increase industrial efficiency and avert strikes by giving labor a voice in the management of industry. Roosevelt, however, rejected the plan. Calls for the ICP continued throughout World War II, but declined sharply in the post-War years.

The reason was the huge economic boom that elevated labor into the middle class after 1945. Workers now had greater job security, union recognition, higher wages, and pensions. With prosperity, Catholics wondered if social reconstruction, even based on papal teachings, was desirable. One Catholic analyst offered a sober assessment of Catholic reconstruction in an age when secular politics brought such widespread abundance: "Since World War II, we have been living in an era in which American capitalism, even if not in theory the best of all possible worlds, seems in practice highly preferable to any but the most remote alternatives."(Ferkiss 1958: 30) As a result, Catholic social action in the 1950s and 1960s attacked racial injustice and poverty. In short, Catholic laborites left the union hall in the 1960s to join the Great Society's anti-poverty fight.

John Cort, a staunch Democrat and ICP advocate, played a complicated role in this transition. In the early post-World War II years he helped soothe Catholic-liberal relations, which had soured during the 1930s. He explained to fellow Catholics that liberals of good will, even if they did not believe in God, were part of an invisible sainthood. He also surprised Catholics by arguing that they were really more liberal than they might have guessed: "Any Catholic who really believes and practices the teachings of his Church must—of necessity and by definition be a liberal—in the sense of being concerned about justice between classes and races and between nations."(Cort 1950: 244) Cort's attitude indicated a new post-War Catholic pluralism that embraced American institutions. This weakened Catholic parochialism and opened Catholics up to mainstream social ideas.

While pro-liberal, Cort also remained faithful to papal-inspired forms of social reconstruction. Even when other Catholics questioned the relevancy of the social encyclicals, Cort still supported the Industry Council Plan. "It is now fashionable for Catholic liberals," he wrote, "to ignore encyclicals as exercises in irrelevance, but time was when they smote their enemies with them with all of the enthusiasm of Samson smiting the Philistines."(Cort 1976: 203) This was true, but Cort was describing a change that had taken place two decades before. Since the late 1940s, working-class Catholics had moved into the suburbs and begun enjoying some of the good life. For Catholic social action this seemed to obviate the need for radical social change. I explain Cort's reaction to this in more detail in the biographical portrait below.

John Cort was born in Woodmere, New York, a small town on Long Island, about twenty miles from New York City, on December 3, 1913. He was the last child in a family of five boys. His father, Ambrose, was a public school principal who spoke out against political corruption in the school department and was denied, his family believed, a promotion to superintendent. His mother, Lydia, a graduate of the New England Conservatory of Music, raised well-mannered boys with gentle tastes (Cort mss.: 5, 11).[1]

John was baptized and raised in the Episcopalian Church, but his family except perhaps for his mother, was plainly disdainful of organized religion. His father was a deist. His eldest brother, David, whom the other boys looked up to for his intellectual gifts, also had a strong bias against religion which John shared. Still, for reasons that are unclear, the boys attended church regularly and even sang in the choir. John had a fine soprano voice and received a scholarship to the Cathedral Choir School of St. John the Divine in New York City. He later attended Taft, a prep school in Connecticut, and enrolled at Harvard in the fall of 1931(Cort mss.: 9-10; McGowan 1961: 3-4).

Cort stunned his family during his junior year when he announced that he was converting to Catholicism. He later explained that his decision had been influenced by his freshman tutor, Paul Doolin. His father was furious and wrote the dean complaining about Doolin and threatened to pull him out of school. Cort, then, waited until after he graduated before being received into the Church (Cort mss.: 7; Cort 1987: 1-19).

Later in 1935 Cort was a young Catholic living in Boston and writing for a small newspaper. He was contemplating a career in journalism when, one Sunday after mass, someone handed him a copy of *The Catholic Worker.* After reading about other young Catholics performing the works of mercy, he helped out at the Boston Catholic Worker. He sold copies of the paper in his spare time and attended roundtable discussions at the Boston Campion headquarters on Washington Street. In April 1936, Dorothy Day came up from New York City to talk about St. Joseph's House of Hospitality. Cort arrived late. He was, however, so taken with Day's sense of humor and fun that he decided to join the Catholic Worker in New York City before she finished speaking. He asked Day, and she invited him to the Catholic Worker farm in Easton, Pennsylvania that summer. In the meantime, Cort turned down a job at WBZ radio. Cort worked at the farm for a month, then moved to St. Joseph's House, located on Mott Street, just north of Chinatown. There he helped feed the hungry and care for the sick while also reporting on the upheaval in the city's labor movement.[2]

The Catholic Worker and the country itself was then buzzing about the recent rash of CIO-led strikes. Day reported on strikes in the steel and auto industries. In Flint, Michigan, she wrote a dramatic account of the sit down strikers who allowed her into the captured plants. Cort was fascinated with these reports. He gleaned national papers for labor news and read all that he could find on labor history. He even took a job making brass cocktail trays to experience assembly line work. When seamen shut down the New York City docks, halting traffic on the Atlantic and Gulf coasts, Day set up a soup kitchen, where Cort ate and slept, around the corner from the strikers' headquarters.

Cort experienced his second conversion during the seamen's strike: to the labor movement. He talked with the men and learned about the hard life of a seaman. The shape-up, low wages, and corrupt union officials—these conditions were contrary to basic human dignity. Yet the Church which recognized the workers' right to organize was not on the docks showing its solidarity with the longshoremen. At this time Cort was also teaching a class on the papal letters and the labor movement and, inspired by one line from *Quadragesimo Anno,* he decided that Catholics had to play a more conspicuous role in the labor movement. He and ten other men, mostly trade unionists, met at the Catholic Worker to start an organization that would bring the Church to the labor movement (Cort mss.: 79-95; Bernstein 1971: 572-589).

These men founded the Association of Catholic Trade Unionists (ACTU) on February 27,1937. Put simply, ACTU's goal was to infuse the labor movement with Christian principles. Cort later credited a line from *Quadragesimo Anno* for the group's inspiration: "Side by side with these trade unions there must always be associations which aim at giving their members a thorough moral and religious training, that these in turn may impart to the unions to which they belong the upright spirit which directs their entire conduct." ACTU members, called Actists, knew working class families who had suffered fighting for union recognition. Martin Wersing and Ed Squitieri had known a Consolidated Edison employee who, after being fired for union organizing, killed himself leaving a wife and seven children (Cort 1939: 35).

Yet, it was the CIO itself that prompted Wersing, Squitieri and Cort. The CIO leadership talked about working class unity and transforming industrial relations. Cort could hardly contain his excitement: "The CIO will determine the future of the American labor movement and the American labor movement will determine the future of America," he wrote (Cort 1937). ACTU picketed with striking workers and advertised consumer boycotts. On street corners and at union meetings, Actists preached that the Church supported the workers' right to join an independent union. In case some Catholics had doubts, ACTU printed a weekly newspaper, *Labor Leader,* that contained long quotes from the Popes on labor and social reconstruction.

In 1938, while Americans anxiously waited for an upswing in the economy, the *Labor Leader* declared that what the country needed was not a National Regulatory Administration (NRA)[3] (ACTU 1937: 2) but the application of Pope Pius XI's vocational group plan: "We accept the program of our Popes and Bishops for the organization of industries and professions into national guilds for the self-regulation and self-government of the economy. We say that unlike NRA such a guild set-up must give labor equal representation with capital..." (ACTU 1938: 2) This view was typical of Catholic activists. While they supported the President—Cort endorsed Roosevelt in 1940, despite his "imperfections,"—most thought that some version of Pius' vocational group plan was the only way to ensure economic recovery and lasting social harmony (*Commonweal* 1940: 361). It was difficult, however, to convince liberals of this. Liberal-Catholic relations at the time were terribly strained. Liberals distrusted Catholic laborites. Catholics distrusted liberals, especially those sympathetic with the Spanish government which had executed priests and nuns and razed churches (McGreevy 1997: 97-131; Gleason 1994: 60-64;). Richard Rovere summarized liberal suspicions about Catholics in the labor movement in an article on the ACTU: "Catholics, like Communists, are often controlled by forces beyond the vision of most Americans; Rome, like Moscow, has its own interests..."(Rovere 1941: 13)

Meanwhile, Cort, who was diagnosed with tuberculosis, had to leave the Catholic Worker. By this time, however, the ACTU had become the center of his "hopes and ambitions."(Cort letter 1939) He explained to Day that trying to bring workers back to the land was hopeless. Day disagreed. She disputed the idea that a Christian form of industrialism was possible, and, years later, even rejected the Industry Council Plan: "We don't believe in those industrial councils," she wrote, "where the heads of United States Steel sit down with the common man in an obscene agape of luxury, shared profits, blood money from a thousand battles all over the world."(*CW* 11/1949: 2) Incredulous, Cort retorted in a letter that the Catholic Worker was "committing itself more and more to a position that can never in the world be reconciled with the [papal] encyclicals, or with the gospel or with natural law. On what Christian ground," he continued, "can you refuse to cooperate with employers who want to change their ways—assuming they do—and to bring some order and justice into the capitalist jungle."(Cort letter 1949) He had warned Joseph Zarrella, a friend at the Catholic Worker, that the ACTU-Catholic Worker split was inimical to the cause of Christ: "Satan has sown this disunity among us to prevent us from doing the more effective work for Christ that united we could certainly accomplish." (Cort letter 1940)

Cort, however, agreed with Day that the ACTU focused too much on bread-and-butter union issues without trying to bring more workers to Christ. He complained that ACTU should do more to Christianize the labor movement. When at one meeting he pointed to Jesus on the cross and remarked that what the group needed was more men willing to suffer like that, he was generally dismissed. Most Actists were basically interested in spreading democracy in the labor unions, and they thought that brother Cort was something of a dreamer who did not have much experience in union politics. Still, Cort tried to lead a revival of sorts within the ACTU using a technique known as *see–judge–act.* Developed by Father Joseph Cardijn, *see–judge–act,* which was more popular in Europe and Canada, involved small groups of Catholics resolving family and social problems by studying relevant passages from the Gospel. Cort formed a cell at the Newspaper Guild, but most Actists resisted what was perceived as a diversion from the more important task of educating and organizing workers. Disappointed, Cort lamented in a letter to Day around 1939 that he had failed to "make the ACTU what I—and you—wanted it to be."(Cort letter 1939; Zotti 1990: 387-400) [4]

The above letter was written from a Bronx hospital. Cort lay on his back for most of the next 12 years. He still, however, managed to edit the *Labor Leader and* write a regular labor column for *Commonweal.* By 1950 he was nearly recovered and moved his wife and family to Boston, where he became Executive Director of the Newspaper Guild. They choose to live in a lower working class area of the city, and Cort tried to form an ACTU-like group at the Boston Catholic Labor Guild. In 1962, Cort, now twice defeated for the

Massachusetts House, became Associate Director of a Peace Corps project in the Philippines. When he returned to Massachusetts two years later, Governor Endicott Peabody asked him to head the Commonwealth Service Corps, the state's anti-poverty initiative.

These years marked the high point of modern liberalism. Economic growth continued at a steady pace. Democrats and Republicans used Keynesian ideas about government spending to stimulate economic growth. A modest amount of public debt was then considered acceptable. The Great Society expanded the welfare state and even gave poor people a chance to run their own anti-poverty programs (Brinkley 1995: 267-269; Matusow 1984: 243-270).

Cort was a staunch liberal. His support for Keynesian economics at the time is evident. In his presidential address before the National Catholic Social Action Conference, in 1967, for example, he endorsed the Freedom Budget. Written by Leon Keyserling, the Freedom Budget intended to spend billions of dollars on anti-poverty, education, and other domestic programs. Cort's endorsement was couched in unmistakably liberal language, even citing the great Keynes himself:

> With the unemployed working for decent wages (lifting the minimum wage to $2.00 an hour is part of the program) millions of Americans would be making and spending billions of dollars more for food, clothing, housing, etc. This in turn would mean a further expansion of these industries, more wages for their workers, more purchasing power, so onward and upward in that lovely ascending spiral Lord Keynes taught us about some 30-odd years ago, but which so many of us still cannot bring ourselves to accept. (Cort 1967)

Cort, however, still pushed for the ICP. He was frustrated with Catholics who ignored it. Why, Cort complained, did Catholic activists not protest the dissolution of labor–management committees after World War II: "For some reason, the Catholic element in the labor movement, which should have been the most interested, has shown an outstanding lack of enthusiasm for this American expression of the encyclicals."(Cort 1954)

Elsewhere, Catholics cared less about social reconstruction, even the vocational group plan. With the post-World War II economic boom, there was greater confidence in liberalism to redistribute wealth and end poverty. Like the Keynesians, Catholic activists believed that with the economy operating at or near maximum capacity, the poor would eventually be lifted up into the middle class. Benjamin Masse, labor editor at *America,* underscored Catholic interest in the "New Economics": "Though economic growth itself may not change the social fabric or the pattern of income distribution, it does assure a bigger pie—with bigger pieces for everyone, the poor as well as the rich. In fact, in a system that combines political democracy and private economic enterprise, a growing economy is generally considered an absolutely essential condition for a successful war on poverty." (Masse 1966) Few Catholics now talked about industrial councils. The U.S. Catholic bishops, who have not referred to the vocational group plan since 1948, in the 1950s and 1960s spoke out against racial segregation and endorsed Great Society anti-poverty legislation (U.S. Bishops 1984: 91). Looking back on a long career in social activism, John F. Cronin, S.S., explained the reason for the demise of the vocational group plan: "Interest in [*Quadragesimo Anno*] and in social action began waning in the United States during the 1950s. The rather sustained surge in economic growth after World War II and the Korean war left many of us with the illusion that our major problems were solved."(Cronin 1971: 317; Greeley 1958)

The marriage between Catholicism and social liberalism was consummated, according to Jay Dolan, in the late 1950s (Dolan 1992: 407).

Yet, since the 1970s, we have seen a gradual erosion of Catholic-liberal relations. "Social" issues such as abortion, feminism, and homosexual rights have weakened Catholic ties to liberal politicians. Recently, the stand of Clinton Democrats toward welfare reform has further alienated progressive Catholics from the Democratic party. John Cort, however, is still a stalwart Democrat, committed to moving the party to the left as a member of Democratic Socialists of America. Others in the Catholic left might turn to third party candidates, the Greens, for example, or abandon politics completely. The Catholic Worker movement, still the outstanding example of a Catholic counter-culture, eschews formal party politics. Regardless, John Cort's life should interest today's activists who are involved in creative efforts at social change at a time when the liberal state, created at the start of John Cort's career, is being torn down.

Acknowledgement

The author thanks his wife, Elizabeth, and sister, Anne, for assistance with research and editing.

Notes

[1] *New York Times* February 18, 1928: 2; Cort letter to author September 28, 1995.

[2] *The Brookline Citizen* October 4 and 25, 1935. Rosalie R. Troester interview with John Cort, Roxbury, MA, June 13, 1988, Dorothy Day–Catholic Worker Collection, Marquette University, Series W-9, Box 3. Cort to the Catholic Worker, February 23, 1936; Cort to Dorothy Day, May 1, 1936; Dorothy Day–Catholic Worker Collection, Series W-2.1, Box 2. Esso Reporter at WBZ from author's interview with Cort, August 9 1996. Cort articles: "Period of Strife and Suffering for Farm and Factory," *The Catholic Worker* (September 1936): 1,4. "Globe Strikers Cause is Right, Strike is Wrong," *The Catholic Worker* (November 1936): 1,3.

[3] Editor's note: the acronym NRA can be confusing because it was used for several depression-era federal programs; perhaps the best known is the National Recovery Administration (1933), which created the National Industrial Recovery Act (1935). This NRA, the National Regulatory Administration, came when Americans were increasingly concerned about the massive intervention of the federal government into the economy.

[4] Author interviews with George R. Donahue, Brooklyn, New York, May 5, 1996, and with John C. Cort, Nahant, MA, August 9, 1996.

Dorothy Day and the Transformation of Work: Lessons for Labor

David L. Gregory

St. John's University

Dorothy Day, Peter Maurin and the members of the Catholic Worker movement practiced what they preached. Day consistently emphasized the dignity and the importance of work while encouraging the solidarity of labor with the unemployed, and ever-present poor; an approach reflecting both Depression-era realities, and perhaps even more compelling, the Catholic Church's preferential option for the poor. Dorothy's writing was eloquent and her personal commitment to, and solidarity with, workers was magnificent. In her autobiography, *The Long Loneliness*, Day recounted how her awareness of labor issues first emerged during her college years:

> There was Eugene Debs. There were the Haymarket martyrs who had been "framed" and put to death in Chicago in 1887. They were martyrs! They had died for a cause.
>
> There had been in the past the so-called "Molly Maguires" in the coal fields, a terrorist organization, and the Knights of Labor, made up of union men working for the eight-hour day and the cooperative system. My heart thrilled at those unknown women in New England who led the first strike to liberate women and children from the cotton mills.
>
> Already in this year 1915 great strides had been taken. In some places the ten-hour day and increased wages had been won. But still only about 8 per cent of the workers were organized, and the great mass of workers throughout the country were ground down by poverty and insecurity. What work there was to be done! (Day 1959: 44-45)

In recounting her first experiences as a journalist with the socialist paper, the *New York Call*, Dorothy noted her ever-increasing awareness of the labor union movement and the major players within it, including the American Federation of Labor, the Industrial Workers of the World, and the newly formed Congress of Industrial Organizations (C.I.O.), whose members were said to be the remainder of the larger group which had signed up with the "reds."(Day 1959: 52) Dorothy Day's first signs of a maturing labor consciousness, thus, were initially formed far from the contours of Catholic teaching or the influence of the Catholic Church. In her autobiography she summarized these early social influences on her thought:

> I wavered between my allegiance to socialism, syndicalism (the I.W.W.'s) and anarchism.
>
> When I read Tolstoi, I was an anarchist. Ferrer with his schools, Kropotkin with his farming communes, the I.W.W.'s with their solidarity, their unions, these all appealed to me.... The I.W.W. had an immediate program for America so I signed up with them.
>
> I do not remember any antireligious articles in the *Call*.... []I was surprised to find many quotations from *Rerum Novarum* of Pope Leo XIII and a very fair exposition of the Church's social teachings. I paid no attention to it at the time. Catholics were a world apart, a people within a people, making little impression on the tremendous non-Catholic population of the country.
>
> There was no attack on religion because people were generally indifferent to religion. They were neither hot nor cold. They were the tepid, the materialistic, who hoped that by Sunday churchgoing they would be taking care of the afterlife, if there were an afterlife. Meanwhile they would get everything they could in this.
>
> On the other hand, the Marxists, the I.W.W's who looked upon religion as the opiate of the people, who thought they had only this one life to live and then oblivion—they were the ones who were eager to sacrifice themselves here and now, thus doing without now and for all eternity the good things of the world which they were fighting to obtain for their brothers. It was then, and still is, a paradox that confounds me. (Day 1959: 60-61)

After her conversion, Dorothy Day began writing for *Commonweal* and other Catholic periodicals. In December 1932, a piece she wrote about the Hunger March in Washington, DC, appeared in the Jesuit publication *America*. She recalled the demonstration in her autobiography:

On a bright sunny day the ragged horde triumphantly with banners flying, with lettered slogans mounted on sticks, paraded three thousand strong through the tree-flanked streets of Washington. I stood on the curb and watched them, joy and pride in the courage of this band of men and women mounting in my heart, and with it a bitterness too that since I was now a Catholic, with fundamental philosophical differences, I could not be out there with them. I could write, I could protest, to arouse the conscience, but where was the Catholic leadership in the gathering of bands of men and women together, for the actual works of mercy that the comrades had always made part of their technique in reaching the workers?....

The demands of the marchers were for social legislation, for unemployment insurance, for old-age pensions, for relief for mothers and children, [and] for work. I remember seeing one banner on which was inscribed, "Work, not wages," a mysterious slogan having to do with man's dignity, his ownership of and responsibility for the means of production. (Day 1959: 160-161)

In reflecting on her early work, Dorothy experienced shame and remorse over her abstraction, her absence of solidarity, and her detachment from workers:

How little, how puny my work had been since becoming a Catholic, I thought. How self-centered, how ingrown, how lacking in sense of community! My summer of quiet reading and prayer, my self-absorption seemed sinful as I watched my brothers in their struggle, not for themselves but for others, How our dear Lord must love them, I kept thinking to myself. They were His friends, His comrades, and who knows how close to His heart in their attempt to work for justice. (Day 1959: 161)

It was in that galvanizing epiphany experience that Dorothy Day's labor and social consciousness as a Catholic was fused, rejuvenated, and revivified in a new, different, transforming way. She poignantly recounted

When the demonstration was over and I had finished writing my story, I went to the national shrine at the Catholic University on the Feast of the Immaculate Conception. There I offered up a special prayer, a prayer which came with tears and with anguish, that some way would open up for me to use what talents I possessed for my fellow workers, for the poor.

> As I knelt there, I realized that after three years of Catholicism my only contact with active Catholics had been through articles I had written for one of the Catholic magazines. Those contacts had been brief, causal. I still did not know personally one Catholic layman. (Day 1959: 161-162)

The first issue of *The Catholic Worker*, printed on May 1, 1933, gave Day the opportunity she desired. Dorothy described the solidarity of *The Catholic Worker* as follows: "*The Catholic Worker*, as the name implied, was directed to the worker, but we used the word in its broadest sense, meaning those who worked with hand or brain, those who did physical, mental or spiritual work. But we thought primarily of the poor, the dispossessed, the exploited."(Day 1959: 199-200) This posture was evident from the start. One of the articles appearing in the first edition addressed the exploitation of African-American labor in the South. The second issue focused on farmer strikes in the Midwest and the poor working conditions of restaurant workers in urban areas. The third issue dealt with textile strikes, and child labor in the textile industry. The fourth issue dealt with strikes in the coal and milk industries (Day 1959: 201).

The Catholic Worker movement also gave Day the opportunity to really become an integral part of the stories she and her colleagues had been writing. Throughout the volatile period of labor organizing which accompanied the Great Depression, Dorothy Day constantly supplemented her journalistic efforts in *The Catholic Worker* by physically joining workers at job sites and on picket lines. In 1934, Dorothy and other Catholic Workers directly practiced the labor solidarity which the paper urged by picketing the Ohrbach Department Store in Manhattan, side by side with the store's own striking employees. Day recalled

> [T]here was mass picketing every Saturday afternoon during the Ohrbach strike, and every Saturday the police drove up with patrol wagons and loaded the pickets into them with their banners and took them to jail. When we entered the dispute with our slogans drawn from the writings of the popes regarding the condition of labor, the police around Union Square were taken aback and did not know what to do. It was as though they were arresting the Holy Father himself, one of them said, were they to load our pickets and their signs into their patrol wagons. The police contented themselves with giving us all injunctions. One seminarian who stood on

> the side lines and cheered was given an injunction too, which he cherished as souvenir. (Day 1959: 201-202)

"The most spectacular help" Dorothy Day and the Catholic Worker gave to assist a strike was through providing housing and food to strikers during the formation of the National Maritime Workers Union in May, 1936:

> The seamen came and went and most of them we never saw again....For the duration of the strike we rented a store on Tenth Avenue and used it as a reading room and a soup kitchen where no soup was served, but coffee and peanut butter and apple butter sandwiches. The men came in from picket lines and helped themselves to what they needed. They read, they talked, and they had time to think. (Day 1959: 204)

Day and others went to Pittsburgh "to write about the work in the steel districts," and to cover the organizing drives by the Congress of Industrial Organizations (Day 1959: 205). On another occasion, the group directly supported a dairy workers strike. According to Day, "when the Borden Milk Company attempted to force a company union on their workers, *The Catholic Worker* took up their cause, called public attention to the use of gangsters and thugs to intimidate the drivers and urged our readers to boycott the company's products while unfair conditions prevailed." Day also reported that she "spoke to meetings of the unemployed in California, to migrant workers, tenant farmers, steelworkers, stockyard workers, [and] auto workers."(Day 1959: 208)

With the support of the Archbishop of Detroit, who urged her to "go to them, to write about them," Dorothy travelled to Flint, Michigan to cover a sit-down strike being staged in a number of General Motors' factories there. Speaking of the Archbishop, Day wrote, "He had one of his priests reserve and pay for a Pullman berth for me so I would be fresh the next day for my work....I visited strike headquarters during the Little Steel strike and talked with the men."(Day 1959: 213-214) For more than two decades, beginning in 1937, the Catholic Worker was the intellectual home for the Association of Catholic Trade Unionists (Troester 1993: 12-13). At its zenith, the Association maintained fourteen chapters and one hundred labor schools, most of which were concentrated in New York and Detroit. Perhaps Dorothy's most direct advocacy on behalf of labor was her challenge to Cardinal Francis Spellman, Archbishop of New York. In 1949, the unionized "grave diggers of Calvary Cemetery, [represented by] Local 293 of the International Food, Tobacco and Agricultural Workers Union, went on strike against their employer, the trustees of St. Patrick Cathedral, principal among whom was Cardinal Spellman."(Miller 1982: 404) The strike continued for over a month, until it was crushed by the Cardinal, who personally ordered and led his seminarians into the cemetery as replacement workers (Miller 1982: 223). Cardinal Spellman stated that the strike was "communist inspired," and that he was "proud and happy to be a strike breaker."(Miller 1982: 404) He said "his resistance to the strike was `the most important thing I have done in my ten years in New York." While he eventually broke the strike, Dorothy Day and the Catholic Worker bore profound and direct witness to his egregious repudiation of Catholic social teaching on the rights of workers. Dorothy Day had decided that "the strike was justified," and members of the Catholic Worker joined striking workers on the picket line at the cemetery. Cardinal Spellman and Dorothy Day, in spite of, or perhaps because of this confrontation, had deep respect for one another, strengthened by Dorothy Day's manifest practices as a Catholic in impeccably good theological standing (Miller 1982: 405). She was theologically and liturgically traditional, while radical in her social justice activism. She once stated, "When it comes to labor and politics...I am inclined to be sympathetic to the left, but when it comes to the Catholic Church, then I am far to the right."(Troester 1993: 63)

Dorothy, called to witness, confronted the Cardinal directly, and she made real and living the Catholic Church's powerful and eloquent social teaching on the rights of workers. She later said of the strike

> [It] "could have been headed off in the very beginning. The trustees could have shown the books to the workers if justice was on their side, proven in black and white that they were incapable of paying what the strikers asked. . . ." It was "all yesterday's news now, those strikers who had to drop their life insurance because they couldn't meet payments." The "terrible significance" of the strike was that "here in our present peaceful New York, a Cardinal, ill-advised, exercised so overwhelming a show of force against a handful of poor working men." (Miller 1982: 405)

Day wrote a very eloquent letter to Cardinal Spellman on March 4, 1949.

> I am deeply grieved to see the reports...of your leading Dunwoodie seminarians into Calvary cemetery, past picket lines, to "break the strike."...Of course you know that a group of our associates at the Catholic Worker office in New York, have been helping the strikers, both in providing food for their families, and in picketing....[Y]ou have been misinformed. I am writing to you, because this strike, though small, is a terribly significant one in a way. Instead of people being able to say of us "see how they love one another," and "behold, how good and how pleasant it is for brethren to dwell together in unity" now "we have become a reproach to our neighbors an object of derision and mockery to those about us." It is not just the issue of wages and hours as I can see from the conversations which our workers have had with the men. It is a question of their dignity as men, their dignity as workers, and the right to have a union of their own, and a right to talk over their grievances. It is no use going into the wages, or the offers that you have made for a higher wage (but the same work week). A wage such as the Holy Fathers have talke[d] of which would enable the workers to raise and educate their families of six, seven and eight children, a wage which would enable them to buy homes, to save for such ownership, to put by for the education of the children,—certainly the wage which they have in these days of high price prices [sic] and exhorbitant [sic] rents, is not the wage for which they are working. Regardless of what the board of trustees can afford to pay, the wage is small compared to the wealth of the men represented on the board of trustees[.] The way the workers live is in contrast to the way of living of the board of trustees....Regardless of rich and poor, the class antagonisms which exist between the well-to-do, those who live on Park [A]venue and Madison [A]venue and those who dig the graves in the cemetery,—regardless of these contrasts, which are most assuredly there, the issue is always one of the dignity of the workers. It is a world issue. (DD-CW, W-6.2, Box 1)

Even near the end of her life, Dorothy Day continued her commitment of physical presence with the organization of workers.

> Her last major adventure came in August, 1973, when she went to the San Joaquin Valley in California to join Cesar Chavez's United Farm Workers in its demonstration against the Teamsters Union.

> In her support of Chavez and the Mexican itinerant workers, she, along with a thousand-or-so others, was arrested and briefly jailed. "If it weren't a prison, it would be a nice place to rest," she commented. (Miller 1982: 500)

From a lifetime of fifty years of direct and immediate solidarity with workers and with the poor, Dorothy Day wrote of the absolute imperative of the fusion of labor practice and labor theory.

> Going around and seeing such sights is not enough. To help the organizers, to give what you have for relief, to pledge yourself to voluntary poverty for life so that you can share with your brothers is not enough. One must live with them, share with them their suffering too. Give up one's privacy, and mental and spiritual comforts as well as physical....
>
> We have lived with the unemployed, the sick, the unemployables. The contrast between the worker who is organized and has his union, the fellowship of his own trade to give him strength, and those who have no organization and come in to us on a breadline is pitiable.....
>
> Going to the people is the purest and best act in Christian tradition and revolutionary tradition and is the beginning of world brotherhood. (Day 1959: 210-211)

The struggle for workers' dignity must be perpetual and incessant. Although the poor will always be with us, Dorothy Day reminds us, by her personal witness, to struggle valiantly to improve the status of workers everywhere:

> In the labor movement every strike is considered a failure, a loss of wages and man power, and no one is ever convinced that understanding between employer and worker is any clearer or that gains have been made on either side; and yet in the long history of labor, certainly there has been a slow and steady bettering of conditions. Women no longer go down into the mines, little children are not fed into the mills. In the long view the efforts of the workers have achieved much. (Day 1959: 212)

Throughout her half century of direct personal commitment to workers, throughout a half century of participation in labor strikes and solidarity on picket lines, Dorothy Day always kept in mind the dignity of all persons—including the employees, with an emphasis on peace and conciliation, and the imperative of charity, decency, and kindness to all.

Her March 4, 1949 letter to Cardinal Spellman, urging him to negotiate with the graveyard workers rather than break their strike, perhaps best and certainly most poignantly summarizes her practice and her theory.

> You are a Prince in the Church, and a great man in the eyes of the world, and these your opponents are all little men, hard working, day laborers, hard handed and hard headed men, filled with their grievances, an accumulation of their grievances. They have wanted to talk to you, they have wanted to appeal to you. The[y] felt that surely their Cardinal would not be against them. And oh, I do beg you so, with all my heart, to go to them, as a father to his children; do not go to a court, do not perpetuate a fight, for ages and ages. Go to them, conciliate them. It is easier for the great to give in than the poor. They are hungry men, their only weapon has been their labor, which they have sold for a means of livelihood, to feed themselves and their families. They have indeed labored with the sweat of their brows, not lived off the sweat of anyone else. They have trully [sic] worked, they have been poor, they are suffering now. Any union organizer will tell you that it is not easy to get men out on strike and it is not easy to keep them out on strike. But the grievance has grown, the anger has grown here. If there were only some way to reach peace. I am sure that the only way is for you to go to them. You have been known to walk the streets among your people, and to call on the poor parishes in person, alone and unattended. Why cannot you go to the union, ask for the leaders, tell them that as members of the mystical body, all members are needed and useful and that we should not quarrel together, that you will meet their demands, be their servant as Christ was the servant of [H]is disciples, washing their feet. (DD-CW, W-6.2, Box 1)

Because of her personal witness, commitment and solidarity with workers everywhere, whether expressed on picket lines or in her newspaper, Dorothy Day's lessons for labor have profound practical and theoretical significance. It is to her theory of labor that we will now turn.

The Labor Theory of Dorothy Day

Because of her unequivocal and courageous personal commitment to literally walk the picket lines with striking workers and to be a member of the labor community in this most real and dramatic way, Dorothy Day's theory of labor has special resonance and genuine meaning. Like her personal philosophies regarding the role and rights of workers, Day's conceptualization of labor theory is best articulated and appreciated through her articles appearing in *The Catholic Worker*, which she edited from its founding on May 1, 1933. When *The Catholic Worker* was founded, the United States was in the depths of the Great Depression. Dorothy's statements on labor throughout the period reflect a rich, complex and sophisticated mind (Roberts 1984: 1). They also reflect, at least equally, and perhaps in an even more compelling way, her deep, personal and lifelong commitment to workers as human beings. Day's essays and columns in *The Catholic Worker* from1933 until the immediate post-World War II period of the late 1940s best reflect her fused praxis and theory.

From its inception, *The Catholic Worker* focused upon the universal world of work. Of the view of one of its co-founders, Day noted, "In Peter's [Maurin] vision, work is a *gift*. Given for the common good,—And the reason why one works is to share gifts and talents, in common with others, to help create a better kind of society." (Troester 1993: 104) Emphasizing the "catholicity" of the paper, in both the religious and universal sense of that word, *The Catholic Worker* sought the unity of workers (Troester 1993: 104-105). In a direct, working class language the newspaper promulgated to workers the social teaching of the Catholic Church, a social justice language that is thoroughly integrative and truly universal: "We try to stress the duty of the worker towards God and himself first of all. And the Catholic neglects those duties when he does not work for social justice."(*CW* 11/1934: 4) *The Catholic Worker* unsparingly criticized the aristocracy of organized labor, repudiated the influences of atheistic communism within labor, and thoroughly condemned the materialism of the capitalist ownership elites:

> One of the difficulties of the labor movement in the United States is that there has been an aristocracy of labor, union men getting high wages in various trades, and ignoring their poorer comrades who have not had the benefits of unionization such as in the textile and mining fields. There is graft and racketeering in labor organi-

> zations which has justly prejudiced not only the employer but the poorer worker against them so that they are more willing very often to accept the radical trade unions than they are the old established ones. There is always a rank and file fight going on against existing trade unions and their technique. (*CW* 11/1934: 4)

Throughout *The Catholic Worker* essays is an ongoing call for pride and care in work on the part of each individual worker:

> I agree too that the attitude of the worker towards his labor is not correct. There is a loss of pride in craftsmanship which is due to the mechanization of industry. Pride in doing to the best of one's ability the work that God has given him to do, is a lesson which the American worker will have to relearn. (*CW* 11/1934: 4)

The organized labor union was a major focus of Day's attention throughout the years of her advocacy. Wherever possible, Dorothy Day urged Catholic employees to strengthen the Catholic solidarity between one another by seeking each other out both within the union structure and outside of it, in the non-unionized workplace. She pointed to a third and better path, transcending both atheistic Marxism and capitalist materialism, to which members of labor unions in a capitalist political economy could look to attempt to solve the problems of society. In her February, 1936 *Catholic Worker* column, she stated

> *The Catholic Worker* does not believe that unions, as they exist today in the United States, are an ideal solution for the social problem, or for any part of it.
>
> We do believe that they are the only efficient weapon which workers have to defend their rights as individuals and Christians against a system which makes the Christ-life practically impossible for large numbers of workers. We believe that Catholic workers must use unions in their efforts to heed the exhortations of the Popes to "de-proletarianize" the workers. (For we too are working toward a classless society, one in which all may become owners, instead of none as the Marxian would have it, or only the ruthless few as capitalism decrees.)
>
> In this measure unions are a form of propaganda for more constructive measures toward a truly Catholic social order. As Pius XI has said in speaking of the work of Catholic unions and of Catholics in unions: "Thus they prepare the way for a Christian renewal of the whole social life." (*CW* 2/1936: 4)

Unions must be autonomous and independent, with each individual constituent member contributing to the collective common good. In language eerily prescient of the contemporary debate regarding whether to repeal section 8(a)(2) of the National Labor Relations Act, Dorothy stated

> It seems obvious that a union instigated and controlled by the company, whose officers are paid for their "union work" by the company, is not likely to meet with success in gaining these benefits for the workers.
>
> It should be obvious, too, that a union cannot function effectively in an "open shop"—a plant where the union represents only some of the men, and where the company is at liberty to hire non-union men. Such a condition means that the presence of men who will have no protection in the event of wage-cutting or any form of exploitation will act as an obstacle to union efforts and will tend to lower the general wage level. (*CW* 2/1936: 7)

She particularly emphasized the critical importance of a collective consciousness:

> There must... be a sacrifice of individual freedom for the common good. We regret that, in the present instance of the Borden [milk company strike] dispute, we have found some Catholics both too short sighted to see the advantages of organization to the workers as a whole, and unwilling to make the sacrifices or take the risks involved in fulfilling their duty of charity.
>
> We believe it is the duty of every Catholic worker to inform himself of the Church's teaching on labor, and to strive for the common good of himself and his fellow workers by applying them to labor situations in which he may be involved....
>
> We believe that strikes are a grave danger to the common good, and that we as Catholics have a duty to use every means in our power to prevent them.(*CW* 2/1936: 7)

The Catholic Worker always focused on the international human rights dimension of unionization. In a September 1937 page one article, *The Catholic Worker* emphasized

> *The Catholic Worker* is a workingman's paper which is published to bring Catholic social principles to the workers in industry, to men and women and young people in mills, in factories, in mines

> and lumber camps, on ships that sail all over the world, and on docks where men unload those ships. *The Catholic Worker* is not a local paper. It doesn't just go to the workers in New York, where it is published, but goes all over the United States and Canada and even all over the world.....
>
> Our paper is addressed especially to Catholics, because we are Catholics, and because a great number of the workers of this country, those who have come from the other side as well as those whose families have been here for generations, are Catholics. We are all Catholics first of all, whether we are French or Irish, Lithuanian or Italian. Nationalities make no difference. Catholic principles remain the same. And the Church has a great deal to say about these principles in regard to the rights and duties of labor. Your right and your duty to organize, to join a union, is an elementary right, a natural right, but it is also a duty. As long ago as 1891 Pope Leo XIII wrote a great letter to labor in which he told the workers of the world that the only way to better their position was to organize into unions so that they could achieve better wages and hours of labor, better working conditions, and the right to be recognized as men, creatures of body and soul, temples of the Holy Ghost.
>
> Pope Pius XI followed that great letter on labor by another one in 1931 when he repeated all Leo XIII had said and pointed out again in even stronger terms the duty as well as the right of labor to organize. He wanted the workers to have such good salaries that they could save enough to buy homes, to educate their children, and to put by for their old age. He wanted them to have enough even so that they could buy a share in industry, so that they could become part owners and share in the responsibilities of industry. *(CW* 9/1937: 1)

The Catholic Worker emphasized the imperative of collective action, not for its own sake, but for the ultimate enhancement of human dignity.

> We all know that by himself, the worker can do very little. He has to join into association with his fellows in order to have the strength to meet with his employer and to bargain collectively.
>
> As Catholics we do not like especially that word "bargain." It assumes that labor is a community [sic] to be sold by the worker at the highest possible price, and to be bought by the employer at the lowest possible price. It degrades labor and takes away from it the

> dignity it has as a vocation as well as a task by which we earn our daily bread.
>
> We would rather say that labor must organize so that they will have the strength to make their voice heard, not only by the employer but by the public. So that they can bring pressure to bear, if needs be on the employer, to force him by this moral pressure to give better conditions to the workers.
>
> Without this combined strength the worker can get nowhere. He must join with others to form a union to better his condition. (*CW* 9/1937: 1)

Thus, the labor union is more than a means of organizing the workplace and benefitting those who return to the job site each day; it has the additional imperative of seeking broader social justice. Day elaborated on this point:

> If you have a strong union and good conditions in one town, you would have to help another town achieve those same conditions, by both moral and physical support. And only a national organization can do this.
>
> As Catholics you certainly ought to realize the necessity to work as a body. You are all members of the Mystical Body of Christ and St. Paul's saying was that when one member suffers, the health of the whole body is lowered. If some of you, in other words, are satisfied with your wages and hours, you have no right to sit back and be comfortable while great masses of workers are suffering under deplorable conditions—poor wages that are not sufficient to maintain a family and keep them in decent health, let alone afford them education and other needs. As long as the great mass of workers have to live in unsanitary, unheated tenements, no one has a right to his comfort while his brother is in misery. (*CW* 9/1937: 2)

Throughout, *The Catholic Worker* continually emphasized the example of Christ as worker and his solidarity with, and position as liaison to, the poor:

> Christ was a worker Himself, and He set an example to us all. He was a worker and He loved the workers. The last words He said to His disciples, the last commandment He gave them, which comprised all the rest, was that we were to love one another. We cannot, in other words, love God unless we love our neighbor. And if we love our neighbor, we have to show our love by trying to help him.

> Of ourselves we can do nothing. We must band together, and with God's help, fight for better conditions for the workers throughout the country, not only in one town. If we are not working together, we are denying Christ and His poor. And He said, "inasmuch as you have not done it unto the least of these my brethren, you have not done it unto me." He was talking then of ministering to others, and seeing to it that they have food and drink, and visitors when they were in prison or sick in the hospital. An association of workers can do these things for each other. (*CW* 9/1938: 2)

Solidarity with, liaisons to, and preferential options for the poor have long been essential elements of Catholic social teaching. Jesus Christ is the source of these teachings, through His life and many parables on themes of wealth and poverty. In the social justice encycicals of the modern Papacy, the fetishisms and pathologies of gross materialism are uniformly and severely criticized, and solidarity with the poor is powerfully urged. Pope John Paul II's consistent exhortations against materialism and for the poor are grounded in *Rerum Novarum* (1891) the first great social encyclical of Pope Leo XIII, who wrote, "the poor and unfortunate seem to be especially favored by God." The 1971 Synod of Bishops echoed this theme in their document, *Justice in the World*, a theme repeatedly articulated and affirmed by the Catholic bishops of the United States in 1986 in their pastoral letter, *Economic Justice for All.*

Perhaps Dorothy Day's greatest synthesis of her labor theory was set forth in the June 1939 issue of *The Catholic Worker*, in an essay entitled "*The Catholic Worker* and Labor." The emphasis throughout was on the example of Christ, and the teaching of the Church through the great social and labor encyclicals of 1891 and 1931:

> We are not only urging the necessity for organization to all workers...but [are] also stressing over and over again the dignity of labor, the dignity of the person a creature composed of body and soul made in the image and likeness of God, and a Temple of the Holy Ghost. It is on these grounds that we fight the speed-up system in the factory, it is on these grounds that we work toward de-proletarianizing the worker, working toward a share in the ownership and responsibility.
>
> We pointed out again and again that the issue is not just one of wages and hours, but of ownership and of the dignity of man. It is not State ownership toward which we are working, although we believe that some industries should be run by the government for

> the common good, it is a more widespread ownership through cooperative ownership. (*CW* 6/1939: 1)

The immediate post-World War II era saw an increasing sophistication and awareness of the corroding effects of industrial production on the human psyche. These trends became increasingly evident to Catholic Workers as did the themes which drove them. However, no attempt to commercialize the newspaper was made. *The Catholic Worker* continued to be sold for a penny and Dorothy Day's theory of labor never became idealized or romanticized beyond the hard lessons of the Christian Gospel. In fact, Day took great pains to expose the false romanticism that upper middle class, distanced intellectuals often attached to organized labor:

> I wish to fling down the challenge at once, that what is the great disaster is that priests and laity alike have lost the concept of work, they have lost a philosophy of labor, as Peter Maurin has always said. They have lost the concept of work, and those who do not know what work in the factory is, have romanticized both it and the workers....(*CW* 9/1946: 1)

Mass production de-emphasized the role of the individual, and compelled one to submit oneself to a dehumanizing work process. This was the reality of the industrial assembly line era and the newspaper warned its readers against the growing false consciousness:

> In the great clean shining factories, with good lights and air and the most sanitary conditions, an eight-hour day, five-day week, with the worker chained to the belt, to the machine, there is no opportunity for sinning as the outsider thinks of sin. No, it is far more subtle than that, it is submitting oneself to a process which degrades, dehumanizes. To be an efficient factory worker, one must become a hand, and the more efficient one is, the less one thinks. Take typewriting, for instance, as an example. . . or driving a car, or a sewing machine. These machines may be considered good tools, an extension of the hand of man. We are not chained to them as to a belt, but even so, we all know that as soon as one starts to think of what one is doing, we slip and make mistakes. One IS NOT SUPPOSED TO THINK. TO THINK is dangerous at a machine. One is liable to lose a finger or a hand, and then go on the scrap heap and spend the rest of one's life fighting for compensation for one's own carelessness, as the factory owners say, for not using the safety devices invented and so plentiful.

> AND HERE IS THE DANGEROUS PART, it is not so much the loss of the hand or the arm, but the loss of one's soul. When one gives one's self up to one's work, when one ceases to think and becomes a machine himself, the devil enters in. We cannot lose ourselves in our work without grave danger. (*CW* 9/1946: 1,3)

Dorothy Day shattered romanticism; she urged reality, and professed that, in reforming reality, ideals can be envisioned and perhaps even achieved:

> Yes, I accused the leaders, the teachers, the intellectuals, the clergy, of having a romantic attitude towards the workers. They write with fervor and glowing words—they dramatize the struggle, they are walking on picket lines, they love the man in the dungarees and the blue or plaid shirt, they write glowingly of his calloused hands—they take these leaves from the communist notebook—they are glorifying the proletariat, the dispossessed, the propertyless, the homeless, and the workers can hang a holy medal on their machine, or over their bunk in the fo'castle and pray as they begin and finish their work and go home to their two-room or three-room apartment and surrounded by children and an exhausted wife, sanctify their surroundings—or forget them in the nearest tavern with polluted beer, adulterated wine or hard liquor....
>
> In 1939, in an address to the International Congress of Catholic Women's League, the Holy Father said: "In this age of mechanization the human person becomes merely a more perfect tool in industrial production and how sad it is to say it, a perfected tool for mechanized warfare. And at the same time material and ready-made amusement is the only thing which stirs and sets the limits to the aspirations of the masses.. . . In this disintegration of human personality efforts are being made to restore unity. *But the plans proposed are vitiated from the start because they set out from the self same principle as the evil they intend to cure. The wounds and bruises of individualistic and materialistic mankind cannot be healed by a system which is materialistic in its own principles and mechanistic in the application of its principles....*" (*CW* 9/1946: 3)

Day quoted letters to *The Catholic Worker* written by Eric Gill in 1940 in which he decried the use and abuse of mechanization:

> I should like to say simply that fundamentally the problem of the machine is one which should be dealt with by those who actually use machines.. . . In a broad way it may be said that the first

> thing to be done (first in the sense of most important) is for the workers to recapture control of industry....
>
> This, of course, is the communist idea but, unfortunately, the communists couple this [their] very crude materialist philosophy and their equally crude idolatry of the machine....
>
> The worker is a man and not simply a "hand." Work done by a man is human work to be valued and thought of as such and not merely as a "cost in the account books."
>
> To labor is to pray—that is the central point of the Christian doctrine of work.... Communism and Christianity are moved by "compassion for the multitude," the object of communism is to make the poor richer but, the object of Christianity is to make the rich poor and the poor holy.
>
> This supernaturalized ideal of labor must needs be accompanied by a supernaturalized ETHIC of labor, by a proper morality in working conditions. Such influences as self interest, hatred and violence have no place in it. Catholic teaching on this point is in direct opposition to that of the atheist, the agnostic, and the materialist, and it is these who have the ear of the laboring classes in the matter of work. (*CW* 9/1946: 7)

Dorothy was not nearsighted by any means and saw her lessons as enduring ones. In an analysis prescient of the high technology computer age, Dorothy Day concludes her September 1946 article on labor by stating:

> Cities have fallen in the past and they will fall again. Perhaps that will be the judgment of God on the machine which has turned man into a hand, a part of a machine. He who lives by the sword will fall by the sword and he who lives by the machine will fall by the machine. (8)

These continuing themes powerfully resonate in the express mission of the Catholic Worker, as set forth in the annual mission statement in each May issue of *The Catholic Worker*:

> *In labor*, human need is no longer the reason for human work. Instead, the unbridled expansion of technology, necessary to capitalism and viewed as "progress," holds sway. Jobs are concentrated in productivity and administration for a "high-tech," warrelated, consumer society of disposable goods, so that laborers are trapped in work that does not contribute to human welfare. Furthermore, as jobs become more specialized, many people are

> excluded from meaningful work or are alienated from the products of their labor. (Troester 1993: 577-578)

Conclusion

What, therefore, are Dorothy Day's lessons for the transformation of work? Her life, her work, and her writing certainly are important parts of labor history. Does her life with workers and with the poor, her many essays on workers' rights and on the dignity of work stand only as eloquent, but ultimately irrelevant, witness to twentieth century labor history? On the contrary, study of, and reflection on, Dorothy Day's life and work is very valuable from the standpoint of labor history alone. History, especially labor history, can teach many lessons with contemporary relevance. I submit that Dorothy Day's lessons for the future of work both encapsulate and transcend history. The challenge is to translate her personalism and subsidiarity into new forms of political and social organization, focusing on human relationships for the communal good.

Although the domestic and international economies of the Depression, mid-century, and century's end are each quite different and distinct from one another, dramatic parallels exist between them. Economic volatility is as unsettling as ever. Work collapsed during the Great Depression. Work in the late twentieth century, as a defining thread of the social contract, is unravelling. Many domestic and international economies no longer rely on manufacturing or industrial models to provide the sources of wage jobs and growth in the private sector. The workplace has increasingly stratified itself into a camp of highly skilled, knowledgeable workers who are served by the other, a large population of precariously situated and low paid service workers. All are surrounded by vast seas of the underemployed and unemployable. The unemployed and the unemployable possess no viable concept of, nor realistic aspiration to acquire, a dignity providing, meaningful work experience. It is very difficult to speak realistically, or even sanely, of the nobility of work in such dire circumstances.

Passage of the National Labor Relations Act was a response to express findings that the individual worker, without protection of the right to unionize, was helpless and atomized in the face of the formidable power of major corporate employers. The current situation is no different and, in many quarters, is even more egregiously stratified than in 1935. Today, individual workers are also atomized in the face of the concentrated power of multi-national corporations who, unlike their early capitalist predecessors, have the ability to execute instantaneous transfers of massive amounts of wealth into the international bond and finance markets through computer technology.

When Dorothy Day was born in 1897, the concept and reality of a job with an eight hour day and a forty hour work week was only an idealized union dream (and an employer's nightmare). Now, the concept of the eight hour day, forty hour work week job, briefly achieved through the efforts of organized labor in mid-century, is rapidly fading away. Most workers are working harder and longer for less money, with disturbing stagnation in wages for the past two decades, and more ominously, with dramatic stratifications of wealth on levels not seen since the days of the robber barons. Currently, the top one percent of the United States population controls forty percent of the national wealth. Today, in the face of transnational corporate employer power how can an atomized and relatively helpless worker seek meaningful dignity and community in work? Technology may be both opening and closing doors, but it is probably not the primary means to new work communities.

Peter Maurin's high romance of the beauty of agriculture, of the imperative of physical labor, and of the return to the land, remains utopian. This is not to say that physical work in agricultural environments is not worth consideration. The New York Catholic Workers continue Peter Maurin's commitments, via the Peter Maurin Farm in Marlboro, New York, along with other such farms. This approach, however, is simply not capable of mass realization in urban regions, or in any other areas dominated by agribusiness. "A return to the land, a living out of Peter Maurin's vision of decentralism, a re-creation of the medieval village with its self-sustained economy based on craft—these are regularly unrealized dreams of many Catholic Workers."(Troester 1993: 249) Agricultural employment, the dominant source of output and work in the pre-industrial age, represented less than three percent of all jobs in the 1990s.

The increasing disappearance of the workplace, with increasing numbers of people working in highly decentralized environments, without central offices, and telecommuting from their homes, seems to make the physical reality of organizing community networks literally impossible. Does the community of the computer offer "frictionless capitalism" or are we in the Darwinian, pioneering environment of the new "Wild West?" In either environment, achieving worker dignity in the new electronic, computerized workplace remains a largely unfulfilled aspiration.

Dorothy Day was an internationalist, like her universal Catholic Church. She was not just another Luddite, although there are Luddite themes in many of today's aspects of Catholic Worker philosophy. "Katharine Temple of the Catholic Worker movement has said it, calling on her comrades to `find even more ways to be latter-day Luddites.'"(Sale 1995: 228) Day clearly warned against the dehumanizing aspects of technology, which, in her day, was exemplified by the assembly line and the typewriter. As a journalist and a writer, she put the technology of the typewriter and the printing press to very good and valuable use. What, therefore, would Dorothy Day say regarding high technology and computerization in the workplace today? Her healthy apprehensions would no doubt be part of the fabric. She would also see, however, some means within computerized work environments for the realization of dignity and human fulfillment. The Catholic Worker movement, indeed, has several web sites.

As an internationalist seeking to manipulate technology to the benefit of workers, she sought protections for the rights of all workers in the domestic and international regimes. The world of work is clearly and increasingly global in its dimensions and ramifications.

There is bitter truth to many of Dorothy Day's lessons, such as her understandable wariness of employer domination of unions, a specter currently resurrected with the initiatives for the statutory modifications of the National Labor Relations Act. She would no doubt see the need for the continuing independent voice of workers in protecting workers' rights. The world of workers is part of the larger world of all persons, including employers, each entitled to maximum human dignity. Therefore, Dorothy Day would also see the need for the maximization of human dignity as inextricably interwoven with the need for community coherence and fruition beyond work and the workplace.

Dorothy Day, however, did not offer formulaic prescriptions for the achievement of strategic objectives. She was a journalist who had identified her life and her living with the workers and with the poor and not with the ruling elites. She was an eloquent voice, a visionary, and perhaps a saint. Saints are those who lived in the world, but were not fully of the world. Therefore, one must not be surprised by those aspects of Dorothy's thinking that were based primarily on exhortation, as they were grounded on ideal aspirations and visions for a world not yet realized; a world that ought to be. Saints and labor organizers have much in common; they see the world as it is and urge the continuance of the struggle to create the world as it one day ought to be. These aspects of her life certainly merit admiration and emulation. Her labor theory, however, is much more problematic, and must be adjusted to contemporary circumstances.

If workers are not to decline into an irredeemable state of helplessness and shattered individualism or to prostrate themselves before transnational corporate employer power, perhaps, through the revitalization of Dorothy Day's lessons, the workplace can once again be made the focus of possibilities for achieving lives of dignity and worth for all and a place to promote the consciousness of the unemployed and the underemployed. Meaningful work of dignity is as difficult to obtain as it was a century ago. Work is a delicate and precious thing; an important means to the attainment of the maximization of fundamental human dignity. If traditional, industrial work is no longer the unifying thread of the social contract, some third way of work, such as nonprofit community service, still incorporating fundamental notions of work and transcending the capitalist political economy of individual profit maximization, may become the central focus of meaningful social life, and informed by the enduring lessons of Dorothy Day.

Dorothy Day stood up for workers who stood up to their bosses (Miller 1973: 134-135). She thus focused primarily on the labor-management relationships, and probably less so on the nature of work itself. The courage and activism of organized workers, standing against corporate employers, was perhaps perceived by Dorothy Day as a means of empowerment, and as more politically ennobling than the work itself. Now, in the "post-work" world, workers and the vast masses of former workers and the unemployables must stand together politically to find means of social reconstruction for meaningful lives for all, including those precluded from the realms of conventional employment.

Jeremy Rifkin, in his powerful book, *The End of Work*, addressed the problems that face labor today and set forth an agenda for dramatically expanding the non-profit community work sector which already accounts for six percent of the domestic economy. This future non-profit community work draws implicitly but thoroughly upon the personalism, subsidiarity, and labor solidarity themes of Dorothy Day and the Catholic Worker. It is a compelling agenda that Dorothy Day would have endorsed, and it merits serious attention.

> Now that the commodity value of human labor is becoming increasingly tangential and irrelevant in an ever more automated world, new ways of defining human worth and social relationships will need to be explored....
>
> Our corporate leaders and mainstream economists tell us that the rising unemployment figures represent short-term "adjustments" to powerful market-driven forces that are speeding the global economy into a Third Industrial Revolution. They hold out the promise of an exciting new world of high-tech automated production, booming global commerce, and unprecedented material abundance....
>
> Millions of working people remain skeptical. Every week more employees learn they are being let go. In offices and factories around the world, people wait, in fear, hoping to be spared one more day. Like a deadly epidemic inexorably working its way through the marketplace, the strange, seemingly inexplicable new economic disease spreads, destroying lives and destabilizing whole communities in its wake. In the United States, corporations are eliminating more than 2 million jobs annually. (Rifkin 1995: xviii)

Rifkin suggests that "those with leisure hours and those with idle time could be effectively directed toward rebuilding thousands of local communities and creating a third force that flourishes independent of the marketplace and the public sector." Like Dorothy Day and Peter Maurin, he recognizes the importance of the relationship between community and work:

> The foundation for a strong, community-based third force in American politics already exists. Although much attention in the modern era has been narrowly focused on the private and public sectors, there is a third sector in American life that has been of historical significance in the making of the nation, and that now offers the distinct possibility of helping to reshape the social contract in the twenty-first century. The third sector, also known as the independent or volunteer sector, is the realm in which fiduciary arrangements give way to community bonds, and where the giving of one's time to others takes the place of artificially

> imposed market relationships based on selling oneself and one's services to others. (273-274)

The stability of industrial employment in the post-war era is disintegrating. Manufacturing accounted for 33% of the United States' workforce in the 1950s. "Today, less than 17% of the workforce is engaged in blue collar work." In whatever forms the future of work will manifest itself, certain ineluctable truths will remain. But hard truths are being challenged, paradigms are shattered, and fundamental questions that have historically incorporated meaningful work into the dignity of the identity of the person are being radically reformulated (Rifkin 1996: 8).

Work is a fundamental dimension of human existence. How work remains may be influenced in some measure by Dorothy Day's lessons for the transformation of work. If her lessons are lost or dismissed as completely irrelevant, and if workers fail to find new ways of social organization, the future may be grim indeed.

Peter Maurin, The Distributists and the Nature of Work

Nicholas C. Lund-Molfese

University of Illinois at Chicago

The title of my paper, "Peter Maurin, the Distributists and the Nature of Work" contains rather self-explanatory terms with the exception of "Distributist." At a gathering such as this, Peter Maurin needs no introduction, but what is a "Distributist?" It sounds like a car part. As Stratford Caldecott has said: "The name is not important. What is important is that ideas once called 'distributist' are now more current than ever." Few would deny that for most of a century "the world has seen massive over-centralization, either by the monolithic state or by [multinational corporations].... The [British] Distributists—led by G. K. Chesterton, Hilaire Belloc, [Eric Gill] and Fr. Vincent McNabb were defenders of the idea of small states and local government" in England during the first half of the twentieth century (Caldecott 1994: 29).

Peter Maurin recommended at least five books by Distributist authors: (Maurin 1936: 111): *The Outline of Sanity* (1926) by G. K. Chesterton, *Work and Leisure* (1935) and *Art in a Changing Civilization* (1934) by Eric Gill, and *The Servile State* (1913) and *The Restoration of Property* (1936) by Hilaire Belloc. It is fair to say then that Maurin found something, or perhaps several things, of value in the writings of the Distributists. Like Maurin, Chesterton, Belloc and Gill argued for the elimination of usury, decentralization in production, and the intrinsic value of human work. However, the differences between Maurin and the Distributists are substantial. And even on the points of seeming agreement, there is a great divergence between Maurin and the Distributists in the methods they employed and how they understood these problems. The principal difference is that Peter Maurin lived his ideas while the Distributists, for the most part, were satisfied with the mere promotion of theirs.[1] Further, Peter

Maurin was considered to be a saint by many who knew him during his life, and was often compared to Saint Francis of Assisi. None of the Distributists has ever been so compared. Chesterton, Belloc and Gill, whatever the merits of their ideas, had substantial personal flaws.[2] Still, there is in fact much merit to be found in their ideas. As a comprehensive study of the Distributists is not possible here, I will confine myself to discussing the contribution of one Distributist, Eric Gill, to the development of one idea, the intrinsic value of work.

Maurin's own understanding of work forms the foundation of his critique of capitalism. For Maurin, work performed as a gift is creative and as such is central to Christian Humanism (Miller 1982: 448). Work, performed in accordance with human dignity, would enable persons to have vocations rather than merely jobs. As Maurin said in one of his Easy Essays, "But they say that there is no work to do. There is plenty of work to do, but no wages. But people do not need to work for wages. They can offer their services as a gift."(Maurin 1936: 68) The great dignity of the person is made manifest when a person makes a gift of him or herself, to others, through work.

Three of Maurin's Easy Essays, "Capital and Labor," "Selling Their Labor," and "Industrialism and Art" (Maurin 1936: 69, 70, 83) touch on the heart of the matter:

Capital and Labor

"Capital," says Karl Marx,
"is accumulated labor,
not for the benefit of the laborers,
but for the benefit of the accumulators."

And Capitalists succeed,
in accumulating labor,
by treating labor
not as a gift
but as a commodity,
buying it as any other commodity
at the lowest possible price.

And organized labor
plays into the hands
of the capitalists
or accumulators of labor
by treating their own labor
not as a gift,
but as a commodity,
selling it as any other commodity
at the highest possible price.

Selling Their Labor

And when the capitalists
or accumulators of labor
have accumulated so much
of the laborer's labor
that they no longer
find it profitable
to buy the laborer's labor
then the laborers
can no longer
sell their labor
to the capitalists
or accumulators of labor.

And when the laborers
can no longer
sell their labor
to the capitalists
or accumulators of labor
they can no longer buy
the products of their labor.

And that is
what the laborers get
for selling their labor
to the capitalists
or accumulators of labor.

Industrialism and Art

Eric Gill says:
the notion of work
has been separated
from the notion of art.

The notion of the useful
has been separated
from the notion of the beautiful.

The artist,
that is to say,
  the responsible workman,
  has been separated
  from all other workmen.

The factory hand
has no responsibility
for what he produces.

He has been reduced
to a sub-human condition
of intellectual irresponsibility.

Industrialism
has released the artist
from the necessity
of making anything useful.

Industrialism
has also released the workman
from making anything amusing.

The essence of Maurin's teaching on work is that work is a gift of self by one person to another, and as such it is inherently creative.[3] It was in expounding this "creative" aspect of work, Maurin believed, that Eric Gill's writings were of the most use. In one of his essays, Gill describes work as:

> in itself good and may be and should be holy and sacred.... At every turn our object must be to sanctify rather than to exclude physical labor, to honor it rather than to degrade it, to discover how to make it pleasant rather than onerous, a source of pride rather than of shame.... [I]n a Christian society, there is no kind of physical labor, no kind whatsoever, none, which is either derogatory to human beings or incapable of being sanctified and ennobled. (Gill 1947: 22-23)

As for the attitude that "manual work is, of itself, subhuman drudgery," Gill called it "not only untrue but subversive of the whole Christian doctrine of man." He recognized that some working conditions are in fact "sub-human," but he held this attributable not to the labor itself but due to "the proletarianism by which men and women become simply 'hands'—simply instruments for the making of money by those who own the means of production."(Gill 1947: 24) This instrumentalization of persons, the use of persons as tools, is fundamentally opposed to the dignity of the human person and the dignity of work.

Gill's reflections on the intrinsic value of labor complements, and in many ways anticipated, the teaching of the Catholic Church on the intrinsic value of work. The most important contemporary Catholic teaching on labor is found in Pope John Paul II's encyclical, *Laborem Exercens (On Human Work).* The encyclical explains that work is a fundamental dimension of human existence on earth (John Paul II 1981: 11). The pope argues that human persons are created in the image of God partly through the mandate we received from our Creator to complete the work of creation through the exercise of our freedom through labor. In and through our labor we share in the work of God our Creator, we continue to develop God's work, and even bring it to perfection. We imitate God both in working and also in resting, since God willed to present his own creative activity under the form of work and rest in the book of Genesis (John Paul II 1981: 57-59).

Work has both an exterior and an interior dimension. The exterior dimension concerns what is produced while the interior dimension concerns the self-realization of the worker. People realize their God-given potential and develop themselves in and through working. "The basis for determining the value of human work is not primarily the kind of work being done but the fact that the one who is doing it is a person. The sources of dignity of work are to be sought primarily in the subjective dimension, not the objective one."

The Christian attitude towards work directly contradicts that of the ancient world where people were put into classes based on the type of work performed: "work which demanded from the worker the exercise of physical strength ...was considered unworthy of free [persons], and was therefore given to slaves....Christianity brought about a fundamental change of ideas in this field especially the fact that the one who, while being God, became like us in all things devoted most of the years of His life on earth to manual work at the carpenter's bench."(John Paul II 1981: 16-17)

Remembering Peter Maurin's admonition, "always they, never I," I'll close with two suggestions as to how we can put into practice in our daily lives an authentically human understanding of work, a spirituality of work.

First, beginning with what is closest to us, let us restore the dignity and respect due to domestic labor which was denigrated in stages, primarily through two sins: sexism and pride. In the first stage, domestic labor, commonly known as "housework" (the cooking and the cleaning, the washing and the sewing, the educating and caring for children) was treated with disrespect by men because, since the later stages of the industrial revolution, it happened to be done by women. This denigration of the intrinsic value of domestic labor, because it is done by women, is one of the evils wrought by sexism. Today most well educated American women and men are in agreement that domestic labor is mindless drudgery, to be done by low paid workers and machines. Here is the contempt of the educated intellectual for manual labor: that is to say the sin of pride.

There is also the pride of the artist who might wish to be freed from household work for "higher" forms of production. The proud artist (or intellectual) might say, "Bread should be made by bread making machines to free persons for painting (or studying)." The false assumption is that "In the fine arts the thing made depends for its quality on the actual personality of the maker, while in ordinary objects of use this is not so." Gill demolishes this assumption with a quick line: "in a normal society the artist is not a special kind of [person], but every [person] is a special kind of artist." He goes on to say that "there is no hard distinction between fine arts and base ones.... It is only [a] dullness of mind and a lack of imagination which prevents [people] from seeing that all things made could be, and should be, regarded as we regard the products of 'artists.'"(Gill 1947: 26-27)

So consider bread-making an art and give the same respect to the baker in the shop and those who bake at home as we do to artists or intellectuals. Bread takes on a deeper value and meaning when it is made out of love for those persons who will be nourished by it. In the same way, children have a right to be fed, bathed and clothed by those who love them, rather than by machines or by the employees of an institution. What is more intellectual than the spiritual and what is more spiritual than love, for as the Apostle Saint John tells us, "God is love."(1 John: 4:8) But in our society where power (and hence production) are valued over loving, over the personal, then we should expect prestige and respect to be given to those who produce rather than those who create through domestic labor. As Gill said, "the root of the matter is in the dishonoring of physical work, and until we have eradicated the prevailing notion that some kinds of work are, of their nature, subhuman drudgery, all discussion of human labor is futile."(Gill 1942: 26)

Second, work is for the benefit of persons; that is to say, work is for the benefit of the worker and those the worker serves by the fruit of that labor. Therefore, people who cannot work, such as very small children, the severely disabled, those suffering from grave illness or the elderly, fully retain their personal dignity (Grisez 1993: 758). In a society where the order of values is inverted, where persons are valued not for themselves but for the material wealth they produce, we should not be surprised that the life of a nuclear weapons designer is seen as more important, of more value, than the life of a farmer or a street cleaner or an unborn child. This is a defining characteristic of a materialistic culture.

Let us each act to protect and defend the dignity of every human person, especially those persons who do not produce material wealth; those the Nazis might have referred to as "useless eaters:" persons with disabilities and the unborn, the elderly and the unemployed. In all we do, we must uphold the value of the human person as primarily creative and not merely for use. That is to say, we must learn to see persons as works of art rather than as instruments for the production of wealth: the simple existence of a person is a thing of beauty. If this change of mind and heart would take place then the desire to eliminate (or even kill) persons who our society increasingly finds to be inconvenient—like the poor, the prisoner, the elderly, the disabled and the unborn—would be replaced by an attitude of solidarity with those we would then recognize as "the least of our brothers:" as Christ himself (Matt. 25: 31-40).

Notes

[1] This comment might be unfair to G. K. Chesterton since his "work" was writing, arguing, urging and he did quite a bit of this for "the cause." Chesterton had capital enough in the form of talent to write, and outlets for his beliefs. He used that capital to argue for those things he believed in; that is to say, he used it to exercise his creativity in free work.

[2] Of the three, this statement most deservedly applies to Eric Gill whose sexual injustices, even judged by contemporary, liberal standards, remain disgusting—at least if Fiona MacCarthy, *Eric Gill: A Lover's Quest for Art and God* (New York: E.P.Dutton, 1989) is ultimately judged to be accurate and reliable. According to A. N. Wilson's extensive study, *Hilaire Belloc* (New York: Atheneum, 1984), 257-259, Belloc "knew perfectly well that his baser nature was dominated by a strong streak of the crude anti-Semitism which he dissects so mercilessly in The Jews." For a more positive (and much more brief) portrayal of Hilaire Belloc see Robert Hamilton, *Hilaire Belloc, An Introduction to his Spirit and Work* (London: Douglas Organ, 1947). For a comprehensive biography of G. K. Chesterton see Joseph Pearce, *Wisdom and Innocence: A Life of G.K. Chesterton* (London: Hodder & Stoughton, 1996). Peter Maurin was likely unaware of these personal failings.

[3] It is remarkable how closely Maurin's attitude is mirrored in the thought of Pope John Paul II: "That educators and teachers may bear witness credibly so that young people may discover the meaning and the beauty of a life lived as a gift for others." (See "Our Holy Father's Prayer Intentions for 1997," *Osservatore Romano,* January 31, 1996.)

Into Their Labors: Work, Technology, and the Sacramentalism of Dorothy Day

Eugene McCarraher

Villanova University

The plentiful photographic chronicle of Dorothy Day and the Catholic Worker movement relates a tale of American Catholic pastoralism in dubious but noble battle with the forces of technological modernity. Here, Day sits serenely by the jenny, spinning wool for her dutifully quiescent if somewhat baffled grandchildren. ("Grandma, why don't you just *buy* some shirts?") There, earnest, bespectacled young men chase an errant cow through hay and manure after a morning spent with a volume of Maritain, Gill, or Dawson. Eventually, these pastoral experiments come to naught, Day and other Workers attend to the issues of race relations and peace, and placards replace plows as the tools of Catholic radicalism.

Nathaniel Hawthorne might have sighed that he could have told her so. In *The Blithedale Romance* (1852), his fictional portrayal of Brook Farm, Hawthorne had asserted that the union of manual and mental labor was a paradise impossible. "We had pleased ourselves with delectable visions of the spiritualization of labor," Miles Coverdale reflects. "It was to be our form of prayer, and ceremonial of worship." But their sweat was more annoying than baptismal, and their calloused hands did not rise to heaven. "The clods of earth, which we so constantly belabored and turned over and over, were never etherealized into thought," Miles Coverdale reflects. "Our thoughts, on the contrary, were fast becoming cloddish." "The yeoman and the scholar," Hawthorne's fictional persona concludes, "are two distinct individuals, and can never be melted or welded into one substance." Day's story becomes another chapter in the social imagination of American romanticism (Hawthorne 1983: 65-66).

I think we need to tell this story in a rather different way, one that provides a richer and wider account of Day's reflections on work and technology. Richer, in that Day's reflections are seen to have roots in her own experience of work and in her desire to close the gap between physical and mental labor. Wider, in that Day's aspersions on factory work and industrial technology dovetail with a broader, motley current of anti-industrialism that includes not only Catholic Distributists such as Eric Gill and G. K. Chesterton but also the anarchist Peter Kropotkin, American populists, the "Southern Agrarians," Lewis Mumford, Paul Goodman, Ivan Illich, and E. F. Schumacher. Day's theological understanding of the nature of human creativity—her "sacramentalism," what I would describe as a "materialist religiosity"—represented an important reformulation of Protestant producerism and determined the possibilities and limitations of the Catholic Worker experiment.

Day's first lessons about work came from her parents. Her father's vagabond journalistic career entailed a prolonged, unsettling, and financially precarious itineracy that shuttled the Days all across the United States, from Brooklyn to San Francisco to Chicago. The Day family life owed much of its dreariness to the circumstances of John's work. Dorothy's later pursuit of journalism as a career reflected her emotional ambivalence toward her father. Day drew upon the literary interests piqued by her father's library and emulated the mobility that both enriched her writing and made a stable family life extraordinarily difficult. Moreover, Day always harbored a moral unease about her writing, a feeling that, like her father's work, it set her against people whose needs were more pressing and legitimate than her own. "The sustained effort of writing, of putting pen to paper so many hours a day when there are human beings around who need me is a harrowingly painful job."(Day 1952: 11)

On the other hand, her mother Grace lay behind her bestowal of salvific significance upon work, her preference for handicraft production, and her suspicion of labor-saving machinery. Day credited Grace with exposing her to the beauties of pre-industrial craftsmanship. "In a day when there were no washing machines, electric irons, vacuum cleaners and electric sewing machines," Grace Day sewed shirts and dresses whose every hem and button demonstrated love, diligence, and artistry. Half a century later, Day wrote that she could still see "the sheen of our ginghams, pale blue and pink, and feel the flowered challis."(Day 1952: 27)

A domestic servant made Grace's sewing somewhat easier, of course, but once the Days could no longer afford this pretension to gentility, Dorothy and her sister undertook most of the household chores. "I took my dishwashing very seriously and I remember scouring faucets until they shone." While tiresome and sometimes boring, washing, scrubbing, sweeping, and cooking provided Dorothy with a genuine if limited fulfillment. The house was easier to clean, in Day's view, because it was an abode of memory and love, however tense, dismal, and fleeting: "we loved the house," she wrote later, "so we loved the work." Fortunately, the housework also afforded ample time for reading, daydreaming, and reflection. "There was time to think, to think about fundamental things." Day later surmised that she had "imbibed a 'philosophy of work,' enjoying the creative aspect of it as well as getting satisfaction from a hard and necessary job well done."(Day 1952: 24)

These early workdays coincided with the commencement of her "long loneliness," her haphazard but indomitable spiritual journey. While the Episcopalianism of her adolesence reinforced her aesthetic and intellectual inclinations, Day recalled in *The Long Loneliness* her attractions to Wesleyan evangelicalism and to Christian Science (Day 1952: 29). Without attributing an inordinate biographical significance to these religious cultures, I think one can assert that Day's Episcopalian romanticism was not at all incompatible either with an evangelical work ethic or with a therapeutic orientation toward the practical, healing fruits of faith. Together they molded Day's lifelong conviction that proximity to material reality brought one closer to God.

Day's early experience of labor left an indelible mark on her views of work, tools, and machines. Developing a talent for what Margaret Miles has called "carnal knowing"—an "experiential understanding that is aware and respectful of the particular and concrete"(Miles 1989: 185)—she acquired an abiding appreciation of the material world, a feel for its intractibility and a keen awareness of the sensual pleasure and disgust it could offer. Housework in a beloved community of people and surroundings gave Day a social and material model of satisfying labor. Moreover, the leisure time left over after her chores—leisure time lost or corrupted, Day would later believe, by "labor-saving devices"—demonstrated that physical labor was fully compatible with intellectual and aesthetic pursuits, that they could even be united.

Day's domestic union of manual and mental work with spiritual fulfillment was a feminine counterpart to the masculine producerist ideal that occupied the center of the 19th-century moral imagination: the industrious, republican, evangelical Protestant proprietor. Lacking the aesthetic sensibility Day would later consider central to felicitous labor, this hale specimen of white male omnicompetence nonetheless exemplified the coordination of hand and brain achieved in the web of family proprietorship, political democracy, and Protestant faith. Since the Civil War, however, as capital sought greater control over the pace and material design of production, skilled workers fought a valiant, often violent, but ultimately futile battle against the appropriation of their craft knowledge by a distinct class of technical and managerial experts. Professionalism as a form of cultural authority cast in terms of credentialled expertise—an authority forged in part in the smithy of liberal Protestant religious culture—is inseparable from this expropriation of skilled workers. Yet with its at least putatively genderless ideal of merit, professionalization also marked a significant break with the gendered work ethos common both to producerism and to Victorian domesticity.

Day has an ambiguous and ambivalent location in this history. Along with other Progressive women such as Jane Addams and Ida Tarbell, she embodied the new gender and class politics implicit in the culture of professionalism. Her first battle—just getting into the journalistic world—ended in triumph over her father, who orchestrated an altogether sleazy effort to keep her out of the loop. As a reporter for the *Call*, a socialist newspaper in New York, Day's roving all over the city ensured that "the daily 'foot' work covering assignments kept me healthy." The work, she later wrote, could be "hard and rigorous" and "for that very reason made mental activities all the more stimulating." As an editor of *The Masses*, Day employed intellectual, aesthetic, and manual skills in the daily process of editing copy and supervising lay-out. She also enjoyed the presence of talented comrades whose company she could keep because "what work I did took not more than a few hours every morning. . .and in the afternoons we had picnics."(Day 1938: 90; 1952: 69)

At the same time, Day's inclination toward anarchism and syndicalism grew more pronounced (Day 1952: 54-56; 1938: 67-68). She found the syndicalist I.W.W. more attractive than the Socialists, and considered Tolstoy's Levin, the prince who sweats in the fields with his peasants in *Anna Karenina,* to be a more compelling figure than

Marx's proletarian in *Capital.* Having read a little of Kropotkin before entering college, she familiarized herself with the whole corpus of the anarchist prince, especially with *Fields, Factories, and Workshops*, where he sketched out a decentralized system of farms and urban communes that enabled a balanced development of city and country and an integration of intellectual and physical labor. Thus, Day's sojourn among the "lyrical left" provided both a beloved community of labor and a significant theoretical education in the possibilities of work and technology.

Yet despite the radical left's celebration of the possibilities generated by corporate technology for material abundance and genderless sexual relations, Day remained wary about these possibilities. Her wariness stemmed from her own work as a reporter. Day couched her reactions to working class poverty in terms which, though strongly gendered, conveyed her estimation of the human costs of industrialization. Every day she would see "exhausted men with all the manhood drained from them by industrialism." Paying homage to the producerist ideal, Day implied that the industrial regime of subdivided work and technology emasculated men by depriving them of creative power and autonomy. Moreover, life as a journalist, she later observed, made her "lose all sense of perspective" and left her "with no time at all for thought or reflection." She also deliberately thwarted the spiritual development she had cultivated. "I felt at the time that religion would only impede my work."(Day 1938: 72; 1952: 43, 45)

Tired of "playing at writing," Day compiled a decidedly wayward, downscale resume over the next decade and a half: nurse, cashier, library assistant, dancer, artist's model. Still, the most satisfying moments of her life during this time (significantly christened "natural happiness" in *The Long Loneliness)* were those that combined strenuous physical and mental labor with spiritual joy. As a nurse, Day immersed herself in the quotidian paraphernalia of hospital work—sheets, needles, douches, enemas, bedpans—attended lectures that complemented the physical work of caring for patients, and renewed her spiritual quest. A decade later, the birth of her daughter Tamar hastened her conversion to Catholicism and inspired a moving *New Masses* article in which she satirized the industrialization of reproduction. Impatient with Tamar's tardiness in entering the world, Day's doctor induced labor in the interests of obstetrical efficiency. "Here I was," she remembered, "conducting a neat and tidy job, begun in a most businesslike manner, on the minute." In these episodes, Day linked together an intimacy with material life, intellectual or aesthetic stimulation, and closeness to divinity in a sacramental or materialist religiosity. As she recalled of her stint as a nurse, "one thing I was sure of, and that was that the fellow workers and I were performing an act of worship."(Day 1952: 99-93; 1928: 5-6)

Thus, Day had been developing a philosophy of work out of her own experience for some time before her fateful meeting with Peter Maurin in 1932. Indeed, the founding of the Catholic Worker movement marked a resolution of her interwoven vocational and spiritual crises: her search for fulfilling work that combined hand and brain and her yearning to end her "long loneliness." Both began in separation, both ended in "community"—often a treacly and obscurantist piece of rhetoric, but in Day's usage a religious materialism encoded in Catholic religious culture and embodied in the labor of daily life. How Day, in tandem with Maurin and other Catholic Workers, set about defining this "community" of labor proved crucial in marking out the subsequent direction of American Catholic radicalism.

A Catholic body of anti-industrial social and cultural criticism had been forming for some time before the 1930s. In *Art and Scholasticism* (1920), Jacques Maritain condemned both industrial technology and the professionalization of work for reducing thought and bodily activity to "the rapidity of a taylorized gesture." Maritain's book became an ur-text among critics of mass production such as the Liturgical Arts Society, the nascent liturgical movement, and artists such as Ade Bethune and Graham Carey. In the work of G. K. Chesterton, Hilaire Belloc, Vincent McNabb, and especially Eric Gill, Catholics could find an even more virulent indictment of industrialism, one that came, in Gill's case, with a host of illustrations that figured a voluptuous spirituality (Maritain 1949: 16; also White 1990; Marx 1956; Corrin 1981; McCarthy 1984).

Day's own relationship to this body of thought is ambiguous. She read Maritain (though only after meeting Maurin and Bethune) and never cottoned to the Chesterbelloc: Chesterton "wearied me," and Belloc "did not inspire me."(Day 1938: 136-137) While much of her anti-industrial polemic resembles that of McNabb and Gill, most of their writing on industrialism appeared after the founding of the Catholic Worker. Day's significance appears more clearly when we locate her in an American tradition of anti-industrialism. While indebted to and even prefigurative of European critics as well, Day and the Catholic Worker inherited the tattered threads of Protestant producerism and rewove them on the loom of Catholic sacramentalism.

"Cult, culture, and cultivation," the trinity of Catholic Workerism, signalled the movement's commitment to the revival of small-scale family farming and handicraft production in the setting of "village communes," "garden communes," or "farming communes." These villages would feature "agronomic universities" where the wedding of manual labor to intellectual training would foster both a personal integration of hand and brain and a related erasure of class divisions. I'll consider the problems with this program in a moment. (In practice, these rural experiments turned out to be, in James Fisher's laconic judgment, "unmitigated disasters.") What I want to stress at this point is that this artisanal critique of industrialism was not historically idiosyncratic. Certainly, the disassembly of the production line, factory decentralization, revival of handicrafts and small farming, and the reunion of scientific, technical, and humanistic education comprised the marrow of Kropotkinesque anarchism. But the ideal of direct producer control over work and technology had galvanized the populist movements at the turn of the century: the Knights of Labor, the Farmers' Alliances, the syndicalist I.W.W. of the early 20th century. Especially among the Knights and the Alliances, a strong evangelical Protestant conviction of the religious significance of labor persisted. Among Day's contemporaries, the Southern Agrarians of *I'll Take My Stand* (1930) identified industrialism as the chief culprit both in the South's subaltern economic position and in the decline of religious faith in the modern world (Day 1952: 220-228; *CW* 1/1937: 1, 7; Coddington 1936: 15; Lasch 1991: 209-225; Gutman 1976; Fink 1983; Palmer 1980: 37-38, 127-128; Winters 1985; Twelve Southerners 1977: 155-175).

But the most revealing comparison among Day's contemporaries would be with Lewis Mumford. In *Technics and Civilization* (1934) Mumford asserted that "the fresh integration of work and art and life" was the desideratum "we must seek and create." Harkening back to the 19th-century Romantic critique of industrialism best articulated by John Ruskin and William Morris, Mumford lauded their "attempt to restore the essential activities of human life to a central place" in the modern world, "instead of accepting the machine as a center." Romanticism encapsulated for Mumford "those vital and historic and organic attributes that had been deliberately eliminated from the concepts of science and from the methods of the earlier technics." More inclined than Day to welcome technological change, Mumford saw in the technology of electrical power transmission a way both to undermine the concentration of industry and to materialize the Romantic vision of the Country and the City balanced and reunited. At the same time, like Day, Maurin, and other Catholic Workers, Mumford both upheld medieval guild production as a model of social organization and aesthetic quality—the production of tangible goods reflecting "high standards of design and workmanship," as he asserted in *The Story of Utopias* (1922)—and lauded medieval religion and philosophy for their approach to labor and technics as moral issues (Mumford 1934: 267, 286; 1922: 207-208).

The celebration of guilds and of "tangible goods" by both Mumford and Day points us toward the Protestant work ethic and its rearing, ugly head in America. In making diligence, methodicalness, and productivity into the cardinal virtues of labor, the Protestant ethic rendered the social organization and material implements of work only tenuously connected, if not wholly irrelevant, to the moral evaluation of its performance. It has tended to de-materialize the moral evaluation of work because its virtues are consonant with almost any regime of work and technology; it can flourish in a field, on an assembly line, or in an office cubicle. Thus, artisanal production proved accidental to rather than indissolubly wedded to the Protestant work ethic. Moreover, thanks in large measure to the Protestant ethic, issues of workplace power relations and technical design came to be considered "utilitarian" and "neutral," less "moral" or "aesthetic." Hence, the liberal Protestant baptism of professional expertise drew from the same font as the evangelical Protestant anointment of proprietary producerism.

Hence, we should see the importance of Day's sacramentalist gospel, not simply as an American outpost of Catholic Distributism, but as a transfiguration of the American Protestant producerist tradition. (It might be worth noting that Paul Tillich, the Protestant intellectual most appreciative of the "Catholic substance," was also the most insistent on the religious significance of art and the sacramentality of technology.) The alchemy of this transfiguration lay in Day's sacramental understanding of work and technology as both divinely conferred creative powers and as emblems of the state of our relationship with God. Through labor on farms or in small workshops, the worker pursued a "vocation" in which he or she "shares in God's creative activity." "Using mind and body to work on beautiful things," Day wrote in 1946, gave men and women "a sense of the sacramentality of life, the holiness, the symbolism of things." Sharing in divine creativity also possessed enormous therapeutic value, since "a man who works with his hands as well as with his head is an integrated personality."(*CW* 5/1947: 1; *CW* 11/1946: 4; Day 1938: 150) The restoration to work and technology of the sacramental quality desecrated by industrial capitalism became for Day and other Catholic radicals a paramount religious duty as well as a radical social commitment.

Day's Catholic radicalism posed a direct religious challenge to the Fordist regime of work and technology: the standardized, mechanized production of consumer goods, conducted under routinized conditions of semi-skilled, subdivided labor, whose abundant commodities compensated for workers' loss of skill, control, and fulfillment in the workplace. In Day's beatific vision of "integrity," the design and materiel of production technology became matters every bit as politically and morally significant as the quantity and substance of its fruits. The ideal of the integration of bodily and mental labor stands against the ideal of professionalism, at least as it has been rooted in the separation of production and planning common both to corporate capitalism and to state socialism. Furthermore, Day's imprecations against "materialism" take on a strange but trenchant meaning when considered in the context of her sacramentalism. "When this dear flesh of ours is denied"—denied, that is, creative work, one of the flesh's most powerful needs—"this," Day declared, "is the worst materialism of all," because industrialism withheld from the worker a felicitous integrity of body, mind, and soul (Day 1938: 136-137).

Yet if we grant to Day a significance in the American anti-industrial tradition, we must also consider the limitations of her position. Except for McNabb, none of the other figures I've mentioned exhibited either her indifference to science or her implacable animosity toward technological development. Kropotkin believed that separating handicraft production from modern technological and scientific methods would bring "the decay of both." Both Kropotkin and Mumford believed that the decentralization of factories and farms depended on sophisticated electrical power systems and biodynamic agricultural techniques. Mumford's "neotechnics" required a "new worker" who was an "all around mechanic" characterized by "alertness, responsibility, [and] an intelligent grasp of the operative parts."

The balanced urban/rural community imagined by Paul and Percival Goodman in *Communitas* (1948) featured plenty of advanced technology. Even Schumacher, himself often dismissed as another guru of the granola set, wrote of *intermediate* technology (Kropotkin 1974: 186; Mumford 1934: 227; Goodman 1960; Schumacher 1973: 181-201).

Day could not envision any sort of technological development that was not insidious. The possibility that technological development (dare I say technological progress?) could proceed in a manner that preserved and even enhanced the artisanal character of production seems never to have entered her mind. Why did Day never consider the possibility that work could be fulfilling, artisanal, and sacramental outside the ambit of traditional handicraft and farming? Let me suggest three reasons.

Reason #1 is named Peter Maurin. Maurin's "Easy Essays" went a long way toward obscuring rather than clarifying some important theoretical and political issues regarding work and technics. Day appeared at times to see this: Maurin, she once observed, "never filled in the chasms, the valleys, in his leaping from crag to crag of noble thought."(Day 1952: 195) Day's ideological deference to Maurin helped to ensure that the Catholic Worker would plunge headfirst into these abysses.

A second reason is a glaring weakness in Day's *curriculum vitae*: no work experience in a factory. Compare Day on this score to Simone Weil, who worked for a year in the Paris Renault plant and participated in the great strike there in 1935. Having taken the measure of the industrial beast, Weil could contemplate the possibilities that resided in newer, more advanced forms of workshop and production technology. All Day could see in "the symbolism of the machine" was something "ugly and devilish."(*CW* 11/1946: 4; Weil 1973: 37-124; Panchias 1977) If she had spent more time there, she might, like Weil, have remembered that the devil was a fallen angel, and that the redemption of technology lay in the politics and blueprints of its design.

We can also trace Day's limitations to the Catholic Worker's highly ambivalent relationship to the labor movement. Day did at one time hope that unions could be cells for a sacramental gospel, arguing in 1938 that they "can be indoctrinated and taught to rebuild the social order." John Cort, founder of the Association of Catholic Trade Unionists, was a protege of Day's. Still, the Catholic Worker never established firm links to the labor unions (or to farmers, for that matter). Thus, its ideals never underwent the sort of popular scrutiny that would have occasioned self-criticism, reformulation, and renewed engagement, in short, a vigorous Catholic discourse on work and technology. While Mumford himself lacked even Day's tenuous connections to workers, he recognized that the "romanticism" he prized had to partake of the "energies" recumbant in "the mass of new machine-workers themselves."(*CW* 7/1936: 2; Cort 1948: 16; Cort 1973: 476; Mumford 1934: 287)

Indeed, it is in the politics of work and technology that we may find Day's most resonant contemporary significance. Like Day, we are living through another wrenching transformation in the nature of work and technology, one that, like its predecessor, holds promise as well as peril for the integration of mental and physical labor. Day's sacramentalism offers a way to discuss issues of class not simply as matters of distributive justice—that is, in the venerable but exhausted tradition of John Ryan and the Catholic bishops' letters—but as matters of technics, workplace relations, aesthetics, and personal fulfillment. It is a long way from the jenny to the computer, from the workshop to the automated plant, from the dung-textured air of the Easton farm to the antiseptic aridity of cyberspace. While Dorothy Day would not see her way clear to a new world of work and technology, she can still guide us in this post-industrial though not post-capitalist moment, and beckon, somewhat despite herself, toward a new stage in the permanent revolution.

Jeff Poniewaz

(a poem in solidarity with the workers of the world
& in liquidarity with the oceans, lakes, rivers,
streams, clouds, and rain...)

Wildcat Musings

Everyone wants more.
Free-enterprise free-for-all.
Free-for-all at collective-bargaining
bargain counter too. Slow down,
turn off the tickertapes for a few days,
close down the Stock Exchange for a few weeks,
so we can hear ourselves think.
Free-enterprise free-for-all
at the collective-bargaining bargain counter
enslaves everyone. Cosmic blinders
help us chase the economic carrot
of diminishing returns
toward spiritual & ecological bankruptcy.
Everyone wants more.
More want more than ever before.
And the more there are,
the more there are wanting more.
When enough was enough, and still is.
And all this represented in dollars
each of which is a warbond
in the war against the Earth.
Industry one vast titanic milkingmachine
clamped to Mother Earth breast,
each dollar a deed to that Deed,
money a vast illusion
destroying everything real.
Overpaid baseball players & screenwriters
walk out on strike just like
Polish factory workers & Canadian mailmen.

Airtraffic controllers go on strike
going buggy overworked preventing collisions
in the pinball machine of
late 20th Century hurlyburly.

If all the poets went on strike
would the President invoke
the Taft-Hartley Act?
Would there be a Haymarket Riot?
How can the people live without poems?
(A poem a day keeps the doctor away.
A poem a day keeps the straitjacket at bay.)
Aren't poems more popular than *TV Guide,*
National Enquirer & the Sports Page?
The people send more letters to President & Congress
protesting the Poetry Shortage than a meat shortage
was ever protested during or after or just before a war.
The President calls out the National Guard
to keep mobs from looting the Poetry warehouses.
Poets are ordered *back* to their poems
for the National Security...

Poets of the World, Unite!
March on the capitals of Earth with placards that say:
"Poets Are the REAL National Guard
the Ancient Order of the Natural Guard,
& Deserve a Kinder Reward Than
Socrates Got from the Republic!"
March on the United Nations with placards that say:
"WORKERS OF THE WORLD,
RELAX!
SOLDIERS OF THE WORLD,
AT EASE!"
Shout it in the streets and to the whole world
via satellite from the General Assembly:
"Quit working yourselves to death,
quit working over the Earth
like a nailbiter's fingernails.
Take a break for a few years.
Retire while you're alive.

You just won a jackpot bigger than Las Vegas:
all your rich dead relatives' wills
have located you at last &
all your poor dead relatives' compensation.
Baby you a rich man,
the green stuff is growing on trees.
  Pennies from heaven better
than plastic pokerchip Acid Rain.
Lilies are better dressed than Oleg Cassini
and no computer is wiser than the whales."

Do poets need a Eugene Debs
to wangle their years of back pay?
Good thing poets aren't on strike–
otherwise I'd be a scab
to write this poem.

PART VI

DOROTHY DAY'S WRITING AND RHETORIC

House of Hospitality dust jacket illustration by Ade Bethune dates from 1939.

The Radical's Paradox: A Reflection on Dorothy Day's "Legendary" Resistance to Canonization

Carol J. Jablonski

University of South Florida

Dorothy Day resisted the notion that she might one day be canonized a saint. "I don't want to be dismissed that easily," she said (Forest 1986: 113, 206; O'Grady 1993: 103; Egan 1983: 19; Wills 1994: 250-52; Farrell 1980: D1; Ellsberg 1980; DD-CW: D-8, Box 4). Day did not want to be remembered (or forgotten) the way she believed Catholics typically remember (or forget) saints. She was uncomfortable with sentimental piety of any sort, and the devotional practices associated with the Catholic cult of saints have often reeked of sentimentality. Instead of seeing Christ exemplified in the lives of saints, Day believed Catholics too often appropriated the saints' images and stories for their own purposes.

It is not easy, of course, to comprehend sanctity, and Day understood this. In a pamphlet that summarized the Catholic Worker retreats from the late 1930s and 1940s, she wrote of the problems of communicating the reality of a saint's life:

> In all secular literature it has been so difficult to portray the good man, the saint, that a Don Quixote is a fool; the Prince Myschkin is an epileptic, in order to arouse the sympathy of the reader, appalled by unrelieved sanctity…The lives of the saints…are too often written as though they were not in this world. We have seldom been given the saints as they really were, as they affected the lives of their times. We get them generally, only in their own writings. But instead of that strong meat we are too generally given the pap of hagiographical writing. (Day 1946)

Dorothy Day in 1946 intuitively sensed the dilemma of inventing and remembering saints. How can portrayals of holy people earn the sympathy and emulation of audiences so as to impel them to saintliness without at the same time diminishing the hard challenges the saints' lives pose?

Day's admirers certainly have been torn by this question. Not long after her death in 1980, the Claretian fathers, a missionary order that also publishes *US Catholic* and, until recently, *Salt,* started to collect materials for what is commonly referred to as "Dorothy's cause."(DD-CW: D-8, Box 4)[1] Published and unpublished responses to their efforts reflect profound ambivalence over the prospects of officially recognizing Day as "Saint Dorothy." Those who favor Dorothy's cause see her not only as worthy of sanctification, but as a saint who is needed in our place and time (DD-CW: D-8, Box 4; Higgins 1983; Fehren 1988; Chittister 1988). Those who question the effort, on the other hand, do not doubt her worthiness or the continuing need for her prophetic witness, but regard the campaign as contrary to Day's own wishes; as a waste of money and time that would be better spent on behalf of the poor; and as unwittingly playing into the hands of those who would soften her message much as they have softened her image (DD-CW: D-8, Box 4).[2]

The question of Day's canonization is fraught with difficulty, for it raises the question not only of why she is to be remembered, but how, and for whose interests. Who is to decide how she is to be remembered? Father Theodore Hesburgh, in correspondence with me about Day's reluctance to receive the University of Notre Dame's Laetare Medal, commented diplomatically that she should be canonized, if only by acclamation (letter to author, 1992). Protestant theologian Martin Marty, writing in a recent collection of stories about saints, was even more careful, calling her "Exemplar Dorothy" instead of "Saint Dorothy."(1994: 286-303)

Day's reaction to the prospects of being canonized, and the ongoing debate over the appropriateness of making a case for her sanctification, reflect the personality and spirituality of a unique public woman. They are also emblematic of Day's stance and strategy as a persuader. My aim is to shed some light on why she stands out as a public figure, which I believe is the outcome of her characteristic use and embodiment of irony. Dorothy Day's legendary resistance to canonization, I believe, epitomizes her ironic posture and furnishes a satisfying way for us to memorialize her.

In what follows, I explore Day's use of irony as a response to her situation as a public woman, the political environment of her time, and her chosen profession of journalism. Day's use of irony was also informed by the dialectic mode of inquiry Peter Maurin taught her. Moreso than Peter (whose customary strategy was to engage in disputation to "make his points"), Dorothy made the *interdependence* of contrary points of view central to her communication strategy. Her rhetoric is marked by a form of *dialectical* irony which, in its characteristic form, acknowledges that *enemies need one another*. Drawing on Kenneth Burke's insightful treatment of the "true" or "humble" ironist, I show how Day's use of dialectical irony gives her discourse a humble, inclusive, and confrontational quality. After examining appeals Day made for racial and ethnic tolerance during the 1930s, I analyze an essay she wrote as a political prisoner following her release from prison in 1957. I conclude by suggesting that concerns over Day's possible canonization may be understood, in part, as anxiety about whether representations of "Saint Dorothy" could adequately show her as the complex and provocative ironist that she was.

To her biographers and others who have observed and written about her, Dorothy Day has been a marvelous and complicated study in contradiction. She was a radical who converted to Roman Catholicism; an anarchist who willingly submitted to ecclesiastical authority; a self-described disciple whose writings practically invented Peter Maurin as her "master," making him the visionary of a movement that she, more than anyone else, made possible; a single mother who espoused traditional family values while spending long periods of time away from home on public speaking tours; a person who reminded Christians that we are all called to be saints, and who spent much of her life in search of spiritual perfection, yet who was adamant in her objection to being canonized. Were she to be canonized, she could easily become the Patron Saint of Paradox.

Like Robert Coles, the psychiatrist who spent over fifty hours interviewing her and has written several books about her, I find myself drawn to Dorothy Day because of her complexity and her contrariety (Coles 1973, 1987). At least part of Day's contradictory nature can be traced to her gender. Communication scholar Karlyn Kohrs Campbell argues that historical prohibitions against women speaking in public created a fundamental contradiction in women's talk. Even in our century, women speakers have had to reckon with the paradoxical requirement that they act like—and yet not like—a woman (Campbell 1983: 101-108). Day's anxiety and physical distress over speaking in public may have been a somatic response to this dilemma (Miller 1982: 308).

The rhetorical constraints of gender were also apparent in her writing, where she made a point of deferring to a system that privileged male speech, particularly that of bishops and clergy. From the beginning of the Catholic Worker movement, she acknowledged that there were those who might question why she, a lay woman and convert, could have anything to say (Day 1933, 1934; DD-CW: D-7, Box 1). Day's references to herself as Peter Maurin's disciple may have been an effort not only to acknowledge Maurin as her teacher but to authorize herself to speak (Piehl 1982: 64-66). Her perplexity over people who treated her as though she could not understand family life because she was not married (and her reminders to readers that she did, indeed, have a family) suggest that she regularly dealt with the dilemma of seeming to be—and not to be—what audiences expected of a woman in public life.

Another indication that Day was affected by the contradictory demands placed on public women was her use of what Campbell calls "feminine style."(Campbell 1989: 13) "Feminine" style is not determined by one's gender, but is a form of rhetorical adaptation that women and other oppressed peoples have used to express themselves in situations that would otherwise silence them. "Feminine" style may be an attempt to overcome barriers to persuasion with audiences that view women's speech as a violation of social norms. Day's use of personal narrative, present in her writing from the beginning of her career, and her legendary "charm and bite" (as Garry Wills phrased it) exemplify feminine style. Day noted early in her career that audiences were more responsive to personal narratives and that editors expected her, as a woman, to produce such stories. Her gracious yet discomfiting way of handling people is noteworthy as behavior that appears on one level to be submissive or accommodating, yet is subversive.

In telling the story of their first meeting, Coles, for example, explains how he stood by waiting for the longest time to introduce himself while Day patiently listened to an intoxicated woman go on and on about something that was concerning her. Day finally interrupted the woman to ask if it would be all right if she stopped for a minute to see what the gentleman wanted. Day then turned to Coles and asked, "Did you want to speak to one of us?" Coles describes how the words, "one of us,"effectively subverted the definition of the situation that he (and anyone in similar circumstances) was working under when he sought her out. Her response to Coles' presence was both hospitable and deadly, illustrative of a pattern of submissive/subversive communication that was in Day neither inadvertent nor coy (Coles 1987: xviii). The presence of contradiction in a woman's communication situation oftentimes demands irony or paradox in response. This situational effect may explain, at least in part, why Day was also perceived by so many not only as a vivid study in contrasts, but as illogical and incapable of abstract thinking.

Day's contrariety cannot be explained by the circumstances of her gender alone, however. Day was drawn to—and came of age in—an intellectual climate marked by an almost nihilistic sense of irony. The nihilist views life as made up of contradictions that reveal its essential meaninglessness; in such a world, maintaining a sense of detachment gives one a sense of coherence if not superiority over others who are not so "enlightened." Social nihilism in the early twentieth century derived from the realization that the effects of modernity—centralization, and the accompanying loss of personal and local autonomy; rationalization, and the accompanying loss of personal control over the meanings and processes of human work; and individualism, and the accompanying loss of community—could not, in the final analysis, be stopped short of total revolution. And, despite radicals' hopes that the Great Depression would mobilize the masses to revolt, the prospects of that happening in the US were not very great. Thus, twentieth century American radicalism has a strong nihilistic aspect, which we see in perhaps greater relief in the social movements of the 1960s.

Day's religious conversion did not erase her nihilistic sensibility but channeled it into a religious mysticism that found its most characteristic expression in her references to the "folly of the cross." St. Paul's description of Christ's redeeming sacrifice gave Day a figure of contradiction around which she could organize her beliefs and appeal for personal action. Rather than seeing the need for a "radical restructuring of society" as a confirmation of the hopelessness of the human condition, she saw it as a confirmation of the Fall. Christ's life and death on the cross gave meaning to suffering and injustice, direction and purpose for personal efforts to effect social change, and a model for activism. No matter how difficult the circumstances one might encounter, victory over evil had already been won. As with St.

Paul, the apparent failure of Christ provided a basis for confidence for Day. Participating in the folly of the cross made it possible for her and her followers to find religious meaning in working with the poor and the destitute, including those whose lives and situations could not be improved so much as "eased," and in taking an absolute stand against war. It was absurd, for example, to talk of prayer as a weapon capable of stopping the conflagration spreading through Europe in the late 1930s, yet that is what Day did (DD-CW: W-1, Box 1). The absurdity of the cross dovetailed with, yet transformed, the absurdity of life as seen by social nihilists. Day's references to the absurd suggest a melding of the two perspectives into what we now recognize as her distinctive brand of Catholic radicalism.

Day's identity and work as journalist served to routinize her ironic perspective. Journalists frequently use irony; contrasts and contradictions grab readers' attention and sustain interest. Irony also gives the illusion of detachment; in mainstream journalism, it creates a sense of "objectivity" or disinterestedness (Glasser and Ettema 1993: 322-338). In advocacy journalism, a sense of irony can intensify polemical argument yet allow the writer's judgment to appear to be untainted by excessive emotionalism. A common use of irony in journalism is the exposure of incongruities between expectations and outcomes. This ironic trope may facilitate insight into common human experiences and failures, as, for example, when we plan carefully for circumstances that end up being wildly beyond our control. Or we plan for A so that B will not occur; yet B does occur, *in spite of* our planning, or perhaps *because* we planned A! The comic potential of this incongruity is celebrated in humor and in "slice of life" reporting. Articles that build a sense of unavoidability are especially appealing in the comic mode because we are encouraged to see the protagonists as well meaning or blameless. The tragic potential of this ironic trope is exploited in articles that point up the needlessness and the cruel consequences of the incongruity. Incongruities between expectations and outcomes are particularly outraging to readers when institutions, organizations, governments, or individuals who should "know better" are portrayed as the disappointing or failing party. Such disparities evoke indignation over what might be seen as inadequate planning, wasteful spending, economic gain at the expense of others, incompetence, misplaced values or hypocrisy.

Piehl has commented on how Day's early writings in the *Call, The Masses,* and the *Liberator* exhibited the telltale style of muckraking journalism: vivid description and dramatization that was calculated to elicit readers' outrage (Piehl 1982: 11). The logical force at work in muckraking, as in all journalism, is irony; muckrakers invited audiences to see that authorities were initiating or permitting things to happen that were the opposite of what both the authorities and the newspapers' audiences said they valued. When Day converted to Roman Catholicism, she did not abandon her muckraking style, though she had occasion later to regret its excesses; in *From Union Square to Rome,* for example, she wrote that as a reporter for the *Call* and *The Masses* she had exaggerated too much (Day 1938: 74). The irony of the radical journalist continued to appear in her writing, however, and helped her to forge a public identity as the editor of *The Catholic Worker* and as the chief spokesperson for the movement.

In *The Catholic Worker,* Day regularly used irony to draw attention to the injustices she saw around her, such as unfair employment practices, housing evictions, child labor laws, racial discrimination, and the treatment of the poor. Ironies she saw and explored in her previous life she now elaborated and supported with papal encyclicals and other Catholic teachings. Day wrote and published others who wrote of the irony of capitalism producing great wealth at the expense of the poor, and the irony of the modern state undermining personal dignity and freedom in attempting to civilize its peoples. Her rich, descriptive reporting and her personal stories offered ways for readers to see for themselves the contradiction between accepted values and actual conditions and practices.

Sometimes Day's irony was abrupt and pointed: her references to "holy mother state" invited ironic comparisons between the church and the state *and* the state and the church that were probably best left to the imagination. Similarly, her statements of how the neediest and most difficult victims of destitution were "dumped" by state bureaucracies at the Catholic Worker left no doubt about the irony of the Catholic Worker doing what the church or the state were supposed to do and yet could not bring themselves to do. Day also had a lighter side, which was perhaps most evident in the early years of the Catholic Worker movement.

The first issues of *The Catholic Worker* were sprinkled with playful irony. In the inaugural issue distributed on May 1, 1933, Day tells readers that the utility company has unwittingly "helped" the enterprise by "taking" their bill late (*CW* 5/1933: 4). The improbability of a utility company allowing a late payment to go unharrassed, and the inadvertence of its helping out a radical newspaper by doing so, makes for an amusing use of irony. But the effect is cleverly amplified in a way that helps the fledgling paper constitute its audience as supportive and involved. The disclosure of the editor's decision to not pay the utility bill on time functions as a kind of "wink" to readers. No doubt they can relate to juggling bills to make ends meet; no doubt they have their own rationalizations for doing so. "We all do this, don't we?" seems to be what the column is asking. But there is more, something that is suggested by the irony of the utility company being in cahoots with the CatholicWorker. Taking readers into their confidence makes readers share in some way in the "complicity" of the editors' delinquency. For irony to work, there needs to be a common ground between the writer and readers; Day's irony drew attention to and creatively strengthened the commonality between herself and readers.

The first "To Our Reader" columns in *The Catholic Worker* imbued the paper's creation with a sense of adventure and danger and added a sense of suspense and involvement over its prospects (the stories behind the production of the first papers read like a serial drama). As its circulation and outreach increased, Day merrily celebrated the ironies of God's Providence appearing in the least likely of moments and circumstances to help the fledgling movement along. Even in its ideological and political tug-of-war with its communist competitor, *The Daily Worker, The Catholic Worker* often showed a playful sense of irony, as when Day responded to the *Daily Worker*'s request that she send them a message of peace for inclusion in a holiday issue of the paper: Day sent them a message that fulfilled their request but that also made it clear that the Catholic Worker saw the communists' espousal of class war as inimical to peace. "THE CATHOLIC WORKER JOINS IN APPEAL FOR DEMOCRACY AND PEACE. THEREFORE ASKS YOU TO JOIN PROTEST AGAINST ALL DICTATORSHIPS... AGAINST ALL SUPPRESSION OF CIVIL LIBERTIES..AND AGAINST ALL WAR, WHETHER IMPERIALIST, CIVIL, OR CLASS. MERRY CHRISTMAS."(*CW* 1/1937: 5)

In the difficult years leading to World War II, as it became clear to her that neither prayer nor conscientious objection would defeat the forces that were leading the nation to war, Day's public communication began to show a more bitter sense of the ironic. Perhaps there is no more bitter irony than that Day expressed in a speech she gave to the Liberal-Socialist Alliance in New York on the evening of the Pearl Harbor attack or in the column she wrote after President Truman exultantly announced dropping the atom bomb. Day points up the ironies in what she called a failed foreign policy on the part of the United States: (1) the US would respond with the same kind of aggression they were damning in the Japanese attack on Pearl Harbor if "Japan…face[d] us from Cuba"; (2) the US and other Western nations were in no position to criticize Japan's colonization of the Pacific, since these nations had also colonized there; and (3) Hitler's expected declaration of war on the US (because of a treaty among the Axis nations) will result in the US defending Stalin ("an ideological crime") (Day 1941). Irony was also the dominant motif of her response to President Truman's jubilation over the killing of so many civilians in the bombing of Hiroshima and Nagasaki. How could Truman or any American celebrate the "saving of American lives" by ending the war with the "mass murder of Japanese civilians"? (*CW* 9/1945: 1)

Day's ironic strategy came to define her stance as a persuader. Her being-in-the-world and her self-expression correlated in a posture of humility. Kenneth Burke describes true irony as "humble" because there is a recognition that each of the opposing elements of contradiction need or depend on the other (Burke 1945: 514). The humble ironist, Burke writes, recognizes that she *needs* her enemies. Burke invites us to consider ideas (as well as persons and groups) as characters in the "drama" of social life. To suggest that opposing ideas are in need of one another is, in some way, to understand Peter Maurin's idea of the utility of discussing contrary perspectives to achieve a "clarification of thought." Day often remarked on the need for differences to exist and to be aired. Our own perspective may not be clear to ourselves or others if we are not aware of, or do not test it in relation to, an antagonistic point of view.

Day's characteristic use of "true" or "humble" irony seems to pivot around her understanding of the Mystical Body of Christ. From the earliest years of the movement, she called for a recognition of all people as members of (or potential members of) the One Body. This included enemies of the nation (such as communists) and enemies of the movement's ideals (capitalists). "As Christ is our Brother," she wrote in the January, 1936 issue of the *CW*, "so are all men our brothers, even the sinning brother capitalist and bourgeoisie." Though she adds, parenthetically, "we prefer the Communist."(*CW* 1/1936: 2)

In a column written later that year and published as a pamphlet, she argues that "Because of [the] dogma of the Mystical Body, Catholics may not allow their souls to be clouded with greed, selfishness and hate. They may not hate Negroes, Jews, Communists. When they are guilty of prejudice, they are injuring the Mystical Body of Christ." Day never missed an opportunity to show Catholic readers how Communists were providing models for Catholic Action in their work with laborers, the poor, and with blacks; at the same time, she pointed out that "Communists and radicals of all descriptions" who valorize political martyrs "should realize the mystery of the tremendous sacrifice of Christ."(Day 1936)

For Day, the Mystical Body of Christ provided a symbolic "container"where all enemies or opposing ideas could be meaningfully brought together and made to appear functionally interdependent. Love was the method by which the Mystical Body was made possible: not only the love of Christ for all, but the love of each member for the other (Merriman 1994).

Day actively sought to overcome readers' obstacles to loving others. She frequently noted how mistaken we are about those who differ from us, particularly those we use as our dramatic "foils." The dramatic foil is a figure that represents the antithesis of our beliefs and values: "we" are who we are because we are *not* "them." Day's voluntary poverty was a way of establishing solidarity with those with whom she worked (a "humbling" way of life in itself) but it was also a dramatic enactment of a role that "played" on the stage of American Catholic social life. Dorothy Day embodied and performed what upwardly mobile Catholics wanted most *not* to be, or to remember being. She confronted each Catholic with the continuing reality of poverty, making it difficult to ignore. In both her personal demeanor and her writing, she opposed popular conceptions of poverty as squalor and the impoverished as morally inferior. The witness of Dorothy Day and the Catholic Workers directly challenges the complacent self-regard and self-righteousness of prospering Catholics, while goading them to revision the characterological "foil" (the poor) by which they define themselves as living moral lives of abundance.

Day's experiences as a political prisoner furnished another opportunity for her to confront American Catholics' understandings of their "enemies" and to demonstrate the commonality of all in Christ. In an article published in *Liberation* shortly after she was released from prison in 1957 for refusing to participate in New York's civil defense drill, for example, Day explores how perceptions of innocence and guilt separate people and keep them from loving one another. Day's rhetorical posture in the piece shifts from being a "foil" to members of the "outside" world to being a "foil" to other prisoners. Both stances catch the reader short, challenging him or her to re-examine his or her moral perspective.

She begins by describing what it is like to pass through the boundary of "inside" and "outside" prison: each side represents a morally superior perspective. Explaining her surprise at being exhausted and disoriented on her release, Day reflects a prisoners' perspective. "One comes out of jail into a world where everyone has problems...and the first thing that strikes me is that the world today is almost worse than jail."(5) In assuming the role of a "foil" for the "free" and "lawabiding" citizen, Day shows how the world we take for granted as normal and sane is, to the sensitive eyes of the prisoner, worse than confinement. Our relative freedom is purchased by a righteousness that the prisoner, particularly, a prisoner of conscience, sees right through: "the world today is...worse than jail."

Later in the piece, she probes the perceptions prisoners had of her when she first arrived at the prison, using it as an object lesson in the human frailty we all share and as a parallel to how "law abiding" citizens might have viewed her. Prisoners viewed Day and the other women who were involved in the protest as prostitutes and drug addicts because they had been arrested in a park. "It seemed to me to indicate more clearly our common humanity—this misconception of theirs; also that our fellow prisoners feel in a way innocent by contrast to the world where 'everyone is dishonest...everyone drinks, plays around...and is trying to get a kick, even if not with dope."(6) At this point, the article is likely to create sympathy for Day and the others who were arrested in the park because *their* foils, the "real" criminals, "mistook" them for moral deviates. As readers, we expect to hear how Day "straightened out" the prisoners' misconceptions, but before she does that, she tells us that those misconceptions are signs of our common humanity, i.e., we *all* feel innocent next to the accused. In this regard, those who are "free" are no better than those who are incarcerated. Day catches us in our own superiority even as she notes the irony of prisoners thinking they are better than the latest arrivals and the world from whence they came.

Day concludes with a story about how the prisoners came to recognize the protesters' ideals and to respect their religious sincerity.

She provides a contrasting vision for the prisoners' eventual release that might be read as a prescription for our own entry into a world without bars (the bars, for example, of our own superiority and cynicism):

> There was no prohibition against talking quietly. I told two Negroes from Florida ...that one way they could help when they got out would be by sending funds to Martin Luther King to further his work of non-violent resistance all through the South....[A] prevailing sin of the age is this feeling of the futility of any endeavor. There is too much analyzing. We look too far ahead. If we do the right thing, unquestioningly; if we pray that God will water the seed we plant; then we can have faith that He will give the increase. Certainly, 'without Him we can do nothing,' and yet 'with Him we can do all things.' (7)

Day shows us the need for opposites in this piece even as she embodies them. The incarcerated prisoner "clarifies" the vision of the prisoner of complacency and superiority; the prisoner of conscience "clarifies" the vision of both the incarcerated prisoner and the prisoner of complacency. Day needs to appear joined to other prisoners in order for her "saintliness" to have the effect of calling us to conscience; if she does not stand with the incarcerated, then we are not challenged to acknowledge prisoners as our moral *"foils."* Similarly, if she is not verbally aligned with sanctity, her function as a "foil" to prisoners' misplaced sense of innocence is compromised. Day's prophetic witness requires that she enact the role of a dramatic ironist. In such a role, she is able to use a distinctive and powerful persuasive appeal (1) to help forge bonds of affection between people who regard themselves as moral opposites, (2) to bring about a closer, more trusting relationship between disparate people and the God of their creation; and (3) to encourage personal activism despite seemingly overwhelming odds against making widespread social change.

Dorothy Day's strategy and stance as a persuader may explain why she made a point of resisting the idea of canonization. It is hard to imagine or to remember saints *ironically.* Canonization literalizes sanctity; it flattens the dynamic interplay of piety and impiety that animate an ironist's life and that, in Day's case, helped to define her prophetic witness. Communication scholars have argued that radicals encounter a paradox when they try to adapt their message to a hostile or indifferent public: to the extent that they succeed in adapting to their audience, they lose their radical separateness that gives their message its challenge and force. But if they do not adapt, their message will not be heard at all (Branham and Pearce 1985: 19-36). Day seems to me to have been masterful in accommodating the radical's paradox. She knew the importance of communicating with an audience. Yet she was also wary of what audiences might make of her. She used irony to keep her sympathizers from domesticating her and her hostile or indifferent audiences from dismissing her. Remembering her as an ironist provides a satisfying way for us to honor her *as* a gifted writer and as a perpetually fiesty saint. Her ironic strategy and stance continues to invite audience participation as we listen to her message. It fuels a continuing challenge to our complacency and an urgent, hopeful call to activism.

Acknowledgments

This work was supported, in part, by the University of South Florida Research and Creative Scholarship Grant Program under Grant Number 1217-932-RO, and by a University of South Florida College of Arts and Sciences Faculty Development Travel Grant.

I am grateful for the assistance of Phil Runkel, whose generous help when I was working with the Dorothy Day-Catholic Worker Collection at the Marquette University Archives made this work possible.

Notes

[1] Dorothy Day–Catholic Worker Collection, Series D-8, Box 4. In an editorial in Sept, 1983 issue of *Salt*, Fr. Henry Fehren called for Day's canonization. *Salt* acted as a clearing house for eyewitness accounts of her influence. Bruce Buursma, "Catholic Magazine Sets Drive for Sainthood for Dorothy Day," Chicago *Tribune,* August 23, 1983, 2, 5; Bart Pollack, "Effort Begun to Declare Catholic Worker Founder a Saint," Syracuse *Herald Journal*, Sept. 3, 1983, A4. See also Kenneth L. Woodward, *Making Saints: How the Catholic Church Determines Who Becomes a Saint, Who Doesn't, and Why* (New York: Simon and Schuster, 1990), 29-36.

[2] One of the major concerns about efforts to canonize Day comes from followers who believe that canonization would domesticate her radicalism and take her away from ordinary people. See, for example, Daniel Berrigan, S.J., "Letter to Editor," *Salt*, January 1984; Gayle Catinella, "Say No to Sainthood," *At the Door*, Spring 1988; Jim Forest, "We Are Called to Be Saints," *Pax Christi* 10 (March 1985): 18. Dorothy Day-Catholic Worker Collection, Series D-8, Box 4.

The Last Word Is Love: Activism, Spirituality, and Writing in the Life of Dorothy Day

Markha G. Valenta

Leiden University (The Netherlands)

Much attention has been given to Dorothy Day's intense desire to fully experience this human world as well as to know and respond to God. Much less attention has been given to her equally deep hunger to communicate, to write of her experiences of the world and of God. Yet it was Day's writing which to a significant extent sustained her social activism, her spirituality, and, in particular, her notable integration of them.

Before discussing Dorothy Day's writing, however, I need to first take a detour to consider Dorothy Day as a reader, for it was her reading which generated and shaped not only her desire to write, but also her yearning to change the world and her strong sense of God. More than 40 years later, Dorothy Day still vividly recalled her first significant reading experience. It was a rainy Sunday afternoon in a Berkeley attic. Dorothy was six years old and reading aloud to her sister from an ancient and imposing Bible they had found. Suddenly, in the midst of play, Dorothy was overcome with a profound feeling of intimate awe. While a moment earlier she had merely been imitating her teachers, her recitation was utterly transformed as "a new personality [impressed] itself on me. I was being introduced to someone and I knew almost immediately that I was discovering God."(Day 1938: 20; Day 1952: 20) It was "a rich, deep feeling" that revolutionized the event into a sumptuous metaphysical moment.

The moment was all the more remarkable for Dorothy Day since she came from a family in which emotion was rarely expressed. At best, Dorothy and her sister could hope for "a firm, austere kiss from my mother every night" but "never a close embrace." They were never "handholders," never "fresh and spontaneous" but "always withdrawn and alone." (Day 1952: 35) Correspondingly, her sudden and thorough inundation in emotion that afternoon marked what would become a lifelong anchoring point. Not only was it a time from which in hindsight she traced her first intimate, meaningful connection to Christianity and religion, but specifically she felt deeply implanted within her the sense of "having a book which would be with me through life."(Day 1938: 20) That is, from the first Dorothy's spirituality was closely linked to both emotional expression and literature, to individual metaphysical communion and inspiration through printed mediums.

Dorothy's awakening to radicalism during her last year of high school, like her religious awakening a decade earlier, was equally mediated through written narratives. These included articles in the socialist newspaper for which her older brother Donald worked, the books of Upton Sinclair and Jack London, biographies of American radicals, the works of the Russian anarchist Prince Peter Kropotkin and of Vera Figner. Upton Sinclair's *The Jungle* left a particularly strong impression because it was about Dorothy's own city, Chicago. In response to her readings, Dorothy began to take long walks in the immigrant neighborhoods close to her home, imagining the scenes of Sinclair's book taking place in the houses she passed by. She compared their poverty with the luxury of the rich neighborhoods along Lakeshore Drive. Believing firmly that the destitution and misery she had read about and now witnessed personally were utterly unnecessary and wrong, she wished she could do something, could play her part in righting this injustice. At this time too, in response to reading Sinclair and London, Dorothy stopped attending the Episcopal church, though she did continue her extensive ecumenical religious readings, including the Christian Science lesson, the New Testament in its original Greek, Wesley's sermons, and Thomas a Kempis' *Imitation of Christ.*

Already as an adolescent, Dorothy translated what she read into concrete actions. The result was that the moment she walked around the corner to explore immigrant neighborhoods like those described in Sinclair's book, the literary reality of his novel took on a material identity. It was embodied in specific buildings and streets, in the smells of bread and tar floating from those buildings and streets, in the brightness of marigolds, and in all the other myriad sense impressions touching Dorothy. Simultaneously, the real, concrete neighborhoods through which Dorothy walked were narrativized, viewed and understood along the lines of the social-realist stories that so impressed her. For Dorothy, the reality of these neighborhoods, and her understanding of them, derived not simply from their physical existence and her personal experience of them, but from their ability to be inserted into the narratives she had read, to be made a part of the stories and the stories a part of them. So the streets and her reading existed not independently of each other as separate islands of experience, one as "real life" and the other as "fiction", but as integrated extensions fusing and diffusing through each other. Through her novels she "read" her social world and personal experience, and through these in turn she read her novels. Dorothy Day's approach to each blended together story and history, undermining the border between the written world and the material, the read world and the lived.

This intimate blending required first, however, that what Dorothy read and what she experienced in the social, material world would be able to be compared to and tested against each other. Dorothy's second concrete action in response to her readings, stopping her church-attendance after several years of intense religious consciousness and activity, resulted from her inability to do just that. Sinclair's novel contains a strong critique of the Roman Catholic Church as the ultimate symbol of religious institutions' oppression of the poor; but it also includes a counter to that critique in the form of a Protestant socialist hobo-minister championing the image of Jesus as radical worker. At the time that Day read Sinclair's novel, she felt conflicted about the interim religious sensibility she had developed as a young adolescent, but she continued to juxtapose religious readings and radical narratives critical of religion. She was unable, however, to accept the resolution to the tensions between them which Sinclair's novel offered in the form of a radical Protestantism. Though a middle class Protestant socialist movement was active at this time (with its own publication, *The Christian Socialist*), it is likely that no such entity as a radical minister existed in Day's immediate environment. That is, she could not walk around the corner and find one as she had been able to discover the immigrant communities portrayed in Sinclair's novel. Lacking the concrete presence of a Protestant radicalism she could personally experience and with which she could confront the criticisms of religion to which her reading exposed her, Dorothy had trouble relating to the example found in Sinclair's novel. It failed to come alive for her, literally as well as metaphorically, so she herself could not bring it to life. This lack of an immediate living example which integrated Protestant Christianity and social radicalism resulted both in Dorothy's failure to respond to the literary example Sinclair presented and in her intensifying sense of opposition between the social critique she read and the religious experiences that had fascinated her since childhood. While her readings were so clearly relevant to the social world around her, her religiosity came to seem increasingly distant, self-indulgent, and hypocritical.

Within a few years, the absence of Christian social action in Day's environment brought the tension between her faith and her radicalism to a climax. She tells us in *The Long Loneliness*

> I did not see anyone taking off his coat and giving it to the poor. I didn't see anyone having a banquet and calling in the lame, the halt, and the blind....I wanted, though I did not know it then, a synthesis. I wanted life and I wanted the abundant life. I wanted it for others too. I did not want just the few, the missionary-minded people like the Salvation Army, to be kind to the poor, as the poor. I wanted everyone to be kind. I wanted every home to be open to the lame, the halt and the blind. (Day 1952: 39)

For a time Dorothy clung to her faith in God after reading Dostoyevsky and Tolstoy during her first year of university; but not knowing anyone who lived out the Bible narratives, Day found it impossible to have the pages of the New Testament come into being, into living action:

> Religion...had no vitality. It had nothing to do with everyday life....Christ no longer walked the streets of this world, He was two thousand years dead and a new prophet had risen up in His place....The masses...were...the new Messiah, and they would release the captives. (Day 1938: 48)

So Dorothy rejected religion and the Bible, if not Biblical metaphors, for the time being.

When, a decade later, Dorothy returned to religion, it would be to the Roman Catholic Church, one of the central religious and social institutions in the immigrant communities she had come to love via her involvement with the socialist, radical labor, and Communist movements. Here too, as with the Protestant churches, Day had no examples before her who combined religion and radical social critique. But she did have before her the example of the crowds of impoverished workers from Eastern and Southern Europe who daily flocked to Mass. Though they did not critique society (from a specifically Catholic perspective, that is), they were a far cry from the self-satisfied, Protestant bourgeoisie Dorothy had known as a child in California and Chicago. Day as yet knew nothing of Catholic social teaching but she "felt that the Church was the Church of the poor, that St. Patrick's had been built from the pennies of servant girls, that it cared for the emigrant."(Day 1952: 150) The simultaneous recognition that as an institution the Roman Catholic Church was "lined up with property, with the wealthy, with the state, with capitalism, and with all the forces of reaction" was a painful one; but the example of Catholic immigrants around her combined with her recent religious readings, offered enough of a counter to allow her return to an explicit religious faith and practice.

During her conversion, Dorothy Day followed her life-long pattern in which each new phase was marked by new readings linked to new actions. In the years immediately prior to her baptism she immersed herself in a new religious literature, beginning in the early 1920s with the autobiographical novels of the famous French symbolist Joris-Karl Huysman, whom Dorothy credited with making her at home in the Catholic Church. She reread Kempis, St. Augustine, the New Testament, as well as Dostoyevsky. Around 1926 and 1927, by then taking catechism lessons and despairing of the saccharine, pious material with which she was presented by Sister Aloysia, Dorothy turned to the great, if agnostic, psychologist William James' *Varieties Of Religious Experience*. This, in turn, led her to the autobiographies of the activist saints Teresa of Avila and John of the Cross.

Dorothy noted at this point in her autobiographical accounts that she was not introduced to the "good" contemporary Catholic literature, because the Catholics she knew did not read anything besides newspapers and secular magazines. While this is an accurate reflection of her experience, what Dorothy Day failed to note is how utterly unusual her literary inclination is for a lay Catholic of that generation. This is particularly true regarding her close personal familiarity with and reliance on the Bible in an age when some priests still prohibited laypeople from reading the Bible without a priest being present. While Dorothy Day was committed to joining the church of the poor, she never even considered abandoning her literary habits or standards, despite the extent to which they by and large differentiated her from the poor.

Peter Maurin's verbal indoctrination of Dorothy five years later, leading to the foundation of the Catholic Worker, was closely accompanied by a long reading list whose purpose was to educate her in the Catholic radical tradition, including papal encyclicals, 19th and 20th century French radical Catholic thought and the lives of more saints, particularly Catherine of Siena and Francis of Assisi. These readings, illustrated by the living example of Peter Maurin, whom Day described as a modern St. Francis, and Peter's specific plan to bring together cult and culture and cultivation, would finally enable Dorothy to find the synthesis for which she had been looking: "to make a synthesis reconciling body and soul, this world and the next, the teachings of Prince Peter Kropotkin and Prince Demetrius Gallitzin, who had become a missionary priest in rural Pennsylvania." (Day 1952: 151)

Though Day (and many others) phrased that synthesis in terms of integrating radical social critique and traditional Catholic religiosity, the material and the spiritual, an equally important but unnamed synthesis consisted of her integrating her readings, her written and her lived life. No longer was she excluding much of her (religious) reading and experience from her public writing as she had prior to her conversion (the most pronounced example of her editing is to be found in the critical ellipses pock-marking *The Eleventh Virgin*), and no longer was she writing predominantly about what she observed. Now Day wrote about her own actions, about her faith, about her readings and about the relation among the three. Much as her readings had been (and would continue to be) both stimulant and response to her life, from now on her writing would do the same, explicitly shaping as well as shaped by her spirituality and radicalism. A critical, early example of this link lies in the founding moments of the Catholic Worker movement. Originally, Dorothy and Peter had called for parish houses of hospitality. Almost immediately, however, in the very process of putting together and distributing the paper, a community came into being all on its own. Not only did this community consist of those involved with *The Catholic Worker*, but, most importantly, it arose in direct response to Day's (and Maurin's) writing. The phenomenal growth of the movement (within six months circulation rose from 2,500 to 100,000 and by 1941 there were 33 Catholic Worker homes and farms spread throughout the country) was not only generated but critically sustained by the presence of the *Catholic Worker* (Day 1952: 182, 186). Dorothy Day's writing was much more than simply the original impetus to the movement; it was her primary way of touching people, of connecting with them, of creating a community of readers to sustain the community of Catholic Workers.

Dorothy Day's writing continued to be influenced by her prolific reading of many of the new books by Emmanuel Mounier, Jacques and Raissa Maritain, Leon Bloy, Charles Peguy and Chaim Potok, but also the same books she had first discovered in childhood and reread tens of times until she could quote whole pages and chapters. These works included the Psalms, *The Imitation of Christ*, the Gospel of St. Matthew, St. Augustine's *Confessions*, lives of the saints (notably Teresa of Avila, Catherine of Siena, John of the Cross, Francis of Assisi and Therese of Lisieux), and the works of the great Russian novelists, particularly Dostoyevsky and Tolstoy. Reading these books, Dorothy once said, gave her the feeling of returning to visit old friends,

Throughout her writings, Day uses the lives of both fictional and historical characters as the standard against which to relate, compare, and evaluate her own experiences and the world around her. Often what Dorothy read in her books seemed more real to her and offered her greater insight into her experiences of the world than what the living people around her had to say. At times this relation was based on direct historical and cultural correspondences, as in the case of London and Sinclair; but it could also derive from broadly philosophical, spiritual, or emotional correspondences, as in the case of nineteeth-century Russian novelists. In college, for example, she found the narratives of Tolstoy and Dostoyevsky to be more "related to life as [she] saw it" than what she was being taught in the classroom by her professors (Day 1952: 43). It was this correspondence which made the books into such good friends and which led Dorothy later in her life to describe reading as a form of prayer. When Sister Peter Claver, for example, first tried to interest her in the talks of Fr. Roy, Dorothy told her that she preferred to go for her spiritual guidance to the lives of the saints. These she could trust to be interesting and insightful.

Significantly, in her own writing Dorothy Day took on the same role of a friend speaking directly to the reader. The germ of Dorothy's writing lay in her hunger, present from very early on, to communicate and by communicating to find community (Day 1952: 49). In her autobiographical novel, *The Eleventh Virgin*, Dorothy writes of her alter ego June chasing her brothers through the house, wielding a knife at them, after they had discovered the hiding place of her diary yet once again and teased her by reciting parts of it out loud. Despite the constant threat of exposure and the recurrent violation of her privacy, Dorothy continued to keep a diary throughout her childhood and early adolescence. The diary provided companionship to the young June: "As furious as [she] became...she never ceased keeping [her diary], because she was lonesome and the little red book was her only comfort."(Day 1924: 20) Writing made happiness last longer, while it dramatized sorrow and took away its bitterness. Writing was a way to work through a problem (Day 1952: 115). Writing modified Dorothy's lived, experienced reality, compensating for it, intensifying it, softening it, ordering it, and providing an audience (even if that audience was originally only her diary) to validate her experiences and to nurture her as much as the books she read.

Dorothy cited a story told in Dostoyevsky's *The Insulted and the Injured* to explain why she herself wrote as an adult. In the book, a young author reads his own new book to his foster father, who responds: "It's simply a little story, but it wrings your heart. What's happening all around you grows easier to understand and to remember, and you learn that the most downtrodden, humblest man is a man, too, and a brother."

Dorothy Day thought when she read those words, "That is why I write."(Day 1963: 71) Significantly, while Dorothy's audience has perceived the humanity of the downtrodden in the process of reading Dorothy's work, Day herself came to perceive humanity more clearly in the process of writing. Writing was both an end as well as a means for Day. She tells us:

> Whenever I felt the beauty of the world in song or story, in the material universe around me, or glimpsed it in human love, I wanted to cry out with joy. The Psalms were an outlet for this enthusiasm of joy—and I suppose my writing was also an outlet. (Day 1952: 29)

Inverse to her reading process, where she translated the written word into lived actions, in her writing Day converted her lived experiences into language. Writing, like reading, could at times be a form of prayer, of spiritual communion for Dorothy. Among Day's most successful examples of this are her descriptions and citations of the destitute visitors to the Catholic Worker, as well as more broadly her description of the slum neighborhoods in which she lived and which she visited.

Reading Day's descriptions of these slums and of the destitute, one can be tempted to find them naively innocent, absent of gritty reality when compared for example to the rampant violence, sexuality, and oppression to be found in Mike Gold's description of these same neighborhoods in *Jews without Money* (1930). Yet, we know that Dorothy explicitly sought out and confronted herself with that grittiness. Understanding her writing (like her reading) as a form of prayer, however, explains the paradox, if we remember that a central component of Day's spirituality and activism consisted of seeing the Christ in those we would be most likely to spurn. In providing these humanizing portraits of the ghettoes and of the destitute, in discovering their beauty rather than ugliness, Dorothy was in fact expressing her own spiritualized understanding and enabling her readers to see with new eyes, hoping that this new vision would lead to new actions.

This close connection between writing and action was far from accidental. In an interview with Robert Coles, Dorothy explained:

> We write in response to what we care about, what we believe to be important, what we want to share with others. I have never stopped wanting to do so. I have been reached so many times by certain writers. What is this distinction between writing and doing that some people make? Each is an act. Both can be part of a person's *response*, an ethical response to the world. (Coles 1973: xi-xii)

In her early diaries, Dorothy is generally her own ideal audience, though at times she also directly addresses her sister, who might snoop at any moment, and indirectly addresses her friend Henrietta. Day's three autobiographical narratives written as an adult are each framed within the context of a dialogue, though the listening reader becomes an increasingly public and complex one. This shift can be witnessed first on a small scale within Dorothy's first book, *The Eleventh Virgin.* Beginning in the voice of a neutral limited-omniscient narrator simply observing June's life, the book gradually shifts into an internal dialogue within June—beginning interestingly enough the moment that the narrator describes June's adolescent religiosity—and culminates in a dialogue between June and her sister in which June offers an explicitly anti-feminist, traditionalist interpretation of the story of her life as told in the novel. Day's second autobiographical book, *From Union Square to Rome*, is explicitly framed in the beginning as a letter to her younger brother John, a Communist, explaining her conversion to Catholicism. But as a public letter the book is also intended for all her Communist friends who cannot understand her decision, as well as for all those Catholics who suspect her of being an enemy boring from within. Having to a large degree found the value system for which she (as well as June) so desperately sought in the first narrative, her own position is more stable, though not necessarily entirely consistent. More dramatic is her attempt to balance multiple audiences, and it is in relation to this that we see the first blossoming of her collage narratives; that is, they begin to depart from the serial dialogues and sets of oppositions in *The Eleventh Virgin* in favor of integrating multiple, previously contradictory, standpoints into one whole so that, for example, Day can cite the New Testament, Communists, the I.W.W. and St. Teresa within a paragraph of each other (Day 1938: 160).

Day's third autobiographical work, *The Long Loneliness*, begins by being framed as a confession (to herself, to her audience, perhaps to God), detailing her life and work and implicitly her sins. While the first two-thirds of the book are narrated in the first person "I," in the final third of the book Day's individual voice becomes increasingly interspersed by the plural subject "we," as she shifts from personal history to a history of the movement, culminating in her famous postscript, beginning "We were just sitting there talking." Which, by the way, I think would have been more accurate, though less poetic, if she had written "We were just sitting there writing." This "we" broadens to include the entire audience two paragraphs from the end when Day writes in universal terms: "We cannot know God unless we love each other, and to love we must know each other." In the final sentence of the book, repeating, "It all happened while we sat there talking," the "we" shifts from universal back to referring only to Catholic Workers. But by the fact that the entire audience has been included just a moment before the possibility has opened for that audience, now or in the future, to be once again included; the boundary between the narrator and reader, the "I "and the "you," can be abolished in the communal "we."

Importantly, this is a "we" characterized by multiple voices rather than a representative one. Throughout her writings, but with increasing refinement as times went on, Dorothy Day made extensive use of quotations to capture the viewpoint and personality of other characters. In *The Long Loneliness*, she put together perhaps her most complex and nuanced collage by interspersing anonymous destitutes, famous secular radicals, radical Christians and Catholics, Catholic Workers, and her own lightly edited diary entries, letters, and more polished narratives, at times even plagiarizing (borrowing without telling us) from her own previous books, including *The Eleventh Virgin*.

Dorothy Day's readings and writing sustained a community of voices, crossing borders of history, religion, class, politics, mental and physical health. She revivified ancient and medieval lives thought irrelevant to our modern, capitalist society. She brought contradictory modern voices and ideas, religious and radical, factual and fictional, in touch with each other. And the special thing is that in bringing this community together on paper as well as in life, making fluid the boundaries separating the written and the lived, the past and the present, the spiritual and the radical, Dorothy both found the integration and community she so yearned for and made it possible for others to do so as well.

Jeff Poniewaz

Well Paid Slaves

Just because some
slaves are well paid
doesn't mean they
aren't slaves,
doesn't mean
they're free.
Just because some
concentration camps
pay a higher minimum wage
and have a few more
"creature comforts"
than Dachau
doesn't mean they aren't
concentration camps.
Almost the whole human race
is slaves
to the world
they've imposed
(super imposed)
over the real world
and all the eons of Creation–
bricking up our natural souls
in Gothic walls of Civilization.
All the skeletons
in all the dark closets of History!

Poetry brings light,
visions bring sight–
human race getting ready for
a giant step of the Mind
that dwarfs the baby step to the Moon.
A Giant Step,
a gentle giant step
more daring than stealing fire
or a goose that lays golden eggs.
A far step, a vast step,
a step in the right direction–
an evolutionary sport
more thrilling than the Olympics.
A daring step out of the Dark Ages
into the Ages of Light!

PART VII

DOROTHY DAY'S SPIRITUALITY

Ade Bethune's Pray & Work/Ora et Labora first appeared in the January 1937 *Catholic Worker.*

Identity, Community, and Crisis: The Conversion Narratives of Dorothy Day

Catherine Faver

University of Tennessee

Conversion may be conceptualized as a crisis of identity because it entails a choice of self-definition. Moreover, recent research suggests that for women in particular, the development of both identity and spirituality is rooted in relationship and community. Focusing on the concepts of identity and community in Dorothy Day's conversion narratives highlights the links between her construction of self, her understanding of God, and her vision of social transformation.

Theoretical Perspectives: Women's Identity and Spirituality

Recent theory and research on women's psychological development suggests that healthy development of identity occurs not through separation from attachments, but through differentiation of self within significant relationships. The notion of the relational self of women challenges the conventional, male-biased developmental models by emphasizing relationship and connection over autonomy and separation in the process of individuation (Gilligan 1982; Chodorow 1985). In short, the development of a unique self is achieved in and through the context of relationships.

Recent research on spirituality among women also affirms the centrality of relationship, connection, and community in women's lives. For example, Winter, Lummis, and Stokes (1994) found that many women who rejected the patriarchal authority of the institutional church nevertheless remained in the church because they found "continuity...community, and connection" (p.196) through congregational participation. The researchers referred to the stance of these women, both Catholic and Protestant, as "defecting in place," a paradoxical position in which women are both true to themselves and committed to the church. Among women dissatisfied with the institutional church, "defecting in place" is a strategy chosen because community is so critical in their lives. Yet, because the institutional church does not completely meet their needs for community, many "defectors in place" are also members of women's spirituality groups, which provide support, alternative forms of worship, and opportunities to work for social change. Indeed, recent scholarship suggests that social justice is a central value in many forms of women's spirituality, and that women often use the resources of religious institutions to support their efforts for change (Winter, Lummis and Stokes, 1994; Eck and Jain, 1987; Plaskow and Christ, 1989).

Taken together, the research and theory on women's identity development and spirituality alert us to the significance of relationships and community in women's spiritual autobiographies. Of course, much attention has been given to Day as co-founder of a community. The focus of this paper is on identity and community in the conversion narratives of Day.

Dorothy Day's autobiographical writings include narratives of two conversions: a conversion away from her childhood faith in late adolescence and her conversion to Catholicism more than a decade later. The narratives of each conversion reflect two crises: a crisis of identity and a crisis of community.

Method

The method of this study is narrative analysis in the tradition of interpretive social science. The interpretive tradition does not assume a direct correspondence between lived experience and the oral or written accounts of experience. Instead, it is assumed that all accounts are representations of experience, and the researcher interprets the representations in the source documents (Denzin 1989; Riessman 1993). As Denzin reminds us, the biographical project is an interpretive process.

Narrative analysis does not aim to determine the truth about a person, but rather how the person constructed her identity or "self." Personal narratives are keys to understanding the construction of identity because, as Riessman explains, "Individuals construct past events and actions in personal narratives to claim identities and construct lives." (p. 2)

The chief primary sources for this analysis are *From Union Square to Rome* (1938) and *The Long Loneliness* (1952). In addition, the analysis is informed by some of Day's other writings and by other biographical accounts of her life (e.g., Forest 1986/1994; Day 1983).

Two points should be made about these sources. First, Dorothy did not write her narratives as autobiographies, but as accounts of coming to faith. As she put it, "I have never intended to write an autobiography. I have always wanted instead to tell of things that brought me to God and that reminded me of God" (Day 1952: 94). Moreover, in his biography of Day, Forest (1986/1994: 157) cites a note Dorothy wrote about *The Long Loneliness*:

> It is always called my autobiography but it is really a selection of periods of my life searching for God and not a story giving the whole truth... .I feel, to put it simply, that it is not the truth about me...[but] only part of the truth.

Second, Day recognized that knowledge, even self-knowledge, is constructed. Our interpretations of the past change as we change. Self-knowledge is particularly elusive because self-deception is a constant danger. Thus she wrote

> I am afraid, too, of not telling the truth or of distorting the truth. I cannot guarantee that I do not, for I am writing of the past. But my whole perspective has changed and when I look for causes for my conversion sometimes it is one thing and sometimes it is another that stands out in my mind. Much as we want to, we do not really know ourselves (1938, in Day 1983: 3-4).

She added: "A conversion is a lonely experience. We do not know what is going on in the depths of the heart and soul of another. We scarcely know ourselves" (1938, in Day 1983: 9).

Analysis

Using citations from Day's writings, the analysis will demonstrate how her accounts of both her rejection of childhood faith during adolescence and her conversion to the Catholic Church during early adulthood represent crises of identity and community.

Childhood Faith

In order to analyze Day's two conversions, we must begin with her childhood faith, which is clearly documented in her autobiographical narratives. In fact, in writing of her conversion to Catholicism in adulthood, she states: "I will try to trace for you the steps by which I came to accept the faith that I believe was always in my heart." (1938, in Day 1983: 3)

As a child Dorothy was baptized and confirmed in the Episcopal church in Chicago, where she "studied the catechism," and "learned the formal prayer of the Church in her Psalms." (Day 1952: 29) Her spirituality, however, was not confined to formal religious training.

She describes experiences of meeting God in solitude as well as periods of melancholy and loneliness, an acute awareness of the beauty of nature and the transience of life, and moments of comfort, peace, and security within her family.

Most prominently, her narratives convey a straining toward union with God and others:

> I always felt the common unity of our humanity; the longing of the human heart is for this communion.... All beauty, all joy, all music thrilled my heart and my flesh, so that they cried out for fulfillment, for union. (Day 1952: 29, 35)

Ironically, however, she summarizes her childhood faith in terms of intellect and reason rather than emotion and relationship: "All those years I believed. I had faith. The argument of authority, of conscience, of creation—I felt the validity of these."(Day 1952: 36)

Youth: Identification with the Poor

During adolescence, Day's evolving identity was centered on an aspiration to fight injustice, initially through writing. Her reading began to be "socially conscious,"creating in her an identification with the poor and giving a direction to her life:

> Kropotkin especially brought to my mind the plight of the poor, of the workers, and though my only experience of the destitute was in books, the very fact that *The Jungle* was about Chicago where I lived, whose streets I walked, made me feel that from then on my life was to be linked to theirs, their interests were to be mine; I had received a call, a vocation, a direction to my life. (Day 1952: 38)

First Conversion: Rejection of Faith

Her growing identification with the poor created a crisis of faith which revolved around the issues of identity and community, and resulted in an active rejection of faith. She was identified with the poor, and she believed that the gospels mandated kindness to the poor, and beyond kindness, justice. She wrote

> I felt even at fifteen, that God meant man to be happy, that He meant to provide him with what he needed to maintain life in order to be happy, and that we did not need to have quite so much destitution and misery as I saw all around and read of in the daily press. (Day 1952: 38).

She had her own vision of what community meant, based on her family's experience following the San Francisco earthquake:

> I wanted, though I did not know it then, a synthesis. I wanted life and I wanted the abundant life. I wanted it for others too. I did not want just the few, the missionary-minded people like the Salvation Army, to be kind to the poor, as the poor. I wanted everyone to be kind. I wanted every home to be open to the lame, the halt and the blind, the way it had been after the San Francisco earthquake. Only then did people really live, really love their brothers. In such love was the abundant life and I did not have the slightest idea how to find it. (Day 1952: 39)

But she saw a sharp contrast between Christian ideals and Christian practice because the institutional church was often aligned not with the poor but with the wealthy and powerful. Indeed, the church seemed to be the antithesis of what the Gospel demanded:

> Children look at things very directly and simply. I did not see anyone taking off his coat and giving it to the poor. I didn't see anyone having a banquet and calling in the lame, the halt and the blind. (Day 1952: 39)

When she went to the University of Illinois, the crisis deepened: "In spite of my studies and my work, I had time to read, and the ugliness of life in a world which professed itself to be Christian appalled me."(Day 1952: 42)

Thus we see that the conflict she experienced was between her understanding of herself and the Christian message, on one hand, and the actions of so-called Christian people, on the other. The context in which she experienced this crisis of identity is critical. Away at college, she was homesick and lonely. She needed a community, but the church community, oblivious to injustice, was unacceptable.

The self Dorothy had constructed—identifed with the poor and poised to fight injustice—was consistent with the God of Dostoevsky and Tolstoy, who had awakened her own social conscience. But to Dorothy the community that claimed to be Christian seemed "comfortably happy in the face of the injustices in the world."(Day 1952: 41) She articulated her conflict:

> Both Dostoevsky and Tolstoi made me cling to a faith in God, and yet I could not endure feeling an alien in it. I felt that my faith had nothing in common with that of Christians around me. (Day 1952: 43)

Here we see the intense loneliness Day experienced in her faith. Her identity was consistent with the Christian message as she understood it, but other Christians did not share her perspective. And her need for community was particularly strong in the transition from home to the university. She wrote: "I was tearing myself away from home, living my own life, and I had to choose the world to which I wanted to belong."(Day 1952: 42) She rejected the Methodist youth group because it seemed antithetical to the self she was constructing:

> I did not want to belong to the Epworth League which some of my classmates joined. As a little child the happy peace of the Methodists who lived next door appealed to me deeply. Now that same happiness seemed to be a disregard of the misery of the world. (42)

Instead, she responded to the call of the radicals whose purposes she shared, adamantly distancing herself from those maintaining the status quo:

> The Marxist slogan, "Workers of the world, unite!" … seemed to me a most stirring battle cry. It was a clarion call that made me feel one with the masses, apart from the bourgeoisie, the smug, and the satisfied. (42)

Thus she rejected religion:

> I felt at the time that religion would only impede my work. I wanted to have nothing to do with the religion of those whom I saw all about me...I felt it indeed to be an opiate of the people and not a very attractive one, so I hardened my heart. It was a conscious and deliberate process. (42)

Day's rejection of faith was both an assertion of identity and a choice of community. There is an inextricable link between identity and community because identity cannot be forged in isolation. As philosopher Carol Ochs (1986) notes, "Alone we are not fully ourselves, for our self lies in relationship to other beings" (p.69). In other words, the establishment of identity requires community.

Interlude

After two years Day left the university and began her career as a radical writer and journalist in association with like-minded friends. The ensuing years brought much sadness, including the suicide of a friend, an unhappy love affair, and the tragedy of abortion. A lonely period of "restless searching" (Day 1983: xxi) ended finally on Staten Island, where she found "natural happiness" (Day 1952) with the man she loved. In the joy of pregnancy and the birth of her daughter, she turned increasingly to God in prayer. These experiences culminated in her own conversion to the Catholic Church, a step she felt compelled to take and never regretted, but one which brought her no immediate consolation.

The Second Conversion: Becoming Catholic

Day's decision to enter the Catholic Church, like her rejection of the church during late adolescence, can be seen as a dual crisis of identity and community. Both crises ultimately were resolved in the Catholic Worker movement.

Crisis of identity

In becoming a Catholic, Day felt that she was deserting the cause of the workers, the poor, all those whose causes gave her own life meaning, in favor of the church that was still aligned with wealth and worldly power. She articulated these feelings explicitly:

> I had become convinced that I would become a Catholic; yet I felt I was betraying the class to which I belonged, the workers, the poor of the world, with whom Christ spent His life. (Day 1952: 144)

> I was just as much against capitalism and imperialism as ever, and here I was going over to the opposition, because of course the Church was lined up with property, with the wealthy, with the state, with capitalism, with all the forces of reaction. (Day 1952: 149)

Yet, in the years since she had rejected the church because of its indifference to the plight of the poor and its substitution of charity for justice, she had come to understand two things clearly. First, she had learned that God was identified with the poor: in the Incarnation God became one of the poor, and God can be found in the poor. Indeed, Dorothy herself was drawn to God through the poor:

> Better let it be said that I found Him through His poor, and in a moment of joy I turned to him. (1938, in Day 1983: 7)

> Because I sincerely loved His poor, He taught me to know Him. (1938, in Day 1983: 6)

> The mystery of the poor is this, that they are Jesus, and what you do for them you do to Him. (Day 1983: xxxvi)

> "Inasmuch as ye have done it unto one of the least of these My brethren, ye have done it unto Me." Feeling this as strongly as I did, is it any wonder that I was led finally to the feet of Christ? (1938, in Day 1983: 7)

Second, Day had learned that the church was literally the church of the poor. Those she saw going to and from Mass were a diverse lot of poor people; the poor were in church.

> I know now that the Catholic Church is the church of the poor, no matter what you say about the wealth of her priests and bishops. I have mentioned in these pages the few Catholics I met before my conversion, but daily I saw people coming from Mass....They were of all nationalities, of all classes, but most of all they were the poor. (1938, in Day 1983: 8)

Still, while she saw the church as the church of the poor, she was deeply distressed at its failure to stand against an unjust social order:

> The scandal of businesslike priests, of collective wealth, the lack of a sense of responsibility for the poor, the worker, the Negro, the Mexican, the Filipino, and even the oppression of these, and the consenting to the oppression of them by our industrialist-capitalist order—these made me feel often that priests were more like Cain than Abel. "Am I my brother's keeper?" they seemed to say in

> respect to the social order. There was plenty of charity but too little justice. (Day 1952: 150)

Thus her inner conflict persisted even after she became a Catholic:

> No wonder there was such a strong conflict going on in my mind and heart. I never regretted for one minute the step which I had taken in becoming a Catholic, but I repeat that for a year there was little joy for me as the struggle continued. (Day 1952: 151)

Crisis of Community

For Day, becoming Catholic entailed not only a crisis of identity, but also a crisis of community. This is true because she was leaving the man she loved, and she had no alternative community of support. Years earlier, in rejecting faith, she had sought companions who shared her identification with the poor. But she had not found the satisfying community she sought. Indeed, she suggests somewhat lightly that her disappointing alliance with Communists was a catalyst to faith:

> I have said, sometimes flippantly, that the mass of bourgeois smug Christians who denied Christ in His poor made me turn to Communism, and that it was the Communists and working with them that made me turn to God. (1938, in Day 1983: 7)

Nevertheless, at the point of decision to become a Catholic, she found it very painful to leave the man with whom she had found "natural happiness." She did not want to be alone:

> Becoming a Catholic would mean facing life alone, and I clung to family life. It was hard to contemplate giving up a mate in order that my child and I could become members of the church. (1938, in Day 1983: 33).

Yet she had realized, even before her child was born, that the natural love of husband and child was not enough. Finally, she wrote, "it got to the point where it was the simple question of whether I chose God or man" (Day 1983: xxii). So she made the break, but it left her alone with her child.

Later she reflected on the need for a community beyond the family. While working in California to support herself and her daughter, she had been isolated and bored. Of this period she wrote

> I was lonely, deadly lonely. And I was to find out then, as I found out so many times, over and over again, that women especially are social beings, who are not content with just husband and family, but must have a community, a group, an exchange with others. A child is not enough. A husband and children, no matter how busy one may be kept by them, are not enough. Young and old, even in the busiest years of our lives, we women especially are victims of the long loneliness. (Day 1952: 157-158)

The Crises Resolved

The crises of identity and community merged when Dorothy, working as a journalist, went to Washington, DC, late in 1932 to cover the Hunger March of the Unemployed Councils and the Farmers' Convention, both of which were led by Communists (1939, in Day 1983: 40). Of her experience watching the march, she wrote:

> I watched that ragged horde and thought to myself, "These are Christ's poor. He was one of them. He was a man like other men, and He chose His friends amongst the ordinary workers. These men feel they have been betrayed by Christianity. Men are not Christian today. If they were, this sight would not be possible. Far dearer in the sight of God perhaps are these hungry ragged ones, than all those smug, well fed Christians who sit in their homes, cowering in fear of the Communist menace."
>
> I felt that they were my people, that I was part of them. I had worked for them and with them in the past, and now I was a Catholic and so could not be a Communist. I could not join this united front of protest, and I wanted to. (1939, in Day 1983: 41)

The crises of identity and community were inextricably linked because identity must be actualized in community. Day identified with the protesters, but she could not unite with them because she was Catholic and they were participating in a Communist led movement. At the same time, she felt no kinship with the "smug, well fed Christians" who feared the Communists. The pain must have been particularly acute for Day because since childhood she had "felt the common unity of our humanity"(Day 1952: 29) and had longed for union.

The end of the story accounts for our celebration of Day's life today. While in Washington, DC, she went to the national shrine at the Catholic University to pray "that some way would open up"(Day 1952: 166) for her to work for the poor. She returned to New York, met Peter Maurin, and together they began the endeavor that became the Catholic Worker.

For Day, love of God and neighbor were united finally in community, dispelling the loneliness that had plagued her:

> We cannot love God unless we love each other, and to love we must know each other. We know Him in the breaking of bread, and we know each other in the breaking of bread, and we are not alone any more. Heaven is a banquet and life is a banquet, too, even with a crust, where there is companionship. We have all known the long loneliness and we have learned that the only solution is love and that love comes with community. (Day 1952: 285-286).

The Catholic Worker movement resolved Day's crises of identity and community by uniting her understandings of self, the sacred, and social transformation. Specifically, the Catholic Worker demonstrated that God can be known through the poor; it embodied a vision of justice as a community in which all are welcomed and loved; and it enabled Day to express her own identity, which could only be realized in community.

Conclusion

Recent scholarship (e.g., Winter, Lummis, and Stokes, 1994; Plaskow and Christ 1989) suggests that many Christian women today are challenging the institutional church in their search for identity and community. What do such women have in common with Dorothy Day, who was ever loyal to her church while leading a revolution within it?

First, we often find that women's understanding of the sacred is at odds with the prevailing practices of their churches, challenging the church to examine the radical potential of the Christian message. Second, the search of many women for self and the sacred has led them into deeper, more satisfying experiences of community. Finally, women today are forming small communities to express their understandings of self and God, to embody their vision of social justice, and to foster social transformation.

Dorothy Day's life is a witness to the social mandate of the Gospel and continues to challenge the institutional church. The impact of Christian women today, who in a less conspicuous way are forming communities to assert their understanding of God and to seek social justice, remains to be seen.

Dorothy Day and Thomas Merton: Overview of a Work in Progress

Julie Leininger Pycior

Manhattan College

The historian Raymond Grew wrote, "To call for comparison is to call for a kind of attitude—open, questioning, searching,"(Woodward 1986: 124) and it seems to me that modern pilgrims struggling to live out their beliefs can glean important insights from a study that weaves together the many strands of the Dorothy Day/Thomas Merton relationship.

Organization

I envision a book of two parts plus a coda. Part One will compare Dorothy Day and Thomas Merton's journeys to faith, from childhood into young adulthood. Similarities include their early identification of themselves as writers, their bohemian adventures in New York City, their conversion experiences, and the discovery of their Christian vocations. Differences include her birth in 1897, his in 1915, Merton's loss of his parents, and Day's situation as a single mother. They forged their first tenuous links in the 1940s, reading each other's works and sharing acquaintanceships such as that with Baroness Catherine De Hueck Doherty, founder of the Harlem-based Friendship House. Longtime Catholic Worker Tom Cornell suspects that a conversation with Dorothy Day contributed to Merton's decision to work there (interview 1997). The similarities, differences, and initial interactions are being treated not as determining categories, so much as waves-now big, now small—in their lifelong spiritual voyages.

Part Two will trace Day and Merton's growing interaction from the 1950s onward. Her friendships with people rejected by society and her protests against militarism profoundly inspired him, while no one supported him more fervently in his decision to become a hermit who was increasingly devoted to meditation. Through it all these two prophetic figures read each other's works and wrote to each other and to the world at large: of turning to prayer, the Mass, and the sacraments; of the call to meet Christ in every person, every tradition; of concern about materialism, militarism, and intolerance; of life in their all-too-human Catholic communities; of struggles with their own interior demons. For example, on January 29, 1967 she wrote him

> Do please forgive my long silence. I do not remember if I ever thanked you for your wonderful article on Camus ["Albert Camus and the Church," in the previous month's *CW*] which had wide repercussions, teachers writing for a score or so copies for their classes, and many individual responses.. . . I am at present enjoying your *Conjectures of a Guilty Bystander.* We all feel that way. I am enclosing the last issue of the *CW* in which I had to write about Cardinal Spellman [a staunch supporter of the U.S. military in general and of its role in Vietnam] not only to cry out in grief, but to point [out] the fact that we are all guilty. We can never do enough praying, fasting, penance and I'm glad and happy as usual that Lent is beginning, and I can start anew and try harder. A rather childish feeling because I know how comfort seeking I am. (Klejment and Roberts 1996: 116-117)

Two weeks later Merton replied

> Thanks so much for your good note of January 29th. I have read your piece in the latest *CW* on Cardinal Spellman and the war. It is beautifully done, soft-toned and restrained, and speaks of love more than of reproof. It is the way a Christian should speak up, and we can all be grateful to you for speaking in this way. It has to be done. The moral insensitivity of those in authority, on certain points so utterly crucial for man and for the Church, has to be pointed out and if possible dispelled. It does not imply that we ourselves are perfect or infallible. But what is a Church after all but a community which is truth shared, not a monopoly that dispenses it from the top down. Light travels on a two-way street in our Church, or I hope it does. . . Yes, Lent is a joy. And we do not have to be worried about relishing the cleanness of it. It feels better not to be stuffed. A little emptiness does one good, and I think it is better now that it is something one can simply choose without any sense of legal obligation. More of a gift. Not that I am terribly ascetic myself, I assure you. Far from it. (Merton 1985: 152)

At the same time they differed in some paradoxical ways that deserve exploring. For example, people remarked on the warmth and sociability of Thomas Merton, the hermit in the woods of Kentucky, while many observers noted the self discipline, even asceticism of Dorothy Day, the one immersed in the lives of poor New Yorkers and frequently on the road to lecture or to visit other Catholic Worker houses (Forest 1986: 170, 173; 1991).

The last section, the coda, will examine the ways in which this relationship remains vital. Some years after Merton's death his Trappist confidant John Eudes Bamberger, by then Abbot of Our Lady of the Genesee, invited Dorothy Day to address that community. Abbot John Eudes recalls

> Dorothy Day spoke to us about her work, and the importance of the cross of Jesus which is the one way to salvation and the resurrection. At that time she had a special interest in the "bag women," the homeless women, and was beginning the new home for them. As I'd told you, she herself mentioned to me that giving such a talk was an ordeal, she found it anxiety provoking, though that was not at all evident to others. She was an effective speaker, used a conversational tone and style, not oratorical, and was well received by our community. (Bamberger 1997)

While Thomas Merton's fellow Trappists have continued the Catholic Worker connection since his death, the converse is true as well. In later years Dorothy Day continued to write about him, as do other Catholic Workers to this day. For example, in the March 1997 issue of the *Catholic Agitator*, published by the Los Angeles Catholic Worker, six of the seven articles make reference to Thomas Merton. In her article which recounts her route to membership in the Los Angeles Catholic Worker community, Joyce Parkhurst writes

> When Jim (her husband) retired, we moved to a rural area, a place of silence, solitude, and beauty.... As the years went by, our life took on a monastic rhythm of Eucharist, shared prayer, meditation, and work. We began to read books on intentional community, liberation theology, peace and justice, and everything we could find by Thomas Merton. We used books suggested by the Catholic Worker community in Los Angeles for our scripture study. The Holy Spirit seemed to suddenly explode into our consciousness with such force that we began to pray with a renewed vigor. Slowly, we became aware that we needed to do more; we

> needed to make a deeper commitment of our lives to God. We began to pray for direction and discernment. When Jim responded by spending several weeks at a time living and working with the Catholic Worker community, I decided to try to *really* live a hermit life. I felt that I could participate in Jim's outreach by praying for him and for those he was serving.... After a year and a half of this listening and waiting, both Jim and I felt we had no choice but to move into community in order to try to live out the gospel message to be servants of all, and to follow a life of discipleship.. . . I know for certain that the kingdom does live within me, and that even though I may become busy, be overtired, distracted, interrupted, or overwhelmed by my own failures, that the Spirit continues to pray within me at all times, even though, as Thomas Merton wrote, "I may know nothing about it." (*Catholic Agitator*, March 1997)[1]

The relationship continues to resonate well beyond their respective Trappist and Catholic Worker circles. Take, for example, Maryknoll Father Roy Bourgeois. While in jail for civil disobedience, he was placed in solitary confinement and was on the brink of despair, beginning to doubt the usefulness of his actions. Suddenly Father Bourgeois' spirits rose when he remembered Dorothy Day's dictum that we should hope in God and not become preoccupied with our own effectiveness. For his part, Merton wrote, "Do not depend on the hope of results . . . just serve Christ's truth." Upon his release Bourgeois himself entered a Trappist monastery but did not end up becoming a monk. The Maryknoller decided that he was called to continue speaking out against the U.S. Army's "School of the Americas," which he accuses of training foreign officers on behalf of military dictatorships, but now he is more careful to balance action with meditation (Richter 1996).

Moreover, Day and Merton's shared appeal is not limited to Catholics. Others drawn to both of their examples range from folksinger/activist Joan Baez to television journalist Bill Moyers to writers such as Robert Coles and Kathleen Norris. *New York Review of Books* caricaturist David Levin portrayed Day, Merton, and their friend Daniel Berrigan, and all three also ended up as three of the four people featured on the signature poster for the social action magazine *Sojourners*, which is Christian but non-denominational. (The fourth person was Dr. Martin Luther King.)

Sources

Hundreds of articles and books have been published about Day and Merton. Biographies range from detailed accounts such as William Miller, *Dorothy Day* and Michael Mott, *The Seven Mountains of Thomas Merton* to meditative profiles such as Robert Coles, *Dorothy Day: A Radical Devotion* and William H. Shannon, *Thomas Merton's Dark Path*. For his part, Jim Forest, friend of both Day and Merton, has written insightful biographies of each. In a lengthy interview with me he reflected on the various ways their relationship resonates for us to this day.

In addition, numerous works, while not comparing the two figures, do look at both of them. Such sources include Kenneth L. Woodward, *Making Saints*; Robert Ellsberg, *All Saints: Daily Reflections on Saints, Prophets, and Witnesses for Our Time;* Dan Wakefield, *Returning: A Spiritual Journey;* and Daniel Berrigan, *Portraits—Of Those I Love*. The few writers who have linked Day and Merton have done so in a limited way, as part of another story. For example, Patricia McNeal (1992) perceptively compares their views of war and peace, while Annice Callahan (1991) analyzes the Day/Merton correspondence and compares their published writings. For her part, Sister Brigid O'Shea Merriman (1994) breaks important new ground by demonstrating the ways in which Day's interest in monasticism intersected with Merton's vocation. Also, Sister Brigid is the first writer to note that while they did not begin corresponding until probably 1959, they were influenced by each other's writings from the late 1940s onward.

Thomas Merton wrote prodigiously: over 60 books as well as numerous poems, articles, and prefaces, while Dorothy Day contributed to nearly every issue of the *Catholic Worker* newspaper for some 45 years and published outside pieces and books despite the hectic life at the Catholic Worker house and her frequent travels. Their vivid autobiographical writings shed much light, particularly on their early experiences. Merton's many contributions to the Catholic Worker starting in 1948, together with her many commentaries on his work, are all essential, as is their correspondence to each other, of course, all of which has been published.

Other important correspondence includes their letters to mutual friends and the letters between their mutual friends. Fortunately for us historians, this may have been the last generation of colleagues to write to each other constantly. They also had the presence of mind to save their mail: not only letters, but also notes, picture postcards, flyers, and other ephemera, which are on deposit at various archives.[2]

Oral history interviews also provide insights. Interviews in 1996 and 1997 with people who knew them both, such as Jim Forest, Tom Cornell, and Abbot John Eudes Bamberger, contribute important firsthand reflections on their similarities, differences, and combined significance. At the same ime, the thoughts of influential Americans of various walks of life, from Robert Coles to Joan Baez, can shed light on the relationship's enduring legacy in general.

Day and Merton were intensely involved in a number of worlds, and books about those worlds can locate the relationship in larger contexts. For example, Mark Silk, *Spiritual Politics: Religion and America Since World War II* provides overviews of religious issues in general. Works such as those by Philip Gleason (1987) and David O'Brien (1972) can situate the relationship in the panorama of modern Catholicism, as in the book *The Renewal of American Catholicism,* where O'Brien featured Day and Merton in his analysis of Catholic radicalism, while O'Brien's *Public Catholicism* showed how they both questioned John Courtney Murray's application of the just war theory in the nuclear age. Studies such as Todd Gitlin, *The Sixties: Years of Hope, Days of Rage* can help to locate the relationship in a particular era, while works such as Linda Kerber et. al., *U.S. History as Women's History* can facilitate the examination of Day and Merton as female and male.

Finally, one needs to ask what sources Dorothy Day and Thomas Merton would suggest. I suspect that they would downplay the famous acolytes they shared and instead emphasize the novelists, the poets, the saints, and the prophets from various traditions that inspired them both. Of paramount importance for them, even more than their own writings, would be the Bible, and at the heart of the Bible the teachings of Jesus, to Whom they devoted their lives.

Methodology

The sheer volume of material is daunting, but the vast array of sources can be made more manageable when approached with Day and Merton's relationship always at the center of the investigation. Moreover, given the powerful yet subtle nature of the relationship, themes must develop organically, emerging as much through description as through interpretation. In his memoir, *Thinking Back: The Perils of Writing History*, C. Vann Woodward notes, "portraying and explaining inevitably go together. They should not be confused, but they are difficult to keep apart, and one should not be allowed to crowd out the other. How events happen can be as important as why." Woodward, inspired by Southern novelists, says that they wrote "to illuminate, to explain the past.... (They had] no theory about the past, present, or future...but rather supported the historian's concern for the particular, the concrete, the individual." Woodward quotes Robert Penn Warren as saying, "History is not truth. The truth is in the telling."(Woodward 1986: 56-57).

In other words, Day and Merton's own compelling writings will provide much of the narrative, along with books that inspired them, observations from people who knew them both, and reflections from contemporary observers who continue to be influenced by both of them. Like a quilter, I will endeavor to stitch into a pattern the many colorful evocations, and I hope and pray that in the process a story will emerge that does them justice.

Notes

[1] The authors and their articles are: Joyce Parkhurst, "The Spirit Continues to Pray within Me At All Times"; Jeff Dietrich, "Resisting the False Self"; Lisa Nollette, CSJ, "Waiting Upon the Lord"; Michael Courtright, "Prayer and Control"; Eric Debode, "Praying as a Subversive Action"; Dorothy Day, "Dorothy Day on Prayer."

[2] The Dorothy Day and Catholic Worker Collection at Marquette University, the Thomas Merton Collection at Columbia University, the Thomas Merton Center at Bellarmine College, the Daniel Berrigan Collection at Cornell University, the Catholic Peace Fellowship papers and related collections at the University of Notre Dame, the Henri Nouwen papers at Yale, and the James Forest papers at Boston College and Nazareth College.

Dorothy Day: Citizen of the Kingdom

Roger A. Statnick

Diocese of Greensburg, PA

Sometimes the roots of living things are deeper than first imagined. Dorothy Day has been viewed as a social reform journalist who used her talents and the vehicle of print media to advance her cause for a new society. She seems a feminist to some, a community organizer to others, and a religious reformer still to others. She is difficult, if not impossible, to pigeon hole within the usual categories of various disciplines, and when attempts are made to do so, the treatments are enlightening, yet incomplete. Something remains hidden from the viewpoint of the historian, journalist or sociologist about Dorothy Day and the Catholic Worker.

This buried root, I contend, is the religious foundation of her life and work. This paper will try to uncover this root by unearthing various levels of her story. First, I will present a morphology of Day's and the Worker's religious vision and lifestyle under the rubric of Ernst Troeltsch's categories of Christian tradition. Then, I will move to the theological dynamics underlying this morphology and disclose how the basic principles of the Catholic Christian faith serve to interpret the descriptions Dorothy Day offers for her life and the Catholic Worker movement.

Troeltsch's Typology

In 1912, Ernst Troeltsch published a classic socio-historical analysis of Christianity through the centuries entitled *The Social Teaching of the Christian Churches* (1931). This study was framed in a threefold typology to describe the development of Christian thought, organization and life-style: the Church, the sect, and mysticism (Troeltsch 1960: Vol. 2, 993-1013).

The Church type is Christianity in its most organized and established form. This configuration of the Gospel tradition of Jesus the Christ emphasizes the institutionalization of the message and ministry of the Kingdom of God in this world. Christianity is realized in clear dogmatic teachings, explicit ritual formulas, and a highly developed and centralized organizational structure. The Church model objectifies the reality and workings of grace for the sake of carrying on in time what began in Jesus' life and Easter victory, namely, the transformation of the world into the Kingdom of God in our midst. To accomplish this goal, Christianity takes on the trappings of the social order in which it lives with the purpose of dominating that order in the name and through the underlying power of God. The medieval synthesis known as Christendom is the classic example of this "Church" category.

Yet, despite the attempts of this form to be all inclusive of the full reality of Christian belief, it remained incomplete and limited when measured against the scriptures and sources of primitive Christianity. Thus arose the sectarian dimension of Christian history. The sect realizes a different direction in Christian faith and life-style. Here, community is formed by commitment to a distinct and separate way of life. Rather than moving into the center of societal power and authority, the sect lives on the fringe of the social order, denying its power and appealing to a higher authority. Instead of working to transform the present order that is judged corrupt in its motives, the sect transcends this order by a distinctive life-style which witnesses to God's new order of grace and salvation. Sectarian Christianity exhibits a clarity of belief and practice, but one marked by its eccentric, unconventional and distinctive character. It shows that God is in charge of this world, and our job is to live by the rules of this divine Kingdom, not those of this world.

The third typology which Troeltsch drew from the history of Christianity is mysticism. Here the focus turns inward. While capturing the subjective dimension of Christian belief expressed in the sect, mysticism's subjectivity is one of the private, personal, direct and immediate experiences of the divine rather than personal commitment to a communal life-style, mission, and its witness. The social order has no direct significance to a person's authenticity in faith, but holiness through personal asceticism purifies the clarity of the Gospel reality. The Kingdom of God is within us, and we are called to abandon all the distractions of the sensible, external world and the desires they create to experience the intimacy of divine union when God takes possession of one's life. While mysticism and the sect sometimes overlap in this history of developments in Christianity, the dimensions of the Gospel tradition which each captures are certainly distinct.

Dorothy Day and The Catholic Worker

Elements of the Church, the sect and the mysticism types constitute Day's personal story and the saga of the Worker movement. Let us take a moment to sample these.

Dorothy Day's biography is like a river of varying currents all finally drawn together in the whirlpool of her conversion to the Catholic Church and the Catholic Worker. The peace and security she seems to find whenever she visits a church building or attends a worship service signals "the Church" dimension of her story. Even before she is a Catholic and understands the Church's beliefs and practices, she is attracted to the solemnity of its ritual, the solidity of its social presence and the clarity of its peoples' practices and beliefs. The Church was the center of life in the immigrant ghettos where she lived and worked, and this dominance and established presence drew her to be a part of such a powerful and influential organization.

> I felt that the Church was the Church of the poor, that St. Patrick's had been built from the pennies of servant girls, that it cared for the emigrant, it established hospitals, orphanages, day nurseries, houses of the Good Shepherd, homes for the aged. (Day 1952: 150)

Dorothy Day admired the bold character of the church institution around which people gathered their life's aspirations and found a place to nourish them and link them to make a better life for themselves and their neighbors. Still, she was not to be co-opted by the big, bold and beautiful Church triumphant:

> I felt that [the Church] did not set its face against a social order which made so much charity in the present sense of the word necessary. I felt that charity was a word to choke over. Who wanted charity? And it was not just human pride but a strong sense of man's dignity and worth, and what was due to him in justice, that made me resent, rather than feel proud of so mighty a sum total of Catholic institutions. (Day 1952: 150)

She asserted "one must live in a state of permanent dissatisfaction with the Church." (Day 1938: 133)

Dorothy Day possessed a bohemian spirit that was more than the exuberance and rebellion of youth. Her passion for life could not be contained in any one structure, theory or plan. Her spirit was expansive, always reaching to the limits of the present situation for something better, greater, more inclusive, just and compassionate. The sectarian rebel was in her blood so deeply, that she never felt at home with the simply conventional or with following the usual paths to success and happiness. There was a restlessness within her that drew her always to the fringes of life where she found kindred spirits in artists, political radicals, the poor, and ultimately, the saints: "Maybe if I stayed away from books more this restlessness would pass."(Day 1952: 34; Miller 1982: 61-62, 98, 145, 198-199)

Finally, Dorothy Day's biography would certainly remain incomplete without acknowledging the mystical moments that become reference points in her telling of her own story. For instance, she attests to a felt sense of the divine mystery while reading the scriptures in the attic of her family's Berkeley home at age six (Day 1952: 20). The mystical lure of nature speaks to her of the creator God while she lived on Staten Island after Tamar's birth (Day 1952: 133-135).[1] And later, when involved with the works of mercy at the Worker, it is Christ Dorothy sees when kissing the woman with cancer of the face on the steps of Precious Blood Church (Day 1963: 79). These experiences relate a personal intimacy and immediacy with the divine. Such "mystical" moments drive her life's journey as much as the Church's peace and stability attracted her loyalty, and the Worker's identity wIth the marginalized captured her imagination. Clearly, Dorothy Day's faith commitment is more than a passion for a better world where all people are valued as members of the human family. It is a marriage to the divine lover who lures her away from any lesser love by drawing her more deeply into His Mystical Body (Miller 1987: 3-4).

The same dimensions of the Church, sect and mysticism converge in the Catholic Worker as well. Certainly, the movement is solidly ensconced as a part of the Roman Catholic Church. It self-consciously identified itself with this institution and accepted its authority as binding upon its methods and members. As a lay movement, the Worker could be freer in its life-style and the focus for its mission than a religious order. Nevertheless, Day and Maurin always conceded respect and final approbation to the local bishop whenever a disagreement arose. Similarly, the heritage, tradition, ritual and formal teaching of the Catholic Church were the backbone of its religious practice and understanding. The works of mercy taught in the Baltimore Catechism were a quick summary of the "program," and the Church's sacraments, popular devo-tions, and liturgy of the hours were the mainstay of its spiritual exercises. The Catholic Worker was firmly anchored in the institutional Church, even while it assumed a wide berth to stay afloat in the harbor of humanity.

A certain freedom from accepted ways and expectations distinguishes the Catholic Worker within the Church. Voluntary poverty, uncompromising pacifism, the agronomic university, the principle of personal responsibility as the foundation for social revolution, and the roundtable discussions for the clarification of thought were all elements of the movement that set it apart from the mainline of Church life and practice. These distinguishing marks of the Worker pushed at the edges of Catholic thought and gave witness to the radical roots of the Church tradition.

Unusual for its day, the Worker appealed to the Beatitudes as the source for its distinctive identity. The Catholic Worker saw a new world order and worked at putting it into practice. This vision and lifestyle segregated it from both the Church and civil society at large. It was a sectarian fellowship formed by the commitment to this new way. Yet, while its members were often jailed by civil authorities and dismissed by popular regard, they remained witnesses to the Church and attached to its life and heritage. On the fringe of the institution, the Worker still remained firmly attached. It wanted a quiet revolution from within.

In the general course of Christian history, the church/sect relationship affected by the Catholic Worker was hard to maintain. In the Protestant heritage, usually such a group would simply break away from the mainline and start its own autonomous Christian tradition. In the Catholic heritage, the sectarian renewal consolidated under the rubric of a religious order or institute, allowing it to assume a distinct identity and freedom while remaining attached to the institutional Church. The Worker followed neither of these directions. It took a different course which was spiritually motivated, yet also rather precarious for its survival.

The mystical tradition of the Church with its appeal to spiritual perfection allowed the Worker to retain its sectarian uniqueness as a lay movement never formalized in Church structures, while remaining firmly identified with the institution. Two primary avenues were used for this purpose. First, Pius XII's encyclical, *Mystici Corporis*, provided institutional justification for a vision that was broader and more inclusive than any institutional framework could incorporate. Every human being potentially offered an encounter with the divine mystery of Christ, and so hospitality, respect for personal freedom, and the bonds of human love were more than humanitarian ideals. They were the grounds for grace, for an immediate, personal experience of this divine reality. Day summarized its importance to her: "What God has done for Christ He is going to do for us because we are in the Mystical Body." and "The doctrine which is behind all our effort, the Mystical Body of Christ." (Miller 1987: 150)

The mystical perspective also penetrated the Catholic Worker through the Lacouture retreat. The point of this spiritual revival was to lead the ordinary believer's vision and lifestyle beyond the conventional beliefs and practices of the Catholic Church. It advocated an asceticism that would focus one's desires on the things of the spirit, in the hope of quieting any lesser need. Its objective was to integrate the material and spiritual dimensions of the human condition by penetrating ordinary reality to its heart and revealing there the divine order. The silence, solitude and discipline of the retreat—while sometimes misunderstood and misleading for some followers—were never meant to be ends in themselves, to which one rigorously adhered. Instead, these practices were ways to invite the divine mystery to show itself as the common bond creating community and giving meaning to whatever came in the course of one's life (Day 1952: 243-263; Miller 1987: 51-60).

So all three of Troeltsch's types were incorporated into the journey of Dorothy Day's personal faith and the development of the Catholic Worker movement. Descriptively, the characteristics of the Church, the sect and mysticism are easily verified in Day's life and the Worker's efforts. However, this picture does not explain how such disparate elements can be held intact both within one life and one movement. How was the struggle and tension these conflicting forces generated negotiated in a positive and constructive manner? What was the secret to this spirituality that could reach so thoroughly into this world to address its needs and hurts from a common human identification, yet never compromise its transcendent origin, purpose, and goal? To answer these questions a more analytical approach to this spirituality is needed, one that uncovers the theological premises on which Day built her life and the Worker built its vision of a place "where it is easier for people to be good." (Day 1952: 280)

A Theological Perspective

How much can humankind know and realize in this earthly realm? How a person responds to this question sets the course for what will follow in his or her life. If the possibilities are limited to this time and space, to what is empirically verifiable and exhausted in the intellectual, emotional and social responses it elicits, then one's biography will be drawn within these boundaries. Its significance and accomplishments will be marked in these terms. Dorothy Day and the Worker are not so self-contained. Her life and the Catholic Worker movement were about knowing and working to realize the divine potential within our human condition. The mystical strain we described above arises from this desire and effort, but it rests upon a theological principle that is foundational.

Nature is the substratum for grace. The created order has as its character and purpose to reveal the Creator and serve the divine intentions. There is a congruence between nature and grace, such that the truth of each is shown only through the other. The character of God is good, true, beautiful and one, and the true nature of our human condition is to reflect this goodness, beauty and unity. Since God is all, any reflection of the divine must be as inclusive as possible. To exclude anyone or anything is to contradict the divine movement and frustrate the deepest intentions of our human nature, namely, to be one with God and as God is one. There is no opposition between the created order and the divine order, but rather creation at its roots is ordered to God and is the way the divine order becomes informed in history. Therefore, the spiritual journey is not about overcoming humanity, but disclosing its true nature as made in God's image and destined for God's Kingdom. It is about assuming the human enterprise under the light of grace, such that the individual is free to exercise one's responsibility as co-creator of the Kingdom. In sharing this responsibility, people together can reshape the social order into the Kingdom.

Finitude limits this human enterprise; evil sometimes counters its intentions and tears it apart; and sin distorts the desires of the human heart to follow lesser ends. These themes permeate Day's writings (1938: 123, 132; 1952: 34; 1963: 177-178). So life is often experienced as a struggle full of the tension of opposing forces. Dorothy Day certainly knew this dimension of the human condition and described the efforts at grace in these terms as "a harsh and dreadful love."(Day 1983: 264) But she and the Worker were firmly and resiliently committed to the transformation possible for individuals and society when grace prevails. She staked her life and the Worker movement on this vision. Christian faith for Dorothy Day was certainly not about denying or escaping the sordid side of humanity, but penetrating its harshness and darkness with the power of divine love that can make it whole once again. The discipline of the retreat coupled with the vision of *Mystici Corporis* had this transformation as its purpose. Far from the world-denying, nature-disfiguring tactic of earlier Jansenist spiritualities, Day and the Worker were respectful and accepting of the human condition as the material for a new creation in Christ.

Yet, this point of making "space for grace" gives a peculiar twist to the Worker's efforts. As a reform, or even radical, movement, the Catholic Worker was exceptionally non-pragmatic, and even ineffectual, in its revolution. In this world's terms, it would look at best odd and at worst foolish when measured by concrete and lasting results. Voluntary poverty has done little to re-distribute wealth in this country. Worker pacifism during World War II decimated support for the movement and certainly did little to restrain the war effort. The agronomic university rarely generated even a subsistence living. And personal responsibility for direct action often left many tasks unattended or carried only by a few. Even cast against their sectarian commitment to a different and separate way, these efforts seem misguided, for they did not provide very well for the sect's own needs. At times, they even jeopardized its survival. What is the point?

Dorothy Day often repeated "Love is the measure by which we are judged,"(Forest 1986) and by this she spoke of divine love, God's way of caring for and nurturing the human condition. This way of Providence is not the way of this world. Its viewpoint values reality differently, such that things are inserted or positioned oddly in the ordering of life. Like the Beatitudes to which the Worker often appealed as its justification, an eschatological logic is at work shaping judgment here. Things are measured against their source in divine creation and their destiny in the eternal Kingdom. Existence is God's gift of divine life into our own. Therefore, every person's life holds infinite value. Eternity has no boundaries of time and space, therefore, our hospitality must be as universally inclusive as humanly possible. Divine love welcomes every one as "equally unique." This oxymoron discloses that the rules are different here, because this is no ordinary place, this is the Kingdom of God in our midst. Dorothy Day and the Catholic Worker intended to make the Kingdom a concrete reality for themselves and others in the world, and in so doing they often looked strange and did not add up in ordinary terms.[2]

But the Catholic Church provided an anchor for both the transforming mysticism and the eschatological, sectarian logic of Dorothy Day's and the Catholic Worker's vision and lifestyle. The sacramental principle was the linchpin connecting Day to the Church in her personal conversion and keeping the movement attached to the Church in its many efforts and causes. Building on the potential of nature for grace and on the peculiar power of grace's transformation, the Catholic Church offered an elaborate system of ritual actions as its normal form of worship.

Ritual's intent is to give an ordered form to those dimensions of our human condition which grace can consecrate to show forth and realize the Kingdom in our midst. The sacraments are particular actions in a specific time and place with certain people assembled to participate in them that allow one to stay in touch with graced-nature and its eccentric logic. Their formality and order are important to Day and the Worker, for otherwise the mystic and sectarian dynamics could become completely idiosyncratic and out of touch with the ordinary dimensions of life. In turn, these rituals nourish and sustain this mystical vision and sectarian life-style by offering a tradition that is rooted in the same principles of nature's potential in grace and the eschatological freedom of measure.

At the height of the United States mobilization for World War II, Dorothy Day wrote

> We must prepare to suffer, building up reserves of endurance. Daily Mass and Communion is now more than ever an absolute essential of the work. Without this daily food we are weak. We can do nothing. *The sacraments are our weapons.* [Italics added] (Day 1942)

A movement as loosely organized as the Catholic Worker and a life as free in spirit and broad in scope as Dorothy Day's needed the focus of the Church's sacramental life and tradition to stay on task. Furthermore, the sacramental character of the Catholic Church directs a member to involvement with the world as the place where the ritual transformation continues in daily life. Sacraments are to grow in one's consciousness until every involvement in living becomes an encounter with the transforming power of Christ, and ultimately, like Christendom in its idyllic form, "All is Grace." The Church anchored this vision for Dorothy Day and the Worker by providing institutional forms to support, sustain, and protect its clarity.

Conclusion

Dorothy Day and the Catholic Worker are a fascinating story which captures the imagination of many people of various religious persuasions. Part of the reason is the anomaly this person and the movement present: Catholic, but unconventional; traditional yet radical; spiritual but street-wise; broad and tolerant yet intense and principled; intellectually sophisticated but with a simple, uncluttered lifestyle; attuned to art and beauty, but involved with the ugliness of poverty and disease. There is something for everyone in the Catholic Worker, yet it avoids the trap of the typical populist movement which panders to the attraction of the moment.

This movement was able to join what in much of Christian history was separated: the Church, sect and mystical elements of the primitive tradition. It could do so because it engaged a spirituality firmly rooted in foundational principles of the faith. These principles allowed Day and the Worker to be flexible in meeting changing circumstances while never losing the original intent of the movement, to "make the kind of society where it is easier for people to be good."(Day 1952: 280) Because nature provides the substance for this project, grace the transformative power and logic to rule it, and the Church's sacramental tradition the guidance to carry it through, the spirituality is ever new and renewable. It also provides the means for self-correction when facing the various drifts of human contingency. No one principle should dominate the spiritual journey, for none is sufficient to encompass the full truth of the tradition. Each is necessary and complements the others by showing them how to reach beyond the aspect of the Kingdom they intend.

The roots here are deep. The understanding of nature and grace as congruent and cooperative sets a metaphysics from which all reality can be read. The eschatological logic of the Kingdom assures the priority of grace in ordering human life. The sacramental principle specifies the workings of grace in nature, bringing to bear the weight of an historical tradition as a ready reference and source for continuity in the midst of a changing world.

Dorothy Day happened into these foundational elements of her spirituality not by any formal theological training, but by reflecting upon her experience through the lens of the secular and sacred texts and teachers which fed her spiritual life. These widely varying sources converged in her thought and lifestyle. While she never articulated the underlying foundations here in any formal theological categories, her self-descriptions and the stances she takes reflect these categories in her life and work. Like any exemplar of ultimate truths, she showed us one view of what the world looks like when grace prevails in nature to create the new order of God's Kingdom.

People today are often on the same search for the Kingdom, but they too often remain locked in categories or exercises without understanding their fundamental character. Such spiritualities are houses built on sand. They rest on a particular experience of grace realized in a certain form without being able to identify the dynamics which transcend any particular experience and form. What Dorothy Day and the Worker show us is the divine foundation for all life and its implications for how we live. While not everyone can do specifically what she did through the Worker, all are called to style their lives on the grace of the Kingdom. With such critical foundational elements as Day and the Worker unearth, the potential for ongoing conversion, both as individuals and as a society, is built into one's spiritual journey. It is a dynamic moving between the nature/grace cooperation, its eschatological logic, and its sacramental manifestation. In other words, any moment of grace will take something of the human condition and transform it as a sign of divine presence and power in our midst, and in so doing will mark it out as peculiar in the ordinary affairs of life. Spiritualities are ways to order and articulate these moments within the Christian tradition.

Dorothy Day is a citizen of the Kingdom because she knew how to live at this level of reality, and it changed the world in some ways. To accept anything less is to settle for only a part of her story and only a part of the Gospel tradition she followed.

Notes

[1] In his collection of Day's notes and reflections, William Miller wrote that she used the following statement on several occasions: "I was 'born again by the word of the Spirit,' contemplating the beauty of the sea and the shore, wind and waves, the tides. The mighty and the minute, the storms and peace, wave and wavelets of receding tides, sea gulls, and seaweed and shells, all gave testimony of a Creator, a Father almighty, made known to us through His Son." (Miller 1987: 62)

[2] In his dissertation John Sandberg takes up this eschatological element of the Worker from an ethical viewpoint and analysis. Here he recognizes the unusual character of the Worker's vision and lifestyle by describing its morality as "parabolic" and its relations with the world as "critical," confronting the alienation of ordinary life with the possibility of the Kingdom of God (Sandberg 1979).

M.L. Liebler

Proverb

after Dorothy Day

The beauty of this
Life is so much
More than the world
Ever lets us see.

PART VIII

PETER MAURIN

St. Isidore of Seville and His Guardian Angel, by Ade Bethune, first appeared in the June 1936 *Catholic Worker.*

Peter Maurin's Ideal of Farming Communes

William J. Collinge

Mount Saint Mary's College

"They started a newspaper," Daniel Berrigan writes of Dorothy Day and Peter Maurin, "and the rest is history. They started houses of hospitality; that too is history. Peter was forever talking about something he called 'agronomic universities.' They started one, on the land; and that is something rather less than history."(Day 1981: xvii) This paper is part of a proposed larger project in which I would like to examine the original ideal of Catholic Worker farming communes, trace the history, or the "rather less than history," of Catholic Worker farms, focusing on several specific examples, and discuss what Catholic Worker farming may have to offer to contemporary American society. I will sketch Peter Maurin's general idea of farming communes, discuss some of its elements and their sources, and note some of the tensions among these elements and sources. A concluding section briefly addresses some of the concerns of the longer project.

Preliminaries

I want to begin with four points about the *sort* of idea Maurin had. First, if your academic training, like mine, was in philosophy, when you study someone's idea of something you carefully analyze the texts in which it is expressed, follow out its links with other ideas, spin out its inner logic, and trace its roots in its sources. But with Maurin, you have to lay aside much of that cast of mind. Maurin, as Anthony Novitsky points out, was essentially a public speaker, not a writer. He would declaim his ideas in catchy "Easy Essays," with repetitive phrasing and word plays, an oral rather than literary mode of composition. He would frequently quote or refer to other authors and tell his audience to read them, but, as Novitsky says, "Citation of an author was often shorthand for an idea or an argument, without any implication of total acceptance of the author's developed thought."(Novitsky 1976: 38)

Second, Maurin didn't claim, and didn't want, to offer a blueprint (Maurin 1949: 195). Rather, his listeners were to give shape to his vision from their own ideas and experience as well as from his own. This is what actually happened, and it accounts in large part for the divergent histories of actual Catholic Worker farms.

Third, though Maurin presented farming communes as a plank in his three-part program of roundtable discussions, houses of hospitality, and farming communes, they were more than *part* of a program; they really represented the concrete form of Maurin's ideal of the good human life and the good human community, his vision of what Aristotle called *eudaimonia* or happiness.

Fourth, we need to keep in mind that Maurin's ideal was often a negative one. Farming communes in his mind were solutions to problems, and he was often clearer on the problems than on the shape of the solutions. At the heart of Maurin's thought was a religious critique of the capitalist and industrialist social order, and farming communes were his alternative to that order. They were to be the way of "building a new society in the shell of the old," to quote the IWW slogan he adopted.

Four problems in particular were to be solved by the farming communes: the problems of labor, work, community, and education, and I will address these in what follows. Maurin makes little mention of communes as solutions to the problem of agriculture, but I will consider the relevance of his ideal to that problem also.

Farms As Solutions to the Problem of Labor

By the problem of labor, I mean the whole complex of problems caused for workers by industrialism. Workers were driven from the land and craft shops to live in poverty in industrial cities (Maurin 1949: 182). Then they were replaced by machines and became unemployed, deprived of both property and income (128). Mechanization led to overproduction, which in turn led domestically to an artificial stimulation of consumption by those who did possess wealth, an expansion of personal debt, and finally to depression (109, 183); internationally it led to competition for markets and thus to colonialism (65) and war (65, 99). Socially, industrialism destroyed local communities, as workers moved to cities to sell their labor as a commodity. People turned to the state for works of mercy, which individuals, churches, and local communities formerly had provided (90). Putting the means of production into the hands of the government, as Socialism proposed, solved few of these problems and exacerbated some of them (54).

Maurin was fond of saying, "There is no unemployment on the land," a statement which might meet with derision from the many displaced farmers in America in his day and our own. Such a statement, however, did not refer to the industrialized agriculture already well established in the United States. Rather, Maurin had in mind agriculture in a radically reconstructed social and economic order. In his conception of such an order, he was indebted to the tradition of European Catholic social thought, especially the French tradition he had learned as a young man, and the English Distributism that to some extent grew out of the continental tradition.

A reactionary medievalism was common in nineteenth century Catholic social thought, and Maurin absorbed it deeply, integrating it with memories of his early years in a peasant community not so different from those of medieval times. Anthony Novitsky has shown the importance of reactionary French social Catholicism on Maurin's thought, though he and others overstate somewhat how reactionary Maurin was. When Maurin first came to Paris as a Christian Brother in the late 1890s, he was involved in a "study club" that was associated with the Oeuvre des Cercles Catholiques d'Ouvriers (OCCO). The OCCO was founded in 1871 by Albert de Mun and Rene de la Tour du Pin. The circles promoted a corporatist social order, one based in trade guilds or corporations which combined labor and capital. Guilds protected both employment and ownership by limiting competition; no entrepreneur could grow at the expense of all the others, buying their equipment and putting them out of work. De Mun and la Tour du Pin opposed the French Revolution, and sought a restoration of monarchy; la Tour du Pin, at least, inclined toward anti-Semitism. Maurin endorsed la Tour du Pin as an exponent of social reconstruction based on Catholic social teachings (Maurin 1949: 204), but he was indifferent toward monarchism and opposed to authoritarianism and anti-Semitism.

Also associated with the OCCO was Leon Harmel (1829-1915), an industrialist who developed an idea of the "Christian Factory," or "Christian corporation" which would be administered by a joint worker-management body along Christian lines. His own woolens mill at Val-des-Bois near Reims was run successfully along those lines for many years. Maurin speaks favorably of Harmel's conception of authority and his management in the spirit of *noblesse oblige* (Maurin 1949: 109, 203). Maurin does not mention Harmel's later turn toward trade unionism and social democracy, but Maurin himself was involved for five or six years in the Christian democratic organization, Marc Sangnier's Sillon. Maurin's sole mention of the Sillon in the Easy Essays is to repeat Abbe Leclercq's criticism of it for thinking democracy was the only social order compatible with Catholicism (164). Perhaps not, but Maurin nonetheless apparently preferred a Jeffersonian or personalist democracy (122, 144-145) and a pluralist state (100-101).

Agrarianism did not play a significant part in the program either of the OCCO or the Sillon. Novitsky takes note of a movement for "workers' gardens," which won the support of the prominent Christian democratic priest and deputy Jules-Auguste Lemire, who had some connections with the Sillon, but that is as close as he brings the idea into association with Maurin (Novitsky 1976: 176-177; Misner 1991).

Much more closely related to Maurin's agrarianism was English Distributism, a movement which included many figures Maurin cites often, such as Hilaire Belloc, Gilbert K. Chesterton, Arthur J. Penty, and Eric Gill. What has been called "the bible of Distributism"(Magill 1965: 755) was Belloc's *The Servile State* (1912). Belloc saw both capitalism and socialism as leading to a "servile state" in which the many would be forced to labor for the few. Against both of these, he contrasted the "mediaeval system, based upon highly divided property in the means of production" and advocated "Property, or the re-establishment of a Distributive State, in which the mass of citizens should severally own the means of production."(Belloc 1912: 5-6) In his emphasis on private property Belloc sometimes sounds like a modern libertarian. For instance, he argued against a minimum wage, unemployment compensation, and employer liability for on-the-job accidents. But he did not favor freedom for unlimited acquisition of property; rather, he favored social arrangements, such as guilds, that promoted the widest distribution of land and capital. Distributism was popularized by Gilbert K. Chesterton, especially in *The Outline of Sanity* (1927), a work which Maurin recommended. More explicitly than Belloc, Chesterton urged a return to the land. To inaugurate the establishment of a peasantry in England, he called for "a popular appeal for volunteers to save the land; exactly as volunteers in 1914 were wanted to save the country." (Chesterton 1927: 134)

Farms As Solutions to the Problem of Work

The Distributists Arthur Penty and Eric Gill were Maurin's guides in addressing the problem of work. Penty, an architect who never belonged to a church, nonetheless advocated what he called a Christian sociology, of which human dignity would be the foundation. He called for a "post-industrial" society, whose foundations would rest, "as all stable societies rest, upon agriculture" and crafts. Penty favored restrictions on the use of machinery. Machinery was to be avoided when it would "turn men into robots," injure health or the family, interfere with distributed property, displace labor, conflict with the crafts and arts, require the artificial stimulation of consumption, or damage the world's supply of irreplaceable raw materials (Kiernan 1941: 112; Penty 1937). "With Penty, the problem of production and the problem of art are the same," Edward Kiernan says (37). The machines that caused people to lose their jobs also caused those who retained jobs to lose the dignity of work.

Maurin drew more on Gill than on Penty on the subject of restoring the dignity of work. Gill, an artist and sculptor whom Maurin called the "best of all" the Englishmen—including Belloc, Chesterton, and Penty—who had "got rid of their blinkers," dedicated his life to overcoming the division between the artist and the worker (Maurin 1949: 187). The artist, Gill said in a passage Maurin quoted, is simply "the responsible workman."(Maurin 1949: 78) But in mechanized factory labor the worker has no responsibility. There is no *product* in which he can take satisfaction. He does not *make* anything, but rather performs a repetitive motion, like a machine.

Being back here in Milwaukee brings to mind my two summers 30 years ago in the old Hotpoint plant on South 43rd St. in West Milwaukee. I spent the day doing small tasks of sub-assembly of dishwashers, made all the worse because each task was Taylorized—described in terms of supposedly scientific "motion and time study," without any indication of how it fit into the construction of a dishwasher as a whole or that it was a human being performing the motions. The latch of a dishwasher has to be attached to a switch, so that the dishwasher shuts off when you open it. Maybe 800 times a day I'd take the latch out of one box, the switch out of another, take two zinc-plated screws and set them in the holes of the switch lined up with those in the latch, drive the screws with a compressed-air screwdriver, put the assembly on a gauge to test it, then toss it into a box. I preserved whatever limited degree of sanity I had by singing Bob Dylan songs in my head. When some years later I drew on my experience to elaborate Gill's point at the Los Angeles Catholic Worker, I was astonished to learn I was the only one in the room who had ever worked in a factory.

In farming and crafts, Maurin agreed with Gill that work rejoined art; the worker had genuine responsibility for making something, whose quality or shoddiness he could directly see.

Farms As Communities or Homesteads?

America has its own agrarian tradition, looking back to Thomas Jefferson's ideal of a democratic society of small landholders and to the experience of frontier homesteading. In Maurin's time, this ideal was revived by the Southern Agrarians, a group mostly composed of literary figures. For instance, Allen Tate and Robert Penn Warren defended the traditional Southern way of life against industrialism. Maurin quoted and recommended their manifesto, *I'll Take My Stand* (Twelve Southerners 1930), but in his usual selective way, showing no attraction at all to their segregationism. Allen Tate was a once and future friend of Dorothy Day (Huff 1996: 70-71), though I've found no evidence he ever met Maurin. Tate and his co-editor, Herbert Agar, later brought together Southern Agrarianism and English Distributism in the 1936 collection, *Who Owns America?* (Agar and Tate 1936), which included a contribution by Belloc and was recommended by Maurin.

Also linked to Distributism was Ralph Borsodi, a former New York advertising executive who moved with his family to a farm near Suffern, New York, in 1927. Borsodi is a good example of Maurin's selectivity in recommending others' works. Maurin recommended Borsodi's *Flight from the City* (1933), doubtless because of its agrarian ideal and its extensive practical advice for setting up a homestead, and Borsodi used language that resembled Maurin's, for example, "Green Revolution." Maurin often visited Borsodi's school in Suffern (Sheehan 1959: 190). But Borsodi was an extreme example of "rugged individualism," as Paul Goodman notes in introducing a 1972 reissue of Borsodi's book, not a communitarian, and Maurin did not share his enthusiasm for household machinery, still less his Nietzschean social philosophy and his contempt for traditional religion (Borsodi 1929).

Borsodi points to an area of tension in Maurin's ideal. Despite the fact that he endorsed the works of the American agrarians and spoke admiringly of Jefferson, his ideal was the peasant and not the yeoman farmer, the village and not the homestead.[1] As he said in an interview in 1943

> I always make a case for communal ownership, which is the ideal. Here in America people homesteaded but they became the victims of their isolation and their children left the farms and went to the cities. They forgot the village idea which was in Europe but went off by themselves. It was really the spirit of individualism which came from the Reformation, and Catholics unfortunately followed it forgetting the community, the liturgical idea. (Maurin 1949: 196)

Maurin's ideal commune reflected his own origins in a peasant village in the south of France, where families owned their own homes and gardens and fields, and worked communal pastures and ovens (Maurin 1949: ii, 200-201). He drew theoretical support for this ideal from the Russian anarchist Peter Kropotkin, whose work he encountered in France in 1907. Dorothy Day, also influenced by Kropotkin, said that Maurin came to her with Saint Francis in one pocket and Kropotkin in the other. The Kropotkin book that Maurin had in his pocket was *Fields, Factories and Workshops* (1901). Against the centralization of industry and the displacement of people from the land, Kropotkin argued that a regional self-sufficiency was possible. He promoted intensive cultivation of the land, including the use of machinery and chemical fertilizers. Much manufacturing would be done in workshops and small, village factories by people who also worked the land. The most efficient cultivation of the land required communal institutions (Kropotkin 1901: 123), and Kropotkin singled out for praise those which prevailed in France:

> Owing to a wide maintenance of the communal spirit, ... support is found in the communal shepherd, the communal wine-press, and various forms of "aids" amongst the peasants. And wherever the village-community spirit is maintained the small industries persist, while no effort is spared to bring the small plots under higher culture. (Kropotkin 1901: 141)

But such institutions and spirit never took root in America, and this has remained a source of difficulty for Catholic Worker farms. As Brian Terrell of Strangers and Guests CW Farm in Maloy, Iowa, says

> The farm idea has been one of the most neglected [parts of the movement], part because most Worker farms have started in the shape of the American family farm. And in most Worker farms, there might be a community instead of a family, but in relation to its neighborhood, it's just another isolated family. (Troester 1993: 253-254)

Farms As Universities

One of Maurin's favorite names for his farming communes was "agronomic universities." Besides the problems of labor, work, and community, the communes were to solve the problem of higher education. Professors, according to Maurin, concentrated in specialized disciplines and had lost interest in problems of society. "College professors were too busy teaching subjects to be interested in mastering situations."(Maurin 1949: 18) Students were taught to "think in terms of jobs, not in terms of work" (72), but once graduated they could not find jobs. On the farms, Maurin said, unemployed college graduates would learn "how to build houses, how to gather their fuel, how to raise their food, how to make their furniture."(73-74) They would unlearn "the ideal that working with your head is superior to working with your head and your hands," which Maurin saw as "how we get so many crazy ideas in society today."(197) Instead, they would "learn to use both their hands and their heads."(Maurin 1949: 74) Education would not stop with crafts but would include a more theoretical component: "Unemployed college graduates must be told why the things are what they are, how the things would be if they were as they should be and how a path can be made from the things as they are to the things as they should be."(73) Maurin says little in his essays about what would be taught and read, but it is clear from all accounts that it would be the same sort of thing that he taught and read wherever he was.[2]

This is another area where Maurin clearly shows the influence of Kropotkin. Kropotkin's ideal society would be "composed of men and women, each of whom is able to work with his or her hands as well as with his or her brain."(Kropotkin 1901: 183) Everyone would be educated in both science and handicrafts, and also, as he occasionally notes, the humanities. Such an educational system would be healthy for individuals, overcome destructive class divisions in society, be beneficial to scientific discovery, and produce better manufactured goods.

> Be it handicraft, science, or art, the chief aim of the school is not to make a specialist from a beginner, but to teach him the elements of knowledge and the good methods of work and, above all, to give him that general inspiration, which will induce him, later on, to put in whatever he does a sincere longing for truth, to like what is beautiful both as to form and contents, to feel the necessity of being a useful unit amidst other human units, and thus to feel his heart at unison with the rest of humanity. (Kropotkin 1901: 199-200)

Another primary source for Maurin's idea of farms as universities is monasticism, which also shaped his idea of farms as communities. He particularly idealized the Irish monasticism of the sixth and seventh centuries, contrasting the Red Revolution of Communism with his own Green Revolution, based on the Christian Communism of the Irish monks. He credited the Irish monks with the synthesis of cult, culture, and cultivation he promoted. He even ascribed to them his three-part program of houses of hospitality, roundtable discussion, and farming communes (Maurin 1949: 49-50, 62, 114).

I agree with Novitsky that Maurin seems not to have known John Ryan's *Irish Monasticism* (1931), the best scholarly source of the day. Sheehan mentions Maurin's use of Benedict Fitzpatrick's *Ireland and the Making of Britain* (1927), which is cited in the reading list in *Catholic Radicalism.*[3] This is certainly an example of "romantic medievalism," as well as of history in the service of Irish nationalism, crediting Ireland with every positive development in Western civilization, especially those to which England might lay claim.

But the great Irish monasteries and their early medieval foundations on the European continent genuinely were "agronomic universities" of a sort. They blended a native Irish scholarly tradition with the Greek and Latin classical tradition and for a time were the chief agents in keeping the study of the classics alive. They taught not only Christianity but also literacy to the surrounding population. They combined learning with agriculture; the stories of the founders are full of examples of their dedication to manual labor (Ryan 1931: 362-364). And they taught improved techniques of farming to the people (Fitzpatrick 1927: 78-81). It was to the monks, says Christopher Dawson, that "the conversion of the peasants was really due, for they stood so near to the peasant culture that they were able to infuse it with the spirit of the new religion."(Dawson 1932: 178) Here is Fitzpatrick's picture, which also supplies you with an example of his style:

> Round forest wells, and on the banks of rivers, spaces were cleared, and roads and bridges made, houses built, and handicrafts set going, while the catechism sounded amid the trees, and sometimes the solemn choral chant of barbarian voices, clumsily learning the melodies of religion and civilization. (Fitzpatrick 1927: 280)

At times, approaching even closer to Maurin's ideal, the lines between the tenants of the monastic lands and the monks themselves were blurred. Speaking of sixth-century Ireland, Ryan says, "So intimate, indeed, was the union between the monastic principality and its lay clients that the latter are called, like the community, *manaig*, and in many records are distinguished only with difficulty from the religious family."(Ryan 1931: 316) Still, this is not exactly Christian Communism, as the tenants did not own the lands they worked nor even share in their ownership, but rather were bound to the monastery by various feudal rights and duties.

Maurin rightly credits the monks with establishing houses of hospitality. Taking seriously the Gospel injunction that in the stranger Christ was met, the Irish monks, like other medieval monks, established hospices in prominent sites within the monastery and devoted much attention to the needs of their guests (Ryan 1931: 318-319). Special care, Ryan says, was to be given to poets, who otherwise might make the monastery the target of their satires. However, I have found nothing that looks much like roundtable discussions. Conversely, Maurin makes no mention of some characteristic features of Irish monasticism, such as its extreme asceticism and its penitential disciplines.

Maurin does not speak directly of the authority of the abbot, who often held ecclesiastical power like that of a bishop and who to some extent succeeded to the role of the chieftain (Dawson 1965: 178-179). However, it seems clear that authority on the farming commune would be something like that of an abbot. Maurin's own anarchist sympathies and emphasis on each person's responsibilities made him reluctant to say much about authority on the farms. "A leader," he said, "must be a personalist. If he is a personalist, he will not be a dictator. He will change the attitude of others through the power of example. It takes an awful lot of patience." (Maurin 1949: 193) Maurin tried this method, without much success, on the Easton farm, and authority has remained a source of problems within Catholic Worker farms.

There are other tensions between the monastic ideal and the idea of a community of families. Monasteries are voluntary organizations, and while families may join communities voluntarily, their subsequent children do not. Moreover, while monasteries can run colleges, family farms cannot. Many Catholic Worker farms have sponsored lectures and discussions, but the capital investment needed in order to run anything like an institution of higher education has been far beyond their reach.

Farms As Farms

Though Maurin saw the farming communes as solutions to the problems of labor, work, community, and education, he had surprisingly little to say about them as solutions to the problems of agriculture. By the 1920s, the industrialization of American agriculture was already well advanced, with the concomitant problems of the destruction of rural communities and the depletion of the soil (Danbom 1979).[4] Still, though the English language of his time did not include the term "sustainability" as we use it today, Maurin seemed to possess much of the concept.

Contrary to Kropotkin and Borsodi, Maurin opposed the use of tractors and farm machinery. "Let the machines rust," he said. He combined nostalgia ("On my farm when I was a child we used oxen to plow the field") with conservationism: "Not only do oxen work but they give manure to enrich the soil."(Vishnewski: 1984) Again parting ways with Kropotkin, he promoted Sir Albert Howard's *An Agricultural Testament* (1943), which was among the early works to sound the alarm about the effects of chemical fertilizers on the long-term health of the soil. Maurin said, "Our farmers too often aren't farmers at all. They are land miners. They just take stuff out of the soil and don't replace it right...It's really soil robbing, and practices of this kind don't make for good character."(Maurin 1949: 201)

Like Kropotkin, Maurin favored local self-sufficiency. "Eat what you raise and raise what you eat," he would say (Day 1952: 176). He opposed cash crops and world trade in foodstuffs, and in fact went so far as to oppose canning. "Can the can," he said (Vishnewski 1984:

204), favoring eating fruits and vegetables in season, drying them or storing them in root cellars for use out of season. He ignored the nutritional consequences of such a diet (Danbom 1995: 10). He admitted that even his native village fell short of the ideal of self-sufficiency. Though the villagers raised calves, chickens, and sheep, they sold them and "ate pork and sausages and the different pork meats."(Maurin 1949: 202)

In his ideas about agriculture as in the rest of his work, Maurin is both backward-and forward-looking. He romanticized the peasant society of the middle ages and his own childhood, but he also accurately perceived the tendencies of contemporary agriculture. In his emphases on protection of the soil, on rural community, and on local self-sufficiency, he anticipated the ideas of such contemporary critics of industrialized agriculture as Wendell Berry.

Conclusion

The Catholic Worker "movement's rural experiments [were] virtually unmitigated disasters," James T. Fisher has said (Fisher 1989: 121). Certainly, no Catholic Worker farm has fully realized all the elements of Maurin's ideal. There is, in the first place, an inherent tension between two parts of Maurin's program: houses of hospitality and farming communes. Though Maurin saw these as separate institutions (or maybe like monasteries with guest houses), actual Catholic Worker farms, as the history of the New York community's farms shows especially well (Vishnewski 1984: 175-207),[5] have tried to be both. It is not easy simultaneously to keep a farm running and to take in everyone who comes to the door.

There are also tensions within Maurin's ideal, and among its sources, as I have sketched above. Should farm machinery and chemicals be rejected entirely or used in the service of local self-sufficiency? Can a voluntary monastic-style community also provide for the needs of families? Can anything like peasant villages thrive in an American culture that venerates the frontier homesteader? Can leadership be exercised in a large, diverse community in the manner that an abbot exercises it in a monastery? Does any sort of farming community have the resources to support a university?

Even so, Fisher's judgment is much too harsh. Catholic Worker farms exist to this day. Eleven are listed in the May 1996 *Catholic Worker*. The New York community has kept some sort of farm, five in succession, going almost continuously since 1936. Its current enterprise at Marlboro, New York, has been a viable small farm and rural guest house since 1979. In Sheep Ranch, California, a Catholic Worker farm has existed continuously since 1976. It is the family farm of Chris and Joan Montesano and their children, but it also comprises an AIDS hostel and a candle crafting business with a multicolor glossy catalogue and a web site. It has served as a meeting place for Catholic Workers throughout the West Coast region. A farm near Alderson, West Virginia, has existed since 1984, raising food and providing rural refuge for the Washington, DC, Catholic Worker community. I doubt the Catholic Worker's batting average is much worse than that of other people who have tried their hand at starting farms in twentieth century America.

More important, the problems for which Peter Maurin envisioned his farming communes as a solution remain with us. And the memory of Maurin and the example of continuing Catholic Worker farms remind us that these problems are interconnected. We have not solved the problem of surplus labor and meaningful work. Machines may now do what I once did at Hotpoint, but the sorts of workers who did those jobs perhaps now earn their living doing telephone solicitation or entering data into computers (at least we still have Bob Dylan). Community, urban as well as rural, has continued to disintegrate in America since Maurin's time. Higher education is no better linked to the promotion of the common good, probably much less linked as education for careers has displaced what was left of the ideal of education for citizenship. Our dominant farming practices continue to deplete the soil and water reserves and to pollute the air and the water.

Maurin would often refer to an author or a book as a shorthand way of making an argument, and so will I: read Wendell Berry (1977, 1993, 1995). The very grandiosity of Maurin's ideal, a new America reconstructed as a network of agricultural colonies that look like monasteries, overwhelms the imagination. But who would say it wouldn't be a better America if the resources we have spent since the 1930s on pesticides and chemical fertilizers, interstate highways and suburban sprawl, we had instead spent on fostering self-sufficient communities practicing sustainable farming and pausing to study and to pray?

Notes

[1] Borsodi describes in much detail an experiment in the Dayton, Ohio, area for an agrarian village system, but announces its failure and takes comfort in the thought that individual farmsteads can still succeed. On Maurin's ideal, see Novitsky 220-221. I find it interesting that Maurin never mentions the American tradition of communal experiments, though this tradition influenced other Catholic Workers, such as Stanley Vishnewski (1984: 175).

[2] Stanley Vishnewski mentions Karl Adam's *The Son of God,* Christopher Dawson's *The Making of Europe,* and Harold Robbins' *The Sun of Justice* as readings assigned by Peter at the Easton farm (Vishnewski 1984: 203).

[3] Sheehan (1959, 158) mistakenly cites the title as *Ireland and the Foundations of Europe.*

[4] The depopulation of the land was temporarily reversed during the Depression of the 1930s, but the depletion of the soil was accelerated by the Dust Bowl.

[5] See also articles in *The Catholic Worker* 1976–1979 on closing of the farm at Tivoli, New York, by Deane Mary Mowrer, March-April 1976, September 1978, October-November 1978, and by Peggy Scherer, September 1979.

Why Peter Maurin Matters

Paul Magno

Peter Maurin is an important but highly underappreciated voice from our past and for our future. Our society doesn't have a clue who he was or what he had to say, which is a pity at the moment, a moment of contentious discourse on the direction of society, a moment of ponderous moralizing, and a moment, for all that, of tremendous spiritual and intellectual barrenness. America, for what it's worth, could use a Peter Maurin. But he is also barely known among the social or political radicals, secular and religious, who ought to be better informed, and among Catholics, among whom his name should at least be recognizable. Scholar and worker, these days, are oblivious to Peter Maurin, and much diminished for it.

I am concerned, too, that he's a bit of a relic and curiosity to the Catholic Worker movement as well. Some of the folks in the movement are doing very admirable work with his "back to the land" idea and, while I recognize that, I am not going to dwell on it here. But I seldom see him cited authoritatively to the extent that Dorothy Day is, or the Scriptures are. How often do we hear someone in our discussions weigh in with, "Dorothy said this..." or "Dorothy would not agree..." or "the Gospel calls us to..." or "Jesus said that....?" Much less often do we hear "Peter said," or "Peter Maurin would have advocated this."

Peter Maurin is the intellectual author of the Catholic Worker Movement and Dorothy Day's primary teacher.

One is tempted, especially in a conference such as we're holding here at Marquette, to identify the Catholic Worker movement exclusively or predominantly with Dorothy Day, or with whatever version of Dorothy we might be partial to. I'm aware that some folks speak only of Dorothy's piety, or only of her devotion to the poor or only of her loyalty to the church, or only of her radicalism, or only of her fire and brimstone denunciation of the "filthy, rotten system." Dorothy

Day is not so easily caricatured, I think, and the movement's origins and identity likewise defy simplistic presentation. I propose that there is no getting around the significance of Peter Maurin as the intellectual author of the Catholic Worker by virtue of the program he propounded, which Dorothy Day amplified through the newspaper and other forums for years while Peter was alive and held up as the movement's agenda and purpose for many, many years after his death. There is also the small matter of her insistence that it was Peter who educated her as a Catholic, and who significantly influenced her intellectual growth and development. It is a mistake to dismiss her deference to Peter as a kind of caginess on her part in order to compensate for the supposed disadvantages of being a woman, a convert, a social radical. Her habitual affirmation of "Peter's Program," was too enduring and too pervasive to warrant such skepticism. The fact that she advocated his program so staunchly, and arguably with greater fervor after his death that before, has to be appreciated by us. If we cherish Dorothy Day and respect her wisdom, then we need to trust her judgement in embracing the program Peter Maurin called the Catholic Worker movement to.

In going through some of Dorothy Day's writing in the *Worker*, especially in the 1940s and 1950s, one finds that often as not in the anniversary issue of the newspaper she makes it a point to emphasize Peter's name and the agenda he promulgated. I would posit, too, that in the early decades of the newspaper its style and focus gradually moved more in the direction of what Peter envisioned. For example, where the 1930s saw a great deal of reporting and involvement in labor activism (strikes and organizing and the like), later decades saw more reflection on the meaning of work.

Peter Maurin articulates a substantial critique of modern society and a vision of what society could be instead.

Peter spoke and wrote in the 1930s and the 1940s at a time when great social calamities, the Great Depression and the Second World War, engulfed our society. As these totalizing social phenomena seized us, Peter warned, in vain, against totalizing institutional answers. The society turned anyway to what Dorothy Day came to call "Holy Mother State." Peter's warnings against dependency on mass institutions were prescient then and they're relevant now. It's taken our society until the 1990s to tire of Big Brother, and it's taken the political right no time at all to effect a shallow mimicry of Peter. Today, our political leaders join Peter in saying that "the Federal Government was never intended to solve people's economic problems," and many a voice would get air time to lament that "modern society has separated the Church from the State," but no one's going to be caught following that lament by adding, "but it has not separated the State from business."(Maurin 1984: 6-7) When Peter Maurin tells us that "when the bank account is the standard of values, the class on top sets the standard," and "cares only for money,... not for culture," he's diagnosing the 1990s even though he wrote that in the 1930s (5-6).

When Peter goes to town one of his favorite economic questions, the lending of money at interest, we see the difference a coherent philosophy makes. Not only does he call us back to the ethics of the "prophets of Israel and the Fathers of the Church" on the question, but he underscores the way in which loan sharking is a treacherous mechanism, economically and ethically, in our social system because it licenses "the acquisitive society" at the expense of "the functional society,"—that is, it is an economic mechanism that drives us collectively to unfettered greed. "Living off the sweat of someone else's brow," he teaches us, somehow damages our capacity for any kind of ethical restraint, and prohibits us from living as "gentlemen."(Maurin 1984: 17-18)

Peter could see in this, as in so many questions that he spoke incessantly about, that what captivates us by way of materialism, be it accumulation of money, the products of industrial capitalism or the opportunities of an affluent society, also takes possession of us spiritually. And, if our society is captivated by mass production, or the omnipotent state, or impressive bank accounts, or even accelerating "progress" be it social, political or technological, then it is held captive against the possibility of benefitting from what manual labor, or holy poverty, or prayerfulness might have to offer if it had any worthwhile contact with them. This is what is fundamental and holistic about so much that he talked about. It's a basic and simple contribution to the common good of our society and I submit, the Catholic Worker movement's gift to our society, if our movement can learn to meaningfully embody and articulate it ourselves.

"To be radically right," Peter Maurin maintained,

> is to go to the roots
> by fostering a society

> based on creed,
> systematic unselfishness
> and gentle personalism.
> To foster a society
> based on creed
> instead of greed,
> on systematic unselfishness
> instead of systematic selfishness,
> on gentle personalism
> instead of rugged individualism,
> is to create a new society
> within the shell of the old. (Maurin 1984: 108)

Even America does not have to rot and die for its sins. Peter Maurin saw and lived a way to be "a new society in the shell of the old" and was so confident of its appeal that he just kept talking it up. We, intellectuals and rabble-rousers alike, can take a dose of that medicine and offer a like gift to our society, our world, and even our church, if we heed Peter Maurin.

Peter Maurin challenges us to form and inform our intellects through clarification of thought and to share that thought with all manner of people.

The very method of the Easy Essays is a method of indoctrination, of summarizing ideas in a way that allows them to inculcate themselves into our intellects. That was the virtue of their simplicity and their catchiness. But that does not mean the teaching of Peter Maurin was simplistic. Not at all. If we attend to the ideas he presents and to the scholarship he recommends to us, we come away with exactly what he advocated: minds that are not only informed but well formed, that have a coherent world view and philosophy, the value of which we cannot underestimate. Broad philosophical unity—vision—is hard to come by, even in the best of learning institutions. It needs to be worked at and cultivated.

Peter isn't satisfied to have us simply memorize his Easy Essays. He wants us to grasp what he is pointing to, and he believes that the exchange of ideas through roundtable "clarification of thought" is absolutely valuable. Dorothy Day emphasizes over and over that "clarification of thought" is the first point in the Catholic Worker program, and the reason for the roundtable discussions, the newspaper, the constant effort to educate people that both Peter and Dorothy undertook.

That is a vital part of our work in sustaining their legacy, I submit. We need to return to serious study of Peter Maurin, through his Easy Essays, through the literature that he recommended, through his summaries of so many intellectuals. In the early years of the paper, he often ran a "books to read" list along with his Easy Essays and easy essay style summaries of the thought of such writers as Maritain, Berdyaev, Belloc. My immersion in Peter Maurin led me to monopolize Georgetown University's library copies of two very early books of Easy Essays, the 1936 Sheed and Ward edition and the 1949 Catholic Worker Books edition, for two years! These both had similar book lists in the back and I read several of those also. Penty, Chesterton, Furfey, and Maritain come to mind.

If we study and discuss just a few of these we'll have a much stronger capacity to think through how to "bring the social order to Christ," how to "build a new society in the shell of the old."

Peter Maurin provides us with a wonderful example of what it means to be a practicing Catholic.

Peter Maurin, without a doubt, was deeply conversant with his religious tradition and able to speak of its spiritual, social and political implications in his day. It is on this basis that he was able to apply the Church's social teachings to modern problems. He was also as devout and pious and loyal to the Church as he could be, but barely ever spoke of obedience or orthodoxy.

Peter Maurin matters as a Catholic because he shows us how to be faithful to Christ and to his church. He does so in personalist terms, taking his own advice to "be what you want the other fellow to be." Without a doubt he advocates that we know our Catholic heritage, that we know the example of the saints and the teachings of the Holy See, that we see the applicability of the Benedictine motto, "Labor and Pray," to our own lives and to our mission in the world. We'd have, then, a primarily spiritual outlook and motivation for all that we do. So, too, if we took to heart the example of St. Francis in practicing poverty

But a deeper lesson impresses me in the remembrances of Peter Maurin, particularly those offered by Dorothy Day. We see that he insisted that the Works of Mercy, or a philosophy of poverty, a philosophy of work, such as he proposed, are rooted in the "primacy of the spiritual." More significantly, he lived them, "at a personal sacrifice." Dorothy Day reports that he never had a second coat, that he often gave away his bed, he never had his own desk, that he always "ate what was set before him." He's the one who brought every Tom, Dick and Harry in from Union Square or the Bowery and thus prompted the first hospitality.

I'm impressed that this wasn't all done to show up or shame anyone or out of any egotistical posturing, nor to impose some "truth" on others, but out of a simple straightforward fidelity to Christ. As such all these practices were primarily devotional acts, offered to God as found in daily prayer and in his brothers and sisters. And as an offering of gifts, it was all done with complete freedom.

I notice, too, that this is the heart of Peter Maurin's adherence to the Church, these acts of love, a very impressive fidelity that speaks so much truer than the voices in our church that clamor on the one hand for order, orthodoxy and obedience, and on the other equality, democracy and inclusion. We who want to call ourselves Catholic Workers need to take this to heart if we are to keep to the principle of "pure means" that Peter advocated. We are all passionate about what we think the Church should be like, and what we think God wants the church to be. And for that reason we can easily takes sides and name enemies. Wearing the name "Catholic Worker" doesn't protect us from this temptation to reduce our church life to politics. Indeed, one of Peter's more critical messages is that life is about higher things than politics, and the Catholic Worker movement's charism is, too.

Peter calls us to a deeper understanding and practice of what it means to be Catholic, a practice that responds to the Christ in his most glorious persona. He captures this beautifully in one of his most "religious" Easy Essays, "The Spirit of the Mass, The Spirit for the Masses":

> The central act of devotional life
> in the Catholic Church
> is the Holy Sacrifice of the Mass.
> The Sacrifice of the Mass
> is the unbloody repetition
> of the Sacrifice of the Cross.
> On the Cross of Calvary
> Christ gave His life to redeem the world.
> The life of Christ was a life of sacrifice.
> The life of a Christian must be a life of sacrifice.

We cannot imitate the sacrifice of Christ
on Calvary
by trying to get all we can.
We can only imitate the sacrifice of Christ
on Calvary
by trying to give all we can. (Maurin 1984: 45)

Conclusion

Let me finish by sharing one of my favorite passages from Dorothy Day on Peter Maurin, one that really underscores his approach to his apostolate. It is taken from *The Long Loneliness*.

> Peter made you feel a sense of his mission as soon as you met him. He did not begin by tearing down, or by painting so intense a picture of misery and injustice that you burned to change the world. Instead, he aroused in you a sense of your own capacities for work, for accomplishment. He made you feel that you and all men had great and generous hearts with which to love God. If you once recognized this fact in yourself you would expect and find it in others. (Day 1952: 171)

I submit that being conversant with Peter Maurin's spirit and his thought and teaching is part and parcel of participation in the Catholic Worker movement. We ought not to disregard him as too quaint or too simplistic to be taken seriously. We need to insure that his legacy is a living legacy, for the vitality of our movement, for the life of our church and for the redemption of our society.

Down on the Farm and Up to Heaven: Catholic Worker Farm Communes and the Spiritual Virtues of Farming

Jeffrey D. Marlett

The College of Saint Rose Albany, New York

Communal life maintains a thin but distinctive line through American religious history. Perhaps because its starting principle—life shared in community—departs dramatically from the American ideal of individualism, communal living exudes a certain exotic character that continually attracts new adherents with innovative lifestyles. Much like Notre Dame in college football, Catholics participated in this alternative lifestyle wholeheartedly as with any other aspect of American culture. In 1941 a young Catholic Worker living outside of Cleveland wrote: "... I know with certainty that we with others will be able to prove to others by our way of life that one may attain happiness and a human manner of life here and now. It is no Utopia but reality." With his wife Dorothy, Bill Gauchat founded Our Lady of the Wayside Farm as one of the attempts during the 1930s and l940s to realize the vision of "farm communes" affiliated with the Catholic Worker. These were agriculturally-based communities established by Catholics convinced that "life on the land" possessed virtues unattainable in the city (Gauchat to Carlos [Cotton], Sept. 5, 1941, DD-CW: W-46, Box 1.).

More than any other attempt by Catholics, the farm communes demonstrated the extent to which what might be called a "Catholic agrarian theology"could shape American experience. The National Catholic Rural Life Conference (NCRLC) had sought to preserve and improve rural life since its emergence in 1923. This "landward movement" had received the NCRLC's blessing during the Depression's worst days. All the standards of Catholic agrarianism which it supported were present in the farm communes: an acknowledgment of the spiritual, physical, and economic benefits of rural life coupled with the sobering recognition that Catholics in the United States were overwhelmingly urban. The rural-to-urban population drift was likewise decried as harmful to the nation's health. By gaining what *The Catholic Worker* called a "toehold on the land," the farm communes embodied the belief that farming God's creation was a more preferable alternative to modem living in the over-crowded and spiritually-bereft city. Beyond that, environmentally sensitive farming methods would separate these new Catholic rural communities from the agribusiness methods which had led to the Dust Bowl (Marlett 1997; Bovée 1987; Shapiro 1977).

Catholic Worker Farm Communes

Historian R. Laurence Moore has noted that, in America "if you do not commodify your religion, someone else will do it for you." The farm communes, though, were not quite the successful commodification that NCRLC leaders envisioned. Despite their insistence that "great caution should be observed to avoid indiscriminate herding of families back to the land regardless of their fitness to carry on as farmers," a number of Catholic Worker farm communes sprang up independent of the suggested authorities.(NCRLC 1933: 84). However, given the Catholic Workers' propensity (led by Day herself) for being "fools for Christ," the communes most often became, according to historian Jim Fisher, yet another Catholic "sign of contradiction" which Americans inside or outside the Church struggled to comprehend (Moore 1994: 11).

Widespread unemployment sparked by the Great Depression provided a rather millenialist flashpoint for the farm communes. An essential part of Peter Maurin's Green Revolution of "cult, culture, and cultivation," the farming communes offered to unify those broken by modernity. Restoring the unemployed and impoverished to a meaningful existence underlay the Catholic Workers' houses of hospitality, and communal subsistence farming would sustain these people until they either found work or awoke to the spiritual virtues of farming. A 1936 "Easy Essay" by Maurin targeted the problem as well as its solution "on the land."

> The industrial revolution
> did not improve things;
> it made them worse.
> The industrial revolution

has given us
technological unemployment.
And the best way
to do away
with technological unemployment
is to place idle hands
on idle land.

The Catholic Worker actually began examining Maurin's idea for farm communes soon after publication began in 1933. However, historian Mel Piehl notes, Dorothy Day "had a city girl's doubts about the value of rural life," and Maurin seemed happy with the Workers' one acre vegetable garden on Staten Island. Nevertheless, inspired by the decentralist treatise *Nazareth or Social Chaos* by English Dominican priest Vincent McNabb, a number of younger Workers soon lost their reserve. Larry Heaney, Marty Paul, and Bill Gauchat, from the Milwaukee, Chicago, and Cleveland houses, respectively, and others clamored to try Maurin's Green Revolution on for size. Day admitted *The Catholic Worker* should not "write about farming communes unless we had one."(*CW* 2/1936: 1; Day 1952: 183, 185; Maurin 1961: 93-94; Fisher 1989: 42)

When land near Easton, Pennsylvania, became available in 1936, Day and others had an opportunity to practice what they had been preaching. Named "Maryfarm," the first Catholic Worker farm commune was soon joined by Worker farms in Illinois, Michigan, Ohio, and Massachusetts. By 1939 farms also existed in eight other states. After the Second World War farm communes sprouted again in New York and Missouri, while individual families influenced the Catholic Worker furthered the Green Revolution by purchasing their own farms (Piehl 1982: 128-129, 132). In the 1950s Dorothy Day and *The Catholic Worker* received a stream of mail from individuals pursuing the farm commune ideal of the 1930s, but it was not until the 1960s that this became popular (DD-CW: W-4, Box 1).

When the Workers obtained Maryfarm, Day wrote that it overlooked "the cultivated fields of New Jersey." Often such a distanced view was as close to farming as the Catholic Workers came. The farm communes were not the successful agricultural reclamation projects that their instigators envisioned, despite all the exuberance. Still, the farm communes were perhaps the most avant-garde expression of the Catholic Revival in America. By taking Maurin's "Green Revolution" at its most literal interpretation, the Catholic Workers convinced of agriculture's moral and spiritual superiority united the Revival's confidence in self sustaining Catholic traditions with the American agrarian and naturalist traditions of Thoreau, Whitman, and Jefferson (Day 1952: 197; Ahlstrom: 491-509).

Since the farm communes were communities united by agricultural work, they exhibited the Catholic unity lauded by the Revival's Neo-Scholastic basis. "Communal life on the land," wrote Milwaukee Catholic Worker Larry Heaney, "is not simply a medieval reality that has ceased to be practical. An organic functional society would have as units self-governing, self-subsistent communities. Healthful inter-course between men is effected by the sharing in common of land, goods and work." In the first year Maryfarm "sheltered about thirty people at a time—unemployed, invalids, strikers, children,—all races, colors, denominations." During the Second World War, Bill Gauchat used his Ohio farm to shelter Latino immigrants and detained Japanese Americans; beginning in 1946, he and his wife began welcoming mentally handicapped children and adults (*CW* 9/1941: 8; *CW* 1/5/1938: 8; *CW* 6/1949: 5).[1]

Maryfarm's name was not mere coincidence. Since the Nativity took place in a stable, the insistence on Mary's mediation of the Incarnation was extended to farming itself. Mary's mediatory role came, of course, through her motherhood, and a noticeable feature of all Catholic Worker farm communes were large families. Maurin and the Catholic agrarians, along with Popes and other Catholic intellectuals, had always insisted that the family was the basic societal unit.

Since Catholic agrarianism espoused farming as the elementary societal occupation, raising a family "on the land" preceded monetary gain as the surest sign of a farm's Catholicity. In the period after Pius XI's *Casti Conubii*, which condemned artificial birth control, the size of commune families often reached tragicomic proportions. "Holy Family Farm," started by members of the Chicago and Milwaukee houses of hospitality, observed this in name and reality: two couples produced nine children between them. In a fit of Catholic Revival fervor, St. Joseph's Farm at Cape May Courthouse, New Jersey proposed the "Congregation for the Holy Family," a "Religious Order for married folks living in community." Marycrest, a post war effort affiliated with the editors of *Integrity* magazine, became known locally for its herd of dirty children. Mario and Estelle Carota, who established the Agnus Dei farm near Aptos, California, had by 1958 two daughters and twelve sons. Day's own daughter Tamar and her husband David Hennessy began a large family on a West Virginia farm (Day 1952: 179, 234, 239; Novitsky 1976; Schuck 1991: 79, 91; DD-CW: W-4, Box 3; Fisher 1989: 101-130).

The farm communes also followed the lead of Catholic agrarianism when it came to farming itself. "Biodynamic" farming, or the integrated use of land, natural fertilizer, and crops, fell on familiar ears among the Catholic Workers, who had practiced forms of it since acquiring Maryfarm. The integrated use of all available farm land embodied in agriculture what the entire farm commune experiment sought to accomplish—that a "community" (in this case, a community of crops, fruit trees, and vegetables) upheld the Christian family far better than the artificiality of city living. The Catholic Worker often reserved its last page for articles on "THE LAND," wherein bio-dynamic farming and homesteading received regular attention. A Catholic Worker in rural Missouri wrote a letter in 1947 about long-range plans to use the ubiquitous "Osage orange" (a bushy native tree with thorns) as a natural alternative to steel wire fencing (Marty Paul to Luigi Ligutti, Sept. 21, 1947, LGL, Box D-1). In May 1950 sixty-five year old Louis McCauley from Washington, Indiana, commented to two Catholic Workers: "But why is a Catholic Worker interested in the laws of plant growth? because a well filled contented body is the greatest place in the world for a holly [sic], God fearing soul."(Letter to Gauchat and Marty Paul, May 7, 1959, DD-CW: W-46, Box 1)

Bio-dynamics enabled those who practiced it to live out Maurin's incessant advice to, "Eat what you raise and raise what you eat."(Day 1952: 176) In 1938 Day wrote that Maryfarm residents still were living off the potatoes and carrots raised last summer. From the St. Benedict farm near Upton, Massachusetts, Arthur Sheehan wrote in "A History of St. Benedict's," that "during the first winter, Monsignor Ligutti of the Catholic Rural Life Conference visited us and spent a day with us. He went over the land and estimated that we should be able to support a hundred persons. He advised getting sheep."(Sheehan to Day, April 7, 1939, DD-CW: W-4, Box 2) Another farm resident, Don Palmer, nicknamed "Missouri" for his native state, achieved some notoriety by making four hundred pounds of sauerkraut for the winter rations. Larry Heaney urged all readers of *The Catholic Worker* to "grow your own food," since "You do not manufacture food then—you grow it or raise it...Somebody must grow your food. You might think about growing your own and even raising some animals. That's a lively thought." (*CW* 6/1949: 4)

Nevertheless, this enthusiasm often found itself confused by the realities of farming. Bill Gauchat diligently studied local edible plant life but wrote in a letter to Leo Branick that he found it "hard discouraging work. The simple things that our grandparents knew, are for us hard won discoveries."(To Branick, Feb. 11, 1942, DDCW: W-46, Box 1)

As with any agricultural endeavor, bio-dynamic farming required constant work, but the farm communes invited failure since often too few persons did the needed work. Further, if only one or two families had established the commune, they often buckled under an enormous workload. Larry Heaney, Marty Paul, Bill Gauchat, and Arthur Sheehan all wrote Dorothy Day their bewilderment at the variety of tasks simultaneously requiring completion. Carmen Welch, a native Midwesterner who ran Nazareth farm near Vandalia, Illinois, often included advice for Day concerning the agricultural and societal difficulties at Maryfarm. She reassured Day, "We don't feel that your work with Maryfarm is a failure. Even we who are experienced farmers make mistakes, too—everyone does. You have just made a start there—and what has been done, will just be stepping stones to the future."(DD-CW: W-4, Box 1; LGL, Box D-1; Paul 1953: 328).

Maryfarm had indeed set an inauspicious example for the other communes. Although many, including seminarians, children on vacation, and college students, crowded in during summers, the permanent residents were a motley crew of families, unemployed laborers, and the urban homeless. A more volatile group unprepared for the tensions of communal living could scarcely be found. Relations soon became strained at best. Residents more than once took Day's monetary gift intended for food and spent it instead on liquor. Other drinking binges included at least one visiting priest. Local school boards and social services fretted about the farm's insufficiencies as an environment for raising children. Day's patience finally reached its limits, and the farm was deeded to three families in 1946. Another Maryfarm was subsequently established at Newburgh, New York, much closer to the paper's headquarters (Day 1963: 55; Piehl 1982: 130).[2]

Not surprisingly, almost anything else would be counted as success, and the tribulations concerning Maryfarm were compensated by some earnest attempts to realize Maurin's Green Revolution. The

Catholic Workers' appropriation of Catholic agrarianism enabled them to invite the marginalized to participate in projects of "Christian social reconstruction." The return of Americans to the land, of course, not only restored the nation but gradually moved it towards the realization of its role in the divine plan of creation. Catholic agrarian theology insisted that subsistence farming in community was a precursor to the heavenly kingdom. The more people participating in this only brought that next world closer. On the other hand, the sheer number of unemployed Americans rendered obsolete theoretical discussion. Action was required, and "the land" appeared, to the Catholic Workers as well as other Catholic and non-Catholic agrarians, as the best solution to the nation's problem. Much as accepting one's salvation at an antebellum revival removed one from the terrors of impending divine judgment, a quick solution through a return to subsistence farming might avoid the economic and spiritual catastrophe sparked by the Depression (Hatch 1989).

The Green Revolution on Rocky Soil: The Gauchats, Heaneys, and Pauls

As mentioned earlier, Bill and Dorothy Gauchat took the Catholic Worker concern for the unemployed to an unprecedented level (*CW* 9/1938: 7). This is not to say that the seventy-six acre Our Lady of the Wayside Farm operated in pristine fashion, without glitches or financial precariousness. The Waysiders' lack of farming expertise led to some potentially deadly gaffes. The Cleveland Department of Public Health and Welfare judged the farm's well water to be "polluted with intestinal type bacteria," from improperly drained barns (W. H. Hay to Gauchat, July 11, 1940, DD-CW: W-46, Box 2). It took a neighbor's repeated pleas for the Waysiders to receive electricity. Raising food for the Cleveland house of hospitality's consumption won some unsolicited advice from F. W. Vincent, the Acting Commissioner of Health for the county Department of Health:

> Farmers who ship their milk to places outside our district are supervised by health authorities in the places using such milk, but we look after what is used here. If you think you want to continue we shall stop and give you an idea of the requirements. (Vincent to Gauchat, Aug. 31, 1945, DD-CW: W-46, Box 2)

The list that followed included a clean barn with cement floor, a clean water supply, and an annual veterinarian examination for the cattle. These concerns appeared minor to Day when she faced the boiling conflicts at Maryfarm. "One of the reasons you don't hear," she wrote Gauchat, "is because your's is one of the places where we are confident everything is going well....Your letters bring us only happiness and inspiration. You get along far better than we do in many ways. You are a good manager." Gauchat apparently saw otherwise. In a 1953 article in *The Catholic Worker* he reflected that Wayside "was the sorriest CW farm ever conceived. I ought to know—I live here."(*CW* 5/1953: 5)

The Catholic "culture of suffering," which blossomed between the world wars, could scarcely have found a better venue than the farm communes. Even martyrdom was readily available. Holy Family Farm, a tragically short-lived colony near Starkenburg, Missouri, revealed the bottomless pit into which any twentieth-century homesteading project could drag its creators. In 1947 Larry Heaney, Marty Paul, and their families moved to the 160 acre farm in central Missouri. Ruth Heaney later recalled that Missouri offered cheap land, and "there were lots of rural Catholic parishes."(Interview with Troester, DD-CW: W-9, Box 4) A shrine for Our Lady of Sorrows, the oldest Marian shrine west of the Mississippi, and St. Martin's parish were about a quarter mile walk away. The Blessed Mother's sorrows would in time come to symbolize the fortunes of the rural living experiment. Heaney wrote to Dorothy Day that they had some experience with communal farming, but "as farmers we are yet greenhorns and consider ourselves apprentice agrarians."(*CW* 6/1947: 3) The apprenticeship turned out to be fatal: Heaney died two years later from work-induced pneumonia while living with eleven people in an unheated farmhouse lacking both electricity and plumbing (Woltjen to *CW* 1955, DD-CW: W-6.1, Box 1).

Before then, though, "our little experiment in saving a shell-shocked social order," as Marty Paul described Holy Family Farm, demonstrated how even "fools for Christ" could participate in the Catholic agrarian appreciation of rural America (*CW* 9/1947: 3). Heaney wrote in *The Catholic Worrker*

> We are not here merely to farm. We are living and working on this farm in order to build a community—a community about a church. It is a new society we desire, based on Holy Mass and

> personal sacrifice for the common good....Our pioneering is unique. Those Nineteenth Century pioneers came west to conquer a wilderness—to harness the natural forces of God's creation. We Twentieth Century pioneers are out to conquer ourselves—to harness all our natural powers and have them supernaturalized by God and His Church. (*CW* 1/1948: 8)

Heaney and Paul might have been better off had their pioneering been less unique. Much like the Gauchats, the sheer amount of farm work that they insisted on doing by hand threatened to bury them, and their lack of agricultural skill magnified this. "Our limited knowledge and even more limited funds didn't make it feasible for us to buy livestock, so for several months we farmed without horses or livestock of any kind."(Paul 1953: 328) Their assumption that "life on the land" would, by some supernatural means inherent to living in a rural location, sustain them through difficulties shattered against successive waves of failure. Unclean conditions wiped out the first flock of chickens. Ironically, Patrick Quinlan's *Standing on Both Feet*, a post-war NCRLC pamphlet which extolled rural homesteads, included the following in its "Practical Points for Homesteaders:" "Let no man tempt you to go into the chicken business unless you have had much experience. Inexperienced chicken farmers often lose small fortunes which have been acquired throughout the greater part of a life time."

While Heaney and Paul put up hay by hand in a time when most of their neighbors were shifting to tractor-drawn balers. The farm's garden, which produced most of the food, took up so much time that "we were learning gardening instead of the rudiments of farming, which we set out to do," wrote Paul. Logs were sawed by hand into boards in order to built additional housing for all the children. Ruth Ann Heaney, a native of rural Nebraska, later remarked "I knew more how to run the farm when we went down there than anybody, just because I knew something about the seasons and what kind of crops."(Troester 1993: 33)

The anti-machine farming practices seemed to approach the Protestant work ethic as well as the Catholic "culture of suffering" in which the Holy Family farmers had been formed before coming to Missouri. The hard work sacramentally conferred grace, much like the daily Mass for which they walked a quarter mile each day (Paul 1953: 328). However, in February 1949, after a train ride back from St. Louis, Heaney arrived at Hermann with a blizzard coming down.

Since Holy Family Farm lacked a telephone, he walked the ten miles back wearing only street clothes. Stricken with severe pneumonia, Heaney was hospitalized for three months at St. Mary's Hospital in St. Louis, but died after a failed operation. Dorothy Day attended the funeral in Rhineland, Missouri, and wrote Heaney's obituary for *The Catholic Worker*: "I remember how shocked everyone was when they saw Larry and his wife living up to the ideas Peter Maurm was always talking about in connection with farming communes."(*CW* 6/1949: 4) Heaney's obituary shared the front page with two other obituaries, one of which was Peter Maurin's.[3]

Such heroism contradicted what outsiders might have dismissed as an avoidably unnecessary sacrifice:

> "No, we do not believe that Larry died of hardships and overwork, but because he had reached that stage of perfection pleasing to God, as his pastor said at his funeral Mass and so he took him. And we rejoice in the suffering and know it to be the gentle rain to water the crop. He is with God." (*CW* 6/1949:6)

Still, in 1940 John Magee wrote Dorothy Day, "anyone who takes responsibility in this work gets it in the neck."(Aug. 4, 1940, DD-CW: W-4, Box 2) The Heaneys and Pauls discovered paradigmatically the painful limits of what that might entail.

Conclusion

Writing about the "communitarian impulse" in American religious history, Sydney Ahlstrom remarked that "most of the new communities, of course, remained simply the ideas of 'reading men,' yet...a few dozen of them became celebrated though transient successes, and...became a major American cultural force."(Ahlstrom 1972: 491) The Mormons, not the Catholic Worker farm communes of the mid-twentieth century were what Ahlstrom had in mind, but they might have qualified as "celebrated through transient successes." They certainly offered examples of how Catholics could participate in a truly "American" form of religious practice while maintaining, often stridently so, Catholic identity.

The communes embodied many of the hallmarks of American communitarianism, yet they did so within the context of the Catholic Church, better known for its "otherness." *The Catholic Worker* at its roots was a separatist Catholic publication, and the farm communes, from Easton to Avon to Rhineland, followed this pattern.

The "green revolution," in all its millenial fervor, seemed impending, and the Catholic Church's most avant-garde farmers appeared to be poised to show the nation the way (Veysey 1973: 71, 110-125; Fisher 1989: 71, 110-125).

Nevertheless, urban Catholics captivated by "life on the land" soon awoke to the realities of that life—physically and spiritually. Most discovered what their neighbors, who never left, knew all along: the benefits of rural living could often be garnered in the suburbs, where private gardens might be tended relatively risk-free. In a way, then, Heaney's death closed the final chapter of American Catholic agrarianism. Scarcely forty-five years earlier, Catholics began settling in southern Missouri's Bootheel and the Catholic rural life movement emerged soon afterwards. In the middle of the state, the Holy Family farm failed, though, largely because the exhausting labor, which earlier colonists did out of necessity, the Heaneys and Pauls did out of spiritual desire. The difference was that such works of supererogation had become more an American identity-forming narrative than reality. What was significant is that Heaney, a third generation Irish-American from the streets of Milwaukee, became as enraptured with that narrative as any other American; what was tragic was its, and Heaney's, short life. The priest who started the first Catholic colony in 1905 lived in the bootheel's slowly drying swamps another seven years after Heaney's death.

Agrarianism and the projects of communal living it inspired were fated to fall out of favor. In 1952 Father H. A. Reinhold, an emigre German priest working in the Seattle shipyards, concluded glumly, but not without some relief, that "there is no longer room, where I live, for sustenance and richly diversified farming, except someone decided to be a martyr of his conviction or has so much capital that he can afford time and labor to make his farm into something like an educational institution." In 1950 Allen Tate, a member of the Vanderbilt Agrarians, had converted to Catholicism. Just as he entered the Church only to stumble upon a vast reorganization, Catholics intoxicated with the spiritual virtues of farming rushed back to the land to find, more often than not, that such virtues came only with the exorbitant price of hard labor and deprivation, and that the very people living closest to those same virtues seemed unaware of their sacred surroundings (Reinhold 1952: 254; Corrin 1996: 436-458).

Notes

[1] William Gauchat, "Our Lady of the Wayside Farm." *The Catholic Worker* 15 (June 1949): 5. For Catholic Worker assistance with Japanese-American relocation, see Ralph M. Galt to William Gauchat, 8 December 1942; DD-CW, W-46, Box 1. In contrast, Ligutti's WHO radio talks across central Iowa prompted one listener to ask: "Could you tell me where or how I could get some Jap help or would Mexican help be better? I have heard the Japs are fine help." A. J. Corrigan to Ligutti, 8 December 1937, LGL, Box C-l.

[2] Day wrote in "Idea for a Farming Commune," p. 8, that, working side by side, "no one knows which are the unemployed workers and which the student or scholar." Eva Gretz to Dorothy Day, 16 March 1942; DD-CW, W-42, Box 1. Rev. Joseph Wood to Dorothy Day, 4 August 1940; DD-CW, W-42, Box 1. Grace Branham to Easton school board, 10 September 1941; DD-CW, W-42, Box 1. Piehl wrote: "Although they admitted that this failure showed there was a 'contradiction' between the two ideas of performing the works of mercy at a personal sacrifice and saving to provide for one's own,' the Workers felt that there was more 'glory' in 'suffering for a cause' than in making a living as farmers." (Piehl 1982: 131)

[3] Heaney interview (Troester 1993: 30); Paul interview with Deane Mowrer, Gauchat interview with William Miller (DD-CW, W-9, Box 1). By comparison, in an interview with Francis Sicius, 17 June 1976 in Boyne City, Michigan, Paul simply remarked "Larry died shortly after we got started there." (DD-CW, W-9, Box 2).

Dorothy Day's View of Peter Maurin

Francis J. Sicius

St. Thomas University

The way to begin this paper about the "gentle personalist" Peter Maurin, is with the personal. Four Octobers ago, I received a phone call from my dear friend and mentor, Bill Miller. "Frank" he began with none of the preliminaries, "Do you think St. Thomas University would like to have my papers and notes on Dorothy and the Worker?" He had taught for two years at St. Thomas and I think the way our little college muddled through its daily life amused him and was maybe a refreshing change from the well ordered university life he had come to know through his entire teaching career. "Sure," I told him in the name of the university without consulting anyone, but my instincts were correct.

I remember quite well the autumn drive with our Library Director Margaret Elliston. Avoiding the interstate, we chose to drive along the old highway 27 which took us through the orange groves of central Florida, then into gently rolling hills of the Ocala horse country, across the Suwanee River through the old cotton land of Madison and Jefferson counties, and finally up to the old Bond plantation in Lloyd, the familial house of Bill's wife Rhea, the home where he had written *A Harsh and Dreadful Love* twenty years prior.

We spent a lovely weekend in the gracious hospitality of the Millers and on Sunday afternoon we packed six boxes of notes into our rented car. As we put the last papers into the trunk, Bill looked at me and said quite sincerely, "You know there are at least two or three books here." His words remained with me on the long drive south. The following Monday morning I put the papers in an 8 by 12 foot room which serves as our archives. Margaret bought some archival boxes and I did a preliminary organizing of the papers, and there they sat for about two years.

Bill died a little over a year after he donated his papers, and my old professor's voice spoke so clearly to me through his neatly written notes that emotionally it became very difficult for me to read them. Then during the summer of 1996 I participated in an NEH Summer Institute on Religious Diversity. During one session I spent some time talking about the Worker movement and Bill's papers and how St. Thomas University had obtained them. When I finished one of the participants said, "I think you owe it to Bill to work on those papers."

The following September when I returned to St. Thomas, I began to go through our new collection in a more systematic manner. The majority comprised Bill's notes which he took from letters written to Day and the Worker, books contained in Peter Maurin's lengthy bibliography, and interviews. Also included were copies of Dorothy's journals from the fifties and sixties which Bill's daughter Carol had typed from the originals. Among these typed manuscripts, I found one that especially intrigued me. It was simply called "Peter Maurin Biography by Dorothy Day, Her Manuscript."

I had never done any research on Peter Maurin in the Marquette Archives, so when I found this document I thought I had found something unique. I talked to some friends and acquaintances whom I consider to be very excellent Catholic scholars and they too were impressed. I thought, and my friends concurred, that this manuscript by Dorothy might be edited and published. What I should have done was consult Miller's biography on Dorothy Day in which he used her manuscript to write his chapter on Maurin (1982: 228). When I asked Phil Runkel about it, I received my first hint that I had not made such a great discovery. He told me that he was aware of the document and some scholars had looked at it and concluded that most of what was in the manuscript had been already published in articles in *The Catholic Worker* and elsewhere. But I remained headstrong and convinced that I had a worthwhile project. After reading the manuscript, however, I learned what an editor at Adair publishing house told David Hennessy in 1944:

"Dorothy Day has in my opinion not written a real biography of Peter Maurin here. The material is very sketchy, disorganized and anything but a finished manuscript." But I am glad that I was not discouraged from reading the document. Although it was "sketchy and disorganized," I was still drawn to the manuscript and I re-read it several times. There are numerous accounts of Dorothy's first meetings with Peter Maurin, and his influence on her, but the profound spiritual impact that Peter had on Dorothy was not conveyed to me until I read this manuscript.

Although roughly written, this document revealed a man of tremendous spiritual and intellectual strength. This apparently simple man gave Dorothy a vision of the infinite and provided a spiritual beacon which illuminated her own unique pilgrimage. It was this part of the document which had been left out of the published accounts of Peter's life. Although Dorothy always paid homage to Peter as her mentor and teacher, the collective published memory of Peter as an oddity or at best an unorthodox philosopher overshadowed the deep spirituality of the man. Arthur Sheehan had made the same observation. He complained that he had to leave much of the spiritual out of Peter's biography, because the publishers felt that readers were more interested in the vignettes of Peter's life which emphasized his eccentricities. But much of Dorothy's manuscript showed that in Peter she saw the face of God. The experience of reading this manuscript has left me with the commitment to write another biography of Peter which will attempt to illuminate the spiritual and intellectual development of this man who had such a profound impact on Dorothy Day. This large task begins with this short paper entitled "Dorothy Day's View of Peter Maurin"

A paper on "Dorothy's view" must of course begin with her. In 1972 I walked into the New York Catholic Worker house for the first time. Someone asked if they could help me and I mumbled quite self consciously that I was there to see Dorothy Day. "Up the stairs first door on your left," they said, and went about their work.. I climbed the stairs, and heard a typewriter, and wondered if I should interrupt her.

"Don't bother her" said an inner voice and I was frozen in front of the door listening to the steady rhythm of thoughts flowing from mind to printed page. But another instinct overcame my fear, and I knocked on the door. Inside the room the typing stopped, a chair scrapped across the floor, and the door opened. There she was, Dorothy Day! I don't really know in actuality if she was taller than me, but that day she was. Apologetically I said something about being a graduate student interested in Catholic pacifists and World War II.

"Oh yes," she said, "Bill Miller's student. "I'm very busy now but we can talk later, go down stairs ask Arthur Lacey for a broom, you can sweep the front sidewalk." This person whom I already held in awe grew even more. She saw that I was nervous out of place, and with those few words she took all that away. She gave me a job that made me part of the community. I'm not the only person to be impressed by the sheer presence of Dorothy Day. In 1936 she was not quite forty years old, but John Cogley never forgot his first meeting with her. Although she "had not yet achieved the spiritual authority that marked her later years," Cogley recalled, "she was well on her way."(Cogley 1976: 11)

These characteristics which left such a great impression on me, on John Cogley and thousands of others were not always part of Dorothy Day's demeanor. In the twenties, in Chicago, her literary friends at the Dill Pickle Club referred to her as "The Madonna of Oak Street Beach," and kidded her about playing the leading part in the film version of her autobiographical novel, *The Eleventh Virgin.* In the late twenties Dorothy was a single mother, and a recent convert to Catholicism. She had a strong social conscience and a reputation as an activist. To her dismay, the various important issues in her life did not mesh. She remained especially uncertain about where her new faith and growing spirituality would take her. She confessed this nervousness to Llewellyn Jones, the literary editor of a Chicago newspaper. Writing from her beach house in 1926 she said, "You see I'm still religious, reading my missal faithfully, pinning medals on the baby and going to mass." But in the same letter, she complained to Jones that despite her spiritual growth, "I guess I am still lacking."(DD-CW: W-6.4, Box 2) Her faith was strong and her commitment to social justice held fast, but the inability to connect these two passions caused a chasm in her life which she could not bridge. This reconciliation would not come until 1932 when Peter Maurin's pilgrimage brought him to her door.

A few years after his death, Dorothy wrote to Brendan O'Grady that "Peter Maurin is most truly the founder of the Catholic Worker movement. I would never have had an idea in my head about such work if it had not been for him. I was a journalist, I loved to write, but was far better at making criticism of the social order than of offering any constructive ideas in relation to it. Peter had a program," Dorothy affirmed, "[and]I tried to follow it...He opened our minds to great horizons, he gave us a vision."(DD-CW: W-10, Box 1)

Dorothy always acknowledged her spiritual and intellectual debt to Peter. When Bill Miller first suggested to Dorothy Day that he wanted to write her biography she insisted that he write about Peter. Of course Miller got around that mandate and wrote about Dorothy reasoning that the best way to get to Maurin was through Day (Miller 1982: xii).

Maybe Dorothy did give too much credit to Maurin. To assume that the movement came solely from his mind and energy would be to ascribe characteristics to Maurin that simply were not his. Peter had already decided on his mission in life. He was an agitator and a motivator. He was not an organizer. His goal was to awake in people a vision of Christian community so they might utilize their specific skills to bring this vision closer to reality. In this way, in Peter's words, the one man revolution becomes a two man revolution and so on. Many people in writing about Peter give the impression that he was doctrinaire. Joseph Brieg, who wrote a fine article about Peter in *Commonweal* in the late thirties, helped create this image. "When Peter started talking," he wrote, "there was nothing to do but lean back and listen." Brieg boasted that one night at a meeting he became the first person in history to quiet Maurin. "Just a minute Peter," he interrupted, "and repeated it louder and louder until he closed his mouth....What we've got to do is Christianize the world we're in,"Brieg argued, "not try to go back to some world of the past. There was a hushed pause," he recalled. "Then Peter pointed a rigid finger at [him] and said 'Young man, if that's what *you* think, that's *your* job....You do it!'"(Brieg to Sheehan, 1958, DD-CW: W-15, Box 3)[1]

Dorothy saw Peter differently. According to her he was "the most meek and submissive of men." She had "seen him again and again at meetings cut short by the chairman and with no sign of resentment, even when he has been stopped in the middle of a word. He will just say, 'Oh' in a little apologetic tone and take his seat." Dorothy described him as being "entirely unsuspicious, and never think[ing] ill of anyone." On the contrary, she wrote, "he sees their good points to so extravagant an extent that his friends say, 'he has no judgment in regard to people'... How beautiful an attribute," she pointed out, "always to see the good." From Dorothy's point of view, Peter was not doctrinaire, nor did he ever stifle someone's inherent passion or talent. On the contrary, Day recalled, "his encouragement sent many young men off on a career of writing and study, inspiring them to become propagandists and agitators for the Christian cause."(Day mss.: 307)

In Brieg's case, Peter saw his passion for modern industrialism and encouraged him to Christianize it. When he first met Dorothy Day, Peter did not say "you will be a journalist and publish my ideas on

Catholic social thought;" that was not his nature. He simply saw her talent for journalism and passion for social justice and helped her to order her life by putting these predilections at the service of Christianity. "You should start a paper," was not a command by Peter, merely a recognition of Dorothy's abilities. As Dorothy pointed out, "undoubtedly it is proof of his genius that he left much for people to find out for themselves by their own reasoning. He leaped as if it were from crag to crag of thought expecting his listeners to fill in the gaps...."Dorothy noted that Peter did not dictate, he simply "held before [people] a vision."

Part of the reason for writing a biography of Peter she explained was "to point to the nature of Peter's influence over [her]." She denied that the attraction was "physical, spiritual or mental." At least not in the usual sense of the word. "It was hard for me to understand him," she recalled. "I had a hard time connecting with him as a peasant, a man and a Frenchman." The early months were a struggle for both of them. "It was amazing," Day wrote in *The Long Loneliness,"* how little we understood each other at first."(Day 1952: 175) Given the fact that Day's instruction in Catholicism had never included the social message of the Church, Peter had to begin her education by making these connections. In her manuscript on Peter, she recalled the first books he brought her to read. "Besides Kropotkin, Fr. Vincent McNabb and Eric Gill, there were Jacques Maritain, Leon Bloy, Charles Peguy, Don Sturzo, Karl Adam, [and] [Nicholas] Berdyaev. It was hard on us both," she recalled. "Many a time I listened and listened unwillingly. I could only go one step at a time."

His style of teaching eventually began to intrigue her. "He never preached. He never talked about the spiritual life as he did the life of the world around him." She emphasized that he was a materialist, an apostle to the world of the poor and the worker whom Dorothy was professing to love, and whose life she wished to share. Peter's Christianity was not simply spiritual, she noted, for it laid out a practical plan which reconciled the apparently fragmented design of her heart and mind. She immediately saw that Peter's view of Christianity provided an alternative to industrial capitalism and communism which helped to remove a serious conflict which had troubled Dorothy since her conversion. Dorothy was anti-capitalist and her new Church was strongly anti-Communist. Yet Communism, she wrote, had provided the new torch that set the world afire (Day mss.: 40).

Because of her conversion to Catholicism, she felt she had to venture carefully into areas where she had previously tread fearlessly. The Christianity that she knew from her conversion had been made safe for the capitalists. She had learned nothing of the social dynamite of the church, Peter told her, because it had been placed in a "hermetically sealed container."

"Peter's great mission," Dorothy wrote, "was to bring back the communal aspects of Christianity to rescue the communal from communism." Maurin believed that the Church was right in attacking the "heresy" of Communism, but they were wrong in simply attacking the heresy and not the cause. People fall into heresy, he explained, when the Church neglects or ignores one aspect of the truth. The "heresy" of Communism had emerged because the church had ignored the message of social responsibility inherent in the Gospels. Dorothy liked Maurin's expression "exploding the dynamite of Christianity, so that it could once again become the socially dynamic force that it once was." She was a writer; she would blow the dynamite with her pen.

The obvious fact that Peter lived his philosophy also affected Dorothy profoundly. He had taken his theory of voluntary poverty and of Christian love and had literally put it on. Soon Dorothy created the paper Peter suggested, or at least as historians tell us a reasonable facsimile, and she began to present Peter's ideas to the world.

In *The Catholic Worker* she introduced not only Peter's life and ideas, but also her own vision, which he had inspired, of a dynamic social Christianity. Dorothy especially liked the idea that Peter was a worker. Describing Peter, she wrote: "He looks as though he were rooted to the ground, gnarled, strong, weather-beaten. He reminds me of a tree trunk, of a rock. His shoulders are broad, he has a chest like a barrel, his head is square and so is his face. Down at the Easton farming commune," she wrote, "he likes to break rocks to mend the road, [and] dig ditches to pipe the water from the spring." Inherent in her description is an important message for the poor. This man who is writing these truths of Christianity in *The Catholic Worker* is not a bishop or a university professor. Our founder is one with you, she told her audience, "he is a simple man who wears workers shoes that he buys on the Bowery for three dollars, [who] wears heavy underwear [and who] washes out the cuffs and the collar of his blue work shirt, dries it over night and puts it on again unironed."(Day mss.: 137-38) Peter dignified the poor to whom he had given the title "Ambassadors of God." Very few of the poor whom Dorothy encountered possessed the dignity and demeanor of Peter Maurin, but she continued to see Peter in all of them.

Peter became so immersed in his mission that outer appearance or his personal material condition meant little to him. In this state he became a special target for Dorothy's universal concern for the poor and downtrodden. In her biography of him she wrote, "I've seen him setting out [with ashes all over him from tending the fire] to give a lecture somewhere all unbrushed and uncombed and have run after him to refurbish him a bit for company. It's for the sake of the others, I tell him."(Day mss.: 349)

One very cold February morning she asked Peter if he was warm enough. "'No,' he answered matter of factly," And Dorothy went right away to reconcile the problem. It angered her to learn that someone had taken his blankets and he was sleeping in his clothes, under his overcoat, and leaving the oil burner going all night to keep warm (Day mss.: 167).

Although she cared for many of his material needs, Dorothy found many of Peter's habits disconcerting. For example, manners were not important to Peter. She noticed that "he would precede others through the door, forget to take off his hat, not give up his seat to an old woman unless he was told, nor say thank you when given anything. He was unconscious of the need for such courtesies. He was not self-conscious about his lack of manners either," Dorothy observed, because to Peter "a gentleman was one who did not live off of the sweat of someone else's brow."(Day mss.: 28) Another aspect of his personality which bothered Dorothy was his profligacy with money. Writing to a priest once, she told him that Peter would be very glad to come up and spend a week with him. But she asked him please "when you send his fare be sure and send him a return ticket to New York; if you gave him the money he is liable to spend it and go someplace else. As you mention making him an offering," she continued, "I also ask you not to give him that but send it to the Catholic Worker—if you give it to him he might decide to visit Bishop O'Hara in Montana or some equally distant place as he is very impulsive."(Letter to Stanley Murphy, Dec. 6, 1934: DD-CW: W-10, Box 1)

Peter's puns and other eccentricities in his writing also bothered Day. Speaking English as a second language, Peter saw rhythms and peculiarities in words which would not occur to a native speaker, and they amused him. He liked to share these oddities with his listeners.

He wanted to make the "papal encyclicals click" he would say, or people bought "stocks till they got stuck." He would be very pleased with his clever verbal gymnastics, but they caused the writer Day to shudder. But this became for Day another lesson from the man who lived his vision. "His puns and paradoxes used to make me blush," she confessed, "but they were as much a part of Peter as his clothes." She soon realized that her intellectual disdain was almost as bad as the snobbish disdain of those who made fun of Peter's clothes or appearance. Or the clothes and appearance of any one for that matter (Day mss.: 22).

Against those who attacked Peter for his appearance, Dorothy defended him strongly as she would any of the poor. She particularly objected to those who called him a bum. Referring to a *Commonweal,* article on Peter entitled "Apostle on the Bum," she admitted that the article painted a very good picture of him. She objected to the word bum. "Peter gave his labor" she pointed out "where it was needed [and] well earned his living with the sweat of his brow. We saw how he could work at manual labor on our farms." In later years "Peter was to speak at seminaries and colleges. But he never received more than modest offerings," she pointed out, "or his fare paid from place to place."

Dorothy's description of Maurin may well have fit any of the exploited working poor. "If he had worn a dress suit, carried a suit case, stayed at a good hotel," she noted, "the offerings would have turned into fees, and the respect accorded him would have been greater." She wrote "these things not with bitterness," Day stated, "but to make the point that Peter often made, that poverty should be respected, that we should see Christ in every man regardless of [his] clothes." Dorothy "thanked God" that "Peter's intelligence and sanctity were apparent to many, in spite of clothes. His old suit cast off of someone else, his dollar suitcase full of books and pamphlets..., his bearing, radiant, serene face, these," she noted, "all came to be loved in many a circle around the country."(Day mss.: 21)

Peter's faith which meshed so completely with his life affirmed all of Dorothy's spiritual inclinations. Solidarity with the poor remained at the core of Peter's message. Dorothy knew this was what set him apart, what distinguished him from other great contemporary teachers and philosophers. Dorothy Day may or may not have known Antonio Gramsci, but she recognized in Peter what Gramsci described as an "organic intellectual," one whose message can no longer consist solely in eloquent words, which are exterior and momentary movers of feelings and passions, "but in active participation in the practical life as constructive organizer, permanent persuader, not just simple orator."(Gramsci 1971)[2] At some point in his life (historians tell us around the age of 50) Maurin underwent a profound conversion. Ideas he had been working out all his adult life took on a new reality for him. He came to the conclusion that he must live as he believed and that if there were to be a revolution of values it must begin with him. He believed that everyone had the potential to realize goodness; through the example of his own life, he believed that he would exhort others to follow their best instincts. He came to believe that working for wages was wrong so he stopped working for wages. In an age that glorified the rugged individual he advocated community. In a system that measured success in terms of material goods, he owned nothing. Rejecting the bourgeois concept of the nuclear family, he sought his family among kindred spirits which included simple workers, investment bankers, and university professors.

"In a time when we are living in an acquisitive society," Dorothy observed, "Peter Maurin is the poor man. Perhaps that is what makes Peter so important a person, this tremendous faith he had not only in God but in man. He was an Apostle to the world. It is this which sets him apart from other men, from other saints of the Church of God who went around preaching penance, reminding men of their relationship with God and eternity." Peter's very being was a demonstration of his faith. "Peter," Dorothy observed "thought not only in terms of eternity, but of the present life where we are actors, where we are placed as though on a testing ground, to prove ourselves for eternal life."(Day mss.: 35) Dorothy recognized the unique genius of Maurin. Peter's life represented a cohesive intellectual, spiritual and practical synthesis which stood as a positive alternative to the rapidly unraveling philosophic fabric of the Enlightenment. He represented the very order of spirit, intellect and action Dorothy had been seeking all her life. It took a while, but she soon realized that this man held a special truth and a spiritual sense she had not found in other sources of her new religion. Dorothy was stubborn, questioning, and skeptical, certainly a difficult student, but once she understood the significance of Peter's message she dedicated herself to understanding and living the ideal which he presented.

Dorothy observed that all of the subjects on which Peter wrote in *The Catholic Worker*—history, philosophy, sociology, economics—

had a truly religious foundation. But none of this writing was ethereal; it all had to do "with the world and this life which we know and love and with the needs of our bodies for food, clothing and shelter." Peter provided for Dorothy Day the connection between the eternal and the finite. He "so felt the tremendous importance of this life," she wrote, that even though this life is "but a second[,]... he made one feel the magnificent significance of our work, our daily lives, the material of God's universe and what we did with it and how we use it."(Day mss.: 35)

"The dignity of the worker. The dignity of work. The goodness of God's goods. Man as co-creator. These were the things he believed in. He had faith in himself, in his own importance as a lay apostle, and that faith was sufficient for him to rise above any and all rebuffs from whatever source they came."(Day mss.: 35) Dorothy admired his confidence in the message he presented. "It was inconceivable to Peter," she noted, "that anyone should be uninterested [in his program]. That is part of the secret to his success. He had a gentle insistence, an enthusiastic generosity, an assumption that one was intellectually capable of grasping the most profound truths and was honestly ready to change one's life to conform thereby."(Day mss.: 26)

According to Dorothy Day, Peter's life epitomized the first letter of John in the New Testament. In this letter John discusses seeing the face of God in our love for one another. John wrote, "No man hath seen God at any time. If we love one another, God abideth in us; and His charity is perfected in us. "If any man say I love God and hateth his brother he is a liar. For he that loveth not his brother whom he seeth how can he love God whom he seeth not?"(Day mss.)

Peter profoundly influenced Dorothy Day because he made the Gospels come alive through his every action. "When people come into contact with Peter Maurin," she wrote, "they change, they awaken, they begin to see, things become as new, they look at life in the light of the Gospels. They admit the truth he possesses and lives by, and though they themselves fail to go the whole way, their faces are turned at least toward the light. And Peter was patient," she observed. "Looking at things as he did in the light of history, taking the long view, he was content to play his part, to live by his principles and to wait."(Day mss.: 358) He always reminded her of the necessity of the long view, of the vision. He taught her to see all things in the light of eternity. Dorothy felt that it was this "longer view that connected them to the infinite and made the work of the day, what

[they] did here and now so important that each thought, each decision, each step [they] took determined the future, not only for themselves but for the world."

Dorothy believed that "Peter was so conscious of the overwhelming fact that he was a child of God, and an heir to heaven, that he made others feel it." His actions and words often reminded Dorothy that we are all partakers of Divine Life and Peter frequently told her that "the Christ life was in all of us." Maybe it was, she admitted, "but not as [great] as it was in Peter." He taught her "the joy and life giving qualities of the works of mercy." "He has brought Christ to us in the face of the poor," Dorothy observed, "as surely as the Blessed Mother brought Christ to Elizabeth." She concluded, "He has shown us the way, with his poverty and his works of mercy, and that way is Christ."(Day mss.: 35-36) From Peter she learned how to live out the vision of eternal community in time. As Robert Coles pointed out, "It was almost as if one of the many poor and ragged and unassuming men who frequented the Depression era streets had suddenly become possessed by God and turned into a ragged disciple." "Without him," Dorothy concluded, "I would never have been able to find a way of working that would have satisfied my conscience. Peter's arrival changed everything, I finally found a purpose in my life and the teacher I needed."(Coles 1987: 72- 73)

Dorothy Day's biographers concur that she constantly sought the truth. But for Day, truth had to be reconciled with her intellect, her spirituality, and the real world around her. When she was thirty years old she felt she found this unity of thought, spirit and action in the Catholic Church, but as her own letters and autobiography tell us, she was often frustrated in her new found religion. Not until she met Maurin did the uneasiness end. With his inspiration she founded the Catholic Worker movement where, as she tells us, her longing was fulfilled. It is absolutely certain that without Dorothy Day there would have been no Catholic Worker, but it is also certain that without the spiritual influence of Peter Maurin, there would not have been a Dorothy Day with the perspective capable of creating that movement. Dorothy Day acknowledged this. She had no doubt of Peter Maurin's spirituality and she knew that the Divine Life existed within him (Day mss.: 37).

Notes

[1] This story also appears in an article Brieg wrote for *Ave Maria* (20 January 1962), but the final quotation differs: "'Young man...if that's what you think, you go ahead and Christianize the modern world. I want to go back.'"

[2] George Lipsitz (1988) helped me make the connection between Maurin and Gramsci's "Organic Intellectuals."

Jeff Poniewaz

The Hundred-Foot Fiberglass Hiawatha

the hundred-foot fiberglass Hiawatha
looming over Ironwood, Michigan
to attract tourists and industry
is not what Longfellow had in mind

*

MINNEHAHA:
LAUGHING WATER

*

the bass & northern pike of pristine Lac La Croix
laced with mercury
leached from rocks by acid rain

Bethlehem Steel gives birth
to the death of lakes in Ontario

birches of Upper Michigan
dying from acid rain

smokestacks cannonade
the amniotic atmosphere
that continually gives birth
to the world

besides getting
outboard motors for their canoes
the Chippewa got
mercury in their fish

Minnehaha
Meets
Minamata

no laughing matter

PART IX

AMMON HENNACY

Christ and the Moneychangers, by Ade Bethune, first appeared in the May 1935 *Catholic Worker.*

An Anarchist Joins the Catholic Church: Why Ammon Hennacy Became a Catholic

James Missey

University of Wisconsin-Stevens Point

The Christian anarchist, Ammon Hennacy, was baptized according to the rite of the Roman Catholic Church on November 17, 1952, by Father Marion G. Casey, in Saint Anastasia's Church, Hutchinson, Minnesota (To Whom It Concerns 2/15/57, MU).[1]

The question as to why Hennacy joined the Catholic Church has long intrigued me, because of Hennacy's hostility towards organized religion and because, without being a member of the Church, for sixteen years or so he had a strong relationship with the Catholic Worker movement. For several years he had the support of a number of priests in Phoenix, where he lived at the time of his conversion.

One can see the opposition of Hennacy to organized religion throughout his career as an anarchist. The opposition, however, often was not directed at organized Christianity itself but at its failure to be truly Christian. More particularly, the church failed to be fully Christian because it had become the faithful servant of the warmaking state. The state made the wars, but its servant had bloody hands.

In the letters that Hennacy wrote in the late 1940s and early 1950s, just before he joined the Catholic Church, one can find evidence of his opposition to organized Christianity on the grounds that it condoned the state's violence, especially its war-making. In a letter to a Henry and Trude (surname unknown), for example, Hennacy wrote that most pacifists and radicals do not belong to an organized church, but that their struggle is not so much with organized religion anyway, but rather with the state that uses the church to sanctify its wars (2/ 20/49, UW). In a letter to William Stuart of Internal Revenue, moreover, about his nonpayment of taxes, Hennacy wrote that the church is immoral "in upholding war and [the] return of evil for evil

This essay originally appeared in Edward J. Miller and Robert P. Wolensky (editors), *Proceedings of the Conference on the Small City and Regional Community* (Volume 13), Stevens Point, WI: UWSP Foundation Press, 1999.

by the state."(1/10/50, UW) Hennacy sounded a similar note in a letter to Jim [Lee?] that condemned "the National Catholic Welfare Council...Jewish religious leaders[,] and the Protestant Federation"for supporting the Korean War (5/20/51, MU). He added with characteristic wryness that "they could hardly have picked out a worse war to praise." Writing to Mr. Manning, the cartoonist for *The Arizona Republic*, Hennacy referred to the rulers in this country only caring about being able to "subsidize organized religion to justify their evil."(Thanksgiving 1951, NAU) Touching on, finally, not only the church's condoning of war but implicitly of capitalism as well, Hennacy said, in a letter to Joseph Breig, that the Church had been a betrayer "in upholding the wealthy classes and supporting their wars."(4/24/52, NAU)

That Hennacy joined the Catholic Church is intriguing not only because he opposed organized religion for its sanctioning of the state's war-making, but also because he did not need to be a member to have a strong relationship with the Catholic Worker movement, according to Hennacy the second great influence in his life (Hennacy 1968: 43). The first was, presumably, reading the Bible and converting to Christianity while he was in prison for agitating against the First World War. Although the precise date of Hennacy's link with the Catholic Worker movement is not clear, Catholic Workers did serve as ushers at the fiftieth anniversary meeting, on November 19, 1937, of the hanging of the Haymarket anarchists, which Hennacy organized in Milwaukee (Hennacy 1968: 49). In a letter to W. I. Fisher, Hennacy said that he had been associated with the Catholic Workers for fifteen years, putting his first affiliation with them in 1936 (7/12/ 51, MU). In a letter written to Herbert A. Leggett, Hennacy said that he had been associated with the Catholic Worker movement for fourteen years, putting his first affiliation with the group in 1937 (9/9/51, MU). Whether he dated his first affiliation with the Catholic Worker movement in 1936 or 1937, Hennacy at the time of his joining the Catholic Church had long been associated with the group.

The long association by Hennacy with the Catholic Worker movement took several forms. He wrote Rita Hologa that in 1937 he helped to begin a Catholic Worker house in Milwaukee (4/15/52, NAU). *The Catholic Worker* also was the first paper to "support [his] non payment of taxes," according to a letter that Hennacy wrote William Stuart of the Internal Revenue Service in 1952 (1/13/52, NAU). The

Worker also published many articles by Hennacy. Writing to a Rev. Greene in 1949, he said he had four articles that the *Worker* would run (3/2/49, UW). In the same letter, Hennacy said that, at churches and in front of Walgreen's, he sold three hundred copies of the *Worker* each month.

In addition to having long been affiliated with the Catholic Worker movement, Hennacy had, without being a member of the Catholic Church, the support of several priests in Phoenix. In a letter to his banker friend, Frank Brophy, Hennacy said that he had told the tax man that seven priests supported what he did, whereas "six chase[d him,] so [he was] one ahead."(6/26/50, UW) Writing to Rita Hologa in 1952, Hennacy said that he was on good terms with five priests, some of whom at mass publicized his picketing and some of whom "sa[id] mass for [his] success."(4/15/52, NAU)

Among the priests supporting Hennacy in Phoenix, one in particular stands out: the Jesuit, Father George Dunne. According to a letter Hennacy wrote Platt Cline in 1951, Father Dunne had said in church the previous Sunday that he sometimes thought that the response to war of his friend, Ammon Hennacy, was the right way (Thanksgiving 1951, NAU). Hennacy wrote Platt Cline in another letter, in 1952, that at three masses in early December Father Dunne had lauded Hennacy's work (1/1/52, NAU). Dunne had gone so far, according to Hennacy's 1950 letter to Agnes Inglis (curator of the Labadie Collection at the University of Michigan), as to say that he thought the Catholic Worker's anarchism and pacifism to be correct but that he had some Jesuit obstacles to overcome "and wanted further conversation with [Hennacy] on the subject."(7/31/50, UM)

Why, then, in view of his opposition to organized religion and his having, without being a member of the Catholic Church, a long-term relationship with the Catholic Worker movement and the support of several priests in Phoenix, did Ammon Hennacy convert to Catholicism?

According to his own testimony, Hennacy was attracted to the Catholic Church because he wanted to gain a greater access of spirituality. In an article, "Fasting and Picketing," Hennacy wrote that, during his annual Hiroshima fast, he "went to St. Mary's to mass" and added that, in his "search for truth and [out of] respect for the CW staff [,he had] for some time [been] attend[ing] mass and sa[ying his] own prayers each Sunday."(CW 9/50: 6) In the same article, he said that he had been heartened by getting from Dorothy Day and others at the Catholic Worker a telegram whose "spiritual emphasis…strengthened [him]." Hennacy also wrote about attending a service at Saint Mary's and reflecting on the special significance to him of the crucified Jesus and on the quality of love that Dorothy Day had and that he was missing. He added that, as he surveyed those gathered in the church, he "desire[d] to be one of them and to help them" and thought that "[m]aybe this [experience was] the beginning," although of what it was a beginning he did not specify. He concluded the account of the experience by saying that, although he did not agree with the "church['s] support of war and capitalism," he would not allow the disagreement to keep him "from God.. . and. . . that Jesus who was a true rebel."

Further evidence from the early 1950s shows that, for spiritual reasons, Hennacy was attracted to the Catholic Church. In the 1951 manuscript "Thoughts on Religion," Hennacy said that he might enter a Catholic Church to say a prayer, "ask[ing] for grace and wisdom, for [himself], a sinner. "(Hennacy 1951) Writing to Platt Cline, moreover, Hennacy referred to the necessity for "spiritual food."(10/12/51, NAU) Finally, in his annual letter to the IRS collector, William Stuart, Hennacy said that he was not a member of any church "but attend[ed] mass and pray[ed] for grace and wisdom…."(1/13/52, NAU)

With the advantage of hindsight, then, one could say that, step-by-step, Hennacy was moving closer to converting to Catholicism. In Chapter Twelve of his autobiography, *The Book of Ammon*, Hennacy describes the immediate steps which led him into the Church. In the late summer or early fall of 1952, Hennacy was in New York at the Catholic Worker. One event that affected him was Dorothy Day's reaction to the singing of the "Star Spangled Banner."(Hennacy 1968: 264) Day had attended mass in a big Catholic Church, and, after communion, the organ began playing the national anthem. Everyone except Dorothy Day stood; she knelt. Later, upon hearing about the experience, Hennacy was powerfully moved, thinking about how superior Day's response was to his own response, in 1941, to the singing of "Onward Christian Soldiers" at an event in a Congregational Church in Milwaukee, where Hennacy had debated the head of the American Legion. Hennacy "sat stubbornly in front of [the assembled people] while they stood and sang. [He] felt mean…."(264)

In addition to being moved by Dorothy Day's example, Hennacy experienced, probably on the Sunday following Day's kneeling during the singing of the "Star Spangled Banner," three further decisive events that seemed to lead him into the Catholic Church. On the afternoon of the Sunday referred to, a communist, whom Dorothy Day and Hennacy knew, with his family visited Peter Maurin Farm near New York City, where Hennacy was staying. Day, Ammon, the communist, his wife, and his teen-aged children went to the library over the chapel and talked for hours. They talked about "communism, anarchism, pacifism,. . . [and] capitalism." They disagreed on the issues yet were cordial and, Hennacy felt, linked in a "spirit of brotherhood" or what "the Catholics call Grace." The second event of the day was Hennacy's reading a short story by Tolstoy, "The Diary of an Insane Man," which illustrated the great writer's ideas on pacifism and Christian anarchism. The final event happened when Hennacy went to the barn, where he was sleeping. By accident he walked into the chapel, where a candle burned next to the Little Flower, near which Dorothy Day had placed a rose. Hennacy said that he "prayed and meditated" for about an hour. He said that he concluded that "the Catholic Church was the true Church" and that he was "only hurting [him]self" by not joining it. He summarized the significant elements of this crucial day: the communist family symbolized his Marxist socialist past; the story by Tolstoy reminded him of his tax resistance and anarchism; the rose, one may infer, reminded him that Dorothy Day was opening to him a door into "deeper spirituality," which for him meant becoming a Catholic (Hennacy 1968: 264-266). Hennacy learned more about the beliefs of the Catholic Church, which he joined on November 17, 1952.

John Cort wrote a contemporary account of Hennacy's move towards Catholicism for *Commonweal,* under the title "The Charms of Anarchism," *Charms* being used, one surmises, in the sense of beguilements. Cort, who was the magazine's labor columnist and had hosted Hennacy sometime in the fall of 1952, began his column by saying that Hennacy "seems to be on his way into the Catholic Church." Later in the article, Cort added, rather presciently in light of Hennacy's withdrawal from the Church towards the end of his life, that, although he hoped Hennacy would continue on his path into the Church, he did not think there were "aid and comfort for anarchism in the wisdom of the Church."(Cort 1952: 139-140)

In addition to what Ammon Hennacy gave as the reason for joining the Catholic Church, we must consider also his attraction to Dorothy Day. In a memoir of the years with Hennacy, Joan Thomas,

Hennacy's widow, said that Hennacy, by his own account, was a Catholic because he was infatuated with Dorothy Day (Thomas 1974: 12). Thomas claimed that Hennacy went to New York in 1952 or 1953 to be with Day and to marry her (183). Twenty-three years after publishing her memoir, Thomas had not changed her view. In a note to the author, Thomas said that, "as far as [she] can tell [and] after [five] months of reading his papers, [Hennacy] became an R. C. out of love for D.D...."(To Missey, 5/24/97)

Other people who knew or knew about Hennacy in the early 1950s corroborated Thomas's view. Draft resister and historian Larry Gara thought that Hennacy was probably sexually attracted to Dorothy Day. Gara wrote in a letter to the author that he "dimly recall[s] Marion Bromley [a woman who was active in the Peacemakers] referring to [Hennacy's] propositioning Dorothy Day."(To Missey 7/21/97) Sam Dolgoff, the anarchist writer, said that it "was hinted that Ammon [Hennacy] was unsuccessfully courting [Dorothy Day]."(Dolgoff 1986: 99)

In *The Book of Ammon* Hennacy himself attested to being infatuated with Dorothy Day and implied that it was the reason that he moved to New York to work at the Catholic Worker headquarters. Although he admitted to having had a "crush on Dorothy" for "a few years," he did not, however, say that he joined the Catholic Church for that reason (Hennacy 1968: 319).

Regardless of the degree of his romantic attraction to Dorothy Day, we may safely conclude that Ammon Hennacy was attracted to her in the sense that he was attracted to a number of strong women, like Mother Bloor, Mother Jones, his own mother, Emma Goldman, and the Doukhobor Helen Demoskoff. Perhaps the thread that unites these women is their courage, according to Hennacy (paraphrasing Samuel Johnson) the greatest of the virtues, because without it one could not practice any of the others (Johnson and Biron 1989: 113). In his chapter of the autobiography on leaving Catholicism, Hennacy strongly implied that he became a Catholic because of the integrity of Dorothy Day (Hennacy 1968: 474).

If Hennacy joined the Catholic Church because of his attraction to the integrity of Dorothy Day, he was repeating a pattern that he had exemplified earlier in his life. In an article, "One Man Revolution,"(*CW* 7-8/1952: 1, 6) he implied that he had been a member of the Communist Party for three years, in the early 1920s, because of his admiration for Charles Ruthenberg, who was then the

Party's general secretary (Zipser 1998: 710-711). If Hennacy had been a communist because of his admiration for Ruthenberg, it is not too difficult to believe that he joined the Catholic Church because he respected Dorothy Day.

Further evidence of the appeal to Hennacy of Dorothy Day's courage is contained in a 1951 letter to Herbert A. Leggett in which Hennacy said that, Gandhi being dead, Dorothy Day was the most virtuous public figure (9/9/51, MU). At about the same time Hennacy wrote someone named Krieg that Dorothy Day was the only person of the day who lived a life similar to that of Saint Francis or Gandhi (9/30/51, NAU). Or, as Hennacy wrote the following April in a letter to Randall Dodson, Dorothy Day was the one person living who was in a league with Debs, Vanzetti, and Gandhi (4/14/52, NAU). Putting his admiration for Day in a different context, Hennacy said in a letter to a Mrs. Riggs that he would only accept criticism from someone, for example, Dorothy Day, whose standard "in courage and wisdom" was "equal [to] or above" Hennacy's own (10/20/51, NAU).

To understand his attitude towards Dorothy Day, we might consider the comments of two people who have written about Hennacy. In a biography of Dorothy Day, William Miller concluded that Hennacy found in Dorothy Day someone "whose radicalism was more ordered and more deeply rooted than his own."(Miller 1982: 41) Joan Thomas took a more sweeping view than Miller's (Thomas 1974: 121). Her memoir referred to a range of women whom Hennacy admired: his great grandmother, his grandmother, his mother, and Mother Bloor. These women were perhaps symbolized for Hennacy by Joan of Arc, one of the saintly rebels of Catholicism whom he held on to even after he left the Church (Hennacy 1968: 475). Miller reported that, after being baptized, Hennacy began "wear[ing] a Joan of Arc medal."(Miller 1982: 425)

Finally, we may consider, not strictly reasons for, but some analogues to Hennacy's joining the Catholic Church. Hennacy had some models of people who were anarchists and Catholics. One model was the English artist Eric Gill, a Catholic anarchist to whom Hennacy referred in a letter to William Stevens (2/2/53, MU). More pertinent so far as Hennacy's particular experience is concerned was the career of Byron Bryant, a friend of Hennacy's whose trajectory somewhat anticipated Hennacy's own. As Hennacy reported in a letter to a Sister Agnes (10/9/49, UW) (probably Sister Agnes de Sales, whom

Hennacy mentioned in his autobiography) (Hennacy 1968: 81), Byron Bryant had been a communist, then became an anarchist, and then, through the appeal to him of the Catholic Worker movement, became a Catholic, identifying himself as an anarchist to church authorities when he joined the Church. The steps by which Bryant became a Catholic anticipated closely those of Hennacy.

In a way that would mirror Hennacy's thoughts about being a Catholic, Bryant wrote an article on the Catholic Worker movement for the anarchist journal *Retort* in 1951. In the course of discussing the anticapitalist tradition within Catholicism during the Middle Ages, Bryant urged that individuals within contemporary Catholicism who wanted to revive that tradition, like Catholic Workers, remain within the Church (Bryant 1951: 9).

In a curious way, what Bryant said sounded like a justification that Hennacy offered for being a member of the Catholic Church. Joan Thomas recalled Hennacy saying that, as long as he was a member of the Church, he may as well remain "'and fight it out with the bastards.'"(Thomas 1974: 12) Thomas also recalled Hennacy took the stance that, although the Church could not assist him, he could help the Church, if its members would hear him (Thomas 1974: 12). Thomas also noted that Hennacy thought that the Catholic Church was the most objectionable church around and that, perhaps through being a member, he could change it (Thomas 1974: 30).

Perhaps, then, we might think that the conversion of Hennacy was not so much about his becoming a Catholic as about his wanting to radicalize the Church along Christian anarchist lines. Patrick Coy (1988: 163) makes the point well, in saying that "Hennacy worked tirelessly to move his adopted church closer to the social demands of the gospel."

Note

[1] The letters of Ammon Hennacy cited in this paper can be found in several collections. References in the text include a notation designating the specific collection. Letters in the Dorothy Day-Catholic Worker Collection, Marquette University Archives, are noted as MU. Letters in the American Heritage Center, University of Wyoming, are noted as UW. Letters in the Platt Cline-Ammon Hennacy Collection, Cline Library, Northern Arizona University, are noted as NAU. Letters in the Labadie Collection, Special Collections Library, University of Michigan, are noted as UM. Letters in private hands are cited as separate entries in the bibliography.

PART X

CATHOLIC WORKER PACIFISM, 1933-1945

The Mystical Body of Christ by Ade Bethune first appeared in the October 1934 *Catholic Worker.*

The Way of Love: Pacifism and The Catholic Worker Movement, 1933-1939

John L. LeBrun

Kent State University-Salem

Since its founding in 1933 by Dorothy Day and Peter Maurin, the Catholic Worker movement has regarded war and the use of violence as immoral. One of the main planks of the Catholic Worker platform was and is an unshaken commitment to absolute pacifism, a complete and total rejection of the use of violence. During the 1930s, when anti-war sentiments were extensive in the United States, the Catholic Worker's pacifism was not out of harmony with a large segment of public opinion. But the rise of the dictators and the coming of the war in Europe changed that mood to one of necessity for preparedness for war. As *The Catholic Worker* continued to reject violence as a solution for international problems, its pacifism became boldly apparant to its readers. What then is the history of Catholic Worker pacifism from the founding of the movement in 1933 to the end of the Spanish Civil War in 1939?

During this six-year period, *The Catholic Worker* developed its position on nonviolence and pacifism in reaction to the political situations in Mexico, Ethiopia, and Spain. In this same period it formulated a theory of absolute pacifism by literally applying the Counsels of Perfection to all Catholics, and it assessed international events using the criteria of the traditional Catholic Just War Theory. Although a new paper and unsure of itself and sometimes contradictory at first, by 1939 it and the movement stood firmly in the pacifist camp.

Apparently, the editors of *The Catholic Worker* did not consider pacifism a topic of concern in the early thirties. Labor relations, strikes, race, and unemployment were the principle subjects discussed in the early issues. As befitting a Catholic paper founded in the depths of the Great Depression and determined to show that the Church had relevant social programs, *The Catholic Worker* had no reason to treat the issue of pacifism until its fifth issue in October 1933 (*CW*: 2) . This issue clearly shows that absolute pacifism has been a basic tenet of the Catholic Worker movement from the very beginning. An article entitled "Catholic Worker Delegates to Attend Peace Conference" stated that Catholic Workers would be among those present at the United States Congress against War to be held in New York City from September 29 to October 1, 1933. The article went on to say that Catholic Workers had been unable to attend a peace meeting called by the Workmen's Ex-Service League in September 1933 because they could not find the meeting place. One of the members, probably Dorothy Day herself, did however find the meeting in Union Square on her way home and "marched with it for a few blocks as a representative of Catholic pacifism."(*CW* 10/33: 2)

During the 1930s *The Catholic Worker* treated war in a way one would expect of any liberal or radical group at that time. It condemned war preparations, especially what it called the pseudo-patriotism and flag-waving of munitions manufacturers (*CW* 5/39: 2). Moreover, its pacifist position was well known to other pacifist groups. A. J. Muste and Marion Frenyear both reported in great detail to the membership of their organization, the Fellowship of Reconciliation, the stand of the Catholic Worker on war (Muste 1937: 4-6; Frenyear 1937: 11). Still the Catholic Worker movement cannot be considered a part of the general peace movement in the 1930s because of the positions it took on the problems in Mexico, Ethiopia, and Spain (LaFarge 1937: 275).

The Mexican Revolution predated the founding of the Catholic Worker movement. Judging from the Catholic press of the time, it must have seemed to many Catholics that Russian Communism-or at least European Masonry—had taken over the Mexican government. *The Catholic Worker* reacted as did other American Catholic publications. At a time when most American liberals were supporting the Mexican government and the Good Neighbor Policy, *The Catholic Worker* appeared to be following the line of the Catholic hierarchy and the Knights of Columbus (Quigley 1965: passim).

The Catholic Worker published many articles on Mexico calling on American Catholics to show solidarity against Mexican atheism and to engage in active protest against the persecution of Mexican Catholics. To coordinate their protests, some Catholic Workers, headed by Tom Coddington, formed the Campion Propaganda Committee, named for the great Jesuit propagandizer and martyr of the Elizabethan persecution, Edmund Campion. The purpose of this group was to study and apply Catholic social doctrine to the social order. The Campions tried to build up a militantly-active and organized laity who would not only know Catholic social principles but also follow this knowledge with Catholic Action. In short, they were to act as the "strong right arm of the Catholic Worker Movement."(*CW* 6/35: 8; 7-8/35: 2)

Under the aegis of the Campion Propaganda Committee, Catholic Workers began an active program of nonviolent protest against the Mexican government for its persecution of Catholics. Beginning with a November 15, 1934 mass march of about 1,000 people, the Campions daily picketed the Mexican Consulate on West 34 th Street in New York City. These protests culminated on December12, the feast of Our Lady of Guadeloupe, the patroness of Mexico, when twenty groups, organized by the Campion Propaganda Committee, marched on the consulate and engaged in a mass demonstration and a prayer rally. In an editorial, *The Catholic Worker* claimed that this was the first time that Catholics in this country had ever picketed as Catholics. This editorial included a statement that embodied the principles of passive resistance, a position that the paper was beginning to express. "It is only by passive resistance that we can oppose our enemies. Picketing is a form of passive resistance to injustice."(*CW* 12/34: 1,6; 4, 7).

On the question of passive resistance and picketing Dorothy Day stood with Peter Maurin. She believed that these activities could lead Catholic Workers away from their core beliefs of personalist daily living to the excitement of crusades and action. As she said at the time, "I allowed this though I was not in favor of it." For a while the Campions were strong, with groups not only in New York City but also in Boston and Washington. In time the Campions were excluded from the Catholic Worker movement. Dorothy Day believed that their actions "sounded too much like Communist tactics to me."(Miller 1973: 69-70, 106).

Although the Mexican protests were nonviolent, they could scarcely be called pacifist. The paper was new and still unsure of itself. Later, Dorothy Day was somewhat critical of the Worker's Mexican position (Miller 1975). The Catholic Worker had yet to enunciate fully a theory of pacifism. Then in March 1935 Father Paul Hanly Furfey of the Catholic University of America wrote "Christ and the Patriot," the first article in *The Catholic Worker* voicing a pacifist theory for the movement.

James Forest, who included this article in his anthology of *Catholic Worker* articles, has claimed that with this single article "the Catholic peace movement in America was born." (Quigley 1968: 44) Father Furfey, a distinguished sociologist and one of America's leading personalists, had been attracted to the Catholic Worker movement because of its personalism. By the time the article was printed he had already given one of his weekend retreats for Catholic Workers. The article was very short, running only to nine column-inches. It consisted of a dialog between the Patriot, a nationalist who believed that a strong defense was the best assurance of peace, and Christ, who simply repeated the New Testament injunctions about loving one's enemies, perishing by the sword, and offering the other cheek. The article ended with a short prayer to the "Lord Jesus Christ, Lover of Peace," and petitioned Him to kindle in the reader a fire of heroic love so that "we may rather suffer injury than protect our rights by violence."(Cornell and Forest 1968: 26-28)

In the same issue, in a letter to the editor, Father Furfey explained that he had tried, in his article, to show that Christian social thought should be based on Christ's maximum standard of love rather than some minimalist position of moral theology. According to Furfey, moral theology permits spending vast sums on armaments, military training, and the like. This permission represents the Church's minimum standard. "But why should we be content with a minimum standard? The charity of Christ is diametrically opposed to militant nationalism." Father Furfey went on to claim that Christians ought to strive for the ideal that was embodied in Christ's command to love one's enemies. He said that he was distinguishing clearly between the two positions of merely avoiding mortal sin and of striving for perfection. He ended his letter by observing "it seems to me that this thought is very much in line with the thought of your group."(*CW* 3/35: 12)

The ideals embodied in Furfey's article and letter and expressed by the Catholic Worker movement were based on a literal interpretation of the Counsels of Perfection. The Catholic Church has traditionally separated the Commandments, rules of conduct for all, from the Counsels of Perfection, exhortations to those who felt called to strive for perfection.

The Catholic Worker has always called all Catholics to the higher life of religion that is typified by the Counsels of Perfection. This life takes literally the command of Christ to be perfect even as God in heaven is perfect. From its very founding in 1933, Peter Maurin's personalist beliefs have formed the philosophical core of the Catholic Worker movement. Catholic Worker personalism believes in the importance of the person, and consequently Catholic Workers have always refused to do violence to others. As personalists, Catholic Workers have always placed great emphasis on each person's moral responsibility for her or his own actions. Therefore, a Catholic Worker can never use the excuse of a military order to absolve himself or herself from moral responsibility. It is clear that Catholic Workers have been led to reject violence and war absolutely.

The Catholic Worker perfectionist tradition opposes war on the grounds that war violates the Sermon On the Mount as a Counsel of Perfection. In doing so, it sees itself as returning to the original Christian witness on war, the pacifism of the pre-Constantine Church. But because the Catholic Worker also wants society to do away with war, it takes nonviolent direct action as a tactic to urge others to seek peace.

Catholic Workers believe that making peace requires an active commitment on the part of those who strive for peace. (Most Catholic Workers of the time preferred the term "peacemaker" to "pacifist" because the former term had a more active connotation.) For them, peacemaking arises from the obedience to the urges of conscience. Nonviolence, a virtue to be sought like voluntary poverty, is the capacity to endure and accept suffering without becoming antagonistic and hostile. In the January 1935 issue of her paper, Dorothy Day summarized this approach:

> When asked what is the program of *The Catholic Worker* by those who are interested in political action, legislation, lobbying, and class war, we reply—It is the program set forth by Christ in the Gospels. The Catholic Manifesto is the Sermon of the Mount. And when we bring *The Catholic Worker* into the streets and public squares, and when we picket the Mexican Consulate, it is to practice the spiritual works of mercy-to instruct the ignorant and comfort the afflicted. (*CW* 1/35: 4)

In 1939, she more fully explained her ideas in her book *House of Hospitality*:

> The day calls for a new technique. We must make use of the spiritual weapons at our disposal, and by hard work, sacrifice, self discipline, patience and prayer (and we won't have any of the former without the latter), work from day to day in the tasks that present themselves. We have a program of action and a philosophy of life. The thing is to use them.
>
> We have been criticized for holding up the counsels of perfection as norms of human conduct. It is sad that it is always the minimum that is expected of lay people. On the other hand we get too much praise from some for performing work which is our plain duty... Indeed we deserve censure for not having done more....
>
> As Leon Bloy wrote: "There is only one unhappiness, and that is *not to be one of the saints.*"
>
> And we could add: the greatest tragedy is that not enough of us desire to be saints. (1939: 226-227)

The second international situation of the 1930s that *The Catholic Worker* confronted was the Ethiopian War. This crisis was caused by the attack on that African state by Mussolini's Italy in 1935. *The Catholic Worker*'s greatest concern was that the church and the papacy itself seemed to approve and to bless the actions of the Italian government. In a September 1935 editorial condemning the war as imperialistic, the paper allied itself with liberal and radical elements in the United States while most other Catholic spokesmen either remained silent or supported Italy. This editorial closed with a statement that the answer to the League of Nations' inaction would be the application of Christian ethics to the international situation. "It is not Christianity which has failed to solve the problem. It is, rather, as someone said, that Christian ideals in international relations has [sic] not yet been tried."(*CW* 10/35: 12)

In October 1935, immediately after the outbreak of the Ethiopian War, *The Catholic Worker* stated that "this war is clearly immoral when judged by Catholic ethics."(*CW* 10/35: 1,6) The paper based its condemnation on the theory of the Just War. This Just War Theory is the traditional Catholic response to the question of war. The article analyzed the Ethiopian War by applying the theory's seven points necessary to justify war.

According to this theory, a war can be considered moral only when it satisfies all seven of the points. A properly constituted authority must declare it. It must be fought for a just cause. The war must be fought for a legitimate reason and with a desire to do good for the opponent. The war must be properly conducted; that is, no immoral actions can be allowed. Any action must be judged by the rule of proportionality; any bad result of a warlike act cannot exceed the good hoped for when the act is committed. Last, the war must be fought only as a last resort; all other methods of resolving the conflict must have already been tried and failed (*CW* 10/35: 1,6).

Though it is not the present day Catholic Worker approach to pacifism, many Catholic Workers did pragmati-cally accept the Just War Theory rather than the perfectionist approach of absolute pacifism. During the 1930s and early 1940s, *The Catholic Worker* ran a large number of articles analyzing events based on the Just War approach to the morality of war. The reason for this seems to have been a belief that while Catholic pacifism was the ideal, an appeal to the traditional approach would be more acceptable and better received by a larger number of American Catholics.

The third major event of the pre-World War II period that shaped the development of Catholic Worker pacifism was the Spanish Civil War. For the Catholic Worker movement, this was the most important of the three because of the unique response the Catholic Worker took within the American Catholic tradition and because of the hostility this response evoked.

The Civil War began in July 1936, with a revolt of the army chiefs in Morocco. The feelings aroused in the United States by this war were both intense and deep. From the very beginning, Catholics found themselves at odds with their fellow Americans. The roster of Loyalist supporters reads like a "Who's Who" of the American Left. Many Protestant and most Jewish leaders also backed the Loyalist regime. But the entire Catholic hierarchy and virtually all prominent Catholic laymen saw the war in a different light. To Catholics, the Spanish Nationalists were defending traditional Spanish Catholicism from attack by the atheistic communist conspiracy. Defense of the nationalists became defense of the Church. Anything less became an attack on the Church (Taylor 1967: 90-100).

The American Catholic press became virtually paranoid on the subject of Spain. Support of the Loyalists by the secular press was seen as but another manifestation of anti-Catholicism. All those who did not favor the Nationalist cause were automatically considered enemies of the Church and hence supporters of communism. Nearly all Catholic periodicals followed this thinking. No Catholic periodical supported the Loyalists and only *The Catholic Worker* consistently took a neutralist position on the war (Darrow 1953: 63-67, 77, 105-110, 180, 191-193; Valaik 1964: 73-82, 91-105, 206-211).

The Catholic Worker praised neither the Franco nor the Loyalist faction. As early as September 1936, the paper outlined editorially what was to be its unchanging position. The editor lamented the disaster of "blood soaked Spain." To Catholic Workers, who abhorred violence, the war was not a struggle of Christ versus Communism but was one in which the members of the Mystical Body of Christ were tearing each other apart. The Spanish people were caught in "a whirlpool of political ambitions" and forced to kill, maim, and torture. Right and wrong existed on both sides of this war, and the editor believed that the issues were "not so clear as to enable either side to condemn the other justifiably." In a statement that must have been meant as an appeal to other Catholic periodicals as much as to *The Catholic Worker*'s readers, the editor continued

> Spain doesn't need favorable publicity for the rebels. She doesn't need condemnation of the Loyalists. What she needs is the prayers of the rest of the Mystical Body. Pleas to God that Members will stop hating each other. Appeals to His Son for an appreciation of the Love that He taught.
>
> The Catholic Worker makes this appeal to its readers: Forget your anger. Let your indignation die. Remember only that the Body is being rent asunder, and the only solution is love. Let us show ours by humbly praying the Source of Love that He intervene in the cause of the Body of which He is the Head. (*CW* 11/36: 4)

The reason for this appeal to forgiveness and love, so Christian in principle and, to its critics, so unrealistic in practice, lay in *The Catholic Worker*'s interpretation of the basic nature of Christianity. Force, it declared, was alien to Christianity. Christ never forced anyone to believe in His doctrines. He did not coerce. His way was to become the servant, emptying Himself completely and suffering the death of the cross. "He set the example, and we are supposed to imitate Him." But, the paper stated, the whole world was turning from Christ's example to the use of force. Fascists and Communists alike believed that only by shedding blood could they conquer. In contrast, *The Catholic Worker* believed that Catholics should be willing to die but not to kill for their faith, for this was Christ's way (*CW* 11/36: 4).

As the Spanish War intensified both on the battlefield and as an issue in the United States, *The Catholic Worker* held steadfast to a neutral position. The entire front page of the December 1936 issue reprinted an article from *Esprit,* the small monthly French journal edited by the noted Catholic Personalist, Emmanuel Mounier. Although the article was unsigned, the paper later identified the author as Alfredo Mendizabal, a noted Spanish Catholic writer and educator (*CW* 12/36: 1,8; 2/37: 6). The article, *The Catholic Worker* editor said, was reprinted in its entirety because it explained the position of the Catholic Worker movement on the Spanish War.

Mendizabal felt that he could not take sides in the civil war in his country. To do so he would have to renounce his independence and independence was the mark of the Christian in his power over the world. He knew full well that his neutral position was an uncomfortable one since he would receive blows from both sides. But this nonpartisan position was necessary if he were to do his duty as a Christian. Applying the Just War system of ethics, he bluntly stated

> If one considers the conditions laid down by theologians on the right of insurrection, it would be very difficult for the partisans of the insurgents to plead their case....
>
> It is always necessary to recall, to those who forget it, the permanent vigor of the fifth commandment of the Divine Law. What are we to think of so-called Catholics who believe themselves free from its observance because their particular concept of patriotism is at stake? (*CW* 12/36: 1)

The Catholic Worker's stand on the Spanish Civil War brought harsh reactions. Mendizabal's article cost the Catholic Worker movement much of the support it had gained among the Protestant and secular left (Chatfield 1971: 239-244). Joseph Zarrella recalled that "We were torn apart by both sides. We were anathema because of our pacifist, neutral position."(Roberts 1984: 119)

But more important to the paper's future was the disapproval of many Catholics. Not until the Spanish Civil War did *The Catholic Worker* come into conflict with the dominant opinion within the Church. Groups that had supported *The Catholic Worker*'s social action programs rejected its stand on nonviolence (Day 1952: 212-214). *The Catholic Worker* came under attack from other Catholic periodicals for compromising on the Spanish issue. Chief among the attackers were *The Brooklyn Tablet* and *Social Justice*, the organ of Father Charles E. Coughlin's National Union for Social Justice. In a front-page editorial on July 5, 1937, *Social Justice* claimed that *The Catholic Worker* "urges compromise with Reds," and then went on to say "hundreds of priests have fallen hook, line and sinker for *The Catholic Worker* program." *Social Justice* damned the "gullibility" of the priests of one Detroit parish who purchased copies of *The Catholic Worker* in bulk for the church book rack (*CW* 7/37: 1). Because of its stand on the Spanish Civil War and pacifism in general, the paper's circulation plummeted from a high of 190,000 in early 1938 to a low of 50,500 during World War II. Almost this entire drop came from the cancellation of bulk orders. Individual subscriptions actually rose during this period (Day 1952: 212-214; LeBrun 1973: 397-400).

Undeterred by the attacks of the liberals or by those rightists like Father Coughlin, or by the drop in its circulation, *The Catholic Worker* stood by its principles. In discussing Spain, many articles used the Just War Theory to condemn the war. One example of this approach was the statement that

> War has become not a conflict of army vs. army but the reciprocal attack of people on people: its object is not to win a battle but to exterminate a people or at least destroy their economic life. Defense as such has ceased to exist. The only defense . . . is offense that means that you have to kill women and children more quickly than the enemy can kill your women and children. All of which makes war today morally indefensible. C. W. applies this vigorously to the Spanish War. (*CW* 8/37: 1)

While the emphasis in many of *The Catholic Worker* articles during these years was on the Just War Theory, Dorothy Day consistently took the perfectionist position of pacifism in her articles on the Spanish War. She condemned the use of force as Christ had condemned Peter when he drew his sword in the garden on the night of Christ's arrest. Instead, Miss Day proposed weapons other than violence. She thought that prayer was the one effective weapon that could bring peace. She recognized the violence, the destruction of churches, the torture of nuns, and the murder of priests in Republican Spain. In September 1938, Day wrote

> In the light of this fact it is inconceivably difficult to write as we do. It is folly—it seems madness, to say as we do—"we are opposed to the use of force as a means of settling personal, national, or international disputes." As a newspaper trying to effect *[sic]* public opinion, we take this stand. We feel that if the press and the public throughout the world do not speak in terms of the counsels of perfection, who else will? (*CW* 9/38: 1)

Dorothy Day obviously recognized that this approach was folly. And truly it was folly. But it was the folly of the cross, the folly of Christ's nonviolent sacrifice of Calvary. The way to follow Christ, she stated, was not to reject the example of Christ but to become fools for Christ (*CW* 9/38: 1,4).

In the same article, Day also wrote that while *The Catholic Worker* took this stand, it did not self-righteously condemn those who were engaging in war or supporting the combatants. From the human standpoint, she said, men do good to defend their faith and country. "But from the standpoint of the Supernatural there is a 'better way'—the way of the Saints, the way of love." The way of love, she insisted, should be emphasized. Again and again in the history of Christianity, she stated, love conquered force. Love and prayer to her and to the Catholic Worker movement were not passive resistance "but the most active glowing force."(*CW* 9/38: 4)

In March 1939, when the Spanish Civil War ended, World War II was only five months away. The six years since the founding of the Catholic Worker movement in 1933 had been very turbulent. During these six years individual Catholic Workers had organized and participated in nonviolent direct-action protests. The paper had condemned war and the use of violence as immoral. It also criticized international events by applying the criteria of the traditional Just War Theory. But, more important, the Catholic Worker movement had for the first time in American history promulgated a theory of Catholic absolute pacifism by applying literally the Counsels of Perfection to all Catholics. In an editorial celebrating the third founding of the paper, *The Catholic Worker* summed up its program and its ideals: "*TheCatholic Worker* is sincerely a pacifist paper."(*CW* 5/36: 2)

As World War II approached, *The Catholic Worker* continued to oppose war and the preparations for war. In 1940 Dorothy Day testified before Congress against the introduction of the peacetime draft. Catholic Workers organized the Association of Catholic Conscientious Objectors that set up and ran Catholic Civilian Public Service Camps during the war. Articles on the Just War Theory became fewer and, by the time the war ended, had completely disappeared from the paper.

Following World War II, the Catholic Worker movement strengthened its pacifist stand and developed a pacifist theology. Catholic Workers participated in the Civil Defense Drill protests of the fifties and the draft card burnings in the sixties. Catholic Worker pacifism and the commitment to nonviolent direct action begun in the thirties formed the basis for these later actions and became the fountainhead of Catholic pacifism in the United States.

Dorothy Day and the Mystical Body of Christ in the Second World War

William T. Cavanaugh

University of St. Thomas
St. Paul, MN

The Mystical Body of Christ was all the rage in Catholic theology in the first half of this century, most especially in the 1930s and 40s. The image penetrated not only academic circles but more popular lay Catholicism as well, being especially prevalent in Catholic Action. The Mystical Body was also central to Dorothy Day's vision of the Catholic Worker movement. What I hope to display in this paper is that Dorothy—as she had such a gift for doing—shared a common vision of the doctrine with others in Catholic circles during World War II, but drew out more profound implications for Christian action. My argument in short is this: While most saw the Mystical Body as that which united Christians in spirit above the battle lines which pitted Christians in Europe against one another, Dorothy interpreted the Mystical Body as that which made Christian participation in the conflict simply inconceivable. The Mystical Body does not hover above the national borders which divide us; it dissolves them.

I will examine the first approach as exemplified in Pius XII's encyclical *Mystici Corporis Christi,* then look at Dorothy Day's approach, and suggest that she reappropriated an older tradition of the Mystical Body rooted in the thought of the early Church Fathers.

A Distinction of Planes

As one commentator has written of the period between the wars, "Few other phrases in theology occasioned so much passion and spilled ink during these years as did the Pauline description of the church as the 'Body of Christ.'"(Walden 1975: 63) The movement would begin around World War I, reach its zenith with *Mystici Corporis* in 1943, and not subside until the Second Vatican Council put the phrase "People of God" front and center. The popularity of the image of the Mystical Body after World War I is largely explained as an attempt to counterbalance the emphasis on the juridical, institutional nature of the Church which had been the cornerstone of seminary education on the Church since Robert Bellarmine's definition of the Church as a *societas perfecta* analogous to the Kingdom of France. After World War I accelerated the crumbling of what remained of Constantinian church-state relations in Europe, Bellarmine's institutional definition of the Church became increasingly difficult to square with reality. The term Mystical Body seemed to capture a new feeling that the Church was more than an institution, a semi-divine bureaucracy, but rather a communion that united in spirit Catholics of all nation-states despite the irrevocable disappearance of a united Christendom (Walden 1975: 44-45, 52-53, 67-69; Dulles 1987: 47-55).

The popes of the nineteenth and early twentieth centuries had, for the most part, clung tenaciously to a certain nostalgia for that Christendom as a way to resist the decay brought on by the liberal state. After his election in 1922, however, Pope Pius XI took a different course. Europe was in a volatile situation of new nation-states and dictatorships, rabid anticlericalism and social upheaval on both left and right. Pius XI decided that the most prudent course under such circumstances would be for the Church to stop fighting the separation of Church and state, which had consumed so much of the Church's energies in the previous two decades. The Church would also withdraw support from Catholic political parties, and remove the Church as much as possible from the political sphere. As the British ambassador to the Vatican put it, "Pius XI wishes to withdraw the Church as far as possible from politics, so that Catholics may unite on a religious and moral basis."(Russell in Rhodes 1973: 15) The Mystical Body of Christ was the key image employed by Pius XI to express this unity (Pius XI in Benedictine Monks of Solesemes 1961: 347-348, 383, 401). It was not that Pius XI wanted to retreat into a purely privatized version of Christianity; rather, he wanted to hew to a distinction between the political and the social. The Church would stay out of attempts to influence the state directly, and would instead concentrate on being a moral and religious influence within civil society. Pius XI dissolved Catholic political parties opposed to Mussolini in Italy in 1924, and Hitler in Germany in 1933, in exchange for assurances that Catholic Action groups could continue their religious and educational activities unhindered in the social sphere. Both Mussolini and Hitler took advantage of the Church's withdrawal from politics to consolidate their power, and then turned on the Church's religious and social activities, directly attacking Catholic Action and harrassing Catholic schools (Rhodes 1973: 11-52, 103-111, 173-210).

As Pius XI's nuncio in Germany and later secretary of state,. Cardinal Eugenio Pacelli, the future Pius XII, would have a key role to play in the Church's strategy of withdrawal from the political, a strategy he would continue as Pope following the outbreak of World War II. The Mystical Body of Christ played a key role in Pius XII's approach to the war and hopes for peace. During the darkest days of the war, in June 1943, Pius XII issued his famous encyclical on the Mystical Body with the expressed purpose of uniting in spirit those divided by politics. As he writes, "towns and fertile fields are strewn with massive ruins and defiled with the blood of brothers"; these tragedies "naturally lift souls above the passing things of earth to those of heaven that abide forever."(Pius XII in Carlen 1990: para. 4) In such a situation the world turns to the Church for a glimmer of hope, for while nations are rent with violence, the Mystical Body of Christ retains a "divinely-given unity"; even those outside the Church "will be forced to admire this fellowship in charity, and with the guidance and assistance of divine grace will long to share in the same union and charity."(Pius XII para. 5) The war itself has necessitated the proclamation of the doctrine of the Mystical Body:

> We have had the great consolation of witnessing something that has made the image of the Mystical Body of Jesus Christ stand out most clearly before the whole world. Though a long and deadly war has pitilessly broken the bond of brotherly union between nations, We have seen Our children in Christ, in whatever part of the world they happened to be, one in will and affection, lift up their hearts to the common Father, who, carrying in his own heart the cares and anxieties of all, is guiding the barque of the Catholic Church in the teeth of a raging tempest. This is a testimony to the wonderful union existing among Christians; but it also proves that, as Our paternal love embraces all peoples, whatever their nationality and race, so Catholics the world over, though their countries may have drawn the sword against each other, look to the Vicar of Jesus

> Christ as to the loving Father of them all, who, with absolute impartiality and incorruptible judgment, rising above the conflicting gales of human passions, takes upon himself with all his strength the defence of truth, justice and charity. (Pius XII para. 6)

There has been much debate concerning Pius XII's silence—especially concerning the Holocaust—during World War II. He has been presented as aloof and uncaring in the face of such tremendous human tragedy (Hochhuth 1964). Other scholars have painted a portrait of a man who agonized over the war and worked behind the scenes to give refuge to thousands of Italian Jews (Conway 1994: 105-120). Regardless of how he is judged, Pius XII's personal failings and virtues are just one facet of a much broader failure of the Church in Europe. This failure was theorized as a distinction between the spiritual or moral and the political. Pius XII saw the Church as Mystical Body, an overarching source of unity which could inspire peace through strict political impartiality. Though individual Catholics needed to serve their own particular countries through military service and other means on the political plane, on the spiritual plane they should unite and listen to the moral guidance of the Pope urging them to find peaceful means of settling their differences. Pius XII tried desperately, and almost completely unsuccessfully, to broker peace among the warring nation-states through diplomatic channels, offering the Church to serve as an impartial forum above the political fray (Conway 1994: 107-110; Garzia 1994: 121-136). He did not, however, seriously call into question the political loyalty of the individual Christian to the nation-state, that being beyond the scope of the Church's spiritual authority. As Pius XII's secretary of state Giovanni Montini, the future Paul VI, understood it, "while, from a *moral* stance the Vatican could only be in favor of good against evil, and of the law against force, from a *political* viewpoint 'it could only be an impartial witness to the war.'" (Garzia : 127)

The practical effect of such distinctions was to allow the possibility of being a good Catholic and a good Nazi at the same time; Austrian peasant Franz Jagerstatter's questioning of that possibility was met with incredulity and indignation by laity, clergy, and bishops alike (Zahn 1964: 160-179). Pius XII's intent was to offer the image of the Mystical Body of Christ as a symbol of unity to a world rent by conflict. Nevertheless, one's membership in the Mystical Body did not seem to override one's loyalty to the state. To know that the person shooting at you is a fellow member of the Mystical Body of Christ would be slight comfort indeed.

Dorothy Day and the Mystical Body

In Dorothy Day's America, the Catholic Church hierarchy and laity largely supported the American effort in the war. It is important to see, however, that the Church in America obeyed the same distinction between the spiritual and the political as put forth by Pius XII. It was assumed that the nation-state was the supreme authority in political matters, of which war was the most prominent. Thus even the official Catholic peace organization, the Catholic Association for International Peace, refused to support conscientious objection and continued to assume that the nation-state, as the supreme political authority, was the arbiter of war and peace (McNeal 1996: 33-44). Dorothy Day, on the other hand, consistently drew upon the doctrine of the Mystical Body of Christ to oppose any Catholic participation in the war. For Dorothy, this was not a matter of direct opposition to any official Church positions; she often quoted Pius XII in *The Catholic Worker* in his repeated denunciations of the war (*CW* 12/1943: 2; *CW* 6/1943: 1,10). Dorothy shared the common Catholic sensibility of the mystical union of Christ in his Body, supremely effected in the Eucharist. But Dorothy, with the authority of Scripture and the Church Fathers behind her, resolutely drew out the consistent implications of this doctrine for human action, refusing to segregate the spiritual from the rest of life and death, and refusing to acknowledge a separate sphere of hegemony for the nation-state. Quoting St. Cyprian, Dorothy said that war was "the rending of the Mystical Body of Christ."(*CW* 11/1949: 2; www. catholic worker. org/dorothyday) It is such because, as Dorothy repeatedly reminded her readers in the words of St. Paul, paraphrasing I Cor. 12:26, "We are all members, one of another. Where the health of one member suffers, the health of the entire body is lowered."(*CW* 7-8/ 1962: 7) She quoted Pope St. Clement of Rome: "Why do the Members of Christ tear one another, why do we rise up against our own body in such madness...?" (*CW* 10/1934: 3) War, in this view, is a triple offense. First, it is an attack on the body of another. Second, it is an attack on one's own body. Third, it is an attack on Christ, who bleeds anew from these fresh wounds. In the writings of Dorothy Day, the emphasis in the phrase "Mystical Body" is put rather more on "body" than "mystical," if mystical is taken to mean something beyond the realm of the physical. Dorothy conveys a very concrete and sacramental sense that war is about the destruction of real bodies, the ripping and bleeding of flesh, which even the noncombatant feels in her own flesh. There can be no unity in spirit when we attack one another in body.

What the Mystical Body of Christ produces in Dorothy's thought is a radical effacing of the difference between us and them. As she repeatedly emphasized, citing St. Augustine, "we are all members or potential members of the body of Christ."(*CW* 10/1934: 3) At the height of the Cold War, she added to this reminder "And since there is no time with God, this includes Chinese, Russians, Cubans, and yes, even those who profess Marxism-Leninism."(*CW* 7-8/1962: 7) There can be no question, therefore, of a religious provincialism which made it impossible to kill fellow Christians, but not-so-impossible to kill those of other faiths. Even less is it possible to privilege the category of nationality over one's participation or potential participation in Christ's very Body. To kill members of Christ on behalf of nation-states of whatever stripe is to obey a rival god. The Mystical Body, therefore, does not merely transcend the borders of nation-states; it radically denies their very legitimacy, especially when the nation-state claims the power to force its citizens to kill and die for it. As Robert Ludlow wrote in *The Catholic Worker* in 1948, "As the ideals of Christianity are realized, as they become exteriorized in society, so will national states wither away as being impediments to the realization of human brotherhood. And so will war be outlawed as rendering asunder the mystical body of Christ."(Ludlow in Cornell et al. 1995: 65)

It is absolutely essential to note that this radical effacing of the difference between me and you, and us and them, is not simply a sentimental belief in the inherent goodness of all, but rather calls us to acknowledge the guilt of all and therefore our own complicity in the structures that produce war. Dorothy's approach to war was resolutely penitential, as a logical consequence of her belief in the Mystical Body. As she wrote in *From Union Square to Rome*, "We are bowed down with [Christ] under the weight of not only our own sins but the sins of each other, of the whole world. We are those who are sinned against and those who are sinning. We are identified with Him, one with Him. We are members of His Mystical Body." (Day 1938: 12) It was therefore possible and necessary for a 1939 editorial in *The Catholic Worker* to be entitled "We Are to Blame for New War in Europe." Nationalism and materialism, in which Americans manifestly shared, were listed as the primary causes of the war (*CW* 12/1939: 1, 4). This sharing of blame was invoked not to elicit resignation but penance among Catholics. What was necessary was to heal the Mystical Body through concrete, direct, and personal action. One must begin with conscientious objection, the simple refusal to participate in the killing. One must also give up any job which directly or indirectly contributed to the war effort (Coy 1996: 49). Peace is not the effect of political negotiations among nation-states, but is rather brought about by the simple refusal to divide the Body of Christ through loyalty to Caesar.

Dorothy Day's understanding of the Mystical Body of Christ depended on her very keen and almost instinctual sense that the soul is not to be separated from the body, and the spiritual is not to be separated from the political. She was by no means a materialist. As she wrote in 1940, "This work of ours toward a new heaven and a new earth shows a correlation between the material and the spiritual, and, of course, recognizes the primacy of the spiritual... Hence the leaders of the work, and as many as we can induce to join us, must go daily to Mass, to receive food for the soul."(*CW* 2/1940: 7) It is Christ in the Eucharist, after all, who builds His Mystical Body; we can only witness to what Christ is doing in His Body. The Body of Christ is therefore "mystical" in the sense that the work is accomplished not by human effort but by the grace of Christ whose Spirit works within us. The Body of Christ is *not* mystical in the common twentieth-century usage of the word, in which it has come to mean an essentially individual spiritual experience transcending space and time. For Dorothy Day, the Mystical Body of Christ did not hover above history either as a purely interior spiritual experience or an experience of communion after death. The Mystical Body of Christ was a real, concrete communion of human bodies which directly challenged other, violent attempts to organize human bodies to do one another harm, specifically the configuration of the nation-state. Dorothy refused therefore to claim the soul for Christ and hand the body over to the state, or claim that we could be "mystically" united in spirit while our bodies fought and bled.

In this construal of the Mystical Body of Christ, Dorothy Day was in fact close to the more traditional usage of the term *corpus mysticum* in Eucharistic theology. As Henri de Lubac's classic study *Corpus Mysticum* showed, in the early Church the term "mystical body" referred not primarily to the Church but to the Eucharistic elements. The term *corpus verum,* or real body, referred to the Church. Christians and their actions are the *real* body of Christ, and the Eucharist is where the Church *mystically* comes to be. The term "mystical" indicated the "mystery" of the Eucharist, its hiddenness from ordinary sense experience, which nevertheless assumed the real presence of Christ in the Eucharistic elements. De Lubac documents a gradual inverssion of meaning, however, beginning in the late middle ages, in which the Church exclusively has come to be identified as the *corpus mysticum* and the Eucharistic elements are the *corpus verum.* The shift in terminology is significant because it occurs at a time when the Church is becoming increasingly institutionalized and the spiritual life is becoming increasingly individualized. The Eucharist is less an ecclesial action and more an extrinsic miracle which invites individual devotion (Lubac 1949). The danger is that the real life of grace in the Church will now be seen as "mystical," with "mystical" redefined as that which is hidden in the recesses of the individual heart, or that which can be realized only outside of history. The true life of Christian charity realized in the Eucharist is then potentially relegated to a "spiritual" realm cordoned off from the "political," the business of the world.

Although Dorothy Day was one with the Catholics of her age in speaking of the Church as the Mystical Body of Christ, she in fact was closer to the patristic and early medieval theologians who saw the Church as the *corpus verum,* the true body of Christ. Here was a sacramental sensibility which felt the Body of Christ as an almost physical reality. The strained sinews, the open wounds, the contorted face, the purplish blood of the crucifixes adorning Catholic Churches were reflected and manifested in a very real sense in the broken and torn bodies which were appearing both on the doorsteps of the Catholic Worker houses and in far greater magnitude on the battlefields of Europe. For Dorothy, in Christ there was no separation of his Body and the Spirit that gave it life. The political and the spiritual were therefore inseparably one, and the peace of Christ should be embodied not only in the hearts of people, but in their tortured limbs as well.

"We Are Still Pacifists": Dorothy Day's Pacifism during World War II

Sandra Yocum Mize

University of Dayton

> We are still pacifists. Our manifesto is the Sermon on the Mount, which means that we will try to be peacemakers. (Day 1983: 262)

This declaration announcing the Catholic Worker's commitment to an absolute pacifism appeared in the January 1942 edition of the New York *Catholic Worker.* The author was the newspaper's editor, Dorothy Day. Despite her use of "we," Day indicated that "there will be great differences of opinion even among our own groups as to how much collaboration we can have with the government in times like these."(Day 1983: 263)

In retrospect, the differences of opinion were far greater than the matter-of-fact tone of the statement indicates. Day's uncompromising position on non-cooperation with the war effort against Nazi and Japanese militarism cost the movement dearly. Subscriptions declined by nearly 75%, from a high of 190,000 in 1938 to 50,500 by 1945. Similarly, the number of houses of hospitality declined from 32 to 10, at least in part because of Day's unyielding commitment to pacifism during World War II. No other occasion rivals this 1942 declaration against warfare for bringing into stark relief the radical posture encountered in Day's pacifism. The dropping of two atomic bombs at the end of this global conflagration to some extent obscures the position. Activism on behalf of peace in a post-nuclear world appears far more sensible than a refusal in 1942 to cooperate in any way with military efforts to stop the real threats posed by the Axis powers.

Noting here the startling nature of Day's 1942 declaration of peace should not be interpreted as a claim that members of the Catholic

Worker movement had no prior indication of Day's pacifism. As early as 1933, Day had made known her, and thus the movement's, pacifist commitment (McNeal 1992: 37). The Spanish Civil War provoked clear statements denouncing the violence produced on both sides of the conflict, and proclaiming the Worker's neutrality, despite U.S. Catholics' overwhelming support for Franco. The position on the Spanish Civil War diminished her paper's popularity, although that negative reaction pales in comparison to the one precipitated by the pronouncements denouncing cooperation in efforts to halt the Axis forces. Even for some clearly committed to the Catholic Worker movement or perhaps especially for them, Day's resolute stance with minimal explanation was frustrating in its stark simplicity.

Of course, Day's numerous biographers and commentators have already identified the source from which she drew her position—the Gospel. Absenting herself from the centuries old conversation on the just war theory, Day drew upon the "Sermon on the Mount" with its clear demands for love of enemy as the Catholic Worker manifesto of pacifism and peacemaking. Pacifism excluded any cooperation with the war including registering for the draft, and peacemaking here meant continuing with the Works of Mercy. Compared to the Catholic Worker activities associated with the 1950s civil defense protests and the 1960s anti-war movement, few direct actions were orchestrated to raise people's consciousness concerning the folly of the war. The only major activity centered on garnering financial support for the camps inhabited by Catholic conscientious objectors.

The war years, rather than a time of public protest, proved to be a period in Day's life of intense and life-transforming spiritual activity and deep personal angst as a single mother of an adolescent daughter. This period, in fact, shares similar elements to her time with Forster Batterham at the beach house on Staten Island: the joys and sorrows of motherhood and the deep urge to love God above all else even if it cost a break with those she loved, in this case the Catholic Workers who could not agree with her absolute pacifism. The relationship of mother and maturing daughter is beyond the scope of this paper; the focus here will be on Day's spiritual renewal, especially through the Lacouture retreat movement and its influence on her articulation of her pacifist stand during World War II.

This paper will attempt to demonstrate the influence of "the retreat"on her articulation of her pacifist commitment by comparing her accounts of the retreats with Father Pacifique Roy and Father

John Hugo, especially as found in *The Long Loneliness*, with the phrasing of the argument employed in Day's public declaration of peace in early 1942. The method is admittedly problematic in that Day wrote the retreat recollections more than a decade after the experience, and she does not explicitly discuss pacifism in the context of discussing "the retreat" though the next chapter does feature the Worker's opposition to war. Yet, the accounts indicate what Day found most memorable, most influential for her own spiritual growth. That the power of these retreat messages remained so vivid in Day's own mind long after their occurrence provides a reasonable basis for looking at least for traces of influence in what was uppermost in her mind at the actual time of the retreats: the preparing for and waging of war.

I want to make very clear from the beginning that I am *not* arguing cause (retreat) and effect (pacifism). The retreats functioned more like the Catholic Workers' round table discussions for clarification of thought. These austere New Testament-inspired retreats, which became part of Day's life around 1939, provide the personal context and to some extent the theological content which inspired Day in the particulars of her defense of pacifism during World War II rather than convince her to embrace pacifism. These links are especially evident in Day's identifying pacifism with penance and mortification or, as she often liked to say, "the folly of the cross."

Dorothy Day's first transforming encounter with the Lacouture retreat movement was through a Josephite priest, Father Pacifique Roy, who had worked with the poor in the South. He himself had been inspired by the message of Father Onesimus Lacouture, a fellow French Canadian, "to see all things new."(Day 1983: 133) This resurrection vision did not forget its necessary antecedent, the cross. In *The Long Loneliness*, Day recalled

> When Father spoke of mortifying, he spoke of putting to death, using the literal meaning of the word. We have been baptized in Christ' s death, he reminded us. We are buried with Christ and we will rise with Christ; we must seek the things which are above, not the things which are below. (253)

Day also noted that a certain suspicion hovered around this emphasis as Jansenist, but she still found inspiration in his words even as she found it in Martin Scheeben's on the glories of nature on which grace builds.

Dorothy Day had endured the daily trials of Catholic Worker life for some six years, and she wrote of it often: the smells, the sounds, the tasteless food, the difficult or emotionally wounded people, the lack of privacy. She was also well aware of a world where people bore the burden of economic destitution and where leaders were dragging the destitute into the madness of war. Father Roy's message provided a sort of lens from which to view these trying experiences, and it seems that when Dorothy Day gazed through that lens the meaning in her life became crystal clear. Recalling the retreat experiences with Father Roy in *The Long Loneliness*, she declared

> Those were beautiful days. It was as though we were listening to the gospel for the first time. We saw all things new. There was a freshness about everything as though we were in love, as indeed we were. (250-251)

Day later notes that the joy with which Father Roy spoke of trials gave the Catholic Workers a deep understanding of Paul's rejoicing in tribulations, "just another of those paradoxes, that needed to be experienced to be understood . . ."(Day 1952: 251) Father Roy articulated the paradox of her own experience. The message delivered through this priest provided Day with a new depth of understanding what she already knew and experienced as the demands of love of God and of neighbors. Though never really faltering, her conviction in the correctness of the Catholic Worker's "aims and purposes" had deepened (Day 1983: 91-92).

Father Roy judged himself wanting in expressing the depth of meaning in the Lacourture retreats, though one has to wonder about his standards of excellence, given Day's exuberance. Yet he insisted that the priest who expressed the full meaning of the retreat was Father John J. Hugo, from the Pittsburgh diocese. *The Long Loneliness* provides Day's recollections of Hugo's versions of the Lacouture retreat. Once again appears the Christian witness to a life defined through the paschal mystery.

The witness demanded always more. Day recalls "shivering" upon hearing Father Hugo say, "'He who says he has done enough has already perished,'. . . ."(Day 1952: 255) Yet, the attraction to these demands came not so much from guilt and shame but rather the possibility of living a life that truly reflected the love relationship between God and each human person within a community of believers:

> There was not much talk of sin in this retreat. Rather there was talk of the good and the better. The talk was of the choice we had to make and not that between good and evil. We have been given a share in the divine life; we have been raised to a supernatural level; we have been given power to become the sons of God. (256)

The Catholic Worker, as lived by Dorothy Day, seemed to involve ongoing choices between good and better rather than good and evil, and absolute pacifism seemed better than any compromise in cooperating with the military.

Day's accounts of "the retreat" in *The Long Loneliness*, like the rest of the narrative, provides little chronological precision. So I turn now to William Miller's *Dorothy Day: A Biography* (1982) as a guide. Of special interest are the dates of the two Catholic Worker retreats. The largest occurred at Maryfarm in Easton, Pennsylvania, on Labor Day weekend, 1940, under Paul Hanly Furfey's direction, although Fr. Roy was present. The second, under Father Hugo's guidance, took place in Oakmont, Pennsylvania in August of 1941. As Miller suggests with other quotes from Dorothy, the recollection of "beautiful days" quoted earlier probably is a melding of the 1940 retreat with days of recollection in Baltimore. Miller features one particular quote from some notes which he associates with the Easton retreat: "We were a little flock. We had broken bread together.. Scripture became a love letter and retreat notes we took we kept rereading, going back to them to try to recapture that flow of rapturous assent to Truth."(Miller 1982: 338) Miller points out that this idyllic experience of Christian community stood in stark contrast to a world under the thrall of war, a contrast that he thinks did not escape Day.

Perhaps it did not escape Day because the war and its impact on the Catholic Worker movement itself had to be very much on her mind. Present at this retreat was John Cogley of the Chicago Catholic Worker House. He was the most vocal among the movement's opponents to Day's insistence on absolute pacifism. Earlier in August of 1940, Day had made known through an open letter to all the Catholic Worker houses that "We will expect our Catholic Workers to oppose, alone and single-handedly if necessary . . . the militaristic system and its propaganda."(Piehl 1982: 196) Her letter was in response to objections, particularly at the houses in Chicago, Seattle, and Los Angeles, to the outspoken anti-war position taken in the New York Catholic Worker newspaper. Cogley, who understood the letter as an ultimatum, was ready to quit the movement, but then agreed to Dorothy's request to attend what Mel Piehl describes as "a pacifist oriented retreat," the Easton retreat under Father Furfey's direction (197). The accounts that I have read of this invitation emphasize Day's desire to work out a sort of compromise with Cogley. Frankly, I think Day sought more than compromise; she hoped for conversion. Father Roy had so convinced her to "to aim at perfection; . . . to be guided by the folly of the Cross." I suspect that she thought John Cogley might come to the same conviction (Day 1952: 247).

I have come across no documentary evidence that explicitly affirms my suspicion. Yet Day invited Cogley to a retreat centered upon Father Furfey's talks and long periods of silence; hardly an occasion for debates on pacifism. I am not here accusing Day of duplicity but rather of complete conviction that the Gospel message as articulated in "the retreat" provided a thorough justification for absolute pacifism. Cogley, coming with far different expectations in terms of argumentation, remained unpersuaded.

"The retreat" as presented in *The Long Loneliness* is basically a combination of the reflections of Father Roy and Father Hugo. As Day presents the two priests' talks, they seem to provide a distillation of "the Gospel" on which Day based her absolute pacifism. Miller claims that the second retreat under Father Hugo provided Day with "a new sensitivity to what she took as the piercing truth of the Gospels." (Miller 1982: 339) He concludes this chapter, "The Coming of War" asserting: "It was hearing the Gospel anew that gave a new force to her character. It was a reinforced spirituality. And if there had ever been any questions about her course, they were gone now. She was on the track. Nothing could change her."(Miller 1982: 341)

His next chapter, entitled "Rearing a Daughter," begins with December 7, 1941 and notes not a single mention of the Pearl Harbor attack appears in her journals.

In the next issue of *The Catholic Worker*, January 1942, Day does mention the war with the declaration: "We are still pacifists." The article appears as an act of prayer rather than a disputation. "I am sitting here in church on Mott Street writing this in your presence."(Day 1984: 261) She writes of love of neighbor, Italian and Chinese, and then of the ease with which that is forgotten. "We have all forgotten. And how can we know unless You tell us?" The point parallels a note Day made to herself during the 1941 retreat.

"Actually I think to myself with a touch of bitterness, the ordinary man does not hear the word of God." At least, they had no opportunity to hear this word as she had unless she spoke it in the newspaper.

Perhaps she had in mind Father Roy's first discourse at the Worker, an engrossing exposition of the Sermon on the Mount, when she declared it to be the movement's manifesto. She continues with a focus upon love of enemy and country and president in a way similar to Father Roy, who on that first morning "went on to talk not about the social order but about love and holiness, without which man cannot see God."(Day 1983: 132) Day, most importantly, emphasized that the key to their efforts was prayer bolstered by penitential practices.

> Let us add that unless we continue this prayer with almsgiving, in giving to the least of God's children; and fasting in order that we may help feed the hungry, and penance in recognition of our share in the guilt, our prayer may become empty words. (Day 1983: 262)

Perhaps her silence concerning the attack on Pearl Harbor or the Nazis' imperialism served as mortification for the love of the least as defined by Father Hugo. He often said, according to Dorothy, "'You love God as much as the one you love the least.'"(Day 1983: 248) The remainder of the effective pacifist efforts parallels those demanding spiritual practices associated with "the retreat." In *The Long Loneliness*, Day recalled Father Roy's insistence that "Prayer and fasting always went together,"(250) and that there are demands of penance for those "baptized in Christ's death." Father Hugo reinforced this message when be insisted, "We have been raised above ourselves by baptism, and the law of this supernatural life is love which demands renunciation"(257). Absolute pacifism in the face of a threat as real as that posed by the Axis powers provided an occasion to live the demands placed before Day in the retreat. The arduous demands of the retreat provided clarification or at least reinforcement in her thinking through why those "baptized in Christ's death" must be willing to assent to absolute pacifism.

Pacifism, like other actions of love, is not sheer sentimentality precisely because mortification remains at the heart of it. Day makes very clear in the February 1942 issue of the newspaper that a Catholic Worker's commitment entails absolute love of neighbor that includes more than objections to the world war. To those who patronize with expressions of sympathy for her sentiments, she describes life in the New York house of hospitality where mortification is a way of life. A Worker mortifies the body through exposure to vermin, cold and dirt; sight by "bodily excretions, diseased limbs, eyes, noses, mouth;" the nose with "smells of sewage, decay, and rotten flesh;" the ears "by harsh and screaming voices;" and taste "by insufficient food cooked in huge quantities." Catholic Workers are hardened by "the class war" and the "race war" where the violence against the laborer and the African American "are Pearl Harbor incidents."(Day 1983: 264)

They remain as non-violent warriors, mortifying their very selves not because they choose the good but the better. "Love is not the starving of whole populations. Love is not bombardment of open cities. Love is not killing, it is the laying down of one's life for one's friend."(Day 1983: 265) Yet, Day's final line taken from Scripture is reminiscent of Father Hugo's warning, "He who says he has done enough has already perished...."(Day 1952: 255) Fearing accusations of a "holier than thou" attitude, Dorothy declared: "I am lower than all men, because I do not love enough. O God, take away my heart of stone and give me a heart of flesh."(Day 1983: 266)

Day's final line may indicate her own ambivalence concerning her particular response to the war effort. According to William Miller, "During the war years it seems that at times Dorothy was avoiding the Worker, fleeing to Della's, to John's, visiting Sister Peter Claver, and taking frequent trips, some of which kept her away for months"(Day 1983: 364). While each individual trip could be justified, taken as a whole they raised questions at least for Day. "The world is too much with me in the Catholic Worker. The world is suffering and dying. I am not suffering and dying in the CW; I am writing and talking about it"(Day 1983: 364). Her response was to "organize days of recollection." In fact, she took a year's leave of absence from the Catholic Worker in 1943. Though her absence amounted only to six months, a significant portion of the time was spent in an austere retreat-like setting.

Here she hoped to regroup and re-focus her efforts as a Catholic Worker even as the war raged on in Europe. Reminiscent of the title, "Spiritual Weapons," used by Father Hugo in a Catholic Worker explication of pacifism, she declared, "The only weapons we will develop will be those of prayer and penance." To do so would bring a dismissive response from the world, which Day describes with her inimitable sarcastic flair: "After all, they are not doing anything. Just a bunch of smug fools praying. We will not be as tormented by its scorn as we are by the praise of the world for works of mercy, houses of hospitality, and farming communities."(Miller 1982: 364)

Pacifism as mortification and penance rather than the Works of Mercy as praiseworthy acts confirms her baptism into the death of Christ and the promise of a new life defined only by the love of God.

I am ultimately unsure whether this paper provides anything more than self-evident observations. In the secondary sources that I examined (and the examination was not exhaustive), certainly mention was made of the retreats of 1940 and 1941 in the same context as the absolute pacifism of World War II. Certainly others have already noted the Gospel basis of her pacifism which was explicitly held as a Catholic Worker position in the early 1930s. The Gospel, of course, has been the guest in many a hermeneutical circle, and Day definitely brought it into a particular one, the Lacouture retreat movement *vis a vis* the praxis of six years at the Catholic Worker.

This paper functions more like a footnote that provides further clarification of Day's praxis-oriented, Gospel-based pacifist commitment. Father Roy's and Hugo's emphasis on a redemptive love formed through mortification provided Day with clarification of thought. It suggests that what appears to be a simplistic and overly maudlin response to the Second World War in fact had a more complex context in which love really was the only measure.

An Uneasy Community: Catholics in Civilian Public Service During World War II

John O'Sullivan

World War Two generated virtually universal support in this country. I say *virtually* universal because there were small but significant pockets of resistance. Approximately 25,000 men refused to take up arms in this cause but were willing to serve in the military in a noncombatant capacity. Another 6,000 opponents of the war, unable or unwilling to meet the criteria for conscientious objector status, went to prison. The third position of opposition, those unwilling on grounds of conscience to serve in the military yet willing to provide alternative service under civilian direction, drew 12,000 men (Frazer and O'Sullivan 1996: xiii). This paper deals with the Catholics who chose this third option and entered the Civilian Public Service program during World War Two. My research examines those men who entered a Catholic camp established in the New Hampshire woods, the strains and complexities of trying to form a community there, and their later difficulties in relating to the broader Historic Peace Church community.

The 1940 draft act allowed conscientious objectors unwilling to perform noncombatant military service to engage, instead, in "work of national importance under civilian direction." (Selective Service Act of 1940, Section 5g) The organization created to administer this program, Civilian Public Service, represented a unique and often uneasy collaboration between the Historic Peace Churches (Mennonites, Brethren, and Quakers) and the Selective Service System.

The peace church leadership viewed this relationship with the government as an arrangement that assured better treatment for conscientious objectors than they had received in World War One. Their working assumption was that virtually all of the men in the program would come from their churches, and they would be able to support them for the one year of service required under the draft act. The reality of the Civilian Public Service program proved quite different. Pearl Harbor extended all terms of service to the duration of the war, imposing a far heavier economic burden of responsibility on the churches. In addition, although the majority of the men who entered CPS came from the Historic Peace Churches, more than forty percent came from 200 other denominations and sects, including 162 Catholics (U.S. Selective Service System 1950: 318-320). These unexpected arrivals at CPS's door would be welcomed, but gradually relations would grow testy.

The American Catholic Church had approximately twenty million members in 1940, so the 162 who entered CPS seem a rather paltry number. However, given the language of the draft act, and the Catholic "just war" tradition, it is somewhat surprising that *any* Catholics qualified for CPS. The 1940 draft act defined entitlement to conscientious objector status very specifically: it must be based on "religious training and belief" and it must reflect opposition to participating in war "in any form." Catholic training and belief at that time drew upon the "just war" criteria and did not teach, as the draft law required, categorical opposition to war.

Apart from this theological difficulty, American Catholics belonged to a church that had become largely assimilated into the political culture of this nation. By World War Two, as Charles Morris wrote, "the loyalty of American Catholics was as unquestioned as it was unquestioning."(Morris 1997: ix) Given those circumstances, we shouldn't be surprised that there were only 162 Catholics in CPS. The real surprise may be that 162 Catholics actually managed to get there.

Part of the answer is Dorothy Day and the Catholic Worker movement. Dorothy Day's commitment to pacifism stayed unshaken as the United States entered World War Two. *The Catholic Worker,* in the first issue after Pearl Harbor, asserted, "We are still pacifists." (Morris 1997: ix) That commitment carried a heavy price. Subscriptions to *The Catholic Worker* would fall by three-quarters, and many houses of hospitality would close (Piehl 1982: 150-159; Sicius 1988: 344-354). Many dedicated to the movement's immersion in the corporal works of mercy pulled away from a pacifist response to a war they found just and necessary. A deep and, for some, an enduring split developed in the movement.

Those men who shared Day's pacifist vision and wished to enter Civilian Public Service were assisted by the newly created Association of Catholic Conscientious Objectors. This "impressive sounding organization" was, in Gordon Zahn's words, "really nothing more than a "front" set up by the Catholic Worker movement. (Zahn 1979: ix) The A.C.C.O. administered a camp program, initially at Stoddard, New Hampshire and subsequently at Warner, New Hampshire from July 1941 until March 1943. The program lacked adequate financial support from the outset and that situation quickly worsened. The Catholic Worker raised some funds, but, absent broader Catholic institutional support, could not continue the program. By the final days of the camp, according to Bob Ludlow, the men "were living on canned peaches."(Ludlow 1977) They were soon disbursed to other CPS camps. Ultimately, 90 percent of the support for Catholics in CPS would have to be paid by the Historic Peace Churches (Zahn 1979: 44).

Although the Catholic Worker initiated the Catholic CPS program, many of the men who arrived there had no affiliation with or, in some cases, knowledge of the Catholic Worker movement. They had arrived independently at their pacifist positions, and persuaded their draft boards of the sincerity of their belief. That task became somewhat easier in January 1942 when General Lewis Hershey, Director of the Selective Service System, ruled that Catholic registrants who interpreted the teachings of the Church as supporting pacifism were eligible to claim conscientious objector status (Hershey 1942). This directive from Washington, however, was itself subject to interpretation by the thousands of local draft boards (Westbrock 1978).

One man I interviewed had a Brooklyn draft board that he insisted would not have granted Jesus Christ conscientious objector status. They turned him down, but he proved more successful with his appeal board. Another Catholic applicant, a follower of Father Coughlin, fared better with a different Brooklyn draft board. He described to me his c.o. application, with a ten page statement drawing upon "Suarez, Bellarmine, people like that, of course the Gospels, Saint Martin of Tours, the martyrs who gave their lives rather than fight in armies." Then, without pausing for a breath, he went on "Also I felt this was a Jewish Masonic Zionist plot to destroy Christianity in Europe and all over the world."(O'Hanlon 1977)

The Catholic CPS camp that opened in the New Hampshire woods brought together Catholic Workers as well as Coughlinite Christian

Fronters, along with many other c.o.'s unaffiliated with either position. They were physically and psychologically isolated, lacking pay or financial assistance, and assigned to perform "work of national importance." They were predominantly from the cities of the East and Midwest and found themselves ineffectually clearing forests. One of the men, Dick Leonard, felt that their "work of national importance" had been reduced to getting enough wood in to keep themselves from freezing to death in the winter (Leonard 1978). Frustrations ran high and, when the camp was closed in March, 1943, there was little unhappiness over the ending of this Catholic witness.

Some of the men, particularly Catholic Workers, soured by this experience and having increasing doubts about their decision, ended up going into the military. The remaining men staying in CPS were sent for a short time to a Quaker camp in Maryland before being dispatched to either Rosewood Training School in Maryland or a CPS camp in Trenton, North Dakota.

I referred, in my title for this paper, to Catholic conscientious objectors as "an uneasy community." I mean that in two senses. First, the Catholic camp, small as it was, was fragmented into several, sometimes antagonistic, groups. Those who came up to New Hampshire expecting to find a community with a shared spiritual vision soon learned otherwise. The relatively brief life of the camp can be ascribed to the general inadequacy of needed external support, along with the daunting task of forging a community of persons with such disparate beliefs and personalities.

The second sense in which we can speak of Catholic conscientious objectors as "an uneasy community" is in relation to the broader CPS population. Charles Morris has written about the self-created isolation that marked much of American Catholicism in the 1930s and 1940s. He described an array of "parallel" organizations; "Catholic businessmen's clubs, medical societies, bar associations, teachers' guilds, youth organizations,"(Morris 1997: ix). That separatism intended to "protect" Catholics meant that, for most of the Catholics who went into CPS, this was their first extended encounter with non-Catholics, and particularly with members of the Historic Peace Churches. Conversely, many of the peace church people had perceptions about Catholics that had generally developed without any sustained encounter with Catholics.

Many of the Catholics resented the conditions of Civilian Public Service, particularly the lack of pay, and held the leadership of the

Historic Peace Churches responsible for negotiating those arrangements. Such feelings found ample expression over the next several years.

The Historic Peace Church people, in turn, often found dealing with Catholics a trying experience. When the men from New Hampshire arrived at the Maryland Quaker camp, they were provided with a monthly stipend of $2.50 for stamps and gum. This money, much to the distress of the Quakers, seemed to go mainly for tobacco and beer. Other Catholics, when the opportunity arose at Rosewood, would moonlight at nearby Pimlico Race Track, another point of irritation to some.

Relations between Catholics and other groups in CPS grew most frayed in the camp at Trenton, North Dakota. Ian Thiermann, a Quaker, wrote: "I happened to wind up in a large bunk house at the end of which were a group of Catholic CO's, most of whom were nonpacifists. They objected to everything. They were loud, uncouth, and I just couldn't believe it. They would be shouting around and carrying on until two o'clock in the morning. The rest of us would be getting up at six, they'd sleep in or refuse to get up. It was one continual hassle with these guys, and I couldn't appreciate them one bit."(Hurwitz and Simpson 1983)

Herman Will, assistant director of the camp, had a less harsh assessment of the Catholic presence. They, he said in an interview, "made it a little more interesting than at other camps." He acknowledged that "because of different Catholic mores.. .about drinking," the camp director would often have to deal with Saturday night blowouts. Will, however, appreciated the involvement of some of the men with the local Catholic church in Trenton, particularly Bolton Morris, a gifted artist who sculpted a wooden crucifix (Will interview).

The Catholic contact with other groups in CPS was shaped, to a large extent, by theological and cultural differences that sadly ended up masking their common commitment to Christianity. As much as CPS proved an alienating experience for most Catholics, there were others who emerged from it with deepened commitments. Robert Ludlow came to the Catholic Worker in New York after his discharge from CPS, lived there, and edited the paper for the next eight years. Robert Hovda, an Episcopalian at the time he entered CPS, requested assignment to the Catholic camp. People he met there, such as Gordon Zahn, proved very influential in the steps he took toward becoming a Catholic. Later he was ordained a priest, subsequently becoming one of the leading liturgists in the Catholic Church (Hovda interview). William Everson, raised a Christian Scientist, drifted from those beliefs and, when he sought c.o. status, couched his argument in "a combination of Western humanism and a Buddhist's sense of the sanctity of all things."(Bartlett 1988: 33) Everson served in a CPS camp at Waldport, Oregon, one that became a center for artists and writers in the program. Everson's biographer noted that he "had been raised to believe that the Catholic Church was a rigid, authoritarian organization, but reading issues of *The Catholic Worker* at Waldport...had shown him there was a strain of the Church that was both anarchist and pacifist. Now it was to this Catholic social activism that he was drawn." (Bartlett: 117) Everson would eventually live and work for a time at the Catholic Worker house of hospitality in Oakland, California. But his spiritual journey would not end there. Everson, unlike many who had only found alienation and frustration in CPS, drew strength and focus from it. He wrote of his time in CPS, "I found a community for the first time in my life. It was the best preparation I could have had for the monastery: the sense of common purpose isolated from the world, interested in a new culture, willing to sacrifice for it and to protest against the decimation and destruction of the world."(Hurwitz and Simpson 1983) Everson, once again, found a community when he became a Dominican lay brother, taking the name Brother Antoninus. Antoninus went on to become a leading American poet in the 1950s and 1960s.

Assessing the significance of Catholic participation in the Civilian Public Service program is problematic. For many of the men, the gap between what they hoped for and what they experienced was too wide to allow for much sense of accomplishment. Those men who served for a time at Rosewood Training School or at the Alexian Brothers hospital in Chicago generally saw that as meaningful service. Others, however, saw their assignments as uncompensated make-work, designed especially to isolate them from a nation at war.

However divided the assessments of individual Catholics are about their CPS experience, we need to acknowledge how unexpected it was that there would be any Catholic institutional presence in the Civilian Public Service program. Absent the efforts of the Catholic Worker, there would have been none. Dorothy Day testified against the impending draft act in Congressional hearings in 1940. Once it became law, the Catholic Worker created the Association of Catholic Conscientious Objectors as the sponsoring body for a Catholic camp.

The financial burdens of sponsorship limited the life of that camp to less than two years. Yet, its existence, in Gordon Zahn's words, marked "in a very real sense, the first corporate witness against war and military service in the history of American Catholicism. Indeed, the claim might even be made that it was the first such witness in the entire history of the Church." (Zahn 1979: viii) Maybe what those disgruntled Catholic CPSers saw as make-work in the woods of New Hampshire was, in reality, the planting of mustard seeds.

Jeff Poniewaz

Cultural Exchange

Better to exchange culture
than nuclear missiles.
Better to exchange the best aspects
of our countries, our peoples
than the worst. Benjamin Britten's *War Requiem,*
the searing soaring adagio of Shostakovich's 7th,
Vaughan Williams' 5th & *Dona Nobis Pacem,*
Ravel's "Concerto for the Left Hand,"
Penderecki's *To the Victims of Hiroshima.*
Whitman's "Drum Taps" and Tolstoy's *War and Peace,*
George Butterworth's *A Shropshire Lad*
  gas'd in World War I trenches,
Wilfred Owen and his whole platoon
  having a "Strange Meeting" with an artillery shell
  a week before the War to End All Wars ended,
Picasso's *Guernica,* Goya's *Disasters of War,*
forbid there to be war, demand
there to be peace, every human
who ever died in war demands
there to be peace. Survival Ultimatum.

Penderecki–Polish composer b. 1933

George Butterworth–British Composer b. 1885, killed in World War I; his tonepoem *A Shropshire Lad* (after Housman) was written in 1912.

Wilifred Owen–British Poet b. 1893, killed in World War I in 1918; his powerful war poems served as text for Britten's *War Requiem* (1962). See his poem "Strange Meeting."

Ravel's "Concerto for the Left Hand" was written for a concert pianist who lost his right arm in World War I.

Shostakovich's 7th was composed during the Siege of Leningrad, 1941

Vaughan Willliams' 5th was premiered while parts of England were under blitzkrieg; someone who heard it over the radio in an underground shelter said "It seemed like a blueprint for a possible future." His cantata *Dona Nobis Pacem* (1936) sets to music several poems from Whitman's "Drum Taps" section of *Leaves of Grass.*

PART XI

ECUMENICAL PERSPECTIVES

Corporal Works of Mercy I: Harbor the Harborless, was Ade Bethune's first illustration for *The Catholic Worker* (1 March 1934).

The Shakers and the Program and Practice of the Catholic Worker

Walt Chura

Simple Gifts Catholic Worker Bookstore
Emmaus House
Albany, NY

They came up from New York City in the '70s to the swampy woods, just a few miles north of Albany, not far from where I live now. Their pacifism, essential to Dorothy Day's vision for the Catholic Worker, in the face of the war, got them into trouble immediately. Some of them spent time in jail—not a new experience for them. Dorothy Day had been incarcerated several times during her lifetime. Like Peter Maurin and Dorothy at St. Joseph's House in New York City and on their several communal farms, they lived in poverty, shared the work, the prayer and what little of material value they had. They cleared the land, drained the swamps, planted gardens, though they were inexperienced city people, like so many Catholic Workers who had moved to farming communes in keeping with Peter's program.

Like the Benedictines who inspired the founders of the Catholic Worker, they dedicated themselves to work and prayer. Their motto was, "Put your hands to work and your hearts to God." They were hungry a lot, as poor as early Franciscans, but like the earliest followers of St. Francis whom Peter sought to emulate, they had the gift to be simple.

Eventually, once they got themselves together enough so that they wouldn't starve, they started to reach out in witness to their neighbors, who thought them strange and intriguing—and maybe dangerous. They embraced "a philosophy so old that it looked new," in Peter's phrase, a philosophy that insisted on "the primacy of the spiritual," just as he had taught. They were, in the words of the IWW union slogan so central to the CW vision, "building a new society within the shell of the old," a society, as Peter envisioned, "in which it would be easier for people to be good," by preparing what Peter saw was necessary: "a new synthesis of cult, culture and cultivation," that is, integrating the life of the spirit, the life of the mind and life on the land.

But I am not describing the vision and project of some young band of 1970s Catholic Workers. These were, rather, the first Shakers. It was the mid-1770s. Their war was the American Revolution.

I grew up in primal Shaker territory, a small city north of Albany, New York called Watervliet, which once encompassed what is now the town of Colonie. In the 1770s Colonie was known by the Mohawk name, Niskayuna. Ann Lee first settled in the wilds of Niskayuna with eight followers in 1776.

I was struck by the common points of Catholic Worker and Shaker visions and programs as soon as I met the Shakers of the Sabbathday Lake, Maine community and began seriously to study Shakerism in 1974—the two hundredth anniversary of Ann Lee's arrival in New York City from Manchester, England.

Yet I have not found any writings in the New York *Catholic Worker*, started by Day in 1933 and still publishing, nor in contemporary Shaker writings which examine the shared values of the two religious movements. They are certainly far from carbon copies of one another. Shaker orderliness and hierarchy, to take just one example, are hardly congruent with Catholic Worker "anarchism." These are not minor differences. In fact both are core values of their respective movements. Nevertheless, those aspects of vision and program common to the two movements are also significant and instructive.

Within a couple of years of the move to Niskayuna of this odd band of fresh English immigrants in 1776, the local patriots were sure they were British sympathizers or even spies. Why else would they refuse to bear arms? Their stated religious reason, that it violated the Gospel to do so, was, to the patriots, obviously disingenuous. Mother and others of her company landed in jail for a while, falsely accused of aiding the enemy.

The Shakers, like the Catholic Worker, were founded by a woman. While great chasms of difference, beyond that of more than 150 years in time, separate Mother Ann Lee (d. 1784) and Dorothy Day (d. 1980), there are some important harmonies between Lee, the mystic and Day, the prophet, as well as between their two Gospel movements. They were both, as the title of a one woman show about Day has it, "Haunted by God."

Their social class certainly differed. Lee was born in 1742 at the dawn of the Industrial Revolution in the poor manufacturing town of Manchester, the illiterate daughter of a blacksmith. Probably at a very early age, she began working in the textile mills. Her family were the kind of people Dorothy, from her position of genteel poverty, would have felt a deep compassion for and perhaps attraction to.

While Dorothy Day abandoned her own youthful piety in her teen years when she entered college, Ann Lee was unwaveringly religious from her youngest years, convicted of a tremendous sense of her unworthiness before God. She craved solitude and prayer. She felt called to celibacy, a vocation not understood by her family, who insisted upon her marriage. Lee birthed four children, all of whom died under the age of four. Day reluctantly aborted her first child and rejoiced in her second, whose birth played a culminating role in her conversion to Catholicism.

Lee and Day in the end both gave up husbands and embraced a life of celibacy rather than repudiate their callings, Ann to fulfill her desires, Dorothy in spite of them. Had they known one another as children, Dorothy would probably have been intrigued by Ann's piety, as she was by that of others she encountered as a girl.

For Ann the indifference to the poor of the established Anglican Church of her day signified its spiritual destitution, which, together with her fervent soul, drove her toward the radical, Pentecostal, millennialist movements which stirred among the poor in the slums of cities like Manchester. She became part of a charismatic group first derisively called the Shaking Quakers, some of the members, it was thought, having once been associated with George Fox's Society of Friends.

These religious radicals were arrested more than once for disturbing the Anglican peace on the Sabbath by the non-violent direct action of displaying charismatic gifts, including prophecies of doom, without invitation, during the Sunday services in Manchester Cathedral. Once, when Ann was in solitary confinement for such misdeeds, she had a mystical experience of union with Christ. She emerged proclaiming, "I no longer live, but Christ lives in me." St. Paul had written the same of his own experience in his letter to the Galatians (2:20).

Ann and her millennialist brothers and sisters were sure the Second Coming had been revealed to and through her. Some have claimed the revelation was that she, Ann Lee, was no less than Christ, come again in female form. Others, including the Shakers today, believe that what had been revealed was that the Second Coming is a spiritual experience now available to all who would surrender to Christ. Ann herself declared, "The Second Coming of Christ is in his Church."

The formal name of the Shaker church is the United Society of Believers in Christ's Second Appearing.

Dorothy Day claimed no mystical experience, and in fact said that the only visions she ever had were visions of unpaid bills. But she also said she loved the Church as Christ present in the world today. Catholic theology identifies this belief as "realized eschatology."

From her encounter with Christ onward, Ann was considered the leader of the community, and, like the founder of a Catholic religious order began to be called Mother Ann.

Persecution in Manchester eventually prompted a group of eight followers, including Ann's brother, William Lee, and her husband, Abraham Standerin, to accompany Mother Ann to America in 1774. Standerin, no more than a tagalong who finally despaired of regaining conjugal privileges from Ann, disappeared in New York. For two years Mother worked as a domestic in the city, while others did odd jobs and sought to secure land in the wilderness near Albany. Except for occasional harassment by suspicious patriots, they eventually lived for four years in solitude, prayer and arduous manual labor at Niskayuna.

In April of 1780, in the midst of a religious revival in Eastern New York and Western Massachusetts, the seclusion of the Believers (as Shakers generally refer to themselves) was broken. Two enthusiastic visitors, who had been received with warm hospitality, reported back to their revived congregation in New Lebanon, New York, on the Massachusetts border, about these "strange and wonderful Christians" near Albany. Their pastor, Joseph Meacham, traveled to Niskayuna and was convinced by the "Shaker testimony," as the revelation to Mother Ann was called.

From that day on, many came from the area touched by the religious awakening in New York and New England to meet the Believers and their inspired Mother. These returned home to share the Testimony and gather new Believers into congregations. In May of 1781 Mother Ann, Father William (her brother) and Father James Whittaker, who with Mother Ann constituted the Shaker leadership, set out from Niskayuna to visit the new communities and to evangelize, or "open the Gospel," as they put it. They spread their Testimony well into New England before returning home in September of 1783.

The three had paid dearly for the success of their missionary journey. Besides the arduousness of the undertaking itself, they suffered attacks and beatings in some towns. Within a year of their return, Fr. William and Mother Ann died. Ann was only forty-two. She died on Sept. 8, 1784, the feast of the Birth of Mary in the Catholic Church.

The witness of Mother Ann Lee is not the whole story of Shakerism, but it is obviously as fundamental as Dorothy Day's is to the CW. Of the commonly recognized elements of Shaker belief, celibacy and communal life, only the first can be traced directly to her revelatory experience and her teaching. It does not take Freud to suspect that her attitude toward sexual intercourse is related to her being forced to violate a felt call to celibacy followed by the death of her children. During her mystical experience while in solitary confinement, she reported she had been given a vision of Adam and Eve's first sin—which Mother Ann said was sexual intercourse.

Yet her call for celibacy among Believers has a deeper foundation than her probable neurosis. Like the significance of celibacy in Catholic theology, it is an eschatological sign. If the Parousia has occurred, if Christ has come again in the Church of the Believers, they are living in the Resurrection. Did Jesus not say that, in the Resurrection, there is no giving and taking in marriage, but all "are like angels in heaven?"(Mark 12:25).

According to Brother Theodore Johnson, who joined the Shaker community in Sabbathday Lake, Maine in the 1960s and died in his fifties in 1986, had Mother Ann lived, the Shaker church would probably have been organized along New England congregationalist lines. We owe the communal order of the United Society of Believers in Christ's Second Appearing to Father Joseph Meacham, the revivalist pastor converted on his visit to Niskayuna in 1780. By 1787, as male leader of the Believers, he called them "into Gospel order" on the model of the primitive church described in the second chapter of Acts. Shaker communal farming villages began to be organized under various "Ministries" led by pairs of male and female ministers. Oversight of the entire Church fell to the Central Ministry, also a man and a woman. At their peak, Shaker communities numbered nineteen, spread around New England and the Midwest, as far south as Kentucky (where the Pleasant Hill community was not far from the Trappists of Gethsemani.) Even in the pre-Civil War period, all Shaker communities were racially integrated.

From Mother Ann, herself, came principles which bore fruit in the craftsmanship and ingenuity which made nineteenth century Shakerism so well-admired. They reflect values and visions which both Peter Maurin and Dorothy Day also championed in the movement they founded. The prime example is Mother's motto, practically a translation (unknowingly) of St. Benedict's *Ora et Labora*: "Put your hands to work and your hearts to God." She also taught her followers to "do all your work as though you had a thousand years to live, and as you would if you knew you must die tomorrow." This admonition to attention without anxiety to one's work echoes another monastic aphorism: *Age quod agis*—"Do what you are doing." From such principles, one nineteenth-century Shaker gardener derived the wisdom that, "You can pray as well by hoeing a row of onions as by singing, 'Glory, halleluia.'"

As I have mentioned, Shaker pacifism also stretches back to Mother Ann. Neither she nor her followers retaliated against those who attacked them. One finds little discussion of the theology behind this stance. In the earliest days, it seemed too obvious to need explicating that the Gospel and the Resurrection life repudiated violence. Shakers have maintained this witness for over two hundred years.

When the draft law would have obligated their taking up arms during the Civil War, church leaders went to President Lincoln and explained their life and reasons for their rejection of violence. He granted them the first recognized status as conscientious objectors in the country's history.

While today they maintain a pacifist position, the small community in Sabbathday Lake, Maine, with eight members, three of whom are men, are not anti-war activists. Throughout much of the nineteenth century, however, Shakers were engaged in national and international movements to end war. Elder Frederick Evans, who came to the Shakers after an activist life concerned with many social problems, served as vice president of the Universal Peace Union. In 1905 the community at Mt. Lebanon, New York, hosted a Peace Convention with the stated goal of bringing pressure to bear on the U.S. government to renounce war altogether.

Shakers, like many Catholic Workers, renounced voting. Dorothy and other Catholic Workers refused to vote because they rejected the impersonality of government social programs and denied the legitimacy of the state's coercive power. The Shakers wanted to avoid the violent divisions electoral politics could introduce into community life. As in the CW, however, there has not been a lack of diversity of opinion about even fundamental issues. Round, square and rectangular table discussions for clarification of thought continue to this day in both communities.

While there is not an overt avowal of voluntary poverty among Believers, there has been a consistent dedication to simplicity. Not only Mother Ann, but many Shakers throughout two hundred plus years have come to the community from poverty, sometimes from destitution. As in Catholic religious orders, property among Believers is held in common. The economic goal of the community has always been to allow everyone a decent, dignified standard of living without extravagance. One nineteenth-century Shaker responded to a critic, "The divine man has no right to waste money on what you call beauty in his house or daily life, while there are people in misery." These sentiments share a common spirit with Dorothy Day's pledge that, "While our brothers suffer from lack of necessities, we will refuse to enjoy comforts."

Indeed, one must note that Shakers and Catholic Workers have come closer to faithful observance of voluntary poverty than many canonical orders. The standard of living in these two exemplary movements has served the same purposes: to create a society in which it is easier for people to be good and in which one is able to accord primacy to the spiritual.

In Shaker as well as in CW communities, hospitality has been a special mark. "Open the windows and door and receive whomever is sent," admonishes a nineteenth-century Shaker rule. In the past, there have always been numbers of what came to be known as "winter Shakers." When the weather turned cold there would be an influx of new converts. The Shakers always welcomed the new comers and integrated them into the community. When spring came, apostasy sprouted up. The communities bid the apostates farewell and sent them on their way with a bit of food.

Today, the phenomenon has reversed. The temporary Shakers are those (mostly, as at CW houses, young people, sometimes troubled) who spend summers living with the Sabbathday Lake Shakers. Now, there is no pretense, but simple acceptance of mutual aid and love.

For many years, when I first met the community, an obviously mentally-unbalanced middle-aged man, with no evidence of faith, lived as part of the "family." A few years ago, a young man with AIDS stayed with them for a while before he died, receiving the anointing of acceptance.

In the last century, Shaker communities took in children who were orphaned or otherwise without parents who could provide for them. This was no ploy to snag recruits for a celibate church. Most of the children left when they reached maturity. But they never forgot their Shaker parents. A few years ago, the community invited back a former member who had left the community with health problems, gotten married and been widowed for some time. As she aged her health deteriorated. Sr. Frances Carr, the community Eldress, said to her, "Come home." She did. She died in 1997 and was buried in the Shaker cemetery on what would have been her ninetieth birthday.

In recent years, members of the Sabbathday Lake community have volunteered at a shelter in the city of Portland, Maine, thirty miles from their rural village, cooking and serving a meal every week.

Shaker villages have been more successful "agronomic universities," in Peter Maurin's phrase, than most CW communal farms. Peter Maurin envisioned these farms to be places where "scholars would become workers and workers would become scholars." In Shaker communities, scholars have had to put their time in at manual labor. Laborers have been provided the opportunity to clarify thought with brothers and sisters of astute and wise minds. World renowned paintings, architecture, books and music, have surrounded the Shaker seamstress, the shepherd, the carpenter, the cook, etc. Sometimes these very workers *were* the painters, the architects, the composers, the writers. They were *all* the singers, and, before this century, the dancers. Worship was referred to as *labor,* not as a burden but as opus dei.

In 1965, the Catholic Art Association presented their Medal to the Shakers, in the person of Sr. Mildred Barker, then Eldress of the Sabbathday Lake community. The citation says:

> In the midst of a world in which commercial values were readily superseding religious ones, these devoted [Shakers] demonstrated the practicality of the good life they had chosen. They solved many of the problems that confront industrialist society today, and thus give us hope that we, and other followers of the Gospels, may see the achievement of equally successful solutions. In gratitude we ask

> the remaining members of this great body of religious men and women to accept this token.

According to Sr. Frances Carr, Dorothy Day was present at that convocation, held in Albany, just south of the first Shaker settlement. At this writing the community at Sabbathday Lake includes the "remaining members" of the United Society of Believers in Christ's Second Appearing. They number eight. Two are very elderly and sick and are in a nearby nursing home. The three sisters living in the Village are in their fifties and sixties. The three brothers are in their thirties. The newest member has been in the community for two years. They still read the New York *Catholic Worker.* Sr. Frances says, though, she thinks it's "too political."

Perhaps the most succinct announcement of common vision between these two radical, Gospel movements is how they each exquisitely embody both the statement of William James which was so often quoted by Dorothy Day and the words of the most famous Shaker hymn:

> I am done with great things and big things, great institutions and big success. And I am for those
> tiny invisible molecular forces.... creeping through the crannies of the world like so many
> rootlets [which] will rend the hardest monuments of man's pride. [James]

> 'Tis the Gift to be simple.
> 'Tis the Gift to be free.
> 'Tis the gift to come down
> where we ought to be.
> When we find ourselves in the place just right,
> 'Twill be in the Valley of Love and Delight.

The Catholic Worker, the Jews, and the Future of Ecumenical Religiosity

Marc H. Ellis

Baylor University

Jews have always been central to Christianity and the embrace of the Christian faith. In many ways, even until the middle of the twentieth century, this centrality has been defined negatively and with corresponding results. For Christians this has meant a combination of rigidity and militarism, a triumphalism of the spirit and the crusades. The travail of the Jews is historic within this negative definition, realized in ghettoization, pogroms, and Holocaust.

The Nazi terror, seemingly so distant but reaching closure only some fifty years ago, is seemingly the last expression of this negative definition, for if the death camps were built within the framework of a political fascist ideology, the singling out of the Jews for destruction came from those who claim to believe and participate in the messianic journey of the Jew who Christians name Christ.

Throughout Christian history Jews have been seen in a dual role, as those who prepared the way for the coming of the messiah and those who refused to accept the messiah once he appeared. Carrying the word of God, the Jews also refused that word, and in the body of the messiah crucified it. The promise which Jews once alone embodied among the world's peoples passed with that crucifixion to a new people who walked in the footsteps of the one who brought salvation. The Old Israel was replaced by the New Israel, with catastrophic and dialectical results for Jews. As those who betrayed the messiah and thus God, Jews were condemned for eternity to live with their choice, humbled, chastened, wandering without solace or home. Jews were important as symbolic reminders of the fate of those who reject God, as well as the sign of the end times. In their betrayal and stubborn adherence to their crime, a crime at once human and ontological, they also represented the possibility of recognizing the salvific act of Jesus Christ. For if one day even Jews recognized their mistake and assented to the messiah, if even the stubbornness of Jews broke with a bow to the truth, then the second coming of Christ was assured. Condemned and broken, with license for those of the New Israel to further abuse Jews for their crime, Jews were also to be watched and evangelized so to monitor the closeness of the end times.

Paradoxically, those who held the keys of the Kingdom and then threw them away for thirty pieces of silver continued to hold them for those who accepted the Kingdom but waited for its manifestation on earth. The definition of Jews by Christians, the very designation of Old and New Israel, therefore, held a tremendous tension and anxiety for Christians. Jews embodied failure and must be seen to have failed, hence ghettoization and violence against them. However, the despised also embodied the possibility of salvation, then and now.

Those who followed Jesus were perpetual latecomers, dependent on those despised. Furthermore, the messiah himself was one of those who embodied this tension. Worshiping a Jew and proclaiming one's superiority within that proclamation could only elicit a variety of unresolved tensions and ambiguities. The polemic and violence which occasioned this dilemma force another question as well: How did those who received the messiah and worshiped him act so violently against this lesser and condemned people without incurring the wrath of the one they worshiped? If the covenant was broken with the Jewish people because of their actions and blindness, could the new covenant also be broken by the actions of Christians against Jews?[1]

Suffering and the Question of God

When I first met William Miller, the biographer of Dorothy Day and her Catholic Worker movement, I had encountered various aspects of these understandings. As a Jew and as part of the first generation born after the Holocaust, I knew very little about Christianity. In my college years I majored in Religious Studies and it was through courses in New Testament and the history of Christianity that I learned the details of what had existed in the background of my upbringing but had lacked articulation: that Christianity was foreign and an enemy, at the least to be avoided and, if the situation worsened, to be opposed with our lives. Though this seems a dramatic rendering in the 1950s of America and in North Miami Beach no less, Germany of the 1920s had seemed hospitable to the Jews of that time. Whatever the objective circumstances, the turns and twists of Jewish history served as a caution, certainly in a time when the ovens of Auschwitz were only recently destroyed. With this as background, my meeting with Miller and the importance of his book was in an existential sense connected to the Holocaust in another way. The formative teacher of my college days was Richard Rubenstein, a Holocaust theologian who, in light of the Holocaust, saw the bond between God and the Jewish people severed. If God is a God of history as Jews believed in their trials and tribulations through the centuries, where was God in the death camps? If the rabbis had believed that Jewish suffering in the diaspora was caused by God as a lesson to heed God's word and return to the practice of the Law, could one believe that the massive suffering of the Holocaust was part of that punishment and desire to return? How could one continue to pray to such a God?[2]

The question of God's existence and goodness was complemented by a further and equally disturbing question as to whether Jews could continue to work for an interdependent world where all would be safe and secure. If one of the lessons of the Holocaust was that Jews could not expect help from God in their time of need, another lesson, at least for Rubenstein, was that Jews could not expect solidarity with other human beings and communities in time of need. Rubenstein found a dual violation in the Holocaust by God and humanity, and therefore posited power as the only remedy for Jews, indeed any people, who hoped to survive the vagaries of God and the world. This was the lesson of the Holocaust as Rubenstein saw it, and the vision of a world bereft of solidarity struck his students, as it did me, with a force that to this day remains with us.

As a Holocaust theologian, Rubenstein also explored the realm of Christianity, especially its role in the degradation of Jews and the groundwork it laid for the Holocaust. Here too there were twists and turns as Rubenstein saw the Nazis as anti-Christian but caught in the very dynamic of Christianity itself. As rebels against Christianity, they affirmed its hold on the European continent and battled against its effeminate aspects, which they ascribed to its Judaic background. For the Nazis would accept Christianity masculinized by rejecting its Judaic elements, a step that many Christians were all too willing to take. The other side of this was the laying of the groundwork for singling out Jews, for this obsession with the Jews was similar to and dependent on the Christian obsession. In this respect, Nazis and Christians shared a worldview that converged on the Jews, and thus even those elements of Christianity that resisted Hitler and the Nazis were often anti-Semitic.

My encounter with Miller and the Catholic Worker carried this background but was moving toward the next question posed by Rubenstein's analysis. If Rubenstein understood the world I inherited at mid-century, was this the world I would inhabit and pass on? There was an earned bitterness in Rubenstein's manner and thought which was both attractive and frightening. It was attractive because it called history to task and faced that history unflinchingly; frightening because Rubenstein's world was void of comfort and love. Drawn as I was to Rubenstein's world which I shared, as all great teachers he issued a summons, a two-fold summons: to accompany him on his journey and then to return to our own with the questions his journey posed.

Yet at this moment I was too young to return only to my world or to embark on my own journey, and instead found an equally powerful figure in Miller. Like Rubenstein, Miller had also encountered history and his defining moment could be found in Dorothy Day and the Catholic Worker. As I listened to Miller and read his first biography of Day, *A Harsh and Dreadful Love: Dorothy Day and the Catholic Worker Movement*, the very title proposed another perspective on history. Here in a life and a movement, the horrors of history were confronted by a commitment, especially to those who suffered, a commitment to build a world of mutual solidarity. In this solidarity, a beauty is found, and so too a God who is with those who are suffering and those who are working toward that solidarity. This solidarity is found in the Christian and specifically Catholic faith, but the resources for the journey move within and far beyond those confines. For me, the encounter with Miller and his work, and later hearing and meeting Dorothy Day, had this quality of posing a different perspective and path in the same world Rubenstein had evoked. The broken solidarity could be reestablished and the connection of God and humanity and humans with each other could be affirmed in a committed life. Moreover, the protection of life did not come through the exercise of political power but through a kind of power that no longer existed in Rubenstein's world: the power of love lived in the world.

The People Israel

In Miller's biography of Day a chapter title appears seemingly out of nowhere. Placed between chapters on the depression years and Dorothy Day's pacifist stand during World War II is a chapter titled "Israel." I can remember reading the book after meeting Miller and wondering what that title might refer to. The modern nation-state came immediately to mind, but the first pages made it clear that this was not the case. In fact Israel was the religious definition of the Jewish people and for Miller, at least, the Worker sensibility toward the Jews was as defining of its intent and direction as any other issue. The 1930s and 1940s were of course defining moments for the Jewish people as well and Miller captures this difficult period well by beginning his section on Israel: "As the Jews moved into the most agonizing phase of their history...." (Miller 1973: 138)

My own copy of Miller's biography is well marked, especially in this chapter. Here a range of Catholic thought on the Jews was brought to my attention, from Charles Coughlin, the anti-Semitic priest and radio commentator, to Jacques Maritain, the influential Catholic philosopher. In fact, as Miller points out in that book as well as in his later biography of Dorothy Day, Day's experience with Jews predates the 1930s, as her closest friend in college, Rayna Simons, and a man she was briefly engaged to during her early years on the Lower East Side of New York, Mike Gold, were both Jewish. Both were revolutionaries and atheists wanting to build a society and world where injustice perished and community was established as the essence of human striving (Miller 1982: 31-54; 64-68).

This experience of being drawn to the ideals and personality of Jews is one that served Dorothy Day well and because of this she rarely entered the theological discussion regarding the relationship of Jews and Christians until after the Vatican II Council. In confronting anti-Semitism, however, she was clear and forthright from the beginning. In response to a particularly offensive broadcast of Fr. Coughlin's in December 1938, Day wrote a statement that she circulated to local newspapers and the *New Republic* asking Jews to consider this a case of "extraordinarily bad manners." In May 1939, she helped organize the Committee of Catholics to Fight Anti-Semitism. A paper, *The Voice*, was created to promulgate the views of this committee and was distributed along with *The Catholic Worker* (Miller 1973: 150-151; *CW* 5/1939: 3,5; *CW* 6/1939: 3).

The early discussion of Jews in *The Catholic Worker* was carried forth largely by Peter Maurin and others associated with the movement. One is drawn to the Easy Essays of Maurin on the subject and the startling artwork of Ade Bethune that becomes more and more prominent in the paper as the tragedy of the Holocaust begins to unfold. One thinks here of Maurin's essay, "Let's Keep the Jews for Christ's Sake," which is central to the front page of the July-August 1939 issue, followed by Bethune's depiction of the baby Jesus within a prominent Star of David in December 1939. On top of the star in Hebrew is the statement rendered in English on the bottom of the star, "the Son of God, the son of man, God is with us."

Maurin's essay is interesting in a variety of ways. Combining and condensing insights from Leon Bloy and Jacques Maritain, Maurin first asserts the "mystery" of the Jews. He begins with what they are not:

> They are not a nation
> although the Zionists
> try to build up one
> in Palestine.
> They are not a race
> for they have intermarried
> with many other races.
> They are not a religion
> since their belief
> calls for one Temple
> and the Jewish Temple
> has not been in existence
> for nearly 1,000 years. (*CW* 7-8/1939: 1)

If Jews are not a nation, race, or religion, what are they? That indeed is the mystery. Jews have survived for millennia in their dispersion and remain a mystery even to themselves. Maurin quickly shifts to an abridged history of Jewish survival where the mystery of the Jews is again addressed. In Spain, for example, and later in the Papal states, Maurin asserts that Jews found protection in the "shadow of the Cross." Historically, the attempt to convert Jews went hand in hand with the protection of Jews, which contrasts significantly with the desire of the Nazis to persecute them. The shadow of the Cross compares favorably with the Swastika partly because of what both symbols stand for: the first salvation, the second perfidy. Moreover, the Church recognizes the mystery of the Jews as a "reminder to the world of the coming of Christ." Though they did not recognize Christ, the Jews remain chosen, "for God does not change." Thus the Jews who "refused to accept the Cross find their best protection in the shadow of the Cross" and surely their refusal of the Cross does not excuse actions which are unchristian in their manner and intent. Maurin closes his essay with the contemporary need for Jews to find refuge and even identifies Jews, against their economic stereotype as parasitic middlemen, as those who can work the land and build urban centers. America is "big enough" to welcome Jews who need refuge and their work on the land and in the cities of Palestine shows their ability to contribute to America (*CW* 7-8/1939: 1).

The situation of the Jews continued to weigh on Maurin and in two subsequent essays, "Why Pick on the Jews" and "Judaism and Catholicism," published in the winter of 1940, he again tries to sort out the issue of Judaism and its relation to Christianity and divorce this relationship from the anti-Semitic racial and economic propaganda emanating from Europe and America. The most obvious battle reigned in Europe with the Nazis and their racialism, but Maurin also understands the tendency of Christians to mistake a significant religious dialogue for persecution. Thus in these essays Maurin argues for the superiority of Christianity only insofar as it completes Judaism. When Jacques Maritain, a convert from Protestantism, is accused by some of being a convert from Judaism, Maurin reports that rather than being ashamed of this possibility, Maritain is proud of his Jewish background, as is his wife, Raissa, who is a convert from Judaism. In fact, Raissa claims that in her conversion to Catholicism "she is now 100% Jewish." Other Jewish converts feel the same way, and Maurin names some prominent academics and priests who have become Catholic as a way of completing their Judaism. The converts who have become priests may have been rabbis if they had not accepted the Cross, and Maurin comments on this without denigration. Though as priests "they announce the good news that the Messiah announced by the Prophets died on Calvary" as rabbis they would be "commenting on the Jewish prophets." This corresponds with Maurin's understanding that Judaism contains within it the "doctrine of a personal God as well as sound social ethics."(Royal 1994) Several years later Maurin used Leon Bloy's own words to express his solidarity with Judaism and the Jewish people and to accelerate his outrage at the anti-Semitism of his day (*CW* 1/1940: 1-2; *CW* 2/

1940: 1-2). In an essay titled, "Salvation is of the Jews," Maurin quotes Bloy:

> The history of the Jews
>   damns the history
>   of the human race
>   as a dike
>   dams a river
>   – in order
>   to raise its level.
> The Jews
>   were the only people
>   from which came forth
>   all the recording secretaries
>   of the commandments of God. (*CW* 7-8/1942: 1-2)

Of course, the authenticity of Judaism and the Jews continues when Jews are Jews, or in Maurin's terminology, "when the Jews are themselves." When the Jews are themselves they believe in and live within the framework of the covenant, especially with reference to the prophets. When Jews are no longer Jews, they adopt bourgeois understandings and practices or a belief in being Jewish solely through race identification. Then they become a "nuisance," for Jews were a "chosen people but they were never a superior race." Still, Maurin applies this sensibility to all who come into his purview. A charge laid to the feet of Jews is that they seek to separate religion and business, but for Maurin that is the assertion of many Christians as well. If Jews turn "sharp corners" in business, so do Christians. Capitalism itself is thought to be founded and promulgated by Jews—and here Maurin addresses the larger critique of Jews having created the liberal and rootless society—but as Maurin reports "Adam Smith and Ricardo, the theoreticians of Bourgeois Capitalism were not Jews." Rather than blaming Jews, the basic problem needs to be addressed: the drift of peoples around the world from their roots in religion and ethics. When a separation of religion and economic and political life occurs, the result is totalitarian systems that breed oppression and resentment. When Jews are blamed for a wider and more substantial failure, this simplifies the analysis and excuses those from all communities who have participated in this failure. Though Maurin believes in the Cross as the preeminent salvific act which all are called to share in belief and action, Jewish religion and ethics are sufficient in and of themselves to critique the wayward drift of the world and to provide the foundation for a new society. If the Jewish people were never a superior race, they were a chosen people, Maurin relates, but the Nordic people are neither superior nor chosen: "Hitler needs to read the Old Testament and the New Testament if he wants to lead men into the Promised Land where people no longer try to cut each other's throats and where the lion comes to lie down with the lamb."(*CW* 1/1940: 2)

In this time of great crisis Maurin argues that Jews are tied to the heritage of Christianity, are essential to the faith of Christians and a test for Christianity and individual Christians. Jesus Christ is of the Jews, historically and in the present, and the fate of Christianity is tied to the treatment of Jews by way of Jesus. What is done unto Jews is done unto Christ. Therefore to persecute Jews is to pervert Christianity, in essence to do what Christians accuse Jews of having done in the past, that is to refuse to recognize the messiah. The attempt of Jews to assimilate into German culture is a political and religious failure on par with the attempt of Christians to assimilate to the bourgeois and totalitarian state. Indeed what makes man human, a title of a subsection of an essay Maurin published in September 1939, is exactly this refusal of assimilation and the recovery of the original covenants, Old and New, in what Maurin terms the "unpopular front." In this front are theists, Protestant Christians, Catholics, humanists, and Jews, who can affirm what makes us human: to give and not to take, to serve and not to rule, to help and not to crush, to nourish and not devour. For Maurin it is ideals rather than deals, creed rather than greed, that ensure the possibility of a humane social order. When brought together, these communities can also confront totalitarianism on the verge of triumph. Moreover, each community has something particular to contribute to this unpopular front and the Jewish Jubilee, where every fiftieth year debts were remitted, land returned and slaves set free, features prominently in his analysis. The foundation of that Jubilee is clearly anchored in the Jewish belief in the God who created the world and the "Brotherhood of Man, for God wants us 'to be our brother's keeper.'"(*CW* 9/1937: 1)

If the theological centrality of Israel was primarily carried by Peter Maurin, *The Catholic Worker* made Jews visible in ordinary and political ways. In a March 1934 column, Dorothy Day wrote of meeting with a minister, priest and rabbi who had just finished a speaking tour of the United States to uproot religious prejudice. Though she was encouraged by their stories of people they had met, Day had received earlier in the day a long, three page, single spaced letter "full of carefully reasoned religious prejudice" that left her "pessimistic about attitudes of Gentile to Jew." Futher along in her column, Day thanks Mrs. Gottlieb, who on fast days feeds the Catholic Worker staff with a "pile of potato pancakes or fish and her cooperation saves the editors a great deal of time and effort."(3) In December 1938 an article appeared titled "Catholic Church Has Defended Jews During Times of Stress," which quotes Martin Luther's diatribes against the Jews and counter poses these with a book by a Catholic priest defending Jews (7). *The Catholic Worker* of July/August 1939 reports on a letter written by Archbishop Samuel Stritch of Milwaukee to Rabbi Joseph Baron of the same city decrying anti-Semitism and pledging the sympathy and active work of the Catholic community to confront this "wicked movement."(1-2) The following month a similar story was reported of a priest, Charles Owen Rice, at the Catholic Worker house in Pittsburgh who condemned the exaggerated accusations against Jews as "damnably un-American, un-Christian and anti-social."(1-2) In May 1940 a long article about the Hebrew Immigrant Aid Society appeared which detailed the travail of the Jews of Europe and reflected upon the charity of Jews to one another and concluded affirmatively: "Though HIAS may not call it such, it is what we call the works of mercy. All those who have passed through the agency are benefiting through the charity of others...We cannot praise too much the work that caused this writing and we ask you to think of them in prayer."(10)

The inclusion of Jews on a variety of levels in *The Catholic Worker* at a time when Jews were under increasing pressure in Europe and America made little tactical sense especially as the United States moved toward war and the Worker adopted an unqualified pacifist stance. Why take on the controversial issue of Jews and Judaism and the most popular war in American history? At the same time the seemingly contradictory stance of support for Jews and arguing for their conversion stands out boldly. The situation is even more complicated by the clear sense found in the Worker newspaper that though Jews should be candidates for conversion, they remain the chosen people and are sufficient unto themselves. If the Jews are a mystery to the world and to themselves, Maurin argues that they are candidates to help implement his synthesis of cult, culture and cultivation. Candidates and more, for the centrality of the Jews remains in their physical being today. For Maurin, at least, their destruction and rescue are central signs of the times in which he lived.

The balance of inclusion, respect, rescue, pacifism and conversion has been a difficult one, especially as the years passed and with the discovery of the extent and nature of the Holocaust. Yet the Worker clearly understood the dimensions of the destruction and argued that only a negotiated peace rather than a conclusive victory could save the Jewish communities of Europe. The May 1943 *Catholic Worker* featured a front page article, "Peace Now Without Victory Will Save Jews," that summarized a talk at the Catholic Worker by Jessie Wallace Hughan, secretary of the War Resisters League: "If we persist in our present war aim of unconditional surrender; if we promise only executions, retributions, punishments, dismemberments, indemnities, and no friendly participation with the rest of the world in a post-war world, we shall be depriving not only the German people of all hope, but we shall be signing the death sentence of the remnant of Jews still alive. If, on the contrary, we demand the release of all Jews from the ghettoes of Europe and work for peace without victory. then there is a chance of saving the Jews." The following month in an essay "Where is Sanctuary?" Day directly confronted the blindness of a person who attended her own talk on the subject of Jews and the war and refused to believe the plight of Jews in Europe: "Against such astounding unbelief the mind is stunned. And yet we of America and England who read and believe, do nothing to oppose the restrictions against immigration of Jews, their seeking sanctuary in this country. Who does not remember and shudder at the thought of that ship that sailed the seas, looking for a haven for its load of sufferers and turned away from these shores, refused by England, and finally rescued by such little Christian countries as Belgium and Holland?" Day outlines in vivid detail reported massacres of Jews in, among other places, Bessarabia, Odessa, Kiev, Pinsk, Brest-Litovsk, Mariupol, and Smolensk. Her cry is clear: "Do we believe these facts and then do nothing? Where then is sanctuary for these suffering ones?" (1,9)[3]

Jews and the Critique of Bourgeois Christianity

We know of course that the world did nothing about these "suffering ones," and Jews were not saved for "Christ's sake." Nor was the war fought for the Jews, as is often thought today. The attempted annihilation of the Jews was part of a broader destruction, of civilization, of Europe, of humanity, and this is how the Worker approached the question. This is how we can understand that though the prominence of Maurin's essays on Jews and the art work depicting the Christ child within the context of the Jewish people—as well as the other articles decrying anti-Semitism and even organizing against it—are startling, the central focus of the Catholic Worker was the demise and reconstruction of the social order in its broadest sense. Other issues, the plight of labor and the argument for pacifism for example, played a much larger role in Worker ideology and coverage in the newspaper. In terms of a specific group of people, African-Americans, then called Negroes, had far more attention paid to them than Jews, and after the war ended the dropping of the atomic bombs on Hiroshima and Nagasaki assumed a central place in Catholic Worker concern. A large part of this concentration on African Americans and atomic warfare flowed naturally from the Worker's sense of its own place in the domestic reality of the United States. Though the coverage of world news was extensive, and in many ways remarkable, the struggle of the Catholic Worker was decidedly here.

After the war, coverage of and comments about Jews declined markedly and much was repeats of Maurin's earlier essays and the Christ child drawing. The issue of Zionism was addressed in several issues of the paper, most extensively in the fall of 1948 and summer of 1951. In the first essay, Robert Ludlow contends non-Jews who support Zionism do so as a way of distancing themselves from Jews who remind them of their own vocation to follow Jesus Christ. "There continues to be among some Christians a persistent and never dying detestation of the Jew," Ludlow writes, "Our God, who as a man was a Jew, would be unwelcome in the homes of these Christians." That is why Christians find Zionism acceptable: because they welcome a solution which would "relegate the Jews to some portion of the earth where they would no longer have to rub elbows with them in the subways nor be disturbed that other than Gentile eats, sleeps, walks in white Gentile America." Ludlow is clear on the desire of Christians to distance themselves from Jews which he relates, like Maurin, to the desire to distance themselves from Jesus himself: "Christ walks in white Gentile America, walks as a spectacle to the nation, walks by the side of His Jewish blood brothers, fills the ghetto on Manhattan's Lower East Side, rubs elbows with white Gentile Americans in the subways, eats, sleeps, walks in white Gentile America to the disgust of those who worship him as God."

In fact, the attempt to distance themselves from Jews is more than an attempt to create distance from the one they worship, or rather it is to place this God at such a distance that they do not bother to follow the precepts of Christ's teaching. Many Christians today would not only exclude Jesus from their apartment buildings, occupations and schools, they would lynch him today as a Jewish radical. The only way to redress this calamity and draw closer to the Jewish man they worship as God, is to welcome Jews who live in the United States and those abroad still displaced by the war. The worthy experiments conducted by Jews in Palestine should be conducted here, sparing the survivors of the Holocaust the increasing violence in Palestine. Therefore, immigration of Jews to the United States should be facilitated and land should be given to them free.

This is the demand of the hour. Insofar as Jews are welcome, the God who Christians worship is welcomed. Clearly, however, Ludlow sees the Jews and the God who comes from the Jews as a subversive presence, questioning what Christianity has become and the social order it upholds. To see Christ among the Jews is to subvert the notion of a white Christianity and a white America as dominant and superior. Here Ludlow closes his essay by linking Jews and Negroes in their common subversion of a Christianity in service to race and the state: "The Christian who does not want the Jew or the Negro for his next door neighbor does not want Christ for his next door neighbor. It is as simple as that. There can be no evasion. The Catholic who objects to intermarriage because of race objects to Christianity. It is as simple as that. The Catholic who is to the least degree anti-Semitic denies the incarnation of Christ, profanes the humanity of Christ, and blasphemes the Holy Eucharist. There can be no evasion. On that issue alone we stand or fall in the Judgement. It is as simple as that."(*CW* 9/1948: 1-3)

The second essay on Zionism was written by Hector Black, who went to the new state of Israel to experience life through the agricultural experiments of the moshav and the kibbutz. These were the agricultural settlements to which Maurin and Ludlow had referred, and their existence affirmed Maurin's sense of the need to live in a communal environment. After arriving in Haifa and Tel Aviv and experiencing the frenetic pace of these cities reminiscent of life in America, Black traveled to a kibbutz and experienced first hand community on the land among Jews. Black reports on his acceptance as a person and a Christian and the international atmosphere of the settlement, with volunteers from around the world. His perceptive report on the agricultural and educational methods of Jewish communal life in Israel, and his interpretation of the lack of overt religiosity saw it as a positive connection with Jewish history. After reporting that there was no religion as such on the kibbutz, Black predicted that the concern for one another and the revival of ancient agricultural festivals would gradually become more recognizable as religion. "I shall never forget celebrating Passover with them," Black writes, "It was a beautiful cool evening as we walked out to the fields to meet the community choir in their folk costume.... I thought of how the Israeli folk song embodies the vigor of the spirit of their people as we followed the singing choir out into a field of new wheat where, with choir still singing, four men cut the first of the grain." A feast followed and at the beginning of the meal the traditional reading of the Book of Exodus took place, a reading modified to include the "subsequent movements of Hebrews including the present exodus from Europe to Israel." Black engaged the members of the kibbutz on the subject of nonviolence, a topic he felt because of present circumstances in the country they could not agree on. Regardless, the time Black spent in Israel was quite fulfilling: "Their strong idealism, their sense of mission, their sensitivity and the way they received me, a Christian, among them as so few Christian communities would have received a Jew—these are beautiful memories." (*CW* 7-8/1951: 3,6)

In this same issue is a review by Michael Harrington of Martin Buber's *Paths in Utopia*. Harrington sees this book as containing a "brilliant" analysis of the revolution which *The Catholic Worker* seeks in its own way. Harrington sees Buber as describing in the most "concise and lucid" way the communal ideals that many in the Christian world are now striving for: "Buber's ideas are close to, if not identical with, the concept of the Christian 'leaven' in society of which Maritain has written. And in light of the clear Papal pronouncements on the social and non-political character of Catholic Action, they deserve to be considered as an important contribution to the philosophy of the lay apostolate." In fact what Buber has done intellectually, according to Harrington, is what Black's journey through Israel has done on the practical level: probe and embody what Catholic Workers and others want in reconstructing the social order in a personalist way. While Black links the Jewish expression of community to ancient and contemporary history, Harrington sees Buber as a philosophical mentor in the exploration of the future for all humanity (*CW* 7-8/ 1951: 3,6)

This discussion of Zionism in the context of combating anti-Semitism at home and the embrace of Jewish work on the land held the dynamic of Catholic Worker discussion of the Jews in a pattern similar to its pre-war discussion. The challenge for Christians was to accept those who gave birth to their faith and in that acceptance to redefine the parameters of Christianity itself. Dynamics of Jewish life in the past and the present, with its dialectic of assimilation and recovery of the prophetic, mirrored the course of Christianity and Christian commitment. Those who recover the "dynamite of the Church," as Maurin often expressed it, could recognize the dynamite inherent in the Jewish message and in the Jewish people. Though Christianity furthered and completed the message of the prophets, the faults of the Jewish people, including their inability to recognize the messiah, were no different than the faults of Christians who worshiped the messiah and turned their back on him at the same time. In both the pre-war and post-war era, Jews are presented as Biblical people who bequeathed the messiah to the world and whose history continues into the present in its own authenticity. Thus Jews are not presented as foils for the Christian message or as Biblical fossils whose history ends with the appearance of Jesus. Even with the message of Jesus completing the words of the prophets, Jesus without the prophets becomes an empty abstraction. Jews are necessary as a reminder of the promises of God and serve today as witnesses to Christians in the deep embrace of their own faith and as pioneers in the reconstruction of the social order. As often as they are written about in their relation to theology and salvation, Jews are also addressed in their living reality as models of serving one another and as intellectual pioneers. Through their productivity they represent the very vision that Christians should be embracing.

In the non-theological realm, Jews are seen alongside African-Americans. African-Americans challenge white supremacy as Jews challenge Gentile arrogance. Moreover, when Christianity is discussed in relation to African-Americans, the challenge is to follow the radical teachings of St. Augustine, himself an African, rather than assimilate to white Christianity. Indeed in an essay in May 1938, Maurin made the same point that Ludlow made after the war, calling African-American's back to there roots just as he did with Jews:

The Jews think
 that they are
 better than the Negroes.
The Germans think
 that they are
 better than the Jews.
I don't think
 that the Jews
 are better than the Negroes
 or the Germans
 better than the Jews.
The way for the Jews
 to be better
 than the Germans
 is to behave
 the way the Prophets
 want the Jews
 to behave.
The way for the Negroes
 to be better
 than the Jews
 or the Germans
 is to behave
 the way St. Augustine
 wants everybody
 to behave. (*CW* 5/1938: 1)

The point that Maurin seems to be making by connecting African-Americans and Jews with their enemies, "racist" whites and racist Germans, is that only through a dynamic of recapturing the essence of their history and embodying it in the present can these peoples witness to who they are.

This witness is the way forward for all peoples rather than a superficial assimilation to the ways of the enemy. It is a self-contained witness and always one beyond itself, not as a question of superiority but rather as a mark of authenticity. Authenticity is the way toward a grappling with self and the social order enfolded in a people's history. At the same time it advises the enemy of the distortion of self and community undergone when a sense of superiority leads to domination and oppression. African-Americans and Jews in their history and in the present serve as reminders of the need to acknowledge particularity in the wider umbrella of universality. They call for justice and a new social order which will allow them to fully participate in a newly conceived universality where neither superiority nor inferiority exists.

Toward an Ecumenical Religiosity

The transition, or perhaps better stated, the revolution embodied in Vatican II was relatively easy for the Catholic Worker. In many ways Peter Maurin and Dorothy Day, along with others who affiliated with the Worker over the years, anticipated the Council and, when it was promulgated, radicalized it as well. For many Catholics, at least in the United States, the call of Vatican II was one of modernization and assimilation to a bourgeois mainstream. Openness to modernity and the goodness of the world led to a celebration of affluence and a participation in it without guilt or restraint. The Catholic Worker saw the changes in the Church in a different light, as a further possibility of engaging the world in pursuit of justice and peace. Rather than modernization and assimilation, the Worker embraced Vatican II as a call to witness to the possibility of goodness by being present to those outside the core culture of modernity.

The emphasis on inclusion in the early years of the Worker illustrated a tendency toward ecumenism. Thus Jews, but also Protestants and atheists were encouraged in their sensibilities even as they were called to a deeper reality. So, too, African Americans were encouraged in their struggle for justice and their inclusion into the larger society. In the post-war world this inclusion extended to what later became known as the Third World. Hence Gandhi was venerated and the struggling people of Latin America, Africa and Asia were reported on in sensitive and perceptive ways. The coming of liberation theology was anticipated by the Worker, especially by Day, and her travels to Cuba and reflections on the death of Camilo Torres were an early and moving recognition that an era of revolution was upon us and the only question was whether religion would play a positive role or would be relegated to a peripheral and reactionary role.

What Vatican II did for the Worker is as important as the vanguard role the Worker had with the coming of the Council: it allowed a freedom to name that which it had anticipated and helped create. In relation to Jews, the freedom now was to accentuate the positive side of the tension the Worker had already articulated, with the authenticity of Jews and the Jewish tradition to be emphasized and the calls to conversion to dwindle. The struggle against anti-

Semitism existed from the very origins of the Worker, and crimes against Jews were also seen as theological transgressions against the very substance of Christianity. Now a further embrace could occur as ancient Jewish texts and contemporary Jews were now viewed as distinct and yet part of the Catholic tradition without being anticipated or transfigured by Jesus. Or better stated, even when the anticipation and transfiguration is asserted, the Jewish dimension is retained, is independent and becomes in a way interdependent with the continuing life of the Jewish people.

The declarations on Jews and Judaism in the Vatican Council are taken almost as self evident, and because of this little space in the Worker newspaper is devoted to this momentous event. With Maurin's death in 1949, the theological speculation on Jews and Judaism essentially ended and Day's comments on both are few and interspersed in her reflections on life and her own journeys. Elie Wiesel, the Holocaust survivor and writer, is mentioned, as is the great theologian Abraham Heschel. Their message is for everyone and the assumption is that reading and contemplating Jewish reflections on suffering, celebration, and God are ways of deepening the human and Christian journey. Yet, paradoxically, it is this sense of inclusion which makes it difficult, if not impossible, to engage in a critical dialogue with Jews in the present. Just as the call for Jews to convert to Christianity ends with the Vatican Council, so too the Worker is silent on an increasingly militaristic Jewish state. The critique of Zionism, fashioned in the context of safeguarding the rights of Jews in the diaspora and as a critique of white Christianity, ends as the emergency situation of the Holocaust years grow distant.

Since the Worker showed a mostly positive emphasis on contemporary Jews during their time of crisis and an a atypically even-handed position of dialogue on religious affirmation when most Catholic thinkers and institutional representatives did not, it is paradoxical that this sensibility does not carry over into the period of Jewish empowerment. In fact a reversal is evidenced in the post-Vatican II era of Worker commentary on Judaism and Jews: whereas in the era of crisis the suffering and capability of the Jewish people is emphasized, in the era of empowerment, Jewish suffering is emphasized almost to the exclusion of contemporary Jewish achievement. In this way the other side of Jewish achievement, Jewish militarism and even criminality in the exercise of state power, is downplayed or ignored. Thus the "mystery" of the people Israel, complicated as it was in

Catholic theology and projected so prominently in the 1930s and 1940s in *The Catholic Worker*, remains as the demystification of state power in Israel becomes important. The Worker correctly fought against the myth of Jewish power promulgated by fascists and demagogues, but when Jews achieve an objectively quantified power, the Worker, as happened with many others, is unable to speak to the issue.

In this sense, the Worker's pre-Vatican II solidarity with Jews is, within the context of the historical and theological currents of the time, a critical solidarity, emphasizing the inclusion of a people in distress, whereas the solidarity with Jews after Vatican II is relatively uncritical. At a time when the desire to convert Jews could be combined with respect and protection, the Worker intervened in a forceful and analytical way against a wave of religious and political anti-Semitism; at a time when a desire for conversion would be seen even retrospectively as anti-Semitic, the embrace of Jews is without critical force or content. The very heart of the Worker and its spirituality, to be with the least and the outcast and to criticize the state and economy that cause dislocation and death, focused on Jews during the war years but is almost completely abandoned with regard to Jews after the war.

If Jews provide critical insight into societal exclusion and white Christianity, those days are fading into the past, especially as Jews take on more and more of the attributes the Worker criticizes. During the 1930s and 1940s, Maurin especially called assimilationist Jews back to the prophets as he called assimilationist Christians back to Christ, but the post-war years seem too confusing as almost the entire Jewish community opts, as a religious act, to support and speak for the state of Israel. On the face of it, Maurin's criticism of bourgeois Jews in the 1930s would call forth a similar criticism of state Jews in the 1960s and beyond—that is, calling the Jewish people back to the prophetic task of creating a world where no one is excluded or denied. Perhaps Maurin's death explains the lack of carry through on this obvious point, as from 1949 on in Worker history Jews are not discussed in a theological way. The practical fight against anti-Semitism led by Day was, in the post-Holocaust years, less and less needed in Catholic circles and in the larger Western world. Here must be added the new understanding of Jews and Judaism that emerges from Vatican II, a positive evaluation to be sure, but one which also minimizes critical engagement with the Jewish world in our ecumenical era.

Perhaps it is here that the limits and possibilities of the new ecumenical religiosity are understood. A critical understanding of Judaism and the Jewish people served the Worker well in forcing a critical evaluation of Christianity in the 1930s and 1940s, but a critical understanding today might force yet another evaluation of Christianity beyond the confines of that religion itself. In former times, Jews and Judaism helped in the confrontation with a cultural Catholicism that was increasingly assimilationist. Peter Maurin and Dorothy Day in particular saw Jews and Judaism as a way of proclaiming a radical center to their faith and therefore calling the Catholic community back to that center. Were Christians really following Jesus the Jew, a Jew who also stood in line with the prophets, even when they persecuted Jews and denigrated Judaism? Blaming Jews and Judaism was symbolic of an entire bourgeois ethos that Christians were, at one and the same time, benefiting from and blaming Jews for inaugurating and encouraging. To blame Jews and Judaism was to take one's critical eye off the behavior of Christians themselves and their betrayal of the message of Jesus and the Church. To discuss the chosen people then meant to discuss the ramifications of being the New Israel. Jews and Judaism became a clarion call to the Catholic tradition, to its origins and meaning. The mystery of Israel was really the mystery of the Church.

In a time when the mystery of the Church has been demystified, even abandoned in some quarters by those seeking to be faithful as Christians in the contemporary world, the mystery of the Jews has little meaning. In fact, as Jews and Christians have followed the path to the deepest assimilation (assimilation to power and the state, the very assimilation the Worker warned against), the ability to establish a center of either faith has diminished. This is often passed over because the lack of such a center brings into question the religious enterprise itself. Instead an ecumenical brotherhood and sisterhood is simply asserted, Judaism and Christianity together, as if both religions are joined in a redemptive mission. Refusing to question Jews and Judaism removes Christianity from questioning itself at a fundamental level.

The Jewish covenant remains in place and so, too, does the Christian covenant. These covenants provide a promise to which Jews and Christians are heirs, but the validity of both together or either separately *as demonstrated in the actions of their adherents* is left unaddressed. Whereas Peter Maurin and Dorothy Day risked much in the assertion of the importance of Jews and Judaism to the fidelity of Christians, today it can actually be a protective procedure, part of the banquet circuit, a dialogue which in some cases becomes a deal of silence and complicity. In this sense the Worker has become a passive participant in that which it originally and passionately argued against, a cultural arrangement benefiting both Jews and Christians as a way of bypassing the central questions of both faiths. Perhaps the Worker does this less because of a desire to mainstream itself than it does because it does not know how to take the next step in the journey of faith. In action the Worker is beyond reproach and without fear, but in its own theology it is stagnant. Is the fear that the culpability of Jews and Judaism is neither mythic nor related to redemption but all too normal, understandable, banal, real, objective, pointing to the same demystified culpability of Christians and Christianity? Could it be that to understand and affirm that we have come to the end of Judaism *as we have known and inherited it* is to affirm that we have come to the same end of Christianity?

With these results the future of ecumenical religiosity comes into question. It cannot begin with the mystery of Judaism or Christianity or even their journey together. To claim the center of each as the Worker once boldly did is to retreat into the past. We are somewhere else now as the assimilation of Judaism and Christianity and Jews and Christians attest to. Where is this "somewhere else," and how can it be defined and embraced? What labels will we attach to it and how shall we celebrate its victories and mourn its failures? These are questions that today lie beyond Peter Maurin and Dorothy Day, indeed beyond the Catholic Worker itself.

Notes

1 For an important study of Christian anti-Semitism see Garvin I. LangMuir, *History, Religion, and Antisemitism* and *Toward a Definition of Antisemitism* (Berkeley: University of California Press, 1990).

2 Richard Rubenstiein's statements of his views about God and human solidarity are found in his classic text *After Auschwitz: Radical Theology and Contemporary Judaism* (Indianapolis: Bobbs Merrill, 1966). For William Miller's analysis of the Catholic Worker movement see his introduction to *A Harsh and Dreadful Love: Dorothy Day and the Catholic Worker Movement* (New York: Liveright, 1973), 3-16.

3 See also: Dorothy Day, "Where Is Sanctuary," *The Catholic Worker*, June 1943. Below this column is a review of a book published by the Jewish Agricultural Society which features the ability of Jews to contribute to rural life in the tradition of the Catholic Worker. See also "Room on the Land," in the same issue.

Protestant Responses to Dorothy Day and the Catholic Worker

Mel Piehl

Valparaiso University

My own responses can perhaps be called part of the Protestant "reception" of Dorothy Day's work, since it is quite true that I am a committed Protestant, specifically a Lutheran who works out of the original meaning of "protestore," an affirmation or confession of belief. That experience has made me highly alert to the dangers and pitfalls of this position. A few years back I spoke about some aspect of Catholic Worker history at a Catholic meeting. At the end someone in the audience asked, "Well, that's all very fine, but what should we be doing today about the crisis of authority in the Church?" And my immediate thought was: "Boy, things must be getting a lot worse than I thought if they're starting to ask *Lutherans* how to solve problems of authority in the Catholic Church!" So I will mostly stick to history, which is what I know best, and let others draw what conclusions they may about further lessons.

Probably the place to begin discussing the "Protestant" reception of Dorothy Day is with Dorothy's own conversion and baptism. No, I do not mean her famous conversion to Catholicism in 1927. I mean her conversion and baptism as a Protestant Christian, specifically into the Episcopal Church in 1907, when she was ten years old. Remember that?

It is important to recall that Dorothy's family was from a Protestant background, though of the generally vague and nonpracticing sort that was increasingly common among the American middle classes at the turn of the century. Her father was of southern Presbyterian background, she had cousins who were Campbellites (the denomination that later evolved into the Disciples of Christ and the Churches of Christ), and her mother's family had been Episcopalian. But most of that family religious background had faded, and neither her father nor mother were churchgoers or, evidently, even remotely interested in religion. They were therefore naturally quite skeptical of young Dorothy's seemingly intense childhood piety and curiosity about religion, and specifically her interest in attending the Episcopalian Church services near their home in Chicago; her mother even suspected that it was a way for her to try to get out of the hard work of preparing for their elaborate Sunday dinners.

Yet for Dorothy this childhood encounter with church life and the Scriptures, which happened to occur in the context of the Protestant Episcopal Church, was enormously important, perhaps even more so because of the resistance she had to overcome in pursuing it. She says in *The Long Loneliness:*

> "When we moved to the North Side [of Chicago] I went to the Episcopal Church of Our Savior, on Fullerton Avenue, and studied the catechism so that I could be baptized and confirmed. There too I learned the formal prayer of the Church in her psalms... The songs thrilled in my heart, and though I was only ten years old, through these Psalms and canticles I called on creation to join with me in blessing the Lord. I thanked him for creating me, saving me from all evils, filling me with all good things." (Day 1952: 29)

There were other childhood encounters with Protestantism as well: the neighbors she visited where the whole family gathered to sing evangelical hymns like "The Old Rugged Cross"and the mother got down on her knees to pray, a gesture that particularly impressed Dorothy. In her early teens she was also fascinated by the evangelical sermons of John Wesley and even read essays by Jonathan Edwards—not exactly typical teenage reading fare today, or even then. Of course Dorothy Day had important childhood encounters with Catholics and Catholic practices and piety as well, and these later assumed great importance for her. But it is fair to say that insofar as Dorothy Day had any early childhood spiritual formation, if we can speak that way, it was primarily a Protestant one.

But that childhood "conversion" did not last. Her encounters with organized Protestantism, especially after she went away to the University of Illinois in 1914, were almost entirely negative. She became more aware of the general tendency of churches of the time, especially Protestant ones, to offer easy, pious rationalizations for injustice and the social status quo. In her writing she refers several times to the way that groups like the YMCA and YWCA controlled campus life and insisted on membership in an evangelical Protestant Church as a condition of student employment. These kinds of experiences with rather rigid and not very socially conscious versions of evangelical Protestant piety may have contributed, along with her own social and intellectual awakening, to her youthful disillusion with all religion. And we know that most of her intense involvement in social movements prior to her conversion occurred within the context of an American radical movement that was either skeptical about all religion or deeply hostile to it.

Yet it might be worth asking why this is so, and why Dorothy never again looked to Protestantism for religious guidance. While many Protestants, probably a large majority, disdained social concern, the early twentieth century saw growing social consciousness within some sectors of Protestantism. There were some serious Protestants who were becoming concerned about the very problems of poverty, social justice, and war that so moved Dorothy, and while some of them gradually migrated away from religious faith, others worked hard to discern the proper relationship between church and society, spirituality and social commitment.

Students can often make one see things in a new way, and this happened to me on this question. A few years ago, when one of my classes was reading *The Long Loneliness,* one of the students suddenly asked, "Well, if she was so interested in linking religion with social concern and social action, why didn't she just convert to Methodism?" (Come to think of it, that student may have been a Methodist!) I'm not sure I have a complete answer to that, and it would take a long time to explore why Dorothy's conversion, or her "second" conversion, was to Roman Catholicism rather than back to some kind of Protestantism. But suffice to say today that the reasons were fundamentally religious and intensely personal, though they may have been influenced by her intuition, from her days in the radical movement, that strong characters and strong beliefs require equally strong communities, and that Catholicism seemed far superior on that ground to any available form of Protestant church life.

Whatever the reasons, it is true that the rest of Dorothy Day's life and career was lived out entirely within the structures, faith, and practices of the Roman Catholic Church, and that she never looked back. But it is also true that, unlike many other notable twentieth century converts to Catholicism, Dorothy never exhibited any hostility toward Protestant beliefs, or toward her vaguely Protestant background, or to individual Protestants, or to Protestant churches generally. One of Dorothy's favorite quotes regarding her own conversion, which she borrowed from St. Augustine, is "The bottle still smells of the liquor it once held." (That's an especially interesting quote from Dorothy considering her general views on that subject!) She meant, of course, "the bottle" in relation to the secular social radical movement that she brought with her into the Church. But perhaps one could suggest the saying could also be true of her relation to her Protestant past, and to the larger Protestant past of this country. Could it be that she understood certain things about Protestant dimensions of American culture that many Catholics of the time did not? She certainly did become fervently "Catholic to her fingertips," as it was said, and she often said that "for me the Catholic Church was the one true Church." But she also displayed a kind of openness toward people of other Christian traditions that was not at all common in the pre-Vatican II American Catholicism of those days. I agree with Robert Coles when he reflected, after his conversations with Dorothy in *A Radical Devotion,* that "there was in Dorothy Day a distinct Protestant side that resisted all her years of Catholic loyalty. She emphasized the phrase 'as it came from Christ himself,' as she read [from Dickens]... . She had told me often how much she enjoyed her private moments with Him—away from the Church." But Coles also notes tht "despite her Protestant, anarchist side she loved the rituals and ceremony, even the institutional authority of the Catholic church."(Coles 1987: 157)

I do not want to suggest, even remotely, that Dorothy was some kind of a crypto-Protestant. It is very important to remember, even if things have changed considerably today, that Dorothy Day and the Catholic Worker movement in the 1930s and 1940s were very much a part of a Catholic world that was, in those days, still largely a separate religious subculture within American society. Dorothy and her associates saw her own mission and vocation primarily in relation to that Catholic Church. Yet Dorothy's was a fervent Catholicism that always turned outward as well as inward to the faith and traditions of the Church. She did not confine the movement's impact to the Catholic people alone, but brought them to everyone who was willing to listen.

An approach to the Protestant "reception" of her work must, therefore, begin by imagining all those people on the streets during the Depression and after who parted with their penny in order to buy

The Catholic Worker; all those who came to the roundtable discussions to listen to Dorothy, Peter Maurin, and others; and of course all the poor who came to the Worker houses of hospitality. Certainly a large number of those people were Catholics or ex-Catholics or people of no religion at all. But weren't some of them also practicing or nonpracticing Protestants of various kinds?

What did they think of all those quotes from the popes, accounts of the liturgy, and Ade Bethune pictures of the saints that attracted so many Catholics? It is impossible to know. *The Catholic Worker* certainly did not keep religious statistics of its readers or those they served in the breadlines. Thank God. But surely there must have been men and women from Protestant backgrounds among them, and over the years and decades it is clear that many people originally raised in pious evangelical homes developed admiration for Dorothy Day and those who worked with her. Here and there in the records of the Catholic Worker and in the pages of *The Catholic Worker* it is possible to catch glimpses of such reactions. In 1934, for example, *The Catholic Worker* printed an article by someone identified only as a "Negro Protestant."

It is even possible that a few Protestants may even have ended up becoming Catholic Workers. I recall in my research being startled by a reference to one of the Catholic Workers in the Minneapolis house of hospitality in the 1930s being a Lutheran. How did he get there? Maybe a stray. But he probably was not alone. Certainly there were not a lot of such people, for most of the early Catholic Workers and their houses of hospitality were very Catholic, intensely so, in ways that would not have been comfortable for most Protestants. And many if not all still shared some of the prevalent Catholic view of the time that Protestantism was at best a watered-down, compromising Christianity that had undermined the powerful social vision of ancient and medieval Catholicism, and at worst a fatal capitulation of Christian faith to worldly values. *The Catholic Worker* periodically carried articles that referred in highly critical terms to such things as John Calvin's weakening of the ban on usury, or favorably reviewed books like one that referred to the Reformation as "History's Greatest Catastrophe." While most such critical pieces generally focused on the alleged social consequences of Protestantism rather than doctrines *per se*, they hardly presented a favorable portrait of the Reformers' historical descendants.

Whatever might have been the view on the streets, however, it is probably fair to say that the great majority of Protestants probably did not know or hear of Dorothy Day in the first decades of the Catholic Worker movement. While most Catholics of that time would at least have heard of her, even if only in skeptical or distorted terms, the average Protestant in the pews was almost entirely unaware of this unusual movement. The few exceptions, interestingly enough, were not among ordinary churchgoers but primarily among Protestant religious leadership. By the late 1930s occasional references to Dorothy and the Catholic Worker could be found in some Protestant journals. For example, the *Christian Century,* then as now the leading voice of mainstream liberal American Protestantism, began to take increasing note of what it called "this new social movement that is making headway in this historic church." Like most Protestant observers of the time, however, the *Century* tended simply to view Dorothy Day and the Catholic Worker as part of what is saw as a surprising new social strategy by the Roman Church. At the same time, Protestants tended to imagine the Catholic Worker enjoying a degree of popular support among the Catholic clergy and hierarchy that likely would have startled the Workers themselves, and probably most people in the Catholic Church, had they heard of it. For example, the *Century* referred to "A monthly periodical called *The Catholic Worker*, which has the support of the masses of Catholic clergy throughout the country and, it is reliably reported, the unofficial support of many bishops. It already has a circulation of 115,000." (*Christian Century* 53: 837-38)

This comment, and other published and unpublished reports like it, reflected the nearly universal Protestant tendency of the time to view Catholicism as a tightly organized, monolithic system, and all individual Catholics as essentially foot soldiers in a militant hierarchical organization run by the Pope as commander in chief, the bishops as his top generals, and the clergy as the lieutenants. From this point of view, the appearance of an energetic social movement like the Catholic Worker could only be seen as the result of a strategy conceived on high. It was natural for Protestants to view groups like the Catholic Worker, however visible and active, as essentially tools in the hands of the clergy and the hierarchy for enhancing the social influence of the Catholic Church. Like many leftist and secular observers of the Catholic Worker, therefore, most Protestants tended to see the Worker as simply an unusually vigorous street-level manifestation of the same cleverly conceived social strategy emanating from the papal encyclicals and the official bishops' Conference, primarily taking the form of the many top-down "Catholic Action" groups. It was literally inconceivable that any serious Catholic movement could have been initiated and led by lay people, or that it was not fundamentally an agency of the Church.

Therefore, it is not surprising, given their general views of the Papacy and the Catholic hierarchy, that most Protestant leaders who were aware of it tended to believe that the Catholic Worker and similar movements would finally be handicapped and fail to achieve their objectives because of what they saw as inherent institutional weaknesses. While some admired the attempted entry of the Catholic Church into the social sphere, Protestant observers tended to think that movements for social justice were permanently weakened by what they saw as Catholic doctrinal rigidity and authoritarianism: "This Catholic social movement is not as spectacular as the one developing within Protestantism. There are good reasons for this. Catholic laymen never denounce Catholic clergy as Methodist laymen denounce Methodist clergymen. [Those were the days!] As long as these social movements emanate from the National Catholic Welfare Conference, and operate only with the official support of the hierarchy, then laymen have to take it and like it." Catholic movements like the CW were thus seen, at bottom, as attempts by the hierarchy to keep their religious hold on the Catholic masses, who were supposedly becoming increasingly disillusioned with the Church's social conservatism, as well as an effort to prevent Catholic activists from turning to socialism or communism. So even as they saw growing Catholic social concern as a positive development, many Protestants of the time believed that Catholic action was inherently crippled by conservative Catholic dogma. And some Protestants could not resist the old prejudice that more Catholics were in poverty partly because they followed the Church's teaching on birth control and so had more children than they could support. Still, Protestant leaders admired what they saw as the organizational strategic advantages of the Catholic Worker and similar Catholic movements: "With its remarkable discipline and organization, qualities woefully lacking among Protestants, it can create a social consciousness in America more quickly than any other group." Such remarks suggest why they *really* could not understand an "organization like the Catholic Worker!

If, insofar as they heard of it at all, mainstream Protestants were generally rather confused about Dorothy Day and The Catholic Worker, or tended to view it indiscriminately as just another Catholic Action group, without examining its particular features or understanding its basic character, that was not the case with the second group of Protestants who encountered The Catholic Worker: the historic Protestant peace churches—Mennonites, the Quakers, and the Brethren. These groups were rather startled, in the leadup to World War II, to discover that in addition to their own well established tradition of pacifist refusal to engage in war, which in most cases went directly back to the 16th and 17th century Reformation era, there was now a Catholic group, the Catholic Workers, who also refused to participate in war on religious grounds.

Yet I think it is fair to say that, for most of those in the historic Protestant peace churches who became aware of Dorothy Day and the Catholic Worker in the very early days of their encounter, they were as much a source of bafflement as of admiration. On the one hand, of course, the Quaker and Anabaptist Protestant groups were pleased to see Catholics, who in that period were generally renowned for their militant patriotism and even belligerence, raising questions about war on religious grounds. Yet for most people in the Protestant peace churches, pacifism was a central part of their entire religion in a way that it could not be for Catholics. It was therefore hard to understand how the Catholic pacifists could arise from such a Church, or remain loyal to it.

This was especially so because of the difficulties over the Civilian Public Service Camps, which the Protestant peace churches essentially paid for on behalf of the government. The supposed "compromises" that the peace churches made with the government were another source of some tension with the Catholic conscientious objectors, tensions that were exacerbated by the fact that the Catholic conscientious objectors (COs), unlike the Protestants, were not financially supported by their churches. The Catholics depended strictly on contributions from the Catholic Worker, which was poor as usual. Eventually, some of the Protestant peace churches did pitch in to provide some financial support for the beleaguered Catholics: $6000 from the Mennonites and over $30,000 from the Quakers. But attempts to get payment from the Catholic Church failed (McNeal 1992: 62, 159). The kind of piety and outlook on society and authority, the general religious and spiritual outlook of the historic Protestant sectarians, was simply fundamentally different from that of almost all Catholics, including Catholic Workers, who tended to accept the idea of a basic religious responsibility for society as a whole, rather than to view "the world" in largely hostile terms.

Still, despite their religious differences and considerable mutual incomprehension, it is fair to say that World War II pacifism introduced an awareness of Dorothy Day and the Catholic Workers into the small sectors of American Protestantism originally deriving from the sixteenth-century Anabaptist movement that was sustained through the years. Most of this awareness focused on the CW's pacifism, but there were a few in those circles who came to know and admire Dorothy Day's broader social vision. Moreover, there was certainly some affinity between the Workers' outlook and the practices of simple living and social service that traditionally held sway within denominations like the Mennonites and Brethren. Somewhat later, there was also contact between Catholic Workers and more communal sects like the Hutterites in the Dakotas and Montana and the Doukhobors in western Canada.

If the major encounter between Protestants and the Catholic Worker during WW II was that of the historic peace churches, after the war there was a growing awareness of the CW by more mainstream Protestant pacifists active in movements like the Committee for Nonviolent Action, the Committee for Nonviolent Revolution, andthe Fellowship of Reconciliation. By far the best known of these was the prominent Protestant clergyman Abraham Johannes Muste—A.J. Muste. Muste was a pastor of the Dutch Reformed Church in America who became perhaps the leading Protestant pacifist when he resigned his pastorate in protest against World War I. In the early 1920s he abandoned the Church and religious belief to become involved in radical labor activism, eventually forming his own tiny radical political party, the Musteites, who joined in the fierce and often sectarian left wing political struggles of the 1930s. In 1937, Muste underwent a major religious reawakening, returned to the Church, and began re-focusing much of his abundant energy on the pacifist cause. He eventually became the most prominent leader of the Fellowship of Reconciliation, the leading organization of Protestant religious pacifism. Muste knew of Dorothy Day and the Catholic Workers during the Depression and World War II. Yet it was really after the war, when he attempted to make pacifism a more positive and dynamic movement, that Muste became most interested in Dorothy. His interest occurred partly as he became increasingly critical of the species of radical individualism that seemed almost inevitably to accompany a good deal of Protestant pacifism, an individualism to which Catholics seemed more immune. Muste also came to admire what he saw as Dorothy Day's more *disciplined* way of life, and the way it wove peacemaking into the fabric of both ordinary existence and a wider social vision: "Some of us regard being a Christian pacifist as involving being a'nonviolent revolutionary.' I always thought that to be a Christian pacifist was to be a revolutionist, though one who has put away the sword. There are a few, such as Dorothy Day, who share that position."(Hentoff 1970: 474-75) Yet it was also true that Muste, like other liberal Protestants, tended to admire Dorothy Day's social stance while being puzzled by her commitment to the Catholic Church. Like the historian Lawrence Veysey, they tended to believe that the Catholic Workers retained only "a tentative tie with Catholicism," and suspected that they would eventually leave the Church to turn into something like an independent denomination. Underneath these attitudes we can still detect a certain degree of suspicion of the Catholic Church and even Catholic doctrines. Dorothy Day could certainly be admired as an individual, but insofar as she was a pious, practicing Catholic, there was also an element of distrust. Muste's biographer, Jo Ann Ooiman Robinson, summarizes Muste's generalization of Catholics: "The Catholic Church, with its rigid hierarchy and strict demands of obedience, had never found comfortable acceptance in Muste's usually ecumenical world view. He respected Dorothy Day and the contributions of her Catholic Worker movement; he had especially close relationships with some of the younger pacifists who created the Catholic Peace Fellowship within the FOR. But for the most part Catholic institutions remained beyond his ken."(Robinson 1981:187) Still, despite such differences, there was a large area of cooperation and friendship that developed between Dorothy Day and mainstream Protestant pacifists like A.J. Muste. Even if this represents the views of only a few Protestants, it was an important connection that grew and developed through the years.

A quite different and perhaps more surprising response to Dorothy Day developed in later postwar years among those who are generally labeled conservative evangelical Protestants, the lineal descendants of the older fundamentalists. While it is certainly true that vast sectors of conservative Protestantism knew nothing of Dorothy Day, and would not approve of her if they did, at least a thread of connection did begin to develop between the Catholic Worker and some people from conservative evangelical traditions.

The beginning of this connection, and perhaps a proof of the idea that the great spiritual leaders of any age tend to find one another, involves Clarence Jordan and the Koinonia community. Jordan was the amazing Southern Baptist preacher and Ph.D. biblical scholar who in 1942 established the interracial Koinonia community near Americus, Georgia, an experiment that struggled for many years against the hostility and violence of the local white population. He was also the author of the brilliantly conceived "Cotton Patch Version of the Gospels," which might be called Jordan's translation of the Scripture from Greek into "poor Southern white." Jordan's social and intellectual legacy had a considerable impact within certain small circles of the Southern Baptist Convention and beyond, especially through the work of perhaps his most famous convert and disciple, Millard Fuller, who founded the now well known Christian movement, Habitat for Humanity.

Although Koinonia grew up quite independently of The Catholic Worker, Jordan and his community heard of Dorothy Day quite early on, and admired their Gospel-based way of life. The admiration was mutual, as *The Catholic Worker* began running stories on Koinonia, and publicizing the pecan sales that enabled the fragile interracial community to survive (*CW* 6/1957). The collaboration reached a kind of climax in April 1957, when Dorothy Day spent Holy Saturday night on guard at Koinonia and her station wagon was hit by shotgun fire.

The Koinonia experience and its aftermath was important for several reasons. It brought into admiring contact with the Catholic Worker two very different minority Protestant groups that previously had had little contact with Catholics: conservative southern white evangelical Protestants like Clarence Jordan and Will Campbell, and African-American Protestants. Most southern evangelical Protestants, if they knew any Catholics at all, had never encountered Catholics like Dorothy Day; and to some degree the lack of knowledge was mutual. Yet there was, I think, an unusual affinity between these people and Day because they were, like the Catholic Workers, traditional in their theology and spirituality but radical in their engagement with social justice. It is important to stress that socially active conservative evangelical Baptists and others at that time were themselves a very rare minority, especially in the South—clearly dissenters within their own tradition. Yet, they may have intuitively sensed in the Catholic Worker something that resonated with their own heritage of intense biblicism and evangelical fervor. One conservative Baptist was quoted as saying that he'd lived his whole life among fundamentalist Protestants, but that Dorothy Day was the only *genuine* fundamentalist he had ever known because she was the only one who took Matthew 25 completely literally.

The other category of southern Protestants who came to admire Day and the Catholic Workers, even if they didn't completely understand them either, was African-American Protestants. Prior to the 1950s, most of the African-Americans who experienced or knew of the Catholic Worker were Catholics, members of a minority within a minority. But by the 1940s at least some black Protestants had begun to encounter Day and the Catholic Workers in connection with movements for civil rights and racial justice. I have been unable to discover many published reactions to Day or the Catholic Worker in black Protestant sources, but there is evidence that those blacks who encountered Day and the Workers in the civil rights movement were surprised and impressed. By the 1960s Dorothy Day had become a fixture in civil rights activity, and her commentary on Martin Luther King, Jr.'s death is a superb tribute to those many connections that had developed (*CW* 4/1968).

The story of various evangelical Protestant responses to Dorothy Day should include the development, beginning in the 1970s, of the newer evangelical Protestant movements that explicitly adopted the kind of commitments to social justice and social reform that had earlier taken root in liberal Protestant communities but had previously been dismissed in evangelical circles. The most prominent of several of these like-minded evangelical movements was the Sojourners community in Washington, DC, and its related journal. It is fair to say that Sojourners performed something of the same historical function within evangelical Protestantism that the Catholic Worker has done within Catholicism, i.e., bringing more critical social and economic perspectives to a religious community that once stood rather firmly for the status quo.

Sojourners and other evangelical social activists early on expressed their admiration for Dorothy Day. Although they did not share her Catholic commitments, she was a model of how to engage in radical action for social justice while remaining committed to Christian faith.

Shortly after its founding in 1971, *Sojourners* referred favorably to Dorothy Day and encouraged its readers to learn more about her. In 1976 it printed an interview with her that suggested connections with *Sojourners*' own concerns, and other references appeared as well. After Dorothy's death in 1980 the attention devoted to Day became even more extensive. By 1982 it was referring to Day as a "saint," and on the Catholic Worker's 50th anniversary, in May 1983, the magazine's editorial entitled "Thank God for the Catholic Worker," concluded, "For us at *Sojourners* the Worker's 50th birthday is an occasion for us to express our love and appreciation for a publication and a community without which ours might not exist."

This kind of admiration among socially active Protestants suggests the ways in which what had once been very significant religious differences had diminished since the 1960s, and a more ecumenical religious situation reflecting changes on all sides had begun to develop. Increasingly, Christians who shared similar social concerns found connections across denominational lines and the divisions *within* the various traditions became in some ways deeper than those between like-minded adherents of each tradition.

In the 1960s, the place of Dorothy Day and the Catholic Worker in the anti-Vietnam War movement brought it into further contact not only with venerable Protestant pacifists like A.J. Muste, but with more prominent mainstream antiwar Protestant clergy like Robert McAfee Brown, William Sloane Coffin, and Richard John Neuhaus (who was at that time still a Protestant, before his conversion to Catholicism). While few of these figures endorsed the Catholic Worker's entire interpretation of the social implications of Christian faith, many admired Dorothy Day herself as a pioneer of Catholic social action. Indeed, there was some tendency among antiwar Protestants in the 1960s, as among some sectors of the Catholic left of the time, to view Day as slightly out-of-date, a kind of John the Baptist of Catholic social action who had been important primarily in preparing the way for more political and sweeping forms of social action to come. Perhaps there was also, more subtly, some tendency among male clerical and lay activists of many denominations to patronize Dorothy Day and to ignore the side of her work that had always focused on hospitality, family, and community building, which were much less exciting than movement activism.

Still, on the whole it is fair to say that knowledge and appreciation of Day spread more widely in Protestant circles beginning in the

1960s. Interest in her work has even been a significant stimulus to ecumenical conversation focused not around doctrine but around questions of lay Christians' role and responsibility in the world. This admiration has extended across many of the barriers that have divided Protestants themselves. The liberal Protestant *Christian Century*, which once doubted the staying power of Day and the Workers, increasingly reflected on her surprising impact within the American Catholic Church. As early as 1963, Elizabeth Haselden wrote in the *Christian Century* of "the luminous mind and spirit of Dorothy Day,"and called her "the heart of the Catholic Worker movement." She also spoke favorably of the "miracles" that the Worker had worked in the inner cities over the years—"miracles which quietly demonstrate the primacy of the spirit, the power of ideas, and the redeeming quality of merciful acts." By 1980, at the time of Dorothy Day's death, the *Century* could comment even more positively on what had once been for Protestants the most troubling feature of Day and the Worker movement: its Catholic religious traditionalism. It cited Stanley Vishnewski's remark that Dorothy Day was one of the most conservative Catholic lay leaders in the United States, yet nevertheless hailed her for developing perhaps the most influential "theology of the laity" within American Catholicism.

By the late 1980s, then, Dorothy Day had begun to be regarded as one of the seminal religious figures of twentieth century American history, and it did not much matter if the historian were Catholic, mainstream Protestant, or evangelical Protestant. Catholic historians as diverse as David O'Brien, Jay Dolan and Philip Gleason all praised Day and her movement, although one can detect differences in tone and emphasis in their assessment of her. The most prominent mainstream Protestant historian, Martin Marty, a Lutheran, treated Dorothy Day extensively in the second volume of *Modern American Religion: The Noise of Conflict, 1919-1941* as the most important Catholic figure of the Great Depression. In assessing the Catholic Worker, he said, "in Depression times it was a significant alternative to ordinary Catholicism, Protestant realism, or the apathy and sullenness into which so many lapsed."(Marty 1986: 340) One of the most prominent conservative evangelical Protestant historians, Mark Noll, also lauded the movement, though with a more critical parenthesis.

He said that Day "displayed an unusual kind of piety that combined absolute, [even simplistic], fidelity to Catholic teaching with a passionate desire to bring the message of the Gospel to bear upon the suffering of the modern world."(Noll 1992: 516)

We are now up to contemporary times. My own highly impressionistic reading is that Dorothy Day is still more widely known and better understood among American Catholics than among Protestants or among those without much knowledge or interest in religion. Perhaps, as Catholic Worker Tom Cornell said in the discussion following this paper at the Marquette conference, Dorothy may really be *best* known among "really old Communists"! There is probably some sense in which she remains a distinctively Catholic figure, associated for Catholics with a critical era that saw their transformation from an isolated subculture into an integral part of the American mainstream; some associated with the Catholic Worker would say that integration has been too complete. Dorothy's thoroughgoing "Americanism" makes her seem part of the Church's "updating," but her association with their traditional religion reminds Catholics of the distance between what the Church upholds and what their society practices. Dorothy Day has particular things to say to Catholics about their history, experience, faith, and habits that are not nearly as accessible to Protestants. I find now, however, that I have to explain the opening scene in the confessional in *The Long Loneliness* to my Catholic as well as my Protestant students. The scene seems nearly as strange to young Catholics as it does to Protestants, as do many of the old-time Catholic Workers' relations to the saints.

But for contemporary American Protestants who know of her, Dorothy Day is an equally challenging figure on religious as well as social grounds. Many Protestants are eager to affirm individual conscience and autonomy, and even social action, but they have more trouble with such matters as discipline, prayer, and especially the centrality of church and community. Day shows, I think, the strength of many of those "Catholic" values that some forms of American Protestant theology and tradition have tended to slight or diminish. Many Protestants now recognize the need for some of these lost, or half-lost practices and find in the witness of Dorothy Day and other Workers a form of Catholic Christianity with which they can connect.

So: how will history view her? With high regard, certainly. But I suspect with considerable puzzlement as well. Dorothy Day does not fit many of the ordinary categories of historical analysis. She was passionately religious, yet open to a great variety of people and ideas.

She is one of those people who belongs to a particular religious community, yet transcends that community to become a possession of humanity at large. She is most certainly a figure of the Church, but as I have tried to suggest here, she belongs to the *whole* Christian church, and not simply its Roman Catholic portion, much as Martin Luther King belongs to the whole Christian Church and not simply African-American Baptists, though he certainly will always have a special place in their history and their hearts, just as Dorothy Day certainly will always have for Catholics. We still have not resolved all the serious differences among the great traditions of Christianity, but figures like Dorothy Day may be one way to bridge the gap.

In recent years, as we know, there has been considerable talk and some controversy about whether Dorothy Day should be declared a saint by the Church. I do not want to comment on that discussion except to note that classical Protestant tradition emphasizes that the "saints" are all who have received faith, and it recognizes that we are all simultaneously saints and sinners. Dorothy frequently said that "all is grace," and in this sense, at least, she is surely already among the saints of God.

Who knows? Perhaps in generations to come, as the church struggles to recover its once-cherished unity, Dorothy Day will come to be regarded as one of the true "mothers of the church." Not just a mother of the Roman Catholic Church, either, but of the whole Christian Church, Catholic and Protestant, Roman and Orthodox. And just as the "fathers of the church" belong to Catholics and Protestants alike, so perhaps will Dorothy Day, who lived and worked at an historic time when women began to be fully appreciated, for the first time, as the true leaders of Christian faith they have actually been all along. If that day ever comes, *all* Christians will have a powerful model of what they hope, by God's grace, to be.

The Catholic Worker and Socially Engaged Buddhism: A Dialogue

John Sniegocki

University of Notre Dame

My goal in this paper is to bring the Catholic Worker movement into dialogue with several representatives of what has been termed "socially engaged Buddhism." Socially engaged Buddhists, often simply called "engaged Buddhists," are persons concerned with exploring the significance of the Buddhist tradition in response to pressing contemporary issues such as violence, social injustice, and ecological crisis. These movements within Buddhism have much in common with the Catholic Worker movement. Both Catholic Workers and engaged Buddhists are committed, for example, to nonviolence and to performing what Christians call the "works of mercy," both express appreciation of the intimate connections between spirituality and social action, and both highlight overall social visions emphasizing social justice, community, decentralization, appropriate technology, and a closeness to the land.

While having these many similarities, the social visions of the Catholic Worker movement and of engaged Buddhism arise from very different religious frameworks. This paper provides a brief overview of these frameworks, explores how they shape the social outlook of each tradition, then brings these traditions into dialogue, suggesting several ways that each could be enhanced through conversation with the other.

For the Catholic Worker movement, all activity is properly to be centered upon the following of Jesus Christ, the incarnation of a loving and saving God. "The aim of the Catholic Worker movement," says the Catholic Worker statement of "Aims and Means," "is to live in accordance with the justice and charity of Jesus Christ."(*CW* 5/1990: 5) Catholic Worker commitment to nonviolence and hospitality and concern for social justice flows from the teachings of Jesus and from belief in the presence of the Spirit of Jesus in each person.

With regard to the works of mercy, Dorothy Day wrote: "When the stranger comes to us to be fed we know, because Christ told us so, that inasmuch as we have fed one of His hungry ones we have fed Him."(*CW* 5/1936: 4) To do violence to, to exploit, or to simply ignore the needs of any human person is to do so such a deed to Christ.

Buddhism, in contrast, has a less immediately apparent ground for its social ethics. Buddhists do not profess a belief in a God whose will could serve as the basis for ethical guidance.[1] Moreover, whereas much of Christian ethics is grounded upon the centrality of the human person as created in the image of God, Buddhists proclaim a doctrine of "no-self"*(anatman* in Sanskrit) that at first glance also seems to provide little grounding for social ethics. Yet as we will see Buddhist ethics rest precisely upon "no-self" and related concepts or, more accurately, upon the experience underlying such concepts.

For the Buddha, the most fundamental question facing humanity is the question of human suffering. "Suffering," said the Buddha, "is my teaching...The cessation of suffering is my teaching."(Davids and Carpenter 1947: 189; Saddhatisa 1970: 63) Buddha viewed questions such as whether or not God exists and other questions of a metaphysical nature as leading to unhelpful speculation. When asked such questions, it is said that Buddha would generally maintain silence. On one occasion he compared the asking of these questions to the situation of a person who is shot with an arrow and who before removing the arrow wants to discuss from what direction the arrow came, what kind of wood the bow was likely made of, and what kind of feathers were on the arrow's tip. The proper response, the Buddha suggests, is instead to simply remove the arrow, to put an end to the suffering (Goldstein 1983: 58).

In his experience of enlightenment the Buddha believed that he had discovered the origins of suffering and the way to end it, which he encapsulated in the Four Noble Truths that are at the heart of Buddhist teaching. These truths are

1) Life as generally experienced is characterized by suffering or dissatisfaction;

2) The cause of this suffering is (self-centered) desire or attachment;

3) There is a way to end self-centered desire and hence end suffering; and

> 4) The way beyond suffering is the Noble Eightfold Path, a combination of moral action, mindfulness, and meditation that gives rise to liberating insight into the true nature of reality.[2]

The most fundamental claim of the Buddha is that suffering is due to attachment or desire caused by a false understanding of who we are. We view ourselves as separate, distinct selves and make these selves the center of our universe. Trying to find happiness and security for such a self is, however, a futile task. Thomas Merton states that the Buddha realized that "ego-desire," this attachment to self, "can never culminate in happiness, fulfillment, and peace, because it is a fracture which cuts us off from the ground of reality in which truth and peace are found."(Merton 1968: 85-86) A life centered upon self, asserts the Buddha, gives rise to greed, hatred, anger, pride, jealousy and other ills. The wisdom resulting from the Noble Eightfold Path consists in part of the experiential realization that all reality, including the human person, is in fact devoid of "self" *(anatman).* Later Mahayana Buddhist philosophers would stress that all reality is characterized by "emptiness" *(sunyata).* The experiential realization of "no-self"or "emptiness" is said to liberate one from all selfishness, fear, and anxiety and to issue forth in compassion and lovingkindness. "When your mind is liberated," says Zen Master Thich Nhat Hanh, "your heart floods with compassion."(Nhat Hanh 1975: 58)

What is crucial of course is how these terms such as "no-self"or "emptiness" are understood. If taken literally, especially in their English translations, and if understood merely on a conceptual level, such terms could seem to provide a basis for nihilism and serve to undercut moral action. If the assertion that "all reality is empty," for example, is mistakenly understood as claiming that all of what appears to be reality is ultimately an illusion, then even killing would not be problematic because there is really no one killing and no one being killed.[3] Buddha himself seemed to realize such dangers, claiming that to get caught in the *concept* of "no-self"is in fact in some ways even more dangerous than being caught in the concept of "self". (Nhat Hanh 1995: 55, 160) What "no-self"ultimately points to is an experiential realization and not a concept, an experiential realization that words are not able to adequately express.

However inadequate words may be, they are nonetheless necessary for human communication. Therefore, phrases such as "no-self"are used. In attempting to provide insight into what the term "no-self" seeks to convey, many contemporary Buddhist masters and commentators stress that it points not to nihilism but rather to the fundamental interconnectedness or interdependence of all being. Thich Nhat Hanh (1995) states

> According to the teachings of Buddhism, it is important to look deeply into things and discover their nature of impermanence *(anitya)* and non-self *(anatman)*. Impermanence and non-self are not negative. They are the doors that open to the true nature of reality...Non-self means...interbeing. Because everything is made of everything else, nothing can be by itself alone. [He speaks for example of a flower, which can be seen to be made up of non-flower elements such as clouds, rain, sunshine, soil, the microorganisms that broke down nutrients in the soil for the flower, and so on.] Non-self is also interpenetration, because everything contains everything else. Non-self is also interdependence...Each thing depends on all other things to be...Nothing can be by itself alone. It has to inter-be with all other things. This is non-self. (Nhat Hanh 1995: 183-84)[4]

Nhat Hanh stresses that interdependence or interbeing as a concept or a philosophy is not what Buddhism is about. Thus, his example of the flower should only be seen as dimly pointing to the reality of which he speaks. Concepts as such don't have the power to heal and to bring about the kind of fundamental transformation that Buddhism seeks. Only deep experience arising from mindfulness and meditation can do that. Such experience is viewed as supremely liberating. "When you touch the *reality* of non-self," Nhat Hanh states, "you touch at the same time nirvana, the ultimate dimension of being, and become free from fear, attachment, illusion, and craving."(Hanh 1995: 185) "Buddhahood, or enlightenment, is no-self," states another contemporary Buddhist master. "It is total...peace, openness, selflessness, oneness, joy."(Thondup 1996: 20) Such masters stress that this experience gives rise to "a new way of relating to others, a way imbued with compassion, love, and sympathy with all that live." (Thien-An 1975: 7)

"No-self"or "emptiness" understood in terms of interbeing does not therefore imply that people and other beings really don't exist; it rather means that people and all beings don't exist as individual, self-contained entities, isolated "selves" separate from the wholeness of reality.[5]

Highlighting the Buddhist concern for wholeness, Thomas Merton stated

> Christian charity seeks to realize oneness with the other "in Christ." Buddhist compassion seeks to heal the brokenness of division and illusion and to find wholeness...in Nirvana—the void which is Absolute Reality and Absolute Love. In either case the highest illumination of love is an explosion of the power of Love's evidence in which all the psychological limits of an "experiencing" subject are dissolved and what remains is the transcendent clarity of love itself, realized in the ego-less subject in a mystery beyond comprehension but not beyond consent. (Merton 1968:86-87)

While Buddhism affirms interbeing and interdependence and even speaks at times of the "oneness" of reality, it is important to recognize that this does not imply a type of monism in which all is merged into an undifferentiated whole. Rather, union and particularity are affirmed simultaneously. Christopher Ives explains

> Zen claims that *prajna* [wisdom] is the ability to merge with the other without the least separation of subject and object. But one does not stop there, for one then emerges from that unobjectifiable unity and sees the other as an 'other,' discriminating and reflecting as necessary, though not losing awareness of the not-two-ness of the merging. In other words, I experience myself and the other non-dualistically; *not one* and *not two*. I am fully me and you are fully you, and yet at the same time we are inseparable from each other....Zen...recognize[s] the very real existence of each individual as something unique, unique through—not despite—interrelationship and interdependence with others. (Ives 1992: 46, 122; Aitken 1994: 15)

This experience and understanding of the nature of reality as "empty," devoid of "self," or "interdependent" forms the basis for Buddhist ethics. From the start, ethics has been central to Buddhism. "Right speech," "right action," and "right livelihood," for example, are among the components of the Noble Eightfold Path. At the core of Buddhist ethics are the five moral precepts *(pancasila)* that all Buddhists are expected to adhere to. These include not killing, not stealing, not lying or using false speech, not misusing sexuality, and not using intoxicants that cloud the mind (Nhat Hanh 1993). Stated positively, these precepts entail commitments to nonviolence, generosity, truthfulness, chasteness and sexual fidelity, and mindfulness. Most schools of Buddhism also stress the four "divine abodings" *(brahmaviharas)* or "sublime virtues." (Dharmasiri 1989: ch. 5; Salzberg 1995) These virtues include lovingkindness *(maitri),* compassion *(karuna),* sympathetic joy *(mudita)* and equanimity *(upeksa).* These terms are all rich in meaning. Lovingkindness refers to an attitude of goodwill and active concern for the welfare of all beings. Compassion entails being aware of and open to others' suffering and seeking to help overcome such suffering. Sympathetic joy involves sharing in the joy of others, not being envious or seeking to demean others in comparison with oneself. Equanimity refers to a detached calmness of mind that allows one to be fully present to situations without being overcome by mental states such as attachment, anger, greed, or sadness.

In Mahayana Buddhism, one of the two major existing strands of Buddhism, the religious and ethical ideal is contained in the figure of the "bodhisattva." The bodhisattva is one who vows to work selflessly and endlessly for the welfare of all sentient beings until every being has realized its true nature and is freed from suffering (Dharmasiri 1989: ch. 10).

With regard to an ethic for the organization of society, early Buddhism set forth the ideal of a righteous ruler, selected by consent of the people. A primary duty of the ruler is to assure that the basic needs of all persons in the kingdom are met. Through the meeting of such needs it is believed that social harmony will be fostered. In Buddhist scriptures crime and violence are seen as resulting largely from poverty and the maldistribution of economic goods. For example, the Cakkravatti Sihanada Sutta states: "From not giving to the destitute, poverty grew rife; from poverty growing rife, stealing increased; from the spread of stealing, violence grew apace; from the growth of violence, the destruction of life became common."(Sivaraksa 1990: 84) Qualities of the ideal ruler highlighted in Buddhist literature include generosity, morality, self-restraint, patience, and nonviolence.[6] Despite this social vision, Buddhism historically has been stronger in the realm of personal morality than in social ethics. In practice, the Buddhist leadership has often become allied with rulers whose conduct has strongly contradicted fundamental Buddhist principles. Rarely has prophetic criticism been demonstrated. This is a critique that is made by contemporary engaged Buddhists with regard to their own tradition (Sivaraksa 1992: 68). What such Buddhists emphasize, however, is that the tradition in fact contains rich resources for social ethics. Social concern, they assert, should follow naturally from the desire to alleviate suffering and to foster the welfare of all beings. Specific moral precepts such as not killing and moral virtues such as compassion likewise provide a strong grounding for social ethical concern and action.

Engaged Buddhist Leaders and Movements

Thich Nhat Hanh coined the term "engaged Buddhism." A Vietnamese Zen Master who rose to prominence as a leader of the Buddhist peace movement during the Vietnam War, Nhat Hanh founded the Order of Interbeing, a religious order of monastics and laypersons committed to engaged Buddhist principles. He was was also instrumental in founding a School of Youth for Social Service in Vietnam. Students of the School engaged in work for peace during the Vietnam War and undertook projects such as caring for orphans, rebuilding war-destroyed villages, and providing literacy training and religious and practical education in the countryside.

Members of the Buddhist peace movement were attacked by both sides during the war. Numerous colleagues of Nhat Hanh were imprisoned, tortured, and killed. Nhat Hanh himself was forced into exile, and now lives in a Buddhist community that he founded in rural France. Through his writings and speaking tours he has become one of the most well-known Buddhists in western Europe and North America. Persons from a variety of nations are now associated with the Order of Interbeing, both as core community members and as part of a large extended community of persons who formally commit themselves to the precepts of the Order.[7]

In his commentary on the five central Buddhist precepts, Nhat Hanh focuses attention both on the precepts' personal and social implications, dimensions which he views as being inextricably intertwined. In his discussion of the precept of not killing, for example, he highlights both the need to overcome the seeds of hatred and anger in oneself, and the importance of confronting the problem of killing as systematized in contemporary forms of militarism and in structural injustice (1998: 13-19). He interprets the precept against stealing not only as forbidding theft and as encouraging the virtue of generosity, but also as requiring a commitment to "prevent others from profiting from human suffering or the suffering of other species on Earth."(1998: 20) The precept thus involves an active commitment to social and even inter-species justice.[8]

Other engaged Buddhists provide interpretations of the social significance of core elements of the Buddhist tradition similar to that of Thich Hhat Hanh. Sulak Sivaraksa, a prominent Buddhist social activist in Thailand and co-founder of the International Network of Engaged Buddhists, has stressed the importance of the Buddhist precepts in his work for political and economic democracy in his country. Like Nhat Hanh, he stresses central Buddhist themes of selflessness, interdependence, and compassion, and asserts the importance of mindfulness and meditation as the basis of ethical life. Like Nhat Hanh too he provides a broad social as well as personal and interpersonal interpretation of the Buddhist precepts (Sivaraksa 1992; Nhat Hanh 1998: 110-114; Queen and King 1996: 195-235). With regard to the first two precepts, forbidding the taking of life and stealing, Sulak highlights the many ways in which killing and stealing are in fact embedded in unjust national and international political and economic systems (1992: 73-76). On the basis of the third precept, which prohibits the misuse of sexuality, Sulak argues against the existence of male dominance in society and in the family (1992: 77-78). He devotes particular attention to problems in Thailand such as the widespread commercial sexual exploitation of women, largely by foreign tourists, but suggests that this represents only a more blatant example of the exploitation that women face in numerous other forms in daily life. The precept concerning truthfulness Sulak uses to engage in a critique of advertising, which stimulates false needs, and the media, which he sees as being dominated by the government and by the wealthy and as confusing people with false information (1992: 77-78). With regard to the precept against the use of intoxicants, he suggests that attention needs to be given to the underlying factors which contribute to substance abuse, such as economic inequality, unemployment, meaningless forms of employment, and the destruction of communal bonds and spiritual traditions that result from the pursuit of so-called "economic development." (1992: 78-79)

Overall, Sulak is very critical of the existing social order, particularly global capitalism, which he believes reinforces the fundamental "three poisons" that Buddhism seeks to overcome: greed, hatred, and ignorance/delusion. He highlights the need for an alternative form of society based on spiritual values, the meeting of basic needs, appropriate technology, popular participation, respect for the rights of women and minorities, and ecological harmony. This alternative would build upon the best in traditional cultural values and practices while at the same time allowing for criticism of such practices when they undermine human dignity (1992: chs. 3-5).

The Sarvodaya Shramadana Movement of Sri Lanka has worked for four decades to bring social and spiritual renewal through an alternative model of society similar to that envisioned by Sulak (Bond in Queen and King 1996: 121-146; Macy 1983; Goulet 1981). Founded in 1958 by A.T. Ariyaratne, Sarvodaya, which translates as "the awakening of all" or "the uplift of all," is a village based development movement founded upon Buddhist and Gandhian principles. The movement centers upon the activity of work camps, called *shramadana*, in which people join together to share their labor in various projects benefitting the community: digging wells, planting gardens, building latrines, building roads, etc. During the work camp Buddhist-inspired teachings are shared, often through song and drama, and Buddhist practices such as lovingkindness meditation are taught. The dual goals of the movement are personal awakening and social uplift, understood as having an integral connection. By sharing and working together for the general welfare participants progress in their spiritual development. "The struggle for external liberation," says Ariyaratne, "is a struggle for inner liberation from greed, hatred and ignorance at the same time." (Ariyaratne 1978: 131-135; 1982: 16; 1996)[9]

For the Sarvodaya movement, which seeks to reconstruct society based on Buddhist inspired values, the western model of economic development is viewed as something to be avoided rather than pursued. "In production-centered societies," says Ariyaratne, "the total perspective of human personality and sustainable relationships between [humans] and nature is lost sight of....The higher ideals of human personality and social values are disregarded."[10] With regard to western societies, he states that "we don't want to reach where they are. Instead we believe in a spiritual foundation, moral relationships, small economic and political organizations in a highly decentralized but coordinated way." (Ariyaratne 1996: 93-94) He sets forth the ideal of a village-based society characterized by "nonviolence, sharing, smallness, decentralization, relevant technologies, production by the masses, and unity." (Bond 1996: 132)

During the 1960s and 1970s the activities of Sarvodaya spread throughout much of the Sri Lankan countryside. By 1985 it was active in over 8,000 villages, about one-third of the villages in the country, and had a staff of thousands of volunteers. It had received international acclaim as one of the most widespread and successful grassroots development movements of the century. Building upon its work camps, and aided by funding from foreign donors, it was able to undertake a wide array of projects in education, health care, agriculture, and appropriate technology.

Since the early 1980s, however, Sarvodaya has suffered various setbacks. These have included the impact of ethnic violence which has torn apart much of Sri Lanka, attacks on the movement by the Sri Lankan government, and a major reduction in funding from foreign aid agencies.[11] Despite these setbacks, however, the movement continues its work, seeking to foster reconciliation and alternative forms of development in its troubled country. "Sarvodaya," Ariyaratne recently stated, "will go on. Every village is organized, and our goal is to double the number of places where we work.... In all our Sarvodaya communities our activities are going on despite the prevailing atmosphere."(1996: 96-97)

These three examples provide a good sense of the views and activities of contemporary engaged Buddhists. Numerous other examples could be cited, such as the involvement of engaged Buddhists in the anti-dictatorship struggle in Burma, the efforts to regain the freedom of Tibet, and efforts to improve the plight of untouchables in India. In the U.S. engaged Buddhists have been involved in the peace and ecology movements and have contributed to the founding of hospices for persons suffering from AIDS. They have also established meditation groups in prisons and have worked to provide employment for the homeless. Underlying these various forms of social involvement has been a central emphasis upon the daily practice of spiritual disciplines.

Dialogue: Helping Each Other to Discover Hidden Jewels

Many similarities in both core values and overall social vision exist between engaged Buddhists and members of the Catholic Worker movement. Broad similarities include affirmation of the need for spiritual transformation, commitment to nonviolence, an emphasis on love and compassion, and recognition of the links between spirituality, "works of mercy," and concern for social justice. In overall social vision shared emphases on decentralization, community, appropriate technology, and rural and urban cooperative grassroots projects also exist. To suggest that there are similarities is not to claim that the values and visions are simply interchangeable. I would argue, however, that major areas of overlap do clearly exist and that fruitful dialogue between the members of these traditions is possible.[12]

In a dialogue between engaged Buddhists and Catholic Workers, there are several major areas in which I believe Catholic Workers could be enriched.

Mindfulness and Meditation

Even engaged Buddhists who are known primarily as activists such as Sulak Sivaraksa stress that mindfulness and meditation are the "most important" elements of Buddhism (1992: 72). What is meant by mindfulness? Fundamentally, mindfulness consists of being fully present to the present moment. Without mindfulness, Thich Nhat Hanh suggests, one is not truly alive. "Mindfulness is the miracle which can call back in a flash our dispersed mind and restore it to wholeness.... Mindfulness...makes it possible to fully live each minute of life."(1987: 14-15) "Each act," Nhat Hnah declares, "must be carried out in mindfulness. Each act is a rite, a ceremony...Does the word 'rite' seem too solemn? I use that word to jolt you into the realization of the life-and-death matter of awareness."(1987: 24) When washing the dishes, for example, Nhat Hanh suggests that one seek to give the same care to the task as they would if they were giving the baby Jesus or Buddha a bath (1987: 61). If you're not able to wash the dishes mindfully, he asserts, neither are you likely to be able to drink your tea mindfully or do anything else mindfully. Mindfulness, as he understands it, is the heart of the Buddhist precepts. By being fully present and being fully aware one gradually comes to perceive more and more the true nature of reality, reality which is otherwise clouded by the incessant chatter of our minds and self-centered thoughts.

The Buddhist tradition suggests a variety of ways in which the practice of mindfulness can be fostered. Many methods center upon awareness of breath. The ability to be mindful throughout the day in each task is viewed as a capacity that one builds slowly, over time and with practice. It is closely linked to the practice of daily meditation, which both strengthens mindfulness and is strengthened by it.

The spirit which perhaps best characterizes Nhat Hanh's teachings on mindfulness is that of joyful simplicity. While being deeply aware of the reality of suffering, he stresses that through mindfulness one is nonetheless also able to appreciate the beauty of life. "Life is filled with suffering," he states, "but it is also filled with many wonders, like the blue sky, the sunshine, the eyes of a baby. To suffer is not enough. We must also be in touch with the wonders of life."(1987: ch.1) He stresses that it has been his own practice of mindfulness and meditation that has sustained him in his many years of service, teaching, and work on behalf of justice and peace (1995: 3).

The ability to be truly present is of crucial importance in the life and ministries of the Catholic Worker. To offer hospitality and live in community necessitates such presence and attentiveness. Through mindfulness one can be more truly aware that the others one encounters are in fact Christ and can be able to respond accordingly. Practices such as mindfulness and meditation, by enabling persons to get in touch with their spiritual depths, could play a major role in enabling Gospel faithfulness and in preventing the problems of burnout that are so common among Catholic Workers.

To appreciate and highlight the importance of spiritual disciplines, one of course does not need to be Buddhist. It was in fact Christian spiritual practices of prayer, Bible reading, participation in the Eucharist, and participation in silent retreats which enabled Dorothy Day to persevere in her lifelong ministry.[13] What is striking about engaged Buddhist movements, however, is that spiritual disciplines almost always play a central role. In my experience, this has not always been the case in Catholic Worker communities. Moreover, in engaged Buddhist movements emphasis is placed upon detailed spiritual training and spiritual formation, drawing upon methods of meditation and mindfulness perfected and taught for thousands of years. This training is designed to provide people with the concrete skills and practices needed to be able to participate in the world in a loving manner, without being overcome by the world. Greater attention to such training and formation (including for Catholic Workers training in both specifically Christian spiritual practices and Christian adaptations of Buddhist practices) could I believe greatly enrich the Catholic Worker movement.

If through encounter with engaged Buddhists Catholic Workers are enabled to come to a deepened appreciation of the importance of spiritual practices in their daily lives, including traditional Christian spiritual practices, Thich Nhat Hanh would be very happy. In his book *Living Buddha, Living Christ* he expresses his deep wish that as one fruit of the encounter with Buddhism non-Buddhists may be able to rediscover the jewels in their own traditions.[14]

Broadened conception of nonviolence

A second area in which I believe Catholic Workers could be enriched through dialogue with engaged Buddhism concerns the holistic understanding of nonviolence that engaged Buddhism contains, an understanding which views nonviolence as pertaining to all areas of life. Vegetarianism, for example, is generally seen to follow from engaged Buddhist principles. This is so both because of the benefits of vegetarianism to humans, such as better health, the freeing of grain and other foods for possible consumption by the hungry, and various ecological benefits, and also because of respect for the life of animals.[15] Buddhism seeks at the same time to expand the notion of nonviolence to include respect for nature more generally.

This respect, like respect for the lives of humans and animals, is grounded in Buddhist experience of interdependence or interbeing. Nhat Hanh uses theistic language in his dialogue with Christians:

> To take good care of yourself and to take good care of living beings and of the environment is the best way to love God. This love is possible when there is the understanding that you are not separate from other beings or the environment. This understanding cannot be merely intellectual. It must be experiential, the insight gained by deep touching and deep looking in a daily life of prayer, contemplation, and meditation. (1995: 112)

"We are imprisoned in our small selves," Nhat Hanh says, "thinking only of some comfortable conditions for this small self, while we destroy our large self. If we want to change the situation, we must begin by being our true selves. To be our true selves we have to be the river, the forest, and the ozone layer."(Kotler 1997: 164) While such experience of interdependence may not provide precise detail for how to best balance care for the environment and meeting human needs, it clearly fosters an attitude of humility and respect and a willingness to accept limits to consumption which are direly needed for such balance to be found.

Again, encounter with such ideas and experiences in Buddhism may help Christians to more deeply explore their own tradition for hidden resources. Dorothy Day, for example, often spoke of the "mystical body of Christ." Generally this notion has been understood as only applying to people, and often only to Christians or even just Roman Catholic Christians. Nhat Hanh, along with several contemporary Christian theologians, suggests an understanding of the body of Christ that explicitly includes all of creation (1995: 31; Habito: 130). This suggestion, I believe, is very valuable and worthy of more extensive consideration and elaboration.

Deepened appreciation of spiritual disciplines and a broader understanding of nonviolence are thus two ways in which I think the Catholic Worker movement, and Christianity more generally, could be enriched through dialogue with engaged Buddhism. There are also several ways in which I believe engaged Buddhists could learn from the Catholic Worker:

Deepened social dimension

It has been in part through encounter with Christianity that engaged Buddhism has been led to rediscover and reemphasize the social significance of Buddhism. Many engaged Buddhist leaders acknowledge their debt to Christianity in motivating them to explore more deeply the social resources that Buddhism contains (Queen and King 1996: 21).

One area in which I believe the Catholic Worker could further add to this encounter is through its emphasis on social analysis. When one reads "The Aims and Means of the Catholic Worker Movement," an emphasis on social analysis is quickly apparent. After introductory comments, the first major section of the statement contains broad analysis of the current state of the world in areas such as "economics," "labor," "politics," and "the arms race." Such analysis is often further pursued in articles in *The Catholic Worker*. By contrast, engaged Buddhist writings often remain very much on the level of affirming general principles or values without engaging in detailed social analysis. Some engaged Buddhists acknowledge this weakness. Sulak Sivaraksa states

> Buddhism is a very strong ethical system, supportive of peace. But there is a weakness: strength in personal commitment is combined with a certain weakness in my understanding of the silent mechanisms of evil...The major question is exactly how the ethical inspiration of Buddhism might enlighten politics by being courageous enough to question social structures, not merely the individual acts of people or their governments. (1991: 164)

Sulak speaks positively of various Christian groups who have engaged in more detailed social analysis and suggests that Buddhists can learn from them (in Nhat Hanh 1998: 111). Similarly, Christopher Ives speaks of the need to augment *prajna* [wisdom] with social analysis, creating what he calls "informed wisdom."(1992: ch.5)

A second area in which I believe the Catholic Worker could enrich Buddhism is through its understanding of the need for a "preferential option for the poor," a phrase used in the Catholic Worker's statement of "Aims and Means." Buddhists are generally resistant to such language, fearing that it fosters dualism (a rich vs. poor mentality) and often leads to action motivated by anger. Thich Nhat Hanh states

> In Latin America, liberation theologians speak of God's preference, or 'option,' for the poor, the oppressed, and the marginalized. But I do not think God wants us to take sides, even with the poor.... When we take sides, we misunderstand the will of God... Any dualistic response, any response motivated by anger, will only make the situation worse. (1995: 79-80)

I believe the Catholic Worker can seek to show how a preferential option for the poor is not an alternative to an affirmation of God's love for all persons, but is rather an integral part of the expression of such love. An option for the poor does not imply hatred of the rich or motivation by anger, but rather calls all, both rich and poor, to conversion and healing. By working to minimize or overcome structural injustice, an option for the poor can in fact serve to lessen the obstacles to more universal solidarity that currently exist. It should be acknowledged, however, that motivation by anger and hatred are indeed dangers in such an option. Buddhist insights into ways to transform and channel the energy of anger in positive directions, part of a very highly developed spiritual psychology in Buddhism, can be a very valuable contribution to Buddhist–Catholic Worker dialogue.[16]

Overall, I find both the Catholic Worker and engaged Buddhism to be very inspiring religious and social movements. It is my hope that the type of dialogue discussed in this paper will increasingly come to be reality. All of us, I believe, would benefit from such sharing.

Notes

[1] While not affirming the existence of God, neither does Buddha deny it. As we will discuss, he saw speculation on the existence or non-existence of God as unhelpful. Concerning Buddha's view of God, Thich Nhat Hanh (1995: 151) states: "The Buddha was not against God. He was only against notions of God that are mere mental constructions that do not correspond to reality, notions that prevent us from developing ourselves and touching ultimate reality."

[2] The Noble Eightfold Path consists of right understanding, right thought, right effort, right speech, right action, right livelihood, right mindfulness, and right concentration. For in-depth discussion of the Four Noble Truths and the Noble Eightfold Path, see Antony Fernando and Leonard Swidler, *Buddhism Made Plain: An Introduction for Christians and Jews* (Maryknoll, NY: Orbis Books, 1985).

[3] Zen master Robert Aitken (1984: 5-6, 17-18) states that this mistaken conceptual view of "no-self," is what allowed Japanese samurai to see no conflict between Zen and their acts of killing.

[4] Robert Aitken, in explaining no-self, sometimes speaks of a "multicentered self," another way of affirming the reality of interbeing. For example, in a dialogue with David Steindl-Rast, he states: "A person who has realized herself or himself as the great multicentered self—not just intellectually but through a deep experience—will naturally tend to practice what you're calling 'self-denial.' It's self-denial only from the perspective of the limited self. From the perspective of the multicentered self, it's really 'self-fulfillment.' Aitken and Steindl-Rast (1994:76) In attempting to explain 'no-self' in Christian terms, Nhat Hanh says: "God is within. You are, and yet you are not, but God is in you. This is interbeing. This is non-self." (1995: 168).

[5] Speaking of the Zen form of Buddhism, Christopher Ives explains that "Zen 'selfhood' is relational. All things 'co-arise dependently'; nothing can exist apart from the matrix of interrelationships constituting reality." (1992: 121) Even this way of phrasing it, however, is still inadequate. Ultimately, what Buddhism stresses is the need to transcend the very concepts of existence and non-existence. Thich Nhat Hanh (1995: 135) states: "We have to transcend notions like birth, death, being, and non-being. Reality is free from all notions." Robert Aitken (1994: 14) states: "The popular idea is that in Buddhism there is no self. A more complete expression would be that there is no self, and the self realizes this fact. To put it another way, no-self and self are complementary.... Existence and non-existence, self and no-self ...are complementarities, like the notion of light as waves and the notion of light as particles. Both notions are correct at the same time. But if we get stuck on light as particles, then we can't see it as waves. It we get stuck on matter as eternally substantial, then we can't see it as empty. It's important that we see into the emptiness in order to fully appreciate the substance."

[6] For a discussion of the early Buddhist vision of proper social organization and the traits of the ideal Buddhist ruler, see Gunapala Dharmasiri, *Fundamentals of Buddhist Ethics* (Antioch, CA: Golden Leaves, 1989: ch. 8). The ruler often cited as having come closest to the Buddhist ideal is the emperor Ashoka, who ruled in northern India in the 3rd century BCE. He is said to have forsaken a past of violent conquest and to have embraced nonviolence, ruling in a very benevolent

manner. Numerous "edicts of Ashoka" espousing nonviolence and describing provisions for the welfare of persons inhabiting his kingdom are inscribed in rocks and stone pillars dating from this period. For some additional detail concerning Ashoka, see Ives (1992: 8).

[7] For biographical information and discussion of the teachings of Thich Nhat Hanh, see Sallie King, "Thich Nhat Hanh and the Unified Buddhist Church: Nondualism in Action," in King and Queen (1996: 321-363). Nhat Hanh's books include: *The Miracle of Mindfulness: A Manual on Meditation*, (1987); *Being Peace* (1987); *Interbeing: Fourteen Guidelines for Engaged Buddhism* (1993); *Living Buddha, Living Christ* (1995); *For A Future To Be Possible: Commentaries on the Five Mindfulness Trainings* (1998).

[8] It is very important to stress here that the selflessness that engaged Buddhists speak of does not entail passivity or willingness to allow oneself or others to be exploited. Instead, the vision of selflessness that is affirmed is one which includes setting oneself actively against all that which causes harm, but seeking to do so in a nonego-centered way. Talk of "selflessness" is often criticized by feminist thinkers, who argue that such notions have historically (particularly in Christian-influenced societies) been harmful to women's well-being by leading to self-denigration, low self-esteem, and passivity in the face of abuse on the part of many women. For an explanation of why the Buddhist concept of "no-self" should not be seen as having such implications and should be seen as compatible with basic feminist insights, see Rita Gross' excellent book, *Buddhism After Patriarchy* (Albany, NY: SUNY Press, 1993), especially chapter 11 entitled "Gender and Egolessness: Feminist Comments on Basic Buddhist Teachings." Also helpful is Jack Kornfield, *A Path With Heart: A Guide Through the Perils and Promises of Spiritual Life* (New York: Bantam, 1993), especially chapter 14, "No Self or True Self?"

[9] The movement employs an interesting adaptation of the Four Noble Truths in explaining their goals. In this adaptation the four truths (paraphrased) are:

1) "There is a suffering village," i.e. a village with problems such as poverty, disease, and the exploitation of some members by others.
2) Such suffering is due to selfishness, competition, greed, and similar vices.
3) There is a way to end such suffering.
4) That way is the Noble Eightfold Path, understood in both personal and social terms.

[10] It is important to note that while its values are largely derived from Buddhist principles, the movement makes every effort not to be sectarian. Non-Buddhist Tamils, for example, have been active participants in the movement and have occupied leadership positions. The vision set forth is presented as "Sri Lankan" rather than as narrowly Buddhist in nature. This is of crucial significance in light of the recent violent conflicts between the Buddhist Sinhalese and non-Buddhist Tamil ethnic groupings within Sri Lanka. Having members from both ethnic groups, Sarvodaya has sought to be a mediating force in the conflict.

[11] Ariyaratne attributes the violence largely to governmental policies which have continued to pursue western models of development and which, Ariyaratne asserts, have destroyed much of the social, moral, and cultural fabric of the country. For Ariyaratne's discussion of the violence, see "Waking Everybody Up," 96-97. Also see Bond, "A.T. Ariyaratne," 134-142. Various factors have

contributed to reduced funding, including the fact that the official aid agencies of the major donor nations have come under the influence of those less sympathetic to some of Sarvodaya's major goals. (Ariyaratne 1996: 96-97; Bond in Queen and King 1996: 134-142)

[12] For overlap in Buddhist and Christian visions, see Merton (1968), Ruben Habito (1989, 1993), Mitchell and Wiseman (1997), Walker (1987), Aitken and Steindl-Rast (1994).

[13] Concerning silent retreats, which she liked to attend whenever possible and to which she devoted a whole section of her autobiography, Dorothy Day stated: "It is not only for others that I must have these retreats. It is because I too am hungry and thirsty for the bread of the strong. I too must nourish myself to do the work I have undertaken. I too must drink at these good springs so that I may not be an empty cistern and unable to help others."(1952: 263). Sulak Sivaraksa expresses a similar appreciation of retreats and spiritual practices, also using the imagery of water: "We must practice our meditation, our prayer, at least every morning or evening. In the crises of the present day, those of us who work in society, who confront power and injustice daily, often get beaten down and we become tired. At least once a year, we need to go to a retreat center to regain our spiritual strength, so we can return to confront society. Spiritual masters are like springs of fresh water. We who are in society need to carry that pure water to flood the banks, to fertilize the land and the trees, to be of use to the plants and animals, so that they can taste something fresh, and be revitalized. If we do not go back to the spring, our minds get polluted, just as water becomes polluted, and we are not of much use. Sulak Sivaraksa, "Buddhism in a World of Change," in Kotler 1996: 72. Thich Nhat Hanh also uses water imagery with regard to the spiritual life: "The well is within us. If we dig deeply in the present moment, the water will spring forth." (1995: 179)

[14] "After you study the Five Wonderful Precepts and the Three Jewels [Buddha, Dharma, Sangha], I hope you will go back to your own tradition and shed light on the jewels that are already there." (11) Nhat Hanh stresses the need for persons to be "re-rooted" in their own tradition (1998: 89). At the same time he believes people can benefit from having more than one root, that they can learn from other traditions. Nhat Hanh himself includes a statue of Jesus along with Buddhist statues on his altar and believes that he has leaned from the life and teaching of Jesus and the witness of Christians. With regard to the jewels of the Christian tradition, Nhat Hanh highlights for example the "practice of the presence of God" and the practice of "resting in God"as being somewhat analogous to the practice of mindfulness. When one is mindfull, he suggests, one experiences the healing presence of the Holy Spirit (1998: 20, 28-29, 154).

[15] Engaged Buddhists recognize that it is unavoidable to kill various microorganisms in the activities of daily life, acknowledge that at times killing pests in agriculture may be necessary (after available nonviolent means of control have been attempted), etc. "We cannot be completely nonviolent," says Nhat Hanh, "but by being vegetarian, we are going in the direction of nonviolence. If we want to head north, we can use the North Star. Our effort is only to proceed in that direction." (1998: 16) For detailed discussion of vegetarianism from a Buddhist perspective, see Roshi Philip Kapleau, *To Cherish All Life: A Buddhist View of Animal Slaughter and Meat-Eating* (Rochester, NY: Zen Center, 1981). For a good general

discussion of vegetarianism, see John Robbins, *Diet For a New America* (Walpole, NH: Stillpoint, 1987).

[16] Good presentations of Buddhist spiritual psychology can be found in Jack Kornfield, *A Path With Heart: A Guide Through the Promises and Pitfalls of the Spiritual Life* (New York: Bantam, 1993); Joseph Goldstein, *Insight Meditation: The Practice of Freedom* (Boston: Shambhala, 1994); Sharon Salzberg, *Loving-kindness* (Boston: Shambhala, 1995); Charlotte Joko Beck, *Everyday Zen* (New York: HarperCollins, 1989).

M.L. Liebler

Where Are the Songs of Spring?

(For Allen Ginsberg)

> "Aye, where are they? Think not of them, thou hast thy music too,"
>
> John Keats

I have investigated the cryptic saxophone
Notes of wailing blues and desperate jazz.
Decoded them all into one long,
Wild barbaric yawp that I first
Remember hearing dance across the rooftops
In my neighborhood of silence.

The omnipotent shadow of nationalism
Followed me ready
To smother my dreams within
Bomb-laden clouds of dying
America. The napalm nightmares of my youth.
I stood frightened and alone as America fell,
Realizing that no one would know,
Or hear the howling prayers of the young
Chanting endless Kaddish for the tortured
Burnt spirits of Hue, Mekong, My Lai,
The dried out Midwest: Chicago, Kent.

It was you, holy soul jelly roll, Bard–
Prophet who freed me, liberated us all
From our mysterious illusions of cornerstone
Backyards in suburban new America. I found
You—brother Poet—in the drowned coil
Of America's sleep. Where I, too, could not stand
My own mind. Where I, too, was not tamed
Or translatable. Where I, too, wanted
Only to come to the point of
Civil Rights, Viet Nam, CIA Death

Dance Politics, Dow Chemical Lament
And Plutonium Ode. I needed
To understand Che, Marx, Jesus, Buddha,
Beatnik, MC 5 stage rage, so that I could free
Myself from fitful McCarthyism doldrums,
And television eye snake dance. I needed
To understand that Fordism was fascism
To understand that Sacco & Vanzetti must not die
To understand that Father Ho was not our enemy
To understand that we were the wrong side
To understand that Malcolm X was right
To understand that America killed JFK, RFK, M.L. King,
Chaney, Goodman, Schwerner, Evers, Till, Hampton
To understand COINTELPRO's endless attempts
To silence Fannie Lou, Rosa Parks, Oches,
Sanders, Abbie, Dellinger, Berrigans, Cleaver,
Newton, Seale, Savio, Davis, Steinem, Chavez
To understand that Lt. Calley was a murderer
To understand four dead in Ohio
To understand that for every neighbor boy killed
In Southeast Asia, for every city burned,
For every Wounded Knee, for every Jackson State
For every homosexual murdered and persecuted
On the streets of America—
America could never be
Put back together again.
Allen, you understood
This, and without hesitation
You put your queer shoulder
To the wheel...
Lord, Lord, Lord,
Caw, caw, caw,
  Lord.

published in *Nexus Review*, and in *The Big Scream*, 1997.

PART XII

PERSONAL NARRATIVES

Lady Poverty, by Ade Bethune, first appeared in the October 1936 *Catholic Worker.*

Dorothy Day Stories

John Cort

Association of Catholic Trade Unionists

I have two stories. The first is set in a loft that the Boston Catholic Worker had rented in a poor section of that city. It was May 1936. Dorothy was visiting Boston, and there was a meeting one night to hear her speak.

At that time I was less than a year out of Harvard. At one dinner party I told a Harvard professor's wife that I had been converted to Catholicism while an undergraduate at that highly unCatholic institution, and her reaction was, "How positively bizarre!"

That May of '36 I had been reading *The Catholic Worker* for a few months and was even selling it on Sunday in front of Catholic churches. I was then a reporter on a weekly newspaper, working for $15 a week plus room and board.

I was late for Dorothy's meeting, and by the time I arrived she was already speaking. After listening to her for 15 minutes I decided, bang, without having given it any serious thought before, to give up my $15 a week job and join the Catholic Worker in a vermin-infested building at 115 Mott Street on the Lower East Side of New York City. I worked for nothing plus room and board.

My conversion at Harvard was an intellectual affair. This was more of a Road-to-Damascus affair, getting knocked off my horse in a flash of light. I'm aware that the Bible doesn't mention a horse, but the metaphor is still appropriate.

What was it about Dorothy that could have this effect? It wasn't physical attraction. She was 38 at the time, an attractive woman, but to me, a mere boy of 22, she was old. Besides, I was in love with the most beautiful girl in the senior class at Wellesley, about whom I had the foolish idea that I could join the Catholic Worker and still persuade her to marry me. The $15 a week was not high risk. The

Wellesley girl was high risk, but fortunately I didn't realize it at the time.

Some years ago I wrote about this occasion in *Commonweal*, and I will quote what I wrote, partly because I really missed the mark:

> She was not a forceful speaker in the usual sense of the word.... What moved me was something else. I remember sitting in that dingy hall and saying to myself, "This woman is getting a lot of fun out of life and I would like to get some of that for myself, so maybe I'd better try the same kind of life." As much as anything it was a quality of humor and laughter, but with a deeper base than you might expect from a good comedian. It was a humor and laughter that seemed to reach down to the secret, hidden places of the soul, promising at any moment to explain the mysteries of life and human striving.

Why do I say that I missed the mark? Actually, I didn't miss it entirely. The first part, the fun part, was on target. The last part, about the mysteries of life, was typical of a second-rate writer overreaching and trying too hard to be profound.

The character of Dorothy's appeal was simpler and at the same time more truly profound. Somebody—I don't remember who—once wrote that "joy is a sign of the presence of the Holy Spirit." We also know from St. Paul that joy is one of the fruits of the Holy Spirit. And it was surely that, the joy of the Holy Spirit, that I saw and heard that night in Dorothy's face and in her humor and laughter. It was surely that that persuaded me to join the Catholic Worker.

And so, on to a second story. Though often characterized as anarchists, Peter and Dorothy preferred to call themselves "personalists," a term derived from the French Catholic writer Emanuel Mounier. Peter translated Mounier's highly intellectual formulations into simple injunctions: don't tell anybody to do anything or not to do anything; do it yourself, or don't do it, and the power of your good example will gently but surely persuade others to go and do, or not do, likewise.

The trouble with this idyllic doctrine was that in the real world of Mott Street you could throw good example at some people forever and watch it bounce off them like peanuts off a tank. And so a number of useful things did not get done, and some not-so-useful things did get done, because the people setting the good example were greatly outnumbered by the people setting bad example, or, more likely, just setting.

During much of my time at Mott Street I slept in a four-room apartment with nine other men, most of them guests from the Bowery. There was Tex, for example, a young seaman who joined us during the 1936 strike and then decided, "what the hell, why go back to sea when I can get free eats and a bed right here?" Tex hardly ever spoke to anybody and never did any work that I can recall, but he could sleep like nobody I ever met before or since. He would go to bed at eleven o 'clock or so; eleven or twelve the next day he would still be in bed, head buried under the covers, no sign of life. I figured he needed a psychiatrist. That and a little oxygen. As it turned out, Dorothy informed me years later, what Tex needed was an operation for carbuncles on his backside. When he got it he changed overnight into a productive citizen, a latter-day miracle.

The building had no bathtubs. There were some public baths, and some of us could count on CW fellow travelers who had apartments nearby and who would let us use the bathtub once a week. It was amazing how quickly I adjusted from a life of daily showers to the realization that no great harm would befall if I bathed but once a week.

Most of the men I lived with had long since resigned themselves to the realization that no great harm would befall if they bathed but once a month, once a year, or once a lifetime. Few of them made their beds in the morning, and fewer still ever bothered to take the broom that I left in a conspicuous spot and follow my good example by sweeping up around their beds.

In a word the place grew, with the passing days, sloppy. In addition we had bedbugs, but bad. At one time or another we swept, washed, painted and sprayed the apartment, but we could not destroy the bugs, which seemed to have dug themselves into the building and pulled the covers up over their heads, like Tex. One metal cot they assigned to me was so infested that I took it up on the roof and went over it with a blowtorch. To this day the rich aroma of roasting bedbug still lingers with me, sharp and acrid in my mind's nose.

Somebody pointed out that this obsessive destruction of these poor little creatures was conduct that would not have been approved by St. Benedict Labre, a favorite saint at the CW, who had such a reverence for life and such a love of mortification that when a louse once fell off his clothes, he gently picked it up and put it back on. I was not that kind of varsity material.

Given my middle-class hang-ups, there was no escaping the day when I would try to impose a minimum of order and cleanliness on my companions. As the one staff member on the floor, I was understood to be in charge, whatever that meant beyond doing all the cleaning up myself. I therefore took it upon myself to post three typewritten rules as follows:

1. Everybody out of bed by 9 a.m. [Seemed reasonable.]
2. Each man is expected to make his own bed. [Also reasonable.]
3. Each man is expected to take turns sweeping up. [*Very* reasonable.]

This backfired. My roommate John Griffin, a Bowery type and a good friend who had absorbed more of the CW philosophy than most of our guests, objected to the rules and appealed to Dorothy, who was recognized as the court of last resort. In fact, we called her the Abbess. John thought the rules violated the principles of personalism and said so. Dorothy agreed with him and told me to take them down. At the time I don't think I even argued with her so great was her authority among us. What it came down to was that the Catholic Worker was an extraordinary combination of anarchy and dictatorship.

Do I think she was right in ruling against me and for John Griffin? Of course not. Neither then nor now was I, or am I, a believer in anarchist dictatorships. But I did console myself with the thought that she ruled against me because she believed I was better able than John to take a negative decision and still stick with the Catholic Worker. She was that kind of a personalist more than a personalist in the manner of Emmanuel Mounier.

And I did stick with the Catholic Worker, at least until the tuberculosis I caught from John Griffin forced me to leave. Otherwise I might be there yet, because you always knew that you had to have a very good reason to justify your leaving.

Threads of Life: Telling the Story

Tina Sipula

Clare House of Hospitality
Bloomington, Illinois

The Catholic Worker nabbed me when I was just a teenager. I was only 18 years old, and went to speak with a priest, Fr. Joe Kelly, about death. I'd had enough of death. At such a young age, I had already lost two brothers, three grandparents, and now my favorite uncle, my godfather, was dying of cancer. But Joe Kelly refused to speak of death. Instead, he spoke of life—joy and despair, loneliness and community, hope in a world filled with injustice. After about two hours of stories, this Irishman leaned toward me and said, mysteriously, "Have you ever heard of the Catholic Worker?" "Have you heard of Peter Maurin and Dorothy Day?"

That was it!! That was the beginning, or the beginning of the end. Joe Kelly has taken great pride in "ruining people s lives," as he calls it, when he introduces them to the Worker, or embarks young lives on quests for justice. I walked out of his office that day, in 1972, with books by Catherine de Hueck Doherty, issues of *The Catholic Worker* dating from 1966, 1967, 1968, and his most recent copy, dated February 1970, with the lead story, "Ammon Hennacy Dies In Salt Lake City." Also in tow were William Miller's *A Harsh and Dreadful Love* and *An Essay on Liberation* by Herbert Marcuse.

There was no turning back. I was ruined, and on the path of becoming a "fool for Christ." I read everything I could get my hands on, and found it was Dorothy I was drawn to the most. Perhaps because she was a woman and had been through so much at an early age too, but mostly, I was overwhelmed by her faith.

On December 8, 1932, Dorothy Day entered the crypt in the Shrine of the Immaculate Conception at Catholic University in Washington, DC, and she offered up a prayer—a prayer that God take her and use her special talents for her fellow unemployed workers, for the poor. And so, God did. She was snatched up, her prayer was answered, and we are the inherited ancestors of that whisper to God-over 60 years ago.

When I was only 18 years old, I read about that prayer in William Miller's book, *A Harsh and Dreadful Love*, and I was moved by such a simple yet devout gesture—to kneel and ask God for direction. Such a simple and powerful act!

I entered the chapel at the Newman Center at Illinois State University and mimicked her actions and words, a bit frightened at what might happen at this bold and humble request at such a young age. Six years later, I sat in front of Dorothy Day in the Maryhouse dining room in New York City.

She was looking at pictures of Clare House, an old Victorian home that had been donated to me and a handful of "fools for Christ." It was October 1978. I was ready to open the house in a month, but Stanley Vishnewski insisted I come out and spend time at the New York Worker and with Dorothy. We had dinner in her room every night, but this night she insisted on going down to the dining room in Maryhouse.

She looked closely at the photos of our house, then gazed around the dining room. Her eyes met mine. "This is not Catholic Worker," she said quietly. "What?" I leaned forward. I must have missed something. She was 80 years old, her steely eyes grabbed me, and she said quite clearly, "This is not the Catholic Worker. This is not what Peter and I had in mind." "What do you mean?" I asked, in wonder. "It's way too big." Her hand swept over the table as she shook her head. "The personalism we knew is no longer. It's too big." Then she tapped the photo of Clare House. "Keep it simple. Keep it small and very simple. Then it will be Catholic Worker."

I kept a mental log of suggestions in my impressionable head:

> Keep it simple.
> Stay small.
> Don t give in to pressure about tax-exemption status.
> Stay close to the eucharist.
> Pray daily.
> Keep your house clean and beautiful. Hang paintings on the wall. (And so, we did, and have been dubbed, "The Hilton of the Worker" for the past 19 years!)
> Demand from God what you need if it is for the poor, for you are doing God s work!

> And, "Call or write when you despair, when you want to give up, and we will be there."

In those early years, when Dorothy and Stanley were still alive, I did call and write often, and they were always there. And so were Jeannette Noel, Kassie Temple, Frank Donovan, and they still are there.

There have been times over these 19 years when despair has rattled my faith; I had to conjure up everything I could muster to not only endure, but carry on with hope and promise, and commit again and again to a belief that we can help be co-creators to build a "world in which it is easier to be good."

I give thanks for the example of Dorothy Day's faith, for the dream and a prayer that set fire in her heart and ignited a blaze that will never go out.

A Long Loneliness: Metaphors of Conversion within the Catholic Worker Movement

Rosalie Riegle

Saginaw Valley State University
Mustard Seed Catholic Worker of Saginaw

Conversations about coming to the Worker and becoming a Worker were an important part of almost every interview I gathered for *Voices from the Catholic Worker,* an oral history of the movement published by Temple University Press in 1993.[1] And almost everyone spoke of this coming and becoming as a conversion to a particular religious sensibility, a definition that I now share as a Worker and member of the Mustard Seed community of Saginaw, Michigan.

Following the example of founders Dorothy Day and Peter Maurin, Catholic Workers live with the poor and espouse personalist anarchism, resisting governmental policies which contribute to social inequalities. As such, the Catholic Worker movement has been influential in calling American Catholicism to a more profound social and political involvement, particularly in resisting war and nuclear weapons. It appears to be less successful in calling the church to a simpler lifestyle or in halting the spread of consumerism. And so, the Catholic Worker continues to attract people who wish to live in opposition to an increasingly materialistic culture, to share a simple life in voluntary poverty with the poor they serve, and sometimes to accept jail terms for nonviolent resistance. They see no divisions between the religious and the political in their work, resisting the evils they see in the world with a communitarian philosophy of personalism and nonviolence. As narrator Jo Roberts says, "What we're doing is a political statement in itself. The whole concept of a house of hospitality—of really saying, 'Yes, I am prepared to take personal responsibility for people, prepared to be my sister's or brother's keeper'—that's political." (265-266)

Catholic Workers seem an anomaly; they call themselves radical, yet offer conservative solutions to contemporary dilemmas; seek the transformation of society, yet look to eschatological ends. In examining the reasons given for joining this paradoxical community, I will analyze portions of the 208 interviews I collected from 1986 to 1991, looking particularly at the rhetoric the narrators use to talk about their coming to the Worker. A brief description of the Workers appears in an appendix to this essay.

To paraphrase William James' view of conversion in *The Varieties of Religious Experience: A Study in Human Nature*, it unifies a divided self. Even though he is a secularist, James' view of conversion is echoed by contemporary spiritual writers. Unlike many in the dominant culture, who work to live (or perhaps work to play), Catholic Workers see themselves as integrating life and work, as well as life and religion. One woman said, "What really attracted me to the Worker is that it's religion and life all mixed up together."(513) In it, religion becomes the "hot place," or "habitual centre of personal energy,"(James 1963: 196) and the other interests dividing the self become "cold" or peripheral to the person's vision.

To characterize it more poetically, conversion is a falling in love with God. One's equilibrium changes and God becomes the center of gravity. Traditional conversion, particularly as described in evangelical rhetoric, calls for a turning away from personal sin, often sins of the flesh, and a turning towards the God of forgiveness and salvation. I noted little of this in analyzing the Catholic Worker interviews and heard instead more a turning away from complicity with the sins or ways of the world, with its militarism and materialism and disregard of the poor and marginal.

William James wrote of conversion resulting in a "sense that all is ultimately well with one, the peace, the harmony, the willingness to be." Bob Imholt echoes: "There's a tremendous amount of peace that comes with being where you know you're supposed to be."(156) But James spoke of the peace following conversion almost as a by-product, where I found that most of the narrators came to the Worker searching for that peace, that unity. Gayle Catinella tells us: "I just don't belong anywhere else. This is where the puzzle pieces of my life fit. And why, I have no idea. I can call it God's call or the fulfillment of God's gifts inside of me and all that, but that's too big a mystery for me to try to work out myself." (162)

To what do these people come and why? They come to small and intense communities, sometimes as strangers traveling long distances, sometimes as friends moving into a communal situation with people they have known for years. Why do they come? They come to the Worker for both community and commitment. Living and being identified as Catholic Workers appears to fulfill for them longings unsatisfied in their previous lives, appears to unite divided selves.

Most Catholic Workers are firmly rooted in a larger faith context, attending services at local churches and participating in a variety of religious practices within the houses of hospitality. While it seems that a great number of Catholic Workers are converts to Roman Catholicism, a quick count of the 208 narrators revealed only 12 who came to the Worker after or shortly before formally joining the Catholic Church. Approximately 25 of the 208 have never identified themselves as Catholics and about 10 were cradle Catholics who no longer consider themselves as belonging to the Church. Some, however, seemed to perceive the Worker itself as their church. Robert Ellsberg describes his self-righteousness before he came to the Worker:

> In some way, the [institutional] church was not good enough for me. I felt called to make a supreme sacrifice, and I didn't feel the church challenged me to do that....I went to the Catholic Worker with a kind of smugness toward the rest of the institutional church and [all its] compromises....The Catholic Worker was my church. (147-149)

I would say most of the people I interviewed see their becoming Workers as a conversion to a particular religious sense, even if they don't see Catholic Worker specifically as Church. Some Workers are former priests and nuns who have severed institutional ties with the Roman Catholic Church but still see themselves as Catholic and remain committed to the essence of the Gospel as lived out in a Catholic Worker community.

In his two chapters on conversion in *Varieties of Religion Experience,* William James first distinguishes between conversion by gradual change, even if accompanied by "jerks and starts," and the dramatic and seemingly sudden conversion by "self surrender."(James 1963: 206) He then explains that psychologically both the "fits and starts" of the more gradual kind and the drama of sudden surrender are preceded or interspersed by unknowable but nonetheless real activity in the subconscious (James 1963: 198). In Catholic Worker conversion stories, we see both gradual and seemingly sudden conversions, and from the stories of search, we can sometimes surmise that subcutaneous changes had often been occurring for years. And contrary to the stereotype that sudden converts backslide into their former lives, many Catholic Workers retain their commitment.

In looking at the rhetoric of Catholic Workers as they speak about coming to the Worker, I will address the following questions: What metaphors do Workers use to describe their changing belief systems? Where do these metaphors originate? Do we find gender or generational differences in the Catholic Worker language of conversion? Does the rhetoric of those coming from a Jewish tradition differ in significant ways from the rhetoric of the mainstream Christians who are attracted to the movement? After looking at these questions, I will conclude with a question on the value of community in attracting converts.

Often my first question, "How did you come to the Worker?" would bring forth a long story. Such stories are found throughout the pages of *Voices from the Catholic Worker;* many of them, however, are recounted in the 23 pages of Chapter Seven specifically devoted to the topic: "Coming and Becoming."

What can the metaphors of Catholic Worker conversion stories tell us? Firstly, several narrators mock such metaphors. Kassie Temple, who holds a doctorate in theology but has avoided the university system, says: "Somebody asked me once if I felt I had a calling to the Worker, and I said, 'It sounds like you're hearing voices.'"(139) When I speak of my own coming to live in a Catholic Worker community, I also downplay the particularity of conversion, perhaps because I want to convince my audience that they can become Catholic Workers themselves. Jeannine Coallier, co-founder with me of the Mustard Seed in Saginaw, sees this tendency as natural: "To me, there was a mysterious journey. Once resolved by my coming to the Worker, it all lightened up and seemed to be no more than chopping wood and hauling water." (Private conversation, Saginaw, MI, 1997)

Predictably, however, the sense of compelling mystery inherent in the metaphors of calling and journey hovers over many of the conversion tales. Bob Imholt tells us

> In my twenties...I went to probably ten or twelve different places looking for a spiritual home. Lutheran and Mormon and everything but Catholic, I think. Nothing felt like home. So I got to the point where I said, "Okay, if God is out there, if there really is a God, and he or she really has something for me to do, then he or she will talk to me. And until that time, I'm going to just go on with my life." And here I am. I feel almost like I'm being...I'm being pulled along in this. (156)

Gayle Catinella speaks of "some reason that I'll never understand." Don Timmerman tells of being pulled to Milwaukee's Casa Maria in a drenching rainstorm and walking into a house full of chaos. He stayed for almost three decades.

Several narrators use food metaphors: hunger for community, for meaning, for difference or excitement (152). Oddly for one who resists militarism, Robert Ellsberg uses metaphors of battle: "the supreme sacrifice, getting the crap knocked out, challenge, Christianity on the front lines, the barricades."(147) Meg Hyre also uses a harsh rhetoric:

> [I saw in the Worker] a very hard kind of approach, a real toughness of analysis and a readiness to take things as they came. An ability to...to embrace reality and not to remain blind for the sake of one's peace. That impressed me very much. And also an honesty about the difficulty of the work here, the failures, the vast imperfections. (231-232)

Many speak either with the metaphors of schooling favored by the founders or ones of formation, a nomenclature coming from the novitiate period of traditional religious orders. Almost every conversion story I heard mentioned family, either birth family (as supportive or non-supportive) or Catholic Worker as becoming family, as noted above. Several echo Richard Cleaver who says "I never felt quite so much at home before."(152)

As outsiders who come home to a faith community, the narrators use metaphors in these "coming to the Worker" stories which generally echo those heard in other conversion contexts. Are there other ways to speak of conversion? Perhaps. But the commonality one finds in these stories may in itself help to provide the identity the narrators seek. Maybe the very sameness of imagery gives access to the community, creates a commonality.

Can we find models in founder Dorothy Day's conversion? William James points out that both Roman Catholicism and the mainstream Protestant traditions "set no...store in instantaneous conversion."(James 1963: 227) In *Dorothy Day: A Radical Devotion,* Robert Coles quotes Paul Tillich who says most conversions are gradual (Coles 1987: 41). Coles illustrates that Day's conversion was also gradual, even if it eventually erupted in a rather precipitous baptism the day after her lover Forster Batterham left for good. I see her conversion as partaking of the kind of underground psychological change described by William James, foregrounded by the intense happiness she felt with her lover but subcutaneously changing from below. For example, "she was lonely, a bit unnerved...and prone to moodiness" in the period before the birth of Tamar (Coles 1987: 46).

Present day Worker stories often echo rhetorically Day's journey to Christianity. John Cort describes Dorothy Day's conversion thusly: "Her life became something of a mess, but she was able to learn from that and to decide that she had to straighten it out. I think she came to the Catholic Church partly as a result of tasting the dregs of human experience."(74)

Lynn Lassalle-Klein tells us she herself was "flailing around," a condition one senses strongly in the early pages of Day's biography, *The Long Loneliness.* Day also writes movingly of the tension between herself and Batterham over religion. Lassalle-Klein also tells us that she was alone on a faith journey. She was involved in an alien community, as Day was, but instead of the Greenwich Village literary scene or a Staten Island cottage, Lassalle-Klein's milieu was the high tech world of computers in California.

> Very hip crowd. Eccentric...and the materialism of it was killing me....I was just consuming, consuming. Buying stuff!....And also the...the constant "playing" that I think some middle-class people our age do. I look back now and I realize that it was a real desert time. None of these computer friends of mine understood. I was caught in this thing, and it was killing me...I would get into these intellectual conversations about God, and I remember at one point feeling like the conversation was killing the spirit, the Holy Spirit....It was just a very empty, empty time. (151)

Sin and temptation were seen as primarily sexual when Day's conversion occurred. Perhaps today's temptations are the blandishments of a materialistic culture which Lynn Lassalle-Klein describes. One can see that the parallels between her story and Day's are uncanny.[2]

Does the rhetoric of Catholic Worker conversion stories differ by gender? Of the 23 pages in the conversion chapter itself, only seven contain women's stories. By contrast, men and women are almost equally represented in the text as a whole, although such a balance was not a publishing goal. Does this imbalance mean that the men have more dramatic conversion stories? Perhaps. When I perform other kinds of interview analysis, for example, looking at the publishing history of the narrators or the social dynamics of individual houses of hospitality, I see that the men construct themselves as more individualistic than the women do. Nevertheless, there are some fully dramatized female conversion stories, as Lynn Lassalle-Klein's saga demonstrates.

One can readily see generational differences in the conversion rhetoric. Basically, the older a narrator, the more casual and circumspect his or her rhetoric. The "pioneer" generation, those who knew founders Day and Maurin, often speak of the fun they had at the Worker and downplay any religious sentiment. Joe Zarrella, a master storyteller, tells how he joined the fledgling New York community in an early protest: "That was the beginning—when the bug hit me—and I was captured. And it was exciting! Never a dull moment. (Pause) Always, always exciting."(12) John Cort describes meeting Day: "This woman is getting a lot of fun out of life. And I'd like some of that myself, so maybe I'd better try the same kind of life."(73)

Another consideration: These narrators may have sensed my own fifties-bred reticence in speaking of the interior life and responded accordingly. Or perhaps they shared my reluctance, either from inculturation or because they see their insides and outsides as matching so completely that the conversion isn't worthy of dramatic comment.

Now this reluctance is not seen in convert Day, and part of her continuing appeal lies in the honesty and sincerity with which she spoke of her spiritual life when few lay women did. As someone told me, "Dorothy Day was never too polite to speak of God's love." In *Dorothy Day: A Radical Devotion,* Day reminds us through Coles that hers was not a political conversion as, say, Jim Levinson's was.

> Jesus Christ is the one who is pushing me to the Catholics.... After Forster left, that day, I kept thinking to myself that it was hopeless:

> I believed in Jesus Christ—that He is *real,* that He is the son of God, that He came here, that He entered history, and that He is still here, with us, all the time, through His Church. (Coles 1987 :53-55)

She wrote in *The Long Loneliness,* "I loved, in other words, and like all women in love, I wanted to be united to my love."(Day 1952: 149)

Like Day, members of the younger generation of Catholic Workers are serious and willing to articulate their religious yearnings. We can see this introspection in Lassalle-Klein's narrative and also in the voice of Robert Ellsberg:

> I came to the Worker with a lot of idealism and...a kind of yearning for moral purity. And out of a sense of too much compromise in my life, too much tendency to intellectualize....I had this need to get my hands dirty. (146-147)

Another intellectual who was getting his hands dirty at a farm in western Massachusetts when I spoke with him, Jim Levinson was an economist formerly with the U.S. State Department. He has never left Judaism, but he speaks of his faith in the Catholic Worker with the passion of a Christian charismatic: "We [were] on the wrong side! Something fundamentally had to change."(152) He and his family returned from the Philippines and underwent what he calls an "incredible conversion experience." While participating in a demonstration at the Pentagon, "All of the pain that I had experienced in these other countries…it all came gushing out, and I was just weeping inconsolably."(153) Within six months, he and his family had moved into the Boston Worker community.

Sometimes one hears directly the acceptance of the will of God or the self-surrender type of conversion. Jim Eder talks of moving into St. Francis House in Chicago and being told his bed had just been vacated by a guest hospitalized with tuberculosis. As he tells it, "I said to myself, 'All right, God! This is your bag, and if I get TB, well, that's your problem, not mine.'"(398) Here we see a self surrender and acceptance of an unknown future that one finds in other stories told throughout the movement, particularly as Workers recount the uncertainties of financial support.

Worker David Stein provides a stark contrast to this evangelical rhetoric, particularly when paired with Jim Levinson. Both men remain committed to Judaism, and David defends his coming to the Worker on purely rational grounds: "I don't see the Catholic Worker as having the remotest thing to do with being Catholic. I justify it on logical and rational terms. On terms having to do with the distribution of wealth. Having to do with environmentalism. Having to do with the elevation of human dignity."(vi)

While many Catholic Workers would agree with Stein's statement on rational grounds, most of them use a decidedly eschatological rhetoric when discussing their coming to the Worker.

We find in the Catholic Worker an increasing number of nuns and priests who remain officially connected with the institutional church yet live in Catholic Worker houses of hospitality. Sometimes the rhetoric of priests is more restrained than that of their lay counterparts. Father Tom Lumpkin of Detroit can be seen as an example of this restraint:

> An idea comes into your mind that this or that might be a possible thing. You pray about it, certainly. Talk to other people, people you respect as having a certain amount of holy wisdom, if you will. And then if it's possible, you try it out tentatively. Also....there's something to say about God's call in some way corresponding to the particular gifts you've been given. (516)

Other priests are more passionate. Mike Baxter, a Holy Cross priest, told me: "Getting down to the basics means I've got to do it. We've got to do it. We've all got to make this thing concrete in our lives. And that's all we have to give—our lives."(517) Notice how he sermonizes even as he explains his decision to leave the university for life at a Catholic Worker house in Phoenix. Throughout the interview, his rhetoric echoed the exhortations of the pulpit.

Yet another contrast is Fr. Frank Cordaro, a self-styled "crazy Italian" from the Midwest, who started a Catholic Worker house in Iowa and is frequently jailed for civil disobedience. Coming from a charismatic family, he tells his lively stories in the first person singular, as one person's rather idiosyncratic response to God's call.

> Was being a Catholic going to be important to me or just peripheral? I could be a cultural Catholic like a lot of my relatives...which is all right. These are good people. But I wanted to know whether it was going to be real....I spent [a] summer in the South Bronx, in a black and Puerto Rican parish, and that just

> changed my whole life. I came to the conclusion that if the only poor people in the world existed in the Bronx, there were too many. And because I'm a Gospel person, I'm going to spend the rest of my life trying to address these issues. (371-372)

In these three examples of the rhetoric of the ordained, we see three uses of person. Fr. Lumpkin uses second person as a generalization to avoid the formal "one" of third person singular; Fr. Baxter uses an exhorting first person plural, and Fr. Cordaro speaks in an individualistic first person singular.

To summarize our examination of evangelical rhetoric, we see somewhat dramatic commonalities in the conversion stories of both men and women, irrespective of background, but a muted rhetoric in the coming-to-the-Worker stories of the pioneers. Three conversion stories—Jo Roberts, Larry Purcell, and Charlie Angus—typify what was almost universal in the "coming and becoming" tales: the search for a way of living which would allow for personal commitment. Lawyer Jo Roberts moved to New York City from her native England.

> I almost had a dual career pattern. Sort of carrying on with traditional career training, but also getting involved in other things....I [liked the practice of law] very much, but I began to realize that only a small part of me was actually being fulfilled in doing that sort of work. My mother said, "Well, you could always have a law practice and volunteer in a homeless shelter on a Friday night." No way! I wanted to commit myself to something that was fulfilling in itself rather than dividing myself up. Then it all came to a head, and I decided to leave...and come to the Catholic Worker. (265)

If I had been specifically collecting conversion stories, instead of recording an oral history of the Catholic Worker movement, I would have pushed Roberts on her evasions in the "it all came to a head" statement, and we might have learned if there were a dramatic conversion story lurking under her seeming reasonableness.

Larry Purcell left both the affluence of family and the security of parish work. He tells us

> [Our family was] really close to each other....Very wealthy. (I learned to drive on a Cadillac limousine.) While we had everything you'd ever imagine, my parents were very clear that they put people first and that relationships were the most important thing. I was

> ordained a priest in 1970 and was a diocesan priest for ten years. Worked in a huge parish. After about three years, I became convinced that people were not the number-one priority in parish life, that the rules and the buildings seemed to dominate. So I left parish ministry; it took me four years to find another way to be a priest. [Finally] I went to a Catholic Worker House in San Jose...found I loved working with the poor, loved working out of the principles of the Gospel, loved the voluntary poverty. I learned that you can live simply and live a very rich life. (420)

Charlie Angus and Lauren Griffin are a young married couple with widely differing personalities. When Charlie found Dorothy Day's biography in a used bookstore, he brought it home to Lauren: "I was jumping up and down. 'Lauren, this is the best book I've ever seen!' This is it. This is the real radicalism of the Gospel."(420) Later in the interview, he pointed out

> It took us, I guess, about three more years of reading, of getting our nerve up, of learning to live simply. Like giving up eating meat. And not buying clothes. Giving away a lot of my records. But it took Lauren to get us going. I would say, "Well, when we're Catholic Workers" or "Well, when we have the house." Lauren finally said, "Charlie, there's no when. You either are or [you aren't.] It's not that you don't get on the road. You're on the road!" (421)

In these conversion stories, we hear those reflecting both the gradual and the more stereotypical self-surrender or sudden models. Among those whose conversions I would characterize as gradual are Fr. Tom Lumpkin, Fr. Mike Baxter, Richard Cleaver, John Cort, Jo Roberts, Bob Imholt, Larry Purcell, David Stein, and Robert Ellsberg. Dramatic conversions are recounted by Joe Zarrella, Lynn Lassalle-Klein, Jim Levinson, Jim Eder, Fr. Frank Cordaro, and Gayle Catinella. Charlie Angus and Lauren Griffin give us a story of "jerks and starts," of conversion and temporary backsliding before making a long-term commitment.

In conclusion, as I think about the Catholic Worker, and about my own relationship to this group, I conclude that it may be the committed community itself, not the promise of a personal relationship with God, which gives many of those coming to the Catholic Worker the impetus for conversion. And in this, of course, they differ markedly from Dorothy Day, who had no community to come to and instead wandered spiritually and politically for several years before founding, with mentor Peter Maurin, the community where she could be at home. One could say that Workers feel comfortable constructing themselves as outsiders who find an inside and a home at the Worker, and several Workers used this inside-outside metaphor. Perhaps we all face "the long loneliness" of Dorothy Day's autobiography. And who's to say whether the longing for God that Day describes so movingly is so different from a longing for the companionship of like-minded souls? In addressing both of these needs, the Catholic Worker movement provides a compelling and appropriate response to the limitations of individualism.

Appendix A: The Narrators

Charlie Angus and **Lauren Griffin** live on a Catholic Worker farm in a small mining town in northern Ontario. Charlie plays in a band and is interested in labor history; Lauren formerly practiced law and was very involved in women's issues. When I interviewed them, they were at the Toronto Catholic Worker.

Fr. Mike Baxter is a Holy Cross priest who founded a Catholic Worker in Phoenix, Arizona. He received doctorate in theology at Duke University and is on the faculty at Notre Dame University.

Gayle Catinella is a certified social worker who prefers the personalism and anarchism of a Catholic Worker house. I met her when she was the "mother" of the St. Francis House in Chicago; she and her husband and large family now live on a farm in Nebraska.

Richard Cleaver served first at the New York house, and was later associated with the Des Moines Worker. After several years in Japan, he is now on the staff of Grinnell College in Iowa.

Fr. Frank Cordaro, a priest in the diocese of Des Moines, Iowa, founded a Catholic Worker house there. He is frequently jailed for resistance to nuclear weapons and continues to call the Church to justice and equality for women.

John Cort, another of the pioneers, is a Harvard graduate who converted to Catholicism. A Christian Socialist, he founded the *Religious Socialism* newletter in 1976 and sserved as editor until 2000.

Jim Eder is a former monk who now works for a parish across the street from Chicago's St. Francis Catholic Worker and continues to run the Catholic Worker soup kitchen.

Robert Ellsberg, the son of Daniel Ellsberg of Watergate fame, is now editor-in-chief of Maryknoll Books.

Meg Hyre came back to the New York house after spending two years at Oxford. Our conversation occurred shortly after her return.

Bob Imholt was formerly a second lieutenant in the army and the commander of one of the military teams delegated to react to Catholic Worker resistance to the Trident submarines in Bangor, Washington. When I last had contact with him, he was living at a Catholic Worker farm near Tacoma, Washington.

Lynn Lassalle-Klein left the world of computers for a Catholic Worker house in Oakland, California. She wrote her master's thesis on marriage in the Catholic Worker. No longer living at the house, she and her husband remain close to their local community.

Jim Levinson is a former economic analyst for the U.S. State Department. Jim and his family were living at Noonday Farm in Western Massachusetts when we met. He is now Director of the International Food and Nutrition Center of Tufts University.

Fr. Tom Lumpkin, a priest in the diocese of Detroit, Michigan, founded a Catholic Worker house in that city over twenty years ago. They run a soup kitchen and campaign against street and police violence.

Larry Purcell grew up in a large, loving, and affluent family. Unfulfilled as a parish priest, he tried several avenues of service before finding the Catholic Worker movement. He currently "fathers" the Redwood City Catholic Worker in northern California.

Jo Roberts, a young lawyer from England, is representative of the educated young idealists who find commitment and hope in the Catholic Worker movement. Before coming to the New York house, Jo had spent one summer at an international youth work camp in Germany, and another few weeks in India, working with Mother Teresa. She is now at the Toronto Catholic Worker.

David Stein, a wood carver and autodidact, drifted from New York to Chicago, where he found the St. Francis Catholic Worker.

Kassie Temple is a faithful member of the New York community and a contributing editor of *The Catholic Worker*. She holds a doctorate in theology from the University of Toronto.

Don Timmerman worked actively at Casa Maria in Milwaukee for over 25 years, calling Marquette University to abolish its ROTC program and challenging the city to serve the poor within its borders. Since moving to Park Falls, Wisconsin, he has been campaigning to preserve farmland and forests threatened by a transmission line project.

Joe Zarrella was one of the early members of the movement, joining with founder Dorothy Day in the 1930s. Faithful for over sixty years, he and his wife still work in a soup kitchen in Tell City, Indiana.

Notes

[1] All quotations are taken from this text, unless otherwise attributed. Both verbatim and edited copies of the transcripts are housed in the Catholic Worker Archives at Marquette University. With few exceptions, participants self-identified as Catholic Workers and were either living in a CW community or attached to one as "extended community."

[2] A traditional oral historian, particularly one of a journalistic bent, might have asked Lassalle-Klein to comment on these parallels. My not doing so, of course, brings up the problematic aspect of interview control. After reading Michael Frisch's *Shared Authorizy* (Albany: SUNY UP, 1990) early in the interview process, I began to think of myself as compiler rather than author, and thus attempted to give authority and therefore control of subject and stance to the narrators themselves.

Dorothy Day: Saint and Troublemaker

Jim Forest

Alkmaar, The Netherlands

Can you think of a word that describes a person who devoted much of her life to being with people many of us cross the street to avoid? Who for half a century did her best to make sure they didn't go hungry or freeze on winter nights? Who went to Mass every day until her legs couldn't take her that far, at which point Communion was brought to her? Who prayed every day for friend and enemy alike and whose prayers, some are convinced, had miraculous results? Who went to confession every week? Who was devoted to the rosary? Who wore hand-me-down clothes and lived in cold-water flats? Whose main goal in life was to follow Christ and to see him in the people around her?

A saint.

Can you think of a word that describes a person who refused to pay taxes, didn't salute the flag, never voted, went to prison every now and then for protests against war and social injustice? Who spoke in a plain and often rude way about our way of life? Who complained that the Church wasn't paying enough attention to its own teaching and compared some of its bishops to sharks?

A troublemaker.

Dorothy Day, saint and troublemaker. Mostly saints lived in the distant past, that is before we were born, and have been presented to us with all blemishes removed. We are not surprised to learn that St. Wonderbread of the North Pole, daughter of pious parents, had her first vision when she was four, joined the Order of the Holy Pallbearers at the age of 11, founded 47 convents, received the stigmata when she was 55, and that when she died 20 years later, not only was her cell filled with divine light but the nuns attending her clearly heard the angelic choir.

What has been left out about the actual St. Wonderbread is that she ran away from home, had a voice that could split rocks and a temper that could melt them back together again, experienced more dark nights of the soul than celestial visions, was accused of heresy by her bishop, narrowly escaped being burned at the stake, and, though she lived long enough to be vindicated, felt like a failure on her deathbed. But all this was edited out after she died—facts like that might tarnish her halo.

If Dorothy Day is ever canonized, the record of who she was, what she was like and what she did is too complete and accessible for her to be hidden in wedding cake icing. She will be the patron saint not only of homeless people and those who try to care for them but also of people who lose their temper.

Dorothy Day was not without rough edges. To someone who told her she was too hot-headed, she replied, "I hold more temper in one minute than you will hold in your entire life." To a college student who asked a sarcastic question about her recipe for soup, she responded, "You cut the vegetables until your fingers bleed." To a journalist who told her it was the first time he had interviewed a saint, she replied, "Don't call me a saint—I don't want to be dismissed that easily."

I was 20 years old the first time I saw her. She was ancient, that is to say 62 years old—seven years older than I am today. This means that for 35 years she has been scolding and encouraging me on a daily basis. The mere fact of her having died 17 years ago doesn't seem to get in the way.

I met her at the Catholic Worker Farm on Staten Island in the days when the island still had rural areas, its only link to the rest of New York City being the ferry. She was sitting with several other people at the battered table where the community had its meals. Before her was a pot of tea, a few cups, none of them matching, and a pile of letters. The Catholic Worker received a good deal of mail every day, much of it for Dorothy. She often read the letters aloud, telling a story or two about the people who had written them. This was the Dorothy Day University in fill swing, though I didn't know it at the time. She wrote countless letters and notes in response every year, but some letters she gave to others to answer either because a personal reply wasn't needed or because she wanted to connect the correspondent with someone on staff. A good part of Dorothy's life was spent reading and writing letters—even her monthly columns were usually nothing more than long letters. If ever she is canonized, she will be one of the patron saints of letter writers.

People sometimes think of her as the personification of the simple life, but in reality her days tended to be busy, complicated and stressful. Often she was away traveling—visiting other Catholic Worker communities; speaking at colleges, seminaries, local parishes; and getting around by bus or a used car on its last spark plugs.

Before an audience, she had a direct, unpremeditated, story-centered way of speaking: no notes, no rhetorical polish, a manner that communicated a certain shyness but at the same time wisdom, conviction, faith and courage. She wasn't the kind of speaker who makes those she is addressing feel stupid or without possibilities.

Her basic message was stunningly simple: we are called by God to love one another as He loves us. (These days many of us go to great lengths to avoid saying "He" in such a sentence, but Dorothy steadily resisted a sexually neutral vocabulary.)

If "God" was one key word, "hospitality" was another. She repeated again and again a saying from the early Church, "Every home should have a Christ room in it, so that hospitality may be practiced." Hospitality, she explained, is simply practicing God's mercy with those around us. Christ is in the stranger, in the person who has nowhere to go and no one to welcome him. "Those who cannot see the face of Christ in the poor are atheists indeed," she often said.

A day never passed without Dorothy speaking of the works of mercy: feeding the hungry, giving drink to the thirsty, clothing the naked, giving shelter to the homeless, caring for the sick, visiting prisoners, burying the dead, admonishing the sinner, instructing the ignorant, counseling the doubtful, comforting the sorrowful, bearing wrongs patiently, forgiving all injuries, praying for the living and the dead. She helped us understand a merciful life has many levels: there is hunger not only for food but also for faith, not only for a place at the table but also for a real welcome, not only for assistance but also for listening, not only for kind words but also for truthful words. There is not only hospitality of the door but also hospitality of the face and heart.

Hospitality of the heart transforms the way to see people and how we respond to them. Their needs become primary. Tom Cornell tells the story of a donor coming into the New York house one morning and giving Dorothy a diamond ring. Dorothy thanked her for the donation and put it in her pocket without batting an eye. Later a certain demented lady came in, one of the more irritating regulars at the CW house, one of those people who make you wonder if you were cut out for life in a house of hospitality. I can't recall her ever saying "thank you" or looking like she was on the edge of saying it. She had a voice that could strip paint off the wall. Dorothy took the diamond ring out of her pocket and gave it to this lady. Someone on the staff said to Dorothy, "Wouldn't it have been better if we took the ring to the diamond exchange, sold it, and paid that woman's rent for a year?" Dorothy replied that the woman had her dignity and could do what she liked with the ring. She could sell it for rent money or take a trip to the Bahamas. Or she could enjoy wearing a diamond ring on her hand like the woman who gave it away. "Do you suppose," Dorothy asked, "that God created diamonds only for the rich?"

For all her traveling, most of Dorothy's life was spent in New York City. Before her conversion, in 1924 when she was 26 years old, she had bought a small beach house on Staten Island. It was a simple structure with a few plain rooms and a cast iron stove. Walking on the beach or to the post office, rosary in hand, she prayed her way through an out-of-wedlock pregnancy, prayed her way through the Baltimore Catechism, prayed her way to her daughter Tamar's baptism in a nearby Catholic parish, prayed her way through the collapse of a common-law marriage and to her own baptism, prayed her way through the incomprehension of her atheist friends who regarded all religion as snake oil.

The main part of her New York life was in Manhattan with the urban part of the Catholic Worker community. In the early sixties, St. Joseph's House of Hospitality was on Chrystie Street, a decrepit three-story building a block from the Bowery, in those days the city's grimmest avenue. As there wasn't enough room inside, the down-and-out were often lined up at the door waiting either for food or clothing—men mainly, people often grouped under the heading "bums." Bums had been a major part of Dorothy's life since leaving college in Illinois to come to New York. She rented a room on the Lower East Side and, at age 18, became a reporter for New York's socialist daily newspaper, the *Call.*

Dorothy's office at the Catholic Worker, just inside the front door, was hardly big enough for her desk. Here she and I would sometimes discuss—occasionally argue—about what should be in the next issue of the paper. It wasn't the easiest place for conversation. The ground floor was where food was prepared and meals served, each meal in shifts as there were only a few bench-style tables. From morning till night, it tended to be noisy. Sitting at her desk one afternoon, talking about the next issue, we could hardly hear each other. Dorothy got up, opened her office door and yelled "Holy silence!" For a few minutes it was almost quiet.

On the second floor, the site of the two clothing rooms, one for men, one for women, there was an area used for daily prayer—lauds, vespers, compline—as well as recitation of the rosary every afternoon. None of this was obligatory, but part of the community was always present, the community being a mixture of "staff" (as those of us who came as volunteers were called) and "family" (people who had once come in for clothing or a bowl of soup and gradually become part of the household).

It wasn't a comfortable life. At the time I joined, Dorothy had a sixth-floor walk-up apartment in a tenement on Spring Street. For $25 a month she got two small rooms, a bathtub next to the kitchen sink, and a bathroom the size of a broom closet. This may sound uninviting, but Dorothy regarded the neighborhood as luxury enough. With an Italian bakery across the street, the smell of bread in the oven was often in the air, and there was always the intoxicating perfume of Italian cooking. The San Gennaro Festival was celebrated annually just around the corner. For a week, that part of Manhattan became a village in sight of Naples.

The day finally came when climbing those five flights of stairs became too much for her aging knees, so we moved her to a similar apartment only one flight up on Ridge Street—also $25 a month, but in a seedier neighborhood. The place was in appalling condition. Stuart Sandberg and I went down to clean and paint the two rooms, dragging box after box of old linoleum and other debris down to the street, including what seemed to us a hideous painting of the Holy Family—Mary, Joseph and Jesus rendered in a few bright colors against a battleship gray background on a piece of plywood. We shook our heads, deposited it in the trash along the curb, and went back to work. Not long after Dorothy arrived carrying the painting. "Look what I found! The Holy Family! It's a providential sign, a blessing." She put it on the mantle of the apartment's bricked-up fireplace. Dorothy had a gift for finding beauty where others tended to see rubbish.

If she was one of the freest persons alive, she was also one of the most disciplined. This was most notable in her religious life. Whether traveling or home, it was a rare day when Dorothy didn't go to Mass, while on Saturday evenings she went to confession. Sacramental life was the bedrock of her existence. She never obliged anyone to follow her example, but God knows she gave an example. When I think of her, the first image that comes to mind is Dorothy on her knees praying before the Blessed Sacrament either in the chapel at the farm or in one of several urban parish churches near the Catholic Worker.

One day, looking into the Bible and Missal she had left behind when summoned for a phone call, I found long lists of people, living and dead, whom she prayed for daily.

Occasionally she spoke of her "prayings": "We feed the hungry, yes. We try to shelter the homeless and give them clothes, but there is strong faith at work: we pray. If an outsider who comes to visit us doesn't pay attention to our prayings and what that means, then he'll miss the whole point."

She was attentive to fast days and fast seasons. It was in that connection she told me a story about prayer. For many years, she said, she had been a heavy smoker. Her day began with lighting up a cigarette. Her big sacrifice every Lent was giving up smoking, but having to get by without a cigarette made her increasingly irritable as the days passed, until the rest of the community was praying she would light up a smoke. One year, as Lent approached, the priest who ordinarily heard her confessions urged her not to give up cigarettes that year but instead to pray daily, "Dear God, help me stop smoking." She used that prayer for several years without it having any impact on her addiction. Then one morning she woke up, reached for a cigarette, and realized she didn't want it, and she never smoked another.

Dorothy was never "too polite" to speak about God. Nothing we achieved was ever our doing, it was only God's mercy passing through us. Our own love wasn't our love. If we experienced love for another person, whether wife or child or friend or enemy, it was God's love. "If I have accomplished anything in my life," she said late in her life, "it is because I wasn't embarrassed to talk about God."

People sometimes tell me how lucky I am to have been part of the same community that Dorothy Day belonged to. They picture a group of more or less saintly people having a wonderful time doing good works. In reality Catholic Worker community life in Manhattan in the early sixties had much in common with purgatory. The "staff" was made up of people with very different backgrounds, interests, temperaments and convictions. We ranged from the gregarious to the permanently furious. There was a recluse named Keith living in a back room on the third floor who maintained the mailing list, a big job as *The Catholic Worker* had nearly a hundred thousand subscribers. He was rarely seen and never said a word; communication with him was by notes. Another member of staff was the angry daughter of a millionaire newspaper publisher; the last I heard, she had become a leader of a Marxist sect.

But not everyone was all thorns. There was lean, gentle, long-suffering Charlie Butterworth, a lawyer who had graduated from Harvard but whose pacifism had led him to the Catholic Worker. Arthur J. Lacey, with his matchstick body, was chiefly responsible for the men's clothing room. He called himself "Haberdasher to the Bowery." There was the always-teasing Stanley Vishnewski, who said most of us belonged "not to the Catholic Worker movement but to the Catholic Shirker movement."

Agreement within the staff was as rare as visits by the President of the United States. The most bitter dispute I experienced had to do with how best to use the small amounts of eggs, butter and other treats that sometimes were given to us. Use them for "the line" (people we often didn't know by name who lined up for meals) or the "family," as had been the custom? Though we worked side by side, saw each other daily, and prayed together, staff tension had become too acute for staff meetings. Dorothy or Charlie Butterworth handed out jobs and once you had a job, it was yours until you stopped doing it. The final authority was Dorothy Day, not a responsibility she enjoyed, but no one else could make a final decision that would be respected by the entire staff. When Dorothy returned from a cross-country speaking trip she told the two people running the kitchen that the butter and eggs should go to the family, which led to their resigning from kitchen work. Soon after they left the community trailing black smoke, convinced that Dorothy Day wasn't living up to the writings of Dorothy Day.

One of the miracles of Dorothy's life is that she remained part of a conflict-torn community for nearly half a century. Still more remarkable, she remained a person of hope and gratitude to the end. (She occasionally spoke of "the duty of hope.")

Dorothy was and remains a controversial lady. There was hardly anything she did which didn't attract criticism. Even hospitality scandalizes some people. We were blamed for making people worse, not better, because we were doing nothing to "reform them." A social worker asked Dorothy one day how long the down-and-out were permitted to stay. "We let them stay forever," Dorothy answered. "They live with us, they die with us, and we give them a Christian burial. We pray for them after they are dead. Once they are taken in, they become members of the family. Or rather they always were members of the family. They are our brothers and sisters in Christ."

What got her in the most hot water was her sharp social criticism. She pointed out that patriotism was a more powerful force in most people's lives than the Gospel. While she hated every kind of tyranny and never ceased to be thankful for America having taken in so many people fleeing poverty and repression, she was fierce in her criticism of capitalism and consumerism. She said America had a tendency to treat people like Kleenex—use them and throw them away. "Our problems stem," she said, "from our acceptance of this filthy, rotten system."

She had no kind words for war or anything having to do with it—war was simply murder wrapped in flags. She was convinced Jesus had disarmed all his followers when he said to Peter, "Put away your sword, for whoever lives by the sword will perish by the sword." A way of life based on love, including love of enemies, left no room for killing. You couldn't practice the works of mercy with one hand and the works of vengeance with the other.

No stranger to prison, she was first locked up as a young woman protesting with Suffragettes in front of the White House during World War I and was last jailed in her seventies for picketing with farm workers. She took pride in the young men of the Catholic Worker who went to prison rather than be drafted; it was a "a good way to visit the prisoner," she pointed out. Yet she also welcomed back others who had left Catholic Worker communities in fight in the Second World War. They might disagree about the best way to fight Nazism, but, as she often said, "there is no 'party line' in the Catholic Worker movement."

Dorothy was sometimes criticized for being too devout a Catholic. How could she be so radical about social matters and so conservative about her Church? While she occasionally deplored statements or actions by members of the hierarchy, she was by no means an opponent of the bishops or someone campaigning for structural changes in the Church. What was needed, she said, wasn't new doctrine but living out the existing doctrine. True, some pastors seemed barely Christian, but one had to aim for their conversion, an event that would not be hastened by berating them, but rather by helping them see what their vocation requires. The way to do that was to set an example.

"I didn't become a Catholic in order to purify the church," Dorothy once said to Bob Coles. "I knew someone, years ago, who kept telling me that if the Catholic Workers could purify the church, then she would convert. I thought she was teasing me when she first said that, but after a while I realized she meant what she was saying. Finally, I told her I wasn't trying to reform the church or take sides on all the issues the church was involved in; I was trying to be a loyal servant of the church Jesus had founded. She thought I was being facetious. She reminded me that I had been critical of capitalism and America, so why not Catholicism and Rome? My answer was that I had no reason to criticize Catholicism as a religion or Rome as the place where the Vatican is located....As for Catholics all over the world, including members of the church, they are no better than lots of their worst critics, and maybe some of us Catholics are worse than our worst critics."

Pleased as she was when home Masses were allowed and the Liturgy translated into English, she didn't take kindly to smudging the border between the sacred and mundane. When a priest close to the community used a coffee cup for a chalice at a Mass celebrated in the soup kitchen on First Street, she afterward took the cup, kissed it, and buried it in the back yard. It was no longer suited for coffee—it had held the Blood of Christ. I learned more about the Eucharist that day than I had from any book or sermon. It was a learning experience for the priest as well; thereafter he used a chalice.

Dorothy's sensitivity for the sacred helps explain her love, rare at the time, of the Orthodox Church, which was famous, or infamous, for its reluctance to modernize, rationalize, speed up or simplify its liturgical life. She longed for the reunion of the Church. She occasionally took me to the small meetings of a group in New York City, The Third Hour it was called, that brought together Catholic and Orthodox Christians, as well as at least one Anglican, the poet W.H. Auden. It was Dorothy who brought me to visit the Russian Orthodox cathedral up on East 97th Street where she introduced me to the Russian priest serving there, Father Matvei Stadniuk, now dean of the Epiphany Cathedral in Moscow. In 1988, it was Father Matvei who launched the first project of Christian volunteer hospital service in what was still Soviet Russia, and it was he, not I, who recalled our first meeting 26 years earlier, but only when I had given him a copy of my biography of Dorothy. "Dorothy Day? Did you know her?" And then he looked more closely at my face and said, "I knew you when you were a young man, when Dorothy brought you to our church."

I'm not sure what had given Dorothy such a warmth for Orthodox Christianity in general and the Russian Orthodox Church in particular, but one of the factors was certainly her love of the books of Dostoevsky, and most of all his novel, *The Brothers Karamazov*. Perhaps the most important chapter for Dorothy concerns a conversation between a wealthy woman and an elderly monk, Father Zosima. The woman asks him how she can really know that God exists. Fr. Zosima tells her that no explanation or argument can achieve this, only the practice of "active love." He assures her that there is no other way to know the reality of God. The woman confesses that sometimes she dreams about a life of loving service to others. She thinks perhaps she will become a nun, live in holy poverty and serve the poor in the humblest way. It seems to her such a wonderful thought that it makes tears comes to her eyes. But then it crosses her mind how ungrateful some of the people she is serving will be. Some will complain that the soup she is serving isn't hot enough, the bread isn't fresh enough, the bed is too hard, the covers too thin. She confesses she couldn't bear such ingratitude, and so her dreams about serving others vanish, and once again she finds herself wondering if there really is a God. To this Fr. Zosima responds with the words, "Love in practice is a hard and dreadful thing compared to love in dreams," words Dorothy often repeated. I think of the Orthodox monk Father Zosima as somehow a co-founder of all the Catholic Worker houses of hospitality.

It is in the same book that Dostoevsky relates the story of a woman who was almost saved by an onion. She had been a person of absolute selfishness and so, when she died, she went to hell. After all, she had chosen hell every day of her life. Even after her death, her guardian angel wanted to save her and so approached the Savior, saying a mistake had been made. "Don't you remember? Olga once gave an onion to a beggar." It was left unsaid that the onion had started to rot, and also that it wasn't so much given as thrown at the beggar. The Savior said, "You are right. I bless you to pull her out of hell with an onion." So the angel flew into the twilight of hell—all those people at once so close to each other and so far apart—and there was the selfish woman, glaring at her neighbors. The angel offered her the onion and began to lift her out of hell with it. Others around her saw what was happening, saw the angel's strength, and saw their chance. They grabbed hold of the woman's legs and so were being lifted with her, a ribbon of people being rescued by one onion. Only the woman had never wanted company. She began kicking with her legs, yelling at her uninvited guests, "Only for me! Only for me!" These three words are hell itself. The onion became rotten and the woman and all the others attached to her fell back into the disconnection of hell.

"Hell is not to love anymore," Dorothy said so many times, quoting another author she loved, Georges Bernanos.

Dorothy Day's main achievement is that she taught us the "Little Way" of love, which it so happens involves cutting up a great many onions. The path to heaven, it seems, is marked by open doors and the smell of onions. "All the way to heaven is heaven," she so often said, quoting St. Catherine of Siena, "because He said, 'I am the Way.'"

It was chiefly through the writings of St Therese of Liseux that Dorothy had been drawn to the "Little Way." No term, in her mind, better described the ideal Christian way of doing things. As she once put it, "Paper work, cleaning the house, dealing with the innumerable visitors who come all through the day, answering the phone, keeping patience and acting intelligently, which is to find some meaning in all that happens, these things, too, are the works of peace, and often seem like a very little way."

I'm sometimes asked, "Dorothy Day gives a fine example for people who don't have a family to take care of and mortgages to pay, but what about the rest of us?"

The rest of us includes my wife and me. I don't have enough fingers on one hand to count our children, and the first of the month is mortgage payment day. But every time I open the door to guests, it's partly thanks to Dorothy Day. Every time I think about things in the bright light of the Gospel rather than in the gray light of money or the dim light of politics, her example has had its influence. Every time I try to overcome meanness or selfishness rising up in myself, it is partly thanks to the example of Dorothy Day. Every time I defeat the impulse to buy something I can get along without, Dorothy Day's examples of voluntary poverty have had renewed impact. Every time I try to see Christ's presence in the face of a stranger, there again I owe a debt to Dorothy Day. No one else has made me think so much about the words we will hear at the Last Judgement: "What you did to the least person, you did to me." What I know of Christ, the Church, sacramental life, the Bible, and truthtelling, I know in large measure thanks to her, while whatever I have done that was cowardly, opportunistic or cruel, is despite her.

It isn't that Dorothy Day is the point of reference. Christ is. But I can't think of anyone I've known whose Christ-centered life did so much to help make me a more Christ-centered person.

It's a century since Dorothy Day was born and nearly 20 years since she died, but she continues to touch our lives, not only as a person we remember with gratitude, but also as a saint, if by the word "saint" we mean a person who helps us see what it means to follow Christ.

"It is the living from day to day," she once said, "taking no thought for the morrow, seeing Christ in all who come to us, and trying literally to follow the Gospel that resulted in this work."

M.L. Liebler

The Lazarus Dream Forgiven

(for Todd Duncan)

I have and you have.
We all have had
Our Lazarus dream
Before. Somewhere we've reached
Out like ghosts
With hands as faint and pale
As still water lying
Along the banks of closed
Streams. We have wondered
About children like us
Who remain buried
Within the skin of our own
Weak desires. We never get
Used to the pain that soaks us
Thick like rags, stopping
Dams, holding back
The currents of our futures. Slowly
We want to float, or have
Someone like us float, out
Of ourselves, just like Lazarus
In the darkness of the cave,
As lonely as his once distant soul,
Before the living waters
Nurtured him back
To life. One piece. All
Forgiven.

from *Stripping the Adult Century Bare,* Viet Nam Generation Press, 1995.

Bibliography

Abrams, Ray H. 1933. *Preachers Present Arms.* Philadelphia: Round Table Press.

"Accept the Pope's Program," *Labor Leader* (April 30, 1938): 2.

Achtemeier, Paul J. ed. 1985. *Harper's Bible Dictionary.* New York: Harper and Row.

Adeney, Bernard T. 1988. *Just War, Political Realism, and Faith.* Metuchen, NJ: Scarecrow Press.

Agar, Herbert. 1934. "The Task for Conservatism," *The American Review* 3 (April 1934): 1-22.

Agar, Herbert, and Allen Tate, eds. 1936. *Who Owns America? A New Declaration of Independence.* Boston: Houghton Mifflin.

Ahlstrom, Sydney. 1972. *A Religious History of the American People.* New Haven: Yale University Press.

Aitken, Robert. 1984. *The Mind of Clover: Essays in Zen Buddhist Ethics.* San Francisco: North Point Press.

——— and David Steindl-Rast. 1994. *The Ground We Share: Everyday Practice, Buddhist and Christian.* Liguori, MO: Triumph.

Allaire, James. 1996. "Therese of Lisieux Inspired Dorothy Day," *Houston Catholic Worker* 16 (May-June 1996): 1, 6

Allaire, James, and Rosemary Broughton. 1995. *Praying with Dorothy Day.* Winona, MN: Saint Mary's Press.

Amato, Joseph. 1975. *Mounier and Maritain : A French Catholic Understanding of the Modern World.* Tuscaloosa: University of Alabama Press.

Anderson, Nels. 1961. *Work and Leisure.* New York: Free Press of Glencoe.

Antezana, Jorge Garcia, ed. 1992. *Liberation Theology and Sociopolitical Transformation: A Reader.* Burnaby, BC: Institute for the Humanities, Simon Fraser University.

Aquinas, Thomas. 1947-48. *Summa Theologiae.* American ed. Literally tr. by Fathers of the English Dominican Province. New York: Benziger.

Arendt, Hannah. 1972. *Crises of the Republic: Lying in Politics, Civil Disobedience on Violence, Thoughts on Politics, and Revolution.* New York: Harcourt Brace Jovanovich.

Ariyaratne, A.T. 1978. *Collected Works,* Nandasena Tarnapala, ed. Sri Lanka: Sarvodaya Press.

———.1982. *In Search of Development: The Sarvodaya's Effort to Harmonize Tradition with Change.* Sri Lanka: Sarvodaya Press.

Aronica, Michele Theresa. 1987. *Beyond Charismatic Leadership: The New York Catholic Worker Movement.* New Brunswick, NJ: Transaction Books.

Bailie, Gil. 1995. *Violence Unveiled.* New York: Crossroad.

Bamberger, John Eudes, O.C.S.O. 1997. Letter to Julie L. Pycior, Sept. 5.

Baum, Gregory, and Robert Ellsberg, eds. 1989. *The Logic of Solidarity: Commentaries on Pope John Paul II's Encyclical "On Social Concern."* Maryknoll, NY: Orbis Books.

Bartlett, Lee. 1988. *William Everson: The Life of Brother Antoninus.* New York: New Directions.

Bauerschmidt, Frederick C. 1997. "The Politics of the Little Way: Dorothy Day Reads Therese of Lisieux." In *American Catholic Traditions: Resources for Renewal*, eds. Sandra Yocum Mize and William Portier. Maryknoll, NY: Orbis Books.

Baxter, Michael J., C.S.C. 1996. "In Service to the Nation: A Critical Analysis of the Formation of the Americanist Tradition in Catholic Social Ethics." Duke University: unpublished Ph.D. dissertation.

———. 1997. "Reintroducing Virgil Michel: Towards a Counter Tradition of Catholic Social Ethics in the United States," *Communio* 24 (Fall 1997): 499-528.

Beck, Charlotte Joko. 1989. *Everyday Zen.* New York: HarperCollins.

Beigel, Gerard. 1997. *Faith and Social Justice in the Teaching of Pope John Paul II.* New York: Peter Lang.

Belloc, Hilaire. 1913/1927/1936. *The Servile State.* London: T.N. Foulis, 1913; 3rd edition, London: Constable, 1927; New York: Holt, 1936.

———. 1936. *The Restoration of Property.* New York: Sheed and Ward.

Benedictine Monks of Solesmes, eds. 1961. *The Lay Apostolate: Papal Teachings,* Boston: St. Paul Editions.

Bernstein, Irving. 1971. *Turbulent Years: A History of the American Worker; 1933-1941.* Boston: Houghton Mifflin.

Berrigan, Daniel. 1982. *Portraits–of Those I Love.* New York: Crossroads.

Berrigan, Philip, and Elizabeth McAlister. 1989. *The Time's Discipline: The Beatitudes and Nuclear Resistance.* Baltimore: Fortkamp.

Berry, Wendell. 1977. *The Unsettling of America: Culture and Agriculture.* San Francisco: Sierra Club Books.

———. 1993. *Sex, Economy, Freedom, and Community.* New York: Pantheon.

———. 1995. *Another Turn of the Crank.* Washington, DC: Counterpoint.

Berryman, Phillip. 1987. *Liberation Theology: The Essential Facts About the Revolutionary Movement in Latin America and Beyond.* New York: Pantheon.

The Holy Bible. 1965. Revised Standard Version, Catholic Edition. San Francisco: Ignatius Press.

Boff, Leonardo, and Clodovis Boff. 1994. *Introducing Liberation Theology.* Maryknoll, NY: Orbis Books.

Borsodi, Ralph. 1929. *This Ugly Civilization.* New York: Simon and Schuster.

———. 1933. *Flight from the City: the Story of a New Way to Family Security.* New York: Harper.

Boulton, Agnes. 1958. *Part of a Long Story.* Garden City, NY: Doubleday.

Bourne, Randolph. 1964. "The State." In *War and the Intellectuals: Collected Essays, 1915-1919.* Ed. Carl Resek. New York: Harper and Row.

Bouscaren, Anthony T. 1966. "The Catholic Peaceniks," *National Review* 18 (March 8, 1966): 202.

Bove, Paul. 1995. "Discourse." In *Critical Terms for Literary Study.* Eds. Frank Lentricchia and Thomas McLaughlin, Chicago: University of Chicago Press.

Bovée, David S. 1987. "The Church and the Land: The National Catholic Rural Life Conference and American Society, 1923-1985." University of Chicago: unpublished Ph.D. dissertation.

Branham, Robert J., and W. Barnett Pearce. 1985. "Between Text and Context: Toward a Rhetoric of Textual Reconstruction," *Quarterly Journal of Speech* 71 (February 1985): 19-36.

Brinkley, Alan. 1995. *The End of Reform: New Deal Liberalism, The Recession and War*. New York: Knopf.

Brown, Robert McAfee. 1989. "Reflections of a North American: The Future of Liberation Theology." In *The Future of Liberation Theology*. Eds. Marc H. Ellis and Otto Maduro. Maryknoll, NY: Orbis Books.

———. 1990. *Gustavo Gutiérrez: An Introduction to Liberation Theology*. Maryknoll, NY: Orbis Books.

———. 1993. *Liberation Theology: An Introductory Guide*. Louisville, KY: Westminster/ John Knox Press.

Bryant, Byron. 1951. "The Catholic Worker Movement Confronts the Modern State," *Retort* 4 (1951): 9.

Burke, Kenneth. 1945. *Grammar of Motives*. Berkeley: University of California Press.

Buckley, William F., Jr. 1960. "The Catholic in the Modern World: A Conservative View," *Commonweal* 73 (December16, 1960): 307-310.

Burns, Edward McNall. 1957. *The American Idea of Mission: Concepts of National Purpose and Destiny*. New Brunswick, NJ: Rutgers University Press.

Byers, David, ed. 1985. *Justice in the Marketplace*. Washington, DC: U.S.Catholic Conference.

Caldecott, Stratford. 1994. "Chesterton's Distributism," *Second Spring* (June 1994).

Callahan, Annice. 1991. *Spiritual Guides for Today: Evelyn Underhill, Dorothy Day, Karl Rahner, Thomas Merrton, Simon Weil, Henri Nouwen*. New York: Crossroad.

Callahan, William M. 1935. "Ethics of Modern War Discussed in Brooklyn," *The Catholic Worker* 3 (December 1935): 3, 7.

Campbell, Karlyn Kohrs. 1983. "Femininity and Feminism: To Be or Not to Be a Woman," *Communication Quarterly* 31 (Spring 1983): 101-108.

———. 1989. *Man Cannot Speak for Her*. Volume 1. Westport, CT: Greenwood Press.

Carlen, Claudia. 1990. *The Papal Encyclicals 1939-1958*. Raleigh, NC: The Pierian Press.

Casey, William Van Etten and Phillip Nobile, eds. 1971. *The Berrigans*. NY: Avon.

Catherine of Siena, Saint. *The Dialogue*. Translation and introduction by Suzanne Noffke. New York: Paulist Press, 1980.

Catholic Church. Pontifica Commissio Biblica. 1994. The Interpretation of the Bible in the Church. *Origins* 23 (January 6, 1994); 521.

The Catholic Worker. Articles are cited as *CW* followed by the month/year: page number. E.g., (CW 5/1937: 3). The Dorothy Day-Catholic Worker Collection at Marquette University contains a complete file of *The Catholic Worker*.

Catholic Worker Pamphlets. 1936. *Mystical Body of Christ*, August. Dorothy Day-Catholic Worker Collection, Series W-1, Box 1.

———. 1938. *The Folly of Force*, Catholic Worker Press, Series 1, No. 4; Dorothy Day-Catholic Worker Collection, Series W-1, Box 1.

Cavanaugh, William T. 1995. "'A Fire Strong Enough to Consume the House': The Wars of Religion and the Rise of the State," *Modern Theology* 11 (October 1995): 377-420.

Cave, Alfred A. 1988. "Canaanites in a Promised Land: The American Indian and the Providential Theory of Empire," *American Indian Quarterly* 12 (Fall 1988): 277-97.

Chamberlain, J.P. 1946. "Looking Backward: Ten Years of *Free America*," *Free America* 10 (Winter 1946-1947): 3.

Chatfield, Charles. 1971. *For Peace and Justice: Pacifism in America, 1914-1941.* Knoxville,TN: University of Tennessee Press.

Chesterton, Gilbert Keith. 1926/1987. *The Outline of Sanity*. New York: Metheun, 1926; reprinted San Francisco: Ignatius Press.

Chinard, Gilbert. 1929/1957. *Thomas Jefferson: The Apostle of Americanism.* 2d ed. Ann Arbor, MI: University of Michigan Press.

Chittister, Joan, O.S.B. 1988. "Viewpoint Woman: Do Call Her a Saint," *Pax Christi USA* 13 (Spring 1988): 16.

Chodorow, N. J. 1985. "Gender, Relation, and Difference in Psychoanalytic Perspective." In *The Future of Difference*. Eds. H. Eisenstein & A. Jardine. New Brunswick, NJ: Rutgers University Press.

Cleaver, Richard G. 1993. *New Heaven, New Earth: Practical Essays on the Catholic Worker Program*. Marion, SD: Rose Hill Books.

Clebsch, William. 1973. *American Religious Thought: A History.* Chicago: University of Chicago Press.

Cogley, John. 1976. *A Canterbury Tale: Experiences and Reflections, 1916-1976.* New York: Seabury Press.

Cohn-Sherbox, Dan. 1987. *On Earth As It Is in Heaven: Jews, Christians, and Liberation Theology*. Maryknoll, NY: Orbis Books.

———. 1992. *World Religions and Human Liberation.* Maryknoll, NY: Orbis Books.

Coleman, John A. 1991. *One Hundred Years of Catholic Social Thought—Celebration and Challenge*. Maryknoll, NY: Orbis Books.

Coles, Robert. 1973. *A Spectacle Unto the World: The Catholic Worker Movement.* New York: Viking Press.

———. 1986. *The Moral Life of Children*. Boston: Atlantic Monthly Press.

———. 1987. *Dorothy Day: A Radical Devotion*. Reading, MA: Addison-Wesley.

———. 1990. *The Moral Life of Children and The Spiritual Life of Children*. Boston: Houghton Mifflin.

Commonweal. 1940. "Roosevelt–Wilkie–The Fence," a poll of contributing editors. *Commonweal* 32 (August 23, 1940): 360-363.

Comstock, W. Richard. 1972. *The Study of Religion and Primitive Religions.* New York: Harper and Row.

Conway, John S. 1994. "The Vatican, Germany and the Holocaust." In *Papal Diplomacy in the Modern Age*. Eds. Peter Kent and John F. Pollard. Westport, CT: Praeger.

Cooney, John. 1984. *The American Pope: The Life and Times of Francis Cardinal Spellman*. New York: Times Books.

Cooney, Robert, and Helen Michalowski, eds. 1987. *The Power of the People: Active Nonviolence in the United States*. Philadelphia: New Society Press.

Cornell, Thomas C., Robert Ellsberg, and Jim Forest, eds. 1995. *A Penny a Copy: Readings from the Catholic Worker*, Maryknoll, N.Y.: Orbis Books.

Corrin, Jay P. 1981. *G.K. Chesterton and Hilaire Belloc: The Battle Against Modernity.* Athens: Ohio University Press.

———.1996. "H. A. Reinhold: Liturgical Pioneer and Anti-Fascist," *Catholic Historical Review* 82 (July 1996): 436-458.

Cort, John C. 1939. "Catholics in Trade Unions," *Commonweal* 30 (May 5 1939): 35.

———. 1937. "ACTU Prefers to be Inside, not Outside," *The Catholic Worker* 5 (July 1937): 5.

———. 1948. "Is a Christian Industrialism Possible?" *Commonweal* 49 (October 29, 1948): 60, 62.

———. 1950. "Catholics and Liberals," *Commonweal* 52 (June 16, 1950): 242-244.

———. 1952. "The Charms of Anarchism." *Commonweal* 57 (November 14, 1952) 19: 139-40.

———. 1954. "A Dream of Industrial Peace," *Catholic Digest* 18 (May 1954): 91.

———. 1967. Address at National Catholic Social Action Association Conference, San Francisco, August 25, 1967, National Catholic Social Action Conference Records, Marquette University Archives, Series 6, Box 4.

———. 1976. "Why I Became a Socialist," *Commonweal* 103 (March 26, 1976): 203.

———. 1987. "A Bizarre Conversion." In *The New Catholics: Contemporary Converts Tell Their Stories*. Ed. Dan O'Neil. New York: Crossroad, 1987: 1-19.

———. 1939. Letter. John C. Cort to Dorothy Day, 1939. Dorothy Day-Catholic Worker Collection, Marquette University Archives, Series 2.1, Box 2.

———. 1940. Letter. John C. Cort to Joe Zarrella, May 4, 1940, Dorothy Day-Catholic Worker Collection, Marquette University Archives, Series W-2.1, Box 2.

———. 1949. Letter. John C. Cort to Dorothy Day, November 15, 1949, Dorothy Day-Catholic Worker Collection, Marquette University Archives, Series W-2.1, Box 2.

———. Unpublished autobiography possession of author, Nahant, MA.

Cowan, Michael A., and Bernard J. Lee, S.M. 1997. *Conversation, Risk, and Conversion: The Inner and Public Life of Small Christian Communities.* Maryknoll, NY: Orbis Books.

Cowley, Malcolm. 1951. *Exile's Return; a Literary Odyssey of the 1920s.* New York: Viking Press.

Coy, Patrick G. 1986. "The Incarnational Spirituality of Dorothy Day." *Spirituality Today* 39 (1986): 114-125.

———. 1988. "The One-Person Revolution: Ammon Hennacy." In *A Revolution of the Heart: Essays on the Catholic Worker*. Ed. Patrick Coy. Philadelphia: Temple University Press.

———. 1996. "Conscription and the Catholic Conscience in World War II." In *American Catholic Pacifism: The Influence of Dorothy Day and the Catholic Worker Movement.* Eds. Anne Klejment and Nancy L. Roberts. Westport, CT: Praeger.

Croly, Herbert. 1909/1965. *The Promise of American Life.* Cambridge, MA: Belknap Press of Harvard University Press.

Craig, Kevin. (N.D.) *Easy Essays: A Concordance*. Unpublished manuscript.

Cronin, John F. 1971. "Forty Years Later: Reflections and Reminiscences." *American Ecclesiastical Review* 164 (May 1971): 310-318.
Crosby, Michael. 1981. *Spirituality of the Beatitudes: Matthew's Challenge for First World Christians.* Maryknoll, NY: Orbis Books.
Cullen, Michael, and Don Ranly. 1972. *A Time To Dance: The Mike Cullen Story.* Celina, OH: Messenger Press.
Curran, Charles. 1982. *American Catholic Social Ethics.* Notre Dame, IN: University of Notre Dame Press.
Danbom, David A. 1979. *The Resisted Revolution: Urban America and the Industrialization of Agriculture, 1900-1930.* Ames: Iowa State University Press.
———. 1995. *Born in the Country: A History of Rural America.* Baltimore: Johns Hopkins University Press.
D'Antonio, William V. 1989. *American Catholic Laity in a Changing Church.* Kansas City, MO : Sheed and Ward.
Darrow, Robert M. 1953. "Catholic Political Power: A Study of the Activities of the American Catholic Church on Behalf of Franco during the Spanish Civil War, 1936-1939" Columbia University: unpublished Ph.D. dissertation.
Davids, T. Rhys, and J. Carpenter, eds. 1947. *Dighanikaya,* vol. 1. London: Pali Text Society.
Davidson, Donald. "Agrarianism for Commuters," *The American Review* 1 (May 1933): 238-242.
Dawson, Christopher. 1932. *The Making of Europe: An Introduction to the History of European Unity.* New York: Macmillan.
Day, Dorothy. Personal papers in the Dorothy Day-Catholic Worker Collection, Marquette University Archives.
———. 1924. *The Eleventh Virgin.* New York : Albert and Charles Boni.
———. 1928. "Having a Baby," *New Masses* 4 (June 1928).
———. 1933. "The Catholic Worker," *Rosary* 83 (1933).
———. 1934. "Start of 'Catholic Worker' Described by its Founder," *Oueen's Work* 26 (April 1934): 11, 30.
———. 1934. "The Mystical Body of Christ," *The Catholic Worker* 2 (October 1934): 3.
———. 1935. *An Answer to Some Charges Against the Catholic Worker.* Pamphlet.
———. 1938/1978. *From Union Square to Rome.* Silver Spring, MD: The Preservation of the Faith Press, 1938; reissued New York: Arno Press, 1978.
———. 1939. *House of Hospitality.* New York: Sheed and Ward.
———. 1939. "We Are to Blame for New War in Europe," *The Catholic Worker* 7 (Sept. 1939): 1,4.
———. 1940. "Aims and Purposes," *The Catholic Worker* 7 (February 1940): 7; reprinted in Cornell et al., 1995.
———. 1941. "Address to the Liberal-Socialist Alliance in New York City," Dec. 8, 1941. Dorothy Day–Catholic Collection, Marquette University Archives, Series D-5, Box 5.
———. 1942. *Fight Conscription.* New York: Catholic Worker Press.
———. 1946. *Called to be Saints.* 1946. Dorothy Day-Catholic Worker Collection, Marquette University Archives, Series W-1, Box 1.

———. 1948/1999. *On Pilgrimage.* New York: Catholic Worker Books, 1948; reprinted with introduction by Mark and Louise Zwick. Grand Rapids, MI. William B. Eerdmans Publishing Company, 1999.

———. 1949. "Beyond Politics," *The Catholic Worker* 16 (November 1949): 1-2, 4.

———. 1952/1981/1997. *The Long Loneliness: the Autobiography of Dorothy Day*, NY: Harper, 1952; reprinted in 1981 and 1997; Image Books edition published in 1959.

———. 1957. "Thoughts After Prison," *Liberation* 11 (September 1957): 5-7.

———. 1960. *Therese*. Notre Dame, IN.: Fides Publishers Assn.

———. 1962. "More about Cuba," *The Catholic Worker*, (July-August 1962): 1,7.

———. 1963/1997. *Loaves and Fishes*. New York: Harper and Row, 1963; reprinted with an introduction by Robert Coles, Maryknoll, NY: Orbis Books, 1997.

———. Letter to Thomas Merton, Jan 26, 1967. In *American Catholic Pacifism.* Eds. Anne Klejment and Nancy Roberts. Westport, CT: Praeger, 1996.

———. 1970. *Meditations*. Ed. Stanley Vishnewski. New York: Newman Press.

———. 1972. *On Pilgrimage: The Sixties*. New York: Curtis Books.

———. 1976. Unpublished address to the World Eucharistic Congress. Philadelphia, PA, August 6,1976.

———. 1983/1992. *By Little by Little*. Ed. Robert Ellsberg. New York: Alfred A. Knopf; reprinted with the title *Selected Writings*. Maryknoll, NY: Orbis Books, 1992.

———. "Peter Maurin, A Biography." Unpublished manuscript. Catholic Worker/ William Miller papers, St. Thomas University, Miami, FL.

Dennis, Marie Adele. 1997. *A Retreat with Oscar Romero and Dorothy Day.* Cincinnati, OH: St. Anthony Messenger Press.

Denzin, N. K. 1989. *Interpretive Biography*. Newbury Park, CA: Sage Publications.

Dharmasiri, Gunapala. 1989. *Fundamentals of Buddhist Ethics*. Antioch, CA: Golden Leaves.

Dierks, Sheila D., and Patricia P. Ladley. 1988. *Catholic Worker Houses: Ordinary Miracles*. Kansas City, MO: Sheed and Ward.

Dietrich, Jeff. 1983. *Reluctant Resister*. Greensboro, NC: Unicorn Press.

The Dill Pickler, Newberry Library mss. collection "Dill Pickle Club," 3.

Dolan, Jay P. 1992. *The American Catholic Experience: A History from Colonial Times to the Present.* Notre Dame, IN: University of Notre Dame Press.

Dolgoff, Sam. 1986. *Fragments: A Memoir*. Cambridge, England: Refract Press.

Dorr, Donal. 1983, revised 1992. *Option for the Poor: 100 Years of Vatican Social Teaching*. Maryknoll, NY: Orbis Books.

Doty, William G. 1986. *Mythography: The Study of Myths and Rituals*. University, AL: University of Alabama Press.

Douglass, James W. 1966. *The Non-Violent Cross: A Theology of Revolution and Peace*. New York: The Macmillan Company.

Downey, Michael, ed. 1993. *The New Dictionary of Catholic Spirituality*. Collegeville, MN: The Liturgical Press.

Duffy, Stephen. 1992. *The Graced Horizon: Nature and Grace in Modern Catholic Thought*. Collegeville, Minnesota: Michael Glazier.

Dulles, Avery, S.J. 1987. *Models of the Church,* expanded ed. Garden City, NY.: Image Books.

Dwyer, Judith, ed. 1994. *The New Dictionary of Catholic Social Thought.* Collegeville, MN: The Liturgical Press.

Eck, D. L., and Jain, D., eds. 1987. *Speaking of Faith: Global Perspectives on Women, Religion and Social Change.* Philadelphia, PA: New Society Publishers.

Editorial Staff, Catholic University of America. 1967-79. *New Catholic Encyclopedia.* New York: McGraw-Hill.

Egan, Eileen. 1973. "50 Years of Non-violent Resistance," *Catholic Worker* 39 (September 1973): 1, 8.

———. 1983. *Dorothy Day and the Permanent Revolution.* Erie, PA: Benet Press.

———. 1999. *Peace Be with You: Justified Warfare or the Way of Nonviolence.* Maryknoll,NY: Orbis Books.

Eichenberg, Fritz. 1992. *Works of Mercy.* Maryknoll, NY: Orbis Books.

Ellacuria, Ignacio, S.J,. and Jon Sobrino, S.J., eds. 1993. *Mysterium Liberationis: Fundamental Concepts of Liberation Theology.* Maryknoll, NY: Orbis Books.

Ellsberg, Robert. 1980. "Remarks on the Death of Dorothy Day at Memorial Service at Haley House," Boston, December 17, 1980. Dorothy Day–Catholic Worker Collection, Marquette University Archives, Series D-8, Box 4.

———. 1983. "Introduction." In *By Little and By Little: the Selected Writings of Dorothy Day.* Ed. Robert Ellsberg. New York: Alfred A. Knopf.

———. 1997. *All Saints: Daily Reflections on Saints, Prophets, and Witnesses for Our Time.* New York: Crossroads.

Ellis, Marc. 1978. *A Year at the Catholic Worker.* New York, Paulist Press.

———. 1981. *Peter Maurin: Prophet in the Twentieth Century.* New York: Paulist Press.

———. and Otto Maduro, eds. 1989. *The Future of Liberation Theology: Essays in Honor of Gustavo Gutiérrez.* Maryknoll, NY: Orbis Books.

Epstein, Barbara. 1991. *Political Protest and Cultural Revolution: Nonviolent Direct Action in the 1970s and 1980s.* Berkeley: University of California Press.

Evans, Henry Clay, Jr. 1936. "Liberty Under the Old Order," *The American Review* 6 (March 1936): 546-565.

Fain, John Tyee, and Thomas Daniel Young, eds. 1974. *The Literary Correspondence of Donald Davidson and Allen Tate.* Athens: University of Georgia.

Farrell, William E. 1980. "Drifters, Priests and Nuns Pay Respects to Dorothy Day," *New York Times* (December 3, 1980), D1.

Fehren, Rev. Henry. 1988. "I Was Going to Write a Letter," *U.S. Catholic* 53 (February 1988): 38-40.

Ferkiss, Victor. 1958. "Social Action in the Affluent Society," *Social Order* 8 (September 1958): 330-335.

Ferm, Deane William, ed. 1987. *Liberation Theology: North American Style.* New York: International Religious Foundation.

Fernando, Antony, and Leonard Swidler. 1985. *Buddhism Made Plain: An Introduction for Christians and Jews.* Maryknoll, NY: Orbis Books.

Fisher, James T. 1989 *The Catholic Counterculture in America 1933-1962.* Chapel Hill: University of North Carolina Press.

Fitzpatrick, Benedict. 1927. *Ireland and the Making of Britain.* New York: Funk and Wagnalls.

Flynn, John T. 1995. "A Rejected Manuscript." In *Forgotten Lessons: Selected Essays of John T. Flynn*. Ed. Gregory P. Pavlik. Irvington-on-Hudson, NY: Foundation for Economic Education.

Flynn, Toni. 1989. *Finding My Way: A Journey along the Rim of the Catholic Worker Movement*. Los Osos, CA: Sand River Press.

Forest, James H. 1968. "No Longer Alone: The Catholic Peace Movement." In *American Catholics and Vietnam*. Ed. Thomas Quigley. Grand Rapids, MI: William B. Eerdmans.

———. 1986. *Love Is the Measure: A Biography of Dorothy Day*. New York: Paulist Press; reprinted 1994, Maryknoll, NY: Orbis Books.

———. 1991. *Living with Wisdom: A Life of Thomas Merton*. Maryknoll, NY: Orbis Books.

Frazer, Heather and John O'Sullivan. 1996. "*We Have Just Begun to Not Fight*": *An Oral History of Conscientious Objectors in Civilian Public Service during World War II* . New York: Twayne Publishers.

Fu, Charles Wei-hsun and Sandra Wawrytko, eds. 1991. *Buddhist Ethics and Modern Society*. New York: Greenwood, 1991.

Furfey, Paul Hanly. 1935. "Maximum–Minimum." *The Catholic Worker* 3 (May 1935): 5.

———. 1936. *Fire on the Earth*. New York: Macmillan.

Gara, Larry. Letter to James Missey. July 21, 1997. Personal possession of Dr. Missey.

Garvey, Michael. 1978. *Confessions of a Catholic Worker*. Chicago: Thomas More Press.

Garzia, Italo Garzia 1994. "Pope Pius XII, Italy and the Second World War" In Kent (1994).

Geertz, Clifford. 1973. "Religion as a Cultural System." In *The Interpretation of Cultures*. New York: Basic Books.

Gelb, Arthur and Barbara. 1962. *O'Neill*. New York: Harper and Row.

Gibellini, Rosino, ed. 1979. *Frontiers of Theology in Latin America*. Maryknoll, NY: Orbis Books.

Gill Eric. 1934. *Art in a Changing Civilization*. London: The Bodley Head.

———. 1935. *Work and Leisure*. London: Faber and Faber, Ltd.

———. *Eric Gill, Autobiography*. 1941. New York: The Devin-Adair Company.

———. *Last Essays*. 1942. London: Jonathan Cape.

———. *Essays by Eric Gill*. 1947. Oxford: Alden Press.

Gilligan, Carol. 1982. *In a Different Voice: Psychological Theory and Women's Development*. Cambridge, MA: Harvard University Press.

Gitlin, Todd. 1987. *The Sixties: Years of Hope, Days of Rage*. New York: Bantam.

Glasser, Theodore L., and James S. Ettema. 1993. "When the Facts Don't Speak for Themselves: A Study of the Use of Irony in Daily Journalism," *Critical Studies in Mass Communication* 10 (December 1993): 322-338.

Gleason, Philip. 1987. *Keeping the Faith; American Catholicism, Past and Present*. Notre Dame, IN.: University of Notre Dame Press.

———. 1994. "American Catholics and Liberalism, 1789-1960." In *Catholicism and Liberalism: Contributions to American Public Philosophy*. Eds. R. Bruce Douglass and David Hollenbach. Cambridge: Cambridge University Press.

Goldstein, Joseph. 1983. *The Experience of Insight: A Simple and Direct Guide to Buddhist Meditation*. Boulder: Shambhala.

———. 1994.*Insight Meditation: The Practice of Freedom*. Boston: Shambhala.

Goodman, Paul, and Percival Goodman. 1960. *Communitas: Means of Livelihood and Ways of Life*. New York: Vintage.

Goulet, Denis. 1981. *Survival with Integrity: Sarvodaya at the Crossroads*. Colombo: Marga Institute.

Gramsci, Antonio. 1971. *Selections from Prison Notebooks,* eds. Quinton Hoare and Geoffrey Nowell Smith. New York: International Publishers.

Gray, Francine du Plessix. 1970. "Profiles: Acts of Witness," *New Yorker* 46 (March 14, 1970): 44-121.

Greeley, Andrew. 1958. "Quadragesimo Anno and 'New' Problems," *America* 100 (December 13, 1958): 340.

Gremillion, Joseph, ed. 1976. *The Gospel of Peace and Justice—Catholic Social Teaching since Pope John*. Maryknoll, NY: Orbis Books.

Grew, Raymond. 1986. Quoted in C. Vann Woodword, *Thinking Back: The Perils of Writing History*. Baton Rouge: Lousiana State University Press, 1986

Grisez, Germain. 1993. *The Way of the Lord Jesus*. Quincy, IL: Franciscan Press.

Gross, Rita. 1993. *Buddhism after Patriarchy*. Albany, NY: SUNY Press.

Gudorf, Christine E. 1981. *Catholic Social Teaching on Liberation Themes*. Washington, DC: University Press of America.

Gustafson, James. 1985. "The Sectarian Temptation: Reflections on Theology, the Church, and the University," *Proceedings of the Catholic Theological Society of America* 40: 83-94.

Gutiérrez, Gustavo. 1988, 1973. *A Theology of Liberation: History, Politics, and Salvation*. Trs. and eds., Sister Caridad Inda and John Eagleson. Maryknoll, NY: Orbis Books.

———. 1990. *The Truth Shall Make You Free: Confrontations*. Tr. Matthew J. O'Connell. Maryknoll, NY: Orbis Books.

Habito, Ruben. 1989. *Total Liberation: Zen Spirituality and the Social Dimension*. Maryknoll, NY: Orbis Books.

———. 1993. *Healing Breath: Zen Spirituality for a Wounded Earth*. Maryknoll, NY: Orbis Books.

Haight, Roger, S.J. 1985. *An Alternative Vision: An Interpretation of Liberation Theology*. New York: Paulist Press.

Hatch, Nathan. 1989. *The Democratization of American Christianity*. New Haven, CT: Yale University Press.

Hauerwas, Stanley. 1988. *Christian Existence Today: Essays on Church, World, and Living In Between.* Durham NC: Labyrinth Press.

Hawthorne, Nathaniel. 1852/1983. *The Blithedale Romance*. Boston: Ticknor, Reed, and Fields; reprint 1983, New York: Viking Press.

Hayes, Carlton J. H. 1926. *Essays on Nationalism*. New York: Macmillan.

———. 1960. *Nationalism: A Religion*. New York: Macmillan.

Hayes, Kathleen. 1987. "Gustavo Gutiérrez: Opting For the Poor." *The Other Side* 23 (November 1987): 10-13.

Hebblethwaite, Margaret. 1993. *Base Communities: An Introduction*. London: G. Chapman.

Hellman, John. 1981. *Emmanuel Mounier and the New Catholic Left, 1930 - 1950.* Toronto: University of Toronto Press.

Hennacy, Ammon. 1954. *Autobiography of a Catholic Anarchist.* New York: Catholic Worker Books.

———. 1968. *The Book of Ammon.* [No place of publication listed. No publisher given.]

———. 1951. "Thoughts on Religion," unpublished ms. of Aug. 31, 1951. Platt Cline-Ammon Hennacy Collection. Cline Library, Northern Arizona University.

Hennelly, Alfred T., ed.1990. *Liberation Theology: A Documentary History.* Tr. Alfred T. Hennelly. Maryknoll, NY: Orbis Books.

———. 1995. *Liberation Theologies: The Global Pursuit of Justice.* Mystic, NY: Twenty-Third Publications.

———. 1979. *Theologies in Conflict: The Challenge of Juan Luis Segundo.* Maryknoll, NY: Orbis Books.

Hess, Karl. 1969. "An Open Letter to Barry Goldwater," *Ramparts* 8 (August 1969): 30.

Higgins, Msgr. George. 1983. "Dorothy Day Qualifies for Sainthood as 'Gift of God'." *Catholic Herald* (September 15, 1983).

Hochhuth, Rolf. 1964. *The Deputy.* New York: Grove Press.

Holland, Joe, and Peter Henriot. 1983. *Social Analysis: Linking Faith and Justice.* Maryknoll, NY: Orbis Books in collaboration with the Center of Concern.

Hovda, Robert. 1978. Interview with John O'Sullivan, Chicago, IL, October 16, 1978.

Howard, Sir Albert. 1943. *An Agricultural Testament.* New York: Oxford University Press.

Huff, Peter A. 1996. *Allen Tate and the Catholic Revival: Trace of the Fugitive Gods.* New York: Paulist Press.

Hughes, John. 1865. *Complete Works of the Most Reverend John Hughes.* Vol. 2. Ed. Lawrence Kehoe. New York: Lawrence Kehoe.

Hurwitz, Deena, and Craig Simpson, eds. 1983. *Against the Tide: Pacifist Resistance in the Second World War, An Oral History.* New York: War Resisters League.

Ives, Charles. 1992. *Zen Awakening and Society.* Honolulu: University of Hawaii Press.

James, William. 1963. *The Varieties of Religious Experience: A Study in Human Nature.* Hyde Park, NY: University Books.

Jasperse, Patrick. 1988. "Non-priests Saying Mass at Casa Maria,"*Milwaukee Journal* (September 9, 1988): Metro page.

John Paul II, Pope. 1981. *Laborem Exercens (On Human Work).* Boston: St. Paul Books.

———. 1999. *Ecclesia in America.* Washington DC: U.S. Catholic Conference.

———. 1992. *The Pope Speaks to the American Church: John Paul II's Homilies, Speeches, and Letters to Catholics in the United States.* San Francisco: HarperSanFrancisco.

Johnson, Samuel, and Chartres Biron. 1989. *The Johnson Quotation Book: Based on the Collection of Chartres Biron.* Ed. Philip Smallwood. Bristol, England: Bristol Classical Press.

Kadir, Djelal. 1992. *Columbus and the Ends of the Earth: Europe's Prophetic Rhetoric as Conquering Ideology*. Berkeley: University of California Press.

Kammer, Fred, S.J. 1991. *Doing Faithjustice: An Introduction to Catholic Social Thought.* New York: Paulist Press.

Kapleau, Roshi Philip. 1981. *To Cherish All Life: A Buddhist View of Animal Slaughter and Meat-Eating.* Rochester, NY: Zen Center.

Kennedy, Eugene. 1988. *Tomorrow's Catholics, Yesterday's Church: the Two Cultures of American Catholicism.* New York : Harper and Row.

Kent, Peter, and John F. Pollard, ed. 1994. *Papal Diplomacy in the Modern Age.* Westport, CT: Praeger.

Kerr, Fergus. 1997. *Immortal Longings.* Notre Dame, IN: University of Notre Dame Press.

Kerber, Linda, Alice Kessler-Harris, and Kathryn Kish Sklar eds. (1995) *U.S. History As Women's History: New Feminist Essays.* Chapel Hill: University of North Carolina Press.

Kiernan, Edward J. 1941. *Arthur J Penty: His Contribution to Social Thought.* Washington, DC. The Catholic University of America Press.

Klejment, Anne, and Alice Klejment. 1986. *Dorothy Day and* "The *Catholic* Worker"*: A Bibliography and Index.* New York: Garland.

Klejment, Anne, and Nancy L. Roberts, eds. 1996. *American Catholic Pacifism: The Influence of Dorothy Day and the Catholic Worker Movement.* Westport, CT: Praeger.

Kohl, Clayton Charles. 1914. *Claims as a Cause of the Mexican War.* New York: New York University.

Kohn, Hans. 1957. *American Nationalism: An Interpretative Essay.* New York: Macmillan.

Komonchak, Joseph. 1996. "John Courtney Murray and the Redemption of History: Natural Law and Theology," In *John Courtney Murray and the Growth of Tradition.* Eds. J. Leon Hooper and Todd David Whitmore. Notre Dame, IN: University of Notre Dame Press.

Kornfield, Jack. 1993. *A Path With Heart: A Guide Through the Promises and Pitfalls of the Spiritual Life.* New York: Bantam.

Kotler, Arnold, ed. 1996. *Engaged Buddhist Reader: Ten Years of Engaged Buddhist Publishing.* Berkeley, CA: Parallax.

Kramer, Michael. 1990. "Read My Ships," *Time* 136 (August 20, 1990): 20.

Kropotkin, Petr Alekseevich, kniaz.' 1901. *Fields, Factories and Workshops; or, Industry Combined with Agriculture and Brain Work with Manual Work*, New ed. New York: G. P. Putnam's Sons.

Kropotkin, Petr Alekseevich. 1912/1968. *Fields, Factories, Workshops; Or, Industry Combined with Agriculture and Brain Work with Manual Work.* London: T. Nelson, 1912. Ed. by Cohn Ward. New York: Greenwood Press, 1968.

Küng, Hans, and Jürgen Moltmann, eds. 1990. *The Ethics of World Religions and Human Rights.* London: SCM Press.

LaFarge, John. 1937. "Some Reflections on the Catholic Worker," *America* 57 (June 26, 1937): 275.

Lamb, Matthew. 1997. *National Catholic Reporter,* September 5, 1997.

Land, Philip S., S.J. 1994. *Catholic Social Teaching: As I Have Lived, Loathed and Loved It.* Chicago: Loyola University Press.

Langmuir, Gavin I. 1990. *History, Religion, and Antisemitism* and *Toward a Definition of Antisemitism*. Berkeley: University of California Press.

Larrowe, Dwight. 1941. "The Association of Catholic Conscientious Objectors," *The Catholic Worker* 8 (September 1941): 2.

LeBrun, John. 1973. "The Catholic Worker and American Pacifism." Case Western Reserve University: unpublished Ph.D. dissertation.

Lentricchia, Frank. 1983. *Criticism and Social Change*. Chicago: University of Chicago Press.

Leonard, Richard. 1978. Interview with John O'Sullivan, Philadelphia, PA, July 29, 1978.

Levin, David. 1996. Cartoons reproduced in *American Catholic Pacifism*. Eds. Anne Klejment and Nancy Roberts. Westport, CT: Praeger.

———. 1996. Cartoon. *Sojourners* (Dec.).

Lincoln, Abraham. 1940. *The Life and Writings of Abraham Lincoln*. Ed. Philip Van Doren Stern. New York: Random House.

Lipset, Seymour Martin. 1966. *American Exceptionalism: A DoubleEdged Sword.* New York: W. W. Norton.

Lipsitz, George. 1988. *A Life In the Struggle: Ivory Perry and the Culture of Opposition*. Philadelphia: Temple University Press.

London, Herbert I., and Albert L. Weeks. 1981. *Myths That Rule America.* Washington, DC: University Press of America.

Ludlow, Robert. 1948. "Revolution and Compassion," in Cornell et al. 1995.

———. 1977. Interview with John O'Sullivan, New York, NY, November 22, 1977.

Lubac, Henri de. 1949. *Corpus Mysticum: L'Eucharistie et L'Eglise au Moyen Age,* 2nd ed. Paris: Aubier.

———. 1998. *The Mystery of the Supernatural.* Trans. Rosemary Sheed, New York: Crossroad.

Lukacs, John.1984. *Outgrowing Democracy: A History of the United States in the Twentieth Century*. Garden City, NY: Doubleday.

———. 1990. *Confessions of an Original Sinner*. New York: Ticknor and Fields.

———. 1993. "1918," *American Heritage* 44 (November 1993): 46-50.

Lynd, Staughton, and Alice Lynd, eds. 1995. *Nonviolence in America: A Documentary History*. Maryknoll, NY: Orbis Books.

MacCarthy, Fiona. 1989. *Eric Gill: A Lover's Quest for Art and God.* New York: E.P. Dutton.

Macdonald, Dwight. 1957. "Dorothy Day." In *Memoirs Of A Revolutionist.* New York: Farrar, Straus and Cudahy.

Macy, Joanna. 1983. *Dharma and Development: Religion as Resource in the Sarvodaya Self-Help Movement.* West Hartford, CT: Kumarian Press.

Magill, Frank N., ed. 1965. *Masterpieces of Catholic Literature.* New York: Harper and Row.

Maritain, Jacques. 1920. *Art and Scholasticism*, trans. J. F. Scanlon. New York: C. Scribner's Sons.

Marlett, Jeffrey. 1997. "Fertile Land and Fertile Souls: American Rural Catholicism and the Theological Imagination,1920–1955." St. Louis University: unpublished Ph.D. dissertation.

Marty, Martin. 1994. "Dorothy Day: The Exemplar." In *A Tremor of Bliss: Contemporary Writers on the Saints*. Ed. Paul Elie. New York: Harcourt Brace.

Marx, Paul B., O.S.B. 1957. *Virgil Michel and the Liturgical Movement.* Collegeville, MN: Liturgical Press.

Masse, Benjamin L., S.J. 1966. "How Goes The Poverty War?" *America* 115 (Sept. 17): 282.

Matuso, Alan J. 1984. *The Unraveling of America: A History of Liberalism in the 1960s*. New York: Harper and Row.

Maurin, Peter. 1936. *Easy Essays*, New York: Sheed and Ward.

———. 1949. *Catholic Radicalism: Phrased Essays for the Green Revolution*, New York: Catholic Worker Books.

———. 1961/1977/1984. *Easy Essays*. Chicago: Franciscan Herald Press. (First published under the title *The Green Revolution* by the Academy Guild Press. Fresno, CA.)

McDonough, Peter. 1992. *Men Astutely Trained: A History Of The Jesuits In The American Century*. New York: Free Press.

McGowan, Patricia. 1961. "Grass Roots Idealist," *Today* (May 1961): 3-4.

McGreevy, John T. 1997. "Thinking On One's Own: Catholics in the American Intellectual Imagination, 1928-1960." In *Journal of American History* 84 (June 1997): 97-131.

McNeal, Patricia. 1973. "Origins of the Catholic Peace Movement," *Review of Politics* 35 (July 1973): 346-74.

———. 1992. *Harder Than War: Catholic Peacemaking in Twentieth-Century America*. New Brunswick, N.J.: Rutgers University Press.

———. 1996. "Catholic Peace Organizations and World War II" in Klejment and Roberts.

McPartlan, Paul. 1995. *Sacrament of Salvation.* Edinburgh: T and T Clark.

Mead, Sidney E. 1963. *The Lively Experiment: The Shaping of Christianity in America: An Introduction to Eucharistic Ecclesiology*. New York: Harper and Row.

Merk, Frederick. 1963. *Manifest Destiny and Mission in American History: A Reinterpretation*. New York: Knopf.

Merriman, Brigid O'Shea. 1992. *Called to Be Holy: Dorothy Day and the Retreat Movement.* Notre Dame, IN: University of Notre Dame Press.

———. 1994. *Searching for Christ: The Spirituality of Dorothy Day*. Notre Dame, IN: University of Notre Dame Press.

Merton, Thomas. 1948. *Seven Storey Mountain*. New York: Harcourt, Brace.

———. 1948. "Clairvaux Prison," *The Catholic Worker* 14 (January 1948): 5.

———. 1967. Letter to Dorothy Day, February 9, 1967. In *The Hidden Ground of Love.*

———. 1968. *Zen and the Birds of Appetite*. New York: New Directions.

———. 1976. *Ishi Means Man*. Foreword by Dorothy Day. Greensboro, NC: Unicorn Press.

———. 1985. *The Hidden Ground of Love: the Letters of Thomas Merton on Religious Experience and Social Concerns*. Ed. William H. Shannon. New York: Farrar, Straus, Giroux.

———. 1995-1998. *The Journals of Thomas Merton*. Seven volumes. San Francisco. HarperSanFrancisco.

Milbank, John. 1991. *Theology and Social Theory.* Cambridge, MA: Blackwell.

Miles, Margaret. 1989. *Carnal Knowing: Female Nakedness and Religious Meaning in the Christian West*. Boston: Beacon Press.

Miller, Perry. 1956. *Errand Into the Wilderness*. Cambridge, MA: Belknap Press of Harvard University Press.

Miller, William D. 1973. *A Harsh and Dreadful Love; Dorothy Day and the Catholic Worker Movement*. New York: Liveright.

———. 1975. Letter to John LeBrun (May 22, 1975).

———. 1982. *Dorothy Day: A Biography*, San Francisco: Harper and Row.

———. 1982. "Dorothy Day and the Bible." In *The Bible And Social Reform*. Ed. Ernest R. Sandeen. Philadelphia: Fortress Press; Chico, CA: Scholars Press.

———. 1987. *All Is Grace: The Spirituality Of Dorothy Day*, Garden City, NJ: Doubleday.

Misner, Paul. 1991. *Social Catholicism in Europe: From the onset of Industrialization to the First World War*. New York: Crossroad.

Mitchell, Donald, and James Wiseman, eds. 1997. *The Gethsemani Encounter: A Dialogue on the Spiritual Life by Buddhist and Christian Monastics*. New York: Continuum.

Mitchell, John J., Jr. 1989. *Critical Voices in American Catholic Economic Thought*. New York: Paulist Press.

Moore, R. Laurence. 1994. *Selling God: American Religion in the Marketplace of Culture*. New York : Oxford University Press.

Morris, Charles. 1997. *American Catholic: The Saints and Sinners Who Built America's Most Powerful Church*. New York: Times Books.

Mott, Michael. 1984. *The Seven Mountains of Thomas Merton*. Boston: Houghton Mifflin.

Mournier, Emmanuel. 1938. *A Personalist Manifesto*. London: Longmans.

Moyers, Bill. 1973. *Bill Moyer's Journal* program on Dorothy Day and the Catholic Worker. Bill Moyers, executive editor. Corporation for Public Broadcasting.

———. 1988. Letter to Julie L. Pycior, June 8.

Mumford, Lewis. 1934. *Technics and Civilization*. New York: Harcourt, Brace.

———. 1962. *The Story of Utopias*. New York: Viking Press.

Murray, Harry. 1990. *Do Not Neglect Hospitality: The Catholic Worker and the Homeless*. Philadelphia: Temple University Press.

Murray, John Courtney, S.J. 1960. *We Hold These Truths*. New York: Sheed and Ward.

Muste, A.J. 1937. "Catholic Workers Unite," *Fellowship* 3 (June): 4-6.

——— and Marion Frenyear. 1937. "Catholic Pacifists at Home," *Fellowship* 3 (November 1937): 11.

Myers, Ched. 1988. *Binding the Strong Man: A Political Reading of Mark's Story of Jesus*. Maryknoll, NY: Orbis Books.

———. 1994. *Who Will Roll Away the Stone: Discipleship Queries for First World Christians*. Maryknoll, NY: Orbis Books.

National Conference of Catholic Bishops. 1983. *The Challenge of Peace: God's Promise and Our Response: A Pastoral Letter on War and Peace*. Washington, DC: U.S. Catholic Conference.

———. 1984. *Pastoral Letters of the U.S. Catholic Bishops, 1792-1983*. Ed. Rev. Hugh J. Nolan, Vol. 3. Washington, DC: U.S. Catholic Conference.

———. 1986. *Economic Justice for All: Pastoral Letter on Catholic Social Teaching and the U.S. Economy.* Washington, DC: U.S. Catholic Conference.

———. 1993. *The Harvest of Justice Is Sown in Peace: A Reflection of the National Conference of Bishops on the Tenth Anniversary of the Challenge of Peace.* Washington, DC: U.S. Catholic Conference.

National Catholic Rural Life Conference. 1933. *Proceedings of the Eleventh Annual Convention of the Catholic Rural Life Conference,* Resolution V.1 (1933): 84.

New York Times. 1986. "A School for Love," review of *Love is the Measure.* May 5, 1986.

Nhat Hanh, Thich. 1987. *Being Peace.* Berkeley, CA: Parallax Press.

———. 1993. *Interbeing: Fourteen Guidelines for Engaged Buddhism.* Berkeley, CA: Parallax Press.

———. 1995. *Living Buddha, Living Christ.* New York: Riverhead.

———. 1996. *The Miracle of Mindfulness: A Manual on Meditation.* Boston: Beacon Press.

———. 1998, ed. *For A Future To Be Possible: Commentaries on the Five Mindfulness Trainings.* Berkeley, CA: Parallax Press. (Originally issued in 1993 as *For A Future to Be Possible: Commentaries on the Five Wonderful Precepts*).

Nickoloff, James B., ed. 1996. *Gustavo Gutiérrez: Essential Writings.* Minneapolis: Fortress.

Niebuhr, H. Richard. 1924. "Ernst Troeltsch's Philosophy of Religion." Yale University: unpublished Ph.D. dissertation.

———. 1935. "Toward the Independence of the Church," in *The Church Against the World,* eds. H. R. Niebuhr, Wilhelm Pauck, and Francis P. Miller. Chicago: Willett, Clark.

———. 1951. *Christ and Culture.* New York: Harper and Row.

Niebuhr, Reinhold. 1962. *The Irony of American History.* New York: Charles Scribner's Sons.

— and Alan Heimert. 1963. *A Nation So Conceived.* New York: Scribner's.

Nolan, Hugh, ed. 1984. *Pastoral Letters of the U.S. Catholic Bishops, 1792-1983.* 3 vols. Washington, DC: U.S. Catholic Conference.

Norris, Kathleen. 1996. *Cloister Walk.* New York: Riverhead Books.

Novitsky, Anthony William. 1976. "The Ideological Development of Peter Maurin's Green Revolution." State University of New York at Buffalo: unpublished Ph.D. dissertation.

O'Brien, David J. 1965."American Social Thought in the1930s." University of Rochester: unpublished Ph.D. dissertation.

———. 1972. *The Renewal of American Catholicism.* New York: Oxford University Press.

———. 1989. *Public Catholicism.* New York: Macmillan.

——— and Thomas Shannon, eds. 1992. *Catholic Social Thought—The Documentary Heritage.* Maryknoll, NY: Orbis Books.

Ochs, Carol. 1986. *An Ascent to Joy: Transforming Deadness of Spirit.* Notre Dame, IN: University of Notre Dame Press.

O'Collins, Gerald, S.J., and Edward Farrugia, S.J. 1991. *A Concise Dictionary of Theology.* New York: Paulist Press.

O'Connor, Ann. 1994. "The Catholic Worker: Is It Still Catholic?" *New Oxford Review* 61 (March 1994): 5-8.

O'Connor, June. 1991. *The Moral Vision of Dorothy Day: A Feminist Perspective.* New York: Crossroad.

O'Gara, James. 1954. "The Catholic Isolationist." In *Catholicism In America.* New York: Harcourt Brace.

Ogden, Schubert M. 1989. *Faith And Freedom: Toward a Theology of Liberation.* Nashville, TN: Abingdon.

O'Gorman, Angie, and Patrick G. Coy. 1988. "Houses of Hospitality: A Pilgrimage into Nonviolence," In *A Revolution of the Heart: Essays on the Catholic Worker.* Ed. Patrick G. Coy. Philadelphia: Temple University Press.

O'Grady, Jim. 1993. *Dorothy Day: With Love for the Poor.* Staten Island, NY: Ward Hill Press.

O'Halloran, James, S.D.B. 1991. *Signs of Hope: Developing Small Christian Communities.* Maryknoll, NY: Orbis Books.

———. 1996. *Small Christian Communities: A Pastoral Companion.* Maryknoll, NY: Orbis Books; Dublin: Columba Press.

O'Hanlon, Raymond. 1977. Interview with John O'Sullivan, Sea Cliff, NY, November 25, 1977.

Pastor-Zelaya, Anthony Sean. 1988. "The Development of Roman Catholic Social Liberalism in the United States, 1887-1935." University of California, Santa Barbara: unpublished Ph.D. dissertation.

Patai, Raphael. 1972. *Myth and Modern Man.* Englewood Cliffs, NJ: Prentice-Hall.

Paul, Martin. 1953. "Diary of a Romantic Agrarian," *Commonweal* 57 (January 2, 1953): 328.

Pelikan, Jaroslav. 1985. *Jesus through the Centuries: His Place in the History of Culture.* New Haven: Yale University Press.

Penatar, Michael P. 1952. *The Social Thought of the Catholic Worker on the Negro.* Washington, DC: Catholic University of America Press.

Penty, Arthur J. 1937. *Tradition and Modernism in Politics.* New York: Sheed & Ward.

Perko, F. Michael, S.J. 1989. *Catholic and American: A Popular History.* Huntington, IN: Our Sunday Visitor Publications.

Peter-Raoul, Mar, Linda Rennie Forcey, and Robert Frederick Hunter, Jr. 1990. *Yearning to Breathe Free: Liberation Theologies in the United States.* Ed. Mar Peter-Raoul. Maryknoll, NY: Orbis Books.

Piehl, Mel. 1982. *Breaking Bread: The Catholic Worker and the Origin of Catholic Radicalism in America,* Philadelphia: Temple University Press.

———. 1984. "The Catholic Worker and American Religious Tradition," *Cross Currents* 34 (Fall 1984): 259-69.

Pius XI. 1931. *Quadragesimo Anno* (Commemorating the 40th anniversary of Leo XIII's *Rerum Novarum:* on reconstructing of the social order), Vatican City.

Pius XII. 1990. *Mystici Corporis Christi* in Carlen.

Planas, Ricardo. 1986. *Liberation Theology: The Political Expression of Religion.* Kansas City, MO: Sheed & Ward.

Plaskow, Judith, and Carol P. Christ, eds. 1989. *Weaving the Visions: New Patterns in Feminist Spirituality.* San Francisco: Harper & Row.

Pletcher, David M. 1978. "Manifest Destiny," In *Encyclopedia of American Foreign Policy.* Vol. 2. Ed. Alexander DeConde. New York: Charles Scribner's Sons.

———.1933. "John L. O'Sullivan and Manifest Destiny." *New York History* 14 (July 1933): 213-34.

———.1935. "The Ideology of American Expansion," In *Essays in Honor of William E. Dodd*. Ed. Avery Craven. Chicago: University of Chicago Press.

Pratt, Julius W. 1936. *Expansionists of 1898*. Baltimore: Johns Hopkins University Press.

Pycior, Julie L. 1996. Interview, Jim Forest, Hastings on Hudson, NY, December 2,1996

———.1997. Interview, John Eudes Bamberger, Abbey of Our Lady of Genesee, Piffard, NY, August 12, 1997

———.1997A. Interview, Msgr. William V. Shannon, Rochester, NY, August 12, 1997

———.1997B. Interview, John Peter Grady, Ithica, NY, August 16, 1997

———.1997C. Interview, Thomas Cornell, Peter Maurin Farm, Marlboro, NY, August 21, 1997.

———.1997D. Interview, John Cort, Milwaukee, WI , October 11, 1997.

———.1997E. Interview, Gordon Zahn, Milwaukee, WI, October 11, 1997.

Queen, Christopher, and Sallie King, eds. 1996. *Engaged Buddhism: Buddhist Liberation Movements in Asia*. Albany, NY: SUNY Press.

Quigley, Margaret, and Michael Garvey, eds. 1982. *The Dorothy Day Book*. Springfield, IL: Templegate.

Quigley, Robert Edward. 1965. "American Catholic Opinions of Mexican Anti-Clericalism, 1910-1936. "University of Pennsylvania: unpublished Ph.D. dissertation.

Quigley, Thomas. 1968. *American Catholics and Vietnam*. Grand Rapids, MI: William B. Eerdmans Publishing Co.

Ranald, Margaret Loftus. 1984. *The Eugene O'Neill Companion*. Westport, CT: Greenwood.

Rauschenbusch, Walter. 1916. *The Social Principles of Jesus,* New York: Association Press.

Riegle, Rosalie. See Troester, Rosalie Riegle.

Reinhold, H. A. 1952. "Back to What?" *Worship* 26 (April 1952): 254.

Reissman, Catherine Kohler. 1993. *Narrative Analysis*. Newbury Park, CA: Sage Publications.

Rhodes, Anthony. 1973. *The Vatican in the Age of Dictators, 1922-45*. London: Hodder and Stoughton.

Richardson, James D., ed. 1896. *A Compilation of the Messages and Papers of the Presidents, 1789-1897*. Vol. 1. Washington, DC: United States Congress.

Richter, Robert. 1996. Lecture, "Inside the School of Assassins," Manhattan College, NY, October 10.

———. 1996A. Film, "Inside the School of Assassins." Robert Richter, producer. Richter Productions.

Rieger, Joerg, ed. 1998. *Liberating the Future: God, Mammon and Theology*. Minneapolis: Fortress Press.

Rifkin, Jeremy. 1995. *The End of Work: The Decline of the Global Labor Force and the Dawn of the Post-Market Era*. New York: G.P. Putnam's Sons.

Robbins, John. 1987. *Diet for a New America*. Walpole, NH: Stillpoint.

Roberts, Nancy. 1984. *Dorothy Day and the "Catholic Worker."* Albany, SUNY Press.

Rosswurm, Steve. 1992. "The Catholic Church and the Left-led Unions," In *The CIO's Left-led Unions*. New Brunswick: Rutgers University Press.

Rothbard, Murray N. 1964. "The Transformation of the American Right," In *Continuum* (Summer 1964): 222.

Rovere, Richard H. 1941. "Labor's Catholic Bloc," *Nation* 150 (January 4, 1941): 13.

Rubenstein, Richard. 1966. *After Auschwitz: Radical Theology and Contemporary Judaism*. Indianapolis: Bobbs-Merrill.

Rubenstein, Richard L., and John K. Roth, eds. 1988. *The Politics of Latin American Liberation Theology: The Challenge to U.S. Public Policy*. Washington, DC: Washington Institute Press.

Ruether, Rosemary Radford. 1972. *Liberation Theology: Human Hope Confronts Christian History and American Power*. New York: Paulist Press.

Ryan, John. 1931. *Irish Monasticism: Origins and Early Development.* London: Longmans, Green.

Saddhatisa, H. 1970. *Buddhist Ethics: Essence of Buddhism*. New York: George Braziller.

Sale, Kirkpatrick. 1995. *Rebels Against the Future: The Luddites and Their War on the Industrial Revolution: Lessons for the Computer Age*. Reading, MA: Addison Wesley.

Salzberg, Sharon. 1995. *Lovingkindness*. Boston: Shambhala.

Sandberg, John Stuart. 1979. "The Eschatological Ethic of the Catholic Worker." The Catholic University of America: unpublished Ph.D. dissertation.

de Schrijver, G., ed. 1998. *Liberation Theologies on Shifting Grounds: A Clash of Socio-economic and Cultural Paradigms*. Leuven (Belgium): Leuven University Press/Uitgeverij Peeters.

Sigmund, Paul E. 1990. *Liberation Theology at the Crossroad: Democracy or Revolution?* New York: Oxford University Press.

Schlesinger, Arthur, Jr. 1949. *The Vital Center: The Politics Of Freedom*. Boston: Houghton Mifflin.

Schuck, Michael J. 1991. *That They Be One: The Social Teaching of the Papal Encyclicals, 1740-1989.* Washington, DC: Georgetown University Press.

Schumacher, E. F. 1973. *Small Is Beautiful: Economics As if People Mattered.* New York: Harper and Row.

Seaton, Douglas. 1981. *Catholics and Radicals: The Association of Catholic Trade Unionists and the American Labor Movement, from Depression to Cold War.* Lewisburg: Bucknell University Press.

Selective Training and Service Act of 1940, Public Law Number 783, 76th Congress, 2nd Session.

Shannon, William. 1992. *Silent Lamp: The Thomas Merton Story*. New York: Crossroad.

Shapiro, Edward. 1977. "The Catholic Rural Life Movement and the New Deal Farm Program," In *American Benedictine Review* 28 (September 1977): 307-332.

Sheed, Wilfred. 1980. "Dorothy Day," *Nation* 231 (December 20, 1980): 660-661.

Sheehan, Arthur. 1941. "Work Camp Offered to Catholic C.O's," *The Catholic Worker* 8 (April 1941): 1, 3.

———. 1959. *Peter Maurin: Gay Believer*. New York: Hanover House.

Sicius, Frank. 1988. "The Chicago Catholic Worker." In *A Revolution of the Heart: Essays on the Catholic Worker*. Ed. Patrick Coy. Philadelphia: Temple University Press.

———. 1996. "Prophecy Faces Tradition: The Pacifist Debate During World War II." In *American Catholic Pacifism*. Eds. Anne Klejment and Nancy L. Roberts. Westport, CT: Praeger Publishers.

Silk, Mark. 1988. *Spiritual Politics: Religion and America Since World War II*. New York: Simon and Schuster.

Sivaraksa, Sulak. 1990. "Human Rights in the Context of Global Problem Solving: A Buddhist Perspective." In *The Ethics of World Religions and Human Rights*. Eds. Hans Küng and Jürgen Moltmann. London: SCM Press.

———. 1992. *Seeds of Peace: A Buddhist Vision for Renewing Society*. Berkeley, CA: Parallax Press.

Slotkin, Richard. 1973/1996. *Regeneration Through Violence : The Mythology of the American Frontier, 1600-1860*. New York: Harper Perennial.

Smith, Christian S. 1991. *The Emergence of Liberation Theology: Radical Religion and Social Movement Theory*. Chicago : University of Chicago Press.

Southern, David W. 1996. *John LaFarge and the Limits of Catholic Interracialism*. Baton Rouge: LSU Press.

Spellman, Francis Cardinal. 1946. *Prayers and Poems*. New York: Charles Scribner's Sons.

———. 1948/1968. "Address of His Eminence Cardinal Spellman at Dinner of the Society, March 17, 1948," *In Memoriam: Francis Cardinal Spellman*. New York: Society of the Friendly Sons of St. Patrick in the City of New York, 1968.

Stephanson, Anders. 1995. *Manifest Destiny: American Expansionism and the Empire of Right*. New York: Hill and Wang.

Tate, Allen. 1936. "Notes on Liberty and Property," *The American Review* 6 March 1936): 596-611.

Taylor, F. Jay. 1967. "American Catholic and Protestant Attitudes Toward the Civil War." In *The Spanish Civil War: Domestic Crisis or International Conspiracy?* Ed. Gabriel Jackson. Boston: D. C. Heath.

Teichman, Jenny. 1986. *Pacifism and the Just War*. Oxford: Basil Blackwell.

Theology in the Americas. 1978. *Is Liberation Theology for North America?: The Response of First World Churches to Third World Theologies*. New York: Theology in the Americas.

Thien-An, Thich. 1975. *Zen Philosophy, Zen Practice*. Emeryville, CA: Dharma Publishing.

Thomas, Joan. 1974. *The Years of Grief and Laughter: A "Biography" of Ammon Hennacy*. Phoenix, AZ: Hennacy Press.

———. 1997. Letter to James Missey. May 24, 1997. In possession of Dr. Missey.

Thondup, Tulku. 1996. *The Healing Power of Mind*. Boston: Shambhala.

Tillich, Paul. 1977. *The Socialist Decision*. Trans. Franklin Sherman. New York: Harper and Row.

Timmerman, Don, Gordon C. Zahn, and John F. Baldovin. 1988. "The Eucharist: Who May Preside?" *Commonweal* 115 (September 9, 1988): 460-463, 466.

Tocqueville, Alexis de. 1848/1953. *Democracy in America*. 2 vols. New York: Knopf.

Tracy, David. 1981/1991. *The Analogical Imagination: Christian Theology and the Culture of Pluralism*. New York: Crossroad.

———. 1987. *Plurality and Ambiguity: Hermeneutics. Religion and Hope*. New York: Harper and Row.

———. 1994. *On Naming the Present: Reflections on God, Hermeneutics, and Church*. Maryknoll, NY: Orbis Books.

Troeltsch, Ernst. 1931/1960/1976. *The Social Teaching of the Christian Churches*. Trans. Olive Wyon, with an introduction by H. Richard Niebuhr, New York: Macmillan; 1960, reprinted New York: Harper; 1976, reprinted Chicago: University of Chicago. Original German edition 1911.

Troester, Rosalie Reigle. 1993. *Voices from the Catholic Worker*. Philadelphia: Temple University Press.

Tuveson, Ernest Lee. 1968. *Redeemer Nation: The Idea of America's Millenial Role*. Chicago: University of Chicago Press.

Tyrell, Ian. 1991. "American Exceptionalism in an Age of International History," *American Historical Review* 96 (October 1991): 1031-1055.

Udoindem, S. Iniobong. 1996. *Pope John Paul II on Inculturation: Theory and Practice*. Washington, DC: University Press of America.

Unity Kitchen. 1995. *Christian Personalism: A Manifesto of Unity Kitchen Community of the Catholic Worker*. Syracuse, NY: Unity Kitchen Community.

U.S. Catholic Bishops. See: National Conference of Catholic Bishops.

"U.S. Recognizes Catholic CO's." *The Conscientious* Objector." 4 (January 1942): 8.

U.S. Selective Service System. 1950. *Conscientious Objection,* Special Monograph No. 11, Volume 1. Washington, DC: U.S. Government Printing Office.

Valaik, J. David. 1964. "American Catholics and the Spanish Civil War: 1936-1939." University of Rochester: Unpublished Ph.D. dissertation.

Veysey, Laurence. 1973. *The Communal Experience; Anarchist and Mystical Counter-Cultures in America*. New York: Harper and Row.

Vishnewski, Stanley. 1984. *Wings of Dawn*. New York: Catholic Worker Press

Waardenburg, Jacques. 1980. "Symbolic Aspects of Myth," In *Myth, Symbol, and Reality*. Ed. Alan M. Olson. Notre Dame, IN: University of Notre Dame Press.

Wakefield, Dan. 1997. *Returning: A Spiritual Journey*. Boston: Beacon Press.

Walden, Ron William 1975. "The Concept of the Church in Recent Roman Catholic Theology." Yale University: unpublished Ph.D. dissertation.

Walker, Susan, ed. 1987. *Speaking of Silence: Christians and Buddhists on the Contemplative Way*. Mahwah, NJ: Paulist Press.

Weaver, Jace. 1995. "Original Simplicities and Present Complexities: Reinhold Niebuhr, Ethnocentrism, and the Myth of American Exceptionalism," *Journal of the American Academy of Religion* 62 (Summer 1995): 231-47.

Weber, Max. 1994. "The Profession and Vocation of Politics." In *Weber: Political Writings*. Trans. Ronald Speirs; eds. Peter Lassman and Ronald Speirs. Cambridge: Cambridge University Press.

Weigel, George. 1987. *Tranquillitas Ordinis*. New York: Oxford University Press.

——— and Robert Royal, eds. 1991. *A Century of Catholic Social Thought*. Washington, DC: Ethics and Public Policy Center; revised edition renamed: *Building the Free Society*, Grand Rapids, MI: Wm. B. Eerdmans Publishing Co., 1993.

Weil, Simone. 1973. *Oppression and Liberty*. Trans. Arthur Wills and John Petrie. Amherst: Universiity of Massachusetts Press.
———. "Factory Work." 1977. In *The Simone Weil Reader*. Ed. George Panichas. Mt. Kisco, NY: Moyer Bell, 1977.
Weinberg, Albert K. 1935/1958. *Manifest Destiny: A Study of Nationalist Expansionism in American History*. Gloucester, MA: Peter Smith.
Westbrock, John. 1978. Interview with John O'Sullivan, Brooklyn, NY, June 2 1978.
White, Susan. 1990. *Art, Architecture, and Liturgical Reform: The Liturgical Arts Society (1928-1972)*. New York: Pueblo Publishing.
Wilkes, Paul. "Joan Baez." 1984. In *Merton by Those Who Knew Him Best*. Ed. Paul Wilkes. New York: Harper and Row.
Will, Herman. 1977. Interview with John O'Sullivan, Washington, DC, February 17.
Wills, Garry. 1980. *Confessions of a Conservative*. New York: Penguin.
———. 1994. *Uncertain Trumpets*. New York: Simon and Schuster
Wink, Walter. 1984. *The Powers*. Vol. 1: *Naming the Powers: The Language of Power in the New Testament*. Philadelphia: Fortress.
Winter, Miriam. T., Adair Lummis, and Allison Stokes. 1994. *Defecting in Place: Women Claiming Responsibility for Their Own Spiritual Lives*. New York: Crossroad.
Woodward, C. Vann. 1986. *Thinking Back: The Perils Of Writing History*. Baton Rouge: Lousiana State University Press.
Woodward, Kenneth L. 1990. *Making Saints*. New York: Simon and Schuster.
———. 1997. "Religion, Politics, and the Media." *America* 177 (August 2-9, 1977): 12-14.
Zagano, Phyllis. 1999. *Twentieth Century Apostles: Contemporary Spirituality in Action*. Collegeville, MN: Liturgical Press.
Zahn, Gordon C. 1972. "Leaven of Love and Justice." *America* 127 (11 November): 383-85.
———. 1979. *Another Part of the War: The Camp Simon Story*. Amherst: University of Massachusetts Press.
Zipser, Arthur. 1998. "Ruthenberg, Charles, E." In *Encyclopedia of the American Left*. 2nd ed. Eds. Mari Jo Buhle, Paul Buhle, and Dan Georgakas. New York: Oxford University Press, 1998.
Zotti, Mary Irene. 1990. "The Young Christian Workers," *U.S. Catholic Historian* 9 (Fall 1990): 387-400.

Authors

Rev. Michael Baxter, C.S.C. teaches at the University of Notre Dame.

Fred Boehrer founded the Albany Catholic Worker Community with his wife, Diane Conroy, and is a doctoral candidate at Syracuse University.

William T. Cavanaugh teaches at the University of St. Thomas, St. Paul, Minnesota.

Walter W. Chura ran the Simple Gifts Catholic Worker bookstore in Albany, New York from 1976–1987.

William J. Collinge teaches at Mount St. Mary's College.

John Cort worked in the New York City Catholic Worker house from 1936–1938 and was a co-founder of the Association of Catholic Trade Unionists.

Patrick G. Coy teaches at Kent State University; he edited *A Revolution of the Heart: Essays on The Catholic Worker*, and wrote several articles on Dorothy Day.

Jacqueline Dickey is a poet who lives in South Bend, Indiana.

Marc H. Ellis is University Professor of American and Jewish Studies at Baylor University and the author of *Peter Maurin: Prophet in the Twentieth Century* and *A Year at The Catholic Worker*.

Catherine A. Faver teaches at the University of Tennessee.

Jim Forest was a member of the New York Catholic Worker cummunity in the early 1960s. A peace activist, he wrote *Love Is the Measure* and co-edited *A Penny a Copy: Readings from The Catholic Worker*.

Geoffrey Gneuhs was an associate editor of *The Catholic Worker* for seven years in the 1970s and 1980s. A painter, he lives in New York City.

David L. Gregory teaches law at St. John's University in Jamaica, New York.

Carol J. Jablonski teaches at the University of South Florida.

Bill Kauffman is the associate editor of *American Enterprise* and a widely published author.

Peter King is a leader of the Unity Kitchen Community of the Catholic Worker, Syracuse, New York along with his wife, Ann O'Connor.

Rev. Stephen T. Krupa, S.J. teaches at John Carroll University.

John L. LeBrun is an emeritus professor at Kent State University.

Julie Leininger Pycior teaches at Manhattan College.

M. L. Liebler is a poet who lives in St. Clair Shores, Michigan.

Nicholas C. Lund-Molfese directs the Integritas Institute for Business and Professional Ethics at the University of Illinois in Chicago.

Paul Magno co-founded the Peter Maurin Center and is a long-time member of the Catholic Worker in Washington, DC.

Jeffrey D. Marlett teaches at the College of St. Rose, Albany, New York.

Eugene McCarraher teaches at Villanova University.

Paul Miller is a mentor at Empire State College, Ithaca, New York.

James Missey retired from teaching at the University of Wisconsin - Stevens Point.

Keith Morton teaches at Providence College.

David J. O'Brien is Loyola Professor of Roman Catholic Studies at Holy Cross College.

Ann O'Connor is a leader of the Unity Kitchen Community of the Catholic Worker, Syracuse, New York, along with her husband Peter King.

John O'Sullivan taught at Florida Atlantic University until his death in the summer of 2000.

Mel Piehl, teaches at Valparaiso University, wrote *Breaking Bread: The Catholic Worker and the Origin of Catholic Radicalism in America.*

Jeff Poniewaz is a poet who lives in Milwaukee, Wisconsin.

Rosalie Reigle teaches at Saginaw Valley State University and is a member and co-founder of the Mustard Seed Catholic Worker Community of Saginaw, Michigan.

John Saltmarsh is on the staff of Campus Compact in Providence, Rhode Island.

Francis J. Sicius teaches at St. Thomas University, Miami, Florida.

Tina Sipula founded and heads the Clare House of Hospitality, Bloomington, Illinois.

Matthew R. Smith founded the Buffalo Catholic Worker and recently completed his M.A. at the University of Buffalo.

John Sniegocki is a professor at the University of Notre Dame.

Rev. Roger A. Statnick is a priest of the diocese of Greensburg, Pennsylvania.

Brian Terrell founded the Strangers and Guests Catholic Worker Farm, Maloy, Iowa, along with his wife, Betsy Keenan.

Markha G. Valenta is doing postdoctoral work at the University of Leiden, The Netherlands.

Sandra Yocum Mize teaches at the University of Dayton.

Mark and Louise Zwick founded Casa Juan Diego in Houston, Texas, and edit the *Houston Catholic Worker.*

Essays Published Elsewhere

Michael Baxter. First published in *Houston Catholic Worker*, November 1999.

Patrick Coy. A later version of this essay was published under the title "An Experiment in Personalist Politics: The Catholic Worker Movement and Nonviolent Action" in *Peace and Change* 26 (January 2001): 78-92.

Jim Forest. First published in *U.S. Catholic*, November 1997, under the title "The Trouble with Saint Dorothy." Reprinted with permission from *U.S. Catholic*, Claretian Publications, www.USCatholic.org, 800-328-6515.

David L. Gregory. Abridged from article in *Hofstra Labor Law Journal* 14 (Fall 1996): 57-150.

Carol J. Jablonski. A later version of this essay was published under the title "Dorothy Day's Contested Legacy: 'Humble Irony' as a Constraint on Memory." *Journal of Communication and Religion* 23 (March 2000): 29-49.

Bill Kauffman. First published in *Chronicles* 22 (November 1998): 17-21.

Peter King/Ann O'Connor. First published in *Unity Grapevine*, January/February/March 1998.

Eugene McCarraher. First published in *Records of the American Catholic Historical Society of Philadelphia* 108 (Spring-Summer 1997): 13-27. Reprinted with permission. This journal is now entitled *American Catholic Studies.*

Sandra Yocum Mize. First published in *Records of the American Catholic Historical Society of Philadelphia* 108 (Spring-Summer 1997): 1-12. Reprinted with permission. This journal is now entitled *American Catholic Studies.*

INDEX